Can you reco
  un ristoran
I am hungry,
I am thirsty,
Check, pleas
Is there a h

Where is . . . ?—Dov e . . . .
What is the way to . . . ?—Qual'è la strada pei . . .
Take me to . . .—Mi conduca a . . . .
I need . . .—Ò bisogno di . . . .
I am ill.—Sono malato.
Please call a doctor.—Chiami un mèdico, per favore.
I want to send a telegram.—Vorrèi spedire un tele-
  gramma.
Where can I change money?—Dove posso far cambiare
  del denaro?
Will you accept checks?—Accètta assegni?
What is the postage?—Quanto còsta l'affrancatura?

Right away.—Sùbito.
Help!—Aiuto!
Come in.—Avanti.
Hello (on telephone).—Pronto.
Stop.—Si fermi.
Hurry.—Fàccia prèsto.
Go on.—Avanti.
Right.—A dèstra.
Left.—A sinistra.
Straight ahead.—Sèmpre diritto.

## Signs

| | |
|---|---|
| Attenzione—Caution | Sènso ùnico—One way (street) |
| Perìcolo—Danger | È vietato fumare—No smoking |
| Uscita—Exit | È vietato entrare—No admittance |
| Entrata—Entrance | |
| Alt, Alto, Fermatevi—Stop | Signore—Women |
| Chiuso—Closed | Signori, Uòmini—Men |
| Apèrto—Open | Gabinetto (di decènza), Cèsso—Toilet |
| Rallentatevi—Slow down | |

# The
# Random House
# Italian
# Dictionary

# The Random House Italian Dictionary

---

## ITALIAN–ENGLISH

---

## ENGLISH–ITALIAN

---

*by*

Robert A. Hall, Jr.

*Professor of Linguistics,
Cornell University*

RANDOM HOUSE

NEW YORK

# Concise Pronunciation Guide

| Italian Letter | Pronunciation |
|---|---|
| a | Like English *a* in *father*. |
| b | As in English. |
| c | Before *e* or *i*, and sometimes at the end of words, like English *ch*. |
| | Elsewhere, like English *k*. |
| ch | Before *e* or *i*, like English *k*. |
| ci | Before *a, o,* or *u*, like English *ch*. |
| d | As in English. |
| é | ("close *e*") Like English *ay* in *day*, but with no final y-like glide. |
| è | ("open *e*") Like English *e* in *bet*. |
| e | Like English *e* in *bet*. |
| f | As in English. |
| g | Before *e* or *i*, like English *g* in *gem*. |
| | Elsewhere, like English *g* in *go*. |
| gh | Before *e* or *i*, like English *g* in *go*. |
| gi | Before *a, o,* or *u*, like English *g* in *gem*. |
| gl | Before *i*, normally like English *lli* in *million*. |
| gli | Before *a, e, o,* or *u*, like English *lli* in *million*. |
| gn | Like English *ny* in *canyon*. |
| h | After *c* and *g*, indicates "hard" pronunciation of preceding consonant letter. |
| | Elsewhere, silent. |
| i | After *c, g,* and (normally) *sc*, before *a, o,* or *u*, indicates "soft" pronunciation of preceding consonant letter or letters. |
| | Elsewhere: |
| | When unstressed and before or after another vowel, like English *y*. |
| | Otherwise, like English *i* in *machine*, but with no final y-like glide. |
| j | At the end of words, when replacing ii in some noun plurals, like Italian *i*. |
| | Otherwise, like English *y*. |
| k | As in English. |
| l | Like English *l* in *like*, but with the tongue behind the upper front teeth. |
| m | As in English. |
| n | As in English. |
| ó | ("close *o*") Like English *o* in *go*, but with no final w-like glide. |
| ò | ("open *o*") Like English *o* in *bought*. |
| o | Like English *o* in *bought*. |
| p | As in English. |

5

**Italian
Letter    Pronunciation**

| | |
|---|---|
| qu | Like English *qu* in *quick*. |
| r | Not at all like American English *r;* a quick flap of the tip of the tongue on the gumridge. |
| s | Between vowels, like English *s* in *lease* (in southern Italy); like *s* in *please* (in northern Italy); sometimes like *s* in *lease* and sometimes like *s* in *please* (in central Italy). |
| | Before *b, d, g, l, m, n, r, v,* like English *z.* |
| | Elsewhere, like English *s* in *same, stick.* |
| sc | Before *e* or *i,* and occasionally at the end of words, like English *sh.* |
| | Elsewhere, like English *sk.* |
| sch | Before *e* or *i,* like English *sk.* |
| sci | Before *a, o,* or *u,* like English *sh.* |
| t | As in English. |
| u | When unstressed and before or after another vowel, like English *w.* |
| | Otherwise, like English *oo* in *boot,* but without final *w*-like glide. |
| v | As in English. |
| w | Rare; like English *v.* |
| x | Rare; like English *x.* |
| z | Like English *ts* in *cats* or like English *dz* in *adze.* |

## Consonant Length

All Italian consonants occur both single (short) and double (long); in the latter instance, the time of their pronunciation lasts from one-and-a-half to two times that of the single consonants.

## Italian Accentuation

In most conventional writing and printing, spoken stress is marked by a grave accent (`` ` ``), but only when it falls on the last syllable of a word: *città, vendè, lunedì, cantò, tribù.* An accent is placed over the vowel letter of some words to distinguish them from others having the same spelling and pronunciation but differing in meaning: *è* "is" versus *e* "and". In other instances, stress is usually left unmarked, although it may fall on any syllable up to the sixth from the end.

However, Italians are very sensitive to misplaced stress, even though accent marks are not customarily used in Italian spelling. In this dictionary, therefore, as in most Italian dictionaries, the occurrence of stress is indicated with an accent mark whenever it does not fall on the next-to-the-last syllable, and also in all words ending in -*ia*, -*io*. In addition, the presence of the open varieties of *e* and *o*, to which Italians are also sensitive, is marked by a grave accent (ˋ) in all its occurrences, even in the next-to-the-last syllable.

# Noun and Adjective Plurals

Virtually all Italian nouns form their plurals by changing the final vowel. The following are the principal patterns of noun plural formation:

| Final Vowel | | Examples | |
|---|---|---|---|
| **Singular** | **Plural** | **Singular** | **Plural** |
| -a (*f.*) | -e | ròsa | ròse |
| -a (*m.*) | -i | dramma | drammi |
| -o (*m.*) | -i | libro | libri |
| -o (*m.*) | -a (*f.*) | bràccio | bràccia |
| -e (*m., f.*) | -i (*m., f.*) | fiume | fiumi |
| | | parte | parti |

Nouns ending in unstressed -*i*, in stressed vowels, or in consonants; family names; and abbreviations are normally unchanged in the plural: *crisi, città, tram; Scaglione; auto, ràdio*.

Adjectives ending in -*o* follow the pattern of *libro* for the masculine and that of *rosa* for the feminine; those ending in -*e* follow the pattern of *fiume, parte* for both masculine and feminine.

# Regular Verbs

| Infinitive | Present | Future | Preterite | Past Part. |
|---|---|---|---|---|
| cantare | canto | canterò | cantai | cantato |
| dormire | dormo | dormirò | dormìi | dormito |
| finire | finisco | finirò | finìi | finito |
| temere | temo | temerò | temèi | temuto |
| véndere | vendo | venderò | vendèi | venduto |

# Irregular Verbs

| Infinitive | Present | Future | Preterite | Past Part. |
|---|---|---|---|---|
| accéndere | accendo | accenderò | accesi | acceso |
| andare | vado | andrò | andai | andato |
| aprire | apro | aprirò | apèrsi | apèrto |
| avere | ò (ho) | avrò | èbbi | avuto |
| bere | bevo | berrò | bevvi | bevuto |
| cadere | cado | cadrò | caddi | caduto |
| cìngere | cingo | cingerò | cinsi | cinto |
| cógliere | colgo | coglierò | colsi | colto |
| concèdere | concedo | concederò | concèssi | concèsso |
| condurre | conduco | condurrò | condussi | condotto |
| dare | do | darò | diedi | dato |
| diféndere | difendo | difenderò | difesi | difeso |
| dire | dico | dirò | dissi | detto |
| dovere | devo | dovrò | dovèi | dovuto |
| èssere | sono | sarò | fui | stato |
| fare | fàccio | farò | feci | fatto |
| fóndere | fondo | fonderò | fusi | fuso |
| giacere | giàccio | giacerò | giacqui | giaciuto |
| morire | muòio | morirò | morìi | mòrto |
| nàscere | nasco | nascerò | nacqui | nato |
| parere | paio | parrò | parsi | parso |
| porre | pongo | porrò | posi | posto |
| potere | pòsso | potrò | potèi | potuto |
| rèndere | rèndo | renderò | resi | reso |
| salire | salgo | salirò | sallì | salito |
| sapere | sò | saprò | seppi | saputo |
| stare | sto | starò | stetti | stato |
| scégliere | scelgo | sceglierò | scelsi | scelto |
| tenere | tengo | terrò | tenni | tenuto |
| trarre | traggo | trarrò | trassi | tratto |
| uscire | esco | uscirò | uscìi | uscito |
| valere | valgo | varrò | valsi | valso |
| vedere | vedo | vedrò | vidi | visto *or* veduto |
| venire | vengo | verrò | venni | venuto |
| vìvere | vivo | vivrò | vissi | vissuto |
| volere | vòglio | vorrò | vòlli | voluto |

# Numerals

## Cardinal

| | | | |
|---|---|---|---|
| 1 | uno, una | 32 | trentadue |
| 2 | due | 38 | trentòtto |
| 3 | tre | 40 | quaranta |
| 4 | quattro | 50 | cinquanta |
| 5 | cinque | 60 | sessanta |
| 6 | sèi | 70 | settanta |
| 7 | sètte | 80 | ottanta |
| 8 | òtto | 90 | novanta |
| 9 | nòve | 100 | cènto |
| 10 | dièci | 101 | centuno |
| 11 | ùndici | 102 | centodue |
| 12 | dódici | 200 | duecènto |
| 13 | trédici | 300 | trecènto |
| 14 | quattòrdici | 400 | quattrocènto |
| 15 | quìndici | 500 | cinquecènto |
| 16 | sédici | 600 | seicènto |
| 17 | diciassètte | 700 | settecènto |
| 18 | diciòtto | 800 | ottocènto |
| 19 | diciannòve | 900 | novecènto |
| 20 | venti | 1,000 | mille |
| 21 | ventuno, ventuna | 2,000 | duemila |
| 22 | ventidue | 3,000 | tremila |
| 28 | ventòtto | 100,000 | centomila |
| 30 | trenta | 1,000,000 | un milione |
| 31 | trentuno, trentuna | 2,000,000 | due milioni |

## Ordinal

| | |
|---|---|
| 1st primo | 15th decimoquinto or |
| 2nd secondo | quindicésimo |
| 3rd tèrzo | 16th decimosèsto or |
| 4th quarto | sedicésimo |
| 5th quinto | 17th decimosèttimo or |
| 6th sèsto | diciassettésimo |
| 7th sèttimo | 18th decimottavo or |
| 8th ottavo | diciottésimo |
| 9th nòno | 19th decimonòno or |
| 10th dècimo | diciannovésimo |
| 11th decimoprimo or | 20th ventésimo |
| undicésimo | 21st ventésimoprimo |
| 12th decimosecondo or | 30th trentésimo |
| dodicésimo | 40th quarantésimo |
| 13th decimotèrzo or | 100th centésimo |
| tredicésimo | 1000th millésimo |
| 14th decimoquarto or | |
| quattordicésimo | |

# Abbreviations

| | |
|---|---|
| *abbr.* | abbreviation |
| *adj.* | adjective |
| *adv.* | adverb |
| *Amer.* | American |
| *Brit.* | British |
| *comm.* | commercial |
| *conj.* | conjunction |
| *eccles.* | ecclesiastical |
| *econ.* | economics |
| *f.* | feminine |
| *fam.* | familiar |
| *fig.* | figuratively |
| *geom.* | geometry |
| *gram.* | grammar; grammatical |
| *interj.* | interjection |
| *intr.* | intransitive |
| *lit.* | literally |
| *m.* | masculine |
| *math.* | mathematics |
| *med.* | medicine |
| *mil.* | military |
| *n.* | noun |
| *naut.* | nautical |
| *num.* | number |
| *pl.* | plural |
| *pred.* | predicate |
| *prep.* | preposition |
| *pron.* | pronoun; pronunciation |
| *refl.* | reflexive |
| *sg.* | singular |
| *tr.* | transitive (used only with verbs which also have reflexive use to indicate intransitive meaning) |
| *typogr.* | typography |
| *vb.* | verb |

# ITALIAN - ENGLISH

# A

**a,** *prep.* at; in; to; by.
**àbaco,** *n.m.* abacus.
**abate,** *n.m.* abbot.
**abbàcchio,** *n.m.* lamb.
**abbagliare,** *vb.* dazzle.
**abbaiamento,** *n.m.* bark; barking.
**abbaiare,** *vb.* bark, bay.
**abbaìno,** *n.m.* dormer.
**abbandonare,** *vb.* abandon, forsake, relinquish, vacate.
**abbandonato,** *adj.* abandoned.
**abbandono,** *n.m.* abandon, abandonment.
**abbassamento,** *n.m.* lowering, abasement.
**abbassare,** *vb.* lower, abase; debase; (*refl.*) stoop; subside.
**abbassato,** *adj.* lowered, downcast.
**abbastanza,** *adv.* enough.
**abbàttere,** *vb.* knock down, fell; dishearten; (*refl.*) droop.
**abbattimento,** *n.m.* disheartenment, dismay, dejection.
**abbattuto,** *adj.* despondent.
**abbazìa,** *n.f.* abbey.
**abbellimento,** *n.m.* embellishment.
**abbellire,** *vb.* beautify, embellish.
**abbigliare,** *vb.* dress up, accouter.
**abbigliatura,** *n.f.* accouterments.
**abbonacciare,** *vb.* becalm.
**abbonamento,** *n.m.* subscription. **biglietto d'a.,** season ticket.
**abbonarsi,** *vb.* subscribe.
**abbondante,** *adj.* abundant, plentiful.

**abbondantemente,** *adv.* abundantly.
**abbondanza,** *n.f.* abundance, plenty.
**abbondare,** *vb.* abound.
**abbordare,** *vb.* accost.
**abborracciare,** *vb.* bungle.
**abbozzare,** *vb.* sketch.
**abbòzzo,** *n.m.* sketch, draft.
**abbracciare,** *vb.* embrace, clasp, hug.
**abbràccio,** *n.m.* embrace, clasp, hug.
**abbreviamento,** *n.m.* abridgement.
**abbreviare,** *vb.* abbreviate, abridge, shorten.
**abbreviatura,** *n.f.* abbreviation.
**abbronzare,** *vb.* tan.
**abbronzato,** *adj.* sunburnt.
**abbronzatura,** *n.f.* sunburn, tan.
**abbrustolire,** *vb.* toast.
**abbrutire,** *vb.* brutalize.
**abdicare,** *vb.* abdicate.
**abdicazione,** *n.f.* abdication.
**aberrante,** *adj.* aberrant.
**aberrare,** *vb.* be aberrant.
**aberrazione,** *n.f.* aberration.
**abete,** *n.m.* fir.
**abiètto,** *adj.* abject.
**àbile,** *adj.* skilful, clever, able, adroit, capable, cunning, deft.
**abilità,** *n.f.* ability, skill, cleverness, adeptness, cunning.
**abilmente,** *adv.* skilfully, ably, adeptly, capably.
**Abissinia,** *n.f.* Abyssinia.
**abissino,** *n. and adj.,* Abyssinian.
**abisso,** *n.m.* abyss, chasm.
**abitàbile,** *adj.* habitable.

---

For pronunciation, see the concise guide on pages 5 to 7.

**abitante,** *n.m.* inhabitant, dweller, resident.

**abitare,** *vb.* live, dwell, re-side, inhabit.

**abitazione,** *n.f.* dwelling, ha-bitation, residence.

**àbito,** *n.m.* dress, suit, habit.

**abituale,** *adj.* habitual, usual, accustomed.

**abituare,** *vb.* accustom, ha-bituate.

**abituarsi a,** *vb.* get accus-tomed to.

**abitùdine,** *n.f.* habit.

**abiura,** *n.f.* abjuration.

**abiurare,** *vb.* abjure.

**ablativo,** *n.m. and adj.* abla-tive.

**abluzione,** *n.f.* ablution.

**abnegare,** *vb.* abnegate.

**abnegazione,** *n.f.* abnega-tion.

**abolimento,** *n.m.* aboli-tion.

**abolire,** *vb.* abolish.

**abominare,** *vb.* abominate, loathe.

**abominazione,** *n.f.* abomi-nation.

**abominévole,** *adj.* abomi-nable, loathsome.

**aborrimento,** *n.m.* abhor-rence.

**aborrire,** *vb.* abhor.

**abortire,** *vb.* abort; be abortive.

**abortivo,** *adj.* abortive.

**aborto,** *n.m.* abortion.

**abrasione,** *n.f.* abrasion.

**abrasivo,** *n.m. and adj.* abra-sive.

**abrogare,** *vb.* abrogate.

**abrogazione,** *n.f.* abroga-tion.

**àbside,** *n.f.* apse.

**a buòn mercato,** *adv.* cheap; cheaply.

**abusare di,** *vb* abuse, mis-use.

**abusivamente,** *adv.* abu-sively.

**abusivo,** *adj.* abusive.

**abuso,** *n.m.* abuse.

**acanto.** *n.m.* acanthus.

**a cavalcioni,** *adv.* astride.

**accadèmia,** *n.f.* academy.

**accadèmico,** *adj.* academic.

**accadere,** *vb.* happen, befall, occur, take place.

**accamparsi,** *vb* camp, en-camp.

**accampamento,** *n.m.* camp, encampment.

**accanto,** *adv.* beside, along-side.

**accanto a,** *prep.* beside, next to, alongside.

**accantonamento,** *n m.* can-tonment.

**accaparrare,** *vb.* corner.

**accarezzare,** *vb* caress, fon-dle, stroke.

**accecare,** *vb.* blind.

**accelerare,** *vb.* accelerate, speed up.

**accelerato,** *n.m.* local.

**acceleratore,** *n.m.* accelera-tor.

**accelerazione,** *n.f.* accelera-tion.

**accèndere,** *vb.* light, switch on, ignite, kindle.

**accendisigaro,** *n.m.* cigar-lighter, cigarette-lighter.

**accennare,** *vb* hint.

**accensione,** *n.f.* ignition.

**accentare,** *vb.* accent, stress.

**accènto,** *n.m.* accent, stress.

**accentuare,** *vb.* accent.

**accerchiare,** *vb.* encircle, ring around.

**accertarsi,** *vb.* ascertain.

**accessìbile,** *adj.* accessible.

**accèsso,** *n.m.* access, ap-proach; fit.

**accessòrio, 1.** *n.m.* accessory attachment. **2.** *adj.* acces-sory; adjunct.

**accetta,** *n.f.* hatchet.

**accettàbile,** *adj.* acceptable.

**accettabilità,** *n.f.* accepta-bility.

**accettabilmente,** *adv.* ac-ceptably.

**accettare,** *vb.* accept.

**accettazione,** *n.f.* accept-ance.

**accètto,** *adj.* acceptable.

**acciaio,** *n.m.* steel.

**accidentale,** *adj.* accidental.

**accidentalmente,** *adv.* acci-dentally.

**accigliato,** *adj.* frowning, glum.

**acciuga,** *n.f.* anchovy.

**acclamare,** *vb.* acclaim.

**acclamazione,** *n.f.* acclama-tion.

**acclimare,** *vb.* acclimate.

**acclimatare,** *vb.* acclimate.

**acclività,** *n.f.* acclivity.

**acclùdere,** *vb.* enclose.

---

For pronunciation, see the concise guide on pages 5 to 7.

accoglienza, n.f. reception.

accògliere, vb. receive, entertain.

accòlito, n.m. acolyte.

accollata, n.f. accolade.

accomodante, adj. accommodating.

accomodare, vb. accommodate; mend; (refl.) make oneself comfortable; compromise.

accomodazione, n.f. accommodation.

accompagnamento, n.m. accompaniment.

accompagnare, vb. accompany.

accompagnatore, n.m. accompanist.

acconciare, vb. fix.

acconciatura, n.f. hair-do.

accondiscendènza, n.f. condescension.

accondiscéndere, vb. condescend.

acconsentire, vb. consent.

accontentare, vb. content.

accoppiare, vb. couple; mate.

accorciare, vb. shorten, curtail.

accordare, vb. tune.

accòrdo, n.m. agreement, accord; compact; concord; chord. d'a., in agreement.

accosciarsi, vb. squat.

accreditare, vb. accredit.

accréscere, vb. accrue, increase, boost, enhance, heighten.

accrescimento, n.m. increase, accretion, accrual, boost.

accucciarsi, vb. crouch.

accumulare, vb. accumulate.

accumulativo, adj. accumulative.

accumulatore, n.m. battery, accumulator.

accumulazione, n.f. accumulation.

accuratamente, adv. accurately, carefully.

accuratezza, n.f. accuracy, carefulness.

accurato, adj. accurate, careful.

accusa, n.f. accusation, indictment.

accusare, vb. accuse, arraign, indict. a. ricevuta

di, acknowledge receipt of.

accusativo, n.m. and adj., accusative.

accusato, n.m. accused.

accusatore, n.m. accuser.

acerbità, n.f. acerbity.

acèrbo, adj. sour, unripe.

àcero, n.m. maple.

acetato, n.m. acetate.

acètico, adj. acetic.

acetilène, n.m. acetylene.

aceto, n.m. vinegar.

acidificare, vb. acidify.

acidità, n.f. acidity.

àcido, n.m. and adj. acid sour.

acidòsi, n.f. acidosis.

acìdulo, adj. acidulous.

acme, n.f. acme.

acne, n.f. acne.

acqua, n.f. water.

acquafòrte, n.f. etching.

acquàio, n.m. sink.

acquarèllo, n.m. watercolor.

acquàrio, n.m. aquarium.

acquàtico, adj. aquatic.

acquavite, n.f. brandy.

acquazzone, n.m. heavy shower, cloudburst.

acquedotto, n.m. aqueduct.

àqueo, adj. aqueous.

acquetare, vb. appease, quiet.

acquiescenza, n.f. acquiescence.

acquietarsi, vb. calm down, acquiesce.

acquisitivo, adj. acquisitive.

acquistare, vb. acquire.

acquisto, n.m. acquisition.

acre, adj. acrid, acrimonious.

acre, adj. tart.

acrèdine, n.f. acrimony.

acrimònia, n.f. acrimony.

acro, n.m. acre.

acròbata, n.m. acrobat.

acròstico, n.m. acrostic.

acume, n.m. acumen.

acùstica, n.f. acoustics.

acutamente, adv. acutely, sharply.

acutezza, n.f. acuteness, sharpness.

acuto, adj. acute, sharp, keen, pointed, shrewd.

ad, prep. at; in; to; by.

adàgio, 1. n.m. adage. 2. adv. slowly; gently.

adamantino, adj. adamant.

adattàbile, adj. adaptable.

**adattabilità**, *n.f.* adaptability.

**adattamento**, *n.* adaptation; fitting.

**adattare**, *vb.* adapt.

**adattévole**, *adj.* adaptive.

**adatto**, *adj.* fit, suitable.

**addetto**, **1.** *n.m.* attaché. **2.** *adj.* assigned, employed.

**addio**, *interj.* hello; good-bye, adieu, farewell.

**additare**, *vb.* point out.

**addizionale**, *adj.* additional.

**addizionare**, *vb.* add.

**addizione**, *n.f.* addition.

**addolorare**, *vb.* grieve, *tr.*; (*refl.*) sorrow.

**addolorato**, *adj.* sorrowful.

**addòme**, *n.m.* abdomen.

**addomesticare**, *vb.* tame.

**addomesticato**, *adj.* tame.

**addominale**, *adj.* abdominal.

**addormentarsi**, *vb.* fall asleep.

**addottrinare**, *vb.* indoctrinate.

**addurre**, *vb.* lead up, bring up, adduce.

**adequatamente**, *adv.* adequately.

**adequato**, *adj.* adequate.

**adenòide**, *adj.* adenoid.

**aderènte**, *n.m.* adherent, member (of association, etc.).

**aderènza**, *n.f.* adherence, support; relation.

**aderire**, *vb.* adhere, cling, stick, support, join.

**adescare**, *vb.* allure, entice, lure.

**adescatore**, *adj.* alluring.

**adesione**, *n.f.* adhesion; intention to join (association, etc.).

**adesività**, *n.f.* adhesiveness.

**adesivo**, *n.m. and adj.*, adhesive.

**adèsso**, *adv.* now.

**adiacènte**, *adj.* adjacent, adjoining.

**adirarsi**, *vb.* get angry.

**adirato**, *adj.* angry, cross.

**adolescènte**, *n. and adj.* adolescent.

**adolescènza**, *n.f.* adolescence.

**adoperare**, *vb.* use.

**adoràbile**, *adj.* adorable.

**adorare**, *vb.* adore, worship.

**adorazione**, *n.f.* adoration, worship.

**adornamento**, *n.m.* adornment.

**adorno**, *adj.* adorned.

**adottare**, *vb.* adopt.

**adozione**, *n.f.* adoption.

**adrenalina**, *n.f.* adrenalin.

**adulare**, *vb.* adulate, flatter, fawn upon.

**adulatore**, *n.m.* flatterer.

**adulazione**, *n.f.* adulation, flattery.

**adùltera**, *n.f.* adulteress.

**adulterante**, *n. and adj.* adulterant.

**adulterare**, *vb.* to adulterate.

**adultèrio**, *n.m.* adultery.

**adùltero**, *n.m.* adulterer.

**adulto**, *n.* (*m.*) *and adj.* adult, grown-up.

**adunata**, *n.f.* gathering, meeting.

**aerare**, *vb.* aerate, air.

**aerazione**, *n.f.* aeration.

**aèreo**, **1.** *n.* aircraft, airplane. **2.** *adj.* aerial.

**aeronàutica**, *n.f.* aeronautics.

**affàbile**, *adj.* affable.

**aerodinàmico**, *adj.* streamlined.

**aeroplano**, *n.m.* airplane.

**aeropòrto**, *n.m.* airport.

**aeroscalo**, *n.m* airport.

**affabilità**, *n.f.* affability.

**affabilmente**, *adv.* affably.

**affaccendato**, *adj.* busy.

**affamato**, *adj.* famished, ravenous.

**affare**, *n.m.* affair, concern; bargain, deal; (*pl.*) business.

**affascinante**, *adj.* fascinating, glamorous.

**affascinare**, *vb.* fascinate, allure, captivate, charm.

**affaticare**, *vb.* fatigue.

**afferènte**, *adj.* afferent.

**affermare**, *vb.* affirm, state.

**affermativamente**, *adv.* affirmatively.

**affermativo**, *adj.* affirmative.

**affermazione**, *n.f.* affirmation, statement.

**afferrare**, *vb.* grasp, grip, seize, catch, snatch.

**affettare**, *vb.* affect; slice.

**affettato**, *adj.* affected; finicky, prim.

**affettazione,** *n.f.* affectation; frill.

**affettuosamente,** *adv.* affectionately.

**affettuoso,** *adj.* affectionate.

**affezione,** *n.f.* affection, attachment.

**affibbiare,** *vb.* buckle.

**affidare,** *vb.* entrust.

**affiggere,** *vb.* post.

**affigliare,** *vb.* affiliate.

**affigliazione,** *n.f.* affiliation.

**affine,** *adj.* related, akin, allied.

**affinità,** *n.f.* affinity.

**affissare,** *vb.* affix.

**affisso,** *n.m.* affix.

**affittare,** *vb.* lease, let, rent.

**affitto,** *n.m.* lease, rent.

**affliggere,** *vb.* afflict, distress.

**afflizione,** *n.f.* affliction, distress.

**affluènte,** *n.m.* tributary.

**affluire,** *vb.* rush.

**afflusso,** *n.m.* rush.

**affollare,** *vb.* crowd.

**affollarsi,** *vb.* come together in crowds, flock.

**affondare,** *vb.* sink.

**affrancare,** *vb.* enfranchise.

**affrancatura,** *n.f.* postage.

**affresco,** *n.m.* fresco.

**affrettare,** *vb.* hasten, haste, hurry, quicken, speed.

**affrettatamente,** *adv.* hastily.

**affrettato,** *adj.* hasty.

**affrontare,** *vb.* face.

**aforismo,** *n.m.* aphorism.

**affrontare,** *vb.* face, go to meet; affront, insult.

**affronto,** *n.m.* affront, insult.

**Àfrica,** *n.f.* Àirica.

**africano,** *n.* and *adj.* African.

**àgata,** *n.f.* agate.

**àgave,** *n.f.* century plant.

**agènda,** *n.f.* note-book.

**agènte,** *n.m.* agent. **a. di càmbio,** stockbroker.

**agenzia,** *n.f.* agency.

**agganciare,** *vb.* clasp.

**aggettivo,** *n.m.* adjective.

**aggiornamento,** *n.m.* adjournment.

**aggiornare,** *vb.* adjourn; bring up to date.

**aggiùngere,** *vb.* add.

**aggiunto, 1.** *n.* and *adj.* adjunct. **2.** *adj.* added, extra.

**aggiustamento,** *n.m.* adjustment.

**aggiustare,** *vb.* adjust.

**aggiustatore,** *n.m.* adjuster.

**aggiustatura,** *n.f.* adjustment.

**agglutinare,** *vb.* agglutinate.

**agglutinazione,** *n.f.* agglutination.

**aggravamento,** *n.m.* aggravation.

**aggravare,** *vb.* aggravate.

**aggregare,** *vb.* aggregate.

**aggregato,** *n.m.* aggregate.

**aggregazione,** *n.f.* aggregation.

**aggressione,** *n.f.* aggression.

**aggressivamente,** *adv.* aggressively.

**aggressività,** *n.f.* aggressiveness.

**aggressivo,** *adj.* aggressive.

**aggressore,** *n.m.* aggressor.

**aggrottare,** *vb.* wrinkle. **a. le ciglia,** frown, scowl.

**aggrovigliare,** *vb.* snarl, tangle.

**àgile,** *n.f.* agile, nimble.

**agilità,** *n.f.* agility.

**àgio,** *n.m.* ease, leisure.

**agire,** *vb.* act.

**agitare,** *vb.* agitate; wave, flourish; stir. (*refl.*) fidget, toss.

**agitatore,** *n.m.* agitator.

**agitazione,** *n.f.* agitation.

**àglio,** *n.m.* garlic.

**agnèllo,** *n.m.* lamb.

**agnòstico,** *n.* and *adj.* agnostic.

**ago,** *n.f.* needle. **a. da rammendo,** darning-needle.

**agonìa,** *n.f.* agony.

**agonizzante,** *adj.* agonized.

**agonizzare,** *vb.* be in agony.

**agosto,** *n.m.* August.

**agràrio,** *adj.* agrarian.

**agricoltore,** *n.m.* farmer.

**agricultura,** *n.f.* agriculture, farming.

**agrifòglio,** *n.m.* holly.

**agrimensore,** *n.m.* surveyor.

**aguzzare,** *vb.* sharpen.

**ahi,** *interj.* ouch!

**Aia,** *n.f.* **l'A.,** The Hague.

**airone,** *n.m.* heron.

**aiutante,** *n.m.* assistant, helper, adjutant, aide.

**aiutare,** *vb.* help, aid, assist, befriend.

**aiuto,** *n.m.* help, aid, assistance.

**ala,** *n.f.* wing.

**alacrità,** *n.f.* alacrity.

**alambicco,** *n.m.* still.

**alba,** *n.f.* dawn, daybreak.

**albèrgo,** *n.m.* hotel, hostelry.

**àlbero,** *n.m.* tree; mast, shaft, spar.

**albicòcca,** *n.f.* apricot.

**albino,** *n.m. and adj.* albino.

**album,** *n.m.* album.

**albume,** *n.m.* albumen.

**àlcali,** *n.m.* alkali.

**alcalino,** *adj.* alkaline.

**alce,** *n.m.* elk.

**àlcole,** *n.m.* alcohol.

**àlcool,** *n.m.* alcohol.

**alc(o)òlico,** *adj.* alcoholic.

**alcòva,** *n.f.* alcove.

**alcuni,** *adj.* some.

**alfabètico,** *adj.* alphabetical.

**alfabèto,** *n.m.* alphabet.

**alfalfa,** *n.f.* alfalfa.

**alfière,** *n.m.* ensign.

**àlgebra,** *n.f.* algebra.

**àlias,** *adv.* alias.

**aliante,** *n.m.* glider.

**àlibi,** *n.m.* alibi.

**alienare,** *vb.* alienate, estrange.

**alièno,** *adj.* alien, foreign, strange.

**alimentare,** *vb.* feed, nourish.

**alimentare,** *adj.* pertaining to food, alimentary.

**alimentàrio,** *adj.* alimentary.

**alimento,** *n.m.* food, nourishment.

**allacciare,** *vb.* enlace.

**allargare,** *vb.* broaden, widen.

**allarmare,** *vb.* alarm, startle.

**allarme,** *n.m.* alarm, alert.

**allarmista,** *n.m.* alarmist.

**alleanza,** *n.f.* alliance.

**alleare,** *vb.* ally.

**alleato, 1.** *n.m.* ally. **2.** *adj.* allied.

**allegare,** *vb.* allege.

**allegazione,** *n.f.* allegation.

**alleggerire,** *vb.* lighten.

**allegoria,** *n.f.* allegory.

**allegria,** *n.f.* merriment, cheerfulness, mirth.

**allegro,** *adj.* lively, merry, cheerful, frisky, jolly.

**allenare,** *vb.* train, coach.

**allenatore,** *n.m.* trainer, coach.

**allentamento,** *n.m.* letdown.

**allentare,** *vb.* loosen, relax.

**allergia,** *n.f.* allergy.

**allevare,** *vb.* train, breed, foster, nurture, raise, rear.

**allevatore,** *n.m.* trainer, breeder.

**alleviare,** *vb.* alleviate, allay, relieve.

**allietare,** *vb.* gladden.

**alligatore,** *n.m.* alligator.

**allineare,** *vb.* align, line up.

**allòdola,** *n.f.* lark.

**alloggiare,** *vb.* lodge, put up, accommodate, billet.

**allòggio,** *n.m.* lodging, accommodation, billet.

**allontanarsi,** *vb.* go away, stray.

**allora,** *adv.* then.

**allòro,** *n.m.* laurel.

**allucinazione,** *n.f.* hallucination.

**allume,** *n.m.* alum.

**allumìnio,** *n.m.* aluminum.

**allùdere,** *vb.* allude.

**allungare,** *vb.* lengthen, elongate; reach out.

**allusione,** *n.f.* allusion, reference.

**almanacco,** *n.m.* almanac.

**Alpi,** *n.f.* (*pl.*) Alps.

**alpino,** *adj.* Alpine.

**alt,** *interj.* halt!

**altalena,** *n.f.* seesaw; swing.

**altamente,** *adj.* highly.

**altare,** *n.m.* altar.

**alterare,** *vb.* alter.

**alterazione,** *n.f.* alteration.

**alternare,** *vb.* alternate.

**alternativa,** *n.f.* alternative.

**alternativo,** *adj.* alternative, alternate.

**altezza,** *n.f.* height; Highness.

**altitùdine,** *n.f.* altitude.

**alto,** *adj.* high, lofty, tall; loud. **in a.,** *adv.* on high, aloft.

**altoparlante,** *n.m.* loudspeaker.

**altopiano,** *n.m.* plateau.

**altrimenti,** *adv.* otherwise, else.

**altro,** *adj.* other, else.

**altrove,** *adv.* elsewhere.

**altruismo,** *n.m.* altruism.

---

For pronunciation, see the concise guide on pages 5 to 7.

**altura**, *n.f.* height.
**alunno**, *n.m.* pupil.
**alveare**, *n.m.* beehive.
**alzaia**, *n.f.* hawser.
**alzare**, *vb.* raise.
**alzarsi**, *vb.* get up rise.
**amàbile**, *adj.* amiable, likeable, lovable.
**amaca**, *n.f.* hammock.
**amàlgama** *n.m.* amalgam.
**amalgamare**, *vb.* amalgamate.
**amante**, **1.** *n.m.* lover; *f.* mistress. **2.** *adj.* fond.
**amaramente**, *adv.* bitterly.
**amare**, *vb.* love.
**amareggiare**, *vb.* embitter.
**amarezza**, *n.f.* bitterness.
**amaro**, *adj.* bitter.
**ambasciata**, *n.f.* embassy; message.
**ambasciatore**, *n.m.* ambassador.
**ambedue**, *adj. and pron.* both.
**ambidestro**, *adj.* ambidextrous.
**ambiènte**, *n.m.* environment, habitat.
**ambiguità**, *n.f.* ambiguity.
**ambiguo**, *adj.* ambiguous.
**ambizione**, *n.f.* ambition.
**ambizioso**, *adj.* ambitious.
**ambra**, *nf.* amber.
**ambulanza**, *n.f.* ambulance.
**ambulatòrio**, *n. and adj.* ambulatory.
**Amburgo**, *n.m.* Hamburg.
**amèba**, *n.f.* amoeba.
**amenità**, *n.f.* amenity.
**América**, *n.f.* America.
**americano**, *n. and adj.* American.
**ametista**, *n.f.* amethyst.
**amica**, *n.f.* friend.
**amichévole**, *adj.* friendly, amicable.
**amichevolezza**, *n.f.* friendliness.
**amicìzia**, *n.f.* friendship, amity.
**amico**, **1.** *n.m.* friend. **2.** *adj.* friendly.
**àmido**, *n.m.* starch.
**ammaccare**, *vb.* bruise.
**ammaccatura**, *n.f.* bruise.
**ammalato**, *adj.* sick.
**ammaliare**, *vb.* bewitch.
**ammassare**, *vb.* amass, hoard; lump.
**ammasso**, *n.m.* hoard, pile.

**ammènda**, *n.f.* fine.
**amméttere**, *vb.* admit.
**ammiccare**, *vb.* wink.
**amministrare**, *vb.* administer, manage.
**amministrativo**, *adj.* administrative.
**amministratore**, *n.m.* administrator, executive, manager.
**amministrazione**, *n.f.* administration, management.
**ammiràbile**, *adj.* admirable.
**ammirabilmente**, *adv.* admirably.
**ammiràglia**, *adj.* **nave ammiràglia**, flagship.
**ammiragliato**, *n.m.* admiralty.
**ammiraglio**, *n.m.* admiral.
**ammirare**, *vb.* admire.
**ammiratore**, *n.m.* admirer.
**ammirazione**, *n.f.* admiration.
**ammirévole**, *adj.* admirable.
**ammissìbile**, *adj.* admissible.
**ammissione**, *n.f.* admission, admittance.
**ammobiliare**, *vb.* furnish.
**ammollire**, *vb.* soften, mollify.
**ammonimento**, *n.m.* warning.
**ammonire**, *vb.* admonish, warn.
**ammonizione**, *n.f.* admonition.
**ammontare**, *vb.* amount.
**ammoniaca**, *n.f.* ammonia.
**ammonire**, *vb.* warn, caution.
**ammorbidire**, *vb.* soften; baste.
**ammortire**, *vb.* deaden.
**ammortizzare**, *vb.* amortize.
**ammucchiare**, *vb.* heap, pile, stack.
**ammuffito**, *adj.* musty.
**ammutinamento**, *n.m.* mutiny.
**ammutinarsi**, *vb.* mutiny.
**amnesia**, *n.f.* amnesia.
**amnistìa**, *n.f.* amnesty.
**amorale**, *adj.* amoral.
**amore**, *n.m.* love.
**amorfo**, *adj.* amorphous.
**amoroso**, *adj.* amorous, of love.
**amovìbile**, *adj.* removable.

**ampère,** *n.m.* ampere.

**ampiezza,** *n.f.* breadth.

**ampio,** *adj.* ample; extensive; broad, wide.

**amplèsso,** *n.m.* (sexual) embrace.

**ampliare,** *vb.* amplify.

**amplificare,** *vb.* amplify.

**ampollina,** *n.f.* cruet.

**ampolloso,** *adj.* stilted.

**amputare,** *vb.* amputate.

**amputato, 1.** *n.m.* amputee. **2.** *adj.* amputated.

**anacronismo,** *n.m.* anachronism.

**analfabèta,** *n. and adj.* illiterate.

**analfabetismo,** *n.m.* illiteracy.

**anàlisi,** *n.f.* analysis.

**analista,** *n.m.* analyst.

**analìtico,** *adj.* analytic.

**analizzare,** *vb.* analyze.

**analogìa,** *n.f.* analogy.

**anàlogo,** *adj.* analogous.

**ananàs,** *n.m.* pineapple.

**anarchìa,** *n.f.* anarchy.

**anatomìa,** *n.f.* anatomy.

**anca,** *n.f.* haunch, hip.

**ancella,** *n.f.* handmaid.

**anche,** *adv.* also, too; even.

**anchilòstoma,** *n.m.* hookworm.

**ància,** *n.f* reed.

**ancora,** *adv.* still, yet.

**àncora,** *n.f* anchor.

**ancorare,** *vb.* anchor.

**ancoraggio,** *n.m.* anchorage.

**andare,** *vb.* go; fare; be (health). **a bene a.** fit; become. **a. a zonzo,** loaf, loiter, lounge; saunter.

**andàrsene,** *vb.* go away.

**andatura,** *n.f.* gait.

**anèddoto,** *n.m.* anecdote.

**anèllo,** *n.m.* ring, link.

**anelare,** *vb.* pant.

**anèllo,** *n.m.* ring.

**anemìa,** *n.f.* anemia.

**anestesia,** *n.f.* anesthesia.

**anestètico,** *n.m. and adj.,* anesthetic.

**anestetista,** *n.m.* anesthetist.

**aneto,** *n.m.* dill.

**anfìbio, 1.** *n.m.* amphibian. **2.** *adj.* amphibious.

**anfiteatro,** *n.m.* amphitheater.

**àngelo,** *n.m.* angel.

**angolare,** *adj.* angular.

**àngolo,** *n.m.* angle, corner.

**angòscia,** *n.f.* anguish, heartache.

**anguilla,** *n.f.* eel.

**ànice,** *n.m.* anise.

**anile,** *n.m.* anil, bluing.

**anilina,** *n.f.* aniline.

**ànima,** *n.f.* soul.

**animale,** *n.m. and adj.* animal.

**animare,** *vb.* animate.

**animazione,** *n.f.* animation.

**ànimo,** *n.m.* spirit, animus, mind.

**animosità,** *n.f.* animosity.

**ànitra,** *n.f.* duck.

**annali,** *n.m.* (*pl.*) annals.

**annegare,** *vb.* drown.

**annerire,** *vb.* blacken.

**annessione,** *n.f.* annexation.

**annèsso,** *n.m.* annex.

**annèttere,** *vb.* annex.

**annichilire,** *vb.* annihilate.

**annidarsi,** *vb.* nestle.

**anniversàrio,** *n.m.* anniversary.

**anno,** *n.m.* year.

**annobilire,** *vb.* ennoble.

**annoiare,** *vb.* annoy, bore, harass.

**annotare,** *vb.* annotate.

**annotazione,** *n.f.* annotation.

**annuale,** *n.m. and adj.* annual, yearly.

**annualità,** *n.f.* annuity.

**annunciare,** *vb.* announce.

**annunciatore,** *n.m.* announcer.

**annunciatrice,** *n.f.* announcer.

**ànnuo,** *adj.* annual.

**annullamento,** *n.m.* annulment, cancellation, nullification.

**annullare,** *vb.* annual, cancel, nullify.

**annunziare,** *vb.* announce.

**annunzio,** *n.m.* announcement, advertisement.

**ànodo,** *n.m.* anode.

**anomalìa,** *n.f.* anomaly.

**anòmalo,** *adj.* anomalous.

**anònimo,** *adj.* anonymous.

**anormale,** *adj.* abnormal.

**anormalità,** *n.f.* abnormality.

**anormalmente,** *adv.* abnormally.

**ansando,** *adv.* panting, breathlessly.

For pronunciation, see the concise guide on pages 5 to 7.

**ansante,** *adj.* panting, out of breath.

**ansare,** *vb.* pant, be out of breath

**ànsia,** *n.f.* anxiety.

**ansietà,** *n.f.* anxiety, concern, worry.

**ansioso,** *adj.* anxious.

**antico,** *adj.* ancient, antique.

**antàcido,** *n.m.* antacid.

**antagonismo,** *n.m.* antagonism.

**antagonista,** *n.m.* antagonist, opponent, villain.

**antàrtico,** *n.m. and adj.* antarctic.

**antecedente,** *adj.* antecedent.

**antenato,** *n.m.* ancestor, forebear, forefather.

**antenna,** *n.f.* antenna; (radio) aerial.

**anteprima,** *n.f.* preview.

**anteriore,** *adj.* anterior, previous, fore.

**antiàcido,** *adj.* antacid.

**antiaèreo,** *adj.* antiaircraft.

**anticamente,** *adv.* in ancient times, formerly.

**anticàmera,** *n.f.* anteroom.

**anticipare,** *vb.* anticipate; advance (payment).

**anticipato,** *adj.* anticipated, foregone.

**anticipazione,** *n.f.* anticipation.

**antìcipo,** *n.m.* advance payment; down payment; **in anticipo,** beforehand.

**anticlericale,** *adj.* anticlerical.

**antico,** *adj.* ancient, antique.

**anticòrpo,** *n.m.* antibody.

**antìdoto,** *n.m.* antidote.

**antìfona,** *n.f.* anthem.

**antìlope,** *n.f.* antelope.

**antimònio,** *n.m.* antimony.

**antipasto,** *n.m.* hors d'oeuvres, appetizer.

**antipatìa,** *n.f.* antipathy, dislike.

**antipàtico,** *adj.* disagreeable, nasty.

**antiquato,** *adj.* antiquated.

**antiquità,** *n.f.* antiquity.

**antisèttico,** *n.m. and adj.* antiseptic.

**antisociale,** *adj.* antisocial.

**antitossina,** *n.f.* antitoxin.

**antologìa,** *n.f.* anthology.

**antrace,** *n.m.* anthrax.

**antracite,** *n.f.* anthracite.

**antropologìa,** *n.f.* anthropology.

**antropològico,** *adj.* anthropological.

**apatìa,** *n.f.* apathy.

**apàtico,** *adj.* apathetic.

**ape,** *n.f.* bee.

**apèrto,** *adj.* open, overt.

**apertura,** *n.f.* opening, aperture, gap.

**apiàrio,** *n.m.* apiary.

**àpice,** *n.m.* apex.

**apiàrio,** *n.m.* apiary.

**àpice,** *n.m.* apex.

**apogèo,** *n.m.* apogee, high point, heyday.

**apologìa,** *n.f.* apology.

**apoplessìa,** *n.f.* apoplexy.

**apoplèttico,** *adj.* apoplectic.

**apòstata,** *n.m.* apostate.

**apostòlico,** *adj.* apostolic.

**apòstolo,** *n.m.* apostle.

**appaciamento,** *n.m.* appeasement.

**appannare,** *vb.* tarnish.

**appannatura,** *n.f.* tarnish.

**apparato,** *n.m.* apparatus.

**apparècchio,** *n.m.* apparatus.

**apparènte,** *adj.* apparent.

**apparènza,** *n.f.* appearance, guise.

**apparire,** *vb.* appear.

**apparizione,** *n.f.* apparition.

**appartamento,** *n.m.* apartment, flat.

**appartenènza,** *n.f.* belonging, appurtenance.

**appartenere,** *vb.* belong, pertain.

**appassionato,** *adj.* passionate.

**appassire,** *vb.* fade, wilt.

**appellante,** *n.m.* appellant.

**appellare,** *vb.* appeal.

**appèllo,** *n.m.* appeal, call, roll-call.

**appena,** *adv.* hardly, scarcely, just, barely.

**appendectomìa,** *n.f.* appendectomy.

**appendice,** *n.f.* appendix, appendage.

**appendicite,** *n.f.* appendicitis.

**appetito,** *n.m.* appetite.

**appezzamento,** *n.m.* lot, plot.

**appiattire,** *vb.* flatten.

**appicciare,** *vb.* stick.

For pronunciation, see the concise guide on pages 5 to 7.

**applaudire,** *vb.* applaud, cheer, clap.

**applàuso,** *n.m.* applause, cheer, plaudit.

**applicàbile,** *adj.* applicable.

**applicare,** *vb.* apply.

**applicazione,** *n.f.* application.

**appoggiare,** *vb.* support, back (up), lean.

**appòggio,** *n.m.* support, backing; foothold; footing; furtherance.

**appollaiarsi,** *vb.* roost, perch.

**apportare,** *vb.* bring, fetch.

**appòsta,** *adv.* on purpose, advisedly, deliberately.

**apposizione,** *n.f.* apposition.

**apprendista,** *n.m.* apprentice.

**apprezzàbile,** *adj.* appreciable.

**apprezzamento,** *n.m.* appreciation.

**apprezzare,** *vb.* appreciate, value, prize.

**approfittare,** *vb.* profit.

**approfondire,** *vb.* deepen.

**appropriato,** *adj.* appropriate.

**appropriarsi,** *vb.* appropriate.

**approssimare,** *vb.* approximate.

**approssimativo,** *adj.* approximate.

**approssimativamente,** *adv.* approximately.

**approssimazione,** *n.f.* approximation.

**approvare,** *vb.* approve.

**approvazione,** *n.f.* approval, approbation.

**appuntamento,** *n.m.* appointment, date, engagement, rendezvous, tryst.

**aprile,** *n.m.* April.

**aprire,** *vb.* open, unlock.

**apriscàtole,** *n.m.* can-opener.

**àquila,** *n.f.* eagle.

**aquilino,** *adj.* aquiline.

**aquilone,** *n.m.* kite.

**aquilòtto,** *n.m.* eaglet.

**aràbile,** *adj.* arable.

**àrabo, 1.** *n.* Arab. **2.** *adj.* Arabic.

**aràchide,** *n.f.* peanut.

**aragosta,** *n.f.* lobster.

**aràldica,** *n.f.* heraldry.

**aràldico,** *adj.* heraldic.

**araldo,** *n.m.* herald.

**arància,** *n.f.* orange.

**aranciata,** *n.f.* orangeade.

**aràncio,** *n.m.* orange tree.

**arare,** *vb.* plow.

**aratro,** *n.m.* plow.

**arbitrare,** *vb.* arbitrate.

**arbitràrio,** *adj.* arbitrary, high-handed.

**arbitrato,** *n.m.* arbitration.

**àrbitro,** *n.m.* arbiter, arbitrator, judge, referee, umpire.

**arbòreo,** *adj.* arboreal.

**arbusto,** *n.m.* shrub.

**arca,** *n.f.* ark.

**arcàico,** *adj.* archaic.

**archeologìa,** *n.f.* archaeology.

**archetto,** *n.m.* little bow. **gambe ad archetto,** bow legs.

**architetto,** *n.m.* architect.

**architettònico,** *adj.* architectural.

**architettura,** *n.f.* architecture.

**archiviare,** *vb.* file.

**archìvio,** *n.m.* archives, file.

**arcidiòcesi,** *n.f.* archdiocese.

**arciduca,** *n.m.* archduke.

**arciere,** *n.m.* archer.

**arcipèlago,** *n.m.* archipelago.

**arcivéscovo,** *n.m.* archbishop.

**arco,** *n.m.* arc, arch; bow. **tiro dell'a.,** archery.

**arcobaleno,** *n.m.* rainbow.

**ardènte,** *adj.* ardent, burning.

**àrdere,** *vb.* burn.

**ardèsia,** *n.f.* slate.

**ardimento,** *n.m.* boldness.

**ardire,** *vb.* be bold, dare.

**arditamente,** *adv.* boldly.

**ardito,** *adj.* bold.

**ardore,** *n.m.* ardor.

**àrduo,** *adj.* arduous, difficult.

**àrea,** *n.f.* area.

**àrem,** *n.m.* harem.

**arena,** *n.f.* sand, arena.

**arenarsi,** *vb.* get stranded.

**Argentina,** *n.f.* Argentine.

**argènteo,** *adj.* silvery.

**argenteo,** *adj.* silvery; Argentine.

**argènto,** *n.m.* silver.

**argilla,** *n.f.* clay.

**argilloso,** *adj.* clayey.

**àrgine,** *n.m.* embankment.

**argomento,** *n.m.* argument, topic.

**arguire,** vb. argue; deduce; conclude.

**ària,** n.f. air, (music) aria.

**aringa,** n.f. herring.

**arioso,** adj. airy.

**àrido,** adj. arid.

**aristocrate,** n.m. aristocrat.

**aristocràtico,** adj. aristocratic.

**aristocrazìa,** n.f. aristocracy.

**aritmètica,** n.f. arithmetic.

**Arlecchino,** n.m. Harlequin.

**arma,** n.f. arm (weapon). **a. da fuòco,** firearm.

**armàdio,** n.m. clothes-closet.

**armamento,** n.m. armament.

**armare,** vb. arm.

**armatura,** f. armor.

**armerìa,** n.f. armory.

**armistizio,** n.m. armistice.

**armonìa,** n.f. harmony.

**armònica,** n.f. harmonica.

**armònico,** adj. harmonic.

**armonioso,** adj. harmonious, dulcet.

**armonizzare,** vb. harmonize.

**àrnica,** n.f. arnica.

**aròma,** n.m. aroma.

**aromàtico,** adj. aromatic.

**arpa,** n.f. harp.

**arrabbiarsi,** vb. get angry.

**arrabbiato,** adj. angry.

**arraffare,** vb. grab.

**arrampicarsi,** vb. climb, creep, clamber up, scramble up.

**arrampicatore,** n.m. climber.

**arrèndersi,** vb. surrender.

**arrestare,** vb. arrest, apprehend; (refl.) stall.

**arrèsto,** n.m. arrest.

**arretrato,** adj. out-of-date.

**arricchire,** vb. enrich.

**arricciare,** vb. curl.

**arringa,** n.f. harangue.

**arringare,** vb. harangue.

**arrischiare,** vb. risk.

**arrivare,** vb. arrive.

**arrivista,** n.m. or f. social climber.

**arrivo,** n.m. arrival.

**arrogante,** adj. arrogant.

**rroganza,** n.f. arrogance.

**arrogarsi,** vb. arrogate, assume.

**arrolamento,** n.m. enlistment.

**arrolare,** vb. enlist.

**arrossire,** vb. blush.

**arrostire,** vb. roast.

**arròsto,** n.m. roast.

**arrotolare,** vb. roll up, coil.

**arruffare,** vb. ruffle, bristle.

**arrugginire,** vb. rust.

**arrugginito,** adj. rusty.

**arruolare,** vb. enroll; levy.

**arsenale,** n.m. arsenal; dockyard, navy yard.

**arsènico,** n.m. arsenic.

**arte,** n.f. art, trade, craft, craftsmanship, guild.

**artèria,** n.f. artery.

**arteriale,** adj. arterial.

**arteriosclerosi,** n.f. arteriosclerosis.

**artesiano,** adj. artesian.

**àrtico,** adj. Arctic.

**articolare,** vb. articulate.

**articolato,** adj. articulate.

**articolazione,** n.f. articulation; joint.

**articolo,** n.m. article, item. **a. di fondo,** editorial.

**artificiale,** adj. artificial.

**artificialità,** n.f. artificiality.

**artificio,** n.m. artifice.

**artigiano,** n.m. artisan, craftsman.

**artigliere,** n.m. gunner.

**artiglieria,** n.f. artillery.

**artiglio,** n.m. talon, claw.

**artista,** n.m. or f. artist.

**artistico,** adj. artistic.

**arto,** n.m. limb.

**artrite,** n.f. arthritis.

**arzillo,** adj. spry.

**asbèsto,** n.m. asbestos.

**ascèlla,** n.f. armpit.

**Ascensione,** n.f. (eccles.) Ascension, Assumption.

**ascensore,** n.m. elevator, lift.

**ascèsso,** n.m. abscess.

**ascètico,** n.m. and adj. ascetic.

**àscia,** n.f. axe.

**asciugamani,** n.m. handtowel.

**asciugapiatti,** n.m. dishtowel.

**asciugare,** vb. dry, blot, wipe.

**asciugatòio,** n.m. towel.

**asciutto,** adj. dry.

**ascoltare,** vb. listen to, hearken to, hark.

**ascrìvere,** vb. ascribe.

**asfalto,** n.m. asphalt.

**asfissìa,** n.f. asphyxia.

**asfissiare,** vb. asphyxiate, smother.

**Asia,** *n.f.* Asia.

**asiàtico,** *adj.* Asiatic.

**asimmetria,** *n.f.* asymmetry.

**àsino,** *n.m.* ass, donkey.

**asma,** *n.m.* asthma. **a. del fièno,** hay fever.

**asmàtico,** *adj.* asthmatic.

**aspàrago,** *n.m.* asparagus.

**asperità,** *n.f.* asperity.

**aspettare,** *vb.* await, wait (for); (*refl.*) expect.

**aspettativa,** *n.f.* expectation, expectancy.

**aspètto,** *n.m.* aspect, appearance, look; meaning.

**aspirante,** *n.m.* aspirant.

**aspirare,** *vb.* aspire, aspirate.

**aspirata,** *n.f.* aspirate (consonant).

**aspiratore,** *n.m.* aspirator.

**aspirazione,** *n.f.* aspiration, suction.

**aspirina,** *n.f.* aspirin.

**asprezza,** *n.f.* harshness.

**aspro,** *adj.* harsh.

**assaggiare,** *vb.* test, try, assay, sample.

**assalire,** *vb.* assail, attack, beset.

**assalitore,** *n.m.* assailant, attacker.

**assaltare,** *vb.* assault.

**assalto,** *n.m.* assault, bout, round.

**assassinare,** *vb.* assassinate.

**assassìnio,** *n.m.* assassination, murder.

**assassino,** *n.m.* assassin, murderer.

**asse,** *n.m.* axis, axle.

**asse,** *n.f.* board plank.

**assediante,** *n.m.* besieger.

**assediare,** *vb.* besiege, beset.

**assèdio,** *n.m.* siege.

**assegnàbile,** *adj.* assignable.

**assegnamento,** *n.m.* assignment.

**assegnare,** *vb.* assign, allot, allocate.

**assegnazione,** *n.f.* assignment, allotment.

**assegno,** *n.m.* cheque; allowance.

**assemblèa,** *n.f.* assembly, gathering, meeting.

**assennato,** *adj.* sensible.

**assènso,** *n.m.* assent.

**assente, 1.** *n.* absentee. **2.** *adj.* absent.

**assentire,** *vb.* assent.

**assenza,** *n.f.* absence.

**assènzio,** *n.m.* absinthe.

**asserire,** *vb.* assert.

**asservire,** *vb.* enslave.

**asserzione,** *n.f.* assertion.

**assessore,** *n.m.* assessor.

**asseverare,** *vb.* asseverate.

**asseverazione,** *n.f.* asseveration.

**assicurare,** *vb.* assure, insure.

**assicurazione,** *n.f.* assurance, insurance.

**assiduamente,** *adv.* assiduously.

**assiduo,** *adj.* assiduous.

**assimilare,** *vb.* assimilate.

**assimilativo,** *adj.* assimilative.

**assimilazione,** *n.f.* assimilation.

**assiòma,** *n.m.* axiom.

**assistènte,** *n.* and *adj.* assistant.

**assistènza,** *n.f.* attendance, assistance, relief. **a. sociale,** social work.

**assistere,** *vb.* be present.

**asso,** *n.m.* ace.

**associare,** *vb.* associate, affiliate.

**associazione,** *n.f.* association, affiliation.

**assoggettare,** *vb.* subject.

**assolo,** *n.m.* solo.

**assolutamente,** *adv.* absolutely.

**assolutezza,** *n.f.* absoluteness.

**assolutismo,** *n.m.* absolutism.

**assoluto,** *adj.* absolute.

**assoluzione,** *n.f.* absolution, acquittal.

**assòlvere,** *vb.* absolve, acquit.

**assomiglianza,** *n.f.* likeness.

**assonanza,** *n.f.* assonance.

**assopirsi,** *vb.* drowse.

**assorbènte, 1.** *n.m.* absorbent. **2.** *adj.* absorbent, absorbing.

**assorbimento,** *n.m.* absorption.

**assorbire,** *vb.* absorb.

**assorbito,** *adj.* absorbed.

**assordare,** *vb.* deafen.

**assortimento,** *n.m.* assortment.

**assortire,** *vb.* assort, sort.

**assortito,** *adj.* assorted.

**assorto,** *adj.* absorbed.

For pronunciation, see the concise guide on pages 5 to 7.

**assùmere**, *vb.* assume, take on.

**assurdamente**, *adv.* absurdly.

**assurdità**, *n.f.* absurdity, nonsense.

**assurdo**, **1.** *n.m.* absurdity. **2.** *adj.* absurd, preposterous.

**astèmio**, *adj.* abstemious.

**astenersi**, *vb.* abstain, refrain.

**asterisco**, *n.m.* asterisk.

**asteròide**, *n.m.* asteroid.

**astigmatismo**, *n.m.* astigmatism.

**astinènza**, *n.f.* abstinence.

**àstio**, *n.m.* grudge.

**astrale**, *adj.* astral, of the stars.

**astrarre**, *vb.* abstract.

**astratto**, *adj.* abstract, abstracted.

**astrazione**, *n.f.* abstraction.

**astringènte**, *adj.* astringent.

**astro**, *n.m.* star, aster.

**astrologìa**, *n.f.* astrology.

**astronomìa**, *n.f.* astronomy.

**astruso**, *adj.* abstruse.

**astuccio**, *n.m.* case.

**astuto**, *adj.* astute, artful, clever, canny, cunning, designing.

**astùzia**, *n.f.* guile.

**atassìa**, *n.f.* ataxia.

**àteo**, **1.** *n.m.* atheist. **2.** *adj.* atheistic godless.

**atlèta**, *n.m.* athlete.

**atlètico**, *adj.* athletic.

**atletismo**, *n.m.* athletics.

**atlante**, *n.m.* atlas.

**atlàntico**, *adj.* Atlantic.

**atmosfèra**, *n.f.* atmosphere.

**atmosfèrico**, *adj.* atmospheric.

**atòllo**, *n.m.* atoll.

**atòmico**, *adj.* atomic.

**àtomo**, *n.m.* atom.

**atonale**, *adj.* atonal.

**atroce**, *adj.* atrocious, heinous.

**atrocità**, *n.f.* atrocity.

**atrofìa**, *n.f.* atrophy.

**atropina**, *n.f.* atropine.

**attaccàbile**, *adj.* assailable.

**attaccamento**, *n.m.* attachment.

**attaccapanni**, *n.m.* coat-hanger.

**attaccare**, *vb.* attach, fasten, hitch, tack, stick; attack, assail.

**attaccatìccio**, *adj.* sticky.

**attacco**, *n.m.* attack, onslaught.

**atteggiamento**, *n.m.* attitude.

**atteggiarsi**, *vb.* take an attitude.

**attentamente**, *adv.* attentively, carefully.

**attènto**, *adj.* attentive, careful, thoughtful.

**attenuare**, *vb.* attenuate.

**attenzione**, *n.f.* attention, carefulness, notice.

**atterràggio**, *n.m.* landing. **pista d'a.**, landing strip, runway.

**atterrare**, *vb.* land.

**atterrire**, *vb.* terrify.

**attesa**, *n.f.* wait. **in a. di**, while waiting for, pending.

**attestare**, *vb.* attest, vouch for.

**àttimo**, *n.m.* instant.

**attìnio**, *n.m.* actinium.

**attinismo**, *n.m.* actinism.

**attirare**, *vb.* attract, entice, lure, decoy.

**attitùdine**, *n.f.* aptitude.

**attivamente**, *adv.* actively, busily.

**attivare**, *vb.* activate.

**attivatore**, *n.m.* activator.

**attivazione**, *n.f.* activation.

**attività**, *n.f.* activity.

**attivo**, **1.** *n.m.* asset. **2.** *adj.* active, busy.

**attizzare**, *vb.* stir, poke.

**atto**, **1.** *n.m.* act, deed. **2.** *adj.* apt, fitted.

**attore**, *n.m.* actor; plaintiff.

**attraènte**, *adj.* attractive, engaging, fetching.

**attrarre**, *vb.* attract.

**attraversare**, *vb.* cross, go through, pass through.

**attravèrso**, *adv. and prep.* across, through.

**attrazione**, *n.f.* attraction.

**attrezzare**, *vb.* rig.

**attrezzatura**, *n.f.* rig.

**attribuìbile**, *adj.* attributable.

**attribuire**, *vb.* attribute.

**attribuzione**, *n.f.* attribution.

**attrice**, *n.f.* actress.

**attrizione**, *n.f.* attrition.

**attualità**, *n.f.* reality, current significance; (*pl.*) newsreel.

---

**attuare**, *vb.* actuate.

**attuàrio**, *n.m.* actuary.

**attutire**, *vb.* silence.

**audace**, *adj.* audacious, bold, daring.

**audàcia**, *n.f.* audacity, boldness, daring.

**auditòrio**, *n.m.* auditorium.

**audizione**, *n.f.* audition.

**augurare**, *vb.* augur; wish.

**àula**, *n.f.* hall; classroom.

**aumentare**, *vb.* augment, increase, raise, enhance.

**aumènto**, *n.m.* increase, raise, rise.

**àureo**, *n.m.* golden.

**aurèola**, *n.f.* halo.

**auriga**, *n.m.* charioteer.

**ausiliare**, *n.m.* and *adj.* auxiliary.

**auspìcio**, *n.m.* auspice.

**austerità**, *n.f.* austerity.

**austèro**, *adj.* austere.

**Austria**, *n.f.* Austria.

**austrìaco**, *adj.* Austrian.

**autenticare**, *vb.* authenticate.

**autenticità**, *n.f.* authenticity.

**autèntico**, *adj.* authentic.

**autista**, *n.m.* chauffeur, (auto) driver.

**àuto**, *n.f.* auto.

**autobiografìa**, *n.f.* autobiography.

**àutobus**, *n.m.* bus.

**autocarro**, *n.m.* truck, lorry.

**autòcrate**, *n.m.* autocrat.

**autocrazìa**, *n.f.* autocracy.

**autògrafo**, *n.m.* autograph.

**autòma**, *n.m.* automaton; robot.

**automaticamente**, *adv.* automatically.

**automàtico**, *adj.* automatic.

**automòbile**, *n.f.* automobile.

**automobilista**, *n.m.* motorist.

**automobilìstico**, *adj.* pertaining to automobiles, automotive.

**autolìnea**, *n.f.* bus line.

**automotrice**, *n.f.* railcar.

**autonomìa**, *n.f.* autonomy.

**autònomo**, *adj.* autonomous.

**autoparcheggio**, *n.m.* parking area.

**autopsia**, *n.f.* autopsy.

**autore**, *n.m.* author.

**autorévole**, *adj.* authoritative.

**autorevolmente**, *adv.* authoritatively.

**autorimessa**, *n.f.* garage.

**autorità**, *n.f.* authority.

**autoritàrio**, *adj.* authoritarian.

**autorizzare**, *vb.* authorize, empower, entitle.

**autorizzazione**, *n.f.* authorization.

**autotreno**, *n.m.* trailer-truck.

**autunno**, *n.m.* autumn, fall.

**avambràccio**, *n.m.* forearm.

**avamposto**, *n.m.* outpost.

**avana**, *adj.* brown, beige.

**avanguàrdia**, *n.f.* vanguard.

**avanti**, **1.** *adv.* in front, ahead, onward, forward, before; (clock) fast. **2.** *prep.* before, in front of. **3.** *interj.* come in!

**avanzamento**, *n.m.* advancement.

**avanzare**, *vb.* advance; be left over.

**avanzato**, *adj.* advanced.

**avanzo**, *n.m.* relic, left-over, surplus.

**avarìa**, *n.f.* damage.

**avariare**, *vb.* damage.

**avarizia**, *n.f.* avarice.

**avaro**, **1.** *n.* miser. **2.** *adj.* avaricious, miserly, grasping, stingy.

**avemmarìa**, *n.f.* Hail Mary.

**avena**, *n.f.* oats.

**avere**, *vb.* have.

**aviàrio**, *n.m.* aviary.

**aviatore**, *n.m.* aviator, flier.

**aviatrice**, *n.f.* aviatrix.

**aviazione**, *n.f.* aviation.

**àvido**, *adj.* avid, greedy.

**aviogètto**, *n.m.* jet plane.

**aviolìnea**, *n.f.* air line.

**aviorimessa**, *n.f.* hangar.

**aviotrasportato**, *adj.* airborne.

**avòrio**, *n.m.* ivory.

**avornièllo**, *n.m.* laburnum.

**avvelenare**, *vb.* poison.

**avvenimento**, *n.m.* event, happening, occurrence.

**avvenire**, *n.m.* future, futurity.

**avventato**, *adj.* reckless.

**avventìzio**, *adj.* adventitious.

**avvènto**, *n.m.* advent.

**avventore,** *n.m.* regular customer.

**avventura,** *n.f.* adventure.

**avventurare,** *vb.* adventure; risk.

**avventurière,** *n.m.* adventurer.

**avventurosamente,** *adv.* adventurously.

**avventuroso,** *adj.* adventurous, enterprising, venturesome.

**avverbiale,** *adj.* adverbial.

**avvèrbio,** *n.m.* adverb.

**avversamente,** *adv* adversely.

**avversàrio,** *n.* adversary.

**avversione,** *n.f.* aversion.

**avversità,** *n.f.* adversity, hardship.

**avvèrso,** *adj.* adverse; averse

**avvertire,** *vb.* warn, alert, advert.

**avvicinarsi a,** *vb.* approach.

**avvilimento,** *n.m.* abasement.

**avvilire,** *vb.* abase, debase.

**avviluppare,** *vb.* envelop.

**avvisare,** *vb.* inform, advise.

**avviso,** *n.m.* advice; news, information, notice, notification; warning.

**avvitare,** *vb.* screw.

**avvizzire,** *vb.* wither.

**avvocato,** *n.m.* advocate, lawyer.

**avvòlgere,** *vb.* wrap up, enfold, wind.

**aziènda,** *n.f.* firm, concern.

**azione,** *n.f.* action; share (of stock).

**azionista,** *n.m.* stockholder.

**azzuffarsi,** *vb.* get into a scrap.

**azzurro,** *adj.* blue, azure.

# B

**babbo,** *n.m.* dad, daddy, pop, pa.

**babbuino,** *n.m.* baboon.

**bacca,** *n.f.* berry.

**baccano,** *n.m.* uproar, racket, row.

**baccellière,** *n.m.* bachelor.

**baccèllo,** *n.m.* pod, shell.

**bacchetta,** *n.f.* wand, (conductor's) baton.

**baciare,** *vb.* kiss.

**bacillo,** *n.m.* bacillus.

**bacino,** *n.m.* basin, dock.

  **bacino di carenaggio,** dry dock.

**bàcio,** *n.m.* kiss.

**bada,** *n.* **(a b.)** at bay.

**badare,** *vb.* heed, look out, mind.

**badessa,** *n.f.* abbess.

**badia,** *n.f.* abbey.

**baffi,** *n.m. pl.* mustache.

**bagàglio,** *n.m.* baggage, luggage.

**bagliore,** *n.m.* glare.

**bagnante,** *n.m. or f.* bather.

**bagnare,** *vb.* bathe, soak.

**bagnino,** *n.m.* bath attendant, life-guard.

**bagno,** *n.m.* bath.

**bàia,** *n.f.* bay.

**baio,** *adj.* bay (color).

**baionetta,** *n.f.* bayonet.

**balaùstra,** *n.f.* balustrade.

**balaustrata,** *n.f.* balustrade.

**balbettare,** *vb.* babble, stammer.

**balbettìo,** *n.m.* babble.

**balbuziènte,** *n.m.* stammerer, stutterer, babbler.

**balcone,** *n.m.* balcony.

**baldacchino,** *n.m.* canopy.

**baldòria,** *n.f.* carousing, revelry, spree.

**balena,** *n.f.* whale.

**balenare,** *vb.* flash.

**baleno,** *n.m.* flash.

**bàlia,** *n.f.* nurse.

**ballìstica,** *n.f.* ballistics.

**balla,** *n.f.* bale.

**ballàbile,** *n.m.* dance tune.

**ballare,** *vb.* dance.

**ballata,** *n.f.* ballad, ballade.

**ballatòio,** *n.m.* catwalk.

**ballerina,** *n.f.* dancer, ballerina.

**ballerino,** *n.m.* dancer.

**ballo,** *n.m.* dance, dancing; ballet; ball.

**balneare,** *adj.* pertaining to baths or bathing.

**balsàmico,** *adj.* balmy, balsamous.

**bàlsamo,** *n.m.* balsam, balm.

**baluardo,** *n.m.* bulwark.

**balzare,** *vb.* bound, leap, dart.

**balzo,** *n.m.* bound, leap, dart.

**bambina,** *n.f.* child, little girl.

**bambinaia,** *n.f.* nurse.

**bambinesco,** *adj.* childish, babyish.

**bambino,** *n.m.* child, little boy.

**bàmbola,** *n.f.* doll.

**bambù,** *n.m* bamboo.

**banale,** *adj.* banal, commonplace, hackneyed.

**banalità,** *n.f.* banality, platitude.

**banana,** *n.f.* banana.

**banca,** *n.f.* bank.

**bancàrio,** *adj.* pertaining to banks.

**bancarotta,** *n.f.* bankruptcy.

**banchetto,** *n.m.* banquet, feast.

**banchière,** *n.m.* banker.

**banchina,** *n.f.* pier.

**banco,** *n.m.* bank; bench; counter, stall.

**banconota,** *n.f.* bank note.

**banda,** *n.f.* band, gang; fillet.

**bandièra,** *n.f.* banner, flag, ensign.

**bandire,** *vb.* banish, exile.

**bandista,** *n.m.* bandsman.

**bandito,** *n.m.* bandit, outlaw.

**banditore,** *n.m.* crier, auctioneer.

**bando,** *n.m.* banishment, exile.

**bar,** *n.m.* bar.

**bara,** *n.f.* bier, pall.

**barattare,** *vb.* barter, swap.

**baratteria,** *n.f.* graft.

**baratto,** *n.m.* barter, swap.

**barba,** *n.f.* beard.

**barbabiètola,** *n.f.* beet.

**barbàrie,** *n.f.* barbarism.

**barbarismo,** *n.m.* barbarism.

**bàrbaro,** **1.** *n.* barbarian. **2.** *adj.* barbarous.

**barbazzale,** *n.m.* curb.

**barbetta,** *n.f.* little beard, goatee.

**barbière,** *n.m.* barber.

**barbitùrico,** *n.m.* barbiturate.

**barbuto,** *adj.* bearded.

**barca,** *n.f.* boat.

**barcollare,** *vb.* stagger, totter.

**bardare,** *vb.* caparison, harness.

**bardatura,** *n.f.* caparison; harness.

**barèlla,** *n.f.* litter, stretcher.

**barile,** *n.m.* barrel, cask.

**bariletto,** *n.m.* keg.

**bàrio,** *n.m.* barium.

**barista,** *n.m.* bartender.

**baritono,** *n.m. and adj.* baritone.

**barlume,** *n.m.* glimmer, gleam.

**baròcco,** *adj.* baroque.

**baromètrico,** *adj.* barometric.

**baròmetro,** *n.m.* barometer.

**baronale,** *adj.* baronial.

**barone,** *n.m.* baron.

**baronessa,** *n.f.* baroness.

**barricata,** *n.f.* barricade.

**barrièra,** *n.f.* barrier.

**basare,** *vb.* base, ground.

**base,** *n.f.* base, basis, footing, ground.

**basetta,** *n.f.* whisker.

**Basilèa,** *n.f.* Basel.

**bassezza,** *n.f.* baseness.

**basso,** **1.** *n.m.* bass. **2.** *adj.* low, vile, base; bass.

**bassofondo,** *n.m.* slum.

**bastardo,** *n.m. and adj.* bastard, mongrel.

**bastare,** *vb.* suffice, be enough.

**bastione,** *n.m.* rampart.

**bastonare,** *vb.* club.

**bastone,** *n.m.* baton, stick, club, staff, rod, bat, cane.

**battàglia,** *n.f.* battle.

**battaglièro,** *adj.* bellicose, warlike, combative.

**battàglio,** *n.m.* clapper.

**battaglione,** *n.m.* battalion.

**battèllo,** *n.m.* boat. **b. a remi,** rowboat.

**bàttere,** *vb.* beat, batter.

**batteria,** *n.f.* battery.

**battèrio,** n.m. bacterium; **(battèri,** pl.) bacteria.

**batteriologìa,** n.f. bacteriology.

**batteriòlogo,** n.m. bacteriologist.

**battesimale,** adj. baptismal.

**battésimo,** n.m. baptism, christening.

**battezzare,** vb. baptize, christen.

**battibecco,** n.m. squabble.

**battipalo,** n.m. ram.

**battista,** n.m. Baptist.

**battistèro,** n.m. baptistery.

**bàttito,** n.m. beat.

**battuto,** adj. beaten.

**batùffolo,** n.m. wad.

**baùle,** n.m. trunk.

**bauxite,** n.f. bauxite.

**bava,** n.f. drivel.

**bavaglìno,** n.m. bib.

**bavaglio,** n.m. gag.

**bazàr,** n.m. bazaar.

**bazzècola,** n.f. trifle.

**beatamente,** adv. blissfully.

**beatificare,** vb. beatify.

**beatitùdine,** n.f. bliss, beatitude.

**beato,** adj. blissful, blessed.

**beccare,** vb. peck.

**becco,** n.m. beak, bill; burner; spout.

**Befana,** n.f. old woman who brings presents on Twelfth Night.

**bèffa,** n.f. gibe.

**beffarsi di,** vb. gibe at, jeer at, mock.

**bèlga,** adj. Belgian.

**Bèlgio,** n.m. Belgium.

**belletto,** n.m. make-up.

**bellezza,** n.f. beauty; **(salone di b.)** beauty parlor.

**bellicosamente,** adv. belligerently.

**bellicoso,** adj. bellicose, belligerent.

**belligerante,** adj. belligerent.

**belligeranza,** n.f. belligerence.

**bellimbusto,** n.m. dandy.

**bellino,** adj. cunning, cute, pretty, good-looking.

**bèllo,** adj. beautiful, fine, fair, handsome, lovely.

**bellumore,** n.m. wag, wit.

**benché,** conj. although.

**benda,** n.f. bandage; blindfold; headband.

**bendare,** vb. blindfold.

**bène, 1.** n. good, asset, **b. mobile,** chattel. **2.** adv. well.

**benedetto,** adj. blessed.

**benedire,** vb. bless.

**benedizione,** n.f. benediction, blessing.

**benefattore,** n.m. benefactor.

**benefattrice,** n.f. benefactress.

**beneficare,** vb. benefit.

**beneficiario,** n.m. beneficiary.

**benefìcio,** n.m. benefit.

**benèfico,** adj. beneficent.

**benèssere,** n.m. welfare.

**benevolènza,** n.f. benevolence.

**benevolmente,** adv. benevolently.

**benèvolo,** adj. benevolent, kindly.

**bèni,** n.m. pl. goods, estate.

**benignità,** n.f. benignity.

**benigno,** adj. benign.

**benvenuto,** adj. welcome.

**benzina,** n.f. benzine, gasoline.

**bere,** vb. drink.

**beri-bèri,** n.m. beriberi.

**Berna,** n.f. Bern.

**berretto,** n.m. cap.

**bersàglio,** n.m. target.

**bestémmia,** n.f. blasphemy, curse-word, expletive, oath.

**bestemmiare,** vb. blaspheme, curse, swear.

**bestemmiatore,** n.m. blasphemer.

**bèstia,** n.f. beast.

**bestiale,** adj. bestial, beastly.

**bestiame,** n.m. cattle; animals, livestock.

**béttola,** n.f. (low-class) wine-shop.

**bevanda,** n.f. beverage, drink.

**bevìbile,** adj. drinkable.

**biancherìa,** n.f. linen.

**bianco,** adj. white, blank.

**biancospino,** n.m. hawthorn.

**biasimare,** vb. blame.

**biàsimo,** n. blame.

**Bibbia,** n.f. Bible.

**bìbita,** n.f. drink.

**bìblico,** adj. Biblical.

**bibliografìa,** n.f. bibliography.

**bibliotèca,** n.f. library.

**bibliotecàrio,** n.m. librarian.

**bicarbonato,** *n.m.* bicarbonate.

**bicchière,** *n.m.* glass.

**bicentennale,** *adj.* bicentennial.

**bicicletta,** *n.f.* bicycle.

**bicìpite,** *n.m.* biceps.

**bidèllo,** *n.m.* janitor.

**bidone,** *n.m.* large can.

**biennale,** *adj.* biennial; biannual.

**biènnio,** *n.m.* two-year period.

**bietta,** *n.f.* wedge, cleat.

**bifocale,** *adj.* bifocal.

**biforcazione,** *n.f.* crotch; junction.

**bigamìa,** *n.f.* bigamy.

**bìgamo, 1.** *n.* bigamist. **2.** *adj.* bigamous.

**bighellone,** *n.m.* gadabout, loafer.

**bigliettàrio,** *n.m.* ticket agent; (tram, bus) conductor.

**biglietto,** *n.m.* note; (money) bill; card; ticket. **b. di visita,** calling card.

**bigotterìa,** *n.f.* bigotry.

**bigottismo,** *n.m.* bigotry.

**bigòtto, 1.** *n.* bigot. **2.** *adj.* bigoted.

**bilància,** *n.f.* balance, scales.

**bilanciare,** *vb.* balance.

**bilaterale,** *adj.* bilateral.

**bile,** *n.f.* bile.

**biliardo,** *n.m.* billiards.

**biliare,** *adj.* bilious.

**bilingue,** *adj.* bilingual.

**bilione,** *n.m.* billion.

**bilioso,** *adj.* bilious.

**bimbo,** *n.m.* child, baby.

**bimensile,** *adj.* bimonthly (twice a month).

**bimestrale,** *adj.* bimonthly (every two months).

**bimèstre,** *n.m.* two months' period.

**bimetàllico,** *adj.* bimetallic.

**binàrio,** *n.m.* track.

**binda,** *n.f.* jack.

**binòcolo,** *n.m.* binoculars, spy-glasses. **b. da teatro,** opera-glasses.

**binoculare,** *adj.* binocular.

**biochìmica,** *n.f.* biochemistry.

**biografìa,** *n.f.* biography.

**biogràfico,** *adj.* biographical.

**biògrafo,** *n.m.* biographer.

**biologìa,** *n.f.* biology.

**biologicamente,** *adv.* biologically.

**biològico,** *adj.* biological.

**biondo,** *adj.* blond(e), fair.

**biòssido,** *n.m.* dioxide.

**bìpede,** *n.m. and adj.* biped.

**birichinata,** *n.f.* prank.

**birichino,** *adj.* naughty.

**birra,** *n.f.* ale, beer.

**birraio,** *n.m.* brewer.

**bisbigliare,** *vb.* whisper.

**bisbiglio,** *n.m.* whisper.

**biscòtto,** *n.m.* cracker, biscuit, cookie.

**bisecare,** *vb.* bisect.

**bisestile,** *adj.* **anno b.,** leap year.

**bisettimanale,** *adj.* twice weekly, biweekly.

**bismuto,** *n.m.* bismuth.

**bisognare,** *vb.* be necessary.

**bisogno,** *n.m.* need, want.

**bisognoso,** *adj.* needy.

**bisonte,** *n.m.* bison.

**bistecca,** *n.f.* beefsteak, steak.

**bisticciarsi,** *vb.* quarrel, argue, bicker.

**bisticcio,** *n.m.* quarrel, argument; pun.

**bistrattare,** *vb.* mistreat.

**bivacco,** *n.m.* bivouac.

**bivio,** *n.m.* (road) fork, junction.

**bizzèffe,** *n.f. pl.* **a b.,** galore.

**blandire,** *vb.* blandish, coax.

**blando,** *adj.* bland; suave.

**blatta,** *n.f.* cockroach.

**bleso,** *adj.* lisping.

**blindato,** *adj.* armored; **(carro b.)** tank.

**bloccare,** *vb.* block.

**blòcco,** *n.m.* bloc; block; blockade.

**blu,** *adj.* blue.

**bluff,** *n.m.* bluff (at cards, etc.).

**bluffare,** *vb.* bluff (at cards, etc.).

**bluffatore,** *n.m.* bluffer.

**blusa,** *n.f.* blouse.

**bòa,** *n.m.* buoy.

**bobina,** *n.f.* bobbin, reel, spool; coil.

**bocca,** *n.f.* mouth. **a b. aperta,** open-mouthed, agape.

**boccapòrto,** *n.m.* hatch, hatchway.

**boccheggiamento,** *n.m.* gasp.

**boccheggiare,** *vb.* gasp.

For pronunciation, see the concise guide on pages 5 to 7.

**boccia,** *n.f.* bowl.

**bocciare,** *vb.* fail, flunk.

**boccone,** *n.m.* morsel, swallow.

**boemo,** *n.m. and adj.* Bohemian.

**boia,** *n.m.* executioner.

**boicottàggio,** *n.m.* boycott.

**boicottare,** *vb.* boycott.

**boliviano,** *adj.* Bolivian.

**bolla,** *n.f.* bubble.

**bollare,** *vb.* stamp.

**bollettino,** *n.m.* bulletin.

**bollire,** *vb.* boil.

**bollo,** *n.m.* stamp.

**bòlo,** *n.m.* cud.

**bomba,** *n.f.* bomb; bombshell.

**bombardamento,** *n.m.* bombardment.

**bombardare,** *vb.* bombard, shell.

**bombardière,** *n.m.* bomber, bombardier.

**bomboletta nebulizzante,** *n.f.* aerosol bomb.

**bonifica,** *n.f.* reclamation.

**bonificare,** *vb.* reclaim.

**bontà,** *n.f.* goodness.

**borbottamento,** *n.m.* mumbling, gibberish.

**borbottare,** *vb.* mutter.

**bordata,** *n.f.* broadside.

**bordèllo,** *n.m.* brothel.

**bordo,** *n.m.* board (side of ship); edge, brink, rim. **a b. di,** *prep.* aboard, on board (of).

**borghese,** *adj.* bourgeois, middle-class.

**borghesia,** *n.f.* bourgeoisie, middle class.

**borgo,** *n.m.* village, burg, borough.

**borgognone,** *n.m.* iceberg.

**bòrico,** *adj.* boric.

**borsa,** *n.f.* bag, brief-case, pouch, purse; fellowship; stock exchange. **b. di stùdio,** scholarship.

**borsaiòlo,** *n.m.* pickpocket.

**borsetta,** *n.f.* little bag, purse, handbag.

**boschetto,** *n.m.* grove.

**bosco,** *n.m.* wood.

**boscoso,** *adj.* wooded.

**botànica,** *n.f.* botany.

**botànico,** *adj.* botanical.

**bottaio,** *n.m.* cooper.

**bòtte,** *n.f.* cask, hogshead.

**bottega,** *n.f.* shop.

**botteghino,** *n.m.* box-office.

**bottìglia,** *n.f.* bottle, jar.

**bottino,** *n.m.* booty, plunder, loot.

**bottone,** *n.m.* button.

**bovaro,** *n.m.* cattleman.

**bovino,** *adj.* bovine.

**bòzze,** *n.f.pl.* proof. **b. in colonna,** galley-proof. **b. impaginate,** page-proof.

**bòzzolo,** *n.m.* cocoon.

**braccialetto,** *n.m.* bracelet.

**bracciata,** *n.f.* armful.

**braccio,** *n.m.* arm; fathom.

**brace,** *n.f.* embers.

**brache,** *n.f.pl.* breeches, pants.

**brama,** *n.f.* ardent desire, craving, eagerness, longing.

**bramare,** *vb.* desire ardently, covet, crave, long for, yearn for.

**bramosamente,** *adv.* desirously, covetously, eagerly.

**bramoso,** *adj.* desirous, covetous, eager.

**brànchia,** *n.f.* gill.

**brandire,** *vb.* brandish.

**brano,** *n.m.* passage, excerpt.

**Brasile,** *n.m.* Brazil.

**brasiliano,** *adj.* Brazilian.

**bravata,** *n.f.* bravado.

**bravo, 1.** *n.m.* henchman. **2.** *adj.* fine.

**breccia,** *n.f.* breach.

**brefotròfio,** *n.m.* foundling hospital.

**Brètone,** *n.m.* Briton.

**brève,** *adj.* brief, short.

**brevemente,** *adv.* briefly.

**brevettare,** *vb.* patent.

**brevetto,** *n.m.* patent.

**brevità,** *n.f.* brevity, briefness.

**brezza,** *n.f.* breeze.

**briccone,** *n.m.* rascal, rogue.

**bricconesco,** *adj.* roguish.

**briciola,** *n.f.* crumb.

**brigantino,** *n.m.* brig.

**brigata,** *n.f.* brigade.

**briglia,** *n.f.* bridle.

**brillante,** *adj.* brilliant.

**brillare,** *vb.* shine.

**brina,** *n.f.* frost.

**brindare,** *vb.* toast.

**brindisi,** *n.m.* toast, health.

**brio,** *n.m.* vim, verve.

**brioso,** *adj.* lively, sprightly.

**britànnico,** *adj.* British.

**brivido,** *n.m.* shudder, shiver, chill.

**bròcca,** *n.f.* jug, pitcher.

**broccato,** *n.m.* brocade.

**bròdo,** *n.m.* broth, bouillon. **b. ristretto,** consommé.

**bronchiale,** *adj.* bronchial.

**bronchite,** *n.f.* bronchitis.

**brontolamento,** *n.m.* grumble.

**brontolare,** *vb.* grumble, growl; rumble.

**brontolìo,** *n.m.* rumble.

**bronzo,** *n.m.* bronze.

**brucare,** *vb.* browse.

**bruciare,** *vb.* burn, scorch.

**bruciatura,** *n.f.* burn.

**bruciore di stòmaco,** *n.m.* heartburn.

**bruco,** *n.m.* caterpillar, cankerworm.

**brughièra,** *n.f.* heath, moor.

**bruna,** *n.f.* brunette.

**brunire,** *vb.* burnish.

**bruno,** *adj.* brown.

**bruscamente,** *adv.* brusquely.

**brusco,** *adj.* brusque.

**brùscolo,** *n.m.* cinder.

**brutale,** *adj.* brutal.

**brutalità,** *n.f.* brutality.

**bruto,** *n.m. and adj.* brute.

**bruttezza,** *n.f.* ugliness.

**brutto,** *adj.* ugly, homely.

**buca,** *n.f.* pit, pot-hole.

**bucato,** *n.m.* laundry.

**bùccia,** *n.f.* hull, husk, peel, rind, skin.

**bùccina,** *n.f.* bugle.

**buco,** *n.m.* hole.

**budèllo,** *n.m.* bowel, intestine, gut.

**budino,** *n.m.* pudding.

**bùfalo,** *n.m.* buffalo.

**bue,** *n.m.* ox; beef.

**buffonata,** *n.f.* antic.

**buffone,** *n.m.* buffoon, jester.

**bugia,** *n.f.* lie, fabrication, falsehood.

**bugiardo, 1.** *n.m.* liar. **2.** *adj.* lying.

**buio, 1.** *n.m.* darkness. **2.** *adj.* dark.

**bulbo,** *n.m.* bulb.

**bulletta,** *n.f.* tack.

**bungalò,** *n.m.* bungalow.

**buongustaio,** *n.m.* gourmet.

**buòn mercato,** *n.m.* cheapness.

**buòno, 1.** *n.m.* bond. **2.** *adj.* good.

**burattino,** *n.m.* puppet.

**burla,** *n.f.* trick, practical joke, prank.

**burlone,** *n.m.* joker.

**burro,** *n.m.* butter.

**burrone,** *n.m.* ravine, canyon, gulch, gully.

**bussare,** *vb.* knock.

**bussata,** *n.f.* knock.

**bùssola,** *n.f.* compass.

**busta,** *n.f.* envelope.

**busto,** *n.m.* bust; bodice, corset.

**buttare,** *vb.* throw, toss.

# C

**C** (on water faucets) = **caldo,** *adj.* hot.

**cabina,** *n.f.* cabin, stateroom.

**cablogramma,** *n.m.* cablegram.

**cacao,** *n.m.* cocoa.

**caccia,** *n.m.* fighter plane.

**càccia,** *n.f.* hunt, hunting, chase.

**cacciare,** *vb.* hunt, chase; stick; shove.

**cacciatore,** *n.m.* hunter, chaser.

**cacciatorpedinière,** *n.m.* destroyer.

**cacciatrice,** *n.f.* huntress.

**cacciavite,** *n.m.* screw-driver.

**cachi,** *n.m.* khaki.

**cacio,** *n.m* cheese.

**cacofonìa,** *n.f.* cacophony.

**cacto,** *n.m.* cactus.

**cadauno, 1.** *adj.* each; apiece. **2.** *pron.* each one.

For pronunciation, see the concise guide on pages 5 to 7.

**cadàvere,** *n.m.* cadaver; corpse.

**cadavèrico,** *adj.* cadaverous.

**cadènza,** *n.f.* cadence, cadenza.

**cadere,** *vb.* fall. **lasciar c.,** drop.

**cadetto,** *n.m.* cadet.

**càdmio,** *n.m.* cadmium.

**caduta,** *n.f.* fall.

**caffè,** *n.m.* coffee; café; buffet.

**caffeina,** *n.f.* caffeine.

**cagionare,** *vb.* occasion, cause.

**cagna,** *n.f.* bitch.

**caimano,** *n.m.* cayman.

**calabrone,** *n.m.* bumblebee, hornet.

**calafatare,** *vb.* calk.

**calafato,** *n.m.* calker.

**calamità,** *n.f.* calamity, woe.

**calamitoso,** *adj.* calamitous.

**calapranzi,** *n.m.* dumbwaiter.

**calare,** *vb.* lower.

**calcagno,** *n.m.* heel.

**calcare,** *adj.* calcareous. **pietra c.,** limestone.

**calce,** *n.f.* lime.

**calcificare,** *vb.* calcify.

**calcina,** *n.f.* mortar.

**càlcio,** *n.m.* calcium; kick; football; butt (of gun).

**calcolàbile,** *adj.* calculable.

**calcolare,** *vb.* calculate.

**calcolatore,** *adj.* calculating.

**càlcolo,** *n.m.* calculus; calculation. **c. biliare,** gallstone.

**caldaia,** *n.f.* boiler, caldron, furnace.

**caldo,** **1.** *n.m.* heat. **2.** *adj.* hot, warm.

**caleidoscòpio,** *n.m.* kaleidoscope.

**calendàrio,** *n.m.* calendar.

**caletta,** *n.f.* joggle.

**càlibro,** *n.m.* caliber; calipers.

**càlice,** *n.m.* chalice; calyx.

**calicò,** *n.m.* calico.

**callìfuga,** *n.m.* corn-plaster.

**calligrafìa,** *n.f.* calligraphy, handwriting.

**callista,** *n.m.* chiropodist.

**callo,** *n.m.* callus, corn.

**callosità,** *n.f.* callousness.

**calloso,** *adj.* callous, horny.

**calma,** *n.f.* calm, composure; stillness.

**calmare,** *vb.* calm, soothe; still.

**calmo,** *adj.* calm, composed; still.

**caloria,** *n.m.* heat, warmth.

**caloria,** *n.f.* calorie.

**calorìfero,** *n.m.* heater.

**calòrico,** *adj.* caloric.

**calorìmetro,** *n.m.* calorimeter.

**caloroso,** *adj.* warm.

**calpestare,** *vb.* tread on.

**calùnnia,** *n.f.* calumny, slander, slur.

**calunniare,** *vb.* calumniate, slander, slur.

**Calvàrio,** *n.m.* Calvary.

**calvìzie,** *n.f.sg.* baldness.

**calvo,** *adj.* bald.

**calza,** *n.f.* stocking, *(pl.)* hose.

**calzare,** *vb.* shoe.

**calzetteria,** *n.f.* hosiery.

**calzino,** *n.m.* sock.

**calzolaio,** *n.m.* shoemaker, cobbler.

**calzoni,** *n.m.pl.* trousers.

**camaleonte,** *n.m.* chameleon.

**cambiamento,** *n.m.* change, shift.

**cambiare,** *vb.* change, shift.

**cambiavalute,** *n.m.* moneychanger.

**cambio,** *n.m.* change; relief. **c. di velocità,** *n.f.* gearshift.

**cambrì,** *n.m.* cambric.

**camèlia,** *n.f.* camelia.

**càmera,** *n.f.* room, chamber; (legislative) house.

**camerata,** *n.m.* comrade, buddy, pal.

**cameratismo,** *n.m.* camaraderie, comradeship.

**cameriera,** *n.f.* chambermaid, waitress; stewardess.

**cameriere,** *n.m.* manservant; waiter; bellboy; steward; valet.

**càmice,** *n.m.* smock.

**camicia,** *n.f.* shirt.

**camiciòla,** *n.f.* undershirt.

**camiciòtto,** *n.m.* smock.

**camino,** *n.m.* chimney.

**camioncino,** *n.m.* light truck; utility.

**camione,** *n.m.* truck.

**cammèllo,** *n.m.* camel.

**cammèo,** *n.m.* cameo.

**camminare,** *vb.* walk, step.

**cammino,** *n.m.* road.

**camoscio,** *n.m.* chamois.

**campagna,** *n.f.* country, countryside; campaign.

**campana,** *n.f.* bell.

**campanèllo,** *n.m.* (little) bell.

**campanette,** *n.f.-pl.* glockenspiel.

**campanile,** *n.m.* bell-tower, belfry, steeple.

**campeggiare,** *vb.* camp.

**campeggiatore,** *n.m.* camper.

**campeggio,** *n.m.* camping.

**campionàrio,** *adj.* pertaining to samples.

**campionato,** *n.m.* championship.

**campione,** *n.m.* champion; sample.

**campo,** *n.m.* field.

**camposanto,** *n.m.* cemetery, churchyard, graveyard.

**camuffamento,** *n.m.* disguise, camouflage.

**camuffare,** *vb.* disguise, camouflage.

**Canadà,** *n.m.* Canada.

**canadese,** *adj.* Canadian.

**canale,** *n.m.* canal, channel, duct, inlet.

**canalizzare,** *vb.* canalize.

**cànapa,** *n.f.* hemp.

**Canàrie,** *n.f.-pl.* Canary Islands.

**canarino,** *n.m.* canary.

**cancellare,** *vb.* cancel, erase, delete, efface, obliterate.

**cancellatura,** *n.f.* erasure.

**cancelleria,** *n.f.* chancellery.

**oggetti di c.,** stationery.

**cancellière,** *n.m.* chancellor.

**cancèllo,** *n.m.* gate.

**cancrena,** *n.f.* gangrene.

**cancrenoso,** *adj.* gangrenous.

**cancro,** *n.m.* cancer, canker.

**candela,** *n.f.* candle. **c. d'accensione,** spark-plug.

**candelabro,** *n.m.* candelabrum.

**candelière,** *n.m.* candlestick.

**candidamente,** *adv.* candidly.

**candidato,** *n.m.* candidate, nominee.

**candidatura,** *n.f.* candidacy.

**càndido,** *adj.* candid.

**candito,** *adj.* candied.

**candore,** *n.m.* candor.

**cane,** *n.m.* dog, hound; cock

(of gun). **c. poliziotto,** police dog, bloodhound.

**cànfora,** *n.f.* camphor.

**canguro,** *n.m.* kangaroo.

**canile,** *n.m.* doghouse, kennel.

**canino,** *adj.* canine.

**canna,** *n.f.* reed, cane.

**cannèlla,** *n.f.* cinnamon.

**cannìbale,** *n.m.* cannibal.

**cannone,** *n.m.* cannon.

**cannoneggiamento,** *n.m.* cannonade.

**cannonièra,** *n.f.* gunboat.

**cannonière,** *n.m.* cannoneer.

**cannùccia di paglia,** *n.f.* straw (for drinking).

**canòa,** *n.f.* canoe.

**cànone,** *n.m.* canon; rent.

**canònico, 1.** *n.m.* canon. **2.** *adj.* canonical.

**canonizzare,** *vb.* canonize.

**canovaccio,** *n.m.* canvas.

**cantare,** *vb.* sing, chant; (hen, goose) cackle; (rooster) crow.

**cantatore,** *n.m.* singer.

**cantatrice,** *n.f.* singer.

**canticchiare,** *vb.* hum, croon.

**cantina,** *n.f.* basement; canteen.

**canto,** *n.m.* corner; song, singing, chant.

**cantuccio,** *n.m.* nook.

**canzone,** *n.f.* song.

**càos,** *n.m.* chaos.

**caòtico,** *adj.* chaotic.

**capace,** *adj.* capable, able.

**capacità,** *n.f.* capacity, ability.

**capanna,** *n.f.* cabin, hut, shack.

**capàrbio,** *adj.* wilful.

**capello,** *n.m.* hair.

**capestro,** *n.m.* halter.

**capezzale,** *n.m.* **al c. di,** at the bedside of.

**capézzolo,** *n.m.* nipple.

**capillare,** *adj.* capillary.

**capire,** *vb.* understand.

**capitale, 1.** *n.f.* capital (city). **2.** *n.m.* capital (money). **3.** *adj.* capital.

**capitalismo,** *n.m.* capitalism.

**capitalista,** *n.m.* capitalist.

**capitalìstico,** *adj.* capitalistic.

**capitalizzare,** *vb.* capitalize.

**capitalizzazione,** *n.f.* capitalization.

**capitano**, *n.m.* captain.

**capitare**, *vb.* happen, befall.

**capitolare**, *vb.* capitulate.

**capitolo**, *n.m.* chapter.

**capitombolare**, *vb.* tumble.

**capitómbolo**, *n.m.* tumble.

**capo**, *n.m.* head, chief, chieftain, head-man, leader, principal.

**capobanda**, *n.m.* bandmaster; gang leader.

**capofitto**, *adv.* **a c.**, headlong.

**capolavoro**, *n.m.* masterpiece.

**capolinea**, *n.m.* terminus.

**caporale**, *n.m.* corporal.

**capotreno**, *n.m.* conductor (of train).

**capovòlgere**, *vb.* overturn, upset, capsize.

**cappa**, *n.f.* cape.

**cappèlla**, *n.f.* chapel.

**cappellano**, *n.m.* chaplain.

**cappellièra**, *n.f.* hatbox, bandbox.

**cappèllo**, *n.m.* hat, bonnet.

**càppio**, *n.m.* loop.

**cappone**, *n.m.* capon.

**cappùccio**, *n.m.* hood.

**capra**, *n.f.* goat.

**capraio**, *n.m.* goat-herd.

**capretto**, *n.m.* kid.

**capriccio**, *n.m.* caprice, whim.

**capricciosamente**, *adv.* capriciously.

**capricciosità**, *n.f.* capriciousness.

**capriccioso**, *adj.* capricious, fanciful, flighty, temperamental.

**caprifòglio**, *n.m.* honeysuckle.

**capriòla**, *n.f.* caper, somersault.

**càpsula**, *n.f.* capsule.

**capzioso**, *adj.* captious.

**carabina**, *n.f.* carbine.

**caraffa**, *n.f.* carafe, decanter.

**caramèlla**, *n.f.* caramel.

**caramente**, *adv.* dearly.

**carato**, *n.m.* carat.

**caràttere**, *n.m.* character.

**caratteristica**, *n.f.* characteristic.

**caratteristicamente**, *adv.* characteristically.

**caratterìstico**, *adj.* characteristic.

**caratterizzare**, *vb.* characterize.

**caratterizzazione**, *n.f.* characterization.

**carbónchio**, *n.m.* carbuncle.

**carbone**, *n.m.* charcoal; coal.

**carbònio**, *n.m.* carbon.

**carbonizzare**, *vb.* char.

**carburante**, *n.m.* fuel.

**carburatore**, *n.m.* carburetor.

**carburo**, *n.m.* carbide.

**carcassa**, *n.f.* carcass; hulk.

**càrcere**, *n.m.* jail.

**carcerière**, *n.m.* jailer.

**carciòfo**, *n.m.* artichoke.

**cardellino**, *n.m.* goldfinch.

**cardìaco**, *adj.* cardiac.

**cardinale**, *n.m. and adj.* cardinal.

**càrdine**, *n.m.* hinge.

**carenare**, *vb.* careen.

**carestìa**, *n.f.* famine.

**carezza**, *n.f.* caress; endearment.

**cariarsi**, *vb.* decay.

**càrica**, *n.f.* charge.

**caricare**, *vb.* load, charge; (watch) wind.

**caricatura**, *n.f.* caricature.

**càrico**, **1.** *n.m.* load, cargo, charge, freight. **2.** *adj.* loaded, fraught.

**càrie**, *n.f.* caries, decay.

**cariglione**, *n.m.* carillon.

**carità**, *n.f.* charity, charitableness.

**caritatévole**, *adj.* charitable, benevolent.

**caritatevolmente**, *adv.* charitably, benevolently.

**carlinga**, *n.f.* cockpit.

**carnale**, *adj.* carnal.

**carne**, *n.f.* meat; flesh.

**carnéfice**, *n.m.* executioner.

**carnevale**, *n.m.* carnival.

**carnìvoro**, *adj.* carnivorous.

**carnoso**, *adj.* fleshy.

**caro**, *adj.* dear, expensive.

**carosèllo**, *n.m.* carousel, merry-go-round.

**caròta**, *n.f.* carrot.

**carovana**, *n.f.* caravan, trailer.

**carpire**, *vb.* seize, grab.

**carrettata**, *n.f.* carload.

**carrettière**, *n.m.* carter, drayman.

**carrièra**, *n.f.* career.

**carro**, *n.m.* car; cart, wagon; chariot; dray, van. **c. ar-**

---

**mato,** tank. **c. fùnebre,** hearse. **c. di scorta,** tender.

**carròzza,** n.f. carriage, coach, (railroad) car. **c. ristorante,** sleeper. **c. ristorante,** diner.

**carrozzèlla,** n.f. baby-carriage, perambulator.

**carrozzino,** n.m. side-car.

**carta,** n.f. paper; card; chart; map; charter. **c. a carbone,** carbon paper. **c. assorbente,** blotter, blotting paper. **c. velina,** tissue-paper; onion-skin. **c. da parati,** wall-paper. **c. intestata,** letterhead.

**cartèlla,** n.f. portfolio; folder.

**cartèllo,** n.m. cartel; placard; poster, sign. **c. pubblicitàrio,** billboard.

**cartilàgine,** n.f. cartilage, gristle.

**cartolaio,** n.m. stationer.

**cartoleria,** n.f. stationery store.

**cartoncino,** n.m. thin cardboard.

**cartone,** n.m. cardboard, pasteboard; cartoon (picture).

**cartuccia,** n.f. cartridge.

**carvi,** n.m. caraway.

**casa,** n.f. house, home. **in c.,** indoors. **c. colònica,** farmhouse.

**casàccio,** n.m. **a c.,** haphazard, helter-skelter, at random.

**casalingo,** adj. home; homelike.

**cascata,** n.f. cascade, waterfall.

**casèlla,** n.f. pigeonhole; P. O. box.

**casèrma,** n.f. barracks.

**casetta,** n.f. cottage.

**casimiro,** n.m. cashmere.

**casino,** n.m. casino.

**caso,** n.m. case; happening; chance. **per c.,** by accident.

**cassa,** n.f. case; chest; box; cashier's office or desk. **c. da mòrto,** coffin. **c. di rispàrmio,** savings bank.

**cassafòrte,** n.f. strongbox; safe.

**cassare,** vb. overrule.

**casseruòla,** n.f. casserole.

**cassetta,** n.f. box.

**cassettina,** n.f. casket.

**cassetto,** n.m. drawer; till.

**cassière,** n.m. cashier; teller.

**cassone,** n.m. caisson.

**casta,** n.f. caste.

**castagna,** n.f. chestnut.

**castagno, 1.** n.m. chestnut tree. **2.** adj. tan.

**castèllo,** n.m. castle, château. **c. di prua,** forecastle.

**castigare,** vb. castigate, chastise, chasten.

**castigo,** n.m. chastisement.

**castità,** n.f. chastity.

**casto,** adj. chaste.

**castòro,** n.m. beaver.

**castrare,** vb. castrate, emasculate; geld.

**castrone,** n.m. gelding, wether.

**casuale,** adj. casual; perfunctory.

**casualmente,** adv. casually.

**casùpola,** n.f. hut.

**cataclisma,** n.m. cataclysm.

**catacomba,** n.f. catacomb.

**catàlogo,** n.m. catalogue.

**catapulta,** n.f. catapult.

**catarro,** n.m. catarrh; cold.

**catarsi,** n.f. catharsis.

**catàstrofe,** n.f. catastrophe.

**catechismo,** n.m. catechism.

**catechizzare,** vb. catechize.

**categoria,** n.f. category.

**categòrico,** adj. categorical.

**catena,** n.f. chain; range.

**catenaccio,** n.m. bolt.

**cateratta,** n.f. cataract; flood-gate.

**catino,** n.m. basin.

**càtodo,** n.m. cathode.

**catrame,** n.m. tar.

**cattedrale,** n.f. cathedral.

**cattivèria,** n.f. badness, mischief.

**cattivo,** adj. bad, evil; mischievous.

**cattolicismo,** n.m. Catholicism.

**cattòlico,** adj. Catholic.

**cattura,** n.f. capture.

**catturare,** vb. capture.

**catturatore,** n.m. capturer; captor.

**càusa,** n.f. cause; lawsuit; case; **(a c. di)** because of.

**causalità,** n.f. causality, causation.

**causare**, *v.b* cause, bring about; encompass.

**càustico**, *adj.* caustic.

**cautèla**, *n.f.* caution.

**cautèrio**, *n.m.* cautery.

**cauterizzare**, *vb.* cauterize.

**càuto**, *adj.* cautious; gingerly.

**cauzione**, *n.f.* bail; security.

**cava**, *n.f.* quarry.

**cavalcare**, *vb.* ride (horseback).

**cavalcata**, *n.f.* cavalcade.

**cavalcavia**, *n.m.* overpass.

**cavalière**, *n.m.* knight, cavalier, horseman, rider.

**cavalla**, *n.f.* mare.

**cavalleresco**, *adj.* chivalric.

**cavalleria**, *n.f.* cavalry; chivalry.

**cavalletta**, *n.f.* grasshopper.

**cavalletto**, *n.m.* easel.

**cavallo**, *n.m.* horse; (chess) knight. **c. a dòndolo**, rocking-horse; hobby-horse. **c. da guerra**, warhorse, charger. **c.-vapore**, horsepower.

**cavatappi**, *n.m.sg.* corkscrew.

**cavèrna**, *n.f.* cavern, cave.

**cavezza**, *n.f.* halter.

**caviale**, *n.m.* caviar.

**caviglia**, *n.f.* ankle.

**cavità**, *n.f.* cavity; hole.

**cavo**, **1.** *n.* hollow; cable. **2.** *adj.* hollow.

**cavolfiore**, *n.m.* cauliflower.

**càvolo**, *n.m.* cabbage; kale.

**cecità**, *n.f.* blindness.

**cédere**, *vb.* yield, cede, surrender; give in; back down; subside.

**cèdola**, *n.f.* coupon.

**cèdro**, *n.m.* cedar.

**celamento**, *n.m.* concealment.

**celare**, *vb.* conceal.

**celebrante**, *n.m.* celebrant.

**celebrare**, *vb.* celebrate.

**celebrazione**, *n.f.* celebration.

**cèlebre**, *adj.* celebrated, famous.

**celebrità**, *n.f.* celebrity.

**celerità**, *n.f.* speed, quickness, celerity.

**celèste**, *adj.* celestial.

**cèlia**, *n.f.* joke, banter, chaff.

**celiare**, *vb.* joke, banter, chaff.

**celibato**, *n.m.* celibacy.

**cèlibe**, *adj.* celibate; single, unmarried.

**cèlla**, *n.f.* cell.

**cellòfane**, *n.m.* cellophane.

**cèllula**, *n.f.* cell.

**cellulare**, *adj.* cellular.

**cellulòide**, *n.f.* celluloid.

**cellulosa**, *n.f.* cellulose.

**cèltico**, *adj.* Celtic.

**cementare**, *vb.* cement.

**cemento**, *n.m.* cement, concrete.

**cena**, *n.f.* supper.

**cenàcolo**, *n.m.* coterie; Last Supper.

**céncio**, *n.m.* rag.

**cencioso**, *adj.* ragged.

**cènere**, *n.f.* ashes.

**cenno**, *n.m.* sign, hint.

**censimento**, *n.m.* census.

**censore**, *n.m.* censor.

**censòrio**, *adj.* censorious.

**censura**, *n.f.* censure; censorship.

**censurare**, *vb.* censure.

**centenàrio**, *n.m. and adj.* centenary.

**centennale**, *n.m. and adj.* centennial.

**centèsimo**, **1.** *n.* cent; 100th part. **2.** *adj.* hundredth.

**centigrado**, *adj.* centigrade.

**centinaio**, *n.m.* group of 100.

**cènto**, *num.* hundred.

**centrale**, *adj.* central.

**centralino**, *n.m.* switchboard.

**centralizzare**, *vb.* centralize.

**cèntro**, *n.m.* center. **cèntro da tàvola**, centerpiece.

**ceppi**, *n.m.pl.* fetters.

**ceppo**, *n.m.* log, stump.

**cera**, *n.f.* wax; beeswax; mien.

**ceralacca**, *n.f.* sealing-wax.

**ceràmica**, *n.f.* ceramics.

**ceràmico**, *adj.* ceramic.

**cerbiàttolo**, *n.m.* fawn.

**cercare**, *vb.* seek, look for, hunt for.

**cérchio**, *n.m.* circle; hoop; ring.

**cereale**, *n.m. and adj.* cereal.

**cerebrale**, *adj.* cerebral.

**cerimònia**, *n.f.* ceremony.

**cerimoniale**, *adj.* ceremonial.

**cerimonioso**, *adj.* ceremonious.

---

For pronunciation, see the concise guide on pages 5 to 7.

**certamente,** *adv.* certainly.

**certezza,** *n.f.* certainty, certitude.

**certificare,** *vb.* certify.

**certificato,** *n.m.* certificate.

**certificazione,** *n.f.* certification.

**cèrto,** *adj.* certain, sure.

**cèrva,** *n.f.* doe; hind; roe.

**cervèllo,** *n.m.* brain.

**cervicale,** *adj.* cervical.

**cervice,** *n.f.* cervix.

**cèrvo,** *n.m.* stag; deer.

**cesellare,** *vb.* chisel.

**cesèllo,** *n.m.* chisel.

**cesòie,** *n.f.pl.* shears.

**cespùglio,** *n.m.* bush.

**cespuglioso,** *adj.* bushy.

**cessare,** *vb.* cease, stop, quit.

**cessazione,** *n.f.* cessation.

**cessione,** *n.f.* cession.

**cesta,** *n.f.* basket; hamper.

**cèto,** *n.m.* class.

**cetriòlo,** *n.m.* cucumber.

**che, 1.** *pron.* who; which; what. **2.** *prep.* than. **3.** *conj.* that.

**chè,** *conj.* for.

**cherubino,** *n.m.* cherub.

**chi,** *pron.* who; whom.

**chiàcchiera,** *f.* chatter, chat.

**chiacchierare,** *vb.* chatter, chat, gab.

**chiacchierone,** *n.m.* chatterbox.

**chiamare,** *vb.* call, summon.

**chiamata,** *n.f.* call, summons.

**chiaramente,** *adv.* clearly.

**chiarezza,** *n.f.* clearness.

**chiarificare,** *vb.* clarify.

**chiarificazione,** *n.f.* clarification.

**chiarimento,** *n.m.* enlightenment.

**chiarina,** *n.f.* clarion.

**chiarire,** *vb.* clear, clear up.

**chiarità,** *n.f.* clarity.

**chiaro,** *adj.* clear, bright, lucid, plain. **c. di luna,** moonlight.

**chiarore,** *n.m.* brightness.

**chiaroveggènte,** *n.* and *adj.* clairvoyant; fortune-teller.

**chiaroveggènza,** *n.f.* clairvoyance.

**chiasso,** *n.m.* uproar, fuss, hullabaloo.

**chiassoso,** *adj.* uproarious, obstreperous.

**chiatta,** *n.f.* barge.

**chiave,** *n.f.* key; clef. **c. inglese,** wrench.

**chicco,** *n.m.* grain; seed.

**chièdere,** *vb.* ask for, request, beg.

**chièsa,** *n.f.* church.

**chiglia,** *n.f.* keel.

**chilociclo,** *n.m.* kilocycle.

**chilogramma,** *n.m.* kilogram.

**chilometràggio,** *n.m.* distance in kilometers.

**chilòmetro,** *n.m.* kilometer.

**chilowatt,** *n.m.* kilowatt.

**chìmica,** *n.f.* chemistry.

**chimicamente,** *adv.* chemically.

**chìmico, 1.** *n.* chemist. **2.** *adj.* chemical.

**chimono,** *n.m.* kimono.

**chinino,** *n.m.* quinine.

**chiocciare,** *vb.* cluck.

**chiòdo,** *n.m.* nail; spike; clove.

**chiòsa,** *n.f.* gloss.

**chiosare,** *vb.* gloss.

**chiòsco,** *n.m.* kiosk.

**chiòstro,** *n.m.* cloister.

**chirurgìa,** *n.f.* surgery.

**chirurgo,** *n.m.* surgeon.

**chitarra,** *n.f.* guitar.

**chiùdere,** *vb.* close, shut. **c. a chiave,** lock.

**chiunque,** *pron.* whoever; whomever.

**chiusa,** *n.f.* lock.

**chiusura,** *n.f.* closure; fastening. **c. lampo,** zipper.

**ci,** *pron.* us; to us.

**ci,** *pro-phrase* (replaces phrases introduced by prepositions of place) there; to it; at it.

**ciabattino,** *n.m.* cobbler.

**ciambellano,** *n.m.* chamberlain.

**cianfrusàglia,** *n.f.* gimcrack; trash.

**ciao,** *interj.* hi!; so long!

**ciarlatanismo,** *n.m.* charlatanism.

**ciarlatano,** *n.m.* charlatan, mountebank.

**ciascuno,** *pron.* each one.

**cibo,** *n.m.* food.

**cicala,** *n.f.* cicada.

**cicatrice,** *n.f.* scar.

**cicatrizzare,** *vb.* scar.

**cicisbèo,** *n.m.* gigolo.

**ciclista,** *n.m.* or *f.* bicyclist.

For pronunciation, see the concise guide on pages 5 to 7.

**complicità,** *n.f.* complicity.

**complimentare,** *vb.* compliment.

**complimento,** *n.m.* compliment.

**complòtto,** *n.m.* plot.

**componènte,** *n.m. and adj.* component.

**comporre,** *vb.* compose.

**comportamento,** *n.m.* behavior.

**comportare,** *vb.* entail, involve; (*refl.*) behave, act.

**compositore,** *n.m.* composer.

**composizione,** *n.f.* composition.

**compostezza,** *n.f.* composure.

**composto,** **1.** *n.m.* compound. **2.** *adj.* composed; compound; composite.

**compra,** *n.f.* purchase.

**comprare,** *vb.* buy; purchase.

**compratore,** *n.m.* buyer, purchaser.

**compréndere,** *vb.* comprehend; comprise.

**comprensibile,** *adj.* comprehensible.

**comprensione,** *n.f.* comprehension, understanding.

**comprensivo,** *adj.* comprehensive.

**compreso,** *adj.* comprised; including.

**compressione,** *n.f.* compression.

**comprèsso,** *adj.* compressed.

**compressore,** *n.m.* compressor.

**comprìmere,** *vb.* compress.

**compromesso,** *n.m.* compromise.

**comprométtere,** *vb.* compromise, endanger.

**comprovare,** *vb.* prove.

**compunzione,** *n.f.* compunction.

**computare,** *vb.* compute.

**computazione,** *n.f.* computation.

**comunale,** *adj.* communal.

**comune,** *adj.* common.

**comunella,** *n.f.* master-key.

**comunemente,** *adv.* commonly.

**comunicàbile,** *adj.* communicable.

**comunicante,** *n.m.* communicant.

**comunicare,** *vb.* communicate; (*refl.*) take communion.

**comunicativo,** *adj.* communicative.

**comunicato,** *n.m.* communiqué.

**comunicazione,** *n.f.* communication.

**comunione,** *n.f.* communion.

**comunismo,** *n.m.* communism.

**comunista,** *n.m. or f.* communist.

**comunìstico,** *adj.* communist.

**comunità,** *n.f.* community.

**comunque,** *adv.* however; howsoever.

**con,** *prep.* with.

**concavo,** *adj.* concave.

**concèdere,** *vb.* grant, concede, allow.

**concentramento,** *n.m.* concentration.

**concentrare,** *vb.* concentrate.

**concentrazione,** *n.f.* concentration.

**concepìbile,** *adj.* conceivable.

**concepibilmente,** *adv.* conceivably.

**concepire,** *vb.* conceive.

**concèrnere,** *vb.* concern.

**concertare,** *vb.* concert.

**concèrto,** *n.m.* concert; concerto.

**concessione,** *n f.* concession; grant, bestowal.

**concètto,** *n.m.* concept.

**conchiglia,** *n.f.* conch-shell.

**conciare,** *vb.* tan.

**conciliare,** *vb.* conciliate.

**conciliativo,** *adj.* conciliatory.

**conciliatore,** *n.m.* conciliator.

**conciliazione,** *n.f.* conciliation.

**concime,** *n.m.* compost, manure.

**concisamente,** *adv.* concisely.

**concisione,** *n.f.* concision, conciseness.

**conciso,** *adj.* concise.

**conclave,** *n.m.* conclave.

**conclùdere,** *vb.* conclude.

**conclusione,** *n.f.* conclusion.

**conclusivamente,** adv. conclusively.

**conclusivo,** adj. conclusive.

**concomitante,** adj. concomitant.

**concordare,** vb. agree.

**concordato,** n.m. concordat.

**concorde,** adj. concordant, agreeing.

**concorrènte,** n. competitor; (sports) entrant.

**concorrènza,** n.f. concurrence; competition.

**concórrere,** vb. compete; concur.

**concorso,** n.m. competition; tournament; contribution; concurrence; rush (of people).

**concozione,** n.f. concoction.

**concretamente,** adv. concretely.

**concretezza,** n.f. concreteness.

**concrèto,** adj. concrete.

**concubina,** n.f. concubine.

**concuòcere,** vb. concoct.

**concupiscente,** adj. lustful.

**concupiscènza,** n.f. lust.

**concussione,** n.f. concussion.

**condanna,** n.f. condemnation; doom; conviction; sentence.

**condannàbile,** adj. condemnable.

**condannare,** vb. condemn; doom; sentence.

**condannato,** n.m. convict.

**condensare,** vb. condense; thicken.

**condensatore,** n.m. condenser.

**condensazione,** n.f. condensation.

**condimento,** n.m. condiment, seasoning; dressing; relish.

**condire,** vb. season, use condiments.

**condividere,** vb. share.

**condizionale,** adj. conditional.

**condizionalmente,** adv. conditionally.

**condizionare,** vb. condition.

**condizione,** n.f. condition; status.

**condoglianza,** n.f. condolence.

**condolere,** vb. condole.

**condonare,** vb. condone.

**condotta,** n.f. conduct, behavior; bearing, deportment.

**condotto,** n.m. conduct.

**conducènte,** n.m. driver.

**condurre,** vb. conduct, lead; conduce; (refl.) behave.

**conduttività,** n.f. conductivity.

**conduttivo,** adj. conductive.

**conduttore,** n.m. conductor.

**conduttura,** n.f. flue.

**confederarsi,** vb. confederate.

**confederato,** n.m. confederate.

**confederazione,** n.f. confederation, confederacy.

**conferènza,** n.f. conference; lecture.

**conferenzière,** n.m. lecturer.

**conferire,** vb. confer, bestow.

**conferma,** n.f. confirmation.

**confermare,** vb. confirm.

**confessare,** vb. confess, admit; avow.

**confessionale,** n.m. and adj. confessional.

**confessione,** n.f. confession, admission, avowal.

**confessore,** n.m. confessor.

**confetteria,** n.f. confectionery, confectioner's shop.

**confettière,** n.m. confectioner.

**confetto,** n.m. candy; confection.

**confettura,** n.f. candy; confection.

**confezione,** n.f. confection (dress).

**confidare,** vb. confide, entrust; rely.

**confidènte,** **1.** n.m. or f. confidant. **2.** adj. confident.

**confidentemente,** adv. confidently.

**confidènza,** n.f. confidence.

**confidenziale,** adj. confidential.

**confinare,** vb. abut; border; confine; verge.

**confine,** n.m. boundary, border.

**confisca,** n.f. confiscation.

**confiscare,** vb. confiscate.

**conflagrazione,** n.f. conflagration.

**conflitto,** n.m. conflict, strife.

**confóndere**, *vb.* confuse, confound, addle, bewilder, befuddle.

**conformarsi**, *vb.* conform.

**conformazione**, *n.f.* conformation.

**conforme**, *adj.* in accordance, in conformity.

**conformemente**, *adv.* accordingly, in conformity.

**conformista**, *n.m.* conformer, conformist.

**conformità**, *n.f.* conformity, accordance.

**confortare**, *vb.* comfort; encourage.

**confortatore**, *n.m.* comforter.

**confòrto**, *n.m.* comfort; encouragement.

**confrontare**, *vb.* compare; confront.

**confronto**, *n.m.* comparison; collation.

**confusione**, *n.f.* confusion, blur, mix-up, turmoil.

**confuso**, *adj.* confused, addled, bewildered.

**confutare**, *vb.* disprove, refute.

**confutazione**, *n.f.* disproof, refutation; rebuttal.

**congedare**, *vb.* dismiss.

**congedo**, *n.m.* dismissal; leave.

**congegno**, *n.m.* contrivance, device, contraption, gadget; gearing.

**congelamento**, *n.m.* congealment; frostbite.

**congelare**, *vb.* congeal.

**congenitamente**, *adv.* congenitally.

**congènito**, *adj.* congenital.

**congestione**, *n.f.* congestion.

**congettura**, *n.f.* conjecture, surmise.

**congetturare**, *vb.* conjecture, surmise.

**congiùngere**, *vb.* join, splice.

**congiuntamente**, *adv.* conjointly.

**congiuntivite**, *n.f.* conjunctivitis.

**congiuntivo**, **1.** *n.m.* (*gramm.*) subjunctive. **2.** *adv.* (verbs) subjunctive; (pronouns) conjunctive.

**congiunto**, *adj.* joint.

**congiunzione**, *n.f.* conjunction; join.

**congiura**, *n.f.* conspiracy.

**congiurare**, *vb.* conspire.

**congiurato**, *n.m.* conspirator.

**conglomerare**, *vb.* conglomerate.

**conglomerato**, *n.m. and adj.* conglomerate.

**conglomerazione**, *n.f.* conglomeration.

**congratularsi con**, *vb.* congratulate.

**congratulazione**, *n.f.* congratulation.

**congregarsi**, *vb.* congregate.

**congregazione**, *n.f.* congregation.

**coniare**, *vb.* coin, mint.

**cònico**, *adj.* conic.

**congrèsso**, *n.m.* congress; convention.

**coniglièra**, *n.f.* hutch.

**coniglietto**, *n.m.* little rabbit, bunny.

**coniglio**, *n.m.* rabbit.

**cònio**, *n.m.* coinage.

**coniugale**, *adj.* conjugal.

**coniugare**, *vb.* conjugate.

**coniugazione**, *n.f.* conjugation.

**connessione**, *n.f.* connection.

**connèsso**, *adj.* related.

**connèttere**, *vb.* connect.

**connivènte**, *adj.* conniving.

**connivènza**, *n.f.* connivance.

**connotare**, *vb.* connote.

**connotazione**, *n.f.* connotation.

**connubiale**, *adj.* connubial.

**còno**, *n.m.* cone.

**conoscènza**, *n.f.* acquaintance, knowledge, cognizance.

**conóscere**, *vb.* know, be acquainted with.

**conoscitore**, *n.m.* connoisseur.

**conosciuto**, *adj.* known, acquainted.

**conquista**, *n.f.* conquest.

**conquistàbile**, *adj.* conquerable.

**conquistare**, *vb.* conquer.

**conquistatore**, *n.m.* conqueror.

**consacrare**, *vb.* consecrate.

**consacrazione**, *n.f.* consecration.

**consapévole**, *adj.* conscious, aware.

**consciamente**, *adv.* consciously.

For pronunciation, see the concise guide on pages 5 to 7.

**cònscio,** *adj.* conscious, aware.

**consecutivamente,** *adv.* consecutively.

**consecutivo,** *adv.* consecutive.

**consegna,** *n.f.* consignment, delivery.

**consegnare,** *vb.* consign, deliver.

**consènso,** *n.m.* concurrence, agreement, assent, consent; consensus.

**consentire,** *vb.* consent, accede.

**conseguènte,** *adj.* consequent.

**conseguentemente,** *adv.* consequently.

**conseguènza,** *n.f.* consequence.

**conseguenziale,** *adj.* consequential.

**consèrva,** *n.f.* jam, preserves; compote.

**conservare,** *vb.* conserve, keep, preserve, retain, store.

**conservativo,** *adj.* preservative.

**conservatore,** *n.m. and adj.* conservative.

**conservatòrio,** *n.m.* conservatory.

**conservazione,** *n.f.* conservation, preservation.

**consideràbile,** *adj.* considerable.

**considerabilmente,** *adv.* considerably.

**considerare,** *vb.* consider.

**considerazione,** *n.f.* consideration.

**considerévole,** *adj.* considerable.

**consigliare,** *vb.* advise, counsel.

**consigliatamente,** *adv.* advisedly.

**consigliatore,** *n.m.* adviser, counselor.

**consiglière,** *n.m.* councilor, counselor.

**consiglio,** *n.m.* advice, counsel; council; board.

**consistènza,** *n.f.* consistency.

**consistere,** *v.b.* consist.

**consolare,** *adj.* consular.

**consolare,** *vb.* console, comfort, solace.

**consolato,** *n.m.* consulate; consulship.

**consolatore,** *n.m.* consoler, comforter.

**consolazione,** *n.f.* consolation, solace.

**console,** *n.m.* consul.

**consòlida reale,** *n.f.* larkspur.

**consolidare,** *vb.* consolidate.

**consonante,** *n.f. and adj.* consonant.

**consòrte,** *n.m. and f.,* consort, mate.

**consòrzio,** *n.m.* syndicate; trust.

**consuèto,** *n.m.* customary.

**consuetùdine,** *n.f.* custom.

**consultare,** *vb.* consult.

**consultatore,** *n.m.* consultant.

**consultazione,** *n.f.* consultation.

**consulto,** *n.m.* consultation.

**consumare,** *vb.* consume; expend, wear out.

**consumato,** *adj.* consummate.

**consumatore,** *n.m.* consumer.

**consumazione,** *n.f.* consummation.

**consumo,** *n.m.* consumption; wear.

**contàbile,** *n.m.* bookkeeper.

**contabilità,** *n.f.* accounting, bookkeeping.

**contadino, 1.** *n.* peasant; countryman; farmer. **2.** *adj.* peasant; rustic.

**contagio,** *n.m.* contagion.

**contagioso,** *adj.* contagious.

**contagocce,** *n.m.* dropper.

**contaminare,** *vb.* contaminate; pollute.

**contanti,** *n.m.pl.* cash.

**contare,** *vb.* count; **c. su** count on, rely on.

**contatore,** *n.m.* meter.

**contatto,** *n.m.* contact.

**conte,** *n.m.* count, earl.

**contèa,** *n.f.* county.

**contemplare,** *vb.* contemplate.

**contemplativo,** *adj.* contemplative.

**contemplazione,** *n.f.* contemplation.

**contemporàneo,** *adj.* contemporary.

**contendènte,** *n.m.* contender.

**contèndere,** *vb.* contend.

**contenere,** *vb.* contain.

**contentezza,** *n.f.* contentment, gladness.

**contènto,** *adj.* glad, happy, content.

**contenzione,** *n.f.* contention.

**contesa,** *n.f.* contest.

**contessa,** *n.f.* countess.

**contestàbile,** *adj.* contestable.

**contestare,** *vb.* contest.

**contèsto,** *n.m.* context.

**contiguo,** *adj.* contiguous.

**continentale,** *adj.* continental.

**continènte, 1.** *n.m.* continent. **2.** *adj.* continent, chaste.

**continènza,** *n.f.* continence.

**contingènte,** *adj.* contingent.

**contingènza,** *n.f.* contingency.

**continuamente,** *adv.* continually.

**continuare,** *vb.* continue.

**continuazione,** *n.f.* continuation.

**continuità,** *n.f.* continuity.

**contìnuo,** *adj.* continual, continuous. **corrènte contìnua,** direct current.

**conto,** *n.m.* account; bill; check; count. **rèndere conto dì,** account for. **rèndersi c. dì,** realize.

**contòrcere,** *vb.* contort; (*refl.*) writhe.

**contorno,** *n.m.* contour; side-dish.

**contorsione,** *n.f.* contortion.

**contorsionista,** *n.m.* contortionist.

**contrabbandière,** *n.m.* smuggler.

**contrabbando,** *n.m.* contraband, smuggling.

**contraddicàbile,** *adj.* contradictable.

**contraddire,** *vb.* contradict; gainsay.

**contraddittòrio,** *adj.* contradictory.

**contraddizione,** *n.f.* contradiction.

**contraffare,** *vb.* counterfeit; forge; imitate; impersonate.

**contraffattore,** *n.m.* forger; impersonator.

**contraffazione,** *n.f.* forgery; impersonation.

**contraffòrte,** *n.m.* buttress.

**contralto,** *n.m.* contralto; alto.

**contrappeso,** *n.m.* counterbalance.

**contrariare,** *vb.* spite.

**contràrio,** *adj.* contrary; reverse.

**contrarre,** *vb.* contract; (*refl.*) shrink.

**contrastare,** *vb.* contrast.

**contrasto,** *n.m.* contrast.

**contrattacco,** *n.m.* counterattack.

**contrattatore,** *n.m.* contractor.

**contratto,** *n.m.* contract.

**contravventore,** *n.m.* violator.

**contravvenzione,** *n.f.* misdemeanor, violation.

**contrazione,** *n.f.* contraction.

**contribuènte,** *n.m.* taxpayer.

**contribuire,** *vb.* contribute.

**contributivo,** *adj.* contributive.

**contributo,** *n.m.* contribution.

**contributore,** *n.m.* contributor.

**contributòrio,** *adj.* contributory.

**contribuzione,** *n.f.* contribution.

**contrito,** *adj.* contrite.

**contrizione,** *n.f.* contrition.

**contro,** *prep.* against, versus. **c. assegno,** C.O.D.

**controazione,** *n.f.* counteraction.

**controcurva,** *n.f.* reverse curve.

**controffensiva,** *n.f.* counteroffensive.

**controllàbile,** *adj.* controllable.

**controllare,** *vb.* check, inspect; audit.

**contròllo,** *n.m.* check; restraint; inspection; audit.

**controllore,** *n.m.* controller; inspector; auditor; ticketcollector.

**contromandare,** *vb.* countermand.

**contromarca,** *n.f.* check.

For pronunciation, see the concise guide on pages 5 to 7.

**contropartita,** *n.f.* counterpart.

**Controriforma,** *n.f.* Counter-Reformation.

**controvèrsia,** *n.f.* controversy.

**controvèrso,** *adj.* controversial.

**contumace,** *adj.* defaulting.

**contumàcia,** *n.f.* default.

**contusione,** *n.f.* contusion.

**convalescènte,** *adj.* convalescent.

**convalescènza,** *n.f.* convalescence.

**conveniènte,** *adj.* convenient; advisable; suitable; fitting.

**convenientemente,** *adv.* conveniently.

**conveniènza,** *n.f.* convenience; advisability; suitability; propriety.

**convenire,** *vb.* come together, convene; be suitable; become: befit.

**convènto,** *n.m.* convent; monastery.

**convenzionale,** *adj.* conventional.

**convenzionalmente,** *adv.* conventionally.

**convenzione,** *n.f.* convention; covenant.

**convergènte,** *adj.* convergent.

**convergènza,** *n.f.* convergence.

**convèrgere,** *vb.* converge.

**conversare,** *vb.* converse.

**conversatore,** *n.m.* conversationalist.

**convèrso,** *adj.* converse.

**convertìbile,** *adj.* convertible.

**convertire,** *vb.* convey.

**convertitrice,** *n.f.* converter.

**convèsso,** *adj.* convex.

**convincènte,** *adj.* convincing, cogent.

**convincere,** *vb.* convince.

**convinzione,** *n.f.* conviction.

**conviviale,** *adj.* convivial.

**convocare,** *vb.* convoke.

**convocazione,** *n.f.* convocation.

**convogliare,** *vb.* convoy.

**convòglio,** *n.m.* convoy, train, procession.

**convulsione,** *n.f.* convulsion.

**convulsivo,** *adj.* convulsive.

**cooperare,** *vb.* cooperate.

**cooperativa,** *n.f.* cooperative.

**cooperativamente,** *adv.* cooperatively.

**cooperativo,** *adj.* cooperative.

**coordinare,** *vb.* coordinate.

**coordinatore,** *n.m.* coordinator.

**coordinazione,** *n.f.* coordination.

**coòrte,** *n.m.* cohort.

**copèrchio,** *n.m.* lid.

**copèrta,** *n.f.* cover, blanket.

**copertina,** *n.f.* cover (of book).

**copertura,** *n.f.* cover, covering.

**còpia,** *n.f.* copy; copiousness.

**copiare,** *vb.* copy.

**copiosamente,** *adv.* copiously.

**copiosità,** *n.f.* copiousness.

**copioso,** *adj.* copious.

**copista,** *n.m.* copyist.

**coppa,** *n.f.* cup, mug, flagon, goblet.

**coprifuòco,** *n.m.* curfew.

**coprire,** *vb.* cover.

**coppia,** *n.f.* couple.

**coraggio,** *n.m.* courage, bravery; gameness; gallantry; mettle.

**coraggiosamente,** *adv.* courageously, gamely, gallantly.

**coraggioso,** *adj.* brave, courageous; game; gallant.

**corale,** *adj.* choral.

**corallo,** *n.m.* coral.

**còrda,** *n.f.* string, rope, cord; chord.

**cordiale,** *n.m. and adj.* cordial, hearty.

**cordialità,** *n.f.* cordiality.

**cordialmente,** *adv.* cordially.

**cordiglièra,** *n.f.* ladder; run.

**cordone,** *n.m.* cordon.

**cordovano,** *n.m.* cordovan.

**Corèa,** *n.f.* Korea.

**coreggiato,** *n.m.* flail.

**coreografia,** *n.f.* choreography.

**coreògrafo,** *n.m.* choreographer.

**coriàndoli,** *n.m.pl.* confetti.

**corista,** *n.m.* chorister.

**cornamusa,** *n.f.* bagpipe.

**còrnea,** *n.f.* cornea.

**cornetta,** *n.f.* cornet.

**cornettista,** *n.m.* cornetist.

**cornice,** *n.m.* frame; mantel.

**cornicione,** *n.m.* cornice.

**còrno,** *n.m.* horn.

**cornucòpia,** *n.m. or f.* cornucopia.

**còro,** *n.m.* chorus, choir; chancel.

**corollàrio,** *n.m.* corollary.

**coróna,** *n.f.* crown. **corona nobiliare,** coronet.

**coronàrio,** *adj.* coronary.

**còrpo,** *n.m.* body; corps.

**corporale,** *adj.* corporal.

**corporato,** *adj.* corporate.

**corporazione,** *n.f.* corporation; guild.

**corpòreo,** *adj.* corporeal, bodily.

**corpulènto,** *adj.* corpulent, burly, portly.

**corpùscolo,** *n.m.* corpuscle.

**corredare,** *vb.* equip, outfit, provide.

**corrèdo,** *n.m.* equipment, outfit.

**corrèggere,** *vb.* correct, amend, right.

**correlazione,** *n.f.* correlation.

**corrènte, 1.** *n.f.* current; stream. **c. alternata,** alternating current. **c. contìnua,** direct current. **c. d'ària,** draft. **2.** *adj.* current; (in dates) instant.

**correntemente,** *adv.* currently.

**correntista,** *n.m.* depositor.

**córrere,** *vb.* run; race.

**correttamente,** *adv.* correctly.

**correttezza,** *n.f.* correctness.

**correttivo,** *adj.* corrective.

**corrètto,** *adj.* correct, right.

**correzione,** *n.f.* correction.

**corridoio,** *n.m.* corridor, hallway; lobby.

**corridore,** *n.m.* runner.

**corrière,** *n.m.* courier.

**corrispondènte, 1.** *n.* correspondent. **2.** *adj.* corresponding; correspondent.

**corrispondènza,** *n.f.* correspondence.

**corrispóndere,** *vb.* correspond.

**corroborare,** *vb.* corroborate.

**corroborativo,** *adj.* corroborative.

**corroborazione,** *n.f.* corroboration.

**corródere,** *vb.* corrode.

**corrómpere,** *vb.* corrupt; bribe.

**corrosione,** *n.f.* corrosion.

**corrugare,** *vb.* corrugate, wrinkle.

**corruttibile,** *adj.* corruptible.

**corruttivo,** *adj.* corruptive.

**corruttore,** *n.m.* corrupter; briber.

**corruzione,** *n.f.* corruption; bribery.

**corsa,** *n.f.* race; ride; trip.

**corso,** *n.m.* course.

**còrso,** *adj.* Corsican.

**corte,** *n.f.* court.

**cortéccia,** *n.f.* bark.

**corteggiamento,** *n.m.* courting, courtship.

**corteggiare,** *vb.* court, woo.

**corteggiatore,** *n.m.* wooer, beau, suitor.

**cortèo,** *n.m.* cortege, procession; pageant.

**cortese,** *adj.* courteous, accommodating, polite.

**cortesia,** *n.f.* courtesy, politeness.

**cortigiana,** *n.f.* courtesan, prostitute.

**cortigiano,** *n.m.* courtier.

**cortile,** *n.m.* courtyard, patio.

**cortina,** *n.f.* curtain.

**corto,** *adj.* short; stupid; (of sea) choppy.

**corvetta,** *n.f.* corvette.

**corvino,** *adj.* raven.

**còrvo,** *n.m.* crow; raven.

**còsa,** *n.f.* thing.

**coscia,** *n.f.* thigh.

**cosciènza,** *n.f.* consciousness; conscience.

**coscienziosamente,** *adv.* conscientiously.

**coscienzioso,** *adj.* conscientious, painstaking.

**coscritto,** *n.m. and adj.* conscript.

**coscrizione,** *n.f.* conscription.

**così,** *adv.* so, thus.

**cosmètico,** *n.m. and adj.* cosmetic.

**còsmico,** *adj.* cosmic.

**còsmo,** *n.m.* cosmos.

**cosmopolita,** *adj.* cosmopolitan.

**cóso,** *n.m.* thingumajig.

For pronunciation, see the concise guide on pages 5 to 7.

**cospàrgere**, *vb.* scatter, intersperse, sprinkle, strew.

**cospicuamente**, *adv.* conspicuously.

**cospicuità**, *n.f.* conspicuousness.

**cospìcuo**, *adj.* conspicuous.

**còsta**, *n.f.* coast.

**costante**, *adj.* constant, fixed, firm.

**costantemente**, *adv.* constantly.

**costanza**, *n.f.* constancy.

**costare**, *vb.* cost.

**costellazione**, *n.f.* constellation.

**costernare**, *vb.* dismay.

**costernazione**, *n.f.* consternation, dismay.

**costièro**, *adj.* coastal.

**costituènte**, *adj.* constituent.

**costituire**, *vb.* constitute.

**costituzionale**, *adj.* constitutional.

**costituzione**, *n.f.* constitution.

**còsto**, *n.m.* cost, expense.

**còstola**, *n.f.* rib.

**costoletta**, *n.f.* cutlet; chop.

**costosamente**, *adv.* expensively.

**costosità**, *n.f.* costliness.

**costoso**, *adj.* costly, dear, expensive, valuable.

**costringere**, *vb.* force, coerce, compel, constrict, constrain.

**costrizione**, *n.f.* compulsion, constriction, constraint.

**costruire**, *vb.* construct, build, erect.

**costruttivamente**, *adv.* constructively.

**costruttivo**, *adj.* constructive.

**costruttore**, *n.m.* builder, constructor.

**costruzione**, *n.f.* construction, erection.

**costume**, *n.m.* costume, garb; custom; (*pl.*) mores.

**còte**, *n.f.* hone.

**cotiglione**, *n.m.* cotillion.

**cotone**, *n.m.* cotton.

**cotonina**, *n.f.* cotton cloth, cretonne.

**còtto**, *adj.* cooked; done.

**còttro**, *n.m.* cutter.

**covare**, *vb.* brood, hatch; smolder.

**covata**, *n.f.* brood.

**covo**, *n.m.* den, lair.

**covone**, *n.m.* sheaf.

**crampo**, *n.m.* cramp.

**crànio**, *n.m.* cranium, skull.

**cratère**, *n.m.* crater.

**cravatta**, *n.f.* necktie.

**creare**, *vb.* create.

**creativo**, *adj.* creative.

**creatore**, *n.m.* creator.

**creatura**, *n.f.* creature.

**creazione**, *n.f.* creation.

**credènte**, *n.m.* believer.

**credènza**, *n.f.* belief, credence; cupboard; dresser.

**credenziali**, *f.pl.* credentials.

**crédere**, *vb.* believe, think.

**credìbile**, *adj.* credible, believable.

**credibilità**, *n.f.* credibility.

**crèdito**, *n.m.* credit.

**creditore**, *n.m.* creditor.

**crèdo**, *n.m.* credo, creed.

**credulità**, *n.f.* credulity.

**crèdulo**, *adj.* credulous, gullible.

**credulone**, *n.m.* dupe.

**cremaglièra**, *n.f.* rack.

**cremare**, *vb.* cremate.

**crematòrio**, *adj.* crematory.

**cremazione**, *n.f.* cremation.

**crèma**, *n.f.* cream.

**crema caramèlla**, *n.f.* custard.

**cremerìa**, *n.f.* creamery.

**cremisi**, *adj.* crimson.

**creosòto**, *n.m.* creosote.

**crèpa**, *n.f.* crack, chink.

**crepàccio**, *n.m.* crevasse.

**crepacuòre**, *n.m.* heartbreak.

**crepùscolo**, *n.m.* twilight, dusk.

**créscere**, *vb.* grow.

**créscita**, *n.f.* growth.

**crespo, 1.** *n.m.* crepe. **2.** *adj.* wavy; crisp.

**cresta**, *n.f.* crest, ridge; (rooster's) comb.

**crèta**, *n.f.* clay.

**cricca**, *n.f.* clique, clan.

**cricco**, *n.m.* jack.

**criminale**, *adj.* criminal.

**criminologia**, *n.f.* criminology.

**criminòlogo**, *n.m.* criminologist.

**crine**, *n.f.* hair.

**crinièra**, *n.f.* mane.

**cripta**, *n.f.* crypt.

crisàlide, n.f. chrysalis.

crisantèmo, n.m. chrysanthemum.

crisi, n.f. crisis.

cristallerìe, n f.pl. glassware.

cristallino, adj. crystalline.

cristallizzare, vb. crystallize.

cristallo, n.m. crystal; cut glass.

cristianésimo, n.m. Christianity.

cristianità, n.f. Christendom.

cristiano, n. and adj. Christian.

critèrio, n.m. criterion.

crìtica, n.f. criticism, critique, fault finding.

criticare, vb. criticize.

crìtico, 1. n. critic. 2. adj. critical.

crittografìa, n.f. cryptography.

crivellare, vb. sift; screen.

crivèllo, n.m. sieve; screen.

croccante, adj. crisp.

crocchetta, n.f. croquette.

croce, n.f. cross.

crocefissione, n.f. crucifixion.

crocefisso, n.m. crucifix.

crocevìa, n.f. crossroads.

crociata, n.f. crusade.

crociato, n.m. crusader.

crocicchio, n.m. crossroads.

crocièra, n.f. crusade.

crocifiggere, vb. crucify.

crogiolo, n.m. crucible.

crollare, vb. collapse, crash.

cròllo, n.m. collapse, crash.

cromàtico, adj. chromatic.

cròmo, m. chrome, chromium.

cromosòma, n.m. chromosome.

crònaca, n.f. chronicle.

cronicamente, adv. chronically.

crònico, adj. chronic.

cronista, n.m. chronicler; (newspaper) columnist; (radio) commentator.

cronologìa, n.f. chronology.

cronològico, adj. chronological.

crosta, n.f. crust; scab.

crostàceo, n.m. and adj. crustacean.

crostino, n.m. crouton; canapé.

crostoso, adj. crusty.

crùccio, n.m. chagrin.

crucivèrba, n.m. cross-word puzzle.

crudèle, adj. cruel.

crudeltà, n.f. cruelty.

crudezza, n.f. crudeness.

crudità, n.f. crudity.

crudo, adj. crude, raw.

crumiro, n.m. scab, strikebreaker.

crup, n.m. croup.

crusca, n.f. bran.

cruscòtto, n.m. dashboard.

cùbico, adj. cubic.

cubìcolo, n.m. cubicle.

cubismo, n.m. cubism.

cubo, n.m. cube.

cuccetta, n.f. berth, bunk.

cucchiàia, n.f. spoon; scoop.

cucchiaiata, n.f. spoonful.

cucchiaino, n.m. (small) spoon.

cucciolo, n.m. puppy.

cucina, n.f. kitchen, cuisine; cooking. c. econòmica, range. libro di c., cookbook.

cucinare, vb. cook.

cucire, vb. sew.

cucitura, n.f. sewing; seam.

cuculo, n.m. cuckoo.

cuffia, n.f. cap; hood; earphone.

cugina, n.f. cousin.

cugino, n.m. cousin.

cui, pron. which; to which; whom; to whom; of which; whose.

cùlice, n.m. gnat.

culinàrio, adj. culinary.

culla, n.f. cradle.

cullare, vb. cradle, lull.

culminante, adj. culminating, climactic.

culminare, vb. culminate.

culminazione, n.f. culmination.

cùlmine, n.m. top; summit; climax.

culo, n.m. posterior.

culto, n.m. cult; worship.

cultura, n.f. culture.

culturale, adj. cultural.

cumulativo, adj. cumulative.

cùneo, n.m. wedge.

**cunetta,** *n.f.* gutter.
**cuòco,** *n.m.* cook, chef.
**cuòio,** *n.m.* leather.
**cuòre,** *n.m.* heart.
**cupè,** *n.m.* coupé.
**cupidigia,** *n.f.* greed, cupidity.
**cupo,** *adj.* sullen.
**cùpola,** *n.f.* cupola, dome.
**cura,** *n.f.* care; cure; worry.
**curare,** *vb.* care for, take care of, nurse, nurture, tend; (*refl.*) care.
**curatore,** *n.m.* curator.
**curiosità,** *n.f.* curiosity, curiosity.
**curioso,** *adj.* curious.
**currìcolo,** *n.m.* curriculum.
**curva,** *n.f.* curve.

**curvare,** *vb.* curve, bend, warp; hunch; (*refl.*) stoop.
**curvatura,** *n.f.* curvature; crook.
**curvo,** *adj.* curved; bent; stooped.
**cuscinetto,** *n.m.* pad; stamp pad; (machinery) bearing; **stato c.** buffer state; **c. a rotolamento,** roller bearing; **c. a sfere,** ball bearing.
**cuscino,** *n.m.* cushion.
**custòde,** *n.m.* custodian, guardian, keeper.
**custòdia,** *n.f.* custody, charge.
**custodire,** *vb.* guard.
**cutàneo,** *adj.* cutaneous.
**cutìcola,** *n.f.* cuticle.

# D

**da,** *prep.* from; by; for; fit for, suitable for; characteristic of; at . . .'s (house, shop, etc.).
**dado,** *n.m.* die (*pl.* dice).
**daga,** *n.f.* dagger.
**dàina,** *n.f.* hind.
**dàino,** *n.m.* buck.
**dàlia,** *n.f.* dahlia.
**dama,** *n.f.* lady; checkers.
**damasco,** *n.m.* damask.
**damerino,** *n.m.* dandy, fop.
**damigèlla,** *n.f.* damsel. **d. d'onore,** maid of honor, bridesmaid.
**danese,** *adj.* Danish.
**Danimarca,** *n.f.* Denmark.
**dannare,** *vb.* damn.
**dannazione,** *n.f.* damnation.
**danneggiare,** *vb.* harm, damage, injure; mar.
**danno,** *n.m.* harm, damage, detriment, hurt, injury.
**dannoso,** *adj.* harmful, baneful, detrimental, hurtful, injurious.
**danza,** *n.f.* dance.
**danzare,** *vb.* dance.
**dappertutto,** *adv.* everywhere; throughout.
**dardo,** *n.m.* dart.

**dare,** *vb.* give.
**data,** *n.f.* date.
**datare,** *vb.* date.
**dati,** *n.m.pl.* data.
**datore,** *n.m.* giver. **d. di lavoro,** employer.
**dàttero,** *n.m.* date.
**dattilògrafa,** *n.f.* typist.
**dattilografare,** *vb.* type.
**davanti,** **1.** *n.m.* front. **2.** *adv.* before. **davanti a,** *prep.* before.
**davanzale,** *n.m.* sill.
**davvero,** *adv.* indeed, really.
**dàzio,** *n.m.* excise.
**dèa,** *n.f.* goddess.
**debilitare,** *vb.* debilitate.
**debitamente,** *adv.* duly.
**dèbito,** **1.** *n.m.* debt, debit. **2.** *adj.* due.
**debitore,** *n.m.* debtor.
**dèbole,** *adj.* weak, feeble, faint, frail, puny.
**debolezza,** *n.f.* weakness, feebleness, failing, frailty.
**debolmente,** *adv.* weakly, faintly.
**debuttante,** *n.* debutant(e).
**debutto,** *n.m.* debut.
**decalcomanìa,** *n.f.* decalcomania.
**decadènte,** *adj.* decadent.

**decadènza,** *n.f.* decay, decadence, decline.

**decadere,** *vb.* decay, decline, lapse.

**decano,** *n.m.* dean.

**decapitare,** *vb.* behead, decapitate.

**deceduto,** *adj.* deceased.

**decènnio,** *n.m.* decade.

**decènte,** *adj.* decent.

**decentramento,** *n.m.* decentralization.

**decentrare,** *vb.* decentralize.

**decènza,** *n.f.* decency.

**decìdere,** *vb.* decide; (*refl.*) decide, make up one's mind, resolve.

**decìduo,** *adj.* deciduous.

**decifrare,** *vb.* decipher, decode.

**decimale,** *adj.* decimal.

**decimare,** *vb.* decimate.

**dècimo,** *adj.* tenth.

**decimonòno,** *adj.* nineteenth.

**decimosèsto,** *adj.* sixteenth.

**decimotèrzo,** *adj.* thirteenth.

**decimottavo,** *adj.* eighteenth.

**decisione,** *n.f.* decision, resolve.

**decisivo,** *adj.* decisive.

**declamare,** *vb.* declaim.

**declamazione,** *n.f.* declamation.

**declinare,** *vb.* decline.

**declinazione,** *n.f.* declension.

**decomporre,** *vb.* decompose, decay.

**decomposizione,** *n.f.* decomposition, decay.

**decorare,** *vb.* decorate.

**decorativo,** *adj.* decorative.

**decoratore,** *n.m.* decorator.

**decorazione,** *n.f.* decoration.

**decòro,** *n.m.* decorum.

**decoroso,** *adj.* decorous.

**decrèpito,** *adj.* decrepit.

**decretare,** *vb.* decree; enact.

**decreto,** *n.m.* decree; enactment.

**dèdica,** *n.f.* dedication.

**dedicare,** *vb.* dedicate, devote; (*refl.*) become addicted.

**dedurre,** *vb.* deduce, deduct.

**deduttivo,** *adj.* deductive.

**deduzione,** *n.f.* deduction.

**deferènte,** *adj.* deferent.

**deferènza,** *n.f.* deference.

**defezione,** *n.f.* defection.

**deficiènte,** *adj.* deficient.

**deficiènza,** *n.f.* deficiency.

**dèficit,** *n.m.* deficit.

**definire,** *vb.* define.

**definitivamente,** *adj.* definitely.

**definitivo,** *adj.* definitive.

**definito,** *adj.* definite; finite.

**definizione,** *n.f.* definition.

**deflazionare,** *vb.* deflate.

**deflazione,** *n.f.* deflation.

**deflèttere,** *vb.* deflect.

**deformare,** *vb.* deform.

**deforme,** *adj.* deformed.

**deformità,** *n.f.* deformity.

**defraudare,** *vb.* defraud.

**defunto,** *adj.* defunct, deceased.

**degenerare,** *vb.* degenerate.

**degenerato,** *n.m. and adj.* degenerate.

**degenerazione,** *n.f.* degeneration.

**degènte,** *adj.* bedridden.

**degnarsi,** *vb.* deign.

**degno,** *adj.* worthy.

**degradare,** *vb.* degrade, demote.

**degradazione,** *n.f.* degradation.

**deificare,** *vb.* deify.

**deità,** *n.f.* deity.

**delegare,** *vb.* delegate.

**delegato,** *n.m.* delegate.

**delegazione,** *n.f.* delegation.

**delfino,** *n.m.* dolphin.

**deliberare,** *vb.* deliberate.

**deliberatamente,** *adv.* deliberately.

**deliberativo,** *adj.* deliberative.

**deliberato,** *adj.* deliberate.

**deliberazione,** *n.f.* advisement; deliberation.

**delicatezza,** *n.f.* delicacy.

**delicato,** *adj.* delicate, dainty.

**delineare,** *vb.* delineate.

**delinquènte,** *adj.* delinquent.

**delinquènza,** *n.f.* delinquency.

**delirante,** *adj.* delirious.

**delirare,** *vb.* be delirious, rave.

**delìrio,** *n.m.* delirium.

**delitto,** *n.m.* crime.

**delizioso,** *adj.* delicious.

**delùdere,** *vb.* delude; disappoint.

---

For pronunciation, see the concise guide on pages 5 to 7.

**delusione,** *n.f.* delusion; disappointment.

**demagogo,** *n.m.* demagogue.

**demarcazione,** *n.f.* demarcation.

**demènte,** *adj.* demented.

**demeritare,** *vb.* forfeit.

**demèrito,** *n.m.* demerit.

**democràtico, 1.** *n.m.* democrat. **2.** *adj.* democratic.

**democrazìa,** *n.f.* democracy.

**demolire,** *vb.* demolish.

**demolizione,** *n.f.* demolition.

**demonìaco,** *adj.* demoniacal, fiendish.

**demònio,** *n.m.* demon, fiend.

**demoralizzare,** *vb.* demoralize.

**denaro,** *n.m.* money.

**denaturare,** *vb.* denature.

**denigrare,** *vb.* denigrate, blacken, slander, cast aspersions on, belittle.

**denigrazione,** *n.f.* slander, aspersion.

**denominatore,** *n.m.* denominator.

**denominazione,** *n.f.* denomination.

**densità,** *n.f.* density.

**dènso,** *adj.* dense, thick.

**dentale,** *adj.* dental.

**dentellare,** *vb.* indent.

**dènte,** *n.m.* tooth; cog.

**dentellatura,** *n.f.* indentation.

**dentièra,** *n.f.* denture; gearing. **ferrovia a d.** cog railway.

**dentifrìcio,** *n.m.* dentifrice.

**dentista,** *n.m.* dentist.

**dentro,** *adv. and prep.* inside, within.

**denudare,** *vb.* denude.

**denùncia,** *n.f.* denunciation.

**denunciare,** *vb.* denounce; report.

**deodorante,** *n.m.* deodorant.

**deodorare,** *vb.* deodorize.

**deperìbile,** *adj.* perishable.

**deplorare,** *vb.* deplore.

**deplorévole,** *adj.* deplorable.

**deporre,** *vb.* depose; put down, set down; lay.

**deportare,** *vb.* deport.

**deportazione,** *n.f.* deportation.

**depositante,** *n.m.* depositor.

**depositare,** *vb.* deposit.

**depòsito,** *n.m.* deposit; de-

pot. **d. bagagli,** checkroom.

**deposizione,** *n.f.* deposition, statement.

**depravare,** *vb.* deprave.

**depravazione,** *n.f.* depravity.

**deprecare,** *vb.* deprecate, decry.

**depredamento,** *n.m.* depredation.

**depressone,** *n.f.* depression.

**deprezzare,** *vb.* depreciate, cheapen.

**deprezzamento,** *n.m.* depreciation.

**deprìmere,** *vb.* depress.

**deputato,** *n.m.* deputy, representative.

**deragliare,** *vb.* derail.

**derelitto,** *adj.* derelict.

**deridere,** *vb.* deride, mock, laugh at, ridicule.

**derisione,** *n.f.* derision, mockery.

**derisivo,** *adj.* derisive.

**deriva,** *n.f.* drift. **alla d.,** adrift.

**derivare,** *vb.* derive.

**derivativo,** *adj.* derivative.

**derivazione,** *n.f.* derivation.

**dermatologìa,** *n.f.* dermatology.

**derogatòrio,** *adj.* derogatory.

**derubare,** *vb.* rob.

**descrittivo,** *adj.* descriptive.

**descrizione,** *n.f.* description.

**desecrare,** *vb.* desecrate.

**desensibilizzare,** *vb.* desensitize.

**desèrto,** *n.m.* desert; wilderness.

**desideràbile,** *adj.* desirable.

**desiderabilità,** *n.f.* desirability.

**desiderare,** *vb.* desire, want, wish.

**desidèrio,** *n.m.* desire, wish.

**desideroso,** *adj.* desirous.

**designare,** *vb.* designate, nominate.

**designato,** *n.m.* nominee.

**designazione,** *n.f.* designation.

**desinènza,** *n.f.* ending.

**desìstere,** *vb.* desist.

**desolare,** *vb.* desolate.

**desolato,** *adj.* desolate.

**desolazione,** *n.f.* desolation.

**dèspota,** *n.m.* despot.

---

For pronunciation, see the concise guide on pages 5 to 7.

**destinare,** *vb.* destine.

**destinatàrio,** *n.m.* addressee.

**destinazione,** *n.f.* destination.

**destino,** *n.m.* destiny, doom.

**destituito,** *adj.* destitute.

**destituzione,** *n.f.* destitution.

**dèstra,** *n.f.* right.

**destramente,** *adv.* skillfully, dexterously.

**destrezza,** *n.f.* adroitness, adeptness, dexterity, skill.

**dèstro,** *adj.* adroit, adept, deft, skillful, dexterous, handy; right.

**destrórso,** *adj. and adv.* clockwise.

**desùmere,** *vb.* gather; infer.

**detenere,** *vb.* detain.

**detenzione,** *n.f.* detention.

**detergènte,** *n.m. and adj.* detergent.

**deteriorare,** *vb.* deteriorate.

**deteriorazione,** *n.f.* deterioration.

**determinare,** *vb.* determine.

**determinazione,** *n.f.* determination.

**determinismo,** *n.m.* determinism.

**detestare,** *vb.* detest, abhor.

**detestazione,** *n.f.* detestation, abhorrence.

**detonare,** *vb.* detonate.

**detonazione,** *n.f.* detonation, report.

**detrarre,** *vb.* detract.

**detrimento,** *n.m.* detriment.

**detriti,** *n.m.pl.* debris.

**detronizzare,** *vb.* dethrone.

**dettagliare,** *vb.* detail.

**dèttaglio,** *n.m.* detail. **al d.,** at retail.

**dettare,** *vb.* dictate.

**dettatura,** *n.f.* dictation.

**devastare,** *vb.* devastate, ravage.

**devastazione,** *n.f.* devastation, havoc, ravage.

**deviare,** *vb.* deviate.

**deviazione,** *n.f.* deviation, detour.

**dèvio,** *adj.* devious.

**devitalizzare,** *vb.* devitalize.

**dev.mo** (for **devotissimo,** *adj.*): **Vostro d.,** yours truly.

**devòto,** *adj.* devout, devoted, godly.

**devozione,** *n.f.* devotion.

**di,** *prep.* of; than.

**diabète,** *n.f.* diabetic.

**diàbolico,** *adj.* diabolic, devilish.

**diàccio,** *adj.* icy.

**diàcono,** *n.m.* deacon.

**diadèma,** *n.m.* diadem, coronet.

**diaframma,** *n.m.* diaphragm; midriff.

**diàgnosi,** *n.f.* diagnosis.

**diagnosticare,** *vb.* diagnose.

**diagnòstico,** *adj.* diagnostic.

**diagonale,** *adj.* diagonal.

**diagonalmente,** *adv.* diagonally.

**diagramma,** *n.m.* diagram.

**dialètto,** *n.m.* dialect.

**diàlogo,** *n.m.* dialogue.

**diamante,** *n.m.* diamond.

**diametrale,** *adj.* diametrical.

**diàmetro,** *n.m.* diameter.

**diàmine!,** *interj.* the dickens!

**diàrio,** *n.m.* diary.

**diarrèa,** *n.f.* diarrhea.

**diatermìa,** *n.f.* diathermy.

**diatriba,** *n.f.* diatribe.

**diàvolo,** *n.m.* devil.

**dibàttere,** *vb.* debate; (*refl.*) flounder.

**dibattimento,** *n.m.* debate.

**di buon' ora,** *adv.* early. ✱

**dicèmbre,** *n.m.* December.

**dicerìa,** *n.f.* gossip, rumor.

**dichiarare,** *vb.* declare, explain. **d. ricevuta di,** acknowledge receipt of.

**dichiarativo,** *adj.* declarative.

**dichiarazione,** *n.f.* declaration; explanation.

**diciannòve,** *num.* nineteen.

**diciannovèsimo,** *adj.* nineteenth.

**diciassètte,** *num.* seventeen.

**diciassettèsimo,** *adj.* seventeenth.

**diciottèsimo,** *adj.* eighteenth.

**diciòtto,** *num.* eighteen.

**didàttico,** *adj.* didactic.

**dièci,** *num.* ten.

**dièsis,** *n.m.* sharp (music).

**dièta,** *n.f.* diet.

**dietètica,** *n.f.* dietetics.

**dietètico,** *adj.* dietetic, dietary.

**dietista,** *n.m.* dietitian.

**dìetro a,** *prep.* behind.

**difèndere**, vb. defend, advocate.

**difensìbile**, adj. defensible.

**difensivo**, adj. defensive.

**difensore**, n.m. defender, advocate.

**difesa**, n.f. defense, advocacy.

**difètto**, n.m. defect, fault, flaw.

**difettoso**, adj. defective, faulty.

**diffamare**, vb. defame, libel, malign.

**diffamatòrio**, adj. defamatory, libelous.

**diffamazione**, n.f. defamation.

**differènte**, adj. different.

**differènza**, n.f. difference.

**differenziale**, adj. differential.

**differenziare**, vb. differentiate.

**differire**, vb. defer, put off; differ.

**difficile**, adj. difficult.

**difficoltà**, n.f. difficulty.

**difficoltoso**, adj. fussy.

**diffidare di**, vb. mistrust.

**diffóndere**, vb. diffuse, spread; (refl.) expatiate, dwell upon.

**diffusione**, n.f. diffusion.

**diffuso**, adj. diffuse, widespread.

**difterite**, n.f. diphtheria.

**diga**, n.f. dike, dam, levee.

**digeribile**, adj. digestible.

**digerire**, vb. digest.

**digestione**, n.f. digestion.

**digestivo**, adj. digestive.

**digitale**, n.f. digitalis, foxglove.

**digiunare**, vb. fast.

**digiuno**, n.m. fast.

**dignificare**, vb. dignify.

**dignità**, n.f. dignity.

**dignitàrio**, n.m. dignitary.

**dignitoso**, adj. dignified.

**digredire**, vb. digress.

**digressione**, n.f. digression.

**digressivo**, adj. discursive.

**digrignare**, vb. gnash.

**dilapidato**, adj. dilapidated.

**dilapidazione**, n.f. dilapidation, disrepair.

**dilatare**, vb. dilate.

**dilatòrio**, adj. dilatory.

**dilemma**, n.m. dilemma.

**dilettante**, n.m. amateur.

**dilettévole**, adj. delightful, delectable.

**dilètto**, 1. n. delight. 2. adj. beloved, darling.

**diligènte**, adj. diligent.

**diligènza**, n.f. diligence.

**diluire**, vb. dilute.

**diluviare**, vb. rain cats and dogs.

**dilùvio**, n.m. deluge.

**diluzione**, n.f. dilution.

**dimenare**, vb. wag; (refl.) toss about; flounce.

**dimensione**, n.f. dimension.

**dimenticare**, vb. forget.

**diméntico**, adj. forgetful.

**diméttere**, vb. dismiss; (refl.) resign, quit.

**dimezzare**, vb. halve, cut in half.

**diminuire**, vb. diminish, lessen, abate, decrease, dwindle, let up, subside.

**diminutivo**, n.m. and adj. diminutive.

**diminuzione**, n.f. diminution, lessening, abatement, decrease.

**dimissione**, n.f. resignation.

**dimora**, n.f. abode, dwelling.

**dimostràbile**, adj. demonstrable.

**dimostrare**, vb. demonstrate.

**dimostrativo**, adj. demonstrative.

**dimostratore**, n.m. demonstrator.

**dimostrazione**, n.f. demonstration.

**dinàmica**, n.f. dynamics.

**dinàmico**, adj. dynamic.

**dinamite**, n.f. dynamite.

**dìnamo**, n.f. dynamo.

**dinastìa**, n.f. dynasty.

**diniègo**, n.m. denial.

**dinosàuro**, n.m. dinosaur.

**dintorni**, n.m.pl. environs, surroundings.

**dio**, n.m. god.

**diòcesi**, n.f. diocese, bishopric.

**dipanare**, vb. reel off, unwind.

**dipartimentale**, adj. departmental.

**dipartimento**, n.m. department.

**dipendènte**, n.m. and adj. dependent.

**dipendènza**, n.f. dependence.

**dipèndere**, *vb.* depend.

**dipìngere**, *vb.* paint, depict.

**dipìnto**, *n.m.* painting.

**diplòma**, *n.m.* diploma.

**diplomàtico**, **1.** *n.m.* diplomat. **2.** *adj.* diplomatic.

**diplomazìa**, *n.f.* diplomacy.

**dipòrto**, *n.m.* sport.

**diramazione**, *n.f.* junction.

**dire**, *vb.* say.

**direttamente**, *adv.* directly.

**direttìssimo**, *n.m.* express train.

**direttìvo**, *adj.* directive, directional.

**dirètto**, *adj.* direct; directed; bound; lineal; right; through.

**direttorato**, *n.m.* directorate.

**direttóre**, *n.m.* director; conductor; editor; manager; principal.

**direzione**, *n.f.* direction, management.

**dirìgere**, *vb.* direct; manage; aim; conduct; steer; edit.

**dirigìbile**, *n.m. and adj.* dirigible.

**dirimpètto**, *adv.* **d. a**, *prep.* opposite; facing.

**diritti**, *n.m.pl.* tax; dues. **d. d'autore**, *copyright*.

**diritto**, **1.** *n.m.* right; law. **2.** *adj.*, *adv.* straight; upright.

**disaccòrdo**, *n.m.* discord, variance.

**disadatto**, *n.m.* unfit.

**disagio**, *n.m.* discomfort.

**disapprovare**, *v.b.* disapprove.

**disapprovazione**, *n.f.* disapproval.

**disarmare**, *vb.* disarm.

**disarmo**, *n.m.* disarmament.

**disastro**, *n.m.* disaster, debacle.

**disastroso**, *adj.* disastrous.

**discendènte**, *n.f.* descendant.

**discérnere**, *vb.* discern.

**discesa**, *n.f.* descent.

**disciplina**, *n.f.* discipline.

**disciplinare**, *adj.* disciplinary.

**disciplinare**, *vb.* discipline.

**disco**, *n.m.* disc, record.

**disconóscere**, *vb.* disavow. disclaim, disown.

**disconoscimento**, *n.m.* disavowal, disclaimer.

**discordante**, *adj.* discordant.

**discordare**, *vb.* disagree, be discordant.

**discòrdia**, *n.f.* discord.

**discórrere**, *vb.* discourse.

**discórso**, *n.m.* speech, discourse, talk, address.

**discotèca**, *n.f.* record library.

**discrèdito**, *n.m.* discredit.

**discrepante**, *adj.* discrepant.

**discrepanza**, *n.f.* discrepancy.

**discreto**, *adj.* discreet; moderate; fair.

**discrezione**, *n.f.* discretion.

**discriminare**, *vb.* discriminate.

**discriminazione**, *n.f.* discrimination.

**discussione**, *n.f.* discussion.

**discusso**, *adj.* moot.

**discùtere**, *vb.* discuss.

**discutìbile**, *adj.* debatable.

**disdegnare**, *vb.* disdain, spurn.

**disdegno**, *n.m.* disdain, scorn.

**disdegnoso**, *adj.* disdainful, scornful.

**disegnare**, *vb.* design; draw.

**disegnatore**, *n.m.* designer; draftsman.

**disegno**, *n.m.* picture; cartoon; design; drawing.

**diseredare**, *vb.* disinherit.

**disertare**, *vb.* desert.

**disertore**, *n.m.* deserter.

**diserzione**, *n.f.* desertion.

**disfare**, *vb.* undo.

**disfatta**, *n.f.* defeat.

**disfattismo**, *n.m.* defeatism.

**disfigurare**, *vb.* disfigure.

**disgràzia**, *n.f.* misfortune, mishap, accident; disgrace.

**disgraziato**, *adj.* unfortunate, unlucky.

**disgustare**, *vb.* disgust.

**disgusto**, *n.m.* disgust, distaste.

**disgustoso**, *adj.* disgusting, distasteful, nasty.

**disidratare**, *vb.* dehydrate.

**disillùdere**, *vb.* disillusion.

**disillusione**, *n.f.* disillusion.

**disimballare**, *vb.* unpack.

**disimpegnare**, *vb.* disengage.

**disincanto**, *n.m.* disenchantment.

**disinfettante**, *n.m.* disinfectant.

**disinfettare**, *vb.* disinfect.

**disingannare,** *vb.* undeceive; disabuse.

**disintegrare,** *vb.* disintegrate.

**disinteressato,** *adj.* disinterested.

**dislocamento,** *n.m.* displacement.

**disobbediènte,** *adj.* disobedient.

**disoccupato,** *adj.* unemployed.

**disonestà,** *n.f.* dishonesty.

**disonèsto,** *adj.* dishonest; foul.

**disonorante,** *adj.* disgraceful.

**disonorare,** *vb.* dishonor, disgrace.

**disonore,** *n.m.* dishonor. disgrace.

**disonorévole,** *adj.* dishonorable, discreditable, disreputable.

**disordinare,** *vb.* disorder.

**disordinato,** *adj.* disorderly.

**disòrdine,** *n.m.* disorder, litter.

**disorganizzare,** *vb.* disorganize.

**disparato,** *adj.* disparate.

**dìspari,** *adj.* odd.

**disparità,** *n.f.* disparity.

**disparte: in d.,** *adv.* apart, aloof.

**dispènsa,** *n.f.* pantry.

**dispensàbile,** *adj.* dispensable.

**dispensare,** *vb.* dispense.

**dispensàrio,** *n.m.* dispensary.

**dispensazione,** *n.f.* dispensation.

**dispepsìa,** *n.f.* dyspepsia.

**dispèptico,** *adj.* dyspeptic.

**disperare,** *vb.* despair.

**disperato, 1.** *n.* desperado. **2.** *adj.* desperate; forlorn, hopeless.

**disperazione,** *n.f.* desperation, despair, hopelessness.

**disperdere,** *vb.* disperse.

**dispersione,** *n.f.* dispersal.

**dispètto,** *n.m.* spite.

**dispiacènte,** *adj.* sorry.

**dispiacere, 1.** *n.* displeasure. **2.** *vb.* displease.

**disponìbile,** *adj.* available, disposable.

**disporre,** *vb.* dispose, arrange; range.

**disposizione,** *n.f.* disposition; disposal.

**dispòtico,** *adj.* despotic.

**dispotismo,** *n.m.* despotism.

**disprezzare,** *vb.* despise, disparage, scorn, slight.

**disprèzzo,** *n.m.* contempt, scorn, slight.

**disputa,** *n.f.* dispute.

**disputàbile,** *adj.* disputable.

**disputare,** *vb.* dispute.

**dissecare,** *vb.* dissect.

**disseminare,** *vb.* disseminate.

**dissènso,** *n.m.* dissent, disagreement, dissension.

**dissenterìa,** *n.f.* dysentery.

**dissentire,** *vb.* dissent, disagree.

**disserrare,** *vb.* unlock.

**dissertazione,** *n.f.* dissertation.

**disservìzio,** *n.m.* disservice. bad service.

**dissetare,** *vb.* quench (one's) thirst.

**dissezione,** *n.f.* dissection.

**dissìmile,** *adj.* dissimilar, unlike.

**dissimulare,** *vb.* dissimulate, dissemble.

**dissipare,** *vb.* dissipate, dispel.

**dissipazione,** *n.f.* dissipation.

**dissociare,** *vb.* dissociate.

**dissolutezza,** *n.f.* dissoluteness, dissipation.

**dissoluto,** *adj.* dissolute, dissipated.

**dissoluzione,** *n.f.* dissolution.

**dissòlvere,** *vb.* dissolve.

**dissonante,** *adj.* dissonant.

**dissonanza,** *n.f.* dissonance.

**dissotterrare,** *vb.* unearth.

**dissuadere,** *vb.* dissuade.

**distaccamento,** *n.m.* detachment (*mil.*).

**distaccare,** *vb.* detach.

**distacco,** *n.m.* detachment.

**distante,** *adj.* distant.

**distare,** *vb.* be distant.

**distèndere,** *vb.* distend.

**distesa,** *n.f.* expanse; extent; spread.

**disteso,** *adj.* spread.

**distillare,** *vb.* distill.

**distillatore,** *n.m.* distiller.

**distillatòrio,** *n.m.* distillery.

---

For pronunciation, see the concise guide on pages 5 to 7.

**distillazione,** *n.f.* distillation.

**distìnguere,** *vb.* distinguish.

**distintamente,** *adv.* distinctly.

**distintivo,** **1.** *n.m.* badge. **2.** *adj.* distinctive.

**distinto,** *adj.* distinct.

**distinzione,** *n.f.* distinction.

**distògliere,** *vb.* deter.

**distòrcere,** *vb.* distort.

**distrarre,** *vb.* distract.

**distratto,** *adj.* absent-minded.

**distrazione,** *n.f.* distraction.

**distretto,** *n.m.* district.

**distribuire,** *vb.* distribute, apportion, deal out, dole out.

**distributore,** *n.m.* distributor.

**distribuzione,** *n.f.* distribution; deal.

**districare,** *vb.* disentangle, extricate, unravel.

**distrùggere,** *vb.* destroy.

**distruttìbile,** *adj.* destructible.

**distruttivo,** *adj.* destructive.

**distruzione,** *n.f.* destruction.

**disturbare,** *vb.* disturb, trouble.

**disturbo,** *n.m.* disturbance, trouble.

**disubbidienza,** *n.f.* disobedience.

**disubbidire,** *vb.* disobey.

**disuguale,** *adj.* uneven.

**disunire,** *vb.* disunite.

**disuso,** *n.m.* disuse.

**ditale,** *n.m.* thimble.

**dito,** *n.m.* finger. **d. del piède,** toe.

**ditta,** *n.f.* firm.

**dittàfono,** *n.m.* dictaphone.

**dittatore,** *n.m.* dictator.

**dittatoriale,** *adj.* dictatorial.

**dittatura,** *n.f.* dictatorship.

**diva,** *n.f.* famous singer, diva.

**divagare,** *vb.* ramble, get off the subject.

**divampare,** *vb.* burst into flames.

**divano,** *n.m.* divan, davenport, lounge.

**divenire,** *vb.* become; get.

**diventare,** *vb.* become; get.

**divergènte,** *adj.* divergent.

**divergènza,** *n.f.* divergence.

**divèrgere,** *vb.* diverge.

**diversione,** *n.f.* diversion.

**diversità,** *n.f.* diversity.

**diversivo,** *n.m.* relief.

**divèrso,** *adj.* diverse, different.

**divertimento,** *n.m.* amusement, hobby, recreation, entertainment, fun.

**divertire,** *vb.* amuse, divert, entertain; (*refl.*) have a good time.

**dividendo,** *n.m.* dividend.

**divìdere,** *vb.* divide, split.

**diviéto,** *n.m.* prohibition.

**divinare,** *vb.* divine.

**divinità,** *n.f.* divinity.

**divino,** *adj.* divine, godlike.

**divisa,** *n.f.* uniform.

**divisìbile,** *adj.* divisible.

**divisione,** *n.f.* division.

**divisòrio,** *adj.* dividing.

**divorare,** *vb.* devour.

**divorziare,** *vb.* divorce.

**divòrzio,** *n.m.* divorce.

**divulgare,** *vb.* divulge.

**dizionàrio,** *n.m.* dictionary.

**dizione,** *n.f.* diction.

**dóccia,** *n.f.* shower.

**dòcile,** *adj.* docile, tame, submissive, amenable.

**documentare,** *vb.* document.

**documentàrio,** *adj.* documentary.

**documentazione,** *n.f.* documentation.

**documento,** *n.m.* document.

**dodicèsimo,** *adj.* twelfth.

**dódici,** *num.* twelve.

**dogana,** *n.f.* customs, customs-house.

**doganière,** *n.m.* customs officer.

**dògma,** *n.m.* dogma.

**dogmaticità,** *n.f.* assertiveness.

**dogmàtico,** *adj.* dogmatic, assertive.

**dogmatismo,** *n.m.* dogmatism.

**dolce,** **1.** *n.m.* candy, bonbon. **2.** *adj.* sweet.

**dolcemente,** *adv.* sweetly, soothingly.

**dolcezza,** *n.f.* sweetness.

**dolènte,** *adj.* sore.

**dolere,** *vb.* hurt, pain; (*refl.*) complain.

**dòllaro,** *n.m.* dollar.

**dolore,** *n.m.* sorrow, pain, ache, grief.

**doloroso,** *adj.* dolorous, sorrowful, mournful, painful; grievous.

**domanda**, *n.f.* question; request; application; demand; query.

**domandare**, *vb.* ask; demand; request; query; (*refl.*) wonder.

**domani**, *n.m. and adv.*, tomorrow.

**domare**, *vb.* tame.

**domènica**, *n.f.* Sunday.

**domèstica**, *n.f.* housemaid.

**domesticare**, *vb.* domesticate.

**domèstico**, 1. *n.* servant. 2. *adj.* domestic.

**domicìlio**, *n.m.* domicile.

**dominante**, *adj.* dominant.

**dominare**, *vb.* dominate, sway.

**dominazione**, *n.f.* domination.

**domìnio**, *n.m.* domain, dominion.

**dòmino**, *n.m.* domino.

**donare**, *vb.* donate.

**donatore**, *vb.* giver.

**donazione**, *n.f.* donation.

**donchisciottesco**, *adj.* quixotic.

**donde**, *adv.* whence.

**dondolare**, *vb.* rock, swing.

**dònna**, *n.f.* woman.

**dònnola**, *n.f.* weasel.

**dono**, *m.* gift, grant, present.

**dopo**, 1. *adv.* afterwards. 2. *prep.* after. **d. che**, *conj.* after.

**doppiamente**, *adv.* doubly.

**doppiare**, *vb.* double.

**dóppio**, *adj.* double; duplex.

**dorare**, *vb.* gild.

**dorato**, *adj.* gilt.

**doratura**, *n.f.* gilt.

**dormire**, *vb.* sleep.

**dormitòrio**, *n.m.* dormitory.

**dorsale**, *adj.* dorsal, pertaining to the back.

**dòrso**, *n.m.* back.

**dosare**, *vb.* dose.

**dosatura**, *n.f.* dosage.

**dòse**, *n.f.* dose.

**dòsso**, *n.m.* back.

**dotare**, *vb.* endow.

**dotato**, *adj.* gifted.

**dotazione**, *n.f.* endowment.

**dòte**, *n.f.* dowry.

**dotto**, 1. *n.* scholar. 2. *adj.* learned.

**dottorato**, *n.m.* doctorate.

**dottore**, *n.m.* doctor.

**dottrina**, *n.f.* doctrine; learning.

**dottrinàrio**, *adj.* doctrinaire.

**dove**, *adv.* where.

**dovere**, 1. *n.* duty. 2. *vb.* owe; be supposed to; have to; must.

**dovunque**, *adv.* wherever.

**dovuto**, *adj.* due, owing.

**dozzina**, *n.f.* dozen.

**draga**, *n.f.* dredge.

**dragare**, *vb.* dredge.

**dragone**, *n.m.* dragon.

**dramma**, *n.m.* dram; drama, play.

**drammàtica**, *n.f.* dramatics.

**drammàtico**, *adj.* dramatic.

**drammatizzare**, *vb.* dramatize.

**drammaturgìa**, *n.f.* dramaturgy, play-writing.

**drammaturgo**, *n.m.* dramatist, playwright.

**drappeggiare**, *vb.* drape.

**drappeggio**, *n.m.* drapery, drapes.

**drappèllo**, *n.m.* platoon.

**dràstico**, *adj.* drastic.

**drenàggio**, *n.m.* drainage.

**drizza**, *n.f.* halyard.

**drizzare**, *vb.* straighten.

**dròga**, *n.f.* drug.

**dromedàrio**, *n.m.* dromedary.

**duale**, *n.m. and adj.* dual.

**dualismo**, *n.m.* dualism.

**dùbbio**, 1. *n.m.* doubt. 2. *adj.* doubtful, dubious.

**dubbioso**, *adj.* doubtful.

**dubitare**, *vb.* doubt.

**duca**, *n.m.* duke.

**ducato**, *n.m.* duchy, dukedom.

**duce**, *n.m.* (Fascist) leader.

**duchessa**, *n.f.* duchess.

**due**, *num.* two.

**duellante**, *n.m.* duellist.

**duellare**, *vb.* duel.

**duèllo**, *n.m.* duel.

**duetto**, *n.m.* duet.

**duna**, *n.f.* dune.

**dunque**, *adv.* therefore; so; then.

**duplicare**, *vb.* duplicate.

**duplicazione**, *n.f.* duplication.

**duplicità**, *n.f.* duplicity, double-dealing.

**duràbile**, *adj.* durable, enduring.

**durabilità**, *n.f.* durability.

**collasso,** *n.m.* collapse.

**collaterale,** *n.m.* and *adj.* collateral.

**collaudare,** *vb.* test.

**collazionare,** *vb.* collate.

**collèga,** *n.m.* colleague.

**collegamento,** *n.m.* connection, liaison.

**collegare,** *vb.* connect, link.

**còllera,** *n.f.* choler, anger, wrath.

**collèrico,** *adj.* choleric.

**collettivamente,** *adv.* collectively, jointly.

**collettivo,** *adj.* collective, joint.

**colletto,** *n.m.* collar.

**collezione,** *n.f.* collection.

**collezionista,** *n.m.* collector.

**collina,** *n.f.* hill.

**còllo,** *n.m.* neck; package.

**collocare,** *vb.* locate; place.

**colloquiale,** *adj.* colloquial.

**colloquialismo,** *n.m.* colloquialism.

**colloquialmente,** *adv.* colloquially.

**collòquio,** *n.m.* colloquy; interview.

**collusione,** *n.f.* collusion.

**colombo,** *n.m.* dove.

**colònia,** *n.f.* colony, settlement.

**Colònia,** *n.f.* Cologne.

**coloniale,** *adj.* colonial.

**colonizzare,** *vb.* colonize.

**colonizzazione,** *n.f.* colonization.

**colonna,** *n.f.* column; (*typogr.*) galley.

**colonnèllo,** *n.m.* colonel.

**colòno,** *n.m.* colonist, settler; farmer.

**colorare,** *vb.* stain.

**colorazione,** *n.f.* coloration.

**colore,** *n.m.* color, hue; paint; stain; suit. **di c.,** colored.

**colorire,** *vb.* color.

**colorito,** *n.m.* coloring, complexion.

**coloritura,** *n.f.* coloring.

**colossale,** *adj.* colossal.

**colpa,** *n.f.* fault, guilt.

**colpetto,** *n.m.* little blow, tap.

**colpévole, 1.** *n.m.* culprit. **2.** *adj.* guilty, culpable.

**colpevolmente,** *adv.* guiltily.

**colpire,** *vb.* hit, strike, rap, smite.

**colpito,** *adj.* stricken.

**colpo,** *n.m.* blow; stroke; clout, hit, rap; shot.

**coltèllo,** *n.m.* knife. **c. a serramànico,** jack-knife.

**coltivare,** *vb.* cultivate, till; grow, raise.

**coltivatore,** *n.m.* cultivator.

**coltivazione,** *n.f.* cultivation.

**colto,** *adj.* cultured, cultivated, educated.

**coltrone,** *n.m.* quilt.

**coma,** *n.m.* coma.

**comandamento,** *n.m.* commandment.

**comandante,** *n.m.* commander.

**comandare,** *vb.* command, order, bid.

**comando,** *n.m.* command.

**comare,** *n.f.* godmother.

**combattènte,** *n.m.* combatant, fighter.

**combàttere,** *vb.* combat, fight, battle.

**combattimento,** *n.m.* combat, fight, fray.

**combinare,** *vb.* combine.

**combinazione,** *n.f.* combination; union suit.

**combriccola,** *n.f.* coterie.

**combustìbile, 1.** *n.* fuel. **2.** *adj.* combustible.

**combustione,** *n.f.* combustion.

**come, 1.** *adv.* how. **2.** *prep. and conj.* like; as.

**cometa,** *n.f.* comet.

**còmico, 1.** *n.* comedian. **2.** *adj.* comic, comical, funny.

**cominciamento,** *n.m.* beginning; commencement.

**cominciare,** *vb.* begin, commence, start.

**comitato,** *n.m.* committee, board, commission.

**commèdia,** *n.f.* comedy.

**commemorare,** *vb.* commemorate.

**commemorativo,** *adj.* commemorative, memorial.

**commemorazione,** *n.f.* commemoration.

**commentare,** *vb.* comment.

**commento,** *n.m.* comment; commentary.

**commerciale,** *adj.* commercial.

**commercialismo,** *n.m.* commercialism.

**commercializzare,** *vb.* commercialize.

**commercialmente,** *adv.* commercially.

**commerciante,** *n.m.* business man, merchant, trader.

**commerciare,** *vb.* trade.

**commèrcio,** *n.m.* commerce, trade.

**commesso,** *n.m.* salesman. **c. viaggiatore,** travelling salesman.

**commèttere,** *vb.* commit.

**commiato,** *n.m.* leave.

**commiserare,** *vb.* commiserate.

**commisurato,** *adj.* commensurate.

**commissariato,** *n.m.* commissary.

**commissàrio,** *n.m.* commissioner.

**commissione,** *n.f.* commission; committee; errand.

**commovènte,** *adj.* moving; affecting; touching.

**commozione,** *n.f.* commotion, stir.

**commuòvere,** *vb.* move; affect; touch (emotionally).

**commutazione,** *n.f.* commutation.

**commutare,** *vb.* commute.

**comodamente,** *adv.* comfortably.

**còmodo, 1.** *n.* ease; leisure. **2.** *adj.* comfortable; leisurely; snug.

**compaesano,** *n.m.* compatriot.

**compagna,** *n.f.* companion.

**compagnìa,** *n.f.* company, companionship.

**compagno,** *n.m.* companion; mate; partner.

**comparàbile,** *adj.* comparable.

**comparare,** *vb.* compare.

**comparativamente,** *adv.* comparatively.

**comparativo,** *adj.* comparative.

**compare,** *n.m.* godfather; crony.

**compassione,** *n.f.* compassion.

**compassionévole,** *adj.* compassionate.

**compassionevolmente,** *adv.* compassionately.

**compasso,** *n.m.* compass.

**compatìbile,** *adj.* compatible.

**compatriòta,** *n.m.* compatriot, fellow-countryman.

**compattezza,** *n.f.* compactness.

**compatto,** *adj.* compact.

**compensare,** *vb.* compensate.

**compensativo,** *adj.* compensatory.

**compensazione,** *n.f.* compensation. **stanza di c.** clearing-house.

**compènso,** *n.m.* compensation.

**competènte,** *adj.* competent; (law) cognizant.

**competentemente,** *adv.* competently.

**competènza,** *n.f.* competence, fitness, (legal) cognizance.

**compètere,** *vb.* compete; be within the province of.

**compilare,** *vb.* compilare.

**compimento,** *n.m.* completion, achievement, accomplishment.

**compire,** *vb.* complete, finish, accomplish, achieve.

**compìto,** *adj.* accomplished.

**còmpito,** *n.m.* task, assignment.

**compleanno,** *n.m.* birthday.

**complemento,** *n.m.* complement

**complessità,** *n.f.* complexity.

**complèsso,** *n.m.* and *adj.* complex.

**completamente,** *adv.* completely; altogether; outright; wholly; quite; throughout; utterly.

**completamento,** *n.m.* completion.

**completare,** *vb.* complete.

**completezza,** *n.f.* completeness.

**complèto,** *adj.* complete; thorough; utter.

**complicare,** *vb.* complicate.

**complicato,** *adj.* complicated, involved, intricate.

**complicazione,** *n.f.* complication; intricacy.

**còmplice,** *n.m.* and *f.* accomplice.

**ciclo,** n.m. cycle.
**ciclone,** n.m. cyclone.
**ciclotrone,** n.m. cyclotron.
**cicòria,** n.f. chicory.
**cicuta,** n.f. hemlock.
**ciecamente,** adv. blindly.
**cièco,** adj. blind.
**cièlo,** n.m. heaven; sky.
**cifra,** n.f. cipher; figure.
**cifràrio,** n.m. code.
**ciglio,** n.m. eyelash, cilia.
**cigno,** n.m. swan.
**cigolare,** vb. creak, squeak.
**cigolìo,** n.m. squeak.
**ciliare,** adj. ciliary.
**ciliègia,** n.f. cherry.
**ciliègio,** n.m. cherrytree.
**cilìndrico,** adj. cylindrical.
**cilindro,** n.m. cylinder.
**cima,** n.f. peak.
**cimare,** vb. clip, trim.
**cìmice,** n.f. bedbug.
**ciminièra,** n.f. smoke-stack; funnel.
**cimitèro,** n.m. cemetery; churchyard.
**Cina,** n.f. China.
**cinciglia,** n.f. chinchilla.
**cincona,** n.f. cinchona.
**cinèllo,** n.m. cymbal.
**cìnema,** n.m. cinema, movies; (movie) theater.
**cinematogràfico,** adj. cinematic, of the movies.
**cinematògrafo,** n.m. cinema, movies; (movie) theater.
**cinese,** adj. Chinese.
**cinètico,** adj. kinetic.
**cìngere,** vb. gird.
**cìnghia,** n.f. strap.
**cinguettare,** vb. chirp.
**cinguettìo,** n.m. chirping.
**cìnico, 1.** n.m. cynic. **2.** adj. cynical.
**ciniglia,** n.f. chenille.
**cinismo,** n.m. cynicism.
**cinnamòmo,** n.m. cinnamon.
**cinquanta,** num. fifty.
**cinque,** num. five.
**cintura,** n.f. belt, girdle, sash; waist.
**ciò,** pron. this; that; it.
**ciòcco,** n.m. log.
**cioccolato,** n.m. chocolate.
**cioè,** conj. that is; namely.
**ciòttolo,** n.m. pebble, stone; cobblestone.
**cipolla,** n.f. onion; chive.
**ciprèsso,** n.m. cypress.
**cìpria,** n.f. face-powder.
**circo,** n.m. circus.

**circolare,** n.m. and adj. circular.
**circolare,** vb. circulate.
**circolatòrio,** adj. circulatory.
**circolazione,** n.f. circulation; currency.
**cìrcolo,** n.m. circle, club.
**circoncìdere,** vb. circumcise.
**circoncisione,** n.f. circumcision.
**circondare,** vb. surround, encompass.
**circonferènza,** n.f. circumference, girth.
**circonlocuzione,** n.f. circumlocution.
**circoscrìvere,** vb. circumscribe.
**circonvenìre,** vb. circumvent.
**circonvenzione,** n.f. circumvention.
**circospètto,** adj. circumspect.
**circostanza,** n.f. circumstance.
**circostanziale,** adj. circumstantial.
**circostanziatamente,** adv. circumstantially.
**circùito,** n.m. circuit.
**cirrìpede,** n.m. barnacle.
**cirròsi,** n.f. cirrhosis.
**ciste,** n.f. cyst.
**cistèrna,** n.f. cistern.
**citare,** vb. cite; quote; summon.
**citazione,** n.f. citation; quotation; summons.
**cìtrico,** adj. citric.
**citrullo,** n.m. fool.
**città,** n.f. city, town. **c. universitària,** campus.
**cittadèlla,** n.f. citadel.
**cittadina,** n.f. woman citizen; small city.
**cittadinanza,** n.f. citizenship; citizenry.
**cittadino,** n.m. citizen.
**ciuffo,** n.m. tuft.
**ciuffolòtto,** n.m. bullfinch.
**civètta,** n.f. owl; coquette, flirt.
**civettare,** vb. coquet, flirt.
**civetterìa,** n.f. coquetry.
**cìvico,** adj. civic.
**civile, 1.** n. and adj. civilian. **2.** adj. civil; civilized.
**civilizzare,** vb. civilize.
**civiltà,** n.f. civilization; civility.

**clàcson,** *n.m.* klaxon; horn.

**clamore,** *n.m.* clamor.

**clamoroso,** *adj.* noisy, blatant, clamorous, obstreperous.

**clandestinamente,** *adv.* clandestinely.

**clandestino,** *adj.* clandestine.

**clangore,** *n.m.* clangor.

**claretto,** *n.m.* claret.

**clarinettista,** *n.m.* clarinetist.

**clarinetto,** *n.m.* clarinet.

**classe,** *n.f.* class.

**classicismo,** *n.m.* classicism.

**clàssico,** *adj.* classic; classical.

**classificàbile,** *adj.* classifiable.

**classificare,** *vb.* classify, class; grade.

**classificazione,** *n.f.* classification.

**clàusola,** *n.f.* clause.

**claustrofobìa,** *n.f.* claustrophobia.

**clava,** *n.f.* cudgel, nightstick.

**clavicémbalo,** *n.m.* harpsichord.

**clavìcola,** *n.f.* collarbone.

**clemènte,** *adj.* lenient.

**clemènza,** *n.f.* clemency.

**cleptòmane,** *n.m.* kleptomaniac.

**cleptomanìa,** *n.f.* kleptomania.

**clericale,** *adj.* clerical.

**clericalismo,** *n.m.* clericalism.

**clèro,** *n.m.* clergy.

**cliènte,** *n.m.* client, customer; guest.

**clientèla,** *n.f.* clientele.

**clima,** *n.m.* climate.

**climàtico,** *adj.* climatic.

**clìnica,** *n.f.* clinic.

**clinicamente,** *adv.* clinically.

**clìnico,** *adj.* clinical.

**clistère,** *n.m.* enema.

**clòro,** *n.m.* chlorine.

**clorofilla,** *n.f.* chlorophyll.

**clorofòrmio,** *n.m.* chloroform.

**cloruro,** *n.m.* chloride.

**coagulare,** *vb.* coagulate.

**coagulazione,** *n.f.* coagulation.

**coalizione,** *n.f.* coalition.

**coalizzarsi,** *vb.* coalesce.

**cobalto,** *n.m.* cobalt.

**cobra,** *n.m.* cobra.

**cocaìna,** *n.f.* cocaine.

**cocchière,** *n.m.* coachman.

**còcchio,** *n.m.* coach.

**coccinèlla,** *n.f.* ladybug.

**còcco,** *n.m.* coconut tree.

**coccodrillo,** *n.m.* crocodile.

**coctèl,** *n.m.* cocktail.

**coda,** *n.f.* tail.

**codardìa,** *n.f.* cowardice.

**codardo, 1.** *n.m.* coward. **2.** *adj.* cowardly, craven.

**codeìna,** *n.f.* codeine.

**còdice,** *n.m.* codex; code.

**codificare,** *vb.* codify.

**coeguale,** *adj.* coequal.

**coercitìvo,** *adj.* coercive, compulsive.

**coercizione,** *n.f.* coercion, duress.

**coerènte,** *adj.* coherent; consistent.

**coesione,** *n.f.* cohesion.

**coesistènza,** *n.f.* coexistence.

**coesìstere,** *vb.* coexist.

**coesìvo,** *adj.* cohesive.

**còfano,** *n.m.* coffer; (auto) hood; (Brit.) bonnet.

**còffa,** *n.f.* crow's-nest.

**cogitare,** *vb.* cogitate.

**cògliere,** *vb.* pick, pluck, gather, cull.

**cognata,** *n.f.* sister-in-law.

**cognato,** *n.m.* brother-in-law.

**cognome,** *n.m.* family name, surname.

**coincidènte,** *adj.* coincident; coincidental.

**coincidènza,** *n.f.* coincidence; (transport) connection.

**coincidere,** *vb.* coincide; connect.

**coinvòlgere,** *vb.* involve.

**colare,** *vb.* strain.

**colatòio,** *n.m.* colander.

**colazione,** *n.f.* light meal; lunch. **prima c.,** breakfast.

**colèra,** *n.f.* cholera.

**colino,** *n.m.* strainer.

**còlla,** *n.f.* glue, paste.

**collaborare,** *vb.* collaborate.

**collaboratore,** *n.m.* collaborator.

**collaborazione,** *n.f.* collaboration.

**collana,** *n.f.* necklace.

**collare,** *n.m.* collar.

**collare,** *vb.* glue.

---

For pronunciation, see the concise guide on pages 5 to 7.

**emolumento,** *n.m.* emolument.

**emorragìa,** *n.f.* hemorrhage.

**emorròide,** *n.f.* hemorrhoid, pile.

**emozionàbile,** *adj.* emotional.

**emozione,** *n.f.* emotion.

**emotivo,** *adj.* emotional.

**empiastro,** *adj.* plaster.

**èmpio,** *adj.* impious, blasphemous, godless.

**empìrico,** *adj.* empirical. rimèdio e., nostrum.

**emulare,** *vb.* emulate.

**emulsione,** *n.f.* emulsion.

**encefalite,** *n.f.* encephalitis.

**encèfalo,** *n.m.* encephalon.

**encìclica,** *n.f.* encyclical.

**enciclopedìa,** *n.f.* encyclopaedia.

**endèmico,** *adj.* endemic.

**endòcrino,** *adj.* endocrine.

**endovenoso,** *adj.* intravenous.

**energìa,** *n.f.* energy.

**enèrgico,** *adj.* energetic.

**ènfasi,** *n.f.* emphasis.

**enfàtico,** *adj.* emphatic.

**enimma,** *n.m.* enigma, riddle.

**enimmàtico,** *adj.* enigmatic.

**ennè,** *n.m.* henna.

**enòrme,** *adj.* enormous.

**enormità,** *n.f.* enormity.

**enteroclisma,** *n.m.* enema, colonic irrigation.

**entità,** *n.f.* entity.

**entrare,** *vb.* enter.

**entrata,** *n.f.* entrance, entry; admission; revenue.

**entro,** *prep.* in; within.

**entusiasmo,** *n.m.* enthusiasm.

**entusiasta,** *n.m. or f.* enthusiast, devotee.

**entusiàstico,** *adj.* enthusiastic.

**enumerare,** *vb.* enumerate.

**enumerazione,** *n.f.* enumeration.

**enunciare,** *vb.* enunciate.

**enunciazione,** *n.f.* enunciation.

**epàtica,** *n.f.* hepatica.

**epàtico,** *adj.* hepatic.

**eperlano,** *n.m.* smelt.

**èpico,** *adj.* epic.

**epicurèo,** *n.m.* epicure.

**epidemìa,** *n.f.* epidemic.

**epidèmico,** *adj.* epidemic.

**epidèrmide,** *n.f.* epidermis.

**epigramma,** *n.m.* epigram.

**epilessìa,** *n.f.* epilepsy.

**epìlogo,** *n.m.* epilogue.

**episòdio,** *n.m.* episode.

**epistola,** *n.f.* epistle.

**epitàffio,** *n.m.* epitaph.

**epìteto,** *n.m.* epithet.

**epitomare,** *vb.* epitomize.

**epìtome,** *n.f.* epitome.

**època,** *n.f.* epoch.

**epopéa,** *n.f.* epic.

**equanimità,** *n.f.* equanimity.

**equatore,** *n.m.* equator.

**equatoriale,** *adj.* equatorial.

**equazione,** *n.f.* equation.

**equèstre,** *adj.* equestrian.

**equidistante,** *adj.* equidistant.

**equilaterale,** *adj.* equilateral.

**equilibrare,** *vb.* balance, equilibrate.

**equilibrato,** *adj.* balanced; level.

**equilìbrio,** *n.m.* balance, equilibrium; poise.

**equinòzio,** *n.m.* equinox.

**equipaggiare,** *vb.* rig.

**equipaggio,** *n.m.* crew; equipment; rig.

**equità,** *n.f.* equity.

**equitazione,** *n.f.* equitation, horsemanship.

**equivalènte,** *adj.* equivalent.

**equivalere,** *vb.* be equivalent.

**equìvoco, 1.** *n.m.* mistake. **2.** *adj.* equivocal.

**èquo,** *adj.* equable, equitable, fair, just.

**èra,** *n.f.* era.

**èrba,** *n.f.* grass; herb.

**erbàccia,** *n.f.* weed.

**erbàceo,** *n.m.* herbaceous.

**erbàrio,** *n.m.* herbarium.

**erboso,** *adj.* grassy.

**ercùleo,** *adj.* Herculean.

**erède,** *n.m.* heir.

**eredità,** *n.f.* heredity; heritage; inheritance.

**ereditare,** *vb.* inherit.

**ereditàrio,** *adj.* hereditary.

**ereditièra,** *n.f.* heiress.

**eremita,** *n.m.* hermit.

**eremitaggio,** *n.m.* hermitage.

**eresìa,** *n.f.* heresy.

**erètico, 1.** *n.* heretic. **2.** *adj.* heretical.

**erètto,** *adj.* erect, upright.

---

**erezione**, *n.f.* erection.
**èrgere**, *vb.* raise.
**érica**, *n.f.* heather.
**erìgere**, *vb.* erect, raise.
**ermellino**, *n.m.* ermine.
**ermètico**, *adj.* hermetic.
**èrnia**, *n.f.* hernia.
**eródere**, *vb.* erode.
**eròe**, *n.m.* hero.
**eroicamente**, *adv.* heroically.
**eròico**, *adj.* heroic.
**eroìna**, *n.f.* heroine; heroin.
**eroismo**, *n.m.* heroism.
**erosione**, *n.f.* erosion.
**erosivo**, *adj.* erosive.
**eròtico**, *adj.* erotic.
**èrpete**, *n.f.* herpes, shingles.
**erpicare**, *vb.* harrow.
**èrpice**, *n.m.* harrow.
**errante**, *adj.* errant.
**errare**, *vb.* err, make a mistake, be wrong; wander; rove.
**erràtico**, *adj.* erratic.
**errato**, *adj.* wrong, mistaken.
**erròneo**, *adj.* erroneous, mistaken.
**errore**, *n.m.* error, mistake, blunder, slip.
**èrto**, *adj.* steep.
**erudito**, **1.** *n.* scholar? **2.** *adj.* erudite.
**erudizione**, *n.f.* erudition, scholarship.
**eruttare**, *vb.* erupt.
**eruzione**, *n.f.* eruption; rash.
**esagerare**, *vb.* exaggerate.
**esagerazione**, *n.f.* exaggeration.
**esàgono**, *n.m.* hexagon.
**esalare**, *vb.* exhale.
**esalazione**, *n.f.* fume.
**esaltare**, *vb.* exalt, elate.
**esaltato**, *adj.* exalted, elated.
**esaltazione**, *n.f.* exaltation, elation.
**esame**, *n.m.* examination; canvass; survey.
**esaminare**, *vb.* examine; canvass; survey.
**esangue**, *adj.* bloodless.
**esasperare**, *vb.* exasperate.
**esasperazione**, *n.f.* exasperation.
**esattamente**, *adv.* exactly.
**esatto**, *adj.* exact.
**esauriènte**, *adj.* exhaustive.
**esaurimento**, *n.m.* exhaustion.
**esaurire**, *vb.* exhaust, deplete.

**esca**, *n.f.* bait; tinder.
**eschimese**, *n.m.* Eskimo pie.
**esclamare**, *vb.* exclaim.
**esclamazione**, *n.f.* exclamation.
**esclùdere**, *vb.* exclude.
**esclusione**, *n.f.* exclusion.
**esclusivo**, *adj.* exclusive.
**escogitare**, *vb.* excogitate, devise.
**escoriare**, *vb.* excoriate.
**escremento**, *n.m.* excrement.
**esculènto**, *adj.* esculent.
**escursione**, *n.f.* excursion, jaunt, junket, outing.
**esecràbile**, *adj.* execrable.
**esecutivo**, *adj.* executive.
**esecutore**, *n.m.* executor.
**esecuzione**, *n.f.* execution, enforcement; performance, rendition.
**eseguire**, *vb.* execute, enforce; perform.
**esèmpio**, *n.m.* example.
**esemplare**, **1.** *n.* copy. **2.** *adj.* exemplary.
**esemplificare**, *vb.* exemplify.
**esentare**, *vb.* exempt; dispense.
**esènte**, *adj.* exempt; immune.
**esercitare**, *vb.* exercise; exert; drill, practise.
**esercitazione**, *n.f.* practice, drill.
**esèrcito**, *n.m.* army.
**esercizio**, *n.m.* exercise.
**esibire**, *vb.* exhibit, display.
**esibizione**, *n.f.* exhibition, display.
**esibizionismo**, *n.m.* exhibitionism.
**esigènza**, *n.f.* exigency; requirement.
**esigere**, *vb.* exact, require, demand.
**esilarare**, *vb.* exhilarate.
**esilarare**, *vb.* exile, banish.
**esilio**, *n.m.* exile, banishment.
**esistènte**, *adj.* existent, extant.
**esistènza**, *n.f.* existence, being.
**esistere**, *vb.* exist.
**esitante**, *adj.* hesitant.
**esitare**, *vb.* hesitate, falter, waver.
**esitazione**, *n.f.* hesitation.
**èsodo**, *n.m.* exodus.

---

**esòfago**, *n.m.* esophagus.

**esonerare**, *vb.* exonerate.

**esorbitante**, *adj.* exorbitant.

**esorcizzare**, *vb.* exorcise.

**esortare**, *vb.* exhort; plead with.

**esortativo**, *adj.* exhortatory.

**esortazione**, *n.f.* exhortation.

**esotèrico**, *adj.* esoteric.

**esòtico**, *adj.* exotic.

**espàndere**, *vb.* expand.

**espansione**, *n.f.* expansion.

**espansivo**, *adj.* expansive, effusive.

**espatriato**, *n.m.* expatriate.

**espediènte**, *n.m. and adj.* expedient; makeshift.

**espèllere**, *vb.* expel, drive out, eject, evict, oust.

**esperiènza**, *n.f.* experience.

**esperimentare**, *n.m.* experiment; experience.

**espèrto**, *n.m. and adj.* expert; experienced, practiced, proficient.

**espettorare**, *vb.* expectorate.

**espiare**, *vb.* expiate, atone for.

**espiazione**, *n.f.* expiation, atonement.

**espirare**, *vb.* expire.

**espirazione**, *n.f.* expiration.

**espletivo**, *adj.* expletive.

**esplicativo**, *adj.* explanatory.

**esplìcito**, *adj.* explicit.

**esplòdere**, *vb.* explode.

**esplorare**, *vb.* explore.

**esplorativo**, *adj.* exploratory.

**esploratore**, *n.m.* explorer; scout.

**esplorazione**, *n.f.* exploration.

**esplosione**, *n.f.* explosion, blast.

**esplosivo**, *n.m. and adj.* explosive.

**esponènte**, *n.m.* exponent.

**esporre**, *vb.* expose.

**esportare**, *vb.* export.

**esportazione**, *n.f.* export, exportation.

**espositivo**, *adj.* expository.

**esposizione**, *n.f.* exposition; exposé; exposure; show.

**esposto**, *n.m.* exposé.

**espressamente**, *adv.* expressly.

**espressione**, *n.f.* expression.

**espressivo**, *adj.* expressive.

**esprèsso**, *n.m. and adj.* express; special delivery; coffee 'espresso.'

**esprimere**, *vb.* express.

**espropriare**, *vb.* expropriate.

**espulsione**, *n.f.* expulsion, ejection, eviction, ouster.

**espùngere**, *vb.* expunge.

**espurgare**, *vb.* expurgate.

**essa**, *pron.f.sg.* she; it.

**esse**, *pron.f.pl.* they.

**essènza**, *n.f.* essence.

**essenziale**, *adj.* essential.

**essenzialmente**, *adv.* essentially.

**èssere**, **1.** *n.* being. **2.** *vb.* be.

**essi**, *pron.m.pl.* they.

**essiccatòio**, *n.m.* drier.

**esso**, *pron.m.sg.* he; it.

**essudato**, *n.m.* exudation.

**èst**, *n.m.* east.

**èstasi**, *n.f.* ecstasy, rapture.

**estasiare**, *vb.* send into ecstasies, enrapture.

**estate**, *n.f.* summer.

**estemporàneo**, *adj.* extemporaneous.

**estensione**, *n.f.* extent; extension; range.

**estenuare**, *vb.* extenuate.

**esteriore**, *adj.* exterior, outer outward.

**esteriormente**, *adv.* outwardly.

**estèrno**, *adj.* external, out side.

**èstero**, **1.** *n.* foreign parts. **2.** *adj.* foreign; external.

**estesamente**, *adv.* extensively.

**esteso**, *adj.* extensive; far-flung.

**estètica**, *n.f.* aesthetics.

**estètico**, *adj.* aesthetic.

**estìnguere**, *vb.* extinguish, quench.

**estinto**, *adj.* extinct.

**estinzione**, *n.f.* extinction.

**estirpare**, *vb.* extirpate.

**estivo**, *adj.* of summer.

**estòllere**, *vb.* extol.

**estòrcere**, *vb.* extort.

**estorsione**, *n.f.* extortion.

**estra-**, *prefix* extra-.

**estradare**, *vb.* extradite.

**estradizione**, *n.f.* extradition.

**estràneo**, *adj.* extraneous.

**estrarre**, *vb.* extract.

**estratto**, *n.m.* extract.

**estrazione**, *n.f.* extraction.

**estremamente,** *adv.* extremely, exceedingly.

**estremità,** *n.f.* extremity; end; butt.

**estremo, 1.** *n.* fullback. **2.** *adj.* extreme, utmost.

**estrovertito,** *adj.* extrovert.

**estuàrio,** *n.m.* estuary.

**esuberante,** *adj.* exuberant; ebullient.

**esultante,** *adj.* exultant.

**esultare,** *vb.* exult.

**esumare,** *vb.* exhume; resurrect.

**età,** *n.f.* age.

**ètere,** *n.m.* ether.

**etèreo,** *adj.* ethereal.

**eternamente,** *adv.* eternally, forevermore.

**eternità,** *n.f.* eternity; eon.

**etèrno,** *adj.* eternal.

**eterodossìa,** *n.f.* heterodoxy.

**eterodòsso,** *adj.* heterodox.

**eterogèneo,** *adj.* heterogeneous, motley.

**ètica,** *n.f.* ethics.

**etichetta,** *n.f.* label; docket; sticker; tag.

**ètico,** *adj.* ethical; hectic.

**etìlico,** *adj.* ethyl.

**etimologìa,** *n.f.* etymology.

**èttaro,** *n.m.* hectare.

**ètto,** *n.m.* hectogram.

**ettogramma,** *n.m.* hectogram.

**eucalitto,** *n.m.* eucalyptus.

**eufònico,** *adj.* euphonious.

**eugenètica,** *n.f.* eugenics.

**eugènico,** *adj.* eugenic.

**eunuco,** *n.m.* eunuch.

**Europa,** *n.f.* Europe.

**europèo,** *adj. and n.* European.

**eutanasìa,** *n.f.* euthanasia.

**evacuare,** *vb.* evacuate.

**evanescènte,** *adj.* evanescent.

**evangelista,** *n.m.* evangelist.

**evaporare,** *vb.* evaporate.

**evaporazione,** *n.f.* evaporation.

**evasione,** *n.f.* evasion; escape.

**evasivo,** *adj.* evasive.

**evènto,** *n.m.* outcome.

**evidènte,** *adj.* evident.

**evidentemente,** *adv.* evidently.

**evidènza,** *n.f.* evidence.

**evitàbile,** *adj.* avoidable.

**evitare,** *vb.* avoid, evade, eschew, obviate.

**evocare,** *vb.* evoke.

**evoluzione,** *n.f.* evolution.

**evoluzionista,** *n.m.* evolutionist.

**evòlvere,** *vb.* evolve.

**evviva,** *interj.* hurrah (for).

**extra,** *adj.* extra.

# F

**F** (on water faucets) = **freddo,** *adj.* cold.

**fa,** *adv.* ago.

**fàbbrica,** *n.f.* factory, mill; (architecture) fabric.

**fabbricante,** *n.m.* manufacturer.

**fabbricare,** *vb.* build; manufacture, fabricate.

**fabbricazione,** *n.f.* manufacture; fabrication.

**fabbro,** *n.m.* smith. **f. ferraio,** blacksmith.

**faccendière,** *n.m.* busybody.

**faccetta,** *n.f.* facet.

**facchino,** *n.m.* porter.

**faccia,** *n.f.* face.

**facciata,** *n.f.* façade.

**facèto,** *adj.* facetious, witty, humorous.

**faciale,** *adj.* facial.

**fàcile,** *adj.* easy, facile.

**facilità,** *n.f.* facility, ease, easiness.

**facilitare,** *vb.* facilitate.

**facilmente,** *adv.* easily.

**facoltà,** *n.f.* faculty, knack, power.

**facoltativo,** *adv.* optional.

**facsìmile,** *n.m.* facsimile.

**factotum,** n.m. handy-man; jack-of-all-trades.

**fagiano,** n.m. pheasant.

**fagiòlo,** n.m. string bean.

**faglia,** n.f. faille.

**fagòtto,** n.m. bassoon.

**falce,** n.f. scythe.

**falciare,** vb. mow.

**falco,** n.m. hawk.

**falcone,** n.m. falcon.

**falconeria,** n.f. falconry.

**falegname,** n.m. carpenter.

**falla,** n.f. leak.

**fallace,** adj. fallacious.

**fallàcia,** n.f. fallacy.

**fallibile,** adj. fallible.

**fallimento,** n.m. bankruptcy; failure.

**fallire,** vb. fail; go bankrupt.

**fallito,** adj. bankrupt.

**falò,** n.m. bonfire.

**falsetto,** n.m. falsetto.

**falsificare,** vb. falsify, fake, counterfeit.

**falsificatore,** n.m. faker.

**falsificazione,** n.f. falsification.

**falsità,** n.f. falsity.

**falso, 1.** n. counterfeit, fake. **2.** adj. false, counterfeit.

**fama,** n.f. fame.

**fame,** n.f. hunger; starvation. **aver f.,** be hungry.

**famigerato,** adj. notorious.

**famiglia,** n.f. family; household.

**familiare,** adj. familiar, well-known; acquainted.

**familiarità,** n.f. familiarity.

**familiarizzare,** vb. familiarize.

**famoso,** adj. famous, famed.

**fanale,** n.m. lamp; light. **f. anteriore,** headlight.

**fanàtico,** n.m. and adj. fanatic, fanatical.

**fanatismo,** n.m. fanaticism.

**fanciulla,** n.f. maiden; girl.

**fanciullescamente,** adv. childishly; boyishly.

**fanciullesco,** adj. childish; boyish.

**fanciullezza,** n.f. childhood; boyhood; girlhood.

**fanciullo,** n.m. child; boy.

**fandònia,** n.f. fib; story; tale; (pl.) nonsense.

**fanfara,** n.f. fanfare.

**fanghìglia,** n.f. slush.

**fango,** n.m. mud, mire.

**fangoso,** adj. muddy.

**fantasìa,** n.f. fantasy, imagination. **di fantasia,** fancy.

**fantasma,** n.m. phantom.

**fantasticherìa,** n.f. reverie, daydream.

**fantàstico,** adj. fantastic.

**fante,** n.m. infantryman.

**fanteria,** n.f. infantry.

**fantino,** n.m. jockey.

**fantoccio,** n.m. puppet, dummy.

**faraona,** n.f. guinea fowl.

**fardèllo,** n.m. burden.

**fare,** vb. do; make. **f. a meno di,** go without. **f. finta di,** pretend to.

**farètra,** n.f. quiver (arrowcase).

**farfalla,** n.f. butterfly.

**farina,** n.f. flour; farina; meal.

**farmacìa,** n.f. drug store, pharmacy.

**farmacista,** n.m. druggist, pharmacist.

**faro,** n.m. beacon, lighthouse.

**farsa,** n.f. farce.

**farsesco,** adj. farcical.

**fàscino,** n.m. fascination; charm; glamor.

**fàscio,** n.m. bundle; sheaf; Fascist group.

**fascismo,** n.m. fascism.

**fascista,** n. and adj. fascist.

**fase,** n.f. phase, stage.

**fastìdio,** n.m. annoyance, bother, trouble, unpleasantness, nuisance.

**fastidioso,** adj. fastidious; bothersome, troublesome.

**fasto,** n.m. pomp.

**fastoso,** adj. pompous.

**fata,** n.f. fairy.

**fatale,** adj. fatal; fateful.

**fatalità,** n.f. fatality.

**fatalmente,** adv. fatally.

**fatica,** n.f. fatigue; toil, hard work.

**faticare,** vb. toil.

**fato,** n.m. fate.

**fattibile,** adj. feasible.

**fatto,** n.m. fact; deed, feat.

**fattore,** n.m. maker; factor; steward; granger.

**fattorìa,** n.f. farm; grange; homestead; ranch; station.

**fattura,** n.f. invoice.

**fatturare,** vb. invoice.

**fàtuo,** adj. fatuous.

**fava,** n.f. bean.

**favo,** n.m. honeycomb.

**fàvola**, n.f. fable.

**favoloso**, adj. fabulous.

**favore**, n.m. favor; behalf. **a f. di**, in behalf of. **per f.**, please.

**favorévole**, adj. favorable, auspicious.

**favorire**, vb. favor.

**favoritismo**, n.m. favoritism.

**favorito**, n.m. and adj. favorite.

**fazione**, n.f. faction.

**fazzoletti detergenti**, n.m.pl. facial tissues.

**fazzoletto**, n.m. handkerchief.

**febbraio**, n.m. February.

**fèccia**, n.f. dregs; lees; (pl.) faeces.

**fèbbre**, n.f. fever.

**febbrile**, adj. feverish.

**febbrilmente**, adv. feverishly.

**fecondo**, adj. fecund.

**fede**, n.f. faith, creed.

**fededegno**, adj. trustworthy, reliable.

**fedele**, adj. faithful, true.

**fedeltà**, n.f. faithfulness, allegiance, fidelity.

**fèdera**, n.f. pillowcase.

**federale**, adj. federal.

**federazione**, n.f. federation.

**fégato**, n.m. liver; pluck, guts.

**felce**, n.f. fern.

**felice**, adj. happy, felicitous.

**felicemente**, adv. happily.

**felicità**, n.f. felicity, happiness.

**felicitare**, vb. congratulate; felicitate; compliment.

**felicitazione**, n.f. congratulation; felicitation.

**felino**, adj. feline.

**fellone**, n.m. felon.

**fellonìa**, n.f. felony.

**feltro**, n.m. felt.

**fémmina**, n.f. female.

**femminile**, adj. female, feminine.

**femminilità**, n.f. femininity.

**féndere**, vb. split, cleave, crack.

**fenditura**, n.f. split, cleft, crack.

**fenomenale**, adj. phenomenal.

**fenòmeno**, n.m. phenomenon.

**feriale**, adj. of a weekday.

**ferire**, vb. wound, injure.

**ferita**, n.f. wound, injury.

**ferito**, n.m. wounded person, casualty.

**feritòia**, n.f. loophole.

**ferma biancheria**, n.m. clothespin.

**fermamente**, adv. firmly, fast.

**fermare**, vb. stop, halt, stay.

**fermata**, n.f. stop, halt. **f. intermèdia**, stop-over.

**fermatura**, n.f. fastening.

**fermentare**, vb. ferment.

**fermentazione**, n.f. fermentation.

**fermento**, n.m. ferment.

**fermezza**, n.f. firmness.

**fermo**, adj. firm, fixed, fast, steady. **f. pòsta**, general delivery. **mettere il f. su**, garnishee.

**feroce**, adj. ferocious, fierce.

**ferocemente**, adv. ferociously.

**ferocità**, n.f. ferocity.

**ferramenta**, n.f.pl. hardware.

**ferrare**, vb. shoe.

**fèrreo**, adj. iron.

**ferrièra**, n.f. ironworks.

**fèrro**, n.m. iron. **f. da stirare**, flat-iron. **f. di cavallo**, horseshoe.

**ferrovìa**, n.f. railroad.

**ferroviàrio**, adj. railroad.

**fèrtile**, adj. fertile.

**fertilità**, n.f. fertility.

**fertilizzante**, n.m. fertilizer.

**fertilizzare**, vb. fertilize.

**fertilizzazione**, n.f. fertilization.

**fervente**, adj. fervent.

**ferventemente**, adv. fervently.

**fèrvido**, adj. fervid.

**fervore**, n.m. fervor, fervency.

**fesso**, adj. cracked; crazy.

**fessura**, n.f. split, cleavage, cranny, fissure; slit; slot.

**fèsta**, n.f. feast, festival, fête, holiday, vacation.

**festività**, n.f. festivity.

**festivo**, adj. festive. **giorno f.**, holiday.

**festone**, n.m. festoon.

**fetale**, adj. foetal.

**feticcio**, n.m. fetish.

**fètido**, adj. fetid.

**fèto**, n.m. foetus.

**fetta,** *n.f.* slice, fillet.
**feudale,** *adj.* feudal.
**feudalismo,** *n.m.* feudalism.
**fèudo,** *n.m.* fief, feud.
**fiacco,** *adj.* limp.
**fiàccola,** *n.f.* torch.
**fiamma,** *n.f.* flame, blaze.
**fiammante,** *adj.* flaming.
**fiammeggiare,** *vb.* flame,
blaze; flare.
**fiammìfero,** *n.m.* match.
**fiammingo, 1.** *n.* Fleming.
flamingo. **2.** *adj.* Flemish.
**fiancheggiare,** *vb.* flank.
**fianco,** *n.m.* flank; hip; side.
**di f. a,** beside, abreast of.
**fiasco,** *n.m.* flask; fiasco; flop.
**fiato,** *n.m.* breath.
**fìbbia,** *n.f.* buckle.
**fibra,** *n.f.* fiber.
**fibroso,** *adj.* fibrous.
**ficcare,** *vb.* put; thrust, stick,
shove.
**fico,** *n.m.* fig.
**fidanzamento,** *n.m.* betrothal, engagement.
**fidanzare,** *vb.* betroth, affiance; (*refl.*) get engaged.
**fidanzata,** *n.f.* fiancée.
**fidanzato,** *n.m.* fiancé.
**fidatezza,** *n.f.* dependability.
**fidènte,** *adj.* reliant.
**fido,** *adj.* dependable.
**fidùcia,** *n.f.* trust.
**fièle,** *n.m.* gall. **vescica del
f.,** gall-bladder.
**fienìle,** *n.m.* hayloft.
**fièno,** *n.m.* hay.
**fièra,** *n.f.* fair. **f. campionària,** sample fair.
**figlia,** *n.f.* daughter.
**figliare,** *vb.* litter.
**figliata,** *n.f.* litter.
**figlio,** *n.m.* son.
**figliòccio,** *n.m.* godchild.
**figura,** *n.f.* figure.
**figurare,** *vb.* figure.
**figurarsi,** *vb.* imagine, fancy,
envisage.
**figuratamente,** *adv.* figuratively.
**figurato,** *adj.* figurative.
**figurina,** *n.f.* figurine.
**fila,** *n.f.* file; line; row; rank;
tier.
**filàccia inglese,** *n.f.* lint.
**filamento,** *n.m.* filament.
**filantropìa,** *n.f.* philanthropy.
**filare,** *vb.* spin.
**filatèlica,** *n.f.* philately.

**filato,** *n.m.* yarn.
**filetto,** *n.m.* fillet.
**filiale,** *adj.* filial.
**filigrana,** *n.f.sg.* filigree.
**filo,** *n.m.* thread; string;
clew; wire.
**filobus,** *n.m.* trolley-bus.
**filone,** *n.m.* vein, lode.
**filosofìa,** *n.f.* philosophy.
**filosòfico,** *adj.* philosophical.
**filòsofo,** *n.m.* philosopher.
**filovìa,** *n.f.* trolley-bus line.
**filtrare,** *vb.* filter.
**filtro,** *n.m.* filter.
**filza,** *n.f.* string; collection;
file.
**finale, 1.** *n.* finale. **2.** *adj.*
final, eventual.
**finalista,** *n.m.* finalist.
**finalità,** *n.f.* finality; purpose.
**finalmente,** *adv.* finally.
**finanza,** *n.f.* finance.
**finanziàrio,** *adj.* financial.
**finanzière,** *n.m.* financier.
**finchè,** *conj.* till, until.
**fine,** *n.m.* purpose.
**fine,** *n.f.* end, finish.
**finèstra,** *n.f.* window.
**finezza,** *n.f.* finesse.
**fìngere,** *vb.* pretend, feign,
assume, make believe.
**finire,** *vb.* end, finish.
**fino,** *adj.* fine; pure.
**fino a,** *prep.* as far as; until,
till. **f. dove?** how far? **f. a
quando?** how long?
**finora,** *adv.* up to now, so far,
hereto, hitherto.
**finta,** *n.f.* pretense, make-believe.
**finto,** *adj.* pretended, fictional, mock, make-believe.
**finzione,** *n.f.* fiction; figment.
**fiòcco,** *n.m.* flake; (boat) jib.
**f. da cìpria,** powder-puff.
**fiòcina,** *n.f.* harpoon.
**fiocinare,** *vb.* harpoon.
**fiòco,** *adj.* hoarse.
**fionda,** *n.f.* sling.
**fioraio,** *n.m.* florist.
**fiore,** *n.m.* flower, bloom,
blossom.
**fiorentino,** *adj.* Florentine.
**fioretto,** *n.m.* foil.
**fiori,** *n.m.pl.* clubs (cards).
**fiorire,** *vb.* flower, bloom,
blossom; flourish.
**fiorito,** *adj.* flowery.
**fiòtto,** *n.m.* stream.

**firma**, *n.f.* signature.

**firmare**, *vb.* sign; endorse.

**fisarmònica**, *n.f.* accordion.

**fischiare**, *vb.* whistle.

**físchio**, *n.m.* whistle.

**física**, *n.f.* physics.

**físico**, **1.** *n.m.* physicist; physique. **2.** *adj.* physical.

**fisiologìa**, *n.f.* physiology.

**fisioterapìa**, *n.f.* physiotherapy.

**fissare**, *vb.* fix; set; appoint; assess (a fine); fasten.

**fisso**, *adj.* fixed; set.

**fittiziamente**, *adv.* fictitiously.

**fittízio**, *adj.* fictitious.

**fitto**, *adj.* thick.

**fiume**, *n.m.* river.

**fiumicino**, *n.m.* stream, creek.

**fiutare**, *vb.* smell.

**fiuto**, *n.m.* scent; smell; flair.

**fiscale**, *adj.* fiscal.

**fissazione**, *n.f.* fixation.

**fissione**, *n.f.* fission.

**fisso**, *adj.* fixed.

**flàccido**, *adj.* flaccid.

**flagellante**, *n.m.* flagellant.

**flagellare**, *vb.* flagellate.

**flagrante**, *adj.* flagrant.

**flagrantemente**, *adv.* flagrantly.

**flan**, *n.m.* custard.

**flanèlla**, *n.f.* flannel.

**flàuto**, *n.m.* flute.

**flèmma**, *n.m.* phlegm.

**flemmàtico**, *adj.* phlegmatic.

**flessìbile**, *adj.* flexible; limp.

**flessibilità**, *n.f.* flexibility.

**flessione**, *n.f.* inflection.

**flessuoso**, *adj.* lithe.

**flèttere**, *vb.* flex.

**flirt**, *n.m.* flirtation.

**flirtare**, *vb.* flirt.

**floreale**, *adj.* floral.

**flòscio**, *adj.* soft; flabby.

**flòtta**, *n.f.* fleet.

**fluènte**, *adj.* glib.

**fluidità**, *n.f.* fluidity.

**flùido**, *n.m. and adj.* fluid.

**fluorescènte**, *adj.* fluorescent.

**fluoroscòpio**, *n.m.* fluoroscope.

**flusso**, *n.m.* flux.

**fluttuare**, *vb.* fluctuate.

**fluttuazione**, *n.f.* fluctuation.

**fobìa**, *n.f.* phobia.

**fòca**, *n.f.* seal.

**focaccia**, *n.f.* cake.

**focale**, *adj.* focal.

**focolare**, *n.m.* fireplace, hearth.

**focoso**, *adj.* fiery.

**fòdera**, *n.f.* lining.

**fòdero**, *n.m.* sheath.

**fòggia**, *n.f.* shape, guise.

**foggiare**, *vb.* make; forge; shape.

**fòglia**, *n.f.* leaf; blade (of grass); foil.

**fogliame**, *n.m.* foliage.

**fòglio**, *n.m.* sheet.

**fogliolina**, *n.f.* leaflet.

**foglioluto**, *adj.* leafy.

**fogna**, *n.f.* drain; sewer.

**folclore**, *n.m.* folklore.

**fòlio**, *n.m.* folio.

**fòlla**, *n.f.* crowd; crush; mob.

**folle**, *adj.* crazy; mad.

**folletto**, *n.m.* elf, hobgoblin.

**follìa**, *n.f.* folly.

**follìcolo**, *n.m.* follicle.

**folto**, *adj.* thick; bushy.

**fomentare**, *vb.* foment.

**fondamentale**, *adj.* fundamental, basic.

**fondamento**, *n.m.* foundation.

**fondare**, *vb.* found.

**fondatore**, *n.m.* founder.

**fondazione**, *n.f.* foundation.

**fondènte**, *n.m.* fondant.

**fóndere**, *vb.* melt; (metal) cast; fuse; (ore) smelt.

**fonderìa**, *n.f.* foundry.

**fondina**, *n.f.* holster.

**fonditore**, *n.m.* melter; smelter; caster.

**fondo**, *n.m.* bottom; fund.

**fonètico**, *adj.* phonetic.

**fontana**, *n.f.* fountain.

**fonte**, *n.f.* spring; source.

**foràggio**, *n.m.* forage; fodder.

**forare**, *vb.* bore, pierce, puncture.

**foratura**, *n.f.* puncture.

**fòrbici**, *n.f.pl.* scissors.

**forca**, *n.f.* pitchfork; gallows.

**forchetta**, *n.f.* fork.

**forcina**, *n.f.* hairpin, bobby pin.

**fòrcipe**, *n.m.* forceps.

**forènse**, *adj.* forensic.

**forèsta**, *n.f.* forest, wood.

**forestièro**, **1.** *n.* foreigner. **2.** *adj.* foreign.

**fórfora**, *n.f.* dandruff.

For pronunciation, see the concise guide on pages 5 to 7.

**forma,** *n.f.* form, mold, shape; (shoe) last.

**formàggio,** *n.m.* cheese.

**formaldèide,** *n.f.* formaldehyde.

**formale,** *adj.* formal.

**formalità,** *n.f.* formality.

**formalmente,** *adv.* formally.

**formare,** *vb.* form, mold, shape; (telephone) dial (a number).

**formativo,** *adj.* formative.

**formato,** *n.m.* format.

**formazione,** *n.f.* formation.

**formica,** *n.f.* ant.

**formicolare,** *vb.* swarm.

**formidàbile,** *adj.* formidable.

**fòrmula,** *n.f.* formula.

**formulare,** *vb.* formulate.

**formulazione,** *n.f.* formulation.

**fornace,** *n.m.* furnace; kiln.

**fornaio,** *r.m.* baker.

**fornèllo,** *n.m.* stove.

**fornire,** *vb.* furnish, equip, supply.

**fornitura,** *n.f.* supply.

**forno,** *n.m.* oven; bakery.

**foro,** *n.m.* hole, bore, vent.

**fòro,** *n.m.* forum.

**forse,** *adv.* perhaps, maybe, possibly.

**forsizia,** *n.f.* forsythia.

**fòrte, 1.** *n.* forte. **2.** *adj.* strong; loud. **3.** *adv.* loud.

**fortemente,** *adv.* strongly; hard.

**fortezza,** *n.f.* fort, fortress; fortitude.

**fortificare,** *vb.* fortify.

**fortificazione,** *n.f.* fortification.

**fortùito,** *adj.* fortuitous, chance.

**fortuna,** *n.f.* fortune, luck.

**fortunato,** *adj.* fortunate, lucky.

**forùncolo,** *n.m.* boil; pimple.

**fòrza,** *n.f.* force, strength.

**forzare,** *vb.* force.

**forzato,** *adj.* forced; forcible.

**fóschia,** *n.f.* fog.

**fosco,** *adj.* dark, dreary, dusky, grim, somber.

**fòsforo,** *n.m.* phosphorus.

**fossa,** *n.f.* moat.

**fossato,** *n.m.* ditch.

**fossetta,** *n.f.* dimple.

**fòssile,** *n.m. and adj.* fossil.

**fossilizzare,** *vb.* fossilize.

**fosso,** *n.m.* ditch.

**fotoelèttrico,** *adj.* photoelectric.

**fotogènico,** *adj.* photogenic.

**fotografare,** *vb.* photograph.

**fotografia,** *n.f.* photograph; photography.

**fotògrafo,** *n.m.* photographer.

**fra,** *prep.* between, among, amid. **f. pòco,** soon, by-and-by, presently.

**fracassare,** *vb.* smash.

**fracasso,** *n.m.* uproar, fuss, ado, fracas.

**fràgile,** *adj.* fragile, brittle, frail.

**fràgola,** *n.f.* strawberry.

**fragore,** *n.m.* clang, crash.

**fragrante,** *adj.* fragrant.

**fragranza,** *n.f.* fragrance.

**fraintèndere,** *vb.* misunderstand, misconstrue.

**frammentàrio,** *adj.* fragmentary.

**frammento,** *n.m.* fragment.

**frana,** *n.f.* landslide.

**francamente,** *adv.* frankly, candidly.

**franchezza,** *n.m.* frankness, candidness, directness.

**francese, 1.** *n.m.* Frenchman; *f.* Frenchwoman. **2.** *adj.* French.

**Frància,** *n.f.* France.

**franco,** *adj.* frank, candid, straightforward.

**francobollo,** *n.m.* postage stamp.

**frangènte,** *n.m.* breaker; (*pl.*) surf.

**fràngia,** *n.f.* fringe; (hair-do) bang.

**frangionde,** *n.m.* breakwater.

**frantumare,** *vb.* shatter, smash.

**frase,** *n.f.* phrase; sentence.

**fràssino,** *n.m.* ash-tree.

**frastagliare,** *vb.* indent.

**frastuòno,** *n.m.* uproar, racket.

**frate,** *n.m.* friar.

**fratellanza,** *n.f.* brotherhood.

**fratellastro,** *n.m.* half-brother; step-brother.

**fratèllo,** *n.m.* brother.

**fraternamente,** *adv.* fraternally.

**fraternità,** *n.f.* fraternity.

**fraternizzare,** *vb.* fraternize.

**fratèrno,** *adj.* brotherly, fraternal.

**fratricida,** *n.m.* fratricide.

**fratricìdio,** *n.m.* fratricide.

**frattèmpo,** *n.m.* meantime, meanwhile, interim.

**frattura,** *n.f.* fracture.

**fratturare,** *vb.* fracture.

**fraudolentemente,** *adv.* fraudulently.

**fraudolento,** *adj.* fraudulent.

**frazione,** *n.f.* fraction.

**frèccia,** *n.f.* arrow; directional signal.

**freddamente,** *adv.* coldly.

**freddezza,** *n.f.* coldness.

**freddo, 1.** *n.m.* cold; chill. **2.** *adj.* cold, chilly. **aver f.,** feel cold. **far f.,** be cold.

**freddura,** *n.f.* pun.

**fregare,** *vb.* rub.

**fregata,** *n.f.* rub; frigate.

**frèmito,** *n.m.* thrill.

**frenare,** *vb.* brake; check.

**frenesìa,** *n.f.* frenzy.

**frenètico,** *adj.* frantic, frenzied.

**freno,** *n.m.* brake; check.

**frequentare,** *vb.* frequent, attend, haunt.

**frequentatore,** *n.m.* habitué.

**frequènte,** *adj.* frequent.

**frequentemente,** *adv.* frequently.

**frequènza,** *n.* frequency.

**freschezza,** *n.f.* freshness.

**fresco, 1.** *n.* coolness. **2.** *adj.* cool; fresh.

**fretta,** *n.f.* haste, hurry, hustle, rush.

**frettolosamente,** *adv.* hastily.

**frettoloso,** *adj.* hasty, cursory.

**fricassèa,** *n.f.* fricassee.

**frìggere,** *vb.* fry.

**frigido,** *adj.* frigid.

**frigorìfero,** *n.m.* refrigerator; freezer.

**frittata,** *n.f.* omelet.

**frittèlla,** *n.f.* fritter, pancake.

**frivolezza,** *n.f.* frivolousness.

**frivolità,** *n.f.* frivolity.

**frìvolo,** *adj.* frivolous.

**frizione,** *n.f.* friction; rubbing; (auto) clutch.

**fròde,** *n.f.* fraud.

**frontale,** *adj.* frontal; head on.

**fronte,** *n.m.* forehead; brow; front.

**fronteggiare,** *vb.* face.

**frontièra,** *n.f.* frontier, border.

**fròttola,** *n.f.* fib, canard; (*pl.*) nonsense.

**frugale,** *adj.* frugal.

**frugalità,** *n.f.* frugality.

**fruizione,** *n.f.* fruition.

**frumento,** *n.m.* wheat.

**frusciare,** *vb.* rustle.

**fruscìo,** *n.m.* rustle.

**frusta,** *n.f.* lash, whip.

**frustare,** *vb.* lash, whip.

**frustino,** *n.m.* horsewhip.

**frustrare,** *vb.* frustrate, foil, thwart.

**frustrazione,** *n.f.* frustration.

**frutteto,** *n.m.* orchard.

**fruttificare,** *vb.* fructify.

**frutto,** *n.m.* fruit.

**fruttuoso,** *adj.* fruitful.

**fucilare,** *vb.* shoot.

**fucile,** *n.m.* gun, rifle.

**fucilerìa,** *n.f.* fusillade.

**fucina,** *n.f.* forge, smithy.

**fuco,** *n.m.* drone.

**fùcsia,** *n.f.* fuchsia.

**fuga,** *n.f.* flight, escape, getaway; fugue.

**fugace,** *adj.* fleeting.

**fuggire,** *vb.* flee; elope; run away.

**fuggitivo,** *n.m.* and *adj.* fugitive.

**fulcro,** *n.m.* fulcrum.

**fulgore,** *n.m.* radiance.

**fuliggine,** *n.f.* soot.

**fulminare,** *vb.* fulminate.

**fulminazione,** *n.f.* fulmination.

**fùlmine,** *n.m.* (bolt of) lightning; thunderbolt.

**fumaiòlo,** *n.m.* smokestack.

**fumare,** *vb.* smoke.

**fumetto,** *n.m.* comic strip. **giornalino a fumetti,** comic book.

**fumigare,** *vb.* fumigate.

**fumigatore,** *n.m.* fumigator.

**fumo,** *n.m.* smoke.

**fune,** *n.f.* rope.

**fùnebre,** *adj.* funeral.

**funerale,** *n.m.* funeral.

**fùnebre,** *adj.* funeral.

**fungicida,** *n.m.* fungicide.

**fungo,** *n.m.* fungus; mushroom.

**funivia,** *n.f.* cableway.

**funzionale,** *adj.* functional.

**funzionare,** *vb.* function; work; run.

**funzionàrio,** *n.m.* functionary, official.

**funzione,** *n.f.* function.

**fuochista,** *n.m.* fireman.

**fuòco,** *n.m.* fire, blaze; focus.

**fuòchi d'artifìcio,** fireworks.

**fuòri,** *adv.* out; outside; forth.

**f. di.** outside.

**fuoruscito,** *n.m.* exile.

**furbo,** *adj.* crafty, tricky, sly, shrewd.

**furfante,** *n.m.* blackguard, scoundrel, villain.

**furgone,** *n.m.* van.

**fùria,** *n.f.* fury.

**furioso,** *adj.* furious; wild.

**furore,** *n.m.* furor, fury.

**furtivamente,** *adv.* stealthily.

**furtivo,** *adj.* stealthy.

**furto,** *n.m.* theft, burglary, larceny, robbery.

**fusìbile, 1.** *n.m.* fuse. **2.** *adj.* easily melted.

**fusione,** *n.f.* fusion, merger.

**fuso,** *adj.* molten.

**fusolièra,** *n.f.* fuselage.

**fustigare,** *vb.* flog.

**fùtile,** *adj.* futile.

**futilità,** *n.f.* futility.

**futuro,** *n.m. and adj.* future.

---

# G

**gabardina,** *n.f.* gabardine.

**gàbbia,** *n.f.* cage.

**gabbiano,** *n.m.* gull.

**gabinetto,** *n.m.* cabinet; toilet; closet; office.

**gagliardo,** *adj.* sturdy.

**gaiamente,** *adv.* gaily.

**gaiezza,** *n.f.* gaiety.

**gaio,** *adj.* gay, cheerful, jolly, blithe, debonair.

**gala,** *n.f.* frill; gala.

**galante,** *adj.* gallant.

**galàssia,** *n.f.* galaxy.

**galatèo,** *n.m.* etiquette, good manners.

**galèa,** *n.f.* galley.

**galeone,** *n.m.* galleon.

**galla,** *n.f.* **a g.,** afloat.

**galleggiare,** *vb.* float.

**gallerìa,** *n.f.* gallery; tunnel; arcade.

**gàllico,** *adj.* Gallic.

**gallina,** *n.f.* hen.

**gallo,** *n.m.* rooster, cock.

**gallone,** *n.m.* stripe; chevron; gallon.

**galoppare,** *vb.* gallop.

**galòppo,** *n.m.* gallop.

**galòscia,** *n.f.* galosh.

**galvanizzare,** *vb.* galvanize.

**galvanoplàstica,** *n.f.* electroplating.

**gamba,** *n.f.* leg.

**gamberetto,** *n.m.* shrimp.

**gambo,** *n.m.* stalk.

**gamma,** *n.f.* scale; gamut.

**gancio,** *n.m.* clip; clasp; hook.

**gànghero,** *n.m.* hinge.

**gara,** *n.f.* competition.

**garantire,** *vb.* guarantee.

**garanzìa,** *n.f.* guarantee; guaranty; bail.

**garbùglio,** *n.m.* tangle.

**gardènia,** *n.f.* gardenia.

**gareggiare,** *vb.* vie, compete.

**gargarismo,** *n.m.* gargle.

**gargarizzare,** *vb.* gargle.

**garòfano,** *n.m.* carnation.

**garrotta,** *n.f.* garrote.

**gàrrulo,** *adj.* garrulous.

**garza,** *n.f.* gauze; cheesecloth.

**gas,** *n.m.* gas.

**gassoso,** *adj.* gassy, gaseous.

**gàstrico,** *adj.* gastric.

**gastrite,** *n.f.* gastritis.

**gastronomìa,** *n.f.* gastronomy.

**gastronòmico,** *adj.* gastronomic.

**gatta,** *n.f.* cat.

**gattino,** *n.m.* kitten.

---

**gatto,** *n.m.* cat, tomcat.
**gavòtta,** *n.f.* gavotte.
**gazzèlla,** *n.f.* gazelle.
**gazzetta,** *n.f.* gazette.
**gelare,** *vb.* freeze.
**gelatina,** *n.f.* gelatine; jelly
**gelatinoso,** *adj.* gelatinous.
**gelato,** *n.m.* ice cream.
**gèlido,** *adj.* chilly, frosty.
**gelone,** *n.m.* chilblain.
**gelosìa,** *n.f.* jealousy.
**geloso,** *adj.* jealous.
**gelsomino,** *n.m.* jasmine.
**gemèllo,** *n.m.* twin.
**gèmere,** *vb.* groan, moan.
**gèmito,** *n.m.* moan, groan.
**gèmma,** *n.f.* gem; bud.
**gemmare,** *vb.* bud.
**gène,** *n.m.* gene.
**genealogìa,** *n.f.* genealogy, pedigree.
**genealògico,** *adj.* genealogical.
**generale,** *n.m. and adj.* general.
**generalità,** *n.f.* generality.
**generalizzare,** *vb.* generalize.
**generalizzazione,** *n.f.* generalization.
**generalmente,** *adv.* generally.
**generare,** *vb.* generate, beget, breed, engender.
**generatore,** *n.m.* generator.
**generazione,** *n.f.* generation.
**gènere,** *n.m.* kind, gender, genre, genus. **g. alimentari,** foodstuffs.
**genèrico,** *adj.* generic.
**gènero,** *n.m.* son-in-law.
**generosamente,** *adv.* generously.
**generosità,** *n.f.* generosity.
**generoso,** *adj.* generous.
**genètica,** *n.f.* genetics.
**genètico,** *adj.* genetic.
**genicìdio,** *n.m.* genocide.
**gènio,** *n.m.* genius; engineering.
**genitale,** *adj.* genital.
**genitali,** *n.m.pl.* genitals.
**genitivo,** *n.m. and adj.* genitive.
**genitore,** *n.m.* parent.
**gennaio,** *n.m.* January.
**Gènova,** *n.f.* Genoa.
**genovese,** *adj.* Genoese.
**gènte,** *n.f.* people, folks.
**gentile,** *adj.* gentile; nice, kind.
**gentilezza,** *n.f.* kindness.

**gentiluòmo,** *n.m.* gentleman.
**genuflèttersi,** *vb.* genuflect.
**genuinamente,** *adv.* genuinely.
**genuinità,** *n.f.* genuineness.
**genuino,** *adj.* genuine.
**genziana,** *n.f.* gentian.
**geografìa,** *n.f.* geography.
**geogràfico,** *adj.* geographical.
**geògrafo,** *n.m.* geographer.
**geomètrico,** *adj.* geometric.
**geometrìa,** *n.f.* geometry.
**geopolìtica,** *n.f.* geopolitics.
**gerànio,** *n.m.* geranium.
**gerarchìa,** *n.f.* hierarchy.
**geràrchico,** *adj.* hierarchical.
**gèrgo,** *n.m.* jargon, slang.
**Germània,** *n.f.* Germany.
**germànico,** *adj.* Germanic.
**gèrme,** *n.m.* germ.
**germicida,** *n.m.* germicide.
**germinale,** *adj.* germinal.
**germinare,** *vb.* germinate.
**germogliare,** *vb.* sprout.
**germòglio,** *n.m.* sprout; shoot.
**geroglìfico,** *adj.* hieroglyphic.
**Gerusalèmme,** *n.f.* Jerusalem.
**gesso,** *n.m.* chalk; gypsum.
**gessoso,** *adj.* chalky.
**gestazione,** *n.f.* gestation.
**gesticolare,** *vb.* gesticulate.
**gesticolazione,** *n.f.* gesticulation.
**gèsto,** *n.m.* gesture.
**Gesù,** *n.m.* Jesus.
**gesuita,** *n.m.* Jesuit.
**gettare,** *vb.* throw, hurl; cast; dash; flip.
**gètto,** *n.m.* throw; cast; jet.
**gettone,** *n.m.* token.
**ghèriglio,** *n.m.* kernel.
**ghermire,** *vb.* snatch.
**gherone,** *n.m.* gusset.
**ghiacciaia,** *n.f.* ice-box.
**ghiacciaio,** *n.m.* glacier.
**ghiàccio,** *n.m.* ice.
**ghiaia,** *n.f.* gravel.
**ghianda,** *n.f.* acorn.
**ghiandaia,** *n.f.* jay.
**ghiàndola,** *n.f.* gland.
**ghigliottina,** *n.f.* guillotine.
**ghingano,** *n.m.* gingham.
**ghiotto,** *adj.* gluttonous.
**ghiottone, 1.** *n.m.* glutton; gourmand. **2.** *adj.* greedy.
**ghiottonerìa,** *n.f.* greediness.
**ghirlanda,** *n.f.* garland, wreath.
**ghisa,** *n.f.* cast iron.

**già, 1.** *adj.* former; sometime. **2.** *adv.* already; formerly.

**giacca,** *n.f.* coat, jacket.

**giacchè,** *conj.* since.

**giacchetta,** *n.f.* jacket.

**giàcchio,** *n.m.* dragnet.

**giacere,** *vb.* lie.

**giacinto,** *n.m.* hyacinth.

**giada,** *n.f.* jade.

**giaguaro,** *n.m.* jaguar.

**giallo,** *adj.* yellow.

**giàmbico,** *adj.* iambic.

**Giappone,** *n.m.* Japan.

**giapponese,** *adj.* Japanese.

**giara,** *n.f.* jar.

**giardinetta,** *n.f.* station wagon.

**giardinière,** *n.m.* gardener.

**giardino,** *n.m.* garden. **g. d'infànzia,** kindergarten.

**giarrettièra,** *n.f.* garter.

**giavazzo,** *n.m.* jet.

**giavellòtto,** *n.m.* javelin.

**gibbone,** *n.m.* gibbon.

**giga,** *n.f.* jig.

**gigante,** *n.m.* giant.

**gigantesco,** *adj.* gigantic; giant.

**giglio,** *n.m.* lily.

**gilè,** *n.m.* vest; waistcoat.

**gimnòto,** *n.m.* electric eel.

**ginecologìa,** *n.f.* gynaecology.

**ginepro,** *n.m.* juniper.

**Ginèvra,** *n.f.* Geneva.

**ginevrino,** *adj.* Genevan.

**ginnàsio,** *n.m.* high school.

**ginnasta,** *n.m.* gymnast.

**ginnàstica,** *n.f.* gymnastics.

**ginnàstico,** *adj.* gymnastic.

**ginòcchio,** *n.m.* knee.

**giocare,** *vb.* play. **g. d'azzardo,** gamble.

**giocatore,** *n.m.* player. **g. d'azzardo,** gambler.

**giocàttolo,** *n.m.* toy.

**giòco,** *n.m.* game. **g. d'azzardo,** game of chance; gambling.

**giocondo,** *adj.* jocund.

**giogo,** *n.m.* yoke.

**gìoia,** *n.f.* joy, glee.

**gioiellerìa,** *n.f.* jewelry.

**gioiellière,** *n.m.* jeweler.

**gioièllo,** *n.m.* jewel.

**gioìre,** *vb.* rejoice; gloat.

**gioioso,** *adj.* joyful, happy, blithe, gleeful.

**giornalaio,** *n.m.* news-vendor.

**giornale,** *n.m.* newspaper; journal; daily.

**giornalièro,** *adj.* daily.

**giornalismo,** *n.m.* journalism.

**giornalista,** *n.m.* journalist.

**giornata,** *n.f.* day.

**giorno,** *n.m.* day. **g. feriale,** weekday; workday. **g. festivo,** holiday.

**gióvane,** *adj.* young.

**giovanile,** *adj.* youthful; juvenile.

**giovedì,** *n.m.* Thursday.

**giovènca,** *n.f.* heifer.

**gioviale,** *adj.* jovial.

**giovinezza,** *n.f.* youth.

**giradischi,** *n.m.* record-player.

**giraffa,** *n.f.* giraffe.

**girare,** *vb.* turn, revolve, spin, whirl; crank; endorse.

**girata,** *n.f.* endorsement.

**giretto,** *n.m.* spin.

**giro,** *n.m.* turn; revolution; round. **prèndere in g.,** make fun of; kid.

**giroscòpio,** *n.m.* gyroscope.

**girovago,** *adj.* itinerant.

**gita,** *n.f.* outing; picnic.

**giù,** *adv.* down.

**giubilante,** *adj.* jubilant.

**giubilèo,** *n.m.* jubilee.

**giudaismo,** *n.m.* Judaism.

**giudèo,** *n.m.* Jew.

**giudicare,** *vb.* judge; deem.

**giùdice,** *n.m.* judge.

**giudiziàrio,** *adj.* judiciary; judicial.

**giudìzio,** *n.m.* judgment, discernment.

**giudizioso,** *adj.* judicious.

**giugno,** *n.m.* June.

**giugulare,** *adj.* jugular.

**giuncata,** *n.f.* junket.

**giunchiglia,** *n.f.* jonquil.

**giunco,** *n.m.* rush.

**giùngere,** *vb.* join; arrive.

**giungla,** *n.f.* jungle.

**giuntura,** *n.f.* juncture, joint.

**giuramento,** *n.m.* oath.

**giurare,** *vb.* swear.

**giurato,** *n.m.* juror.

**giurìa,** *n.f.* jury.

**giurisdizione,** *n.f.* jurisdiction.

**giurisprudènza,** *n.f.* jurisprudence.

**giurista,** *n.m.* jurist.

**giustacuòre,** *n.m.* jerkin.

**giustamente,** *adv.* justly, fairly.

**giustezza,** *n.f.* fairness.

For pronunciation, see the concise guide on pages 5 to 7.

**giustificàbile,** *adj.* justifiable.

**giustificare,** *vb.* justify.

**giustificazione,** *n.f.* justification.

**giustizia,** *n.f.* justice; right; eousness.

**giustiziare,** *vb.* execute.

**giusto,** *adj.* just, fair; even-right; righteous; sound.

**gl',** *def. art. n.pl.* the.

**glaciale,** *adj.* glacial. **zona g.,** frigid zone.

**gladiòlo,** *n.m.* gladiolus.

**glàndola,** *n.f.* gland.

**glandolare,** *adj.* glandular.

**glaucòma,** *n.m.* glaucoma.

**gli,** 1. *def. art. m.pl.* the. 2. *pron.* 3. *sg.m.* dative. to him.

**glicerina,** *n.f.* glycerine.

**globale,** *adj.* global.

**glòbo,** *n.m.* globe. **g. dell'òcchio,** eyeball.

**globulare,** *adj.* globular.

**glòbulo,** *n.m.* globule.

**glòria,** *n.f.* glory.

**gloriarsi,** *vb.* glory.

**glorificare,** *vb.* glorify.

**glorificazione,** *n.f.* glorification.

**glorioso,** *adj.* glorious.

**glossàrio,** *n.m.* glossary.

**glucòsio,** *n.m.* glucose.

**glutinoso,** *adj.* glutinous.

**gnòcco,** *n.m.* dumpling.

**gobba,** *n.f.* hunchback (woman); hump; hunch.

**gobbo,** *n.m.* humpback, hunchback.

**góccia,** *n.f.* drop.

**gocciamento,** *n.m.* dripping.

**gocciolare,** *vb.* drip.

**godere,** *vb.* enjoy; (*refl.*) bask in.

**godìbile,** *adj.* enjoyable.

**godimento,** *n.m.* enjoyment.

**goffàggine,** *n.f.* clumsiness.

**gòffo,** *adj.* awkward, clumsy, gawky, uncouth.

**gola,** *n.f.* throat; gorge; gullet.

**golf,** *n.m.* golf; sweater.

**golfo,** *n.m.* gulf.

**gòmena,** *n.f.* hawser.

**gómito,** *n.m.* elbow.

**gomma,** *n.f.* gum; rubber. **g. lacca,** shellac.

**gommoso,** *adj.* gummy.

**góndola,** *n.f.* gondola.

**gondolière,** *n.m.* gondolier.

**gonfiamento,** *n.m.* inflation; swelling up.

**gonfiare,** *vb.* inflate; swell; bloat; (*refl.*) bulge.

**gonfio,** *adj.* inflated; swollen; baggy.

**gong,** *n.m.* gong.

**gònna,** *n.f.* skirt.

**gonnèlla,** *n.f.* gown; petticoat.

**gonorrèa,** *n.f.* gonorrhea.

**gorgogliare,** *vb.* gurgle.

**gorgoglio,** *n.m.* gurgle.

**gorilla,** *n.m.* gorilla.

**gòtico,** *adj.* Gothic.

**governante,** *n.f.* governess.

**governare,** *vb.* govern.

**governativo,** *adj.* governmental.

**governatorato,** *n.m.* governorship.

**governatore,** *n.m.* governor.

**governatoriale,** *adj.* gubernatorial.

**govèrno,** *n.m.* government.

**gozzo,** *n.m.* goiter.

**gozzovìglia,** *n.f.* revel.

**gozzovigliare,** *vb.* revel.

**gracchiare,** *vb.* caw.

**gràcchio,** *n.m.* grackle.

**gracidare,** *vb.* croak.

**gradale,** *n.m.* grail.

**gradatamente,** *adv.* by degrees.

**gradévole,** *adj.* pleasing; acceptable; agreeable.

**gradevolmente,** *adv.* pleasingly; agreeably; acceptably.

**gradino,** *n.m.* step.

**grado,** *n.m.* degree; grade; rank.

**graduale,** *adj.* gradual.

**gradualmente,** *adv.* gradually.

**graduare,** *vb.* graduate.

**graduazione,** *n.f.* foreclosure.

**graffiare,** *vb.* scratch.

**graffiatura,** *n.f.* scratch.

**gràfico,** 1. *n.m.* graph. 2. *adj.* graphic.

**grafite,** *n.f.* graphite.

**grafologia,** *n.f.* graphology.

**grammàtica,** *n.f.* grammar.

**grammaticale,** *adj.* grammatical.

**grammàtico,** *n.m.* grammarian.

**grammo,** *n.m.* gram.

**grammòfono,** *n.m.* gramophone, phonograph.

**granaio,** *n.m.* granary; barn.

**granata,** *n.f.* grenade.

**granatina,** *n.f.* grenadine.

granato, *n.m.* garnet.

Gran Bretagna, *n.f.* Great Britain.

grànchio, *n.m.* crab.

grande, *adj.* big; large; great; grand.

grandezza, *n.f.* greatness, grandeur; size; magnitude.

grandinare, *vb.* hail.

grandinata, *n.f.* hailstorm.

gràndine, *n.f.* hail.

grandiosamente, *adv.* grandiosely, grandly.

grandioso, *adj.* grandiose.

granito, *n.m.* granite.

grano, *n.m.* grain; bead. g. saraceno, buckwheat.

granturco, *n.m.* corn; maize.

granulare, *adj.* granular.

granulare, *vb.* granulate.

granulazione, *n.f.* granulation.

granèllo, *n.m.* granule.

grappa, *n.f.* clamp.

gràppolo, *n.m.* bunch, cluster.

grassatore, *n.m.* highway robber.

grassazione, *n.f.* hold-up.

grassetto, *adj.* chubby; boldface.

grasso, 1. *n.* fat; grease. 2. *adj.* fat; stout; fatty; greasy.

grassòccio, *adj.* plump, buxom.

grata, *n.f.* lattice.

graticola, *n.f.* grate; grill; grid; gridiron; griddle; broiler.

gratificare, *vb.* gratify.

gratificazione, *n.f.* gratification; bonus.

gratitùdine, *n.f.* gratitude.

grato, *adj.* grateful, thankful; pleasing.

grattacièlo, *n.m.* skyscraper.

grattugia, *n.f.* grater.

grattugiare, *vb.* grate.

gratuitamente, *adv.* gratis.

gratùito, *adj.* free, gratis, complimentary, gratuitous.

grave, *adj.* grave; grievous.

gravemente, *adv.* gravely.

gràvida, *adj.f.* pregnant, big with child.

gravidanza, *n.f.* pregnancy.

gravità, *n.f.* gravity.

gravitare, *vb.* gravitate.

gravitazione, *n.f.* gravitation.

gràzia, *n.f.* grace.

graziosamente, *adv.* graciously.

grazioso, *adj.* gracious; pretty; becoming; comely.

Grècia, *n.f.* Greece.

grèco, *adj.* Greek.

gregàrio, *adj.* gregarious.

gregge, *n.m.* flock, herd.

grembiule, *n.m.* apron.

grèmbo, *n.m.* lap.

gretto, *adj.* mean; shabby.

grezzo, *adj.* raw.

gridare, *vb.* cry; shout, yell.

grido, *n.m.* cry; shout, yell.

grigiastro, *adj.* grayish.

grigio, *adj.* gray; drab.

grilletto, *n.m.* trigger.

grillo, *n.m.* cricket.

grisou, *n.m.* firedamp.

gròg, *n.m.* grog.

grónda, *n.f.* eaves.

grondaia, *n.f.* gutter.

grossagrana, *n.f.* grosgrain.

gròsso, *adj.* big; large; fat.

grossolanamente, *adv.* grossly.

grossolanità, *n.f.* coarseness; grossness.

grossolano, *adj.* coarse; gross.

grotta, *n.f.* grotto.

grottesco, *adj.* grotesque.

groviglio, *n.m.* ravel, tangle, snarl.

gru, *n.f.* crane; derrick.

gruccia, *n.f.* crutch.

grugnire, *vb.* grunt.

grugnito, *n.m.* grunt.

gruppo, *n.m.* group; clump; cluster; gang.

guadagnare, *vb.* earn; gain.

guadagno, *n.m.* gain, profit; (*pl.*) earnings.

guado, *n.m.* ford.

guaìna, *n.f.* sheath.

guaio, *n.m.* trouble, woe.

guància, *n.f.* cheek; jowl.

guanciale, *n.m.* pillow.

guanto, *n.m.* glove; gauntlet.

guardacòste, *n.m.* coast guard.

guardare, *vb.* look at; guard; gaze; regard; watch; (*refl.*) beware.

guardaròba, *n.m.* cloakroom; wardrobe.

guàrdia, *n.f.* guard; watch.

guardiano, *n.m.* guardian; caretaker; watchman.

guardina, *n.f.* guard-house.

guardingo, *adj.* guarded.

guaribile, *adj.* curable.

guarigione, *n.f.* cure, recovery.

guarire, *vb.* cure, heal.

---

**guarnigione**, *n.f.* garrison.
**guarnire**, *vb.* garnish.
**guarnizione**, *n.f.* garnishment; gasket.
**guastare**, *vb.* spoil, mar.
**guazzabùglio**, *n.m.* mess; hash.
**guèrra**, *n.f.* war.
**guerresco**, *adj.* warlike.
**guerrièro**, *n.m.* warrior.
**guerriglia**, *n.f.* guerrilla.
**guerriglière**, *n.m.* guerrilla fighter.
**gufo**, *n.m.* owl.
**gùglia**, *n.f.* spire.

**guida**, *n.f.* guide; guidance; leadership; guidebook; directory.
**guidare**, *vb.* guide; drive (auto).
**guinzàglio**, *n.m.* leash.
**gùscio**, *n.m.* shell.
**gustare**, *vb.* taste.
**gustativo**, *adj.* gustatory, involving taste.
**gusto**, *n.m.* taste; gusto; relish.
**gustoso**, *adj.* tasty, appetizing, palatable.
**gutturale**, *adj.* guttural.

---

# H, I

**hascisc**, *n.m.* hashish.
**i**, *def. art. m.pl.* the.
**iato**, *n.m.* hiatus.
**ibernazione**, *n.f.* hibernation.
**ibisco**, *n.m.* hibiscus.
**ibridazione**, *n.f.* cross-fertilization.
**ìbrido**, *adj.* hybrid.
**icòne**, *n.f.* icon.
**iddìo**, *n.m.* god.
**idèa**, *n.f.* idea.
**ideale**, *adj.* ideal.
**idealismo**, *n.m.* idealism.
**idealista**, *n.m.* idealist.
**idealìstico**, *adj.* idealistic.
**idealizzare**, *vb.* idealize.
**idealmente**, *adj.* ideally.
**idèntico**, *adj.* identical.
**identificàbile**, *adj.* identifiable.
**identificare**, *vb.* identify.
**identificazione**, *n.f.* identification.
**identità**, *n.f.* identity.
**ideologìa**, *n.f.* ideology.
**idìllico**, *adj.* idyllic.
**idìllio**, *n.m.* idyll.
**idiòma**, *n.m.* idiom.
**idiòta**, **1.** *n.* idiot. **2.** *adj.* idiotic.
**idiozìa**, *n.f.* idiocy.
**idòlatra**, *n.m. or f.* idolater.
**idolatrare**, *vb.* idolize.
**idolatrìa**, *n.* idolatry.
**ìdolo**, *n.m.* idol.

**idoneità**, *n.f.* fitness.
**idòneo**, *adj.* fit; qualified.
**idrante**, *n.m.* hydrant.
**idrato di carbone**, *n.m.* carbohydrate.
**idràulico**, **1.** *n.m.* plumber. **2.** *adj.* hydraulic.
**idroclòrico**, *adj.* hydrochloric.
**idroelèttrico**, *adj.* hydroelectric.
**idrofobìa**, *n.f.* hydrophobia.
**idrògeno**, *n.m.* hydrogen.
**idropisìa**, *n.f.* dropsy.
**idroscalo**, *n.m.* seaplane airport.
**idroterapèutica**, *n.f.* hydrotherapy.
**idrovolante**, *n.m.* seaplane; hydroplane.
**ièna**, *n.f.* hyena.
**ièri**, *n.m. and adv.* yesterday.
**igiène**, *n.f.* hygiene; sanitation.
**igiènico**, *adj.* hygienic; sanitary.
**ignaro**, *adj.* ignorant.
**ignòbile**, *adj.* ignoble.
**ignominioso**, *adj.* ignominious.
**ignorante**, *adj.* ignorant.
**ignorantone**, *n.m.* ignoramus.
**ignoranza**, *n.f.* ignorance.
**ignòto**, *adj.* unknown.
**il**, *def. art. m.sg.* the.

For pronunciation, see the concise guide on pages 5 to 7.

**ilare**, *adj.* hilarious.
**ilarità**, *n.f.* hilarity.
**illécito**, *adj.* illicit.
**illegale**, *adj.* illegal.
**illeggìbile**, *adj.* illegible.
**illeggibilmente**, *adv.* illegibly.
**illegittimità**, *n.f.* illegitimacy.
**illegìttimo**, *adj.* illegitimate.
**illimitatamente**, *adv.* boundlessly.
**illimitato**, *adj.* unlimited; boundless; limitless.
**illògico**, *adj.* illogical.
**illuminare**, *vb.* illuminate; light up; brighten; enlighten.
**illuminazione**, *n.f.* illumination.
**illusione**, *n.f.* illusion.
**illusòrio**, *adj.* illusory; illusive.
**illustrare**, *vb.* illustrate.
**illustrativo**, *adj.* illustrative.
**illustrazione**, *n.f.* illustration.
**illustre**, *adj.* illustrious.
**imbacuccare**, *vb.* wrap up.
**imballàggio**, *n.m.* packing.
**imballare**, *vb.* pack.
**imbalsamare**, *vb.* embalm.
**imbarazzare**, *vb.* embarrassment.
**imbarazzo**, *n.m.* embarrassment.
**imbarcare**, *vb.* embark.
**imbastire**, *vb.* baste.
**imbavagliare**, *vb.* gag.
**imbecìlle**, *n.m. and adj.* imbecile; half-wit; moron.
**imbèrbe**, *adj.* beardless.
**imbiancare**, *vb.* whiten; bleach.
**imboccatura**, *n.f.* mouthpiece; nozzle.
**imboscata**, *n.f.* ambush; **tendere un' i.** to ambush.
**imbottire**, *vb.* pad; stuff.
**imbottita**, *n.f.* quilt.
**imbottitura**, *n.f.* wadding; padding; batting.
**imbrattare**, *vb.* soil; stain; daub.
**imbrattatura**, *n.f.* daub.
**imbrogliare**, *vb.* embroil; entangle.
**imbuto**, *n.m.* funnel.
**imitare**, *vb.* imitate; mimic.
**imitativo**, *adj.* imitative.
**imitatore**, *n.m.* mimic; imitator.
**imitazione**, *n.f.* imitation.

**immacolato**, *adj.* immaculate.
**immagazzinare**, *vb.* store.
**immaginàbile**, *adj.* imaginable.
**immaginare**, *vb.* imagine; fancy.
**immaginàrio**, *adj.* imaginary.
**immaginativo**, *adj.* imaginative.
**immaginazione**, *n.f.* fancy; imagination.
**immàgine**, *n.f.* image.
**immaginoso**, *adj.* fanciful.
**immane**, *adj.* huge.
**immanènte**, *adj.* immanent.
**immateriale**, *adj.* immaterial.
**immaturo**, *adj.* immature.
**immediatamente**, *adv.* immediately; instantly; directly; forthwith; presently.
**immediato**, *adj.* immediate, instant.
**immènso**, *adj.* immense.
**immèrgere**, *vb.* immerse, dip.
**immigrante**, *n. and adj.* immigrant.
**immigrare**, *vb.* immigrate.
**imminènte**, *adj.* imminent.
**immischiarsi**, *vb.* interfere, meddle, tamper.
**immòbile**, *adj.* immobile, motionless, immovable.
**immobilizzare**, *vb.* immobilize.
**immoderato**, *adj.* immoderate.
**immodèstia**, *n.f.* immodesty.
**immodèsto**, *adj.* immodest.
**immorale**, *adj.* immoral.
**immoralità**, *n.f.* immorality.
**immoralmente**, *adv.* immorally.
**immortalare**, *vb.* immortalize.
**immortale**, *adj.* immortal, deathless.
**immortalità**, *n.f.* immortality.
**immune**, *adj.* immune.
**immunità**, *n.f.* immunity.
**immunizzare**, *vb.* immunize.
**immutàbile**, *adj.* immutable.
**impaginare**, *vb.* arrange in pages.
**impalare**, *vb.* impale.
**impalcatura**, *n.f.* scaffolding.
**impallidire**, *vb.* pale; blanch; fade.
**impantanarsi**, *vb.* bog down.
**imparare**, *vb.* learn.

---

**imparentato,** adj. related, kindred.

**impartire,** vb. impart.

**imparziale,** adj. impartial.

**impastare,** vb. knead.

**impaziènte,** adj. impatient, eager.

**impazientemente,** adv. impatiently, eagerly.

**impaziènza,** n.f. impatience, eagerness.

**impazzito,** adj. gone crazy, deranged.

**impedimento,** n.m. impediment, hindrance.

**impedire,** vb. impede, hinder, hamper, avert, balk, forestall, prevent.

**impegnare,** vb. pledge; pawn.

**impegno,** n.m. undertaking, commitment.

**impèllere,** vb. impel.

**impenetràbile,** adj. impenetrable.

**impenitènte,** adj. impenitent.

**impennarsi,** vb. rear.

**imperativo,** n.m. and adj. imperative.

**imperatore,** n.m. emperor.

**imperatrice,** n.f. empress.

**impercettìbile,** adj. imperceptible.

**imperfètto,** adj. imperfect.

**imperfezione,** n.f. imperfection.

**imperiale,** adj. imperial.

**imperialismo,** n.m. imperialism.

**imperioso,** adj. imperious.

**imperituro,** adj. imperishable; immortal.

**impermeàbile, 1.** n. raincoat. **2.** adj. water-proof.

**impèro,** n.m. empire.

**impersonale,** adj. impersonal.

**impersonare,** vb. impersonate.

**impersonatore,** n.m. impersonator.

**impertinènte,** adj. impertinent.

**impertinènza,** n.f. impertinence.

**impèrvio,** adj. impervious.

**impeto,** n.m. impetus.

**impetuosamente,** adv. impetuously; boisterously.

**impetuoso,** adj. impetuous; boisterous; dashing; heady.

**impiallacciare,** vb. veneer.

**impiantare,** vb. implant.

**impianto,** n.m. installation; plant.

**impiccagione,** n.f. hanging.

**impiccare,** vb. hang.

**impiccatore,** n.m. hangman.

**impìccio,** n.m. jam, fix, pickle, predicament, scrape.

**impiegare,** vb. employ; use.

**impiegata,** n.f. employee.

**impiegato,** n.m. employee, clerk.

**impiègo,** n.m. employment, job.

**implacàbile,** adj. implacable.

**implicare,** vb. implicate; imply; involve.

**implicazione,** n.f. implication.

**implìcito,** adj. implicit, implied.

**implorare,** vb. implore, beg, plead with.

**imponderàbile,** adj. imponderable.

**imporre,** vb. impose; levy.

**importante,** adj. important, momentous.

**importanza,** n.f. importance.

**importare,** vb. import; be important, matter.

**importazione,** n.f. import, importation.

**importunare,** vb. importune.

**importuno,** adj. importunate.

**imposizione,** n.f. imposition.

**impossìbile,** adj. impossible.

**impossibilità,** n.f. impossibility.

**imposta,** n.f. tax, duty, levy.

**impostare,** vb. mail, post.

**impostura,** n.f. imposture, humbug.

**impotènte,** adj. impotent, powerless, helpless.

**impotènza,** n.f. impotence.

**impoverire,** vb. impoverish.

**impregnare,** vb. impregnate.

**imprenditore,** n.m. contractor; entrepreneur. **i. di pompe fùnebri,** undertaker.

**impresa,** n.f. enterprise, undertaking; feat.

**impresàrio,** n.m. impresario, theatrical manager.

**impressionante,** adj. impressive.

**impressionare,** vb. impress.

**impressione,** n.f. impression.

**imprigionare,** vb. imprison.

**imprimere,** vb. impress.

**improbàbile,** adj. improbable, unlikely.

**impronta,** n.f. mark; print. **i. digitale,** fingerprint.

**impròprio,** adj. improper.

**improvvisare,** vb. improvise.

**improvviso, 1.** n. impromptu. **2.** adj. unforeseen; sudden; abrupt.

**impudènte,** adj. impudent, cocky.

**impudicìzia,** n.f. immodesty, shamelessness.

**impùdico,** adj. immodest, shameless; lewd.

**impugnare,** vb. impugn.

**impulsivo,** adj. impulsive.

**impulso,** n.m. impulse.

**impunità,** n.f. impunity.

**impurità,** n.f. impurity.

**impuro,** adj. impure.

**imputare,** vb. impute; accuse; impeach.

**imputato,** n.m. defendant.

**imputridire,** vb. rot; (refl.) go rotten; (egg) addle.

**in,** prep. in; into.

**inàbile,** adj. ineligible; unfitted.

**inalare,** vb. inhale.

**inalienàbile,** adj. inalienable.

**inamidare,** vb. starch.

**inano,** adj. inane.

**inaridire,** vb. parch.

**inaspettatamente,** adv. unexpectedly.

**inaspettato,** adj. unexpected.

**inattivo,** adj. inactive, dormant.

**inaugurale,** adj. inaugural.

**inaugurare,** vb. inaugurate.

**inaugurazione,** n.f. inauguration.

**inavveduto,** adj. inadvertent.

**incandescènte,** adj. incandescent, glowing.

**incandescènza,** n.f. incandescence, glow.

**incantamento,** n.m. incantation.

**incantare,** vb. enchant, charm.

**incantatore,** n.m. enchanter, charmer.

**incantatrice,** n.f. enchantress, charmer.

**incantèsimo,** n.m. spell.

**incantévole,** adj. enchanting.

**incanto,** n.m. enchantment, charm.

**incapace,** adj. unable.

**incapacità,** n.f. incapacity; disability.

**incarcerare,** vb. incarcerate.

**incaricare,** vb. charge, entrust, commission.

**incàrico,** n.m. charge; commission, task, assignment.

**incarnato,** adj. incarnate.

**incarnazione,** n.f. incarnation.

**incartamento,** n.m. dossier.

**incatenare,** vb. chain.

**incatramare,** vb. tar.

**incavo,** n.m. dent.

**incendiàrio,** n.m. and adj. incendiary.

**incèndio,** n.m. fire. **i. doloso** arson.

**incènso,** n.m. incense, frankincense.

**incentivo,** n.m. incentive.

**incerare,** vb. wax.

**incertezza,** n.f. uncertainty, suspense.

**incèrto,** adj. uncertain.

**incespicare,** vb. stumble, falter.

**incessante,** adj. incessant, ceaseless.

**incèsto,** n.m. incest.

**inchièsta,** n.f. inquiry; inquest.

**inchinarsi,** vb. bow.

**inchino,** n.m. bow.

**inchiodare,** vb. nail.

**inchiòstro,** n.m. ink.

**inciampare,** vb. stumble.

**incidentale,** adj. incidental.

**incidentalmente,** adv. incidentally.

**incidènte,** n.m. accident; incident.

**incidènza,** n.f. incidence.

**incìdere,** vb. incise, engrave; record.

**incìnta,** adj.f. pregnant.

**incipiènte,** adj. incipient.

**incipriare,** vb. powder.

**incisione,** n.f. incision; engraving; gravure; recording.

**incisivo,** adj. incisive. **dènte i.,** incisor.

**incisore,** n.m. engraver.

**incitare,** vb. incite.

**inclinare,** vb. incline; list; slant; tilt; tip.

**inclinazione,** n.f. inclination; tilt; list; penchant.

**inclùdere,** vb. include.

**inclusivo,** adj. inclusive.

**incògnito,** adj. incognito.

**incollare**, *vb.* glue, paste.
**incollatura**, *n.f.* sizing.
**incolpare**, *vb.* blame, accuse.
**incolpato**, *n.m.* accused, blamed.
**incolpatore**, *n.m.* blamer, accuser.
**incombènte**, *adj.* incumbent.
**incombustibile**, *adj.* fire-proof, incombustible.
**incominciare**, *vb.* begin.
**incomodare**, *vb.* inconvenience.
**incòmodo**, *adj.* inconvenient.
**incomparàbile**, *adj.* incomparable.
**incompetènte**, *adj.* unqualified.
**incondizionato**, *adj.* unqualified.
**inconscio**, *adj.* unconscious.
**inconsiderato**, *adj.* rash.
**incontrare**, *vb.* meet, encounter.
**incontro**, **1.** *n.m.* meeting, encounter; match. **2.** *adv.* towards; to meet.
**incoraggiamento**, *n.m.* encouragement, urging, abetment.
**incoraggiare**, *vb.* encourage, urge, abet.
**incoraggiatore**, *n.m.* encourager, urger, abettor.
**incorniciare**, *vb.* frame.
**incoronare**, *vb.* crown.
**incoronazione**, *n.f.* coronation.
**incorporare**, *vb.* incorporate; embody.
**incorpòreo**, *adj.* incorporeal; disembodied.
**incorreggìbile**, *adj.* incorrigible.
**incórrere**, *vb.* incur.
**incostante**, *adj.* inconstant, fickle.
**incostanza**, *n.f.* inconstancy, fickleness.
**incredìbile**, *adj.* incredible.
**incredulità**, *n.f.* incredulity.
**incrèdulo**, *adj.* incredulous.
**incremento**, *n.m.* increment.
**increspare**, *vb.* ruffle.
**increspatura**, *n.f.* ruffle; ripple.
**incriminare**, *vb.* incriminate.
**incriminazione**, *n.f.* incrimination.
**incrociare**, *vb.* cross; intersect; cruise.

**incrociato**, *adj.* crossed; criss-cross.
**incrociatore**, *n.m.* cruiser.
**incrocio**, *n.m.* crossing; cross; intersection.
**incrostare**, *vb.* incrust.
**incubatrice**, *n.f.* incubator.
**incubo**, *n.m.* nightmare.
**incudine**, *n.f.* anvil.
**inculcare**, *vb.* inculcate.
**incuneare**, *vb.* wedge.
**incuràbile**, *adj.* incurable.
**incurante**, *adj.* not caring, nonchalant.
**incursione**, *n.f.* inroad, raid.
**indebitato**, *adj.* indebted.
**indebolire**, *vb.* weaken; sap.
**indefinitamente**, *adv.* indefinitely.
**indefinito**, *adj.* indefinite.
**indegnità**, *n.f.* indignity; unworthiness.
**indegno**, *adj.* unworthy.
**indelèbile**, *adj.* indelible.
**indennità**, *n.f.* indemnity.
**indennizzare**, *vb.* indemnify.
**Ìndia**, *n.f.* India.
**indiana**, *n.f.* chintz.
**indiano**, *adj.* Indian.
**indicare**, *vb.* indicate, point to.
**indicativo**, *n.m. and adj.* indicative.
**indicatore**, *n.m.* indicator.
**indicazione**, *n.f.* indication.
**indice**, *n.m.* index; forefinger.
**indietreggiare**, *vb.* back (up); go backwards; recoil.
**indiètro**, *adv.* backwards; aft; behind; slow.
**indifferènte**, *adj.* indifferent, casual, nonchalant.
**indifferentemente**, *adv.* indifferently, casually.
**indifferenza**, *n.f.* indifference, casualness, disregard.
**indìgeno**, **1.** *n.m.* aborigine, native. **2.** *adj.* indigenous, aboriginal, native.
**indigènte**, *adj.* indigent.
**indigestione**, *n.f.* indigestion.
**indignato**, *adj.* indignant.
**indignazione**, *n.f.* indignation.
**indimenticàbile**, *adj.* unforgettable.
**indipendènza**, *n.f.* independence.
**indipendènte**, *adj.* independent.
**indirètto**, *adj.* indirect.

**indirizzare**, *vb.* address.

**indirizzo**, *n.m.* address; direction.

**indiscreto**, *adj.* indiscreet.

**indiscrezione**, *n.f.* indiscretion.

**indispensàbile**, *adj.* indispensable.

**indisposizione**, *n.f.* indisposition; distemper.

**indisposto**, *adj.* indisposed, unwell.

**indistinto**, *adj.* indistinct, blurred.

**individuale**, *adj.* individual.

**individualità**, *n.f.* individuality.

**individualmente**, *adv.* individually.

**individuo**, *n.m.* individual; fellow.

**indivisìbile**, *adj.* indivisible.

**indolènte**, *adj.* indolent.

**Indonèsia**, *n.f.* Indonesia.

**indorare**, *vb.* gild.

**indossare**, *vb.* put on, don.

**indovinare**, *vb.* guess.

**indovinèllo**, *n.m.* riddle, conundrum, puzzle.

**indugiare**, *vb.* delay, loiter, dally, dawdle, lag, linger.

**indùgio**, *n.m.* delay.

**indulgènte**, *adj.* indulgent.

**indulgènza**, *n.f.* indulgence.

**indùlgere**, *vb.* indulge.

**indurire**, *vb.* harden, steel.

**indurre**, *vb.* induce.

**indùstria**, *n.f.* industry.

**industriale**, **1.** *n.* industrialist.  **2.** *adj.* industrial, manufacturing.

**industrioso**, *adj.* industrious.

**induttivo**, *adj.* inductive.

**induzione**, *n.f.* induction.

**inebbriante**, *adj.* inebriating, heady.

**inebbriare**, *vb.* inebriate, intoxicate.

**ineguale**, *adj.* unequal.

**ineleggìbile**, *adj.* ineligible.

**inerènte**, *adj.* inherent.

**inèrte**, *adj.* inert.

**inèrzia**, *n.f.* inertia.

**inespèrto**, *adj.* inexperienced, callow.

**inesplicàbile**, *adj.* inexplicable.

**inespugnàbile**, *adj.* impregnable.

**inestimàbile**, *adj.* priceless.

**inètto**, *adj.* inept.

**inevitàbile**, *adj.* inevitable.

**infallìbile**, *adj.* infallible.

**infame**, *adj.* infamous.

**infàmia**, *n.f.* infamy.

**infante**, *n.m.* infant.

**infantile**, *adj.* infantile, childish, childlike, babyish.

**infantilità**, *n.f.* childishness.

**infànzia**, *n.f.* infancy, childhood.

**infarcire**, *vb.* stuff, cram.

**infastidire**, *vb.* annoy, bother, irk, be troublesome.

**infaticàbile**, *adj.* indefatigable.

**infatuare**, *vb.* infatuate.

**infàusto**, *adj.* ill-omened, ominous.

**infedele**, *n. and adj.* unfaithful, infidel.

**infedeltà**, *n.f.* infidelity.

**infelice**, *adj.* unhappy; unlucky.

**inferènza**, *n.f.* inference.

**inferiore**, *adj.* inferior; lower; under.

**inferiorità**, *n.f.* inferiority.

**inferire**, *vb.* infer.

**infermeria**, *n.f.* infirmary.

**infermièra**, *n.f.* nurse.

**infermità**, *n.f.* infirmity.

**infermo**, *adj.* infirm.

**infernale**, *adj.* infernal, hellish.

**infèrno**, *n.m.* hell.

**inferriata**, *n.f.* grating.

**infestare**, *vb.* infest.

**infettare**, *vb.* infect.

**infettivo**, *adj.* infectious.

**infètto**, *adj.* infected.

**infezione**, *n.f.* infection.

**infiammàbile**, *adj.* inflammable.

**infiammare**, *vb.* inflame.

**infiammatòrio**, *adj.* inflammatory.

**infiammazione**, *n.f.* inflammation.

**infilare**, *vb.* string, thread.

**infiltrare**, *vb.* infiltrate.

**infiltrazione**, *n.f.* infiltration; leakage.

**infinità**, *n.f.* infinity.

**infinitesimale**, *adj.* infinitesimal.

**infinito**, **1.** *n.m.* infinite; infinitive.  **2.** *adj.* infinite.

**infisso**, *n.m.* fixture.

**inflazione**, *n.f.* inflation.

**inflessione**, *n.f.* inflection.

**inflìggere**, *vb.* inflict.

**inflizione**, *n.f.* infliction.

**influènte**, *adj.* influential.

**influènza**, *n.f.* influence; influenza; grippe.

**influsso**, *n.m.* influence.

**infoltire**, *vb.* thicken.

**inforcatura**, *n.f.* crotch.

**informare**, *vb.* inform; acquaint, appraise; (*refl.*) inquire.

**informazióne**, *n.f.* piece of information; (*pl.*) information.

**informe**, *adj.* formless.

**infornata**, *n.f.* batch.

**infossato**, *adj.* sunken.

**inframmettènte**, *adj.* meddlesome, officious.

**inframméttere**, *vb.* interject; (*refl.*) meddle.

**infràngere**, *vb.* infringe.

**infruttuóso**, *adj.* fruitless, unsuccessful.

**infuòri**, *adv.* **all' i. di**, except for, outside of.

**infuriare**, *vb.* become infuriated, rage.

**ingabbiare**, *vb.* cage.

**ingannare**, *vb.* deceive, trick, fool, beguile, cheat, bluff, double-cross, hoax, hoodwink, mislead.

**ingannatóre**, **1.** *n.m.* deceiver, cheater. **2.** *adj.* deceitful.

**ingannévole**, *adj.* deceptive, treacherous.

**inganno**, *n.m.* deceit, deception, trickery, bluff, hocuspocus.

**ingarbugliare**, *vb.* tangle; garble.

**ingegnère**, *n.m.* engineer.

**ingegneria**, *n.f.* engineering.

**ingegnosaménte**, *adv.* cleverly, ingeniously.

**ingegnosità**, *n.f.* cleverness, ingeniousness.

**ingegnóso**, *adj.* clever, ingenious.

**ingènuo**, *adj.* naïve; artless.

**ingerènza**, *n.f.* interference.

**Inghilterra**, *n.f.* England.

**inghiottire**, *vb.* swallow; gulp.

**inginocchiarsi**, *vb.* kneel.

**ingiùngere**, *vb.* enjoin.

**ingiunzióne**, *n.f.* injunction.

**ingiùria**, *n.f.* insult, abuse.

**ingiuriare**, *vb.* insult, abuse.

**ingiuriosaménte**, *adv.* insultingly.

**ingiurióso**, *adj.* insulting, abusive.

**ingiustificato**, *adj.* unwarranted.

**ingiustizia**, *n.f.* injustice.

**ingiusto**, *adj.* unjust, unfair.

**inglése**, **1.** *n.m. or f.* Englishman; Englishwoman. **2.** *adj.* English.

**ingollare**, *vb.* gobble, gulp down.

**ingombrante**, *adj.* cumbersome.

**ingombrare**, *vb.* encumber, clog, clutter.

**ingozzare**, *vb.* guzzle.

**ingranàggio**, *n.m.* gear, gearing.

**ingranare**, *vb.* mesh.

**ingrandimento**, *n.m.* enlargement, aggrandizement.

**ingrandire**, *vb.* enlarge, aggrandize, magnify.

**ingranditóre**, *n.m.* enlarger.

**ingrassare**, *vb.* fatten.

**ingravidare**, *vb.* render pregnant, impregnate.

**ingrediènte**, *n.m.* ingredient.

**ingrèsso**, *n.m.* entrance, entry.

**ingròsso**, *n.m.* **all'i.**, wholesale.

**inguine**, *n.m.* groin.

**inibire**, *vb.* inhibit.

**inibizióne**, *n.f.* inhibition.

**iniettare**, *vb.* inject.

**iniezióne**, *n.f.* injection.

**inimicizia**, *n.f.* enmity; feud.

**inimitàbile**, *adj.* inimitable.

**iniquità**, *n.f.* iniquity.

**iniquo**, *adj.* unrighteous.

**iniziale**, *n.f. and adj.* initial.

**iniziare**, *vb.* initiate, begin, start.

**iniziativa**, *n.f.* initiative.

**iniziazióne**, *n.f.* initiation.

**inizio**, *n.m.* beginning, inception, start.

**innaffiare**, *vb.* water.

**innalzare**, *vb.* raise, hoist.

**innamorare**, *vb.* enamor.

**innamorarsi**, *vb.* fall in love.

**innamorata**, *n.f.* sweetheart.

**innamorato**, *n.m.* sweetheart.

**innàrio**, *n.m.* hymnal.

**innestare**, *vb.* graft.

**innèsto**, *n.m.* graft.

**inno**, *n.m.* hymn. **i. nazionale**, national anthem.

**innocènte**, *adj.* innocent; harmless; blameless.

**innocènza**, *n.f.* innocence.

**innòcuo**, *adj.* innocuous, harmless.

**innovazione**, *n.f.* innovation.

**innumerévole**, *adj.* innumerable, countless, myriad.

**inoculare**, *vb.* inoculate.

**inoculazione**, *n.f.* inoculation.

**inoltre**, *adv.* besides, furthermore.

**inondare**, *vb.* inundate, flood, swamp.

**inondazione**, *n.f.* inundation, flood.

**inorridire**, *vb.* be horrified.

**inossidàbile**, *adj.* rust-proof.

**inquietare**, *vb.* worry; (*refl.*) be concerned.

**inquièto**, *adj.* uneasy.

**inquilino**, *n.m.* occupant, tenant.

**inquisizione**, *n.f.* inquisition.

**insaccare**, *vb.* put in a bag.

**insalata**, *n.f.* salad.

**insanguinato**, *adj.* gory.

**insània**, *n.f.* insanity.

**insano**, *adj.* insane.

**insaporire**, *vb.* flavor.

**insaputa**, *n.f.* **all'i. di**, without the knowledge of.

**insediamento**, *n.m.* installation.

**insediare**, *vb.* install.

**insegna**, *n.f.* standard; signboard; coat of arms; ensign; (*pl.*) insignia.

**insegnante**, *n.m. or f.* teacher.

**insegnare**, *vb.* teach.

**inseguimento**, *n.m.* pursuit.

**inseguire**, *vb.* follow, pursue.

**insensìbile**, *adj.* insensible, insensitive, unfeeling.

**insensibilità**, *n.f.* insensitivity, callousness.

**inseparàbile**, *adj.* inseparable.

**inserire**, *vb.* insert, put in.

**inservìbile**, *adj.* unusable.

**inserzione**, *n.f.* insertion; advertisement.

**inserzionista**, *n.m.* advertiser.

**insetticida**, *adj.* **pólvere i.,** insecticide.

**insètto**, *n.m.* insect, bug.

**insidioso**, *adj.* insidious.

**insième**, **1.** *n.m.* ensemble. **2.** *adv.* together.

**insignificante**, *adj.* insignificant.

**insignificanza**, *n.f.* insignificance.

**insinuare**, *vb.* insinuate.

**insinuazione**, *n.f.* insinuation, innuendo.

**insìpido**, *adj.* insipid, tasteless.

**insistènte**, *adj.* insistent.

**insistènza**, *n.f.* insistence.

**insistere**, *vb.* insist.

**insoddisfazione**, *n.f.* dissatisfaction.

**insoffrìbile**, *adj.* insufferable.

**insolènte**, *adj.* insolent, insulting, abusive.

**insolentemente**, *adv.* insolently.

**insolènza**, *n.f.* insolence.

**insòlito**, *adj.* unusual.

**insònnia**, *n.f.* insomnia.

**instàbile**, *adj.* unsteady.

**installare**, *vb.* install.

**installazione**, *n.f.* installation.

**insù**, *adv.* **all'i.,** uphill; upwards.

**insufficiènte**, *adj.* insufficient.

**insulare**, *adj.* insular.

**insulina**, *n.f.* insulin.

**insulso**, *adj.* dull, insipid.

**insultare**, *vb.* insult, abuse.

**insulto**, *n.m.* insult, abuse.

**insuperàbile**, *adj.* insuperable.

**insurrezione**, *n.f.* insurrection.

**intaccare**, *vb.* notch, nick.

**intangìbile**, *adj.* intangible.

**intascare**, *vb.* pocket.

**intatto**, *adj.* intact.

**integrale**, *adj.* integral.

**integrare**, *vb.* integrate.

**integrità**, *n.f.* integrity.

**intellètto**, *n.m.* intellect; understanding.

**intellettuale**, *adj.* intellectual.

**intelligènte**, *adj.* intelligent, smart.

**intelligènza**, *n.f.* intelligence; wit.

**intellighènzia**, *n.f.* intelligentsia.

**intelligìbile**, *adj.* intelligible.

**intensificare**, *vb.* intensify.

**intensivo**, *adj.* intensive.

**intènso**, *adj.* intense.

**intènto**, *n.m. and adj.* intent.

**intenzionale**, *adj.* intentional.

**intenzionalmente**, *adv.* intentionally, designedly.

**intenzione**, *n.f.* intention.

**interamente,** *adv.* entirely; wholly.

**intercèdere,** *vb.* intercede.

**intercettare,** *vb.* intercept.

**interdetto. 1.** *n.m.* interdict. **2.** *adj.* speechless.

**interdire,** *vb.* interdict.

**interessante,** *adj.* interesting.

**interessare,** *vb.* interest, concern; affect; (*refl.*) concern oneself.

**interèsse,** *n.m.* interest, concern.

**interferènza,** *n.f.* interference.

**interiezione,** *n.f.* interjection.

**interiora,** *f.pl.* entrails.

**interiore,** *adj.* interior, inner, inside.

**interlùdio,** *n.m.* interlude.

**intermediàrio. 1.** *n.m.* intermediary, mediator, go-between. **2.** *adj.* intermediary.

**intermèdio,** *adj.* intermediate.

**intermissione,** *n.f.* intermission.

**intermittènte,** *adj.* intermittent.

**internare,** *vb.* intern.

**internazionale,** *adj.* international.

**internazionalismo,** *n.m.* internationalism.

**intèrno. 1.** *n.* inside. **2.** *adj.* internal; inner, inside; inland.

**intero,** *adj.* entire, whole.

**interporre,** *vb.* interpose.

**interpretare,** *vb.* interpret, construe.

**interpretazione,** *n.f.* interpretation.

**intèrprete,** *n.m.* interpreter.

**interrogare,** *vb.* interrogate, question.

**interrogativo,** *adj.* interrogative.

**interrogazione,** *n.f.* interrogation.

**interrómpere,** *vb.* interrupt; discontinue.

**interruttore,** *n.m.* switch.

**interruzione,** *n.f.* interruption, break.

**intersecare,** *vb.* intersect.

**intersezione,** *n.f.* intersection.

**intervallo,** *n.m.* interval; headway.

**intervenire,** *vb.* intervene.

**intervènto,** *n.m.* intervention.

**intervista,** *n.f.* interview.

**intervistare,** *vb.* interview.

**intestino. 1.** *n.m.* intestine, bowel, gut. **2.** *adj.* intestine.

**intimamente,** *adv.* intimately; inwardly.

**intimidazione,** *n.f.* intimidation.

**intimidire,** *vb.* intimidate, daunt.

**intimità,** *n.f.* intimacy; privacy.

**intimo,** *adj.* intimate; inward. **più i.,** innermost.

**intitolare,** *vb.* entitle.

**intollerante,** *adj.* intolerant.

**intonacare,** *vb.* plaster.

**intònaco,** *n.m.* plaster.

**intonare,** *vb.* intone.

**intonazione,** *n.f.* intonation.

**intontito,** *adj.* groggy.

**intorno,** *adv.* around; about; round. **i. a,** *prep.* around; about; round.

**intossicare,** *vb.* intoxicate.

**intossicazione,** *n.f.* intoxication.

**intràlcio,** *n.m.* hindrance.

**intrappolare,** *vb.* entrap.

**intraprèndere,** *vb.* undertake.

**intravedere,** *vb.* glimpse.

**intrecciare,** *vb.* braid.

**intréccio,** *n.m.* plot.

**intrepidamente,** *adv.* dauntlessly, fearlessly.

**intrepidezza,** *n.f.* intrepidity, fearlessness.

**intrèpido,** *adj.* intrepid, dauntless, fearless.

**intricato,** *adj.* intricate.

**intrigare,** *vb.* intrigue.

**intrigo,** *n.m.* intrigue.

**intrìnseco,** *adj.* intrinsic.

**introdurre,** *vb.* introduce.

**introduttivo,** *adj.* introductory.

**introduzione,** *n.f.* introduction.

**introspezione,** *n.f.* introspection.

**introvertito,** *adj.* introvert.

**intrùdere,** *vb.* intrude, obtrude.

**intruso,** *n.m.* intruder.

**intuire,** *vb.* sense.

**intuitivo,** *adj.* intuitive.

**intuizione,** *n.f.* intuition.

**inumano,** *adj.* inhuman.

**durare,** *vb.* endure, last.
**durata,** *n.f.* duration.
**durante,** *prep.* during.
**duramente,** *adv.* hard.

**durévole,** *adj.* lasting.
**durezza,** *n.f.* hardness.
**duro,** *adj.* hard.
**dùttile,** *adj.* ductile.

# E

**e,** *conj.* and.
**èbano,** *n.m.* ebony.
**ebràico,** *n.* and *adj.* Hebrew; Hebraic; Jewish.
**ebrèo,** *n.* and *adj.* Hebrew; Jew(ish).
**eccèdere,** *vb.* exceed.
**eccellènte,** *adj.* excellent.
**eccellènza,** *n.f.* excellence.
**Eccellènza,** *n.f.* Excellency.
**eccèllere,** *vb.* excel.
**eccentricità,** *n.f.* eccentricity.
**eccèntrico,** *adj.* eccentric.
**eccessivo,** *adj.* excessive.
**eccèsso,** *n.m.* excess.
**eccètto,** *prep.* except; but.
**eccettuare,** *vb.* except.
**eccezionale,** *adj.* exceptional.
**eccezione,** *n.f.* exception.
**eccitàbile,** *adj.* excitable, high-strung, hot-headed.
**eccitamento,** *n.m.* excitement.
**eccitare,** *vb.* excite.
**eccitazione,** *n.f.* excitement.
**ecclesiàstico, 1.** *n.* ecclesiastic, cleric, clergyman. **2.** *adj.* ecclesiastical.
**ècco,** *vb.* here is; there is; lo; behold.
**echeggiare,** *vb.* echo.
**eclissare,** *vb.* eclipse.
**eclissi,** *n.f.* eclipse.
**eco,** *n.m.* echo.
**economìa,** *n.f.* economy, thrift. **e. polìtica,** economics.
**economicamente,** *adv.* economically, cheaply.
**econòmico,** *adj.* economic, economical, cheap.
**economista,** *n.m.* economist.

**economizzare,** *vb.* economize, save.
**eczèma,** *n.m.* eczema.
**ed,** *conj.* and.
**édera,** *n.f.* ivy.
**edificare,** *vb.* edify, build.
**edificio,** *n.m.* edifice, building.
**editore,** *n.m.* publisher.
**editto,** *n.m.* edict.
**editoriale,** *adj.* editorial.
**edizione,** *n.f.* edition, publication.
**edonismo,** *n.m.* hedonism.
**educare,** *vb.* educate, train.
**educativo,** *adj.* educational.
**educazione,** *n.f.* education, breeding, manners.
**educatore,** *n.m.* educator.
**effeminato,** *adj.* effeminate.
**effervescènza,** *n.f.* effervescence.
**effettivamente,** *adv.* effectively; in effect.
**effettività,** *n.f.* effectiveness.
**effettivo,** *adj.* effective.
**effètto,** *n.m.* effect.
**effettuare,** *vb.* effect, bring about, contrive.
**efficace,** *adj.* efficacious, effectual.
**efficàcia,** *n.f.* efficacy.
**efficiènte,** *adj.* efficient.
**efficientemente,** *adv.* efficiently.
**efficiènza,** *n.f.* efficiency.
**effigie,** *n.f.* effigy.
**effìmero,** *adj.* ephemeral.
**egemonìa,** *n.f.* hegemony.
**ègida,** *n.f.* aegis, auspices, protection.
**Egitto,** *n.m.* Egypt.
**egiziano,** *adj.* Egyptian.
**egli,** *pron.* he.

For pronunciation, see the concise guide on pages 5 to 7.

**egoìsmo,** *n.m.* egoism, selfishness.

**egoìstico,** *adj.* selfish.

**egotìsmo,** *n.m.* egotism.

**egotìsta,** *n.m.* egotist.

**eiaculare,** *vb.* ejaculate.

**elaborare,** *vb.* elaborate.

**elaborato,** *adj.* elaborate.

**elasticità,** *n.f.* elasticity.

**elàstico,** *n.m. and adj.* elastic.

**elefante,** *n.m.* elephant.

**elefantesco,** *adj.* elephantine.

**elegante,** *adj.* elegant, smart.

**eleganza,** *n.f.* elegance.

**elèggere,** *vb.* elect.

**eleggìbile,** *adj.* eligible.

**eleggibilità,** *n.f.* eligibility.

**elegìa,** *n.f.* elegy.

**elegìaco,** *adj.* elegiac.

**elementare,** *adj.* elemental. elementary.

**elemento,** *n.m.* element.

**elemòsina,** *n.f.* charity, alms, dole.

**elencare,** *vb.* list, itemize.

**elènco,** *n.m.* list. **e. telefònico,** telephone directory.

**elettivo,** *adj.* elective.

**elettricista,** *n.m.* electrician.

**elettricità,** *n.f.* electricity.

**elèttrico,** *adj.* electric, electrical.

**elettrocuzione,** *n.f.* electrocution.

**elèttrodo,** *n.m.* electrode.

**elettrodomèstici,** *n.m. pl.* electric household appliances.

**elettròlisi,** *n.f.* electrolysis.

**elettromotrice,** *n.f.* electric railcar.

**elettrone,** *n.m.* electron.

**elettrònica,** *n.f.* electronics.

**elettrònico,** *adj.* electronic.

**elettrotreno,** *n.m.* express train of electric railcars.

**elevare,** *vb.* elevate.

**elevazione,** *n.f.* elevation.

**elezione,** *n.f.* election.

**èlica,** *n.f.* propeller.

**elicòttero,** *n.m.* helicopter.

**eliminare,** *vb.* eliminate.

**eliminazione,** *n.f.* elimination.

**èlio,** *n.m.* helium.

**eliocèntrico,** *adj.* heliocentric.

**eliògrafo,** *n.m.* heliograph.

**eliotipìa,** *n.f.* blueprint.

**eliotròpio,** *n.m.* heliotrope.

**elisìr,** *n.m.* elixir.

**ella,** *pron.f.* she; (very formal) you.

**ellènico,** *adj.* Hellenic.

**ellenismo,** *n.m.* Hellenism.

**èlmo,** *n.m.* helmet.

**elocuzione,** *n.f.* elocution.

**elogiare,** *vb.* eulogize.

**elògio,** *n.m.* eulogy.

**eloquènte,** *adj.* eloquent.

**eloquentemente,** *adv.* eloquently.

**eloquènza,** *n.f.* eloquence.

**èlsa,** *n.f.* hilt.

**elucidare,** *vb.* elucidate.

**elùdere,** *vb.* elude, dodge, evade.

**elusivo,** *adj.* elusive.

**emaciato,** *adj.* emaciated.

**emanare,** *v.b.* emanate.

**emancipare,** *vb.* emancipate.

**emancipatore,** *n.m.* emancipator.

**emancipazione,** *n.f.* emancipation.

**ematite,** *n.f.* hematite.

**embargo,** *n.m.* embargo.

**emblèma,** *n.m.* emblem, badge.

**emblemàtico,** *adj.* emblematic.

**embriologìa,** *n.f.* embryology.

**embrionale,** *adj.* embryonic.

**embrione,** *n.m.* embryo.

**emendamento,** *n.m.* amendment.

**emendare,** *vb.* amend, emend.

**emergènte,** *adj.* emergent.

**emergènza,** *n.f.* emergency.

**emèrgere,** *vb.* emerge.

**emètico,** *adj.* emetic.

**emèttere,** *vb.* emit; send forth; issue; utter.

**emicrània,** *n.f.* migraine.

**emigrante,** *n.m. and adj.* emigrant.

**emigrare,** *vb.* emigrate.

**emigrazione,** *n.f.* emigration.

**eminènte,** *adj.* eminent.

**eminènza,** *n.f.* eminence.

**emisfèrio,** *n.m.* hemisphere.

**emissàrio,** *n.m.* emissary.

**emissione,** *n.f.* issue.

**emofilìa,** *n.f.* hemophilia.

**emoglobina,** *n.f.* hemoglobin.

**emolliènte,** *n.m. and adj.* emollient.

---

**inumidire**, vb. dampen, humidify, moisten, wet.
**inùtile**, adj. useless, needless.
**invàdere**, vb. invade, overrun.
**invàlido**, 1. n. invalid. 2. adj. disabled; invalid.
**invano**, adv. in vain.
**invariàbile**, adj. invariable.
**invasione**, n f. invasion.
**invasore**, n.m. invader.
**invecchiare**, vb. grow old, age.
**invece**, adv. instead.
**inventare**, vb. invent.
**inventàrio**, n.m. inventory.
**inventivo**, adj. inventive.
**inventore**, n.m. inventor.
**invenzione**, n.f. invention.
**invernale**, adj. of winter, wintry.
**invèrno**, n.m. winter.
**invèrso**, adj. inverse.
**invertebrato**, n.m. and adj. invertebrate.
**investigare**, vb. investigate.
**investigazione**, n.f. investigation; inquiry.
**investimento**, n.m. investment.
**investire**, vb. invest; run into.
**inveterato**, adj. inveterate.
**invettiva**, n.f. invective.
**inviare**, vb. send.
**inviato**, n.m. envoy.
**invìdia**, n.f. envy.
**invidiàbile**, adj. enviable.
**invidiare**, vb. envy, begrudge.
**invidioso**, adj. envious.
**invigorire**, vb. invigorate.
**inviluppare**, vb. enmesh.
**invincìbile**, adj. invincible.
**invisibile**, adj. invisible.
**invitare**, vb. invite, ask.
**invito**, n.m. invitation; bid.
**invocare**, vb. invoke.
**invocazione**, n.f. invocation.
**involontàrio**, adj. involuntary.
**involucro**, n.m. wrapping.
**invulneràbile**, adj. invulnerable.
**inzuppare**, vb. drench; soak, dunk.
**io**, 1. pron. I. 2. n. ego.
**iòdio**, n.m. iodine.
**iperacidità**, n.f. hyperacidity.
**ipèrbole**, n.f. hyperbole.
**ipercrìtico**, adj. hypercritical.
**ipersensitivo**, adj. hypersensitive.
**ipertensione**, n.f. hypertension.
**ipnòsi**, n.f. hypnosis.

**ipnòtico**, adj. hypnotic.
**ipnotismo**, n.m. hypnotism.
**ipnotizzare**, vb. hypnotize.
**ipocondrìa**, n.f. hypochondria.
**ipocondrìaco**, n.m. and adj. hypochondriac.
**ipocrisìa**, n.f. hypocrisy, cant.
**ipòcrita**, n.m. hypocrite.
**ipòcrito**, adj. hypocritical.
**ipodèrmico**, adj. hypodermic.
**ipotèca**, n.f. mortgage.
**ipotecare**, vb. mortgage.
**ipotenusa**, n.f. hypotenuse.
**ipòtesi**, n.f. hypothesis.
**ipotètico**, adj. hypothetical.
**ippòdromo**, n.m. hippodrome; race-track.
**ippopòtamo**, n.m. hippopotamus.
**ira**, n.f. anger, ire, wrath.
**Iràk**, n.m. Iraq.
**irato**, adj. irate, wrathful.
**iride**, n.f. iris.
**irìdio**, n.m. iridium.
**iris**, n.f. iris.
**Irlanda**, n.f. Ireland.
**irlandese**, adj. Irish.
**ironìa**, n.f. irony.
**irònico**, adj. ironical.
**irradiare**, vb. beam, shine, radiate.
**irradiazione**, n.f. radiation.
**irrazionale**, adj. irrational.
**irrefutàbile**, adj. irrefutable.
**irregolare**, adj. irregular; fitful.
**irregolarità**, n. f. irregularity.
**irreprensìbile**, adj. irreprehensible, faultless.
**irreprensibilmente**, adv. irreprehensibly, faultlessly.
**irrequièto**, adj. restless.
**irresistìbile**, adj. irresistible.
**irresponsàbile**, adj. irresponsible.
**irrevocàbile**, adj. irrevocable.
**irriconoscìbile**, adj. unrecognizable.
**irrigare**, vb. irrigate.
**irrigazione**, n.f. irrigation.
**irrigidire**, vb. stiffen.
**irrispettoso**, adj. disrespectful.
**irritàbile**, adj. irritable, on edge, edgy, fretful.
**irritabilità**, n.f. irritability, fretfulness.
**irritabilmente**, adv. irritably, fretfully.
**irritante**, adj. irritant.

For pronunciation, see the concise guide on pages 5 to 7.

**irritare,** *vb. tr.* irritate, fret, gall, vex.

**irritato,** *adj.* irritated, cross.

**irritazione,** *n.f.* irritation.

**irriverènte,** *adj.* irreverent.

**irsuto,** *adj.* hirsute.

**iscrivere,** *vb.* inscribe; enroll, register.

**iscrizione,** *n.f.* inscription; enrollment, registration.

**isola,** *n.f.* island.

**isolamento,** *n.m.* isolation; insulation.

**isolare,** *vb.* isolate; insulate.

**isolatore,** *n.m.* insulator.

**isolazione,** *n.f.* isolation.

**isolazionista,** *n.m.* isolationist.

**isolotto salvagènte,** *n.m.* safety island.

**isòscele,** *adj.* isosceles.

**ispettore,** *n.m.* inspector.

**ispezionare,** *vb.* inspect.

**ispezione,** *n.f.* inspection.

**ìspido,** *adj.* shaggy.

**ispirare,** *vb.* inspire.

**ispirazione,** *f.* inspiration.

**Israèle,** *n.m.* Israel.

**israelita,** *n.m.* Israelite.

**israelìtico,** *adj.* Israelite.

**istantànea,** *n.f.* snapshot.

**istantàneo,** *adj.* instantaneous.

**istante,** *n.m.* instant.

**istanza,** *n.f.* instance.

**istèrico,** *adj.* hysterical.

**isterismo,** *n.m.* hysteria, hysterics.

**istigare,** *vb.* instigate.

**istillare,** *vb.* instill.

**istintivo,** *adj.* instinctive.

**istinto,** *n.m.* instinct.

**istituto,** *n.m.* institute.

**istituzione,** *n.f.* institution.

**istmo,** *n.m.* isthmus.

**istriònica,** *n.f.* histrionics.

**istriònico,** *adj.* histrionic.

**istruire,** *vb.* instruct.

**istruttivo,** *adj.* instruction.

**istruttore,** *n.m.* instructor.

**istruttrice,** *n.f.* instructress.

**istruzione,** *n.f.* instruction.

**itàlico,** *adj.* Italic.

**italiano,** *n.m. and adj.* Italian.

**Itàlia,** *n.f.* Italy.

**itineràrio,** *n.m.* itinerary.

**itterìzia,** *n.f.* jaundice.

**ittiologìa,** *n.f.* ichthyology.

**iuniore,** *adj.* junior.

**iuta,** *n.f.* jute.

# J, K

**jarda,** *n.f.* yard.

**Jugoslàvia,** *n.f.* Yugoslavia.

**jugoslavo,** *adj.* Yugoslav.

**karakiri,** *n.m.* harakiri.

**kg.** (abbr.) kilogram.

**km.** (abbr.) kilometer.

**kohl,** *n.m.* mascara.

**kw.** (abbr.) kilowatt.

# L

**l',** **1.** *def. art.* the. **2.** *pron.* **3.** *sg.* him; her.

**la,** **1.** *pron.* her; it; you. **2.** *def. art. f.* the.

**là,** *adv.* there.

**labbro,** *n.m.* lip. **l. leporino** hairlip.

**labirinto,** *n.m.* labyrinth, maze.

**laboratòrio,** *n.m.* laboratory.

**laborioso,** *adj.* laborious.
**lacca,** *n.f.* lacquer.
**laccare,** *vb.* lacquer.
**lacchè,** *n.m.* lackey, flunkey.
**làccio,** *n.m.* string; trap; noose; lariat, lasso; loop.
**lacerare,** *vb.* lacerate.
**lacerazione,** *n.f.* laceration.
**lacònico,** *adj.* laconic.
**lacuale,** *adj.* lake.
**ladro,** *n.m.* thief, burglar.
**ladrone,** *n.m.* robber.
**lagnanza,** *n.f.* complaint, grievance.
**lagnarsi,** *vb.* complain.
**lago,** *n.m.* lake.
**làgrima,** *n.f.* tear.
**laguna,** *n.f.* lagoon.
**laicato,** *n.m.* laity.
**làico,** **1.** *n.* layman. **2.** *adj.* lay.
**lama,** *n.f.* blade.
**lambire,** *vb.* lap.
**lamentare,** *vb.* lament, bewail.
**lamentazione,** *n.f.* lamentation.
**lamentévole,** *adj.* lamentable.
**lamento,** *n.m.* lament.
**laminare,** *vb.* laminate.
**làmpada,** *n.f.* lamp.
**lampadàrio,** *n.m.* chandelier.
**lampadina,** *n.f.* light bulb. **l. tascàbile,** flashlight.
**lampeggiare,** *vb.* lighten.
**lampeggiatore,** *n.m.* blinker.
**lampo,** *n.m.* (flash of) lightning.
**lampone,** *n.m.* raspberry.
**lana,** *n.f.* wool; **l. di acciaio** *n.f.* steel wool.
**lancetta,** *n.f.* lancet.
**lància,** *n.f.* lance, spear; launch.
**lanciafiamme,** *n.m.* flamethrower.
**lanciare,** *vb.* hurl, cast, chuck, fling, launch, pitch, sling, throw.
**lanciatore,** *n.m.* pitcher.
**lànguido,** *adj.* languid; lackadaisical.
**languire,** *vb.* languish, pine.
**languore,** *n.m.* languor.
**lanolina,** *n.f.* lanolin.
**lantèrna,** *n.f.* lantern.
**lanugine,** *n.f.* down, fuzz.
**lanuginoso,** *adj.* fluffy, downy; fuzzy.
**lapidare,** *vb.* stone.
**làpis,** *n.m.* pencil.

**largamente,** *adv.* broadly, widely.
**larghezza,** *n.f.* breadth; width.
**largo,** *adj.* broad, wide; (music) largo.
**laringe,** *n.f.* larynx.
**laringite,** *n.f.* laryngitis.
**larva,** *n.f.* larva; grub; ghost.
**lasciare,** *vb.* let; leave; quit; **l. stare,** let alone.
**làscito,** *n.m.* legacy.
**lascivo,** *adj.* lascivious, lecherous.
**lassativo,** *n.m. and adj.* laxative.
**lassitùdine,** *n.f.* lassitude.
**lastra,** *n.f.* plate; sheet; slab.
**latènte,** *adj.* latent.
**laterale,** *adj.* lateral.
**latino,** *n.m. and adj.* Latin.
**latitanza,** *n.f.* hiding (used of criminals.)
**latitùdine,** *n.f.* latitude.
**lato,** *n.m.* side.
**latrare,** *vb.* howl, bay.
**latrato,** *n.m.* howl, bay.
**latrina,** *n.f.* latrine, lavatory, toilet, privy.
**latta,** *n.f.* tin.
**lattaia,** *n.f.* milkmaid, dairymaid.
**lattaio,** *n.m.* milkman, dairyman.
**latte,** *n.m.* milk.
**làtteo,** *adj.* milky.
**latteria,** *n.f.* dairy; milk-bar.
**làttico,** *adj.* lactic.
**lattòsio,** *n.m.* lactose.
**lattuga,** *n.f.* lettuce.
**làudano,** *n.m.* laudanum.
**laudativo,** *adj.* laudatory.
**làurea,** *n.f.* degree.
**laurearsi,** *vb.* graduate.
**laureato,** *adj.* laureate.
**làuro,** *n.m.* laurel; bay.
**lavabiancheria,** *n.m.* washing machine.
**lavabo,** *n.m.* wash-basin.
**lavagna,** *n.f.* blackboard; slate.
**lavanda,** *n.f.* lavender.
**lavandaia,** *n.f.* laundress.
**lavandaio,** *n.m.* laundryman.
**lavanderia,** *n.f.* laundry.
**lavandino,** *n.m.* sink.
**lavare,** *vb.* wash, launder.
**lavorare,** *vb.* work.
**lavoratore,** *n.m.* worker.
**lavoro,** *n.m.* work.

**lavatòio**, *n.m.* washroom.
**laziale**, *adj.* of Latium.
**Làzio**, *n.m.* Latium.
**le**, **1.** *def. art. f.pl.* the. **2.** *pron.* **3.** *sg.* dative to her; **3.** *pl.f.* them.
**leale**, *adj.* loyal.
**lealista**, *n.m.* loyalist.
**lealtà**, *n.f.* loyalty.
**lebbra**, *n.f.* leprosy.
**lebbroso**, **1.** *n.* leper. **2.** *adj.* leprous.
**leccare**, *vb.* lick.
**lega**, *n.f.* league; alloy.
**legale**, *adj.* legal, lawful.
**legalizzare**, *vb.* legalize.
**legame**, *n.m.* tie, bond, link.
**legamento**, *n.m.* ligament.
**legare**, *vb.* bequeath, leave (in will); bind, tie.
**legato**, *n.m.* bequest, legacy.
**legatore**, *n.m.* bookbinder.
**legatorìa**, *n.f.* bindery, book-bindery.
**legatura**, *n.f.* ligature; (music) slur.
**legazione**, *n.f.* legation.
**legge**, *n.f.* law.
**leggènda**, *n.f.* legend.
**leggendàrio**, *adj.* legendary.
**lèggere**, *vb.* read.
**leggerezza**, *n.f.* lightness; levity.
**leggiadro**, *adj.* lovely.
**leggìbile**, *adj.* legible.
**leggieramente**, *adv.* lightly; flippantly.
**leggièro**, *adj.* light; flippant.
**legione**, *n.f.* legion.
**legislatore**, *n.m.* legislator.
**legislazione**, *n.f.* legislation.
**legìttimo**, *adj.* legitimate, lawful.
**legna**, *n.f.* firewood.
**legname**, *n.m.* lumber, timber.
**legume**, *n.m.* vegetable, legume.
**lèi**, *pron.* she; her; you.
**lembo**, *n.m.* hem; flap.
**lentamente**, *adv.* slowly.
**lènte**, *n.f.* lens; eyeglass.
**lentezza**, *n.f.* slowness.
**lentìcchia**, *n.f.* lentil.
**lentìggine**, *n.f.* freckle.
**lentigginoso**, *adj.* freckled.
**lento**, *adj.* slow, slack, sluggish.
**lenzuòla**, *n.f.pl.* sheets, bed-clothes.
**lenzuòlo**, *n.m.* sheet.
**leone**, *n.m.* lion.

**leopardo**, *n.m.* leopard.
**lèpre**, *n.f.* hare.
**lesione**, *n.f.* lesion.
**lèssico**, *n.m.* lexicon.
**letale**, *adj.* lethal.
**letame**, *n.m.* dung, manure, muck.
**letargìa**, *n.f.* lethargy.
**letàrgico**, *n.m.* lethargic.
**lèttera**, *n.f.* letter.
**letterale**, *adj.* literal.
**letteràrio**, *adj.* literary.
**letteratezza**, *n.f.* literacy.
**letterato**, *adj.* literate.
**letteratura**, *n.f.* literature.
**letterecci**, *n.m.pl.* bedding.
**lettièra**, *n.f.* bedstead; litter; (animal's) bed.
**lettino**, *n.m.* cot.
**lètto**, *n.m.* bed; couch.
**lettore**, *n.m.* reader.
**lettura**, *n.f.* reading.
**leucèmia**, *n.f.* leukemia.
**lèva**, *n.f.* lever; levy.
**levare**, *vb.* raise; (*refl.*) get up, arise.
**levatrice**, *n.f.* midwife.
**levigare**, *vb.* smooth.
**levigato**, *adj.* smooth.
**levrière**, *n.m.* greyhound.
**lezione**, *n.f.* lesson.
**li**, *pron.* **3.** *pl.m.* them.
**lì**, *adv.* there.
**libagione**, *n.f.* libation.
**libbra**, *n.f.* pound.
**liberale**, *adj.* liberal, generous, bounteous.
**liberalismo**, *n.m.* liberalism.
**liberalità**, *n.f.* liberality, generosity, bounty.
**liberare**, *vb.* liberate, deliver, free, relieve, release, rescue.
**liberazione**, *n.f.* liberation, deliverance, relief, release, rescue.
**lìbero**, *adj.* free.
**libertà**, *n.f.* liberty, freedom.
**libertino**, *n.m. and adj.* libertine.
**libidinoso**, *adj.* libidinous.
**libraio**, *n.m.* bookseller.
**librerìa**, *n.f.* bookstore.
**libretto**, *n.m.* booklet; (opera) libretto.
**libro**, *n.m.* book.
**licènza**, *n.f.* license; furlough; leave.
**licenziamento**, *n.m.* discharge.
**licenziare**, *vb.* discharge, fire, sack.

For pronunciation, see the concise guide on pages 5 to 7.

licenzioso, *adj.* licentious.
liceo, *n.m.* high school.
lido, *n.m.* beach, shore, sea-shore.
lietamente, *adv.* gladly.
lieto, *adj.* glad, happy.
lievito, *n.m.* leaven.
lignàggio, *n.m.* lineage, ancestry.
lignite, *n.f.* lignite.
ligure, *adj.* Ligurian.
ligustro, *n.m.* privet.
lillà, *n.m.* lilac.
lima, *n.f.* file.
limare, *vb.* file.
limatura, *n.f.* filings.
limbo, *n.m.* limbo.
limitare, *vb.* limit.
limitazione, *n.f.* limitation.
limite, *n.m.* limit, bound.
limonata, *n.f.* lemonade.
limone, *n.m.* lemon.
limpido, *adj.* limpid.
lince, *n.f.* lynx. **l. persiana**, caracul.
linciare, *vb.* lynch.
lindezza, *n.f.* neatness.
lindo, *adj.* neat.
linea, *n.f.* line; figure.
lineare, *adj.* linear.
linfa, *n.f.* lymph; sap.
lingeria, *n.f.* lingerie.
lingua, *n.f.* tongue, language.
linguàggio, *n.m.* language.
linguista, *n.m.* linguist.
linguìstica, *n.f.* linguistics.
linguìstico, *adj.* linguistic.
linimento, *n.m.* liniment.
lino, *n.m.* linen.
liquefare, *vb.* liquefy.
liquidare, *vb.* liquidate.
liquidazione, *n.f.* liquidation.
liquido, *n.m. and adj.* liquid.
liquirizia, *n.f.* licorice.
liquore, *n.m.* liquor; liqueur.
lira, *n.f.* lira; lyre.
liricismo, *n.m.* lyricism.
lirico, *adj.* lyric; operatic.
lisciare, *vb.* smooth.
liscio, *adj.* smooth, sleek.
lista, *n.f.* list; menu, bill of fare; stripe.
listello, *n.m.* lath.
lite, *n.f.* fight, quarrel, struggle, affray, brawl, row.
litigante, *n.m.* litigant.
litigare, *vb.* quarrel, bicker, row.
litigioso, *adj.* quarrelsome, argumentative, rowdy.
litografare, *vb.* lithograph.

litografìa, *n.f.* lithography; lithograph.
litania, *n.f.* litany.
litro, *n.m.* liter.
liturgìa, *n.f.* liturgy.
litùrgico, *adj.* liturgical.
liuto, *n.m.* lute.
livellare, *vb.* level.
livellatrice, *n.f.* bulldozer.
livello, *n.m.* level.
livido, *adj.* livid.
Livorno, *n.m.* Leghorn.
livrèa, *n.f.* livery.
lo, **1.** *pron.* him; it; you. **2.** *def. art. m.* the.
lobo, *n.m.* lobe.
locale, *adj.* local.
località, *n.f.* locality, locale.
localizzare, *vb.* localize.
locanda, *n.f.* inn.
locomotiva, *n.f.* locomotive, engine.
locomotore, *n.m.* locomotive.
locomozione, *n.f.* locomotion.
locusta, *n.f.* locust.
locuzione, *n.f.* expression.
lodare, *vb.* praise, commend, laud.
lode, *n.f.* praise, commendation.
lodévole, *adj.* praiseworthy, commendable, laudable.
lodevolmente, *adv.* praise-worthily, commendably.
loggia, *n.f.* loge.
loggione, *n.m.* top gallery.
lògica, *n.f.* logic.
lògico, *adj.* logical.
logorare, *vb.* wear out.
lògoro, *adj.* worn-out, shabby.
lombàggine, *n.f.* lumbago.
Lombardìa, *n.f.* Lombardy.
lombardo, *adj.* Lombard.
lombata, *n.f.* loin.
lombo, *n.m.* loin; sirloin.
lombrico, *n.m.* earthworm.
londinese, *adj.* of London.
Londra, *n.f.* London.
longevità, *n.f.* longevity.
longèvo, *adj.* long-lived.
longitudinale, *adj.* longitudinal.
longitudine, *n.f.* longitude.
lontano, **1.** *adj.* distant, far. **2.** *adv.* far away, far off, afar.
lòppa, *n.f.* chaff.
loquace, *adj.* loquacious, talkative.
lordo, *adj.* soiled; (weight) gross.
loro, *pron.* they; their; theirs;

them; to them; you; your; yours; to you.

**losanga,** *n.f.* lozenge.

**lòto,** *n.m.* lotus; mud, mire.

**lotta,** *n.f.* struggle, fight.

**lottare,** *vb.* struggle, wrestle.

**lotteria,** *n.f.* lottery, raffle.

**lotto,** *n.m.* lot.

**lozione,** *n.f.* lotion.

**lubrificante,** *n.m. and adj.* lubricant.

**lubrificare,** *vb.* lubricate, grease, oil.

**lucchetto,** *n.m.* padlock.

**luccicare,** *vb.* twinkle.

**lùcciola,** *n.f.* firefly; glowworm.

**luce,** *n.f.* light.

**lucernàrio,** *n.m.* skylight.

**lucèrtola,** *n.f.* lizard.

**lucidare,** *vb.* polish, shine.

**lucidatura,** *n.f.* polish.

**lucidezza,** *n.f.* shininess, gloss.

**luci di città,** *n.f. pl.* parking lights.

**lùcido, 1.** *n.* polish. **2.** *adj.* shiny, glossy.

**lucrativo,** *adj.* lucrative.

**lucrosamente,** *adv.* gainfully.

**lucroso,** *adj.* gainful.

**lùglio,** *n.m.* July.

**lùi,** *pron.* he; him.

**lumaca,** *n.f.* snail.

**luminoso,** *adj.* luminous, bright, light, shining.

**lunare,** *adj.* lunar.

**lunàtico,** *n.m. and adj.* lunatic.

**lunedì,** *n.m.* Monday.

**lunga,** *n.* **di gran lunga.** by far.

**lungamente,** *adv.* long.

**lunghezza,** *n.f.* length.

**lungo, 1.** *adj.* long. **2.** *prep.* along.

**luogo,** *n.m.* place. **l. comune,** cliché. **aver l.,** take place.

**lupa,** *n.f.* she-wolf.

**lupo,** *n.m.* wolf.

**lùppolo,** *n.m.* hop.

**lusingare,** *vb.* flatter, cajole.

**lusingatore,** *n.m.* flatterer.

**lusinghe,** *n.f. pl.* flattery.

**lusinghièro,** *adj.* flattering.

**lusso,** *n.m.* luxury. **di l.,** de luxe.

**lussuòso,** *adj.* luxurious.

**lussureggiante,** *adj.* luxuriant, lush.

**lustrascarpe,** *n.m.* bootblack.

**lustro,** *n.m.* luster.

**luterano,** *adj.* Lutheran.

**lutto,** *n.m.* mourning.

# M

**ma,** *conj.* but.

**màcabro,** *adj.* macabre.

**maccheroni,** *n.m. pl.* macaroni.

**màcchia,** *n.f.* spot, blemish, stain, blot; underbrush, brushwood.

**macchiare,** *vb.* spot, blot.

**macchietta,** *n.f.* fleck.

**macchiettato,** *adj.* spotted, dappled.

**màcchina,** *n.f.* machine; engine. **m. da scrìvere,** typewriter.

**macchinista,** *n.m.* engineer; machinist.

**macellaio,** *n.m.* butcher.

**macellare,** *vb.* butcher, slaughter.

**macèllo,** *n.m.* butchery, slaughter.

**màcina,** *n.f.* grindstone.

**macinare,** *vb.* grind, mill.

**madornale,** *adv.* gross.

**madre,** *n.f.* mother; (cheque) stub.

**madrigale,** *n.m.* madrigal.

**madrina,** \*n.f.* godmother.

**maestà,** *n.f.* majesty.

**maestoso,** *adj.* majestic.

**maestra,** *n.f.* teacher.

**maestro,** *n.m.* master, teacher.

**magari,** *adv.* perhaps even.

**magazzinàggio,** *n.m.* storage.

**magazzino,** *n.m.* storehouse; (arms) depot, armory.

For pronunciation, see the concise guide on pages 5 to 7.

**maggese**, *n.m.* fallow field. **a m.**, fallow.

**màggio**, *n.m.* May.

**maggiordòmo**, *n.m.* butler.

**maggioranza**, *n.f.* majority.

**maggiore**, **1.** *n.* major; elder; senior. **2.** *adj.* greater; elder; greatest; eldest.

**maggiormente**, *adv.* mostly.

**magìa**, *n.f.* magic.

**màgico**, *adj.* magic.

**magistrato**, *n.m.* magistrate.

**magistratura**, *n.f.* judiciary.

**màglia**, *n.f.* mesh; jersey.

**magnànimo**, *adj.* magnanimous, high-minded.

**magnate**, *n.m.* magnate.

**magnèsio**, *n.m.* magnesium.

**magnète**, *n.m.* magnet.

**magnètico**, *adj.* magnetic.

**magnetòfono**, *n.m.* tape recorder.

**magnificènza**, *n.f.* magnificence.

**magnìfico**, *adj.* magnificent.

**magniloquènte**, *adj.* grandiloquent.

**mago**, *n.m.* magician.

**magro**, *adj.* lean, gaunt, meager, spare, thin.

**mai**, *adv.* ever; never.

**maiale**, *n.m.* hog, pig; pork.

**maionese**, *n.m.* mayonnaise.

**malamente**, *adv.* badly.

**malària**, *n.f.* malaria.

**malato**, *adj.* sick, ill, ailing.

**malattìa**, *n.f.* sickness, malady, illness, ailment, disease.

**malaugùrio**, *n.m.* ill omen, jinx.

**malavìta**, *n.f.* underworld.

**maldicènza**, *n.f.* scandal.

**male**, **1.** *n.m.* evil; pain, ache, hurt. **m. di mare**, seasickness. **2.** *adv.* badly.

**maledétto**, *adj.* accursed.

**maledìre**, *vb.* curse.

**maledizióne**, *n.f.* curse.

**malevolènza**, *n.f.* malice.

**malèvolo**, *adj.* malevolent.

**malfattóre**, *n.m.* ruffian.

**malgrado**, *prep.* despite.

**maligno**, *adj.* malignant.

**malincònia**, *n.f.* melancholy.

**malincònico**, *adj.* melancholy.

**malìzia**, *n.f.* mischief.

**malizióso**, *adj.* mischievous.

**malleàbile**, *adj.* malleable.

**mallevadóre**, *n.m.* guarantor; sponsor.

**malóre**, *n.m.* illness.

**malto**, *n.m.* malt.

**maltrattàre**, *vb.* maltreat, mistreat.

**malvàgio**, *adj.* wicked, fell.

**malvagità**, *n.f.* wickedness.

**malvaròsa**, *n.f.* hollyhock.

**mamma**, *n.f.* mother.

**mammèlla**, *n.f.* breast; udder.

**mammìfero**, *n.m.* mammal.

**manàta**, *n.f.* handful.

**mancanza**, *n.f.* lack; failure; shortage. **in m. di**, failing; lacking.

**mancàre**, *vb.* be missing, be lacking; fail.

**mància**, *n.f.* tip, gratuity.

**mancorrènte**, *n.m.* hand-rail.

**mandàre**, *vb.* send.

**mandato**, *n.m.* mandate; warrant.

**mandolìno**, *n.m.* mandolin.

**màndorla**, *n.f.* almond.

**màndorlo**, *n.m.* almond-tree.

**mandra**, *n.f.* herd, drove.

**maneggiàre**, *vb.* handle.

**manétte**, *n.f.pl.* handcuffs.

**manganése**, *n.m.* manganese.

**mangiàbile**, *adj.* edible, eatable.

**mangiàre**, *vb.* eat.

**mangiatòia**, *n.f.* manger.

**manìa**, *n.f.* mania, craze, fad.

**manìaco**, *n.m. and adj.* maniac.

**mànica**, *n.f.* sleeve.

**mànico**, *n.m.* handle, haft.

**manicòmio**, *n.m.* madhouse, (insane) asylum.

**manicòtto**, *n.m.* muff.

**manicùre**, *n.f.* manicure.

**manièra**, *n.f.* manner, way, fashion.

**manierìsmo**, *n.m.* mannerism.

**manifestàre**, *vb.* manifest, evince.

**manifèsto**, **1.** *n.m.* manifesto. **2.** *adj.* manifest.

**manìglia**, *n.f.* handle.

**manipolàre**, *vb.* manipulate.

**mannàia**, *n.f.* axe, chopper, cleaver.

**mano**, *n.f.* hand.

**manodòpera**, *n.f.* labor.

**manoscrìtto**, *n.m. and adj.* manuscript.

**manovèlla**, *n.f.* handle, crank.

**manòvra**, *n.f.* maneuver.

**manovràre**, *vb.* maneuver.

**mansuèto**, *adj.* tame.

**mantèllo**, *n.m.* cloak, mantle, wrap.

**mantenere**, *vb.* maintain, keep.

**mantenimento**, *n.m.* maintenance.

**màntice**, *n.m.* bellows.

**Màntova**, *n.f.* Mantua.

**mantovano**, *adj.* Mantuan.

**manuale**, **1.** *n.* manual, handbook. **2.** *adj.* manual.

**manùbrio**, *n.m.* handle-bar.

**marca**, *n.f.* brand.

**marcare**, *vb.* mark.

**marchese**, *n.m.* marquis.

**marchigiano**, *adj.* of the Marche.

**màrchio**, *n.m.* stamp, hall-mark.

**màrcia**, *n.f.* march.

**marciapiède**, *n.m.* sidewalk.

**marciare**, *vb.* march.

**màrcio**, *adj.* rotten, decayed; (egg) addled.

**marcire**, *vb.* rot, decay.

**mare**, *n.m.* sea.

**marèa**, *n.f.* tide.

**maresciallo**, *n.m.* marshal.

**margarina**, *n.f.* margarine.

**margherita**, *n.f.* daisy.

**marginale**, *adj.* marginal, borderline.

**màrgine**, *n.m.* margin, edge.

**marina**, *n.f.* navy; marine.

**marinaio**, *n.m.* mariner, sailor.

**marinare**, *vb.* marinate.

**marino**, *adj.* marine.

**marionetta**, *n.f.* marionette.

**maritale**, *adj.* marital.

**maritare**, *vb.* marry.

**marito**, *n.m.* husband.

**marmellata**, *n.f.* marmalade; jam.

**marittimo**, *adj.* maritime; marine.

**marmo**, *n.m.* marble.

**marmòcchio**, *n.m.* brat.

**marmotta**, *n.f.* ground hog.

**maroso**, *n.m.* billow.

**marrone**,*n.m.* maroon; chestnut.

**marrubio**, *n.f.* horehound.

**Marsìglia**, *n.f.* Marseilles.

**martedì**, *n.m.* Tuesday.

**martellare**, *vb.* hammer.

**martèllo**, *n.m.* hammer.

**martinèllo**, *n.m.* jack.

**màrtire**, *n.m.* martyr.

**martìrio**, *n.m.* martyrdom.

**marziale**, *adj.* martial.

**marzo**, *n.m.* March.

**mascalzone**, *n.m.* scoundrel; blackguard; crook.

**mascèlla**, *n.f.* jaw.

**màschera**, *n.f.* mask; usher.

**m. antigas**, gas mask.

**mascherare**, *vb.* mask.

**mascherata**, *n.f.* masquerade.

**maschile**, *adj.* masculine.

**maschio**, **1.** *n.* male; cock; buck. **2.** *adj.* masculine; male.

**massa**, *n.f.* mass; bulk; lump.

**massacrare**, *vb.* massacre, slaughter.

**massacro**, *n.m.* massacre, slaughter.

**massaggiare**, *vb.* massage.

**massaggiatore**, *n.m.* masseur.

**massaggio**, *n.m.* massage.

**massaia**, *n.f.* housekeeper; housewife.

**massìccio**, *adj.* massive.

**màssima**, *n.f.* maxim.

**màssimo**, *n.m. and adj.* maximum.

**masticare**, *vb.* chew, masticate.

**masticatore**, *n.m.* chewer.

**mastro**, *n.m.* master. **libro m.**, ledger.

**matassa**, *n.f.* skein, hank.

**matemàtica**, *n.f.* mathematics.

**matemàtico**,*adj.* mathematic.

**materasso**, *n.m.* mattress.

**matèria**, *n.f.* matter; subject.

**materiale**, *n.m. and adj.* material.

**materialismo**, *n.m.* materialism.

**materializzare**, *vb.* materialize.

**maternità**, *n.f.* maternity.

**matèrno**, *adj.* maternal.

**matita**, *n.f.* pencil; crayon.

**matriarcato**, *n.m.* matriarchy.

**matrìcola**, *n.f.* freshman.

**matrigna**, *n.f.* stepmother.

**matrimònio**, *n.m.* matrimony, marriage; match.

**matrona**, *n.f.* matron.

**mattatòio**, *n.m.* stockyards.

**mattina**, *n.f.* morning.

**mattinata**, *n.f.* morning; matinée.

**mattino**, *n.m.* morning.

**mattone**, *n.m.* brick.

**maturare**, *vb.* ripen; mature.

**maturato**, *adj.* ripened; mellow.

**maturità,** *n.f.* maturity.

**maturo,** *adj.* mature; ripe; grown.

**mausolèo,** *n.m.* mausoleum.

**mazza,** *n.f.* bludgeon, cudgel.

**mazzo,** *n.m.* bunch; (cards) pack.

**me,** *pron.* me.

**meccànico, 1.** *n.m.* mechanic. **2.** *adj.* mechanical.

**meccanismo,** *n.m.* mechanism, machinery.

**meccanizzare,** *vb.* mechanize.

**medàglia,** *n.f.* medal.

**medaglione,** *n.m.* medallion, locket.

**mèdia,** *n.f.* average; mean.

**mediano,** *adj.* median.

**medicare,** *vb.* medicate.

**medicina,** *n.f.* medicine.

**mèdico, 1.** *n.* doctor, physician. **2.** *adj.* medical.

**mèdio,** *adj.* middle; average; medium; mean; mid-.

**mediòcre,** *adj.* mediocre.

**mediocrità,** *n.f.* mediocrity.

**medioevale,** *adj.* mediaeval.

**medioèvo,** *n.m.* Middle Ages.

**meditare,** *vb.* meditate, muse.

**meditazione,** *n.f.* meditation.

**mediterràneo,** *n.m. and adj.* Mediterranean.

**medusa,** *n.f.* jellyfish.

**megàfono,** *n.m.* megaphone.

**mèglio,** *adv.* better. **il m.,** (the) best.

**mela,** *n.f.* apple.

**melancònico,** *adj.* melancholy, dismal.

**melanzana,** *n.f.* eggplant.

**melassa,** *n.f.* molasses.

**mellone,** *n.m.* melon; cantaloupe.

**melma,** *n.f.* muck, mire, ooze, slime.

**melo,** *n.m.* apple-tree.

**melodia,** *n.f.* melody, tune.

**melodioso,** *adj.* melodious, tuneful.

**melodramma,** *n.m.* melodrama.

**membrana,** *n.f.* membrane.

**mèmbro,** *n.m.* member; limb.

**memoràbile,** *adj.* memorable.

**mèmore,** *adj.* mindful.

**memòria,** *n.f.* memory; memoir; record.

**memoriale,** *n.m.* memorial.

**menare,** *vb.* lead.

**mènda,** *n.f.* fault, defect, imperfection.

**mendace,** *adj.* mendacious, lying.

**mendicante,** *n.m. and adj.* beggar, mendicant.

**mendicare,** *vb.* beg.

**mèndico,** *n.m.* mendicant.

**menestrèllo,** *n.m.* minstrel.

**meno,** *adv. and prep.* minus; less. **a m. di,** without. **a m. che . . . . non,** unless.

**menomare,** *vb.* diminish, reduce; impair.

**menopàusa,** *n.f.* menopause.

**mensile,** *adj.* monthly.

**mènsola,** *n.f.* bracket.

**menta,** *n.f.* mint.

**mentale,** *adj.* mental.

**mentalità,** *n.f.* mentality.

**mente,** *n.f.* mind.

**mentire,** *vb.* lie.

**mento,** *n.m.* chin.

**mentòlo,** *n.m.* menthol.

**mentre,** *conj.* while.

**menzionare,** *vb.* mention.

**menzione,** *n.f.* mention.

**menzogna,** *n.f.* lie, untruth.

**menzognèro,** *adj.* lying, untruthful.

**meramente,** *adv.* merely.

**meraviglia,** *n.f.* marvel, wonder; amazement, astonishment.

**meravigliare,** *vb.* amaze, astonish; (*refl.*) be amazed, marvel, wonder.

**meraviglioso,** *adj.* marvellous, wonderful, amazing.

**mercante,** *n.m.* merchant.

**mercanteggiare,** *vb.* bargain, haggle.

**mercantile,** *adj.* mercantile.

**mercanzia,** *n.f.* merchandise.

**mercato,** *n.m.* market.

**mèrce,** *n.f.* commodity; ware. (*pl.*) goods; freight.

**mercenàrio, 1.** *n.* hireling; mercenary. **2.** *adj.* mercenary.

**mercerìa,** *n.f.* haberdashery.

**merciàio,** *n.m.* haberdasher.

**mercoledì,** *n.m.* Wednesday.

**mercùrio,** *n.m.* mercury.

**merènda,** *n.f.* light meal, collation.

**meretrice,** *n.f.* harlot.

**meridionale,** *adj.* southern.

**meringa,** *n.f.* meringue.

**meritare,** *vb.* deserve, merit, earn.

**meritèvole,** *adj.* deserving.

**mèrito,** *n.m.* merit.
**meritòrio,** *adj.* meritorious.
**merletto,** *n.m.* lace.
**mèrlo,** *n.m.* blackbird.
**merluzzo,** *n.m.* cod, codfish.
**mèro,** *adj.* mere.
**meschino,** *adj.* mean, petty; paltry, shabby, beggarly, picayune, trivial.
**mescolanza,** *n.f.* mixture, admixture, blend.
**mescolare,** *vb.* mix, blend, mingle; alloy.
**mese,** *n.m.* month.
**messa,** *n.f.* mass.
**messaggèro,** *n.m.* messenger.
**messàggio,** *n.m.* message.
**messicano,** *adj.* Mexican.
**Mèssico,** *n.m.* Mexico.
**mesticcio,** *n.m.* half-breed.
**méstola,** *n.f.* ladle.
**mèstolo,** *n.m.* ladle, dipper.
**mestruazione,** *n.f.* menstruation.
**mèta,** *n.f.* goal.
**metà,** *n.f.* half.
**metabolismo,** *n.m.* metabolism.
**metafìsica,** *n.f.* metaphysics.
**metàllico,** *adj.* metallic.
**metallo,** *n.m.* metal.
**metamòrfosi,** *n.f.* metamorphosis.
**mètano,** *n.m.* methane, firedamp.
**metèora,** *n.f.* meteor.
**meteorologia,** *n.f.* meteorology.
**meticoloso,** *adj.* meticulous.
**mètodo,** *n.m.* method.
**metràggio,** *n.m.* length in meters; footage.
**mètrico,** *adj.* metric.
**mètro,** *n.m.* meter.
**metròpoli,** *n.f.* metropolis.
**metropolitana,** *n.f.* subway.
**metropolitano,** *adj.* metropolitan.
**méttere,** *vb.* place, put, set, lay.
**mezzaluna,** *n.f.* half-moon.
**mezzanino,** *n.m.* mezzanine.
**mezzanòtte,** *n.f.* midnight.
**mezzaria,** *n.f.* center line.
**mèzzo, 1.** *n.m.* middle; medium; means; **in m. a,** amid. **2.** *adj.* half; mid-.
**mezzogiorno,** *n.m.* noon; south.
**mi,** *pron.* me; to me.
**microfilm,** *n.m.* microfilm.

**microscòpico,** *adj.* microscopic.
**microscòpio,** *n.m.* microscope.
**midollo,** *n.m.* marrow.
**mièle,** *n.m.* honey.
**miètere,** *vb.* reap.
**miglio,** *n.m.* mile.
**miglioramento,** *n.m.* improvement.
**migliorare,** *vb.* improve, better, ameliorate, amend.
**migliore,** *adj.* better. **il m.** (the) best.
**migrare,** *vb.* migrate.
**migratòrio,** *adj.* migratory.
**migrazione,** *n.f.* migration.
**milanese,** *adj.* Milanese.
**Milano,** *n.f.* Milan.
**miliare,** *adj.* **pietra m.,** milestone.
**milionàrio,** *n.m.* millionaire.
**milione,** *n.m.* million.
**militante,** *adj.* militant.
**militare,** *adj.* military.
**militarismo,** *n.m.* militarism.
**milite,** *n.m.* soldier.
**milìzia,** *n.f.* militia.
**millantare,** *vb.* bluster, brag.
**millantatore,** *n.m.* braggart.
**millanteria,** *n.f.* bluster, brag.
**mille,** *num.* thousand.
**millìmetro,** *n.m.* millimeter.
**mimetismo,** *n.m.* mimicry; camouflage.
**mimetizzare,** *vb.* camouflage.
**mina,** *n.f.* mine.
**minàccia,** *n.f.* menace, threat.
**minacciare,** *vb.* menace, threaten.
**minare,** *vb.* mine.
**minatore,** *n.m.* miner.
**minerale,** *n.m. and adj.* mineral, ore.
**mineràrio,** *adj.* mining.
**minèstra,** *n.f.* soup.
**miniatura,** *n.f.* miniature.
**minièra,** *n.f.* mine.
**minimamente,** *adv.* least.
**mìnimo, 1.** *n.m.* minimum. **2.** *adj.* least, minimum.
**ministèro,** *n.m.* ministry.
**ministrare,** *vb.* minister.
**ministro,** *n.m.* minister.
**minoranza,** *n.f.* minority.
**minore,** *adj.* minor, lesser; younger, junior.
**minorènne,** *n.m. and adj.* minor.
**minorità,** *n.f.* minority.

**minùgia**, *n.f.pl.* catgut.

**minùscolo**, *adj.* tiny.

**minuto**, *n.m. and adj.* minute. **al m.**, at retail.

**mio**, *adj.* my; mine.

**miope**, *adj.* short-sighted.

**miopìa**, *n.f.* myopia.

**miosòtide**, *n.f.* forget-me-not.

**mira**, *n.f.* aim.

**miràcolo**, *n.m.* miracle.

**miracoloso**, *adj.* miraculous.

**miràggio**, *n.m.* mirage.

**mirare**, *vb.* aim.

**mirìade**, *n.f.* myriad.

**mirto**, *n.m.* myrtle.

**miscellàneo**, *adj.* miscellaneous.

**miscredènte**, *n. and adj.* miscreant; infidel.

**miscùglio**, *n.m.* mixture; medley; hodge-podge.

**misèria**, *n.f.* poverty, want; misery.

**misericòrdia**, *n.f.* mercy.

**misero**, *adj.* miserable, wretched.

**missile**, *n.m.* missile.

**missionàrio**, *n.m. and adj.* missionary.

**missione**, *n.f.* mission.

**misterioso**, *adj.* mysterious.

**mistèro**, *n.m.* mystery.

**mìstico**, *adj.* mystic.

**mistificare**, *vb.* mystify.

**misto**, *adj.* mixed; coeducational.

**mistura**, *n.f.* mixture.

**misura**, *n.f.* measure; size.

**misuramento**, *n.m.* measurement.

**misurare**, *vb.* measure, gauge.

**misuratore**, *adj.* measuring.

**mite**, *adj.* gentle; meek; mild.

**mitemente**, *adv.* mildly, gently.

**mitezza**, *n.f.* mildness, meekness.

**mìtico**, *adj.* mythical.

**mitigare**, *vb.* mitigate, soften, lessen, assuage.

**mito**, *n.m.* myth.

**mitologìa**, *n.f.* mythology.

**mitràglia**, *n.f.* grapeshot.

**mitragliatrice**, *n.f.* machine-gun.

**mòbile**, **1.** *n.* piece of furniture. **2.** *adj.* movable, mobile.

**mobilia**, *n.f.* furnishings.

**mobilitare**, *vb.* mobilize.

**mobilitazione**, *n.f.* mobilization.

**mòda**, *n.f.* mode, fashion. **alla m.**, fashionable, modish.

**modellare**, *vb.* model, mold.

**modèllo**, *n.m.* model, pattern.

**moderare**, *vb.* moderate.

**moderato**, *adj.* moderate.

**moderazione**, *n.f.* moderation.

**modèrno**, *adj.* modern.

**modèstia**, *n.f.* modesty.

**modèsto**, *adj.* modest, demure; plain.

**modificare**, *vb.* modify.

**modìsta**, *n.m. or f.* milliner.

**modisterìa**, *n.f.* millinery.

**mòdo**, *n.m.* manner; mode; way.

**modulare**, *vb.* modulate.

**mòdulo**, *n.m.* blank form.

**moffetta**, *n.f.* skunk.

**mògano**, *n.m.* mahogany.

**mòggio**, *n.m.* bushel.

**mòglie**, *n.f.* wife.

**molare**, *adj.* molar.

**molècola**, *n.f.* molecule.

**molestare**, *vb.* molest.

**molle**, *adj.* soft.

**mòlo**, *n.m.* jetty, mole, pier.

**molòsso**, *n.m.* bulldog.

**moltéplice**, *adj.* multiple; manifold.

**molteplicità**, *n.f.* multiplicity.

**moltiplicare**, *vb.* multiply.

**moltiplicazione**, *n.f.* multiplication.

**moltitùdine**, *n.f.* multitude; host.

**molto**, **1.** *adj.* much; (*pl.*) many, plenty of. **2.** *adv.* very; much.

**momentàneo**, *adj.* momentary.

**momènto**, *n.m.* moment.

**mònaca**, *n.f.* nun.

**mònaco**, *n.m.* monk.

**Mònaco di Bavièra**, *n.m.* Munich.

**monarca**, *n.m.* monarch.

**monarchìa**, *n.f.* monarchy.

**monastèro**, *n.m.* monastery.

**moncone**, *n.m.* stump.

**mondano**, *adj.* worldly.

**mondiale**, *adj.* world-wide.

**mondo**, *n.m.* world.

**monèllo**, *n.m.* gamin, urchin.

**monèta**, *n.f.* coin.

**monetàrio**, *adj.* monetary.

**monitore**, *n.m.* monitor.

**monòcolo**, *n.m.* monocle.

**monòlogo**, *n.m.* monologue.

**monoplano**, *n.m.* monoplane.
**monopolizzare**, *vb.* monopolize.
**monopòlio**, *n.m.* monopoly.
**monosìllabo**, *n.m.* monosyllable.
**monòssido**, *n.m.* monoxide.
**monotonìa**, *n.f.* monotony, dullness.
**monòtono**, *adj.* monotonous, dull, dreary, humdrum.
**monsone**, *n.m.* monsoon.
**montàggio**, *n.m.* assembly.
**montagna**, *n.f.* mountain.
**montagnoso**, *adj.* mountainous.
**montanaro**, *n.m.* mountaineer.
**montare**, *vb.* mount; set.
**monte**, *n.m.* mount, mountain.
**montone**, *n.m.* ram.
**montuoso**, *adj.* mountainous.
**monumentale**, *adj.* monumental.
**monumento**, *n.m.* monument, memorial.
**mòra**, *n.f.* blackberry.
**morale**, **1.** *n.m.* morale. **2.** *n.f. and adj.* moral.
**moralista**, *n.m.* moralist.
**moralità**, *n.f.* morality.
**moralmente**, *adj.* morally.
**mòrbido**, *adj.* soft.
**morbillo**, *n.m.* measles.
**morboso**, *adj.* morbid.
**mordace**, *adj.* scathing.
**mòrdere**, *vb.* bite.
**morfina**, *n.f.* morphine.
**mormorare**, *vb.* murmur.
**mormorìo**, *n.m.* murmur.
**mòrso**, *n.m.* bite; (harness) bit.
**mortale**, *adj.* mortal, deadly, deathly, fatal.
**mortalità**, *n.f.* mortality.
**mòrte**, *n.f.* death, demise.
**mortificare**, *vb.* mortify.
**mòrto**, *adj.* dead.
**mortuàrio**, *adj.* mortuary.
**mosàico**, *n.m.* mosaic.
**mosca**, *n.f.* fly. **m. cavallina**, horsefly.
**mostarda**, *n.f.* mustard.
**mostra**, *n.f.* show, exhibit, exhibition.
**mostrare**, *vb.* show, exhibit.
**mostro**, *n.m.* monster.
**mostruosità**, *n.f.* monstrosity, freak.
**mostruoso**, *adj.* monstrous, freak.

**motivare**, *vb.* motivate.
**motivo**, *n.m.* motive; motif; sake.
**mòto**, *n.m.* motion.
**motocicletta**, *n.f.* motorcycle.
**motocultura**, *n.f.* motorized farming.
**motore**, **1.** *n.m.* motor. **2.** *adj.* motive.
**motorizzare**, *vb.* motorize.
**motoscafo**, *n.m.* motor-boat.
**motto**, *n.m.* motto, quip, slogan.
**movimento**, *n.m.* movement.
**mozione**, *n.f.* motion.
**mozzare**, *vb.* lop off.
**mozzicone**, *n.m.* stub.
**mozzo**, *n.m.* deck-hand.
**mòzzo**, *n.m.* hub.
**mùcchio**, *n.m.* heap, pile, stack.
**muco**, *n.m.* mucus.
**mucoso**, *adj.* mucous.
**muffa**, *n.f.* mold. **m. bianca**, mildew.
**muffito**, *adj.* moldy.
**mugghiare**, *vb.* bellow, low.
**mùgghio**, *n.m.* bellow.
**muggire**, *vb.* bellow.
**muggito**, *n.m.* bellow.
**mughetto**, *n.m.* lily of the valley.
**mugnaio**, *n.m.* miller.
**mulatto**, *n.m.* mulatto.
**mulino**, *n.m.* mill.
**mulo**, *n.m.* mule.
**multa**, *n.f.* fine.
**multare**, *vb.* fine.
**multicolore**, *adj.* multicolored, motley.
**mùltiplo**, *adj.* multiple.
**mummia**, *n.f.* mummy.
**mùngere**, *vb.* milk.
**municipale**, *adj.* municipal.
**munificènte**, *adj.* munificent.
**munizione**, *n.f.* munition, ammunition.
**muòvere**, *vb.* move, stir; (*refl.*) budge.
**murale**, *adj.* mural.
**muratore**, *n.m.* bricklayer, mason.
**muratura**, *n.f.* masonry, bricklaying.
**muro**, *n.m.* wall.
**musa**, *n.f.* muse.
**muschio**, *n.m.* moss.
**muscolare**, *adj.* muscular.
**mùscolo**, *n.m.* muscle.
**musèo**, *n.m.* museum.
**museruòla**, *n.f.* muzzle.

**mùsica**, *n.f.* music.   **m. da camera**, chamber music.
**musicale**, *adj.* musical.
**musicista**, *n.f.* musician.
**muso**, *n.m.* muzzle.
**mussolina**, *n.f.* muslin.
**muta**, *n.f.* pack (of dogs).
**mutabilità**, *n.f.* changeability.

**mutamento**, *n.m.* change.
**mutare**, *vb.* change.
**mutazione**, *n.f.* mutation.
**mutévole**, *adj.* changeable.
**mutilare**, *vb.* mutilate.
**mutilato**, *n.m.* amputee.
**muto**, *adj.* mute, dumb.
**mùtuo**, *adj.* mutual.

# N

**nàcchere**, *n.f.pl.* castanets.
**nafta**, *n.f.* naphtha.
**nàilon**, *n.m.* nylon.
**nano**, *n.m.* dwarf, midget.
**napoletano**, *adj.* Neapolitan.
**Nàpoli**, *n.f.* Naples.
**narciso**, *n.m.* narcissus, daffodil.
**narcòtico**, *n.m. and adj.* narcotic.
**narice**, *n.f.* nostril.
**narrare**, *vb.* narrate, relate.
**narrativo**, *adj.* narrative.
**narrazione**, *n.f.* narration, relation.
**nasale**, *adj.* nasal.
**nàscere**, *vb.* come into being; be born; arise.
**nàscita**, *n.f.* birth.
**nascóndere**, *vb.* hide; (*refl.*) lurk.
**nascondìglio**, *n.m.* hide-out, cache.
**naso**, *n.m.* nose.
**naspo**, *n.m.* reel.
**nastro**, *n.m.* ribbon; tape.
**natale**, *adj.* natal.
**Natale**, *n.m.* Christmas.
**natalità**, *n.f.* birth rate.
**nàtica**, *n.f.* buttock.
**natività**, *n.f.* nativity.
**nativo**, *adj.* native.
**nato**, *adj.* born.
**natura**, *n.f.* nature.   **n. mòrta**, still life.
**naturale**, *adj.* natural.
**naturalezza**, *n.f.* naturalness.
**naturalista**, *n.m.* naturalist.
**naturalizzare**, *vb.* naturalize.
**naufragare**, *vb.* wreck.
**naufràgio**, *n.m.* shipwreck.
**nàufrago**, *n.m.* castaway.

**nàusea**, *n.f.* nausea.
**nauseante**, *adj.* nauseous.
**nàutico**, *adj.* nautical.
**navale**, *adj.* naval.
**navata**, *n.f.* aisle; nave.
**nave**, *n.f.* ship, vessel.
**navigàbile**, *adj.* navigable.
**navigare**, *vb.* navigate; sail.
**navigatore**, *n.m.* navigator.
**navigazione**, *n.f.* navigation.
**nazionale**, *adj.* national.
**nazionalismo**, *n.m.* nationalism.
**nazionalità**, *n.f.* nationality.
**nazionalizzare**, *vb.* nationalize.
**nazionalizzazione**, *n.f.* nationalization.
**nazione**, *n.f.* nation.
**ne**, *pro-phrase* (replaces phrases introduced by **di** and by **da** when meaning "from") some; any; thereof; of it (him, her); about it (him, her); from there.
**nè**, *conj.* neither; nor.
**nébbia**, *n.f.* fog, haze, mist.
**nebbioso**, *adj.* foggy, hazy, misty.
**nebulizzare**, *vb.* atomize (liquids); spray.
**nebulosa**, *n.f.* nebula.
**nebulóso**, *adj.* nebulous.
**necessàrio**, *adj.* necessary, needful, requisite.
**necessità**, *n.f.* necessity.
**necrològio**, *n.m.* obituary.
**nefàrio**, *adj.* nefarious.
**negare**, *vb.* deny.
**negativa**, *n.f.* negative.
**negativo**, *adj.* negative.
**negligènte**, *adj.* remiss.

For pronunciation, see the concise guide on pages 5 to 7.

**negligènza,** *n.f.* oversight.

**negoziante,** *n.m.* dealer.

**negoziare,** *vb.* negotiate.

**negoziazione,** *n.f.* negotiation.

**negozio,** *n.m.* store, shop.

**negro,** *n.m.* Negro.

**nemico,** *n.m. and adj.* enemy, foe.

**neòfita,** *n.m.* neophyte.

**nèon,** *n.m.* neon.

**nepotismo,** *n.m.* nepotism.

**nèrbo,** *n.m.* sinew.

**nero,** *adj.* black.

**nèrvo,** *n.m.* nerve.

**nervoso,** *adj.* nervous, jittery.

**nessuno, 1.** *adj.* no; (after negative) any. **2.** *pron.* nobody, no one; none.

**nèttare,** *n.m.* nectar.

**netto,** *adj.* clean; clear-cut; net.

**neurologia,** *n.f.* neurology.

**neutralità,** *n.f.* neutrality.

**neutralizzare,** *vb.* neutralize, counteract.

**nèutro,** *n.m. and adj.* neutral.

**nevischio,** *n.m.* sleet.

**nevralgia,** *n.f.* neuralgia.

**neve,** *n.f.* snow.

**nevicare,** *vb.* snow.

**nevròtico,** *adj.* neurotic.

**nìbbio,** *n.m.* kite.

**nichel,** *n.m.* nickel.

**nicotina,** *n.f.* nicotine.

**nido,** *n.m.* nest, aerie.

**niènte,** *pron.* nothing. **n. affatto,** *adv.* not at all.

**ninfa,** *n.f.* nymph.

**ninna-nanna,** *n.f.* lullaby.

**ninnolo,** *n.m.* trinket.

**nipote,** *n.m. and f.* nephew; niece; grandson; granddaughter.

**nitrato,** *n.m.* nitrate.

**nitrògeno,** *n.m.* nitrogen.

**nò,** *interj.* no.

**nòbile,** *n. and adj.* noble.

**nobilmente,** *adv.* nobly.

**nobiltà,** *n.f.* nobility.

**nobiluòmo,** *n.m.* nobleman.

**nòcca,** *n.f.* knuckle; fetlock.

**nocciòla,** *n.f.* nut; hazelnut.

**nocciòlo,** *n.m.* hazel; (*fig.*) kernel.

**noce,** *n.* **1.** *m.* nut-tree; walnut. **n. americano,** hickory. **2.** *f.* nut; walnut.

**nocivo,** *adj.* harmful, injurious.

**nòdo,** *n.m.* knot, gnarl, kink.

**n. scorsoio,** slipknot; noose.

**nodoso,** *adj.* knotty.

**noi,** *pron.* we; us.

**nòia,** *n.f.* boredom, ennui.

**noleggiare,** *vb.* hire.

**noléggio,** *n.m.* rental.

**nòlo,** *n.m.* hire.

**nòmade,** *n.m.* nomad.

**nome,** *n.m.* name; given name.

**nomignolo,** *n.m.* nickname.

**nòmina,** *n.f.* nomination, appointment.

**nominale,** *adj.* nominal.

**nominare,** *vb.* nominate, name, appoint.

**non,** *adv.* not.

**noncurante,** *adj.* easy-going.

**nondimeno,** *adv.* nonetheless, nevertheless, all the same.

**nonna,** *n.f.* grandmother.

**nònno,** *n.m.* grandfather.

**nòno,** *adj.* ninth.

**nonostante,** *prep.* notwithstanding.

**non ti scordar di me,** *n.m.* forget-me-not.

**nord,** *n.m.* north.

**nord-èst,** *n.m.* northeast.

**nord-ovèst,** *n.m.* northwest.

**nòrma,** *n.f.* norm; standard.

**normale,** *adj.* normal; standard.

**normalmente,** *adv.* normally.

**norvegese,** *adj.* Norwegian.

**Norvègia,** *n.f.* Norway.

**nostalgìa,** *n.f.* nostalgia; homesickness.

**nòstro,** *adj.* our; ours.

**nostròmo,** *n.m.* boatswain.

**nòta,** *n.f.* note; footnote.

**notaio,** *n.m.* notary.

**notare,** *vb.* note.

**notazione,** *n.f.* notation.

**notévole,** *adj.* notable, noticeable, remarkable.

**notificare,** *vb.* notify.

**notificazione,** *n.f.* notification.

**notizia,** *n.f.* piece of news.

**noto,** *adj.* noted, well-known.

**notorietà,** *n.f.* notoriety.

**notòrio,** *adj.* notorious.

**notturno, 1.** *n.m.* nocturne. **2.** *adj.* nocturnal.

**novanta,** *num.* ninety.

**novantèsimo,** *adj.* ninetieth.

**nòve,** *num.* nine.

**novellistica,** *n.f.* novel-writing, fiction.

**novèmbre,** *n.m.* November.

**novèna,** *n.f.* novena.

**novità,** *n.f.* novelty.

**novìzio,** *n.m.* novice.

**nozióne,** *n.f.* notion.

**nòzze,** *n.f. pl.* wedding.

**nube,** *n.f.* cloud.

**nucleare,** *adj.* nuclear.

**nùcleo,** *n.m.* nucleus.

**nudità,** *n.f.* nudity, bareness.

**nudo,** *adj.* naked, nude, bare.

**nulla,** *pron.* nothing.

**nullità,** *n.f.* nonentity.

**nullo,** *adj.* void.

**numerare,** *vb.* number.

**numèrico,** *adj.* numerical.

**numero,** *n.m.* number.

**numeroso,** *adj.* numerous.

**nùnzio,** *n.m.* nuncio.

**nuòcere,** *vb.* harm, injure.

**nuòra,** *n.f.* daughter-in-law.

**nuotare,** *vb.* swim.

**nuòvo,** *adj.* new. **di n.,** anew; again.

**nutrice,** *n.f.* nurse.

**nutriènte,** *adj.* nutritious.

**nutrimento,** *n.m.* nourishment; feed.

**nutrire,** *vb.* nourish; feed.

**nutrizione,** *n.f.* nutrition.

**nùvola,** *n.f.* cloud.

**nuvolosità,** *n.f.* cloudiness.

**nuvoloso,** *adj.* cloudy.

**nuziale,** *adj.* nuptial, bridal.

# O

**o,** *conj.* or. **o . . . o,** either . . . or.

**oasi,** *n.f.* oasis.

**obbediènte,** *adj.* obedient, compliant.

**obbediènza,** *n.f.* obedience, compliance.

**obbedire,** *vb.* obey, comply.

**obbligare,** *vb.* oblige.

**obbligatòrio,** *adj.* obligatory, binding, compulsory, mandatory.

**obbligazione,** *n.f.* obligation; bond, debenture.

**obelisco,** *n.m.* obelisk.

**obèso,** *adj.* obese.

**òbice,** *n.m.* howitzer.

**obiettare,** *vb.* object, demur.

**obiettivo, 1.** *n.* objective. **2.** *adj.* objective; factual.

**obiezione,** *n.f.* objection.

**oblazione,** *n.f.* fine paid voluntarily.

**oblìo,** *n.m.* oblivion.

**obliquo,** *adj.* oblique, slant.

**oblò,** *n.m.* porthole.

**oblungo,** *adj.* oblong.

**òbolo,** *n.m.* obol; mite.

**òca,** *n.f.* goose.

**occasionale,** *adj.* occasional.

**occasione,** *n.f.* occasion, opportunity, chance; bargain.

**occhiali,** *n.m.pl.* eyeglasses, spectacles.

**occhiata,** *n.f.* glance, look.

**occhièllo,** *n.m.* button-hole; eyelet.

**òcchio,** *n.m.* eye. **o. della mànica,** armhole. **o. pesto,** black eye.

**occidentale,** *adj.* occidental, western.

**occidènte,** *n.m.* Occident, west.

**occulto,** *adj.* occult.

**occupante,** *n.m.* occupant.

**occupare,** *vb.* occupy.

**occupato,** *adj.* busy.

**occupazione,** *n.f.* occupation, job.

**ocèano,** *n.m.* ocean.

**oculare,** *adj.* ocular. **testimone o.,** eye-witness.

**oculista,** *n.m.* oculist.

**od,** *conj.* or.

**odiare,** *vb.* hate.

**òdio,** *n.m.* hate, hatred.

**odontoiatrìa,** *f.* dentistry.

**odore,** *n.m.* odor, scent, smell.

**odioso,** *adj.* hateful, invidious, odious, obnoxious.

**offèndere**, *vb.* offend.
**offensiva**, *n.f.* offensive.
**offensivo**, *adj.* offensive, objectionable.
**offensore**, *n.m.* offender.
**offerènte**, *n.m.* bidder.
**offèrta**, *n.f.* offer; bid.
**offesa**, *n.f.* offense.
**officiare**, *vb.* officiate.
**offrire**, *vb.* offer, tender; bid.
**oftàlmico**, *adj.* ophthalmic.
**oggètto**, *n.m.* object.
**òggi**, *n.m. and adv.* today.
**ogni**, *adj.* each, every.
**ogniqualvòlta**, *adv.* whenever.
**ognuno**, *pron.* everybody, everyone.
**Olanda**, *n.f.* Holland.
**olandese**, 1. *n.m.* Dutchman. 2. *adj.* Dutch.
**oleoso**, *adj.* oily.
**olfattòrio**, *n.m.* olfactory.
**oligarchìa**, *n.f.* oligarchy.
**òlio**, *n.m.* oil.
**oliva**, *n.f.* olive.
**olivo**, *n.m.* olive-tree.
**olmo**, *n.m.* elm.
**olocàusto**, *n.m.* holocaust.
**oltràggio**, *n.m.* outrage.
**oltraggioso**, *adj.* outrageous.
**oltre**, *adv. and prep.* beyond; besides, further.
**oltrepassare**, *vb.* pass beyond; outrun.
**omàggio**, *n.m.* homage; gift, present.
**ombellico**, *n.m.* navel.
**ombra**, *n.f.* shade; shadow.
**ombreggiare**, *vb.* shade.
**ombrèllo**, *n.m.* umbrella.
**ombroso**, *adj.* shady.
**omelìa**, *n.f.* homily.
**omèttere**, *vb.* omit, leave out; overlook.
**omicida**, *n.m.* homicide.
**omicìdio**, *n.m.* homicide; manslaughter.
**omissione**, *n.f.* omission.
**òmnibus**, *n.m.* local (train).
**omogèneo**, *adj.* homogeneous.
**omogenizzare**, *vb.* homogenize.
**omologare**, *vb.* probate.
**omologazione**, *n.f.* probate.
**omònimo**, 1. *n.* homonym; namesake. 2. *adj.* homonymous, of the same name.
**omosessuale**, *adj.* homosexual.
**óncia**, *n.f.* ounce.

**onda**, *n.f.* wave.
**ondare**, *vb.* surge.
**ondeggiare**, *vb.* undulate.
**ònere**, *n.m.* burden, onus.
**oneroso**, *adj.* burdensome.
**onestà**, *n.f.* honesty.
**onestamente**, *adv.* honestly, decently.
**onèsto**, *adj.* honest, decent, above board.
**onnipotènte**, *adj.* almighty, omnipotent.
**onorare**, *vb.* honor.
**onoràrio**, 1. *n.m.* honorarium, fee. 2. *adj.* honorary.
**onore**, *n.m.* honor.
**onorévole**, *adj.* honorable, decent.
**onorevolezza**, *n.f.* honorableness, decency.
**opacità**, *n.f.* opacity.
**opaco**, *adj.* opaque.
**opale**, *n.m.* opal.
**òpera**, *n.f.* work; opera.
**operaio**, *n.m.* worker.
**operare**, *vb.* operate.
**operativo**, *adj.* operative.
**operatore**, *n.m.* operator.
**operazione**, *n.f.* operation; transaction.
**operetta**, *n.f.* operetta; musical comedy.
**operoso**, *adj.* industrious.
**opinione**, *n.f.* opinion.
**opporre**, *vb.* oppose; (*refl.*) object.
**opportunamente**, *adv.* advisably.
**opportunismo**, *n.m.* opportunism.
**opportunità**, *n.f.* desirability; suitability; advisability; expediency.
**opportuno**, *adv.* fitting; desirable; advisable; expedient.
**opposizione**, *n.f.* opposition.
**oppressione**, *n.f.* oppression.
**oppòsto**, *n.m. and adj.* opposite.
**oppressivo**, *adj.* oppressive.
**opprèsso**, *adj.* oppressed, downtrodden.
**oppressore**, *n.m.* oppressor.
**opprimènte**, *adj.* oppressive; burdensome.
**opprimere**, *vb.* oppress.
**optometrìa**, *n.f.* optometry.
**opulènto**, *adj.* opulent, affluent.
**opulènza**, *n.f.* opulence, affluence.

---

opùscolo, *n.m.* pamphlet.

opzione, *n.f.* option.

ora, 1. *n.f.* hour; o'clock; time. che o. è? what time is it? 2. *adv.* now.

oràcolo, *n.m.* oracle.

orale, *adj.* oral.

oràrio, *n.m.* timetable, schedule.

oratore, *n.m.* orator, speaker.

oratòria, *n.f.* oratory.

orazione, *n.f.* oration.

orbare, *vb.* bereave.

òrbita, *n.f.* orbit; socket.

orchèstra, *n.f.* orchestra.

orchidèa, *n.f.* orchid.

òrda, *n.f.* horde.

ordàlia, *n.f.* ordeal.

ordinamento, *n.m.* arrangement.

ordinanza, *n.f.* ordinance.

ordinare, *vb.* order, arrange, array; ordain; tidy, trim

ordinàrio, *n.m.* ordinary.

ordinato, *adj.* orderly, tidy, trim.

ordinazione, *n.f.* ordination.

òrdine, *n.m.* order, array; fiat.

orecchino, *n.m.* ear-ring.

orécchio, *n.m.* ear.

orecchioni, *n.m.pl.* mumps.

orèfice, *n.m.* goldsmith.

òrfano, *n.m.* orphan.

orfanotròfio, *n.m.* orphanage.

orgànico, *adj.* organic.

organismo, *n.m.* organism.

organista, *n.m.* organist.

organizzare, *vb.* organize.

organizzazione, *n.f.* organization.

òrgano, *n.m.* organ.

organza, *n.f.* organdy.

òrgia, *n.f.* orgy, debauch.

orgòglio, *n.m.* pride.

orgoglioso, *adj.* proud.

orientale, *adj.* Oriental; eastern.

orientamento, *n.m.* orientation; bearings.

orientare, *vb.* orient.

orientazione, *n.f.* orientation.

oriènte, *n.m.* Orient; east.

originale, *adj.* original, novel.

originalità, *n.f.* originality.

orìgine, *n.f.* origin.

origliare, *vb.* eavesdrop.

orina, *n.f.* urine.

orinare, *vb.* urinate.

orinatòio, *n.m.* urinal.

orizzontale, *adj.* horizontal; level.

orizzonte, *n.m.* horizon.

orlare, *vb.* hem; edge.

orlatura, *n.f.* edging.

orlo, *n.m.* brink, brim, edge, rim, verge; hem. o. a giorno, hemstitch.

orma, *n.f.* footstep; footprint.

ormeggiare, *vb.* moor.

ormeggio, *n.m.* mooring.

ormone, *n.m.* hormone.

ornamentale, *adj.* ornamental.

ornamento, *n.m.* ornament.

ornare, *vb.* ornament, adorn.

ornato, *adj.* ornate.

ornitologìa, *n.f.* ornithology.

òro, *n.m.* gold.

orologiaio, *n.m.* watchmaker.

orològio, *n.m.* clock; watch. o. a pólvere, hourglass.

or' ora, *adv.* just now.

oròscopo, *n.m.* horoscope.

orrèndo, *adj.* ghastly, gruesome.

orrìbile, *adj.* horrible, grisly.

òrrido, *adj.* horrid.

orrore, *n.m.* horror.

orso, *n.m.* bear.

ortènsia, *n.f.* hydrangea.

orticultura, *n.f.* horticulture.

òrto, *n.m.* orchard; garden.

ortodòsso, *adj.* orthodox.

ortografìa, *n.f.* orthography, spelling.

ortopèdico, *adj.* orthopedic.

orzaiòlo, *n.m.* sty.

orzo, *n.m.* barley.

osare, *vb.* dare; venture.

oscèno, *adj.* obscene.

oscillare, *vb.* oscillate, sway.

oscuramento, *n.m.* darkening; blackout.

oscurare, *vb.* darken, obscure, dim, shade.

oscurità, *n.f.* darkness, obscurity, dimness, gloom.

oscuro, *adj.* dark, obscure, dim, gloomy.

osmòsi, *n.f.* osmosis.

ospedale, *n.m.* hospital.

ospedalizzare, *vb.* hospitalize.

ospedalizzazione, *n.f.* hospitalization.

ospitale, *adj.* hospitable.

ospitalità, *n.f.* hospitality.

òspite, *n.* 1. *m.* host; guest; visitor; lodger. 2. *f.* hostess; guest; visitor.

ossatura, *n.f.* framework.

ossequioso, *adj.* obsequious.

osservanza, *n.f.* observance.

**osservare**, *vb.* observe, notice, remark.

**osservatore**, *n.m.* observer.

**osservatòrio**, *n.m.* observatory.

**osservazione**, *n.f.* observation, remark.

**ossessione**, *n.f.* obsession.

**ossìa**, *conj.* or.

**ossìgeno**, *n.m.* oxygen.

**òsso**, *n.m.* bone.

**ossuto**, *adj.* bony.

**ostacolare**, *vb.* hinder, bar, block, interfere with, obstruct.

**ostàcolo**, *n.m.* obstacle, bar, hindrance, block, snag.

**ostàggio**, *n.m.* hostage.

**òste**, *n.m.* innkeeper.

**ostensìbile**, *adj.* ostensible.

**ostentare**, *vb.* show off, display, flaunt.

**ostentato**, *adj.* ostentatious.

**ostentazione**, *n.f.* ostentation, display.

**osterìa**, *n.f.* tavern.

**ostètrico**, **1.** *n.m.* obstetrician. **2.** *adj.* obstetrical.

**òstia**, *n.f.* Host.

**ostile**, *adj.* hostile, antagonistic.

**ostilità**, *n.f.* hostility.

**ostinato**, *adj.* obstinate, dogged, headstrong; obdurate.

**ostracizzare**, *vb.* ostracize.

**òstrica**, *n.f.* oyster.

**ostruire**, *vb.* obstruct.

**ostruzione**, *n.f.* obstruction.

**ottàgono**, *n.m.* octagon.

**ottanta**, *num.* eighty, fourscore.

**ottantésimo**, *adj.* eightieth.

**ottava**, *n.f.* eighth; octave.

**ottavino**, *n.m.* piccolo.

**ottavo**, *adj.* eighth.

**ottenere**, *vb.* obtain, get.

**òttica**, *n.f.* optics.

**òttico**, **1.** *n.m.* optician. **2.** optic.

**ottimismo**, *n.m.* optimism.

**ottimìstico**, *adj.* optimistic.

**òtto**, *num.* eight.

**ottobre**, *n.m.* October.

**ottone**, *n.m.* brass.

**ottopode**, *n.m.* octopus.

**ottùndere**, *vb.* dull.

**otturare**, *vb.* stop up; fill.

**otturatore**, *n.m.* shutter.

**otturazione**, *n.f.* filling.

**ottusamente**, *adv.* bluntly, obtusely.

**ottusità**, *n.f.* obtuseness, dullness, bluntness.

**ottuso**, *adj.* obtuse, dull, blunt.

**ovaia**, *n.f.* ovary.

**ovale**, *n.m. and adj.* oval.

**ovazione**, *n.f.* ovation.

**ovatta**, *n.f.* wadding.

**òvest**, *n.* west.

**òvvio**, *adj.* obvious.

**oziare**, *vb.* loaf.

**òzio**, *n.m.* idleness.

**ozioso**, *adj.* idle.

# P

**pacca**, *n.f.* smack.

**pacco**, *n.m.* package, pack, parcel.

**pace**, *n.f.* peace.

**pacificare**, *vb.* pacify.

**pacificatore**, *n.m.* pacifier.

**pacìfico**, *adj.* pacific, peaceful.

**pacifismo**, *n.m.* pacifism.

**pacifista**, *n.m.* pacifist.

**padèlla**, *n.f.* pan, frying pan.

**padiglione**, *n.m.* pavilion, stand.

**Pàdova**, *n.f.* Padua.

**padovano**, *adj.* Paduan.

**padre**, *n.m.* father.

**padrino**, *n.m.* godfather.

**padrona**, *n.f.* mistress; landlady.

**padronanza**, *n.f.* mastery.

**padrone**, *n.m.* boss, employer; landlord; master.

**paesàggio**, *n.m.* landscape, scenery.

**paese**, *n.m.* country.

**paga**, *n.f.* pay.

**pagamento**, *n.m.* payment.

**pagano**, *n. and adj.* pagan, heathen.

**pagare**, *vb.* pay, defray.

**pàggio**, *n.m.* page.

**pàgina**, *n.f.* page.

**pàglia**, *n.f.* straw; **p. di acciaio**, *n.f.* steel wool.

**pagliaccesco**, *adj.* clownish.

**pagliàccio**, *n.m.* clown.

**pagnòtta**, *n.f.* loaf.

**pagòda**, *n.f.* pagoda.

**paio**, *n.m.* pair, couple.

**pala**, *n.f.* shovel.

**palafitta**, *n.f.* pile.

**palafrenière**, *n.m.* groom.

**palato**, *n.m.* palate.

**palazzo**, *n.m.* palace; large building; mansion. **p. di giustizia**, courthouse.

**palco**, *n.m.* antler; box (in theater).

**palcoscènico**, *n.m.* stage.

**palèstra**, *n.f.* gymnasium.

**palla**, *n.f.* ball.

**pallacanestro**, *n.f.* basketball.

**pallamaglio**, *n.m.* croquet.

**pallidezza**, *n.f.* paleness.

**pàllido**, *adj.* pale, pallid, wan, pasty.

**pallinacci**, *n.m.pl.* buckshot.

**pallini**, *n.m.pl.* shot.

**pallone**, *n.m.* balloon.

**pallòttola**, *n.f.* bullet; ball.

**palma**, *n.f.* palm.

**palo**, *n.m.* pole, post, stake.

**pàlpebra**, *n.f.* eyelid.

**palpitare**, *vb.* palpitate.

**palude**, *n.f.* swamp, bog, marsh.

**panacèa**, *n.f.* panacea.

**pancetta**, *n.f.* bacon.

**pància**, *n.f.* paunch, belly.

**panciòtto**, *n.m.* vest.

**pane**, *n.m.* bread, loaf. **p. abbrustolito**, toast.

**pànfilo**, *n.m.* yacht.

**pànico**, *n.m.* panic.

**panino**, *n.m.* roll, biscuit.

**panna**, *n.f.* cream.

**pannaiòlo**, *n.m.* clothier; draper.

**pannèllo**, *n.m.* panel.

**pannilino**, *n.m.* diaper; sanitary napkin.

**pannolino**, *n.m.* diaper.

**panorama**, *n.m.* panorama.

**pantaloni**, *n.m.(pl.)* trousers, pants, breeches.

**pantano**, *n.m.* bog.

**pantèra**, *n.f.* panther.

**pantòfola**, *n.f.* slipper.

**pantomima**, *n.f.* pantomime.

**papa**, *n.m.* pope.

**papà**, *n.m.* papa.

**papale**, *adj.* papal.

**pàpera**, *n.f.* goose.

**paperetto**, *n.m.* gosling.

**pàpero**, *n.m.* gander.

**pappa**, *n.f.* gruel.

**pappagallo**, *n.m.* parrot; parakeet.

**paràbola**, *n.f.* parabola.

**parabrezza**, *n.m.* windshield, windscreen.

**paracadute**, *n.m.* parachute.

**paradiso**, *n.m.* paradise.

**paradòsso**, *n.m.* paradox.

**parafango**, *n.m.* mudguard; fender.

**paraffina**, *n.f.* paraffin.

**parafrasare**, *vb.* paraphrase.

**paràfrasi**, *n.f.* paraphrase.

**parafùlmine**, *n.m.* lightningrod.

**parafuòco**, *n.m.* firescreen.

**paragonàbile**, *adj.* comparable.

**paragonare**, *vb.* compare.

**paragone**, *n.m.* comparison.

**paràgrafo**, *n.m.* paragraph.

**parallelo**, *n.m. and adj.* parallel.

**paràlisi**, *n.f.* paralysis.

**paralizzare**, *vb.* paralyze.

**paralume**, *n.m.* shade.

**parapìglia**, *n.m.* scramble.

**parassita**, *n.m.* parasite.

**parata**, *n.f.* parade.

**paratia**, *n.f.* bulkhead.

**paravènto**, *n.m.* screen; windshield.

**parcamento**, *n.m.* parking.

**parcare**, *vb.* park.

**parcheggio**, *n.m.* parking.

**parco**, *n.m.* park.

**parécchio**, *adj.* some; considerable; *(pl.)* several.

**parènte**, *n.f.* relative.

**parentela**, *n.f.* kin, kindred; relationship.

**parèntesi**, *n.f.* parenthesis. **p. quadra**, bracket.

**parere**, **1.** *n.* opinion. **2.** *vb.* appear, seem.

**parrucchière**, *n.m.* hairdresser; barber.

**pari**, **1.** *n.m.* peer. **2.** *n.f.* par. **3.** *adj.* even, equal.

**pària**, *n.m.* pariah, outcast.

**Parigi**, *n.f.* Paris.

**parigino**, *adj.* Parisian.

**parità**, *n.f.* parity.  **p. àurea**, gold standard.

**parlamentare**, *adj.* parliamentary.

**parlamentare**, *vb.* parley.

**parlamento**, *n.m.* parliament, legislature; parley.

**parlare**, *vb.* speak, talk.

**parmigiano**, *adj.* Parmesan.

**parodìa**, *n.f.* parody.

**parodiare**, *vb.* parody.

**paròla**, *n.f.* word.

**parossismo**, *n.m.* paroxysm.

**parròcchia**, *n.f.* parish.

**parrocchiale**, *adj.* parochial.

**pàrroco**, *n.m.* parish priest; parson.

**parrucca**, *n.f.* wig.

**parrucchière**, *n.m.* hairdresser.

**parsimònia**, *n.f.* parsimony.

**parte**, *n.f.* part; share.  **a p.**, apart.  **p. del discorso**, part of speech.

**partecipante**, *n.m.* participant.

**partecipare**, *vb.* participate, partake.

**partecipazione**, *n.f.* participation.

**partènza**, *n.f.* departure.

**particèlla**, *n.f.* particle.

**particìpio**, *n.m.* participle.

**particolare**, *adj.* particular.

**particolareggiato**, *adj.* detailed; circumstantial.

**partigiano**, *n.m.* and *adj.* partisan.

**partire**, *vb.* depart, leave.

**partita**, *n.f.* game.

**partito**, *n.m.* party.

**partitura**, *n.f.* score.

**partizione**, *n.f.* partition.

**parto**, *n.m.* childbirth.

**partorire**, *vb.* bear, give birth to.

**parziale**, *adj.* partial.

**parzialità**, *n.f.* partiality, bias.

**pàscere**, *vb.* graze.

**pàscolo**, *n.m.* pasture; grazing.

**Pasqua**, *n.f.* Easter.

**pasquinata**, *n.f.* lampoon.

**passàbile**, *adj.* passable.

**passàggio**, *n.m.* passage; aisle; crossing.  **p. a livello**, grade crossing.

**passante**, *n.m.* passer-by.

**passapòrto**, *n.m.* passport.

**passare**, *vb.* pass; spend.

**passatèmpo**, *n.m.* pastime.

**passato**, **1.** *n.m.* past; purée.  **2.** *adj.* past, over, bygone.

**passeggiare**, *vb.* walk, stroll; ride.

**passeggiata**, *n.f.* walk, stroll; ride.

**passeggèro**, *n.m.* passenger.

**passeggiatore**, *n.m.* stroller.

**passerèlla**, *n.f.* gangway.

**pàssero**, *n.m.* sparrow.

**passione**, *n.f.* passion; fondness.

**passivo**, *n.m.* and *adj.* passive.

**passo**, *n.m.* pass; pace; step; tread.

**pasta**, *n.f.* paste; dough, batter.  **p. asciutta**, macaroni.  **p. frolla**, frosting.

**pasteurizzare**, *vb.* pasteurize.

**pasticca**, *n.f.* pastille, lozenge, tablet.

**pasticcerìa**, *n.f.* pastry; pastry-shop.

**pasticcio**, *n.m.* mess; pasty.

**pastiglia**, *n.f.* pastille.

**pasto**, *n.m.* meal.

**pastore**, *n.m.* shepherd; pastor.

**patata**, *n.f.* potato.

**patènte**, *n.m.* license.

**paternità**, *n.f.* paternity, fatherhood.

**patèrno**, *adj.* paternal, fatherly.

**patètico**, *adj.* pathetic.

**patìbolo**, *n.m.* scaffold.

**patinoso**, *adj.* furry.

**patologia**, *n.f.* pathology.

**pàtos**, *n.m.* pathos.

**pàtria**, *n.f.* country; fatherland, homeland.

**patriarca**, *n.m.* patriarch.

**patrigno**, *n.m.* stepfather.

**patrimònio**, *n.m.* patrimony, inheritance; estate.

**patriòta**, *n.m.* patriot.

**patriòttico**, *adj.* patriotic.

**patriottismo**, *n.m.* patriotism.

**patronato**, *n.m.* patronage.

**patròno**, *n.m.* patron.

**pattinare**, *vb.* skate.

**pàttino**, *n.m.* skate.

**patto**, *n.m.* pact; compact.

**pattùglia**, *n.f.* patrol.

**paùra**, *n.f.* fear;  **(aver p.)** be afraid.

**pauroso**, *adj.* fearful.

**pàusa**, *n.f.* pause.

**pavimentare**, *vb.* pave.

**pavimentazione**, n.f. flooring.

**pavimento**, n.m. floor.

**pavone**, n.m. peacock.

**pavoneggiarsi**, vb. strut.

**paziènte**, adj. patient.

**paziènza**, n.f. patience.

**pazzìa**, n.f. insanity, madness, lunacy.

**pazzo**, adj. crazy, insane, mad.

**peccaminoso**, adj. sinful.

**peccare**, vb. sin.

**peccato**, n.m. sin; pity; shame. **che p.!** what a pity!

**peccatore**, n.m. sinner.

**pece**, n.f. pitch.

**pechblenda**, n.f. pitchblende.

**pècora**, n.f. sheep, ewe.

**peculiare**, adj. peculiar.

**peculiarità**, n.f. peculiarity.

**pecuniàrio**, adj. pecuniary.

**pedagogìa**, n.f. pedagogy.

**pedagògo**, n.m. pedagogue.

**pedale**, n.m. pedal.

**pedante**, n.m. pedant.

**pedèstre**, adj. pedestrian.

**pediàtra**, n.m. pediatrician.

**pedina**, n.f. pawn.

**pedonale**, adj. pedestrian.

**pedone**, n.m. pedestrian.

**pèggio**, adv. worse. **il p.,** worst.

**peggiore**, adj. worse. **il p.,** the worst.

**pegno**, n.m. pledge; pawn.

**pelare**, vb. skin, peel.

**pèlle**, n.f. skin, hide. **p. verniciata**, patent leather.

**pellegrinàggio**, n.m. pilgrimage.

**pellegrino**, n.m. pilgrim.

**pellìccia**, n.f. fur.

**pellicciaio**, n.m. furrier.

**pellìcola**, n.f. film, movie.

**pellirossa**, n.m. red-skin, (American) Indian.

**pelo**, n.m. hair.

**peloso**, adj. hairy.

**pelùria**, n.f. down.

**pèlvi**, n.f. pelvis.

**pena**, n.f. pain; penalty.

**pèndere**, vb. hang.

**pendènte**, **1.** n.m. pendant. **2.** adj. pending.

**pendènza**, n.f. slope.

**pendìo**, n.m. slope, slant, incline.

**penetrante**, adj. penetrating, discerning.

**penetrare**, vb. penetrate.

**penetrazione**, n.f. penetration, insight.

**penicillina**, n.f. penicillin.

**penìsola**, n.f. peninsula.

**penitènte**, n.m. and adj. penitent.

**penitènza**, n.f. penitence, penance.

**penna**, n.f. feather, plume; pen. **p. stilogràfica**, fountain pen.

**pennèllo**, n.m. brush.

**pennuto**, adj. feathered.

**pensare**, vb. think.

**pensatore**, n.m. thinker.

**pensièro**, n.m. thought.

**pensilina**, n.f. marquee.

**pensionante**, n.m. boarder.

**pensione**, n.f. pension, boarding house.

**pensoso**, adj. pensive, thoughtful.

**pentimento**, n.m. repentance.

**pentirsi**, vb. repent, rue.

**pèntola**, n.f. kettle, pot. **p. a pressione**, pressure cooker.

**penùria**, n.f. penury.

**penzolare**, vb. dangle.

**pepe**, n.m. pepper.

**pepita**, n.f. nugget.

**per**, prep. for; through; by; per.

**pera**, n.f. pear.

**per cènto**, adv. per cent.

**percentuale**, n.m. percentage.

**percettìbile**, adj. perceptible.

**percezione**, n.f. perception.

**perché**, **1.** adv. why. **2.** conj. because; for.

**perciò**, adv. therefore.

**percorrènza**, n.f. distance travelled.

**percorso**, n.m. passage (of time); lapse; route.

**percòssa**, n.f. blow; (pl.) beating.

**percuòtere**, vb. hit, strike, maul; tap.

**pèrdere**, vb. lose; miss; forfeit; leak.

**pèrdita**, n.f. loss; bereavement; forfeiture; leakage.

**perdizione**, n.f. perdition.

**perdonare**, vb. pardon, forgive.

**perdono**, n.m. pardon, forgiveness.

**perènne**, adj. perennial.

**perentòrio**, adj. peremptory.

---

For pronunciation, see the concise guide on pages 5 to 7.

**perfettamente,** *adv.* perfectly.

**perfètto,** *adj.* perfect, flawless.

**perfezionare,** *vb.* perfect.

**perfezione,** *n.f.* perfection.

**perfino,** *adv.* even.

**perforare,** *vb.* punch.

**perforazione,** *n.f.* perforation.

**pergamena,** *n.f.* parchment.

**pergolato,** *n.m.* arbor, bower.

**pericolo,** *n.m.* danger, peril, jeoparody.

**pericoloso,** *adj.* dangerous, perilous.

**priferiea,** *n.f.* periphery, outskirts.

**perimetro,** *n.m.* perimeter.

**periòdico,** 1. *n.m.* periodical; magazine. 2. *adj.* periodical; periodic; serial.

**periodo,** *n.m.* period, term.

**perire,** *vb.* perish.

**pèrla,** *n.f.* pearl.

**permanènte,** *adj.* permanent.

**permanènza,** *n.f.* stay.

**permeare,** *vb.* permeate.

**permesso,** *n.m.* permission, leave, license.

**permèttere,** *vb.* permit, let, allow.

**permissìbile,** *adj.* permissible.

**pernàcchia,** *f.* Bronx cheer.

**pernice,** *n.f.* partridge.

**pernicioso,** *adj.* pernicious.

**pèrnio,** *n.m.* pivot.

**pero,** *n.m.* pear-tree.

**però,** *adv.* however; though.

**perpendicolare,** *n.m.* and *adj.* perpendicular.

**perpetrare,** *vb.* perpetrate.

**perpètuo,** *adj.* perpetual.

**perplessità,** *n.f.* perplexity, bafflement, bewilderment, quandary.

**perplèsso,** *adj.* perplexed, baffled, bewildered.

**persecuzione,** *n.f.* persecution.

**perseguire,** *vb.* pursue.

**perseguitare,** *vb.* persecute.

**perseveranza,** *n.f.* perseverance.

**perseverare,** *vb.* persevere.

**pèrsico,** *adj.* **pesce p.** bass (fish); perch.

**persistènte,** *adj.* persistent.

**persìstere,** *vb.* persist.

**persona,** *n.f.* person.

**personàggio,** *n.m.* personage.

**personale,** 1. *n.m.* personnel, staff. 2. *adj.* personal.

**personalità,** *n.f.* personality.

**personalmente,** *adv.* personally.

**persuadere,** *vb.* persuade.

**persuasivo,** *adj.* persuasive.

**pèrtica,** *n.f.* perch; pole.

**pertinènte,** *adj.* pertinent, relevant.

**perturbare,** *vb.* perturb.

**pervàdere,** *vb.* pervade.

**perversione,** *n.f* perversion.

**pervèrso,** *adj.* perverse.

**pervertire,** *vb.* pervert, debauch.

**pesante,** *adj.* heavy.

**pesare,** *vb.* weigh; balance.

**pesca,** *n.f.* fishing.

**pèsca,** *n.f.* peach.

**pescàggio,** *n.m.* draft.

**pescare,** *vb.* fish; angle.

**pescatore,** *n.m.* fisherman.

**pesce,** *n.m.* fish. **p. rosso,** goldfish. **p. spada,** swordfish.

**pececane,** *n.m.* shark; profiteer.

**peschièra,** *n.f.* fishery.

**pesciolino,** *n.f.* minnow.

**pescivèndola,** *n.f.* fishwife.

**pescivèndolo,** *n.m.* fishmonger.

**pèsco,** *n.m.* peach-tree.

**peso,** *n.m.* weight. **p. màssimo,** heavyweight. **p. lordo,** gross weight.

**pessimismo,** *n.m.* pessimism.

**pestare,** *vb.* pound.

**pèste,** *n.f.* plague.

**pestilènza,** *n.f.* pestilence.

**pesto,** *adj.* pounded, crushed. **òcchio p.,** black eye.

**pètalo,** *n.m.* petal.

**petardo,** *n.m.* firecracker.

**petizione,** *n.f.* petition.

**petròlio,** *n.m.* petroleum. **p. raffinato,** kerosene.

**pettégola,** *n.f.* gossip.

**pettegolare,** *vb.* gossip.

**pettegolezzo,** *n.m.* gossip.

**pettégolo,** 1. *n.m.* gossip. 2. *adj.* gossipy.

**pettinare,** *vb.* comb.

**pettinatura,** *n.f.* coiffure, hair-do.

**pèttine,** *n.m.* comb.

**pettirosso,** *n.m.* robin.

**pètto,** *n.m.* chest, bosom; (meat) brisket.

---

**petulante**, *adj.* petulant.

**petulanza**, *n.f.* petulance, huff.

**pèzza**, *n.f.* patch.

**pezzettino**, *n.m.* little bit, mite.

**pezzetto**, *n.m.* scrap.

**pèzzo**, *n.m.* piece, bit, chunk. **p. di ricàmbio**, spare part. **p. grosso**, big shot.

**piacere**, 1. *n.m.* pleasure. 2. *vb.* please.

**piacévole**, *adj.* pleasing, pleasant, agreeable, genial.

**piacevolezza**, *n.f.* pleasing quality, geniality.

**piacevolmente**, *adv.* pleasingly, agreeably, genially.

**piaga**, *n.f.* sore; wound.

**piagnucolare**, *vb.* whimper, snivel, blubber.

**piagnucolone**, *n.m.* whiner, whimperer, sniveler, complainer.

**piagnucoloso**, *adj.* maudlin.

**pialla**, *n.f.* plane.

**piallàccio**, *n.m.* veneer.

**piallare**, *vb.* plane.

**pianeta**, *n.m.* planet.

**piàngere**, *vb.* weep, cry, bewail, mourn.

**pianista**, *n.m.* pianist.

**piano**, 1. *n.m.* plan; storey; floor; plane. 2. *adj.* level, flat.

**pianofòrte**, *n.m.* piano.

**pianta**, *n.f.* plant; plan, plot; map.

**piantagione**, *n.f.* plantation.

**piantare**, *vb.* plant.

**piantatore**, *n.m.* planter.

**pianto**, *n.m.* crying, weeping.

**pianura**, *n.f.* plain.

**pianuzza**, *n.f.* halibut.

**piattaforma**, *n.f.* platform, dais.

**piattino**, *n.m.* saucer.

**piatto**, 1. *n.m.* dish, plate; cymbal. 2. *adj.* flat.

**piazza**, *n.f.* square.

**piazzale**, *n.m.* large square.

**piccante**, *adj.* piquant.

**picchetto**, *n.m.* picket.

**picchiare**, *vb.* hit, smack, sock, clout, cuff, rap.

**picchiata**, *n.f.* nose dive.

**picchiatore**, *n.m.* dive-bomber.

**picchio**, *n.m.* blow, rap.

**piccione**, *n.m.* pigeon.

**viaggiatore**, homing pigeon; carrier pigeon.

**picco**, *n.m.* peak, crag.

**piccolo**, *adj.* little, small; petty.

**piccone**, *n.m.* pick.

**pidòcchio**, *n.m.* louse.

**piède**, *n.m.* foot. **p. stòrto**, clubfoot.

**piedestallo**, *n.m.* pedestal.

**pièga**, *n.f.* fold, crease, pleat, tuck.

**piegare**, *vb.* fold, bend, crease.

**pieghévole**, *adj.* pliable, pliant.

**Piemonte**, *n.m.* Piedmont.

**piemontese**, *adj.* Piedmontese.

**pienamente**, *adv.* fully.

**pienezza**, *n.f.* fullness.

**pieno**, *adj.* full.

**pietà**, *n.f.* mercy, pity, piety.

**pietoso**, *adj.* merciful, pitiful.

**piètra**, *n.f.* stone. **p. angolare**, cornerstone. **p. focaia**, flint.

**pietrificare**, *vb.* petrify.

**piffero**, *n.m.* fife; fifer, piper.

**pigiama**, *n.m.pl.* pyjamas.

**pigione**, *n.f.* rent.

**pigmènto**, *n.m.* pigment.

**pigro**, *adj.* lazy.

**pila**, *n.f.* battery. **p. a secco**, dry cell.

**pilastro**, *n.m.* pillar.

**pillola**, *n.f.* pill.

**pilone**, *n.m.* pier; pillar.

**pilòta**, *n.m.* pilot.

**pinna**, *n.f.* fin.

**pinnàcolo**, *n.m.* pinnacel.

**pino**, *n.m.* pine.

**pinta**, *n.f.* pint.

**pinze**, *n.f.pl.* pincers, pliers.

**pinzette**, *n.f.pl.* pliers.

**pio**, *adj.* pious.

**pioggerèlla**, *n.f.* drizzle.

**pioggia**, *n.f.* rain.

**piombo**, *n.m.* lead.

**pionière**, *n.m.* pioneer.

**piòta**, *n.f.* turf, sod.

**piòvere**, *vb.* rain.

**piovigginare**, *vb.* drizzle.

**piovoso**, *adj.* rainy.

**pipa**, *n.f.* pipe.

**pipistrèllo**, *n.m.* bat.

**pipita**, *n.f.* hangnail.

**piràmide**, *n.f.* pyramid.

**pirata**, *n.m.* pirate.

**piroscafo**, *n.m.* steamship.

**p. pisèllo**, *n.m.* pea.

**pisolino,** *n.m.* doze, snooze, nap.

**pista,** *n.f.* (race) track; (race) course; (cinder) path. **p. d'atterràggio,** landing strip, runway.

**pistola,** *n.f.* pistol.

**pistone,** *n.m.* piston.

**pittore,** *n.m.* painter.

**pittoresco,** *adj.* picturesque.

**pittura,** *n.f.* painting.

**più, 1.** *adv.* more; **per di p.,** moreover; **per lo p.,** mostly. **2.** *prep.* plus.

**piuma,** *n.f.* plume, feather.

**piumàggio,** *n.m.* plumage.

**piumato,** *adj.* plumed, feathered.

**piumino,** *n.m.* feathers.

**piumoso,** *adj.* feathery.

**piuòlo,** *n.m.* peg, rung.

**piuttosto,** *adv.* rather.

**pizzicòtto,** *n.m.* nip, pinch.

**pizzo,** *n.m.* lace.

**placare,** *vb.* appease, placate.

**placatore,** *n.m.* appeaser.

**plàcido,** *adj.* placid.

**plàgio,** *n.m.* plagiarism.

**planetàrio, 1.** *n.m.* planetarium. **2.** *adj.* planetary.

**plasma,** *n.m.* plasma.

**plàstica,** *n.f.* plastic; **plàstico,** *adj.* plastic.

**plàtino,** *n.m.* platinum.

**plausìbile,** *adj.* plausible.

**plebàglia,** *n.f.* mob, rabble.

**plebiscito,** *n.m.* plebiscite.

**pleurite,** *n.f.* pleurisy.

**plotone,** *n.m.* platoon.

**plùmbeo,** *adj.* leaden.

**plurale,** *n.m. and adj.* plural.

**plutòcrate,** *n.m.* plutocrat.

**pneumàtico, 1.** *n.* tire. **2.** *adj.* pneumatic.

**po', n. un p.,** a little, somewhat.

**pòchi,** *adj. and pron. pl.* few.

**pòco,** *n. and adv.* little. **fra p.,** in a short time, presently, soon.

**poèma,** *n.m.* poem.

**poesìa,** *n.* poem; poetry.

**poèta,** *n.f.* poet.

**poètico,** *adj.* poetic.

**pòi,** *adv.* then.

**poiana,** *n.f.* buzzard.

**poiché,** *conj.* since.

**polacca,** *n.f.* polonaise.

**polacco,** *adj.* Polish.

**polare,** *adj.* polar.

**poligamìa,** *n.f.* polygamy.

**poliglòtto,** *adj.* polyglot.

**polìgono,** *n.m.* polygon.

**polìtica,** *n.f.* politics; policy.

**polìtico, 1.** *n.m.* politician. **2.** *adj.* politic, political.

**polizìa,** *n.f.* police.

**poliziòtto,** *n.m.* policeman, cop.

**polizza,** *n.f.* policy.

**pollame,** *n.m.* poultry.

**pòllice,** *n.m.* thumb; big toe; inch.

**pòlline,** *n.m.* pollen.

**pollo,** *n.m.* chicken, fowl.

**polmonare,** *adj.* pulmonary.

**polmone,** *n.m.* lung.

**polmonite,** *n.f.* pneumonia.

**pòlo,** *n.m.* pole.

**Polònia,** *n.f.* Poland.

**polpa,** *n.f.* pulp.

**polpetta,** *n.f.* meat-ball; croquette.

**polsino,** *n.m.* cuff.

**polso,** *n.m.* wrist; pulse.

**poltrona,** *n.f.* armchair, easy-chair.

**pólvere,** *n.m.* dust; powder.

**polverizzare,** *vb.* pulverize; powder.

**polveroso,** *adj.* dusty.

**pomeriggio,** *n.m.* afternoon.

**pomo,** *n.m.* apple.

**pomodoro,** *n.m.* tomato.

**pompa,** *n.f.* pump; pomp. **p. da incèndio,** fire engine.

**pompare,** *vb.* pump.

**pompèlmo,** *n.m.* grapefruit.

**pompière,** *n.m.* fireman.

**pomposo,** *adj.* pompous.

**pònce,** *n.m.* punch.

**ponderare,** *vb.* ponder.

**ponderoso,** *adj.* ponderous.

**ponte,** *n.m.* bridge; deck; span. **p. levatòio,** drawbridge. **p. sospeso,** suspension bridge.

**pontéfice,** *n.m.* pontiff.

**pontile,** *n.m.* gangplank.

**pontone,** *n.m.* pontoon.

**popelina,** *n.f.* broadcloth.

**popolare,** *adj.* popular.

**popolarità,** *n.f.* popularity.

**popolazione,** *n.f.* population.

**pòpolo,** *n.m.* people, folk.

**poppa,** *n.f.* stern; breast.

**pòrca,** *n.f.* sow; ridge.

**porcellana,** *n.f.* porcelain, china.

**porcellino,** *n.m.* piglet. **p. d' India,** guinea pig.

**porcile,** *n.m.* sty.

pòrco, *n.m.* hog, pig, swine.

pornografìa, *n.f.* pornography.

pòro, *n.m.* pore.

poroso, *adj.* porous.

pórpora, *n.f.* purple.

porre, *vb.* put, place, set, lay.

pòrro, *n.m.* leek.

pòrta, *n.f.* door; gate; gateway; goal.

portabagagli, *n.m.* porter.

portacéneri, *n.m.* ash-tray.

portaèrei, *n.m.* aircraft carrier, flat-top.

portafògli, *n.m.* billfold, wallet; pocketbook.

portafòglio, *n.m.* portfolio.

portafortuna, *n.m.* goodluck charm; mascot.

portale, *n.m.* portal.

portare, *vb.* carry, bear, bring; wear.

portasigarette, *n.m.* cigarette-holder.

portata, *n.f.* reach; range, scope.

portàtile, *adj.* portable.

portatore, *n.m.* carrier, bearer.

portavóce, *n.m.* spokesman, mouthpiece.

pòrtico, *n.m.* portico, porch.

portièra, *n.f.* door.

portière, *n.m.* goal-keeper; porter.

portinaio, *n.m.* doorman, concierge.

portinerìa, *n.f.* concierge's office.

pòrto, *n.m.* port, harbor, haven, inlet.

Portogallo, *n.m.* Portugal.

portoghese, *adj.* Portuguese.

portone, *n.m.* gate.

porzione, *n.f.* portion, helping, share.

pòsa, *n.f.* pose; exposure.

posare, *vb.* pose.

posarsi, *vb.* perch.

posaterìa, *n.f.* cutlery.

posatòio, *n.m.* perch.

poscritto, *n.m.* postscript.

positivo, *adj.* positive.

posizione, *n.f.* position.

posporre, *vb.* postpone.

possedère, *vb.* possess, own.

possènte, *adj.* powerful.

possessivo, *adj.* possessive.

possèsso, *n.m.* possession, belonging.

possessore, *n.m.* possessor, owner.

possìbile, *adj.* possible.

possibilità, *n.f.* possibility.

possibilmente, *adv.* possibly.

pòsta, *n.f.* mail, post.

postale, *adj.* postal.

posteggio, *n.m.* parking.

pòsteri, *n.m.pl.* posterity.

posteriore, *adj.* posterior, rear, back, hind.

posterità, *n.f.* posterity.

postino, *n.m.* mailman, postman.

pòsto, *n.m.* place; post; room; spout.

potàssio, *n.m.* potassium.

potènte, *adj.* powerful, potent, forcible, mighty.

potènza, *n.f.* power, might.

potenziale, *n.m. and adj.* potential.

potere, **1.** *n.m.* power. **2.** *vb.* be able, can, may.

pòvero, **1.** *n.m.* poor man, pauper. **2.** *adj.* poor.

povertà, *n.f.* poverty.

pozione, *n.f.* potion.

pozzànghera, *n.f.* puddle.

pòzzo, *n.m.* well; shaft. **p. nero,** cesspool.

prammàtico, *adj.* pragmatic.

pranzare, *vb.* dine.

pranzo, *n.m.* dinner.

praterìa, *n.f.* prairie.

pràtica, *n.f.* practice.

praticàbile, *adj.* passable; practicable.

praticamente, *adv.* practically.

praticare, *vb.* practice.

pràtico, *adj.* practical, businesslike. **p. di,** skilled in; acquainted with, familiar with.

prato, *n.m.* meadow, field; lawn.

preàmbolo, *n.m.* preamble.

preavvertire, *vb.* forewarn.

precàrio, *adj.* precarious.

precauzione, *n.f.* precaution.

precedènte, **1.** *n.m.* precedent. **2.** *adj.* preceding, former, previous.

precedènza, *n.f.* precedence right of way.

precedère, *vb.* precede, go before, (in time) antedate.

precètto, *n.m.* precept.

precinto, *n.m.* precinct.

precipitare, *vb.* precipitate; (*refl.*) rush.

precipìzio, *n.m.* precipice.

For pronunciation, see the concise guide on pages 5 to 7.

**precisione**, *n.f.* precision.
**preciso**, *adj.* precise.
**precludere**, *vb.* preclude.
**precòce**, *adj.* precocious.
**precursore**, *n.m.* precursor, forerunner, harbinger.
**prèda**, *n.f.* prey.
**predare**, *vb.* plunder, forage.
**predatòrio**, *adj.* predatory.
**predecessore**, *n.m.* predecessor.
**predestinazione**, *n.f.* predestination.
**predicare**, *vb.* preach.
**predicato**, *n.m.* predicate.
**predicatore**, *n.m.* preacher.
**predilètto**, *n. and adj.* favorite, darling.
**predilezione**, *n.f.* predilection.
**predire**, *vb.* predict, foretell.
**predisporre**, *vb.* predispose, bias.
**predominante**, *adj.* predominant.
**predominio**, *n.m.* dominance.
**prefabbricato**, *adj.* prefabricated.
**prefazione**, *n.f.* preface, foreword.
**preferènza**, *n.f.* preference.
**preferibile**, *adj.* preferable.
**preferire**, *vb.* prefer.
**prefètto**, *n.m.* prefect.
**prefisso**, *n.m.* prefix.
**pregare**, *vb.* pray, beg.
**preghièra**, *n.f.* prayer, request, plea.
**pregiudicare**, *vb.* prejudice.
**pregiudizio**, *n.m.* prejudice, bias.
**prègna**, *adj.f.* pregnant.
**pregustare**, *vb.* foretaste.
**pregustazione**, *n.f.* foretaste.
**preistòrico**, *adj.* prehistoric.
**preliminare**, *adj.* preliminary.
**prelùdio**, *n.m.* prelude.
**prematuro**, *adj.* premature.
**premeditare**, *vb.* premeditate.
**prèmere**, *vb.* press.
**premessa**, *n.f.* premise.
**premiare**, *vb.* award (a prize to); reward.
**prèmio**, *n.m.* prize, award, premium.
**premonizione**, *n.f.* premonition.
**premurosamente**, *adv.* considerately.

**premuroso**, *adj.* considerate.
**prenatale**, *adj.* prenatal.
**préndere**, *vb.* take; get; catch.
**prenotare**, *vb.* reserve.
**prenotazione**, *n.f.* reservation.
**preoccupare**, *vb.* worry.
**preoccupazione**, *n.f.* worry.
**preparare**, *vb.* prepare.
**preparatòrio**, *adj.* preparatory.
**preparazione**, *n.f.* preparation.
**preponderante**, *adj.* preponderant.
**preposizione**, *n.f.* preposition.
**prepotènte**, **1.** *adj.* overbearing, tyrannical. **2.** *n.* bully.
**prerogativa**, *n.f.* prerogative.
**presa**, *n.f.* grasp, grip, hold; (electrical) outlet; socket. **p. di tèrra**, (electrical) earth.
**presàgio**, *n.m.* omen, portent.
**presagire**, *vb.* presage, predict, forebode, foreshadow, portend.
**prescrìvere**, *vb.* prescribe.
**prescrizione**, *n.f.* prescription.
**presentàbile**, *adj.* presentable.
**presentare**, *vb.* present, introduce.
**presentazione**, *n.f.* presentation, introduction.
**presènte**, *adj.* present.
**presentimento**, *n.m.* presentiment, foreboding.
**presentire**, *vb.* forebode.
**presènza**, *n.f.* presence.
**preservare**, *vb.* preserve.
**presidènte**, *n.m.* president, chairman.
**presidènza**, *n.f.* presidency, chairmanship.
**presièdere**, *vb.* preside.
**prèssa**, *n.f.* press.
**pressappòco**, *adv.* about, approximately.
**pressione**, *n.f.* pressure.
**prèsso a**, *prep.* near; by.
**prestare**, *vb.* lend, loan.
**prestìgio**, *n.m.* prestige.
**prèstito**, *n.m.* loan.
**prèsto**, *adv.* soon, quickly; early.
**presùmere**, *vb.* presume.

**presuntuosità,** *n.f.* presumptuousness, forwardness.

**presuntuoso,** *adj.* presumptuous.

**presunzione,** *n.f.* presumption.

**presupporre,** *vb.* presuppose.

**prète,** *n.m.* priest.

**pretèndere,** *vb.* pretend; claim.

**pretenzioso,** *adj.* pretentious.

**pretesa,** *n.f.* pretense.

**pretèsto,** *n.m.* pretext.

**prevalènte,** *adj.* prevalent.

**prevalere,** *vb.* prevail.

**prevedere,** *vb.* foresee, forecast.

**prevedìbile,** *adj.* foreseeable.

**preventivo,** **1.** *n.m.* estimate; budget. **2.** *adj.* preventive.

**prevenzione,** *n.f.* prevention.

**previdènza,** *n.f.* foresight.

**previsione,** *n.f.* forecast.

**prezioso,** *adj.* precious, valuable.

**prezzémolo,** *n.m.* parsley.

**prèzzo,** *n.m.* price, charge; fare; rate.

**prigione,** *n.f.* prison, jail.

**prigionìa,** *n.f.* imprisonment, captivity.

**prigionièro** *n.m. and adj.* prisoner, captive.

**prima,** **1.** *n.* première. **2.** *adv.* first; before; beforehand.

**prima che,** *conj.* before.

**prima di,** *prep.* before.

**primàrio,** *adj.* primary.

**primato,** *n.m.* record.

**primavera,** *n.f.* spring.

**primitivo,** *adj.* primitive; original.

**primo,** *adj.* first; foremost; prime.

**principale,** *adj.* principal, chief, main, prime.

**principalmente,** *adv.* principally, chiefly, mainly.

**prìncipe,** *n.m.* prince.

**principéssa,** *n.f.* princess.

**principiante,** *n.m.* beginner.

**principiare,** *vb.* begin.

**princìpio,** *n.m.* beginning; principle.

**priorità,** *n.f.* priority.

**prisma,** *n.m.* prism.

**privare,** *vb.* deprive, bereave.

**privato,** *adj.* private.

**privazione,** *n.f.* deprivation.

**privilègio,** *n.m.* privilege.

**privo,** *adj.* devoid, void, lacking (in); destitute.

**probàbile,** *adj.* probable.

**probabilità,** *n.f.* probability, likelihood.

**probità,** *n.f.* probity.

**problèma,** *n.m.* problem.

**procèdere,** *vb.* proceed.

**procedimento,** *n.m.* proceeding; procedure.

**procedura,** *n.f.* procedure.

**processione,** *n.f.* procession.

**procèsso,** *n.m.* process; trial.

**proclamare,** *vb.* proclaim.

**proclamazione,** *n.f.* proclamation.

**procrastinare,** *vb.* procrastinate.

**procura,** *n.f.* proxy.

**procurare,** *vb.* procure.

**procuratore,** *n.m.* attorney; proxy.

**prodezza,** *n.f.* prowess.

**prodigalità,** *n.f.* prodigality, extravagance.

**prodigare,** *vb.* lavish.

**prodìgio,** *n.m.* prodigy.

**pròdigo,** *adj.* prodigal, extravagant, lavish.

**proditòrio,** *adj.* treacherous.

**prodotto,** *n.m.* product.

**produrre,** *vb.* produce.

**produttivo,** *adj.* productive.

**produzione,** *n.f.* production, output, yield.

**profanare,** *vb.* profane, defile.

**profano,** *adj.* profane.

**proferire,** *vb.* utter.

**professare,** *vb.* profess.

**professionale,** *adj.* professional.

**professione,** *n.f.* profession, calling, occupation.

**professionista,** *n.m.* professional; practitioner.

**professore,** *n.m.* professor.

**profèta,** *n.m.* prophet.

**profètico,** *adj.* prophetic.

**profètizzare,** *vb.* prophesy.

**profezìa,** *n.f.* prophecy.

**profilo,** *n.m.* profile.

**profitto,** *n.m.* profit.

**profondamente,** *adv.* deeply, profoundly.

**profondità,** *n.f.* profundity, depth.

**profondo,** *adj.* deep, profound.

**profumare,** *vb.* perfume.

**profumo,** *n.m.* perfume, scent.

**profuso**, *adj.* profuse.

**progettare**, *vb.* project, plan.

**progetto**, *n.m.* project, plan, scheme. **p. di legge**, (legislative) bill.

**prognosi**, *n.f.* prognosis.

**programma**, *n.m.* program.

**progredire**, *vb.* progress, advance.

**progredito**, *adj.* progressed; advanced.

**progressivo**, *adj.* progressive.

**progresso**, *n.m.* progress, headway.

**proibire**, *vb.* prohibit, forbid, ban.

**proibitivo**, *adj.* prohibitive.

**proibizione**, *n.f.* prohibition, ban.

**proiettare**, *vb.* project.

**proiettile**, *n.m.* projectile.

**proiettore**, *n.m.* projector.

**proiezione**, *n.f.* projection.

**prole**, *n.f.* offspring, issue.

**prolifico**, *adj.* prolific.

**prologo**, *n.m.* prologue.

**prolungamento**, *n.m.* prolongation, extension.

**prolungare**, *vb.* prolong, extend.

**promessa**, *n.f.* promise.

**promettere**, *vb.* promise.

**prominente**, *adj.* prominent.

**promiscuo**, *adj.* promiscuous.

**promozione**, *n.f.* promotion.

**promuovere**, *vb.* promote.

**promulgare**, *vb.* promulgate.

**pronome**, *n.m.* pronoun.

**pronosticare**, *vb.* forecast.

**pronosticatore**, *n.m.* forecaster.

**prontamente**, *adv.* readily.

**pronto**, **1.** *adj.* ready; prompt; quick; willing. **2.** *interj.* (telephone) hello.

**pronuncia**, *n.f.* pronunciation.

**pronunciare**, *vb.* pronounce.

**propaganda**, *n.f.* propaganda.

**propagare**, *vb.* propagate.

**propendere**, *vb.* incline.

**propensione**, *n.f.* propensity.

**propenso**, *adj.* inclined.

**propizio**, *adj.* propitious, favorable.

**proponente**, *n.m.* proponent.

**proporre**, *vb.* propose.

**proporzionato**, *adj.* proportionate.

**proporzione**, *n.f.* proportion.

**proposito**, *n.m.* purpose. **a**

**p.**, apropos. **di p.**, on purpose.

**proposizione**, *n.f.* sentence.

**proprietà**, *n.f.* property, belongings.

**proposta**, *n.f.* proposal; proposition.

**proprietario**, *n.m.* proprietor.

**proprio**, **1.** *adj.* proper; own. **2.** *adv.* just; right; quite.

**propugnare**, *vb.* advocate.

**propugnatore**, *n.m.* advocate.

**propugnazione**, *n.f.* advocacy.

**prora**, *n.f.* prow, bow.

**proroga**, *n.f.* delay; extension.

**prorogare**, *vb.* delay; extend.

**prorompere**, *vb.* burst forth.

**prosa**, *n.f.* prose.

**prosaico**, *adj.* prosaic.

**prosciutto**, *n.m.* ham.

**proscrivere**, *vb.* proscribe.

**prosperare**, *vb.* prosper, thrive.

**prosperità**, *n.f.* prosperity, boom.

**prospero**, *adj.* prosperous.

**prospettiva**, *n.f.* perspective.

**prospettivo**, *adj.* prospective.

**prospetto**, *n.m.* prospect.

**prossimità**, *n.f.* proximity, nearness, closeness.

**prossimo**, **1.** *n.* neighbor. **2.** *adj.* next; nearest; forthcoming.

**prostituta**, *n.f.* prostitute.

**prostrare**, *vb.* prostrate.

**prostrato**, *adj.* prostrate.

**proteggere**, *vb.* protect, shield.

**proteina**, *n.f.* protein.

**protesta**, *n.f.* protest.

**protestante**, *n.m. and adj.* Protestant.

**protestantesimo**, *n.m.* Protestantism.

**protestare**, *vb.* protest.

**protettivo**, *adj.* protective.

**protettore**, *n.m.* protector.

**protezione**, *n.f.* protection.

**protocollo**, *n.m.* protocol.

**protone**, *n.m.* proton.

**protrarre**, *vb.* protract.

**protuberanza**, *n.f.* protuberance, swelling, bulge, lump.

**prova**, *n.f.* proof; test; ordeal; rehearsal; probation; trial. **p. conclusiva**, acid test. **p. generale**, dress rehearsal.

**provare**, *vb.* try; essay; rehearse; test.

**proverbiale**, *adj.* proverbial.

**provèrbio**, *n.m.* proverb, adage.

**provincia**, *n.f.* province.

**provinciale**, *adj.* provincial.

**provocante**, *adj.* defiant.

**provocare**, *vb.* provoke.

**provocazione**, *n.f.* provocation.

**provvedere**, *vb.* provide, supply.

**provvidènza**, *n.f.* providence.

**provvisòrio**, *adj.* temporary, acting, interim.

**provvista**, *n.f.* provision; supply, store, stock.

**prudènte**, *adj.* prudent.

**prudènza**, *n.f.* prudence.

**prùdere**, *vb.* itch.

**prudore**, *n.m.* itch.

**prugna**, *n.f.* plum.

**prurire**, *vb.* itch.

**prurito**, *n.m.* itch.

**pseudònimo**, *n.m.* pseudonym.

**psichiatra**, *n.m.* psychiatrist.

**psichiatrìa**, *n.f.* psychiatry.

**psicoanàlisi**, *n.f.* psychoanalysis.

**psicologìa**, *n.f.* psychology.

**psicològico**, *adj.* psychological.

**psicòsi**, *n.f.* psychosis.

**ptomaìna**, *n.f.* ptomaine.

**pubblicare**, *vb.* publish.

**pubblicazione**, *n.f.* publication.

**pubblicità**, *n.f.* publicity; advertising.

**pubblico**, *n. and adj.* public.

**pugilato**, *n.m.* boxing.

**pugilatore**, *n.m.* boxer.

**pugilìstico**, *adj.* pugilistic, fistic.

**Pùglie**, *n.f.pl.* Apulia.

**pugliese**, *adj.* Apulian.

**pugnace**, *adj.* pugnacious.

**pugnalare**, *vb.* stab.

**pugnalata**, *n.f.* stab.

**pugnale**, *n.m.* dagger.

**pugno**, *n.m.* fist; punch.

**pula**, *n.f.* chaff.

**pulce**, *n.f.* flea.

**pulcino**, *n.m.* chick.

**puledro**, *n.m.* colt.

**pulèggia**, *n.f.* pulley.

**pulire**, *vb.* clean; polish. **p. a secco**, dry-clean.

**pulito**, *adj.* clean; polished.

**pulitore**, *n.m.* cleaner.

**pulitura**, *n.f.* cleaning. **p. a secco**, dry-cleaning.

**pulizìa**, *n.f.* cleanliness.

**pullman**, *n.m.* de luxe bus.

**pùlpito**, *n.m.* pulpit.

**pulsare**, *vb.* pulsate.

**pungènte**, *adj.* pungent, sharp, biting.

**pùngere**, *vb.* prick, sting.

**pungiglione**, *n.m.* sting.

**pùngolo**, *n.m.* goad.

**punire**, *vb.* punish, chastise.

**punitivo**, *adj.* punitive.

**punizione**, *n.f.* punishment, chastisement.

**punta**, *n.f.* tip.

**puntare**, *vb.* point; aim; wager, stake.

**puntata**, *n.f.* installment.

**punteggiare**, *vb.* punctuate.

**punteggiatura**, *n.f.* punctuation.

**puntellare**, *vb.* prop.

**puntèllo**, *n.m.* prop.

**puntina**, *n.f.* needle.

**punto**, *n.m.* point; period; dot; stitch. **p. di vista**, viewpoint; standpoint. **due punti**, colon. **p. mòrto**, stalemate, deadlock. **p. esclamativo**, exclamation point. **p. e virgola**, semicolon.

**puntuale**, *adj.* punctual.

**puntura**, *n.f.* puncture; sting.

**pupàttola**, *n.f.* doll.

**pupillo**, *n.m.* ward.

**purchè**, *conj.* provided that.

**purezza**, *n.f.* purity.

**purga**, *n.f.* purge.

**purgante**, *n.m. and adj.* purgative, laxative.

**purgare**, *vb.* purge.

**purgativo**, *adj.* cathartic.

**purificare**, *vb.* purify.

**purità**, *n.f.* purity.

**puro**, *adj.* pure.

**putrefatto**, *adj.* rotten, decayed.

**putrefazione**, *n.f.* rot.

**pùtrido**, *adj.* decayed, putrid, rotten; (egg) addled.

**pùttana**, *n.f.* whore, tart.

**puzzare**, *vb.* stink, smell.

**puzzo**, *n.m.* stench, smell.

**puzzolènte**, *adj.* stinking, noisome.

**puzzone**, *n.m.* skunk.

---

For pronunciation, see the concise guide on pages 5 to 7.

# Q

qua, *adv.* hither.

quadràngolo, *n.m.* quadrangle.

quadrante, *n.m.* quadrant; dial.

quadrare, *vb.* square.

quadrato, 1. *n.m.* square; ring. 2. *adj.* square.

quadro, *n.m.* picture; table; cadre.

quadrùpede, *n.m.* quadruped.

quàglia, *n.f.* quail.

quagliare, *vb.* curdle.

quagliata, *n.f.* curd, clabber.

qualche, *adj.* some.

qualcosa, *pron.* something; anything.

qualcuno, *pron.* somebody; anybody.

quale, *adj.* which. il q., which; who.

qualìfica, *n.f.* qualification.

qualificare, *vb.* qualify.

qualificazione, *n.f.* qualification.

qualità, *n.f.* quality.

qualunque, *adj.* whatever; whichever.

quando, *adv.* when. di q. in q., from time to time, occasionally.

quantità, *n.f.* quantity, amount.

quanto, *adj. and adv.* how much; how many. in q. che, in so far as.

quantunque, *conj.* although.

quaranta, *num.* forty.

quarantèsimo, *adj.* fortieth.

quarentena, *n.f.* quarantine.

quarésima, *n.f.* Lent.

quartetto, *n.m.* quartet.

quartière, *n.m.* quarter. q. generale, headquarters.

quarto, 1. *n.* quarter. 2. *adj.* fourth.

quarzo, *n.m.* quartz.

quasi, 1. *adv.* almost, nearly. 2. *conj.* as if.

quattòrdici, *num.* fourteen.

quattro, *num.* four.

quegli, *adj.m.pl.* those.

quei, *adj.m.pl.* those.

quel, *adj.m.sg.* that.

quella, *adj. and pron. f.sg.* that.

quelle, *adj. and pron. f.pl.* those.

quelli, *pron.m.pl.* those.

quello, 1. *adj.* that. 2. *pron.* that one; the former.

quèrcia, *n.f.* oak.

questa, *adj. and pron. f.sg.* this.

queste, *adj. and pron. f.pl.* these.

questi, *pron. m.sg.* this man.

questionàrio, *n.m.* questionnaire.

questione, *n.f.* question.

questo, 1. *adj.* this. 2. *pron.* this one; the latter.

quèstua, *n.f.* (church) collection.

qui, *adv.* here.

quietanza, *n.f.* receipt.

quìete, *n.f.* quiet, stillness.

quièto, *adj.* quiet.

quindi, *adv.* hence, therefore.

quindicèsimo, *adj.* fifteenth.

quìndici, *num.* fifteen.

quindicinale, *adj.* fortnightly, bimonthly.

quintètto, *n.m.* quintet.

quinto, *adj.* fifth.

quòta, *n.f.* quota; dues; fee.

quotidianamente, *adv.* daily.

quotidiano, *n.m. and adj.* daily, everyday.

---

# R

**rabàrbaro,** *n.m.* rhubarb.

**rabberciare,** *vb.* botch.

**ràbbia,** *n.f.* anger; rage; rabies.

**rabbino,** *n.m.* rabbi.

**rabbioso,** *adj.* rabid.

**rabbrividire,** *vb.* shudder; shiver.

**racchetta,** *n.f.* racket.

**raccògliere,** *vb.* collect, gather; harvest, reap.

**raccòlta,** *n.f.* collection, gathering; harvest, crop.

**raccòlto,** *n.m.* crop, harvest.

**raccomandare,** *vb.* recommend; commend.

**raccomandazione,** *n.f.* recommendation.

**raccontare,** *vb.* tell, narrate.

**racconto,** *n.m.* story, tale, account, narrative.

**raccorciamento,** *n.m.* abbreviation; shortening.

**raccorciare,** *vb.* abbreviate; shorten.

**raddrizzare,** *vb.* straighten.

**ràdere,** *vb.* shave.

**radiatore,** *n.m.* radiator.

**radicale,** *n.m.* and *adj.* radical.

**radicchiélla,** *n.f.* dandelion.

**radice,** *n.f.* root.

**ràdio,** *n.* **1.** *m.* radium. **2.** *f.* radio, wireless.

**radioattivo,** *adj.* radio-active.

**radiocorrière,** *n.m.* radio news.

**radiofònico,** *adj.* radio.

**radiotelemetria,** *n.f.* radar.

**radiotelèmetro,** *n.m.* radar.

**rado,** *adj.* sparse.

**radunare,** *vb.* gather; muster.

**raduno,** *n.m.* rally.

**radura,** *n.f.* glade, clearing.

**ràfano,** *n.m.* horse-radish.

**raffazzonamento,** *n.m.* re-working; patchwork.

**raffermo,** *adj.* stale.

**ràffica,** *n.f.* gust; squall; blast.

**raffinare,** *vb.* refine.

**raffinatezza,** *n.f.* refinement.

**ràffio,** *n.m.* claw.

**rafforzare,** *vb.* strengthen.

**raffreddare,** *vb.* chill.

**raffreddore,** *n.m.* cold.

**raffrenare,** *vb.* restrain, curb.

**ragazza,** *n.f.* girl, lass.

**ragazzo,** *n.m.* boy, lad.

**raggiante,** *adj.* radiant, beaming.

**ràggio,** *n.m.* spoke; ray; beam; shaft; radius.

**raggiùngere,** *vb.* arrive at, achieve, attain; reach; overtake.

**raggiungìbile,** *adj.* attainable.

**raggiungimento,** *n.m.* achievement, attainment.

**ragionare,** *vb.* reason; talk.

**ragione,** *n.f.* reason. **aver r.,** be right.

**ragioneria,** *n.f.* accounting.

**ragionévole,** *adj.* reasonable.

**ragionière,** *n.m.* accountant.

**raggrumarsi,** *vb.* clot.

**raggruppare,** *vb.* group.

**ragliare,** *vb.* bray.

**raglio,** *n.m.* bray.

**ragnatelo,** *n.m.* cobweb.

**ragno,** *n.m.* spider.

**ràion,** *n.m.* rayon.

**rallegrare,** *vb.* cheer up, rejoice.

**rallentare,** *vb.* slow down, slacken.

**ramaiuolo,** *n.m.* ladle; scoop.

**ramanzina,** *n.f.* scolding.

**rame,** *n.m.* copper.

**rammendare,** *vb.* mend, darn.

**rammendatura,** *n.f.* mend, darn.

**rammentare,** *vb.* remind; (*refl.*) recollect.

**ramo,** *n.m.* branch, bough, limb.

**ramolàccio,** *n.m.* radish.

**ramoscèllo,** *n.m.* twig; sprig.

**rana,** *n.f.* frog.

**ràncido,** *adj.* rancid.

**ràncio,** *n.m.* mess.

**rancore,** *n.m.* rancor.

**rango,** *n.m.* rank.

**rannicchiarsi,** *vb.* huddle.

**rannuvolarsi,** *vb.* cloud over.

**ranòcchio,** *n.m.* frog.

---

**ràntolo,** *n.m.* rattle.

**ranùncolo,** *n.m.* buttercup.

**rapa,** *n.f.* turnip.

**rapidamente,** *adv.* rapidly, quickly, fast.

**ràpido,** **1.** *n.m.* limited (train). **2.** *adj.* rapid, fast, quick, speedy.

**rapimento,** *n.m.* abduction, kidnapping.

**rapina,** *n.f.* rapine, plunder.
**uccèllo di rapina,** *n.m.* bird of prey.

**rapire,** *vb.* abduct, kidnap.

**rapitore,** *n.m.* abductor, kidnapper.

**rappezzare,** *vb.* patch.

**rapporto,** *n.m.* relation; report; rapport; ratio; intercourse.

**rappresàglia,** *n.f.* reprisal, retaliation.

**rappresentare,** *vb.* represent; perform.

**rappresentativo,** *adj.* representative.

**rappresentazione,** *n.f.* representation; performance.

**raramente,** *adv.* rarely, seldom.

**raro,** *adj.* rare.

**raschiare,** *vb.* scrape; scratch out; erase.

**raschino,** *n.m.* eraser.

**rasentare,** *vb.* skirt, skim.

**raso,** *n.m.* satin.

**rasòio,** *n.m.* razor.

**rassegnarsi,** *vb.* resign oneself.

**rassegnazione,** *n.f.* resignation.

**rassicurare,** *vb.* reassure.

**rassomigliare,** *vb.* resemble.

**rastrellare,** *vb.* rake.

**rastrelliera,** *n.f.* rack.

**rastrèllo,** *n.m.* rake.

**rata,** *n.f.* installment.

**ratificare,** *vb.* ratify.

**ratto,** *n.m.* rat; abduction.

**rattoppare,** *vb.* patch.

**rattristare,** *vb.* sadden.

**ràuco,** *adj.* hoarse, raucous.

**ravanèllo,** *n.m.* radish.

**ravvivamento,** *n.m.* revival.

**ravvivare,** *vb.* enliven; revive.

**razionale,** *adj.* rational.

**razionare,** *vb.* ration.

**razione,** *n.f.* ration.

**razza,** *n.f.* race, breed, kind.

**re,** *n.m.* king.

**reagire,** *vb.* react.

**reale,** *adj.* real; royal.

**realista,** *n.m.* realist.

**realizzare,** *vb.* realize; fulfill.

**realizzazione,** *n.f.* realization; fulfillment.

**realmente,** *adv.* really.

**realtà,** *n.f.* reality.

**reame,** *n.m.* realm.

**reattore,** *n.m.* reactor; jet.

**reazionàrio,** *adj.* reactionary.

**reazione,** *n.f.* reaction.

**recare,** *vb.* reach; hand (over); (*refl.*) go, betake oneself.

**recèdere,** *vb.* recede.

**recensione,** *n.f.* review.

**recensire,** *vb.* review.

**recènte,** *adj.* recent; latter.

**recentemente,** *adv.* recently, lately.

**recinto,** *n.m.* enclosure, fence.

**recipiènte,** *n.m.* vessel; beaker; bin; container; holder.

**recitare,** *vb.* act; play; recite.

**recitazione,** *n.f.* recitation; acting.

**reclamante,** *n.m.* claimant.

**reclamare,** *vb.* claim.

**réclame,** *n.f.* advertising.

**reclamizzare,** *vb.* advertise.

**reclamo,** *n.m.* claim.

**reclinare,** *vb.* recline.

**rècluta,** *n.f.* recruit.

**reclutare,** *vb.* recruit.

**rèddito,** *n.m.* income.

**redentore,** *n.m.* redeemer.

**redenzione,** *n.f.* redemption.

**redìgere,** *vb.* draw up, draft; edit.

**redìmere,** *vb.* redeem, reclaim.

**rèdina,** *n.f.* rein.

**regalare,** *vb.* present.

**regale,** *adj.* regal.

**regalità,** *n.f.* royalty.

**regalo,** *n.m.* present.

**reggènte,** *n.m.* regent.

**règgere,** *vb.* hold up; wield.

**reggimento,** *n.m.* regiment.

**reggipètto,** *n.m.* brassière.

**reggiseno,** *n.m.* brassière.

**regime,** *n.m.* regime; rule; diet.

**regina,** *n.f.* queen.

**règio,** *adj.* royal.

**regione,** *n.f.* region.

**registrare,** *vb.* register; record; (luggage) check.

**registratore a filo,** *n.m.* wire recorder.

**registratore magnètico,** *n.m.* tape recorder.

**registrazione,** *n.f.* registration.

**registro,** *n.m.* register; record.

**regnare,** *vb.* reign, rule.

**regno,** *n.m.* kingdom, realm, reign.

**règola,** *n.f.* rule; *(pl.)* menstruation.

**regolamento,** *n.m.* regulation.

**regolare,** *adj.* regular.

**regolare,** *vb.* regulate; rule; set.

**regolarità,** *n.f.* regularity.

**regolatore,** *n.m.* regulator.

**régolo,** *n.m.* ruler. **r. calcolatore,** slide-rule.

**reiterare,** *vb.* reiterate.

**relatività,** *n.f.* relativity.

**relativo,** *adj.* relative.

**relazione,** *n.f.* relation; liaison.

**religione,** *n.f.* religion.

**religioso,** *adj.* religious.

**reliquia,** *n.f.* relic.

**remare,** *vb.* row.

**remata,** *n.f.* row.

**reminiscènza,** *n.f.* reminiscence.

**remo,** *n.m.* oar, paddle.

**remòto,** *adj.* remote.

**rena,** *n.f.* sand.

**rèndere,** *vb.* render; give back. **r. conto di,** account for.

**rendiconto,** *n.m.* statement.

**rène,** *n.f.* kidney.

**reniforme,** *adj.* kidney-shaped.

**rènna,** *n.f.* reindeer.

**renoso,** *adj.* sandy.

**repellènte,** *adj.* repulsive.

**repertòrio,** *n.m.* repertoire.

**rèplica,** *n.f.* reply, rejoinder; repeat performance.

**replicare,** *vb.* reply, rejoin; repeat.

**repressione,** *n.f.* repression.

**reprimere,** *vb.* repress.

**repubblica,** *n.f.* republic; commonwealth.

**repubblicano,** *adj.* republican.

**repulsivo,** *adj.* repulsive; forbidding.

**requisire,** *vb.* requisition, commandeer.

**requisito,** *n.m.* requirement, qualification.

**requisizione,** *n.f.* requisition.

**rescìndere,** *vb.* rescind.

**residènte,** *adj.* resident.

**residènza,** *n.f.* residence.

**residuo,** *n.m.* residue.

**rèsina,** *n.f.* rosin.

**resistènza,** *n.f.* resistance.

**resìstere,** *vb.* resist.

**respingènte,** *n.m.* bumper, buffer.

**respingere,** *vb.* reject, repel, repulse.

**respirare,** *vb.* breathe.

**respirazione,** *n.f.* respiration.

**respiro,** *n.m.* breath, breathing.

**responsàbile,** *adj.* responsible, accountable, answerable, liable; amenable.

**responsabilità,** *n.f.* responsibility, liability.

**responsivo,** *adj.* responsive.

**restare,** *vb.* remain, stay.

**restaurare,** *vb.* restore.

**restaurazione,** *n.f.* restoration.

**restituire,** *vb.* restore; refund.

**restituzione,** *n.f.* restitution.

**rèsto,** *n.m.* remainder, remnant; change.

**restringere,** *vb.* restrict.

**restrizione,** *n.f.* restriction.

**retàggio,** *n.m.* inheritance.

**rete,** *n.f.* net; netting; network.

**reticèlla,** *n.f.* luggage rack.

**reticènte,** *adj.* reticent.

**reticènza,** *n.f.* reticence.

**rètina,** *n.f.* retina.

**retribuzione,** *n.f.* retribution.

**retroattivo,** *adj.* retroactive.

**retroguàrdia,** *n.f.* rear-guard.

**retroscèna,** *n.f.* backstage.

**retrospettivo,** *adj.* retrospective.

**retrotèrra,** *n.f.* hinterland.

**retrovisore,** *adj.* **specchio r.,** rear-view mirror.

**rettàngolo,** *n.m.* rectangle.

**rettificare,** *vb.* rectify.

**rettificatrice,** *n.f.* rectifier.

**rèttile,** *n.m.* reptile.

**rettilìneo,** *n.m.* straightaway.

**rètto,** *adj.* straight.

**rettòrica,** *n.f.* rhetoric.

**rettòrico,** *adj.* rhetorical.

**reumàtico,** *adj.* rheumatic.

**reumatismo,** *n.m.* rheumatism.

**reverèndo,** *adj.* reverend.

**revisióne,** *n.f.* revision.

**revisóre,** *n.m.* (accounts) auditor; (proof) proof-reader.

**rèvoca,** *n.f.* revocation.

**revocàre,** *vb.* revoke.

**riabilitàre,** *vb.* rehabilitate.

**riassùmere,** *vb.* make a résumé of, summarize.

**riassùnto,** *n.m.* abstract, résumé.

**ribadìre,** *vb.* rivet.

**ribàlta,** *n.f.* footlights.

**ribàttere,** *vb.* retort.

**ribellàrsi,** *vb.* rebel, revolt.

**ribèlle,** 1. *n.m.* rebel, insurgent. 2. *adj.* rebellious, insurgent; refractory.

**ribellióne,** *n.f.* rebellion.

**ribes,** *n.m.* gooseberry; currant.

**ricadére,** *vb.* relapse.

**ricadùta,** *n.f.* relapse.

**ricalcitrante,** *adj.* recalcitrant.

**ricamàre,** *vb.* embroider.

**ricambiàre,** *vb.* reciprocate, retaliate.

**ricàmbio,** *n.m.* exchange. **di r.,** spare.

**ricàmo,** *n.m.* embroidery.

**ricapitolàre,** *vb.* recapitulate, sum up.

**ricattàre,** *vb.* blackmail.

**ricattatóre,** *n.m.* blackmailer, extortioner.

**ricàtto,** *n.m.* blackmail.

**ricchézza,** *n.f.* riches, wealth.

**rìccio,** *n.m.* hedgehog.

**rìcciolo,** *n.m.* curl.

**ricciùto,** *adj.* curly.

**ricco,** *adj.* rich, wealthy.

**ricérca,** *n.f.* search, quest; research.

**ricercàre,** *vb.* search.

**ricercàto,** *adj.* recherché; far-fetched.

**ricètta,** *n.f.* recipe.

**ricettàcolo,** *n.m.* receptacle.

**ricettìvo,** *adj.* receptive.

**ricevènte,** *n.m.* recipient.

**ricévere,** *vb.* receive, get.

**riceviménto,** *n.m.* reception; party.

**ricevitóre,** *n.m.* receiver.

**ricevùta,** *n.f.* receipt.

**richiamàre,** *vb.* recall.

**richièdènte,** *n.m.* applicant.

**richièdere,** *vb.* request, ask for; demand; entail; require.

**richièsta,** *n.f.* request; demand.

**ricompènsa,** *n.f.* recompense, reward.

**ricompensàre,** *vb.* recompense, reward.

**riconciliàre,** *vb.* reconcile.

**ricongiùngersi,** *vb.* rejoin.

**riconóscere,** *vb.* recognize; acknowledge.

**riconosciménto,** *n.m.* recognition.

**ricordàre,** *vb.* remember, recollect.

**ricòrdo,** *n.m.* remembrance, souvenir, keepsake, memento; record.

**ricórrere,** *vb.* recur; resort; have recourse.

**ricórso,** *n.m.* recourse, resort.

**ricostruìre,** *vb.* reconstruct, rebuild.

**ricoveràre,** *vb.* shelter.

**ricòvero,** *n.m.* shelter.

**ricuperàre,** *vb.* recover, recuperate; retrieve.

**ricùpero,** *n.m.* recovery.

**ridacchiàre,** *vb.* giggle, chortle.

**rìdere,** *vb.* laugh.

**ridìcolo,** 1. *n.* ridicule. 2. *adj.* ridiculous, laughable, ludicrous.

**ridìre,** *vb.* say again.

**ridótto,** *n.m.* redoubt; foyer.

**ridùrre,** *vb.* reduce, curtail; (music) arrange.

**riduttóre,** *n.m.* adapter.

**riduzióne,** *n.f.* reduction; (music) arrangement.

**riempìre,** *vb.* fill.

**rientrànza,** *n.f.* recess.

**riesàme,** *n.m.* review.

**riesaminàre,** *vb.* re-examine, review.

**riferiménto,** *n.m.* reference.

**riferìre,** *vb.* refer; (*refl.*) relate.

**rifiutàre,** *vb.* refuse, decline.

**rifiùto,** *n.m.* refusal.

**rifiùti,** *n.m.pl.* refuse, garbage.

**riflessióne,** *n.f.* reflection.

**riflèsso,** *n.m.* reflection, glint; reflex.

**riflèttere,** *vb.* reflect.

**rifluìre,** *vb.* ebb.

**riflùsso,** *n.m.* ebb.

**rifórma,** *n.f.* reform, reformation.

---

For pronunciation, see the concise guide on pages 5 to 7.

...form.

...nk.

... refuge.

...gee.

..., shelter,

..., row.

...pl. giblets.

...re, vb. reject.

...idezza, n.f. rigidity, stiffness.

**rigido,** adj. rigid, stiff.

**rigo,** n.m. line; staff.

**rigoglioso,** adj. luxuriant.

**rigore,** n.m. rigor.

**rigoroso,** adj. rigorous, stringent.

**riguardare,** vb. regard, concern.

**riguardo,** n.m. regard. **r. a,** regarding.

**rilassamento,** n.m. relaxation, laxity.

**rilassato,** adj. relaxed, lax.

**rilegare,** vb. bind.

**rilegatura,** n.f. binding.

**rilevamento,** n.m. survey.

**rilevante,** adj. relevant, germane.

**rilucènte,** adj. shiny, lustrous.

**riluttante,** adj. reluctant, loath.

**riluttanza,** n.f. reluctance.

**rima,** n.f. rhyme.

**rimandare,** vb. postpone, put off.

**rimando,** n.m. reference.

**rimanènte,** n.m. remainder, rest.

**rimanere,** vb. remain, stay, abide.

**rimarchévole,** adj. noteworthy, remarkable.

**rimare,** vb. rhyme.

**rimbalzare,** vb. bounce, rebound.

**rimbalzo,** n.m. bounce, rebound.

**rimbambimento,** n.m. dotage.

**rimbambirsi,** vb. grow childish (in old age).

**rimboccare,** vb. tuck.

**rimborsare,** vb. reimburse, repay.

**rimediare,** vb. remedy.

**rimèdio,** n.m. remedy.

**rimèttere,** vb. put back; remit; reinstate; (refl.) get back.

**rimodernare,** vb. modernize, renovate.

**rimorchiare,** vb. tow.

**rimorchiatore,** n.m. tug-boat.

**rimòrchio,** n.m. trailer.

**rimorso,** n.m. remorse.

**rimozione,** n.f. removal.

**rimpatriare,** vb. repatriate.

**rimpiàngere,** vb. regret.

**rimpianto,** n.m. regret.

**rimpiazzare,** vb. replace.

**rimpinzare,** vb. cram, stuff.

**rimproverare,** vb. reprove, chide, rebuke, reproach, reprimand, upbraid.

**rimpròvero,** n.m. rebuke, reproof, reproach, reprimand.

**rimuòvere,** vb. remove.

**rinàscere,** vb. be reborn.

**rinascimento,** n.m. renaissance.

**rinàscita,** n.f. rebirth.

**rinchiùdere,** vb. enclose.

**rincréscere,** vb. cause regret.

**rincrescimento,** n.m. regret.

**rinforzare,** vb. reinforce.

**rinfòrzo,** n.m. reinforcement.

**rinfrescare,** vb. cool; refresh; freshen.

**ringhiare,** vb. snarl.

**ringhièra,** n.f. railing, banister.

**ringiovanire,** vb. rejuvenate.

**ringhio,** n.m. snarl.

**ringraziare,** vb. thank.

**rinnovamento,** n.m. renewal.

**rinnovare,** vb. renew.

**rinoceronte,** n.m. rhinoceros.

**rinomanza,** n.f. renown.

**rinomato,** adj. renowned.

**rintocco,** n.m. knell.

**rintracciare,** vb. trace.

**rinùncia,** n.f. waiver.

**rinunciare,** vb. renounce, forego; waive.

**rione,** n.m. ward.

**ripagare,** vb. repay.

**riparare,** vb. repair, recondition.

**riparazione,** n.f. repair, reparation, redress.

**ripercussione,** n.f. repercussion.

**ripètere,** vb. repeat.

**ripetizione,** n.f. repetition.

**ripetutamente,** adv. repeatedly, again and again.

**ripiano,** n.m. ledge.

**rìpido,** adj. steep; abrupt.

**ripièno, 1.** *n.m.* stuffing. **2.** *adj.* stuffed.

**riposante,** *adj.* restful.

**riposare,** *vb.* rest, repose.

**ripòso,** *n.m.* repose, rest, leisure.

**riprèndere,** *vb.* retake; resume; reprehend.

**riprensibile,** *adj.* reprehensible.

**ripresa,** *n.f.* revival; (music) repeat.

**riprodurre,** *vb.* reproduce.

**riproduzione,** *n.f.* reproduction.

**ripudiare,** *vb.* repudiate.

**ripùdio,** *n.m.* repudiation.

**ripugnante,** *adj.* repugnant, abhorrent.

**ripugnanza,** *s.f.* repugnance, abhorrence, loathing.

**ripulsa,** *n.f.* rebuff, repulse.

**riputare,** *vb.* repute.

**riputazione,** *n.f.* reputation, standing.

**risanare,** *vb.* heal.

**risata,** *n.f.* burst of laughter.

**risatina,** *n.f.* snicker.

**riscaldare,** *vb.* warm up, heat; (*refl.*) warm oneself; bask.

**riscattare,** *vb.* ransom.

**riscatto,** *n.m.* ransom.

**rischiare,** *vb.* risk, hazard; stake; venture.

**rischio,** *n.m.* risk, hazard, venture.

**rischioso,** *adj.* risky, hazardous.

**risciacquare,** *vb.* rinse.

**riscuòtere,** *vb.* shake; collect; cash.

**risèrva,** *n.f.* reserve.

**riservare,** *vb.* reserve.

**riservato,** *adj.* reserved, aloof.

**risièdere,** *vb.* reside.

**riso,** *n.m.* laughter; rice.

**risoluto,** *adj.* resolute, determined.

**risoluzione,** *n.f.* resolution.

**risòlvere,** *vb.* resolve, solve.

**risonante,** *adj.* resonant.

**risonanza,** *n.f.* resonance.

**risonare,** *vb.* resound, ring out.

**risorgènte,** *adj.* resurgent.

**risorsa,** *n.f.* resource.

**risparmiare,** *vb.* save.

**rispàrmio,** *n.m.* saving(s).

**rispettàbile,** *adj.* respectable.

**rispettare,** *vb.* resp—

**rispettivo,** *adj.* respe—

**rispètto,** *n.m.* respe— gard.

**rispettoso,** *adj.* respectful.

**risplendènte,** *adj.* resple— ent, beaming, effulgent.

**risplèndere,** *vb.* be resplend— ent, shine, beam, glitter.

**rispóndere,** *vb.* answer, respond, reply.

**risposta,** *n.f.* answer, response, reply.

**rissa,** *n.f.* brawl, fight, affray.

**ristorante,** *n.m.* restaurant.

**ristorare,** *vb.* restore, refresh.

**ristoratore,** *n.m.* restaurant.

**ristòro,** *n.m.* refreshment.

**risultare,** *vb.* result; appear; be evident.

**risultato,** *n.m.* result, outgrowth.

**risurrezione,** *n.f.* resurrection.

**risvegliare,** *vb.* rouse.

**risvòlta,** *n.f.* lapel.

**ritrasméttere,** *vb.* relay.

**ritaglio,** *n.m.* clipping, cutting.

**ritardare,** *vb.* delay, retard.

**ritardo,** *n.m.* delay, lag. **in r.,** delayed, late.

**ritenere,** *vb.* retain.

**ritenzione,** *n.f.* retention.

**ritirare,** *vb.* retire, withdraw; (*refl.*) retreat, pull back, back out; flinch.

**ritirata,** *n.f.* retreat; toilet.

**rito,** *n.m.* rite.

**ritornare,** *vb.* return; revert.

**ritorno,** *n.m.* return.

**ritrarre,** *vb.* retract, pull back.

**ritrattare,** *vb.* portray; retract.

**ritratto,** *n.m.* portrait.

**ritroso,** *adj.* unwilling, balky.

**ritrovato,** *n.m.* finding.

**ritròvo,** *n.m.* meeting-place, hang-out. **r. notturno,** cabaret.

**rituale,** *n.m.* and *adj.* ritual.

**riunione,** *n.f.* reunion; meeting, assembly.

**riunire,** *vb.* reunite; join; assemble; (*refl.*) meet, foregather.

**riuscire,** *vb.* succeed; turn out.

**riuscita,** *n.f.* success.

**riuscito**, *adj.* successful.

**riva**, *n.f.* bank; strand.

**rivale**, *n. and adj.* rival.

**rivaleggiare**, *vb.* rival.

**rivalità**, *n.f.* rivalry.

**rivedere**, *vb.* see again; review.

**rivelare**, *vb.* reveal, disclose.

**rivelazione**, *n.f.* revelation, disclosure, exposure.

**rivendicare**, *vb.* vindicate.

**riverberare**, *vb.* reverberate.

**riverente**, *adj.* reverent.

**riverenza**, *n.f.* reverence; bow, curtsy, obeisance.

**riverire**, *vb.* revere.

**rivestitura**, *n.f.* facing.

**rivista**, *n.f.* magazine; review; revue; musical comedy; muster.

**rivolta**, *n.f.* revolt.

**rivoltare**, *vb.* revolt.

**rivoltella**, *n.f.* revolver.

**rivoluzionàrio**, *adj.* revolutionary.

**rivoluzione**, *n.f.* revolution.

**ròba**, *n.f.* stuff. **r. da chiòdi**, junk; nonsense.

**robustezza**, *n.f.* hardiness.

**robusto**, *adj.* robust, strong, hardy, hale, stalwart, sturdy.

**ròcca**, *n.f.* fortress; rock.

**roccaforte**, *n.f.* stronghold.

**rocchetto**, *n.m.* reel; spool.

**ròccia**, *n.f.* rock.

**roccioso**, *adj.* rocky.

**ródere**, *vb.* gnaw, champ.

**roditore**, *n.m.* rodent.

**rognone**, *n.m.* kidney.

**Roma**, *n.f.* Rome.

**romano**, *adj.* Roman.

**romàntico**, *adj.* romantic.

**romanzière**, *n.m.* novelist.

**romanzo**, *n.m.* novel; romance.

**romitàggio**, *n.m.* hermitage.

**rómpere**, *vb.* break.

**rompibile**, *adj.* breakable.

**rompicollo**, *adv.* **a r.**, breakneck.

**róndine**, *n.f.* swallow.

**ronzare**, *vb.* buzz, drone; hum.

**ronzino**, *n.m.* nag.

**ronzìo**, *n.m.* buzz, drone, hum.

**ròsa**, **1.** *n.* rose. **2.** *adj.* pink.

**rosàrio**, *n.m.* rosary.

**ròseo**, *adj.* rosy.

**rosicchiare**, *vb.* nibble.

**rosolìa**, *n.f.* German measles.

**rossetto**, *n.m.* lipstick; rouge.

**rosso**, *adj.* red.

**rossore**, *n.m.* blush.

**rosticceria**, *n.f.* grillroom.

**rotaia**, *n.f.* rail.

**rotare**, *vb.* rotate.

**rotatòrio**, *adj.* rotatory.

**rotazione**, *n.f.* rotation. **r. del ginócchio**, knee-cap.

**rotolare**, *vb.* roll.

**ròtolo**, *n.m.* roll; scroll.

**rotondo**, *adj.* round.

**rotta**, *n.f.* rout.

**rotto**, *adj.* broken.

**rottura**, *n.f.* break, breakage; rupture.

**rovesciare**, *vb.* reverse; spill.

**rovèscio**, *n.m.* reverse; downpour. **a rovèscio**, backhand.

**rovina**, *n.f.* ruin, downfall, wreck.

**rovinare**, *vb.* ruin, wreck.

**rovinoso**, *adj.* ruinous.

**rovo**, *n.m.* briar.

**rozzo**, *adj.* rough.

**rubacchiare**, *vb.* pilfer.

**rubare**, *vb.* rob, steal, burglarize, filch.

**rubicondo**, *adj.* rubicund, ruddy, florid.

**rubinetto**, *n.m.* faucet; tap; cock.

**rubino**, *n.m.* ruby.

**rude**, *adj.* rude, rough, curt, abrupt, blunt.

**rùdere**, *n.m.* ruin.

**rudezza**, *n.f.* roughness, curtness, abruptness.

**rudimento**, *n.m.* rudiment.

**ruga**, *n.f.* wrinkle.

**rùggine**, *n.f.* rust.

**rugginoso**, *adj.* rusty.

**ruggire**, *vb.* roar.

**ruggito**, *n.m.* roar.

**rugiada**, *n.f.* dew.

**rugiadoso**, *adj.* dewy.

**rullare**, *vb.* roll.

**rullio**, *n.m.* roll.

**rullo**, *n.m.* roller.

**ruminare**, *vb.* chew the cud.

**rumore**, *n.m.* noise, clatter, din.

**rumoroso**, *adj.* noisy, blatant.

**ruòlo**, *n.m.* list, roll; rôle.

**ruòta**, *n.f.* wheel.

**rupe**, *n.f.* cliff, rock.

**rurale**, *adj.* rural.

**ruscèllo**, *n.m.* brook.

**russare**, *vb.* snore.

For pronunciation, see the concise guide on pages 5 to 7.

**Rùssia,** *n.f.* Russia.
**russo,** *adj.* Russian.
**rùstico,** *n.m. and adj.* rustic.

**ruttare,** *vb.* belch.
**rutto,** *n.m.* belch.
**rùvido,** *adj.* rough.

# S

**sàbato,** *n.m.* Saturday.
**sàbbia,** *n.f.* sand; grit.
**sabbioso,** *adj.* sandy.
**sabotàggio,** *n.m.* sabotage.
**sabotare,** *vb.* sabotage.
**sabotatore,** *n.m.* saboteur.
**saccarina,** *n.f.* saccharine.
**saccarino,** *n.m.* saccharine.
**saccarino,** *adj.* saccharine.
**saccheggiare,** *vb.* sack, pillage, plunder.
**saccheggio,** *n.m.* sack, pillage.
**sacco,** *n.m.* sack, bag.
**sacramento,** *n.m.* sacrament.
**sacrificare,** *vb.* sacrifice.
**sacrificio,** *n.m.* sacrifice.
**sacrilègio,** *n.m.* sacrilege.
**sacrilego,** *adj.* sacrilegious.
**sacro,** *adj.* sacred.
**sadismo,** *n.m.* sadism.
**saggezza,** *n.f.* wisdom.
**saggiare,** *vb.* sample, try, assay, test.
**sàggio, 1.** *n.m.* essay; sample, specimen; assay, test.
**2.** *adj.* wise, sage.
**saggista,** *n.m.* essayist.
**sàgoma,** *n.f.* loading gauge.
**sagrestano,** *n.m.* sacristan, sexton.
**sagrestia,** *n.f.* sacristy, vestry.
**sala,** *n.f.* hall; room.
**salame,** *n.m.* salami; bologna.
**salamòia,** *n.f.* pickle.
**salare,** *vb.* salt.
**salàrio,** *n.m.* wages.
**salato,** *adj.* salty; briny.
**saldare,** *vb.* solder; (comm.) settle; balance.
**saldatura,** *n.f.* solder.
**saldo,** *n.m.* (comm.) balance.
**saldo,** *adj.* steady, steadfast.
**sale,** *n.m.* salt.
**sàlice,** *n.m.* willow.
**salire,** *vb.* go up, ascend, mount.
**saliscendi,** *n.m.* latch.

**salita,** *n.f.* ascent.
**saliva,** *n.f.* saliva.
**salmo,** *n.m.* psalm.
**salmone,** *n.m.* salmon.
**salone,** *n.m.* salon; lounge.
**salottino,** *n.m.* boudoir.
**salòtto,** *n.m.* parlor.
**salpare,** *vb.* set sail.
**salsa,** *n.f.* sauce.
**salsiccia,** *n.f.* sausage.
**salso,** *adj.* salt, salty.
**saltare,** *vb.* jump, leap, bound, hop, gambol, skip, spring, vault.
**salto,** *n.m.* jump, leap, bound, hop, gambol, spring, vault.
**s. mortale,** somersault.
**saltuàrio,** *adj.* desultory.
**salubre,** *adj.* salubrious, healthful.
**salutare,** *adj.* salutary, beneficial.
**salutare,** *vb.* greet, salute, hail.
**salutazione,** *n.f.* salutation.
**salute,** *n.f.* health.
**saluto,** *n.m.* greeting, salute, salutation.
**salvagente,** *n.m.* life-buoy; life-preserver. **isolòtto s.,** safety island.
**salvare,** *vb.* save, salvage.
**salvaguardare,** *vb.* safeguard.
**salvaguàrdia,** *n.f.* safeguard.
**salvatàggio,** *n.m.* salvage.
**salvatore,** *n.m.* savior.
**salvezza,** *n.f.* salvation.
**salvo, 1.** *adj.* safe. **2.** *prep.* except, but, save.
**sambuco,** *n.m.* elder tree.
**sanatòrio,** *n.m.* sanatorium.
**sàndalo,** *n.m.* sandal.
**sangue,** *n.m.* blood; gore.
**sanguinare,** *vb.* bleed.
**sanguinàrio,** *adj.* bloodthirsty, sanguinary.
**sanguinoso,** *adj.* bloody.

**sanguisuga**, *n.f.* leech.

**sanità**, *n.f.* sanity.

**sanitàrio**, *adj.* sanitary.

**sano**, *adj.* healthy, sound, sane, wholesome.

**santificare**, *vb.* sanctify, hallow.

**santità**, *n.f.* holiness, sanctity.

**santo**, **1.** *n.* saint. **2.** *adj.* holy, sainted.

**santuàrio**, *ib.* sanctuary, shrine.

**sanzionare**, *vb.* sanction.

**sanzione**, *n.f.* sanction.

**sapere**, *vb.* know; know how to; savor, taste.

**sapone**, *n.m.* soap.

**sapore**, *n.m.* taste, flavor, savor.

**saporito**, *adj.* savory, tasty.

**saporoso**, *adj.* tasty, luscious.

**sarcasmo**, *n.m.* sarcasm.

**sarcàstico**, *adj.* sarcastic.

**Sardegna**, *n.f.* Sardinia.

**sardèlla**, *n.f.* sardine.

**sardo**, *adj.* Sardinian.

**sarta**, *n.f.* dressmaker.

**sarto**, *n.m.* tailor.

**sasso**, *n.m.* rock, boulder, stone.

**satèllite**, *n.m.* satellite.

**sàtira**, *n.f.* satire.

**satireggiare**, *vb.* satirize.

**saturare**, *vb.* saturate.

**saturazione**, *n.f.* saturation, glut.

**saziare**, *vb.* satiate, sate, cloy.

**sbadato**, *adj.* careless, heedless.

**sbadigliare**, *vb.* yawn.

**sbadìglio**, *n.m.* yawn.

**sbagliare**, *vb.* err, blunder, make a mistake, slip.

**sbàglio**, *n.m.* mistake.

**sbalordire**, *vb.* astound, dumbfound.

**sbalzellone**, *n.m.* jerk.

**sbandare**, *vb.* disband.

**sbarazzare**, *vb.* rid.

**sbarcare**, *vb.* disembark, land.

**sbarco**, *n.m.* disembarkation, landing.

**sbarra**, *n.f.* bar, rail.

**sbarramento**, *n.m.* **fuòco di s.**, barrage.

**sbarrare**, *vb.* bar.

**sbàttere**, *vb.* slam, bang.

**sbavare**, *vb.* drivel.

**sbirciare**, *vb.* peek, look sideways.

**sbocco**, *n.m.* outlet.

**sborsare**, *vb.* disburse, pay out.

**sbraitare**, *vb.* squall.

**sbriciolare**, *vb.* crumble.

**sbrigare**, *vb.* expedite.

**sbrinamento**, *n.m.* defrosting (refrigerator.)

**sbrinare**, *vb.* defrost (refrigerator)

**sbucciare**, *vb.* peel, pare.

**sbuffare**, *vb.* puff, chug.

**sbuffo**, *n.m.* puff, chug.

**scabroso**, *adj.* rugged.

**scacchi**, *n.m.pl.* chess.

**scacchièra**, *n.f.* chessboard, checkerboard.

**scacco**, *n.m.* chessman. **s. matto**, checkmate.

**scadènza**, *n.f.* maturity.

**scadere**, *vb.* fall due.

**scaffale**, *n.m.* shelf; bookcase.

**scafo**, *n.m.* hull.

**scagliare**, *vb.* hurl, sling.

**scaglione**, *n.m.* echelon.

**scala**, *n.f.* staircase; scale. **s. a piuòli**, ladder.

**scalare**, *vb.* scale, climb.

**scalèo**, *n.m.* stepladder.

**scalo**, *n.m.* station. **s. mèrci**, freight station. **s. di smistamento**, marshalling yards, freight yard.

**scalzo**, *adj.* barefoot.

**scambiàbile**, *adj.* exchangeable.

**scambiare**, *vb.* exchange.

**scàmbio**, *n.m.* exchange; (railroad) switch; points.

**scampanare**, *vb.* chime, peal.

**scampanellata**, *n.f.* ring.

**scampanìo**, *n.m.* chime, peal.

**scampo**, *n.m.* escape.

**scandagliare**, *vb.* take soundings, sound out, fathom.

**scàndalo**, *n.m.* scandal.

**scandaloso**, *adj.* scandalous.

**scandire**, *vb.* scan (poetry).

**scanso**, *n.m.* avoidance. **a s. di**, so as to avoid.

**scapaccione**, *n.m.* cuff.

**scappare**, *vb.* escape.

**scappata**, *n.f.* escapade.

**scappatòia**, *n.f.* means of escape, loophole.

**scarafàggio**, *n.m.* beetle.

**scaramùccia**, *n.f.* skirmish.

**scaramucciare**, *vb.* skirmish.

**scàrica**, *n.f.* discharge.

**scaricare**, *vb.* unload, discharge, dump.

For pronunciation, see the concise guide on pages 5 to 7.

**scàrico**, *n.m.* discharge; spill-way.

**scarlattina**, *n.f.* scarlet fever.

**scarlatto**, *n.m. and adj.* scarlet.

**scarpa**, *n.f.* shoe.

**scarseggiare**, *vb.* be scarce.

**scarsezza**, *n.f.* scarcity, dearth.

**scarsità**, *n.f.* scarcity, dearth.

**scarso**, *adj.* scarce, meager, scant.

**scartamento**, *n.m.* gauge.

**scartare**, *vb.* discard, scrap.

**scarti**, *n.m.pl.* rubbish.

**scàtola**, *n.f.* box; can.

**scattare**, *vb.* spring up; burst forth; spurt; dash.

**scatto**, *n.m.* spring; spurt; dash.

**scavare**, *vb.* excavate, dig out; burrow, delve.

**scavo**, *n.m.* excavation.

**scégliere**, *vb.* choose, pick, select.

**scelta**, *n.f.* choice, selection.

**scelto**, *adj.* select, choice.

**scèna**, *n.f.* scene.

**scéndere**, *vb.* descend, go down; get down, alight.

**scervellato**, *adj.* hare-brained; madcap.

**scèttico**, **1.** *n.* skeptic. **2.** *adj.* skeptical.

**scheda**, *n.f.* card; form; ballot.

**schedàrio**, *n.m.* card-file.

**schedina**, *n.f.* (filing card).

**scheggia**, *n.f.* chip, splinter.

**scheggiare**, *vb.* chip, splinter.

**schèletro**, *n.m.* skeleton.

**scherma**, *n.f.* fencing.

**schermidore**, *n.m.* fencer.

**schermire**, *vb.* fence.

**schermo**, *n.m.* screen.

**schernire**, *vb.* mock, scoff at, taunt.

**scherno**, *n.m.* mockery.

**scherzare**, *vb.* joke, jest, banter.

**scherzo**, *n.m.* joke, jest, banter; play; (music) scherzo.

**scherzoso**, *adj.* joking, playful.

**schiaccianoci**, *n.m.* nut-cracker.

**schiacciare**, *vb.* crush, mash.

**schiaffeggiare**, *vb.* slap, buffet, smack.

**schiaffo**, *n.m.* slap, buffet.

**schiarire**, *vb.* clear up.

**schiavitù**, *n.f.* slavery.

**schiavo**, *n.m.* slave.

**schièna**, *n.f.* back.

**schifoso**, *adj.* loathsome.

**schioccare**, *vb.* snap.

**schiuma**, *n.f.* foam, froth, lather, suds.

**schivare**, *vb.* avoid, dodge, shun.

**schizzare**, *vb.* sketch; squirt.

**schizzinoso**, *adj.* squeamish.

**schizzo**, *n.m.* splash, splotch, dab; sketch, outline.

**sci**, *n.m.* ski.

**scìa**, *n.f.* wake.

**sciàbola**, *n.f.* saber.

**sciacallo**, *n.m.* jackal.

**scialacquare**, *vb.* squander.

**scialle**, *n.m.* shawl.

**sciamare**, *vb.* swarm.

**sciame**, *n.m.* swarm.

**sciampagna**, *n.f.* champagne.

**sciampo**, *n.m.* shampoo.

**sciancato**, **1.** *n.* cripple. **2.** *adj.* crippled.

**sciare**, *vb.* ski.

**sciarpa**, *n.f.* scarf, muffler.

**sciàtica**, *n.f.* sciatica.

**sciatto**, *adj.* sloppy; dowdy.

**scientifico**, *adj.* scientific.

**scinza**, *n.f.* science.

**scienziato**, *n.m.* scientist.

**scimmia**, *n.f.* ape; monkey.

**scimpanzè**, *n.m.* chimpanzee.

**scindere**, *vb.* split.

**scintilla**, *n.f.* spark.

**scintillare**, *vb.* sparkle, glitter, glisten.

**scintillìo**, *n.m.* sparkle, glitter.

**sciocco**, *adj.* stupid, foolish, dumb, silly.

**sciògliere**, *vb.* untie; loosen; resolve; dissolve; melt.

**scioglimento**, *n.m.* dénouement.

**sciòlto**, *adj.* loose.

**scioperare**, *vb.* strike.

**sciòpero**, *n.m.* strike.

**scissione**, *n.f.* division; cleavage; split.

**sciupare**, *vb.* spoil; waste; fritter away.

**sciròppo**, *n.m.* syrup.

**sciupone**, *n.m.* spendthrift.

**scivolare**, *vb.* slip; slide; glide.

**scivolone**, *n.m.* slip.

**scodèlla**, *n.f.* bowl.

**scòglio**, *n.m.* reef.

**scoiàttolo**, *n.m.* squirrel.

**scolare**, *vb.* drain.

**scolaro,** *n.m.* pupil.

**scollato,** *adj.* décolleté.

**scolorimento,** *n.m.* discoloration.

**scolorire,** *vb.* discolor.

**scolpare,** *vb.* exculpate.

**scolpire,** *vb.* carve.

**scommessa,** *n.f.* bet, wager.

**scomméttere,** *vb.* bet, wager.

**scomodità,** *n.f.* inconvenience.

**scomparire,** *vb.* disappear.

**scomparsa,** *n.f.* disappearance.

**scompartimento,** *n.m.* compartment.

**scompigliare,** *vb.* disarrange.

**scompiglio,** *n.m.* disarray.

**scomposto,** *adj.* unseemly. **stare s.,** slouch.

**scomùnica,** *n.f.* excommunication.

**scomunicare,** *vb.* excommunicate.

**sconcertante,** *adj.* disconcerting, upsetting, bewildering.

**sconcertare,** *vb.* disconcert, upset, faze, abash.

**sconfiggere,** *vb.* defeat.

**sconfinato,** *adj.* unbounded.

**sconfitta,** *n.f.* defeat, discomfiture.

**scongiurare,** *vb.* conjure.

**sconnèsso,** *adj.* disconnected, disjointed.

**sconnèttere,** *vb.* disconnect.

**sconosciuto,** *adj.* unknown.

**sconsolato,** *adj.* disconsolate, comfortless.

**scontare,** *vb.* discount.

**scontentare,** *vb.* discontent.

**scontènto, 1.** *n.m.* discontent. **2.** *adj.* discontented, disgruntled.

**sconto,** *n.m.* discount, rebate.

**scontrarsi,** *vb.* collide.

**scontrino,** *n.m.* check.

**scontro,** *n.m.* collision.

**sconveniènte,** *adj.* unbecoming, improper, unseemly.

**sconvòlgere,** *vb.* upset, overturn; overthrow; derange; unsettle.

**sconvolgimento,** *n.m.* upset, overturn; overthrow; derangement.

**scopa,** *n.f.* broom.

**scopèrta,** *n.f.* discovery.

**scopèrto,** *adj.* uncovered, bare.

**scopetta,** *n.f.* whisk-broom.

**scòpo,** *n.m.* purpose, aim.

**scoppiare,** *vb.* burst, explode.

**scoppiettare,** *vb.* pop.

**scòppio,** *n.m.* outbreak; explosion.

**scoprimento,** *n.m.* detection.

**scoprire,** *vb.* discover, uncover, bare, detect.

**scopritore,** *n.m.* discoverer.

**scoraggiamento,** *n.m.* discouragement, dejection.

**scoraggiare,** *vb.* discourage, dishearten.

**scoraggiato,** *adj.* discouraged, dejected, downhearted.

**scorato,** *adj.* broken-hearted.

**scòrgere,** *vb.* perceive, discern.

**scórrere,** *vb.* flow; peruse.

**scorrerìa,** *n.f.* foray.

**scorrévole,** *adj.* fluent.

**scorrevolezza,** *n.f.* fluency.

**scorsóio,** *adj.* running.

**scòrta,** *n.f.* escort.

**scortare,** *vb.* escort.

**scortese,** *adj.* discourteous, impolite.

**scortesìa,** *n.f.* discourtesy.

**scorticare,** *vb.* flay.

**scorza,** *n.f.* bark.

**scoscéso,** *adj.* steep.

**scòssa,** *n.f.* jolt; shake; shock.

**scottare,** *vb.* scald.

**scottatura,** *n.f.* scald.

**Scòzia,** *n.f.* Scotland.

**scozzese,** *adj.* Scotch.

**screditare,** *vb.* discredit, debunk.

**scremare,** *vb.* skim.

**screpolare,** *vb.* chap.

**screpolatura,** *n.f.* chapping; crevice.

**scriba,** *n.m.* scribe.

**scribacchiare,** *vb.* scribble.

**scricchiolare,** *vb.* creak.

**scrigno,** *n.m.* strong-box, safe, coffer.

**scritto,** *n.m.* writing.

**scrittore,** *n.m.* writer.

**scrittura,** *n.f.* writing; scripture.

**scrivanìa,** *n.f.* desk.

**scrivere,** *vb.* write.

**scrofa,** *n.f.* sow.

**scròscio,** *n.m.* gust.

**scrostare,** *vb.* scale.

**scrùpolo,** *n.m.* scruple.

**scrupoloso,** *adj.* scrupulous.

**scrutare,** *vb.* scrutinize, scan.

**scudo**, *n.m.* shield, escutcheon.

**sculacciare**, *vb.* spank.

**sculacciata**, *n.f.* spanking.

**scultore**, *n.m.* sculptor, carver.

**scultura**, *n.f.* sculpture, carving.

**scuola**, *n.f.* school.

**scuotere**, *vb.* shake, jog, jar; wag; (*refl.*) bestir oneself.

**scuretto**, *n.m.* shutter.

**scusa**, *n.f.* excuse, apology.

**scusàbile**, *adj.* excusable.

**scusare**, *vb.* excuse; (*refl.*) apologize.

**sdraiarsi**, *vb.* stretch out, sprawl.

**sdrucciolare**, *vb.* slide, slip.

**sdrucciolévole**, *adj.* slippery.

**se**, *conj.* if; whether.

**sè**, *pron.* himself; herself; itself; themselves.

**sebbène**, *conj.* although.

**seccare**, *vb.* dry; bore.

**seccatura**, *n.f.* bore, nuisance.

**secchezza**, *n.f.* dryness.

**sécchia**, *n.f.* bucket, pail, hod.

**secco**, *adj.* dry.

**secolare**, *adj.* secular; century-long.

**sècolo**, *n.m.* century.

**secondàrio**, *adj.* secondary.

**secondo. 1.** *n.* second; half-back; mate. **2.** *adj.* second. **3.** *prep.* according to.

**sèdano**, *n.m.* celery.

**sedativo**, *n.m. and adj.* sedative.

**sede**, *n.f.* seat. **Santa S.**, Holy See.

**sedere**, *vb.* sit.

**sèdia**, *n.f.* chair, seat. **s. a dòndolo**, rocker.

**sedicésimo**, *adj.* sixteenth.

**sédici**, *num.* sixteen.

**seducènte**, *adj.* seductive, alluring.

**sedurre**, *vb.* seduce.

**seduta**, *n.f.* sitting.

**sega**, *n.f.* saw.

**ségale**, *n.f.* rye.

**segare**, *vb.* saw.

**seggiovia**, *n.f.* ski-lift.

**seghettato**, *adj.* jagged.

**segmento**, *n.m.* segment.

**segnalare**, *vb.* signal.

**segnale**, *n.m.* signal.

**segnare**, *vb.* mark; score.

**segno**, *n.m.* sign, cue, mark, token.

**sego**, *n.m.* tallow.

**segregare**, *vb.* segregate.

**segretària**, *n.f.* secretary.

**segretàrio**, *n.m.* secretary.

**segreto**, *n.m. and adj.* secret.

**seguace**, *n.m.* follower, hanger-on.

**seguènte**, *adj.* next.

**seguire**, *vb.* follow.

**séguito**, *n.m.* retinue, suite.

**sèi**, *num.* six.

**selce**, *n.f.* flint.

**selciato**, *n.m.* pavement.

**selettivo**, *adj.* selective.

**selezione**, *n.f.* selection.

**sella**, *n.f.* saddle.

**sellare**, *vb.* saddle.

**selvaggina**, *n.f.* game.

**selvàggio**, *n.m. and adj.* savage, wild.

**selvàtico**, *adj.* wild.

**semàforo**, *n.m.* traffic light.

**semàntica**, *n.f.* semantics.

**semàntico**, *adj.* semantic.

**sembrare**, *vb.* seem.

**seme**, *n.m.* seed.

**semèstre**, *n.m.* semester.

**semicérchio**, *n.m.* semicircle.

**semidìo**, *n.m.* demigod.

**seminare**, *vb.* sow.

**seminàrio**, *n.m.* seminary.

**sempiterno**, *adj.* everlasting.

**sémplice**, *adj.* simple, plain.

**sempre**, *adv.* always, ever; still, yet.

**semplicemente**, *adv.* simply.

**semplicità**, *n.f.* simplicity.

**semplificare**, *vb.* simplify.

**sempreverde**, *adj.* evergreen.

**sènape**, *n.f.* mustard.

**senato**, *n.m.* senate.

**senatore**, *n.m.* senator.

**senile**, *adj.* senile.

**senno**, *n.m.* sense.

**seno**, *n.m.* breast, bosom. **s. frontale**, sinus.

**sensale**, *n.m.* broker.

**sensazionale**, *adj.* sensational, lurid.

**sensazione**, *n.f.* sensation.

**senserìa**, *n.f.* brokerage.

**sensìbile** *adj.* sensitive, sympathetic.

**sensitivo**, *adj.* sensitive.

**sènso**, *n.m.* sense; direction. **s. unico**, one-way (street).

**sensuale**, *adj.* sensual.

**sentièro**, *n.m.* path, trail.

**sentimentale,** *adj.* sentimental.

**sentimento,** *n.m.* feeling, sentiment.

**sentire,** *vb.* feel; hear.

**senza,** *prep.* without.

**separare,** *vb.* separate, part.

**separato,** *adj.* separate.

**separazione,** *n.f.* separation, parting.

**sepoltura,** *n.f.* burial, interment.

**seppellire,** *vb.* bury, entomb, inter.

**sequèstro,** *n.m.* lien.

**sera,** *n.f.* evening.

**serbare,** *vb.* keep, preserve.

**serbatòio,** *n.m.* reservoir; cistern; tank.

**serenata,** *n.f.* serenade.

**sereno, 1.** *n.m.* clear sky. **2.** *adj.* serene; clear; cloudless.

**sergènte,** *n.m.* sergeant.

**seriamente,** *adv.* seriously.

**sèrie,** *n.f.* series; row; array; set; suite; succession.

**serietà,** *n.f.* seriousness, earnestness.

**sèrio,** *adj.* serious, earnest. **sul s.,** earnestly.

**sermone,** *n.m.* sermon.

**sèrpe,** *n.m.* snake.

**serpènte,** *n.m.* serpent.

**sèrra,** *n.f.* greenhouse, hothouse.

**serràglio,** *n.m.* menagerie.

**serratura,** *n.f.* lock.

**servile,** *adj.* servile, menial, subservient.

**servitù,** *n.f.* servitude, bondage; servants.

**serviziévole,** *adj.* helpful, obliging.

**servizio,** *n.m.* service; employ.

**sèrvo,** *n.m.* servant.

**sessanta,** *num.* sixty.

**sessantésimo,** *adj.* sixtieth.

**sessione,** *n.f.* session.

**sèsso,** *n.m.* sex.

**sessuale,** *adj.* sexual.

**sesto,** *num.* sixth.

**seta,** *n.f.* silk.

**setàceo,** *adj.* silken.

**sete,** *n.f.* thirsty.

**sétola,** *n.f.* bristle.

**setoloso,** *adj.* bristly.

**sètta,** *n.f.* sect, denomination.

**settanta,** *num.* seventy.

**settantésimo,** *adj.* seventieth.

**sètte,** *num.* seven.

**settèmbre,** *n.m.* September.

**settentrionale,** *adj.* northern.

**settimana,** *n.f.* week.

**settimanale,** *n.m.* and *adj.* weekly.

**sèttimo,** *adj.* seventh.

**severità,** *n.f.* severity.

**sevèro,** *adj.* severe, dour, stern, strict.

**sezionale,** *adj.* sectional.

**sezione,** *n.f.* section.

**sfacèlo,** *n.m.* breakdown, ruin, debacle.

**sfavore,** *n.m.* disfavor, disgrace.

**sfavorévole,** *adj.* unfavorable.

**sfèra,** *n.f.* sphere.

**sfèrza,** *n.f.* whip, scourge, lash.

**sferzare,** *vb.* lash, whip, scourge.

**sfida,** *n.f.* challenge, dare, defiance.

**sfidare,** *vb.* defy, challenge, dare.

**sfidatore,** *n.m.* defier, challenger.

**sfidùcia,** *n.f.* distrust.

**sfilare,** *vb.* defile; file off.

**sfinito,** *adj.* tired out; jaded.

**sfiorare,** *vb.* touch lightly, brush against, dab at, skim.

**sfogare,** *vb.* vent.

**sfògo,** *n.m.* expression; outlet; scope; vent.

**sfondo,** *n.m.* background.

**sfortuna,** *n.f.* misfortune, bad luck.

**sfortunato,** *adj.* unfortunate.

**sforzare,** *vb.* strain.

**sforzarsi,** *vb.* make an effort, endeavor, strive.

**sforzo,** *n.m.* effort, endeavor, exertion; stress.

**sfregiare,** *vb.* deface.

**sfrontatezza,** *n.f.* effrontery.

**sfruttamento,** *n.m.* exploitation.

**sfruttare,** *vb.* exploit.

**sfuggire,** *vb.* escape.

**sfumatura,** *n.f.* nuance.

**sgabèllo,** *n.m.* stool; footstool.

**sgarberìa,** *n.f.* indignity.

**sgargiante,** *adj.* flamboyant, garish.

**sghignazzare,** *vb.* guffaw.

**sghignazzata,** *n.f.* guffaw.

**sgomberare,** *vb.* clear.

**sgombro,** *n.m.* mackerel.

**sgonfiare,** *vb.* deflate.

**sgorbia,** *n.f.* gouge.

**sgòrbio,** *n.m.* blotch; daub; scrawl.

**sgorgare,** *vb.* empty, disgorge; gush, well forth.

**sgradévole,** *adj.* disagreeable.

**sgranocchiare,** *vb.* munch.

**sgraziato,** *adj.* graceless.

**sgridare,** *vb.* scold, bawl out, berate, chide.

**sguardo,** *n.m.* look, glance.

**si,** *pron.* himself; herself; itself; themselves; yourself; yourselves.

**sì,** *interj.* yes.

**sìa,** *conj.* either; or.

**sibilare,** *vb.* hiss.

**sìbilo,** *n.m.* hiss.

**siccità,** *n.f.* dryness, drought.

**Sicilia,** *n.f.* Sicily.

**siciliano,** *adj.* Sicilian.

**sicuramente,** *adv.* surely; securely; assuredly.

**sicurezza,** *n.f.* safety, security, surety.

**sicuro,** *adj.* sure; secure; assured; safe.

**sidro,** *n.m.* cider.

**sièpe,** *n.f.* hedge.

**sièro,** *n.m.* buttermilk; whey; serum.

**sifilide,** *n.f.* syphilis.

**sifilìtico,** *adj.* syphilitic.

**sifone,** *n.m.* syphon.

**Sig.,** *n.m.* (abbr. for Signore) Mr.

**sigaretta,** *n.f.* cigarette.

**sìgaro,** *n.m.* cigar.

**sigillare,** *vb.* seal.

**sigillo,** *n.m.* seal; cachet.

**significare,** *vb.* signify, mean, betoken, purport.

**significativo,** *adj.* significant.

**significato,** *n.m.* significance, meaning, import, purport.

**signora,** *n.f.* lady; Mrs.; madam.

**signore,** *n.f.pl.* (on toilets) ladies.

**signore,** *n.m.* gentleman; lord; Mr.; sir.

**signorìa,** *n.f.* lordship.

**silenziatore,** *n.m.* silencer, muffler.

**silènzio,** *n.m.* silence.

**silenzioso,** *adj.* silent, quiet, noiseless.

**sìllaba,** *n.f.* syllable.

**silo,** *n.m.* silo.

**silòfono,** *n.m.* xylophone.

**silvicultore,** *n.m.* forester.

**silvicultura,** *n.f.* forestry.

**simbòlico,** *adj.* symbolic.

**simbolo,** *n.m.* symbol.

**similcuòio,** *n.m.* artificial leather.

**simile,** *adj.* similar, alike, like.

**similmente,** *adv.* similarly, alike, likewise.

**simpàtico,** *adj.* likeable, agreeable, pleasant, congenial.

**simpatìa,** *n.f.* sympathy.

**simpatizzare,** *vb.* sympathize.

**simulare,** *vb.* simulate.

**simultàneo,** *adj.* simultaneous.

**sinceramente,** *adv.* sincerely.

**sincerità,** *n.f.* sincerity.

**sincèro,** *adj.* sincere, heartfelt.

**sincronizzare,** *vb.* synchronize.

**sìncrono,** *adj.* synchronous.

**sindacato,** *n.m.* union.

**sìndaco,** *n.m.* mayor.

**sinfonìa,** *n.f.* symphony; overture.

**sinfònico,** *adj.* symphonic.

**singhiozzare,** *vb.* sob.

**singhiozzo,** *n.m.* sob.

**singolare,** *adj.* singular.

**singulto,** *n.m.* hiccup.

**sinistra,** *n.f.* left.

**sinistro, 1.** *n.m.* accident. **2.** *adj.* left; sinister.

**sinistròrso,** *adj. and adv.* counter-clockwise.

**sino,** *prep.* as far as, up to, till. **s. da,** since.

**sinònimo, 1.** *n.* synonym. **2.** *adj.* synonymous.

**sìntesi,** *n.f.* synthesis.

**sintètico,** *adj.* synthetic.

**sìntomo,** *n.m.* symptom.

**sintonizzare,** *vb.* tune in.

**sinuoso,** *adj.* sinuous.

**sipàrio,** *n.m.* curtain.

**sirèna,** *n.f.* siren; mermaid.

**siringa,** *n.f.* syringe.

---

For pronunciation, see the concise guide on pages 5 to 7.

**sistèma,** *n.m.* system.

**sistemare,** *vb.* put in order, arrange, settle, fix up.

**sistemàtico,** *adj.* systematic.

**sito,** *n.m.* site.

**situare,** *vb.* situate.

**situazione,** *n.f.* situation, location.

**slanciarsi,** *vb.* rush, dash.

**slancio,** *n.m.* rush, dash; impetus; élan.

**slavo,** *adj.* Slavic.

**sleale,** *adj.* disloyal.

**slealtà,** *n.f.* disloyalty.

**slitta,** *n.f.* sleigh, sled.

**slittamento,** *n.m.* skid.

**slittare,** *vb.* slide, skid.

**slogare,** *vb.* dislocate.

**sloggiare,** *vb.* dislodge.

**smaltare,** *vb.* enamel, glaze.

**smalto,** *n.m.* enamel, glaze.

**smantellare,** *vb.* dismantle.

**smarrire,** *vb.* mislay, misplace, lose.

**smarrito,** *adj.* stray.

**smascherare,** *vb.* unmask.

**smembrare,** *vb.* dismember.

**smentire,** *vb.* give the lie to, belie.

**smeraldo,** *n.m.* emerald.

**smeriglio,** *n.m.* emery.

**smèttere,** *vb.* stop, quit.

**smilitarizzare,** *vb.* demilitarize.

**smilzo,** *adj.* gangling.

**smobilitare,** *vb.* demobilize.

**smobilitazione,** *n.f.* demobilization.

**smontare,** *vb.* dismount, alight; disassemble.

**smòrfia,** *n.f.* grimace.

**snaturare,** *vb.* denaturalize.

**snervamento,** *n.m.* enervation.

**snervare,** *vb.* enervate.

**sobbalzare,** *vb.* jounce, jolt; throb.

**sobbalzo,** *n.m.* jounce, jolt.

**sobborgo,** *n.m.* suburb, (*pl.*) outskirts.

**sobrio,** *adj.* sober, somber.

**socchiuso,** *adj.* half-closed, ajar.

**soccómbere,** *vb.* succumb.

**soccórrere,** *vb.* succor, relieve.

**soccorso,** *n.m.* succor, relief.

**sociale,** *adj.* social.

**socialismo,** *n.m.* socialism.

**socialista,** *n. and adj.* socialist.

**società,** *n.f.* society; company. **S. delle Nazioni,** League of Nations.

**socièvole,** *adj.* sociable, companionable.

**socio,** *n.m.* member; fellow; partner.

**sociologìa,** *n.f.* sociology.

**sòda,** *n.f.* soda.

**soddisfacènte,** *adj.* satisfactory.

**soddisfare,** *vb.* satisfy.

**soddisfazione,** *n.f.* satisfaction.

**sòdio,** *n.m.* sodium.

**sòdo,** *adj.* hard-boiled.

**sofà,** *n.m.* sofa.

**sofaletto,** *n.m.* davenport.

**soffiare,** *vb.* blow.

**soffietto,** *n.m.* bellows.

**soffitta,** *n.f.* attic, garret.

**soffitto,** *n.m.* ceiling.

**soffocare,** *vb.* suffocate, choke, smother, stifle.

**soffrire,** *vb.* suffer, tolerate, put up with.

**sofìsma,** *n.m.* chicanery.

**sofisticato,** *adj.* sophisticated.

**soggètto, 1.** *n.* subject. **2.** *adj.* subject, liable.

**soggezione,** *n.f.* awe; uneasiness.

**sogghignare,** *vb.* sneer.

**sogghigno,** *n.m.* sneer.

**soggiogare,** *vb.* subjugate, subdue.

**soggiornare,** *vb.* sojourn, stay.

**soggiorno,** *n.m.* sojourn, stay.

**sògliola,** *n.f.* sole.

**sognare,** *vb.* dream.

**sognatore,** *n.m.* dreamer.

**sogno,** *n.m.* dream.

**solaio,** *n.m.* loft.

**solamente,** *adv.* only, alone.

**solare,** *adj.* solar.

**solatìo,** *adj.* sunny.

**solco,** *n.m.* furrow; groove; rut.

**soldato,** *n.m.* soldier. **s. sémplice,** private.

**sòldo,** *n.m.* penny.

**sole,** *n.m.* sun; sunshine.

**solènne,** *adj.* solemn.

**solennità,** *n.f.* solemnity.

**solere,** *vb.* be in the habit of, be accustomed to.

**solidificare,** *vb.* solidify.

**solidità,** *n.f.* solidity.

**sòlido,** *n.m. and adj.* solid.

**solista,** *n.m. or f.* soloist.

**solitàrio,** *adj.* solitary, lone, lonely, lonesome.

**sòlito,** *adj.* usual, habitual, accustomed.

**solitùdine,** *n.f.* solitude, privacy.

**sollecitare,** *vb.* solicit; urge.

**sollécito,** *adj.* solicitous.

**solleticare,** *vb.* ticklish.

**sollevare,** *vb.* raise, lift, heave; relieve, ease.

**sollevazione,** *n.f.* uprising.

**sollièvo,** *n.m.* relief.

**solo,** *adj.* alone, sole, only, single.

**soltanto,** *adv.* only.

**solùbile,** *adj.* soluble.

**soluzione,** *n.f.* solution.

**solvènte,** *n.m. and adj.* solvent.

**somaro,** *n.m.* donkey.

**somiglianza,** *n.f.* likeness, similarity.

**somma,** *n.f.* sum, amount, quantity.

**sommare,** *vb.* sum up, add.

**sommàrio,** *n.m. and adj.* summary.

**sommèrgere,** *vb.* submerge.

**sommergìbile,** *n.m.* submarine.

**sommersione,** *n.f.* submersion.

**sommità,** *n.f.* summit, top.

**sondare,** *vb.* probe; sound.

**sonnecchiare,** *vb.* doze, nap, drowse.

**sonnellino,** *n.m.* nap, doze.

**sonno,** *n.m.* sleep, slumber.

**sonnolènto,** *adj.* somnolent, drowsy, sleepy.

**sonnolènza,** *n.f.* somnolence, drowsiness.

**sontuoso,** *adj.* sumptuous.

**soppiantare,** *vb.* supplant, supersede.

**soppiatto,** *adj.* **di s.,** stealthily.

**sopportàbile,** *adj.* bearable.

**sopportare,** *vb.* support, bear; abide, endure.

**sopportazione,** *n.f.* endurance.

**soppressione,** *n.f.* suppression.

**sopprìmere,** *vb.* suppress, put down, quell.

**sopra,** *adv. and prep.* over, above; upon.

**sopràbito,** *n.m.* overcoat, topcoat.

**sopracciglio,** *n.m.* eyebrow.

**sopraddetto,** *adj.* aforesaid.

**sopraffare,** *vb.* overcome, overwhelm.

**sopraindicato,** *adj.* aforementioned.

**soprannaturale,** *adj.* supernatural.

**soprano,** *n.m.* soprano.

**sopratutto,** *adv.* above all.

**sopravvivènza,** *n.f.* survival.

**sopravvìvere,** *vb.* survive, outlive.

**sorbetto,** *n.m.* sherry.

**sórcio,** *n.m.* mouse.

**sòrdido,** *adj.* sordid.

**sordità,** *n.f.* deafness.

**sordo,** *adj.* deaf.

**sordomuto,** *n.m.* deaf-mute.

**sorèlla,** *n.f.* sister.

**sorgènte,** *n.f.* source; spring; headwater(s).

**sórgere,** *vb.* rise, spring.

**sormontare,** *vb.* surmount.

**sorpassare,** *vb.* pass; surpass; cross over.

**sorpasso,** *n.m.* passing.

**sorprèndere,** *vb.* surprise.

**sorpresa,** *n.f.* surprise, astonishment.

**sorrìdere,** *vb.* smile.

**sorriso,** *n.m.* smile.

**sorseggiare,** *vb.* sip.

**sorso,** *n.m.* swallow; sip.

**sòrta,** *n.f.* sort.

**sòrte,** *n.f.* luck; lot.

**sorteggio,** *n.m.* drawing.

**sorveglianza,** *n.f.* surveillance, supervision.

**sorvegliare,** *vb.* oversee, supervise.

**sospèndere,** *vb.* suspend, discontinue.

**sospensione,** *n.f.* suspension; abeyance; stay.

**sospettare,** *vb.* suspect.

**sospètto,** **1.** *n.m.* suspicion, hunch. **2.** *adj.* suspicious, suspect.

**sospettosamente,** *adv.* suspiciously, askance.

**sospettoso,** *adj.* suspicious, distrustful.

**sospirare,** *vb.* sigh.

**sospiro,** *n.m.* sigh.

**sòsta,** *n.f.* stopping.

**sostantivo,** *n.m.* noun.

**sostanza,** *n.f.* substance.

**sostanziale,** *adj.* substantial.

**sostare**, vb. stop.

**sostegno**, n.m. backing, support; foothold.

**sostenere**, vb. uphold, sustain; maintain; support, back (up).

**sostenitore**, n.m. upholder, backer, sponsor.

**sostituire**, vb. substitute, replace.

**sostituto**, n.m. substitute, alternate.

**sostituzione**, n.f. substitution.

**sottana**, n.f. petticoat; skirt.

**sotterfugio**, n.m. subterfuge.

**sotterràneo**, adj. underground.

**sottile**, adj. subtle; thin; slim.

**sotto**, adv. and prep. under, underneath, below, beneath.

**sottolineare**, vb. underline.

**sottomarino**, adj. submarine.

**sottométtere**, vb. submit.

**sottomissione**, n.f. submission.

**sottopassàggio**, n.m. underpass.

**sottoporre**, vb. subject.

**sottoscritto**, adj. undersigned.

**sottoscrivere**, vb. subscribe; sign.

**sottosopra**, adv. upside down, topsy-turvy.

**sottotenènte**, n.m. second lieutenant.

**sottovalutare**, vb. underestimate.

**sottovènto**, 1. n. lee. 2. adv. leeward.

**sottovèste**, n.f. slip; (pl.) underwear.

**sottrarre**, vb. subtract, deduct; (refl.) get out of, shirk.

**sottufficiale**, n.m. non-commissioned officer.

**sovranità**, n.f. sovereignty.

**soviètico**, adj. soviet.

**sovrano**, n.m. and adj. sovereign, ruler.

**sovrintendènte**, n.m. superintendent.

**sovrumano**, adj. superhuman.

**sovvenzione**, n.f. subvention.

**sovversivo**, adj. subversive.

**sovvertire**, vb. subvert; overthrow.

**spaccare**, vb. split.

**spàccio**, n.m. sale; shop.

**spada**, n.f. sword.

**spadroneggiare**, vb. act as if one owned the place; be bossy, domineer.

**spaghetti**, n.m.pl. spaghetti.

**Spagna**, n.f. Spain.

**spagnuòlo**, 1. n.m. Spaniard. 2. adj. Spanish.

**spago**, n.m. twine.

**spalancare**, vb. open wide.

**spalla**, n.f. shoulder.

**spalleggiare**, vb. back (up).

**spalmare**, vb. smear.

**spanna**, n.f. span.

**spàragi**, n.m. (pl.) asparagus.

**sparare**, vb. fire, shoot.

**spàrgere**, vb. scatter.

**sparire**, vb. disappear.

**sparlare**, vb. speak ill.

**sparo**, n.m. shot.

**sparuto**, adj. haggard.

**spàsimo**, n.m. spasm, pang.

**spasmòdico**, adj. spasmodic.

**spassionato**, adj. dispassionate.

**spauràcchio**, n.m. scarecrow.

**spaventare**, vb. frighten, alarm, appal, scare.

**spavènto**, n.m. fright, scare.

**spaventoso**, adj. fearful, frightful.

**spàzio**, n.m. space.

**spazioso**, adj. spacious, capacious; roomy, commodious.

**spazzacamino**, n.m. chimney-sweep.

**spazzamine**, n. nave s., mine-sweeper.

**spazzare**, vb. sweep.

**spazzatura**, n.f. sweepings, dust.

**spazzino**, n.m. street-cleaner; scavenger.

**spàzzola**, n.f. brush.

**spazzolare**, vb. brush.

**spècchio**, n.m. mirror, looking-glass.

**speciale**, adj. special, especial.

**specialista**, n.m. specialist.

**specialità**, n.f. specialty.

**specialmente**, adv. specially, especially.

**spècie**, n.f. species.

**specificare**, vb. specify.

**specifico,** *adj.* specific.

**speculare,** *vb.* speculate.

**speculazione,** *n.f.* speculation.

**spedire,** *vb.* send, despatch, ship; remit.

**speditore,** *n.m.* sender, shipper, dispatcher.

**spedizione,** *n.f.* expedition; despatch; shipment; remittance.

**spedizionière,** *n.m.* shipping agent.

**spègnere,** *vb.* put out; douse; switch off.

**spèndere,** *vb.* spend; expend.

**spensieratamente,** *adv.* thoughtlessly, heedlessly, carelessly.

**spensieratezza,** *n.f.* thoughtlessness, heedlessness, carelessness.

**spensierato,** *adj.* thoughtless, heedless, careless; happy-go-lucky.

**speranza,** *n.f.* hope.

**sperare,** *vb.* hope.

**spergiurare,** *vb.* perjure oneself.

**spergiuro,** *n.m.* perjury.

**sperimentale,** *adj.* experimental; tentative.

**sperimentare,** *vb.* experiment.

**sperone,** *n.m.* spur.

**spesa,** *n.f.* expense, expenditure.

**spesso,** **1.** *adj.* thick. **2.** *adv.* often.

**spessore,** *n.m.* thickness.

**spettacolare,** *adj.* spectacular.

**spettàcolo,** *n.m.* spectacle, show.

**spettatore,** *n.m.* spectator, onlooker, bystander.

**spèttro,** *n.m.* specter, ghost; spectrum.

**spèzie,** *n.f.pl.* spice.

**spiaccicare,** *vb.* squash.

**spiacévole,** *adj.* unpleasant.

**spiàggia,** *n.f.* beach, shore.

**spiare,** *vb.* spy.

**spiccàgnolo,** *adj.* freestone.

**spidocchiare,** *vb.* delouse.

**spiegare,** *vb.* explain; spread; unfold; unfurl.

**spiegazione,** *n.f.* explanation.

**spiegazzare,** *vb.* crinkle, crease, crumple.

**spietato,** *adj.* pitiless, merciless, ruthless.

**spiga,** *n.f.* ear (of grain).

**spilla,** *n.f.* brooch.

**spillo,** *n.m.* pin. **s. di sicurezza,** safety-pin.

**spina,** *n.f.* thorn; spine; (electric) plug. **s. dorsale,** backbone.

**spinaci,** *n.m.pl.* spinach.

**spinetta,** *n.f.* spinet.

**spingere,** *vb.* push, jostle, shove; thrust; urge.

**spinta,** *n.f.* push, shove; thrust.

**spionàggio,** *n.m.* espionage.

**spione,** *n.m.* spy.

**spira,** *n.f.* spire, coil.

**spirale,** *n.m. and adj.* spiral.

**spiritismo,** *n.m.* spiritualism.

**spirito,** *n.m.* spirit; wit.

**spiritoso,** *adj.* witty.

**spirituale,** *adj.* spiritual.

**splèndere,** *vb.* shine.

**splèndido,** *adj.* splendid, gorgeous.

**splendore,** *n.m.* splendor, brilliance.

**spodestare,** *vb.* dispossess.

**spogliare,** *vb.* unclothe; divest, despoil, strip; harry.

**spoletta,** *n.f.* fuse.

**sponda,** *n.f.* shore.

**spontaneità,** *n.f.* spontaneity.

**spontàneo,** *adj.* spontaneous.

**spopolare,** *vb.* depopulate.

**spòra,** *n.f.* spore.

**sporàdico,** *adj.* sporadic.

**sporcare,** *vb.* foul, soil.

**spòrco,** *adj.* dirty, foul, soiled.

**spòrgere,** *vb.* put out; project.

**sportivo,** **1.** *n.* sportsman. **2.** *adj.* sport.

**sposa,** *n.f.* bride, spouse.

**sposalizio,** *n.m.* wedding, espousal.

**sposare,** *vb.* marry, espouse.

**sposi,** *n.m.pl.* bride and groom; newlyweds.

**sposo,** *n.m.* bridegroom, spouse.

**spostamento,** *n.m.* displacement.

**spostare,** *vb.* displace.

**sprecare,** *vb.* waste.

**sprèco,** *n.m.* waste.

**spregévole,** *adj.* contemptible, despicable, mean.

---

**spregiare**, *vb.* despise.
**spregiudicato**, *adj.* broad-minded.
**sprèmere**, *vb.* squeeze.
**spremuta**, *n.f.* squash.
**sprezzante**, *adj.* contemptuous, despising, scornful.
**sprezzantemente**, *adv.* contemptuously.
**sprigionare**, *vb.* release.
**sprizzare**, *vb.* spray.
**sprofondarsi**, *vb.* subside; sink.
**spronare**, *vb.* spur.
**sprone**, *n.m.* spur.
**sproporzionato**, *adj.* disproportionate.
**sproporzione**, *n.f.* disproportion.
**spruzzare**, *vb.* spout; spurt; splash; spatter.
**spruzzo**, *n.m.* splash, spatter.
**spugna**, *n.f.* sponge.
**spuma**, *n.f.* foam, froth.
**spuntare**, *vb.* appear; dawn.
**spuntino**, *n.m.* snack.
**spùrio**, *adj.* spurious.
**sputacchièra**, *n.f.* spittoon, cuspidor.
**sputare**, *vb.* spit.
**squadra**, *n.f.* squad; gang; team.
**squadrone**, *n.m.* squadron.
**squalifica**, *n.f.* disqualification.
**squalificare**, *vb.* disqualify.
**squàllido**, *adj.* squalid, bleak.
**squallore**, *n.m.* squalor, bleakness.
**squama**, *n.f.* scale.
**squarciare**, *vb.* gash, slash.
**squàrcio**, *n.m.* gash, slash.
**squillare**, *vb.* blare.
**squillo**, *n.m.* blare.
**squisito**, *adj.* exquisite, dainty, delicate.
**squisitezza**, *n.f.* exquisiteness, daintiness, delicacy.
**Sra.**, (abbr. for Signora) Mrs.
**sradicare**, *vb.* eradicate; uproot.
**sradicatore**, *n.m.* eradicator.
**sregolatezza**, *n.f.* dissipation, debauchery.
**stàbile**, *adj.* stable.
**stabilimento**, *n.m.* establishment.
**stabilire**, *vb.* establish; set; appoint; settle.

**stabilità**, *n.f.* stability.
**stabilizzare**, *vb.* stabilize.
**staccare**, *vb.* detach, sever.
**stacciare**, *vb.* sift.
**stàccio**, *n.m.* sieve.
**stàdio**, *n.m.* stadium; stage.
**staffière**, *n.m.* footman; groom.
**stagione**, *n.f.* season.
**stagnante**, *adj.* stagnant.
**stagnare**, *vb.* stagnate.
**stagnino**, *n.m.* tinsmith; plumber.
**stagno**, *n.m.* pond; pool; tin.
**stalla**, *n.f.* stable.
**stallo**, *n.m.* stall.
**stallone**, *n.m.* stallion.
**stame**, *n.m.* stamen.
**stamigna**, *n.m.* bunting.
**stampa**, *n.f.* press; printing.
**stampare**, *vb.* print.
**stampèlla**, *n.f.* crutch.
**stampino**, *n.m.* stencil.
**stampo**, *n.m.* stamp; mold; die.
**stancare**, *vb.* tire.
**stanco**, *adj.* tired, fagged, weary.
**standardizzare**, *vb.* standardize.
**stanga**, *n.f.* shaft.
**stanghetta**, *n.f.* hang-over.
**stantuffo**, *n.m.* piston.
**stanza**, *n.f.* room. **s. da bagno**, bathroom. **s. da lètto**, bedroom.
**stanziamento**, *n.m.* appropriation.
**stanziare**, *vb.* appropriate.
**stare**, *vb.* stand; be.
**starnutire**, *vb.* sneeze.
**starnuto**, *n.m.* sneeze.
**stasera**, *adv.* tonight.
**stàtico**, *adj.* static.
**statìstica**, *n.f.* statistics.
**stato**, *n.m.* state; estate.
**stàtua**, *n.f.* statue.
**statura**, *n.f.* stature.
**statuto**, *n.m.* statute.
**stazionàrio**, *adj.* stationary.
**stazione**, *n.f.* station; resort. **s. balneare**, bathing resort.
**stecca**, *n.f.* stick; cue; slat; splint.
**stella**, *n.f.* star.
**stellare**, *adj.* stellar.
**stelo**, *n.m.* stem.
**stèmma**, *n.m.* coat of arms.
**stèndere**, *vb.* extend; spread; draw up; (*refl.*) span.

For pronunciation, see the concise guide on pages 5 to 7.

**stenògrafa,** *n.f.* stenographer.

**stenografìa,** *n.f.* stenography, shorthand.

**stentatamente,** *adv.* with difficulty.

**stèrco,** *n.m.* dung.

**stereotipìa,** *n.f.* stereotype.

**stèrile,** *adj.* sterile, barren.

**sterilità,** *n.f.* sterility, barrenness.

**sterilizzare,** *v.b.* sterilize.

**sterlina,** *n.f.* pound sterling.

**sterminare,** *vb.* exterminate.

**sterminìo,** *n.m.* extermination.

**stesso,** *adj.* same; self.

**stetoscòpio,** *n.m.* stethoscope.

**stìa,** *n.f.* hen-coop.

**stigma,** *n.m.* stigma.

**stile,** *n.m.* style.

**stima,** *n.f.* esteem, estimate, appraisal.

**stimàbile,** *adj.* estimable.

**stimare,** *vb.* esteem, estimate, appraise, deem, value.

**stìmmate,** *n.f.pl* stigmata

**stimolante,** *n.m. and adj.* stimulant.

**stimolare,** *vb.* stimulate, goad.

**stimolo,** *n.m.* stimulus, goad.

**stinco,** *n.m.* shin.

**stipèndio,** *n.m.* salary.

**stipettaio,** *n.m.* cabinetmaker.

**stìpite,** *n.m.* jamb.

**stipo,** *n.m.* cabinet, deem, value.

**stipulare,** *vb.* stipulate.

**stirare,** *vb.* iron.

**stirpe,** *f.* lineage; stock.

**stitichezza,** *n.f.* constipation.

**stàtico,** *adj.* constipated.

**stiva,** *n.f.* hold (of boat).

**stivale,** *n.m.* boot.

**stivatore,** *n.m.* stevedore.

**stizzoso,** *adj.* peevish.

**Stoccarda,** *n.f.* Stuttgart.

**Stoccolma,** *n.f.* Stockholm.

**stòffa,** *n.f.* cloth, stuff, material, fabric.

**stòico,** **1.** *n.* stoic. **2.** *adj.* stoical.

**stòla,** *n.f.* stole.

**stòlido,** *adj.* stolid.

**stolto,** **1.** *n.m.* fool, dunce. **2.** *adj.* foolish.

**stòmaco,** *n.m.* stomach.

**stòrcere,** *vb.* sprain.

**stordimento,** *n.m.* dizziness.

**stordire,** *vb.* stun.

**stordito,** *adj.* stunned, dizzy.

**stòria,** *n.f.* history; story, yarn.

**stòrico,** **1.** *n.* historian **2.** *adj.* historic, historical.

**stornare,** *vb.* turn away; divert.

**storpiare,** *vb.* maim.

**stòrta,** *n.f.* sprain.

**stòrto,** *adj.* crooked.

**stovìglie,** *n.f.pl.* earthenware, pottery.

**strale,** *n.m.* arrow; shaft.

**stra-,** *prefix,* extra-.

**stràbico,** *adj.* cross-eyed.

**stràccio,** *n.m.* rag; clout.

**straccione,** *n.m.* ragamuffin.

**strada,** *n.f.* road, street. **s. maestra,** highway.

**stradale,** *adj.* pertaining to roads.

**strafottènte,** *adj.* inconsiderate.

**stranezza,** *n.f.* strangeness, oddity.

**strangolare,** *vb.* strangle, choke.

**stranièro,** **1.** *n.* stranger; foreigner. **2.** *adj.* strange; foreign.

**strano,** *adj.* strange, odd, peculiar, queer, quaint, weird.

**straordinàrio,** *adj.* extraordinary; extra.

**strapazzate,** *adj.* uòva s., scrambled eggs.

**strappare,** *vb.* tear, rip, rend; snatch, wrench.

**straripare,** *vb.* overflow.

**stratagèmma,** *n.m.* stratagem.

**strategìa,** *n.f.* strategy.

**stratègico,** *adj.* strategic.

**strato,** *n.m.* stratum, layer; coating.

**stratosfèra,** *n.f.* stratosphere.

**strattone,** *n.m.* jerk.

**stravagante,** *adj.* extravagant.

**stravaganza,** *n.f.* extravagance.

**straziante,** *adj.* heart-rending.

**straziato,** *adj.* heartbroken.

**strega,** *n.f.* witch, hag.

**stregare,** *vb.* bewitch.

**stregone,** *n.m.* wizard.

**stregonerìa,** *n.f.* sorcery.

**strènuo**, *adj.* strenuous.

**streptocòcco**, *n.m.* streptococcus.

**stretta**, *n.f.* clasp; squeeze. **s. di mano**, hand-shake.

**stretto**, 1. *n.m.* strait. 2. *adj.* narrow, tight.

**strìa**, *n.f.* streak.

**strìdulo**, *adj.* shrill, strident.

**strigliare**, *vb.* curry.

**strillare**, *vb.* scream, shriek.

**strillo**, *n.m.* scream, shriek.

**strinare**, *vb.* singe.

**stringere**, *vb.* hold tight; clasp; clench; squeeze; press; tighten. **s. la mano a**, shake hands with.

**striscia**, *n.f.* strip; stripe; band; slip.

**strisciare**, *vb.* creep.

**strofinàccio**, *n.m.* wiper; dustcloth; dishcloth.

**strofinare**, *vb.* rub; wipe.

**strumentale**, *adj.* instrumental.

**strumento**, *n.m.* instrument; implement.

**strutto**, *n.m.* lard.

**struttura**, *n.f.* structure.

**struzzo**, *n.m.* ostrich.

**stucco**, *n.m.* stucco.

**studènte**, *n.m.* student.

**studentéssa**, *n.f.* student.

**studiare**, *vb.* study.

**stùdio**, *n.m.* study; studio.

**studioso**, *adj.* studious.

**stufa**, *n.f.* stove.

**stufare**, *vb.* stew.

**stufato**, *n.m.* stew.

**stuòia**, *n.f.* mat.

**stuoino**, *n.m.* door-mat.

**stupèndo**, *adj.* stupendous.

**stupidità**, *n.f.* stupidity, dumbness, backwardness.

**stùpido**, *adj.* stupid, dumb, backward.

**stupire**, *vb.* amaze, astonish, astound, surprise, daze.

**stupìrsi**, *vb.* be amazed, be astonished, be surprised.

**stupore**, *n.m.* daze, stupor; astonishment, amazement, wonder.

**sturare**, *vb.* uncork.

**su**, *prep. and adv.* on; upon; up.

**subcosciènte**, *adj.* subconscious.

**subire**, *vb.* undergo.

**subito**, *adv.* immediately.

**sublimare**, *vb.* sublimate.

**sublimato**, *n.m. and adj.* sublimate.

**sublime**, *adj.* sublime.

**subnormale**, *adj.* subnormal.

**subordinato**, *n.m. and adj.* subordinate.

**succèdere**, *vb.* succeed; happen, occur.

**successione**, *n.f.* succession.

**successivo**, *adj.* successive; subsequent.

**successo**, *n.m.* success.

**successore**, *n.m.* successor.

**succhiare**, *vb.* suck.

**succhièllo**, *n.m.* auger, gimlet.

**succo**, *n.m.* juice.

**succoso**, *adj.* juicy.

**succursale**, *n.f.* branch.

**sud**, *n.m.* south. **polo s.**, South Pole.

**sudare**, *vb.* sweat, perspire, swelter.

**sudàrio**, *n.m.* shroud.

**suddetto**, *adj.* aforesaid.

**suddito**, *n.m.* subject.

**sud-èst**, *n.m.* southeast.

**sùdicio**, *adj.* dirty, dingy, filthy, grimy.

**sudiciume**, *n.m.* dirt, filth, grime.

**sudore**, *n.m.* sweat, perspiration.

**sud-òvest**, *n.m.* southwest.

**sufficiènte**, *adj.* sufficient, adequate, enough.

**sufficientemente**, *adv.* sufficiently, adequately.

**sufficiènza**, *n.f.* sufficiency, adequacy.

**suggellare**, *vb.* seal.

**suggèllo**, *n.m.* seal.

**suggerimento**, *n.m.* suggestion.

**suggerire**, *vb.* suggest.

**suggeritore**, *n.m.* prompter.

**sùghero**, *n.m.* cork.

**sugo**, *n.m.* sauce. **s. di carne**, gravy.

**suicidarsi**, *vb.* commit suicide.

**suicìdio**, *n.m.* suicide.

**suindicato**, *adj.* aforementioned.

**sultanina**, *adj.* **uva s.**, sultana raisin.

**sunto**, *n.m.* abstract, résumé.

**suo**, *adj.* his; her; hers; its; your; yours.

**suòcera**, *n.f.* mother-in-law.

**suòcero,** *n.m.* father-in-law.
**suòla,** *n.f.* sole.
**suòlo,** *n.m.* soil.
**suonare,** *vb.* sound; ring; play.
**suonatore,** *n.m.* player.
**suòno,** *n.m.* sound; ring.
**superare,** *vb.* overcome; surpass, exceed; excel; top; pass (exam.).
**supèrbia,** *n.f.* haughtiness, pride.
**supèrbo,** *adj.* haughty, proud; superb.
**superficiale,** *adj.* superficial.
**superfìcie,** *n.f.* surface.
**supèrfluo,** *adj.* superfluous.
**superiore,** *adj.* superior; upper.
**superiorità,** *n.f.* superiority.
**superlativo,** *n.m. and adj.* superlative.
**superstizióne,** *n.f.* superstition.
**superstizióso,** *adj.* superstitious.
**superuòmo,** *n.m.* superman.
**supplemento,** *n.m.* supplement.
**sùpplica,** *n.f.* supplication, entreaty.
**supplicare,** *vb.* supplicate, beseech, entreat.
**supplichévole,** *adj.* beseeching.
**supplichevolmente,** *adv.* beseechingly.
**supplire,** *vb.* replace; make up for; eke out.
**supporre,** *vb.* suppose.
**supposizióne,** *n.f.* supposition, assumption.
**suppurare,** *vb.* suppurate, fester.
**supremazìa,** *n.f.* supremacy, ascendancy.

**suprèmo,** *adj.* supreme, paramount.
**surrenale,** *adj.* adrenal.
**susìna,** *n.f.* plum.
**susìno,** *n.m.* plum-tree.
**sussidiare,** *vb.* subsidize.
**sussìdio,** *n.m.* subsidy.
**sussultare,** *vb.* start.
**sussulto,** *n.m.* start.
**svaligiare,** *vb.* rob completely.
**svalutare,** *vb.* devalue.
**svanire,** *vb.* vanish.
**svantàggio,** *n.m.* disadvantage, drawback, handicap.
**svariato,** *adj.* varied.
**svedese, 1.** *n.* Swede. **2.** *adj.* Swedish.
**svegliare,** *vb.* awaken, wake up, arouse; (*refl.*) awake.
**svéglio,** *adj.* awake.
**svelto,** *adj.* quick; slender.
**svenimento,** *n.m.* faint, swoon.
**svenire,** *vb.* faint, swoon.
**sventolare,** *vb.* wave; fan.
**svernare,** *vb.* winter; hibernate.
**svestire,** *vb.* undress; (*refl.*) disrobe.
**Svèzia,** *n.f.* Sweden.
**sviarsi,** *vb.* lose one's way, go astray.
**sviato,** *adj.* lost; stray.
**svignàrsela,** *vb.* (fam.) abscond.
**sviluppare,** *vb.* develop.
**sviluppatore,** *n.m.* developer.
**sviluppo,** *n.m.* development, growth.
**sviscerare,** *vb.* eviscerate.
**svista,** *n.f.* blunder.
**Svìzzera,** *n.f.* Switzerland.
**svìzzero,** *n. and adj.* Swiss.
**svogliato,** *adj.* listless.
**svolazzare,** *vb.* flutter.
**svòlta,** *n.f.* turn.

# T

**tabacco,** *n.m.* tobacco.
**tabernàcolo,** *n.m.* tabernacle.
**tacca,** *n.f.* nick, notch.

**taccagno,** *adj.* niggardly.
**tacchino,** *n.m.* turkey, gobbler.
**tacco,** *n.m.* heel.

**taccuino,** *n.m.* note-book.

**tacere,** *vb.* be quiet, keep quiet.

**tachìmetro,** *n.m.* speedometer.

**tafano,** *n.m.* gadfly.

**tafferùglio,** *n.m.* scuffle, scrap.

**tagliando,** *n.m.* coupon.

**tagliare,** *vb.* cut; carve; chop; clip; hack; hew.

**tagliatèlle,** *n.f.pl.* noodles.

**tagliatore,** *n.m.* cutter.

**tàglio,** *n.m.* cut.

**tale,** *adj.* such.

**talènto,** *n.m.* talent.

**tallone,** *n.m.* heel.

**talpa,** *n.f.* mole.

**tamburo,** *n.m.* drum; drummer. **tamburo maggiore** drum major.

**tana,** *n.f.* burrow, den, lair.

**tànghero,** *n.m.* boor, clod.

**tangìbile,** *adj.* tangible.

**tappare,** *vb.* plug, stop up.

**tappeto,** *n.m.* carpet, rug.

**tappezzare,** *vb.* upholster.

**tappezzerìa,** *n.f.* tapestry, hanging.

**tappezzière,** *n.m.* upholsterer.

**tappo,** *n.m.* cork, stopper, plug.

**tarchiato,** *adj.* squat, stocky.

**tardi,** *adv.* late.

**tardivo,** *adj.* tardy, late.

**tardo,** *adj.* late.

**targa,** *n.f.* plate.

**tariffa,** *n.f.* tariff; fare.

**tarma,** *n.f.* moth.

**tartagliare,** *vb.* stutter.

**tartaruga,** *n.f.* turtle.

**tasca,** *n.f.* pocket.

**tascàbile,** *adj.* pocket-size.

**tassa,** *n.f.* tax; fee.

**tassèllo,** *n.m.* dowel.

**tassì,** *n.m.* taxicab.

**tasso,** *n.m.* badger.

**tastièra,** *n.f.* keyboard.

**tasto,** *n.m.* key.

**tastoni,** *adv.:* **andare a t.,** grope.

**tatto,** *n.m.* tact; feel.

**tàvola,** *n.f.* table; board; plank.

**tavoletta,** *n.f.* tablet.

**tavolòzza,** *n.f.* palette.

**tazza,** *n.f.* cup.

**te,** *pron.* 2. *sg.* thee; you.

**tè,** *n.m.* tea.

**teatro,** *n.m.* theater.

**tècnica,** *n.f.* technique.

**tècnico,** *adj.* technical.

**todesco,** *n. and adj.* German.

**tèdio,** *n.m.* tedium.

**tedioso,** *adj.* tedious.

**tègola,** *n.f.* tile.

**teièra,** *n.f.* tea-pot.

**tela,** *n.f.* cloth; web. **t. cerata,** oil-cloth. **t. da fusto,** buckram.

**telaio,** *n.m.* loom; frame; chassis.

**telefonare,** *vb.* telephone.

**telefonata,** *n.f.* telephone call.

**telèfono,** *n.m.* telephone.

**telegrafare,** *vb.* telegraph.

**telègrafo,** *n.m.* telegraph.

**telegramma,** *n.m.* telegram.

**teleschermo,** *n.m.* television screen.

**telescòpio,** *n.m.* telescope.

**telescrivènte,** *n.f.* teletype.

**televisione,** *n.f.* television.

**televisore,** *n.m.* television set.

**tèma,** *n.m.* theme.

**temerarietà,** *n.f.* rashness, foolhardiness.

**temeràrio, 1.** *n.m.* daredevil. **2.** *adj.* rash, foolhardy.

**temere,** *vb.* fear, dread.

**temperamento,** *n.m.* temperament.

**temperanza,** *n.f.* temperance.

**temperare,** *vb.* temper.

**temperato,** *adj.* temperate.

**temperatura,** *n.f.* temperature.

**temperino,** *n.m.* pen-knife.

**tempèsta,** *n.f.* tempest, storm, gale.

**tempestoso,** *adj.* tempestuous, stormy, gusty.

**tèmpia,** *n.f.* temple.

**tèmpio,** *n.m.* temple.

**tèmpo,** *n.m.* time; weather.

**tenace,** *adj.* tenacious, dogged.

**tènda,** *n.f.* tent; awning; booth.

**tendènte,** *adj.* tending, conducive.

**tendènza,** *n.f.* tendency, trend.

**tèndere,** *vb.* tend, conduce; stretch.

**tèndine,** *n.m.* tendon.

**tènebre,** *n.f.pl.* darkness.

For pronunciation, see the concise guide on pages 5 to 7.

**tenebroso**, *adj.* dark.

**tenènte**, *n.m.* lieutenant.

**teneramente**, *adv.* tenderly, fondly.

**tenere**, *vb.* hold; keep.

**tenerézza**, *n.f.* tenderness, fondness.

**tènero**, *adj.* tender, fond.

**tenóre**, *n.m.* tenor.

**tensióne**, *n.f.* tension, strain.

**tentare**, *vb.* attempt, try; tempt.

**tentativo**, **1.** *n.m.* attempt. **2.** *adj.* tentative.

**tentazióne**, *n.f.* temptation.

**tènue**, *adj.* tenuous, flimsy.

**teologìa**, *n.f.* theology.

**teòlogo**, *n.m.* theologian.

**teorìa**, *n.f.* theory.

**teòrico**, *adj.* theoretical.

**teppista**, *n.m.* hoodlum.

**terapìa**, *n.f.* therapy.

**tergicristallo**, *n.m.* windshield-wiper.

**terminare**, *vb.* terminate, end, finish.

**terminale**, *adj.* terminal.

**tèrmine**, *n.m.* end; terminus; term; deadline; abutment.

**termòmetro**, *n.m.* thermometer.

**termosifóne**, *n.m.* heating system.

**tèrra**, *n.f.* earth, ground, land.

**terrazza**, *n.f.* terrace.

**terremòto**, *n.m.* earthquake.

**terreno**, **1.** *n.* soil, terrain; lot. **2.** *adj.* earthy, earthly.

**terrìbile**, *adj.* terrible, awful, frightful, dire, dreadful.

**terribilmente**, *adv.* terribly, awfully, dreadfully.

**terrìccio**, *n.m.* loam.

**territòrio**, *n.m.* territory.

**terróre**, *n.m.* terror, fear, awe.

**tèrzo**, *adj.* third.

**tèsa**, *n.f.* (hat) brim.

**teso**, *adj.* tight, taut, tense.

**tesorière**, *n.m.* treasurer.

**tesòro**, *n.m.* treasure; treasury.

**tèssera**, *n.f.* card; ticket.

**tèssere**, *vb.* weave.

**tèssile**, *adj.* textile.

**tessitóre**, *n.m.* weaver.

**tessitura**, *n.f.* texture; weaving.

**tessuto**, *n.m.* tissue; textile.

**tèsta**, *n.f.* head. **t. di sbarco**,

bridgehead. **tener t. a.** cope with.

**testaménto**, *n.m.* testament, will.

**testardo**, *adj.* stubborn, headstrong, self-willed.

**testàtico**, *n.m.* poll-tax.

**testimòne**, *n.m.* witness. **t. oculare**, eyewitness.

**testimoniare**, *vb.* testify.

**testimonianza**, *n.f.* testimony.

**tèsto**, *n.m.* text.

**tètano**, *n.m.* tetanus, lockjaw.

**tetraóne**, *n.m.* grouse.

**tètto**, *n.m.* roof.

**tettóia**, *n.f.* shed.

**thè**, *n.m.* tea.

**ti**, *pron.* 2. *sg.* thee; you.

**tièpido**, *adj.* tepid, lukewarm.

**tìfo**, *n.m.* typhus.

**tifoidèo**, *adj.* typhoid.

**tifóso**, *n.m.* fan, enthusiast.

**tìglio**, *n.m.* lime-tree; linden.

**tiglióso**, *adj.* tough, leathery.

**tigre**, *n.m.* tiger.

**timbrare**, *vb.* stamp.

**timbro**, *n.m.* stamp.

**timidaménte**, *adv.* timidly, shyly, bashfully.

**timidézza**, *n.f.* timidity, shyness, bashfulness.

**tìmido**, *adj.* timid, shy, bashful; coy; chicken-hearted; diffident.

**timóne**, *n.m.* helm; rudder; (wagon) pole.

**timonière**, *n.m.* steersman, helmsman; coxswain.

**timóre**, *n.m.* fear, apprehension, dread.

**timoróso**, *adj.* timorous, fearful, apprehensive.

**tìmpano**, *n.m.* ear-drum; kettle-drum.

**tìngere**, *vb.* dye.

**tino**, *n.m.* vat.

**tinta**, *n.f.* tint, shade.

**tintinnare**, *vb.* tinkle, jingle.

**tintóre**, *n.m.* dyer; dry-cleaner.

**tintura**, *n.f.* dye.

**tìpico**, *adj.* typical.

**tipo**, *n.m.* type.

**tirannìa**, *n.f.* tyranny.

**tiranno**, *n.m.* tyrant.

**tirare**, *vb.* draw, pull, tug.

**tirata**, *n.f.* pull.

For pronunciation, see the concise guide on pages 5 to 7.

**tiratura**, *n.f.* printing.

**tirchio**, *adj.* stingy.

**tiro**, *n.m.* trick.

**tisi**, *n.f.* consumption, tuberculosis.

**tisico**, *adj.* consumptive.

**titolare**, **1.** *n.* incumbent. **2.** *adj.* titular.

**titolo**, *n.m.* title, headline, heading, caption.

**tizio**, *n.m.* chap, fellow, guy.

**toccare**, *vb.* touch.

**tocco**, *n.m.* touch.

**togliere**, *vb.* take away, remove.

**tollerante**, *adj.* tolerant.

**tolleranza**, *n.f.* tolerance.

**tollerare**, *vb.* tolerate, stand.

**tomba**, *n.f.* tomb, grave.

**tombale**, *adj.* pertaining to a tomb or grave.

**tondo**, *adj.* round.

**tonfo**, *n.m.* splash; thud.

**tonica**, *n.f.* (music) tonic.

**tonico**, *n.m. and adj.* tonic.

**tonnellata**, *n.f.* ton.

**tonno**, *n.m.* tuna.

**tono**, *n.m.* tone, pitch.

**tonsilla**, *n.f.* tonsil.

**topo**, *n.m.* mouse.

**torcere**, *vb.* twist, wring.

**torinese**, *adj.* Turinese.

**Torino**, *n.f.* Turin.

**torlo**, *n.m.* yolk.

**tormentare**, *vb.* torment; fret; nag; tease.

**tormento**, *n.m.* torment.

**tormentoso**, *adj.* excruciating.

**tornare**, *vb.* return.

**tornasole**, *n.m.* litmus.

**tórnio**, *n.m.* lathe.

**toro**, *n.m.* bull.

**torre**, *n.f.* tower.

**torrefazione**, *n.f.* roasting (of coffee).

**torrènte**, *n.m.* torrent; mountain stream.

**torretta**, *n.f.* turret.

**tórsolo**, *n.m.* core.

**torta**, *n.f.* cake, tart, pie.

**torto**, *n.m.* wrong. **aver t.**, be wrong.

**tortura**, *n.f.* torture.

**torturare**, *vb.* torture.

**tosare**, *vb.* clip, shear.

**tosatore**, *n.m.* clipper.

**tosatura**, *n.f.* clipping.

**Toscana**, *n.f.* Tuscany.

**toscano**, *adj.* Tuscan.

**tosse**, *n.f.* cough.

**tossicomane**, *n.m.* drug addict.

**tossire**, *vb.* cough.

**totale**, *n.m. and adj.* total.

**totalità**, *n.f.* totality, entirety.

**totalitàrio**, *adj.* totalitarian.

**tovàglia**, *n.f.* tablecloth.

**tovagliolino**, *n.m.* little napkin; doily.

**tovagliolo**, *n.m.* napkin.

**tozzo**, *adj.* stocky, chunky.

**tra**, *prep.* between, among, amid.

**traballare**, *vb.* reel, stagger, lurch.

**traboccare**, *vb.* overflow.

**tràccia**, *n.f.* trace.

**tradimento**, *n.m.* betrayal, treason.

**tradire**, *vb.* betray.

**traditore**, *n.m.* traitor.

**tradizionale**, *adj.* traditional.

**tradizione**, *n.f.* tradition.

**tradurre**, *vb.* translate.

**traduzione**, *n.f.* translation.

**tràffico**, *n.m.* traffic.

**trafiggere**, *vb.* transfix, spear.

**traforare**, *vb.* pierce; tunnel.

**traforo**, *n.m.* tunnel.

**tragèdia**, *n.f.* tragedy.

**traghetto**, *n.m.* ferry.

**tràgico**, *adj.* tragic.

**traguardo di puntamento**, *n.m.* bombsight.

**tram**, *n.m.* street-car, trolley-car.

**trambusto**, *n.m.* flurry.

**tramestio**, *n.m.* bustle.

**tramezzino**, *n.m.* sandwich.

**trampolino**, *n.m.* springboard.

**tranne**, *prep.* except.

**tranquillità**, *n.f.* tranquillity.

**tranquillo**, *adj.* tranquil, quiet, peaceful.

**transatlàntico**, **1.** *n.* liner. **2.** *adj.* transatlantic.

**transizione**, *n.f.* transition.

**tranvìa**, *n.f.* tramway, street-car line.

**tranviàrio**, *adj.* tramway.

**trapanare**, *vb.* drill.

**tràpano**, *n.m.* drill.

**trapasso**, *n.m.* death; passage; (property) conveyance.

**tràppola**, *n.f.* pitfall, snare, trap.

**trapunta**, *n.f.* quilt.

**trasalire**, *vb.* give a start.

**trasandato**, *adj.* sloppy.

**trascinare**, *vb.* drag, haul, lug.

**trascinarsi**, *vb.* crawl.

**trascórrere**, *vb.* elapse, pass.

**trascuràbile**, *adj.* negligible.

**trascurare**, *vb.* neglect, disregard, ignore, overlook.

**trascuratamente**, *adv.* negligently, carelessly.

**trascuratezza**, *n.f.* negligence, carelessness.

**trascurato**, *adj.* negligent, careless, frowzy, sloppy, slovenly.

**trasferimento**, *n.m.* transfer.

**trasferire**, *vb.* transfer.

**trasformare**, *vb.* transform.

**trasfusione**, *n.f.* transfusion.

**traslòco**, *n.m.* move; (household goods) moving.

**trasméttere**, *vb.* transmit, broadcast, convey.

**trasmettitore**, *n.m.* transmitter, broadcaster.

**trasmissione**, *n.f.* transmission. **t. radiofònica**, broadcast.

**trasparènte**, *adj.* transparent.

**trasportare**, *vb.* transport, carry, haul, convey.

**trasportatore**, *n.m.* conveyor.

**traspòrto**, *n.m.* transport; transportation; carriage; cartage; haulage.

**trastullare**, *vb.* amuse; (*refl.*) toy.

**trastullo**, *n.m.* toy.

**trasudare**, *vb.* ooze, seep.

**tratta**, *n.f.* draft.

**trattamento**, *n.m.* treatment.

**trattare**, *vb.* treat; deal.

**trattato**, *n.m.* treaty; treatise.

**trattenere**, *vb.* entertain; refrain; restrain; withhold; (*refl.*) forbear.

**trattenimento**, *n.m.* entertainment.

**tratto**, *n.m.* trait; feature; dash; stretch; tract. **t. d' unione**, hyphen.

**trattore**, *n.m.* restaurantkeeper.

**trattoria**, *n.f.* restaurant.

**trattrice**, *n.f.* tractor.

**travasare**, *vb.* scoop; pour off.

**trave**, *n.f.* beam, girder.

**travèrso**, *adv.*: **di travèrso**, awry.

**travestimento**, *n.m.* disguise; travesty.

**travestire**, *vb.* disguise; travesty.

**travicèllo**, *n.m.* joist, rafter.

**tre**, *num.* three.

**tréccia**, *n.f.* braid.

**tredicèsimo**, *adj.* thirteenth.

**trédici**, *num.* thirteen.

**trégua**, *n.f.* truce; respite.

**tremare**, *vb.* tremble, quake, shake.

**tremèndo**, *adj.* tremendous; awesome.

**trèmito**, *n.m.* trembling, quake.

**tremolare**, *vb.* tremble, flicker, quaver.

**tremolìo**, *n.m.* trembling, flicker.

**treno**, *n.m.* train.

**trenta**, *num.* thirty.

**trentèsimo**, *adj.* thirtieth.

**tresca**, *n.f.* intrigue; (illicit) love affair.

**trescone**, *n.m.* reel (dance).

**triàngolo**, *n.m.* triangle.

**tribolazione**, *n.f.* tribulation.

**tribordo**, *n.m.* starboard.

**tribù**, *n.f.* tribe, clan.

**tribuna**, *n.f.* stand, grandstand.

**tributàrio**, *n.m. and adj.* tributary.

**tributo**, *n.m.* tribute.

**trichèco**, *n.m.* walrus.

**trifòglio**, *n.m.* clover.

**trimestrale**, *adj.* every three months, quarterly.

**trimèstre**, *n.m.* three-month period, quarter; (school) term.

**trincèa**, *n.f.* trench; cutting.

**trincerare**, *vb.* entrench.

**trinciante**, *n.m.* carvingknife.

**trinciare**, *vb.* carve, cut up.

**trionfale**, *adj.* triumphal.

**trionfante**, *adj.* triumphal.

**trionfare**, *vb.* triumph.

**trionfo**, *n.m.* triumph.

**triplicare**, *vb.* triple.

**triplice**, *adj.* triple.

**triste**, *adj.* sad, gloomy, depressed, doleful, glum.

For pronunciation, see the concise guide on pages 5 to 7.

**tristezza,** *n.f.* sadness, gloom, glumness.
**tritare,** *vb.* pound, mangle.
**trito,** *adj.* trite.
**triturare,** *vb.* mince.
**trivello,** *n.m.* auger, borer.
**trofèo,** *n.m.* trophy.
**trògolo,** *n.m.* trough.
**tròia,** *n.f.* sow.
**tromba,** *n.f.* trumpet.
**trombaio,** *n.m.* plumber.
**trombettière,** *n.m.* trumpeter.
**tronco,** *n.m.* trunk; log.
**tròno,** *n.m.* throne.
**tròpico, 1.** *n.m.* tropic. **2.** *adj.* tropical.
**troppo, 1.** *adj.* too many; too much. **2.** *adv.* too.
**tròta,** *n.f.* trout.
**trottare,** *vb.* trot.
**tròtto,** *n.m.* trot.
**trovare,** *vb.* find, locate; (*refl.*) be; be located; happen to be.
**trovatèllo,** *n.m.* foundling.
**trucco,** *n.m.* trick.
**trucidare,** *vb.* slay.
**truffare,** *vb.* cheat, swindle.
**truffatore,** *n.m.* cheater, swindler.
**truppa,** *n.f.* troop.
**tu,** *pron.* 2.*sg.* thou; you.
**tuberculòsi,** *n.f.* tuberculosis.
**tubo,** *n.m.* tube, pipe.
**tuffare,** *vb.* plunge; dip; dunk; (*refl.*) dive.

**tuffatore,** *n.m.* diver; dive-bomber.
**tuffo,** *n.m.* dive, plunge.
**tugùrio,** *n.m.* hovel.
**tulipano,** *n.m.* tulip.
**tumore,** *n.m.* tumor.
**tùmulo,** *n.m.* mound.
**tumulto,** *n.m.* tumult, uproar, hubbub, riot.
**tumultuare,** *vb.* riot.
**tuo,** *adj.* thy; your.
**tuonare,** *vb.* thunder.
**tuòno,** *n.m.* thunder.
**turbante,** *n.m.* turban.
**turbina,** *n.f.* turbine.
**turbinare,** *vb.* whirl, gyrate, swirl.
**turbine,** *n.m.* whirlwind.
**turbo-elica,** *n.f.* turbo-prop.
**turbolènto,** *adj.* turbulent, boisterous.
**turboreattore,** *n.m.* turbojet.
**Turchìa,** *n.f.* Turkey.
**turco, 1.** *n.m.* Turk. **2.** *adj.* Turkish.
**turismo,** *n.m.* sightseeing, tourism.
**turista,** *n.m.* tourist.
**turìstico,** *adj.* tourist.
**turno,** *n.m.* turn, shift.
**tuta,** *n.f.* overalls; dungarees.
**tutèla,** *n.f.* guardianship.
**tutore,** *n.m.* guardian.
**tuttavia,** *adv.* however; yet.
**tutto, 1.** *adj.* all; whole. **t. a un tratto,** all of a sudden. **2.** *pron.* everything.

# U

**ubbidire,** *vb.* obey.
**ubbriachezza,** *n.f.* drunkenness, intoxication.
**ubbriaco,** *adj.* drunk, drunken.
**ubbriacone,** *n.m.* drunkard, inebriate.
**uccellièra,** *n.f.* bird-house, aviary.
**uccellino,** *n.m.* fledgling.
**uccèllo,** *n.m.* bird. **u. di rapina,** bird of prey.

**uccìdere,** *vb.* kill.
**uccisore,** *n.m.* killer.
**udibile,** *adj.* audible.
**udiènza,** *n.f.* audience, interview, hearing.
**udire,** *vb.* hearing.
**uditivo,** *adj.* auditory.
**udito,** *n.m.* hearing.
**uditore,** *n.m.* hearer, auditor.
**uditòrio,** *n.m.* audience.
**uditrice,** *n.f.* hearer, auditor.

**ufficiale, 1.** *n.m.* officer, official. **2.** *adj.* official.

**ufficio,** *n.m.* office, bureau.

**ùgola,** *n.f.* uvula.

**uguaglianza,** *n.f.* equality.

**uguagliare,** *vb.* equal, equalize, equate, match.

**uguale,** *adj.* equal.

**ùlcera,** *n.f.* ulcer.

**ulteriore,** *adj.* ulterior, further.

**ùltimo,** *adj.* last, end, hindmost, ultimate.

**umanamente,** *adv.* humanly.

**umanésimo,** *n.m.* humanism.

**umanista,** *n.m.* humanist.

**umanità,** *n.f.* humanity, mankind.

**umanitàrio,** *adj.* humanitarian, humane.

**umano,** *adj.* human.

**umbro,** *adj.* Umbrian.

**umidità,** *n.f.* dampness, humidity, moisture.

**ùmido,** *adj.* damp, humid, moist, wet.

**ùmile,** *adj.* humble, lowly.

**umiliare,** *vb.* humiliate, humble; (*refl.*) grovel.

**umiliazione,** *n.f.* humiliation.

**umiltà,** *n.f.* humility.

**umore,** *n.m.* humor.

**umorismo,** *n.m.* humor.

**umorista,** *n.m.* humorist.

**umorìstico,** *adj.* humorous, jocular.

**unànime,** *adj.* unanimous.

**uncinare,** *vb.* hook.

**uncino,** *n.m.* hook, grapple.

**undicésimo,** *adj.* eleventh.

**undici,** *num.* eleven.

**ùngere,** *vb.* grease; smear; anoint; oil.

**unghérese,** *adj.* Hungarian.

**Unghería,** *n.f.* Hungary.

**ùnghia,** *n.f.* fingernail.

**unguènto,** *n.m.* unguent, salve, ointment.

**ùnico,** *adj.* only; unique; single; sole.

**unificare,** *vb.* unify.

**uniforme, 1.** *n.m.* uniform. **2.** *adj.* uniform, even.

**uniformità,** *n.f.* uniformity, evenness.

**unilaterale,** *adj.* unilateral, one-sided.

**unione,** *n.f.* union.

**unire,** *vb.* unite.

**unità,** *n.f.* unity; unit.

**universale,** *adj.* universal.

**università,** *n.f.* university, college.

**universitàrio,** *adj.* pertaining to a university, collegiate.

**univèrso,** *n.m.* universe.

**uno,** *m.,* **una** *f.* **1.** *art.* a, an. **2.** *num.* one.

**untuoso,** *adj.* greasy.

**uòmo,** *n.m.* man.

**uòpo,** *n.m.* purpose.

**uòvo,** *n.m.* egg. **u. affogato,** poached egg.

**uragano,** *n.m.* hurricane.

**uraninite,** *n.f.* pitchblende.

**urbano,** *adj.* urban.

**urgènte,** *adj.* urgent, pressing.

**urgènza,** *n.f.* urgency.

**urlare,** *vb.* yell, holler, bawl, shout, cry, howl.

**urlo,** *n.m.* yell, shout, howl.

**urna,** *n.f.* urn.

**urtare,** *vb.* bump; shock; clash.

**urto,** *n.m.* bump; shock; impact; clash.

**usanza,** *n.f.* usage.

**usare,** *vb.* use.

**uscière,** *n.m.* usher; bailiff.

**uscita,** *n.f.* exit.

**usignuòlo,** *n.m.* nightingale.

**uso,** *n.m.* use; custom.

**usuale,** *adj.* usual.

**usura,** *n.f.* usury.

**usurpare,** *vb.* usurp, encroach upon.

**utensile,** *n.m.* utensil, tool.

**utènte,** *n.m.* user.

**ùtero,** *n.m.* uterus, womb.

**utile,** *adj.* useful, helpful.

**utilità,** *n.f.* utility, usefulness, helpfulness.

**utilizzare,** *vb.* utilize.

**uva,** *n.f.* grape.

---

# V

**vacante**, *adj.* vacant.
**vacanza**, *n.f.* holiday, (*pl.*) vacation.
**vacchetta**, *n.f.* cowhide.
**vacca**, *n.f.* cow.
**vaccaro**, *n.m.* cowboy, cow hand.
**vaccinare**, *vb.* vaccinate
**vaccinazione**, *n.f.* vaccination.
**vaccinio**, *n.m.* huckleberry.
**vaccino**, *n.m.* vaccine
**vacillare**, *vb.* vacillate, waver.
**vàcuo**, *adj.* vacuous.
**vagabondo**, *n.m.* vagabond, hobo, bum, tramp.
**vagare**, *vb.* wander around, gallivant, ramble, roam.
**vàglia**, *n.m.* money-order.
**vàglio**, *n.m.* sieve.
**vago**, *adj.* vague, dreamy, hazy; (*poetical*) charming.
**vagone**, *n.m.* car; coach. **v. ristorante**, dining car. **v. lètti**, sleeper.
**vaiòlo**, *n.m.* smallpox.
**valanga**, *n.f.* avalanche.
**valere**, *vb.* be worth.
**vàlido**, *adj.* valid.
**valigetta**, *n.f.* little suitcase; handbag.
**valigia**, *n.f.* suitcase, valise.
**valle**, *n.f.* valley.
**valletta**, *n.f.* vale, dale, glen.
**valore**, *n.m.* valor; value, worth.
**valoroso**, *adj.* valiant.
**valuta**, *n.f.* currency.
**valutare**, *vb.* evaluate, estimate, value.
**valutazione**, *n.f.* evaluation, estimate.
**vàlvola**, *n.f.* valve; (radio) tube.
**vàlzer**, *n.m.* waltz.
**vampiro**, *n.m.* vampire.
**vanaglorioso**, *adj.* vainglorious, boastful.
**vàndalo**, *n.m.* vandal.
**vanga**, *n.f.* spade.
**vangèlo**, *n.m.* gospel.
**vaniglia**, *n.f.* vanilla.
**vanità**, *n.f.* vanity, conceit.

**vanitoso**, *adj.* vain, conceited.
**vano**, **1.** *n.m.* room. **2.** *adj.* vain.
**vantaggio**, *n.m.* advantage, benefit, profit. **trarre v. da**, benefit by.
**vantaggiosamente**, *adv.* advantageously.
**vantaggioso**, *adj.* advantageous, beneficial, profitable.
**vantare**, *vb.* boast.
**vantatore**, *n.m.* boaster.
**vanteria**, *n.f.* boast, boasting, boastfulness.
**vanto**, *n.m.* boast.
**vapore**, *n.m.* vapor, steam.
**varare**, *vb.* launch.
**variare**, *vb.* vary.
**variazione**, *n.f.* variation
**varicèlla**, *n.f.* chicken-pox.
**varietà**, *n.f.* variety.
**vàrio**, *adj.* various.
**varo**, *n.m.* launching.
**vasca**, *n.f.* tub.
**vasellame**, *n.m.* crockery, earthenware.
**vaso**, *n.m.* vase. **v. da nòtte**, chamber-pot.
**vassallo**, *n.m.* vassal.
**vassòio**, *n.m.* tray.
**vasto**, *adj.* vast.
**vècchia**, *n.j.* old woman, crone.
**vècchio**, *adj.* old, aged, elderly.
**vedere**, *vb.* see, behold.
**védova**, *n.f.* widow.
**védovo**, *n.m.* widower.
**veduta**, *n.j.* view.
**veemènte**, *adj.* vehement.
**veemènza**, *n.f.* vehemence.
**vegetale**, *adj.* vegetable.
**véglia**, *n.f.* vigil; wake.
**vegliare**, *vb.* be awake.
**veicolo**, *n.m.* vehicle.
**vela**, *n.f.* sail.
**velato**, *adj.* veiled, filmy.
**veleno**, *n.m.* poison, venom.
**velenoso**, *adj.* poisonous, venomous.
**vèllo**, *n.m.* fleece.

**velloso,** *adj.* fleecy.

**velluto,** *n.m.* velvet.

**velo,** *n.m.* veil.

**veloce,** *adj.* swift, fleet, speedy.

**velocista,** *n.m.* sprinter.

**velocità,** *n.f.* velocity, speed.

**vena,** *n.f.* vein.

**vendémmia,** *n.f.* vintage.

**véndere,** *vb.* sell.

**vendetta,** *n.f.* revenge, vengeance.

**vendicare,** *vb.* avenge, revenge.

**vendicatore,** *n.m.* avenger.

**véndita,** *n.f.* sale; **(v. all' asta)** auction.

**venerdì,** *n.m.* Friday. **v. santo,** Good Friday.

**venèreo,** *adj.* venereal.

**Venèzia,** *n.f.* Venice.

**veneziano,** *adj.* Venetian.

**venire,** *vb.* come.

**ventàglio,** *n.m.* fan.

**ventésimo,** *adj.* twentieth.

**venti,** *num.* twenty.

**ventilare,** *vb.* ventilate.

**ventilazione,** *n.f.* ventilation.

**ventina,** *n.f.* score.

**ventura,** *n.f.* venture.

**venuta,** *n.f.* coming.

**vènto,** *n.m.* wind.

**ventoso,** *adj.* windy, breezy.

**ventre,** *n.m.* belly.

**ventríglio,** *n.m.* gizzard.

**veramente,** *adv.* truly, really, actually.

**veranda,** *n.f.* porch.

**verbale,** **1.** *n.m.* minutes. **2.** *adj.* verbal.

**vèrbo,** *n.m.* verb.

**verboso,** *adj.* verbose, wordy.

**verde,** *adj.* green. **al v.,** broke, penniless.

**verdetto,** *n.m.* verdict.

**verdura,** *n.f.* vegetables.

**verga,** *n.f.* rod, switch.

**vérgine,** *n.f.* virgin.

**vergogna,** *n.f.* shame.

**vergognarsi di,** *vb.* be ashamed of.

**vergognoso,** *adj.* ashamed; shameful.

**verídico,** *adj.* truthful.

**verifica,** *n.f.* verification, check, audit.

**verificare,** *vb.* verify, check, audit.

**verità,** *n.f.* truth, reality, actuality.

**vèrme,** *n.m.* worm.

**vermíglio,** *adj.* vermilion.

**vernàcolo,** *n.m. and adj.* vernacular.

**vernice,** *n.f.* varnish, glaze.

**verniciare,** *vb.* varnish, glaze.

**vero,** *adj.* true, real, actual; very.

**vèrro,** *n.m.* boar.

**versamento,** *n.m.* payment.

**versare,** *vb.* pour; pay in; shed.

**versato,** *adj.* versed, conversant.

**versàtile,** *adj.* versatile.

**versificare,** *vb.* versify.

**versione,** *n.f.* version.

**vèrso,** **1.** *n.m.* verse; song; (hen, goose) cackle. **2.** *prep.* toward.

**versucci,** *n.m.pl.* doggerel.

**vertebrato,** *n.m. and adj.* vertebrate.

**verticale,** *adj.* vertical.

**vertígine,** *n.f.* vertigo, dizziness.

**vertiginoso,** *adj.* vertiginous, dizzy.

**verzura,** *n.f.* greenery.

**vescica,** *n.f.* bladder; blister.

**vescovato,** *n.m.* bishopric.

**véscovo,** *n.m.* bishop.

**vèspa,** *n.f.* wasp.

**vespasiano,** *n.m.* public urinal.

**vèspri,** *n.m.pl.* vespers.

**vestàglia,** *n.f.* dressing-gown, bathrobe, négligée.

**vèste,** *n.f.* dress, garb, apparel, robe.

**vestiarista,** *n.m.* costumer.

**vestíbolo,** *n.m.* vestibule, hallway.

**vestígio,** *n.m.* vestige.

**vestimento,** *n.m.* clothing, garb, apparel.

**vestire,** *vb.* dress, clothe, garb, apparel.

**vestito,** **1.** *n.* dress, suit, garment; (*pl.*) clothes, clothing. **2.** *adj.* clad, clothed.

**Vesùvio,** *n.m.* Vesuvius.

**veterano,** *n.m.* veteran.

**veterinàrio,** *n.m. and adj.* veterinary.

**vèto,** *n.m.* veto.

**vetraio,** *n.m.* glazier.

**vetro,** *n.m.* glass, pane.

**vetroso,** *adj.* glassy.

**vetta,** *n.f.* summit.

**vettovàglie,** *n.f.pl.* victuals.

For pronunciation, see the concise guide on pages 5 to 7.

**vettura,** *n.f.* carriage; car.

**vezzeggiare,** *vb.* fondle, coddle, pet.

**vi,** *pron.* 2. *pl.* you.

**vi,** *pro-phrase* (replaces phrases introduced by prepositions of place) there; to it; at it.

**via, 1.** *n.f.* way, road, street. **2.** *adv.* away; off. **3.** *prep.* via.

**viadotto,** *n.m.* viaduct.

**viaggiare,** *vb.* journey, travel, tour, voyage.

**viaggiatore,** *n.m.* traveller.

**viaggio,** *n.m.* journey, trip, travel, tour, voyage.

**viale,** *n.m.* avenue, boulevard; drive(way); (in garden) alley.

**vibrare,** *vb.* vibrate.

**vibrazione,** *n.f.* vibration.

**vicario,** *n.m.* vicar.

**vicinanza,** *n.f.* neighborhood, vicinity.

**vicino, 1.** *n.m.* neighbor. **2.** *adj.* nearby, neighboring, close. **vicino a,** *prep.* near, about. **3.** *adv.* near, close.

**vico,** *n.m.* hamlet.

**vicolo,** *n.m.* alley. **v. cieco,** blind alley, dead end.

**vietare,** *vb.* forbid, veto.

**vietato,** *adj.* forbidden.

**vigilante,** *adj.* vigilant, alert, watchful.

**vigilare,** *vb.* watch, lock out.

**vigile,** *n.m.* policeman.

**vigilia,** *n.f.* vigil; eve.

**vigliacco,** *n.m.* cad.

**vigna,** *n.f.* vineyard.

**vigore,** *n.m.* vigor, force.

**vigoria,** *n.f.* forcefulness.

**vigoroso,** *adj.* vigorous, forceful, lusty.

**vile,** *adj.* vile.

**villaggio,** *n.m.* village.

**villano,** *adj.* inconsiderate.

**villetta,** *n.f.* cottage.

**vincere,** *vb.* conquer, overcome, overpower, beat, vanquish, win.

**vincibile,** *adj.* conquerable.

**vincitore,** *n.m.* victor, conqueror, winner.

**vincolare,** *vb.* bind.

**vincolo,** *n.m.* bond, link.

**vino,** *n.m.* wine. **v. di** Xeres, sherry.

**viola,** *n.f.* viola; viol; violet.

**violare,** *vb.* violate; rape.

**violatore,** *n.m.* violator.

**violazione,** *n.f.* violation, breach.

**violento,** *adj.* violent.

**violenza,** *n.f.* violence.

**violino,** *n.m.* violin, fiddle.

**violoncellista,** *n.m.* cellist.

**violoncello,** *n.m.* cello.

**viottolo,** *n.m.* byway, lane.

**vipera,** *n.f.* adder, viper.

**virare,** *vb.* tack, veer.

**virgola,** *n.f.* comma.

**virile,** *adj.* virile, manly.

**virilità,** *n.f.* virility, manhood.

**virtù,** *n.f.* virtue.

**virtuale,** *adj.* virtual.

**virtuoso,** *adj.* virtuous.

**vischi,** *n.m.* whisky.

**vischio,** *n.m.* bird-lime; mistletoe.

**viscoso,** *adj.* viscous, sticky.

**visibile,** *adj.* visible.

**visione,** *n.f.* vision.

**visita,** *n.f.* visit.

**visitare,** *vb.* visit.

**visivo,** *adj.* of vision.

**viso,** *n.m.* face, countenance.

**visone,** *n.m.* mink.

**vista,** *n.f.* sight; eyesight; view.

**vistare,** *vb.* visa.

**visto,** *n.m.* visa.

**vistosamente,** *adv.* gaudily.

**vistosità,** *n.f.* flashiness, gaudiness.

**vistoso,** *adj.* flashy, gaudy.

**visuale,** *adj.* visual.

**vita,** *n.f.* life; livelihood; living; waist.

**vitale,** *adj.* vital.

**vitalità,** *n.f.* vitality.

**vitalizio,** *adj.* for life.

**vitamina,** *n.f.* vitamin.

**vite,** *n.f.* vine; grapevine; screw.

**vitello,** *n.m.* calf; veal.

**vitreo,** *adj.* glassy, of glass.

**vittima,** *n.f.* victim.

**vitto,** *n.m.* food, victuals, board.

**vittoria,** *n.f.* victory.

**vittorioso,** *adj.* victorious.

**viva,** *interj.* hurrah (for).

**vivace,** *adj.* vivacious, lively, brisk.

**vivacemente,** *adv.* vivaciously, briskly.

**vivacità,** *n.f.* vivacity, liveliness, briskness.

**vivaio,** *n.m.* hatchery, nursery.

**vivènte,** *adj.* living, alive.

**vivere,** *vb.* live, be alive.

**vivido,** *adj.* vivid.

**vivo,** *adj.* live.

**viziare,** *vb.* vitiate.

**vizio,** *n.m.* vice.

**vizioso,** *adj.* vicious.

**vocabolàrio,** *n.m.* vocabulary.

**vocale, 1.** *n.f.* vowel. **2.** *adj.* vocal.

**vocazione,** *n.f.* vocation, calling.

**voce,** *n.f.* voice; word, rumor, report.

**vociare,** *vb.* vociferate.

**voga,** *n.f.* vogue.

**vòglia,** *n.f.* wish; desire; birth-mark.

**voi,** *pron.* 2. *pl.* you.

**volante,** *n.m.* steering-wheel; flounce.

**volare,** *vb.* fly.

**volerci,** *vb.* be necessary.

**volgare,** *adj.* vulgar; common; vernacular.

**volgarità,** *n.f.* vulgarity, commonness.

**volgo,** *n.m.* rabble.

**volo,** *n.m.* flight.

**volontà,** *n.f.* will.

**volontàrio, 1.** *n.m.* volunteer. **2.** *adj.* voluntary.

**volpe,** *n.f.* fox.

**volpino,** *adj.* foxy.

**volta,** *n.f.* time; vault.

**voltafaccia,** *n.m.* about-face.

**voltàggio,** *n.m.* voltage.

**volteggiare,** *vb.* hover; turn; vault.

**volume,** *n.m.* volume, bulk.

**voluminoso,** *adj.* voluminous, bulky.

**vòmere,** *n.m.* colter; plowshare.

**vomitare,** *vb.* vomit, disgorge.

**vòmito,** *n.m.* vomit.

**vòrtice,** *n.m.* vortex, whirlpool, eddy.

**vòstro,** *adj.* your; yours.

**votante,** *n.m.* voter.

**votare,** *vb.* vote.

**votazione,** *n.f.* voting, ballot.

**voto,** *n.m.* vow; wish; mark; grade.

**vulcano,** *n.m.* volcano.

**vulneràbile,** *adj.* vulnerable.

**vuotare,** *vb.* empty.

**vuòto,** *adj.* **1.** *n.* emptiness; vacuum. **2.** empty, blank, vacant.

# W, Z

**W.,** abbr. for **evviva** hurrah for.

**W. C.,** abbr. for water-closet (toilet).

**zaffiro,** *n.m.* sapphire.

**zàino,** *n.m.* knapsack.

**zampa,** *n.f.* paw.

**zampillare,** *vb.* gush; squirt.

**zampogna,** *n.f.* bagpipe.

**zàngola,** *n.f.* churn.

**zanna,** *n.f.* fang.

**zanzara,** *n.f.* mosquito.

**zanzarièra,** *n.f.* mosquito-net.

**zappa,** *n.f.* hoe.

**zappare,** *vb.* hoe.

**zàttera,** *n.f.* raft.

**zavorra,** *n.f.* ballast.

**zebra,** *n.f.* zebra.

**zecca,** *n.f.* mint.

**zèffiro,** *n.m.* zephyr.

**zelante,** *n.m.* zealous.

**zelo,** *n.m.* zeal.

**zènzero,** *n.m.* ginger.

**zeppo,** *adj.* chock full.

**zèro,** *n.m.* zero; cipher.

**zia,** *n.f.* aunt.

**zibellino,** *n.m.* sable.

**zinco,** *n.m.* zinc.

**zìngara,** *n.f.* gypsy woman.

**zìngaro,** *n.m.* gypsy.

**zìo,** *n.m.* uncle.

**zitella,** *n.f.* old maid, spinster.

**zitto,** *adj.* silent.

**zòccolo,** *n.m.* hoof; wooden shoe; baseboard.

**zòlla,** *n.f.* clod, sod.

**zòna,** *n.f.* zone.

**zoològico,** *adj.* zoological.

**zoologìa,** *n.f.* zoology.

**zoppicamento,** *n.m.* limp.

**zoppicare,** *vb.* limp, hobble.

**zòppo,** *adj.* lame.

**zòtico, 1.** *n.* boor. **2.** *adj.* boorish.

**zoticone,** *n.m.* lout.

**zucca,** *n.f.* gourd, pumpkin, squash.

**zùcchero,** *n.m.* sugar.

**zuppa,** *n.f.* soup.

**Zurigo,** *n.m.* Zurich.

For pronunciation, see the concise guide on pages 5 to 7.

# ENGLISH - ITALIAN

# A

**a,** *art.* un *m.*, una *f.*

**abacus,** *n.* àbaco *m.*

**abandon, 1.** *n.* abbandono *m.* **2.** *vb.* abbandonare.

**abandoned,** *adj.* abbandonato.

**abandonment,** *n.* abbandono *m.*

**abase,** *vb.* abbassare, avvilire.

**abasement,** *n.* abbassamento *m.*, avvilimento.

**abash,** *vb.* sconcertare.

**abate,** *vb.* diminuire.

**abatement,** *n.* diminuzione *f.*

**abbess,** *n.* badessa *f.*

**abbey,** *n.* badìa *f.*, abbazìa *f.*

**abbot,** *n.* abate *m.*

**abbreviate,** *vb.* abbreviare, raccorciare.

**abbreviation,** *n.* abbreviatura *f.*, raccorciamento *m.*

**abdicate,** *vb.* abdicare.

**abdication,** *n.* abdicazione *f.*

**abdomen,** *n.* addòme *m.*

**abdominal,** *adj.* addominale.

**abduct,** *vb.* rapire.

**abduction,** *n.* rapimento *m.*, ratto *m.*

**abductor,** *n.* rapitore.

**aberrant,** *adj.* aberrante.

**aberration,** *n.* aberrazione *f.*

**abet,** *vb.* incoraggiare.

**abetment,** *n.* incoraggiamento *m.*

**abettor,** *n.* incoraggiatore *m.*

**abeyance,** *n.* sospensione *f.*

**abhor,** *vb.* aborrire, detestare.

**abhorrence,** *n.* aborrimento *m.*, detestazione *f.*, ripugnanza *f.*

**abhorrent,** *adj.* ripugnante.

**abide,** *vb.* (dwell) abitare; (remain) rimanere; (tolerate) sopportare.

**abiding,** *adj.* permanènte, costante.

**ability,** *n.* abilità *f.*, capacità *f.*

**abject,** *adj.* abiètto.

**abjuration,** *n.* abiura *f.*

**abjure,** *vb.* abiurare.

**abjurer,** *n.* chi abiura.

**ablative,** *adj. and n.*, ablativo (*m.*).

**ablaze,** *adj.* in fiamme.

**able,** *adj.* àbile, capace (di); **(be a.)** potere.

**able-bodied,** *adj.* forte, robusto.

**ablution,** *n.* abluzione.

**ably,** *adv.* abilmente.

**abnegate,** *vb.* abnegare.

**abnegation,** *n.* abnegazione *f.*

**abnormal,** *adj.* anormale.

**abnormality,** *n.* anormalità *f.*

**abnormally,** *adv.* anormalmente.

**aboard, 1.** *adv.* (naut.) a bordo; **(all a.)** in carrozza. **2.** *prep.* a bordo di.

**abode,** *n.* dimora *f.*

**abolish,** *vb.* abolire.

**abolishment,** *n.* abolimento *m.*

**abolition,** *n.* abolizione *f.*

**abominable,** *adj.* abominévole.

**abominate,** *vb.* abominare.

**abomination,** *n.* abominazione.

**aboriginal,** *adj.* indìgeno.

**aborigine,** *n.* indìgeno *m.*

**abort,** *vb.* abortire.

**abortion,** *n.* aborto *m.*

**abortive,** *adj.* abortivo.

**abound,** *vb.* abbondare.

**about, 1.** *adv.* (approximately) pressappòco, all'incirca; (around) intorno; **(be a. to)** stare per. **2.** *prep.* (concerning; around) intorno a; (near) vicino a.

**about-face,** *n.* voltafàccia *m.*

**above,** *adv. and prep.* sopra.

**aboveboard, 1.** *adj.* sincèro, onèsto. **2.** *adv.* apertamente, onestamente.

**abrasion,** *n.* abrasione *f.*

**abrasive,** *n. and adj.* abrasivo (*m.*).

**abreast,** *adv. and prep.* di fianco (a).

**abridge,** *vb.* abbreviare.

**abridgment,** *n.* abbreviamento *m.*

**abroad,** *adv.* all'èstero.

**abrogate,** *vb.* abrogare.

**abrogation,** *n.* abrogazione *f.*

**abrupt,** *adj.* (sudden) improvviso; (steep) rìpido; (curt) rude.

**abruptly,** *adv.* (suddenly) all'improvviso, improvvisamente; (curtly) rudemente.

**abruptness,** *n.* rudezza *f.*

**abscess,** *n.* ascèsso *m.*

**abscond,** *vb.* sparire; (fam.) svignàrsela.

**absence,** *n.* assènza *f.*

**absent,** *adj.* assènte.

**absentee,** *n.* assènte *m.*

**absent-minded,** *adj.* distratto.

**absinthe,** *n.* assènzio *m.*

**absolute,** *adj.* assoluto.

**absolutely,** *adv.* assolutamente.

**absoluteness,** *n.* assolutezza *f.*

**absolution,** *n.* assoluzione *f.*

**absolutism,** *n.* assolutismo *m.*

**absolve,** *vb.* assòlvere.

**absorb,** *vb.* assorbire.

**absorbed,** *adj.* (lit.) assorbito; (fig.) assorto.

**absorbent,** *n. and adj.* assorbènte.

**absorbing,** *adj.* assorbènte.

**absorption,** *n.* assorbimento *m.*

**abstain,** *vb.* astenersi.

**abstemious,** *adj.* astèmio.

**abstinence,** *n.* astinènza *f.*

**abstract, 1.** *n.* (book, article) riassunto *m.*, sunto *m.* **2.** *adj.* astratto. **3.** *vb.* astrarre, riassùmere.

**abstracted,** *adj.* astratto.

**abstraction,** *n.* astrazione *f.*

**abstruse,** *adj.* astruso.

**absurd,** *adj.* assurdo.

**absurdity,** *n.* assurdità *f.*, assurdo *m.*

**absurdly,** *adv.* assurdamente.

**abundance,** *n.* abbondanza *f.*

**abundant,** *adj.* abbondante.

**abundantly,** *adv.* abbondantemente.

**abuse, 1.** *n.* (misuse) abuso *m.*; (insult) insulto *m.*, ingiùria *f.* **2.** *vb.* abusare (di), insultare, ingiuriare.

**abusive,** *adj.* (misusing) abusivo; (insulting) insolente, ingiurioso.

**abusively,** *adv.* abusivamente,

insolentemente, ingiuriosamente.

**abut,** *vb.* confinare.

**abutment,** *n.* tèrmine *m.*

**abyss,** *n.* abisso *m.*

**Abyssinia,** *n.* Abissinia, *f.*

**Abyssinian,** *n. and adj.* abissino.

**academic,** *adj.* accadèmico.

**academic freedom,** *n.* libertà d'insegnamento *f.*

**academy,** *n.* accadèmia *f.*

**acanthus,** *n.* acanto *m.*

**accede,** *vb.* consentire.

**accelerate,** *vb.* accelerare.

**acceleration,** *n.* accelerazione *f.*

**accelerator,** *n.* acceleratore *m.*

**accent,** *n.* accènto *m.*

**accentuate,** *vb.* (lit.) accentare, (fig.) accentuare.

**accept,** *vb.* accettare.

**acceptability,** *n.* accettabilità.

**acceptable,** *adj.* accètto, accettàbile, gradévole.

**acceptably,** *adv.* accettabilmente.

**acceptance,** *n.* accettazione *f.*

**access,** *n.* accèsso *m.*

**accessible,** *adj.* accessìbile.

**accessory,** *n. and adj.* accessòrio (*m.*).

**accident,** *n.* incidènte *m.*, sinistro *m.*; (by a.) per caso.

**accidental,** *adj.* accidentale.

**accidentally,** *adv.* accidentalmente.

**acclaim,** *vb.* acclamare.

**acclamation,** *n.* acclamazione *f.*

**acclimate,** *vb.* acclimare, acclimatare.

**acclivity,** *n.* acclività *f.*

**accolade,** *n.* accollata *f.*

**accommodate,** *vb.* accomodare; (lodge) alloggiare.

**accommodating,** *adj.* accomodante, cortese.

**accommodation,** *n.* accomodazione *f.*; (lodging) allòggio *m.*

**accompaniment,** *n.* accompagnamento *m.*

**accompanist,** *n.* accompagnatore *m.*

**accompany,** *vb.* accompagnare.

**accomplice,** *n.* còmplice *m.* and *f.*

**accomplish,** *vb.* compire.

**accomplished,** *adj.* compito.

**accomplishment,** n. compimento m.

**accord,** n. accòrdo m.

**accordance,** n. conformità f.; **(in a with)** conforme a.

**accordingly,** adv. (correspondingly) conformemente; (therefore) dunque.

**according to,** prep. secondo.

**accordion,** n. fisarmònica f.

**accost,** vb. abbordare.

**account,** n. (comm.) conto m.; (narrative) racconto m.

**accountable for,** adj. responsàbile di.

**accountant,** n. ragioniere.

**account for,** vb. rèndere conto di.

**accounting.** n. (occupation) ragioneria f.; (procedure) glicontabilità f.

**accouter,** vb. abbigliare.

**accoutrements,** n. abbigliatura f.sg.

**accredit,** vb. accreditare.

**accretion,** n. accrescimento m.

**accrual,** n. accrescimento m.

**accrue,** vb. accréscere.

**accumulate,** vb. accumulare.

**accumulation,** n. accumulazione f.

**accumulative,** adj. accumulativo.

**accumulator,** n. accumulatore m.

**accuracy,** n. accuratezza f.

**accurate,** adj. accurato.

**accursed,** adj. maledetto.

**accusation,** n. accusa f.

**accusative,** n. and adj. accusativo (m.).

**accuse,** vb. accusare, incolpare, imputare.

**accused,** n. accusato m., incolpato m.

**accuser,** n. accusatore m., incolpatore m.

**accustom,** vb. abituare.

**accustomed,** adj. sòlito, abituale; (be accustomed to) solere; (become accustomed to) abituarsi a.

**ace,** n. asso m.

**acerbity,** n. acerbità f.

**acetate,** n. acetato m.

**acetic,** adj. acètico.

**acetylene,** n. acetilène f.

**ache,** n. dolore m., male m.

**achieve,** vb. compire, raggiùngere.

**achievement,** n. compimento m., raggiungimento m.

**acid,** n. and adj. àcido (m.).

**acidify,** vb. acidificare.

**acidity,** n. acidità f.

**acidosis,** n. acidòsi f.

**acid test,** n. pròva conclusiva f.

**acidulous,** adj. acidulo.

**acknowledge,** vb. (recognize) riconòscere; **(a. receipt of)** accusare, dichiarare ricevuta di.

**acme,** n. acme f., punto culminante m.

**acne,** n. acne f.

**acolyte,** n. accòlito m.

**acorn,** n. ghianda f.

**acoustics,** n. acùstica f.sg.

**acquaint,** vb. informare, far sapere; (be acquainted with) conóscere.

**acquaintance,** n. conoscènza f.

**acquainted,** adj. conosciuto, familiare.

**acquiesce,** vb. acquietarsi, consentire tacitamente.

**acquiescence,** n. acquiescenza f.

**acquire,** vb. acquistare.

**acquisition,** n. acquisto m.

**acquisitive,** adj. acquisitivo.

**acquit,** v. assòlvere.

**acquittal,** n. assoluzione f.

**acre,** n. acro m.

**acreage,** n. estensione di terra f.

**acrid,** adj. acre.

**acrimonious,** adj. acre.

**acrimony,** n. acrèdine f., acrimònia f.

**acrobat,** n. acròbata, m.

**across,** adv. and prep. attraverso.

**acrostic,** n. acròstico m.

**act,** 1. n. atto m. 2. vb. agire; (stage) recitare; (behave) comportarsi.

**acting,** 1. n. recitazione f. 2. adj. provvisòrio.

**actinism,** n. attinismo m.

**actinium,** n. attìnio m.

**action,** n. azione f.

**activate,** vb. attivare.

**activation,** n. attivazione f.

**activator,** n. attivatore m.

**active,** adj. attivo.

**activity,** n. attività f.

**actor,** n. attore m.

**actress,** n. attrice f.

**actual,** adj. vero.

**actuality,** n. verità f.

**actually,** adv. veramente.

**actuary,** n. attuàrio m.

**actuate,** vb. attuare.

**acumen,** *n.* acume *m.*

**acute,** *adj.* acuto.

**acutely,** *adv.* acutamente.

**acuteness,** *n.* acutezza *f.*

**adage,** *n.* adàgio *m.*, màssima *f.*, provèrbio *m.*

**adamant,** *adj.* adamantino.

**Adam's apple,** *n.* pomo d'Adamo *m.*

**adapt,** *vb.* addattare.

**adaptability,** *n.* addattabilità *f.*

**adaptable,** *adj.* adattàbile.

**adaptation,** *n.* addattamento *m.*

**adapter,** *n.* riduttore *m.*

**adaptive,** *adj.* adattévole.

**add,** *vb.* (join) aggiùngere; (arith.) sommare, addizionare.

**adder,** *n.* vìpera *f.*

**addict,** *n.* (drug a.) tossicòmane *m.*

**addict oneself to,** *vb.* dedicarsi a.

**addition,** *x.* addizione *f.*

**additional,** *adj.* addizionale.

**addle,** *vb.* confòndere; (egg) imputridirsi.

**addled,** *adj.* confuso; (egg) màrcio, pùtrido.

**address,** **1.** *n.* (on letters, etc.) indirizzo; (speech) discorso. **2.** *vb.* (a letter) indirizzare; (a person) indirizzarsi a.

**addressee,** *n.* destinatàrio *m.*

**adduce,** *vb.* addurre.

**adenoid,** **1.** *n.* vegetazione adenòide *f.* **2.** *adj.* adenòide.

**adept,** *adj.* dèstro, àbile.

**adeptly,** *adv.* destramente, abilmente.

**adeptness,** *n.* destrezza *f.*, abilità *f.*

**adequacy,** *n.* sufficiènza *f.*

**adequate,** *adj.* adeguato, sufficiènte.

**adequately,** *adv.* adeguatamente, sufficientemente.

**adhere,** *vb.* aderire.

**adherence,** *n.* aderènza *f.*

**adherent,** *n.* aderènte *m.*

**adhesion,** *n.* adesione *f.*

**adhesive,** *n. and adj.* adesivo (*m.*).

**adhesiveness,** *n.* adesività *f.*

**adieu,** *interj.* addio.

**adjacent,** *adj.* adiacènte.

**adjective,** *n.* aggettivo *m.*

**adjoin,** *vb.* essere adiacènte a.

**adjoining,** *adj.* adiacènte.

**adjourn,** *vb.* aggiornare.

**adjournment,** *n.* aggiornamento *m.*

**adjunct,** *n. and adj.* aggiunto, accessòrio.

**adjust,** *vb.* aggiustare.

**adjuster,** *n.* aggiustatore.

**adjustment,** *n.* (action) giustamento *m.*; (money) aggiustatura *f.*

**adjutant,** *n.* aiutante *m.*, assistènte *m.*

**administer,** *vb.* amministrare.

**administration,** *n.* amministrazione *f.*

**administrative,** *adj.* amministrativo.

**administrator,** *n.* amministratore *m.*

**admirable,** *adj.* ammirévole, ammiràbile.

**admirably,** *adv.* ammirabilmente.

**admiral,** *n.* ammiràglio *m.*

**admiralty,** *n.* ammiragliato *m.*, ministero della marina *m.*

**admiration,** *n.* ammirazione *f.*

**admire,** *vb.* ammirare.

**admirer,** *n.* ammiratore *m.*

**admiringly,** *adv.* con ammirazione.

**admissible,** *adj.* ammissìbile.

**admission,** *n.* (entrance) ammissione *f.*; (entry) entrata; (confession) confessione *f.*

**admit,** *vb.* amméttere.

**admittance,** *n.* ammissione *f.*; (entry) entrata *f.*

**admittedly,** *adv.* lo confèsso.

**admixture,** *n.* mescolanza *f.*

**admonish,** *vb.* ammonire.

**admonition,** *n.* ammonizione *f.*

**ado,** *n.* fracasso *m.*

**adolescence,** *n.* adolescènza *f.*

**adolescent,** *n. and adj.* adolescènte (*m.*).

**adopt,** *vb.* adottare.

**adoption,** *n.* adozione *f.*

**adorable,** *adj.* adoràbile.

**adoration,** *n.* adorazione *f.*

**adore,** *vb.* adorare.

**adorn,** *vb.* adornare, ornare.

**adorned,** *adj.* adorno.

**adornment,** *n.* adornamento.

**adrenal glands,** *n.* ghiàndole surrenali *f.pl.*

**adrenalin,** *n.* adrenalina *f.*

**adrift,** *adv.* alla deriva.

**adroit,** *adj.* destro, àbile.

**adulate,** *vb.* adulare.

**adulation,** *n.* adulazione *f.*

**adult,** *n. and adj.* adulto.

**adulterant,** *n. and adj.* adulterante.

**adulterate,** *vb.* adulterare.

**adulterer,** *n.* adultero.

**adulteress,** *n.* adultera *f.*

**adultery,** *n.* adultèrio *m.*

**advance, 1.** *n.* progresso; (pay) anticipo; **(in a.)** in anticipo. **2.** *vb.* avanzare, progredire; (pay) anticipare.

**advanced,** *adj.* avanzato, progredito.

**advancement,** *n.* avanzamento *m.*

**advantage,** *n.* vantàggio *m.*

**advantageous,** *adj.* vantaggioso.

**advantageously,** *adv.* vantaggiosamente.

**advent,** *n.* avvènto *m.*

**adventitious,** *adj.* avventizio.

**adventure, 1.** *n.* avventura *f.* **2.** *vb.* avventurare, rischiare.

**adventurer,** *n.* avventurière *m.*

**adventurous,** *adj.* avventuroso.

**adventurously,** *adv.* avventurosamente.

**adverb,** *n.* avvèrbio *m.*

**adverbial,** *adj.* avverbiale.

**adversary,** *n.* avversàrio *m.*

**adverse,** *adj.* avvèrso.

**adversely,** *adv.* avversamente.

**adversity,** *n.* avversità *f.*

**advert,** *vb.* avvertire.

**advertise,** *vb.* far réclame per, reclamizzare.

**advertisement,** *n.* réclame *f.*, pubblicità *f.*; (newspaper) annunzio *m.*, inserzione *f.*

**advertiser,** *n.* inserzionista *m.*

**advertising,** *n.* réclame *f.*, pubblicità *f.*

**advice,** *n.* consiglio *m.*; (news) avviso *m.*

**advisability,** *n.* convenienza *f.*, opportunità *f.*

**advisable,** *adj.* conveniente, opportuno.

**advisably,** *adv.* opportunamente.

**advise,** *vb.* consigliare; (inform) avvisare.

**advisedly,** *adv.* consigliatamente, apposta.

**advisement,** *n.* deliberazione *f.*

**adviser,** *n.* consigliatore *m.*

**advocacy,** *n.* difesa *f.*, propugnazione *f.*

**advocate, 1.** *n.* (law) avvocato; (defender) difensore *m.*, propugnatore *m.* **2.** *vb.* propugnare, difèndere.

**aegis,** *n.* ègida *f.*

**aerate,** *vb.* aerare.

**aeration,** *n.* aerazione *f.*

**aerial,** *adj.* aèreo.

**aerially,** *adv.* per ària.

**aerie,** *n.* nido *m.*

**aeronautics,** *n.* aeronàutica *f.*

**aerosol bomb,** *n.* bomboletta nebulizzante *f.*

**aesthetic,** *adj.* estètico.

**aesthetics,** *n.* estètica *f.*

**afar,** *adv.* lontano.

**affability,** *n.* affabilità *f.*

**affable,** *adj.* affàbile.

**affably,** *adv.* affabilmente.

**affair,** *n.* affare *m.*

**affect,** *vb.* (move) commovere; (concern) interessare; (pretend) affettare.

**affectation,** *n.* affettazione *f.*

**affected,** *adj.* affettato.

**affecting,** *adj.* commovènte.

**affection,** *n.* affezione *f.*

**affectionate,** *adj.* affettuoso.

**affectionately,** *adv.* affettuosamente.

**afferent,** *adj.* afferènte.

**affiance,** *vb.* fidanzare.

**affidavit,** *n.* dichiarazione giurata *f.*

**affiliate,** *vb.* affigliare, associare.

**affiliation,** *n.* affigliazione *f.*, associazione *f.*

**affinity,** *n.* affinità *f.*

**affirm,** *vb.* affermare.

**affirmation,** *n.* affermazione *f.*

**affirmative,** *adj.* affermativo.

**affirmatively,** *adv.* affermativamente.

**affix, 1.** *n.* affisso *m.* **2.** *vb.* affissare.

**afflict,** *vb.* affliggere.

**affliction,** *n.* afflizione *f.*

**affluence,** *n.* opulènza *f.*

**affluent,** *adj.* opulènto.

**afford,** *vb.* (have the means to) avere i mezzi di.

**affray,** *n.* lite *f.*, rissa *f.*

**affront, 1.** *n.* affronto *m.* **2.** *vb.* affrontare.

**afield,** *adv.* (far a.) lontano.

**afire,** *adv.* in fiamme.

**afloat,** *adv.* a galla.

**aforementioned,** *adj.* sopraindicato, suindicato.

**aforesaid,** *adj.* sopraddetto, suddetto.

**afraid,** *pred.adj.* **(be a.)** aver paura.

**Africa,** *n.* Àfrica *f.*

**African,** *n. and adj.* africano *m.*

**aft,** *adv.* indiètro.

**after, 1.** *prep.* dopo. **2.** *conj.* dopo che.

**aftereffect,** *n.* effètto *m.*

**aftermath,** *n.* conseguènze *f.(pl.)*

**afternoon,** *n.* pomerìggio, *m.*

**afterthought,** *n.* (as an a.) ripensàndoci.

**afterward,** *adv.* dopo.

**afterwards,** *adv.* dopo.

**again,** *adv.* di nuòvo; (again and again) ripetutamente.

**against,** *prep.* contro.

**agape,** *adv.* a bocca aperta.

**agate,** *n.* àgata *f.*

**age, 1.** *n.* età *f.* **2.** *vb.* invecchiare.

**aged,** *adj.* vècchio.

**ageless,** adj. che non invècchia.

**agency,** *n.* agenzìa *f.*

**agenda,** *n.* òrdine del giorno *m.*

**agent,** *n.* agènte *m.*

**agglutinate,** *vb.* agglutinare.

**agglutination,** *n.* agglutinazione *f.*

**aggrandize,** *vb.* ingrandire.

**aggrandizement,** *n.* ingrandimento *m.*

**aggravate,** *vb.* aggravare.

**aggravation,** *n.* aggravamento *m.*

**aggregate, 1.** *n.* aggregato *m.* **2.** *vb.* aggregare.

**aggregation,** *n.* aggregazione *f.*

**aggression,** *n.* aggressione *f.*

**aggressive,** *adj.* aggressivo.

**aggressively,** *adv.* aggressivamente.

**aggressiveness,** *n.* aggressività *f.*

**aggressor,** *n.* aggressore *m.*

**aghast,** *adj.* sbalordito.

**agile,** *adj.* àgile.

**agility,** *n.* agilità *f.*

**agitate,** *vb.* agitare.

**agitation,** *n.* agitazione *f.*

**agitator,** *n.* agitatore *m.*

**agnostic,** *n. and adj.* agnòstico *m.*

**ago,** *adv.* fa (*always follows*).

**agonized,** *adj.* agonizzante.

**agony,** *n.* agonìa *f.*; (be in a.) agonizzare.

**agrarian,** *adj.* agràrio.

**agree,** *vb.* concordare, èssere d'accordo.

**agreeable,** *adj.* piacévole, gradévole; (of persons) simpàtico.

**agreeably,** *adv.* piacevolmente, gradevolmente.

**agreeing,** *adj.* concòrde.

**agreement,** *n.* accòrdo *m.*

**agriculture,** *n.* agricultura *f.*

**ahead,** *adv.* avanti; (straight a.) sèmpre diritto.

**aid, 1.** *n.* aiuto *m.* **2.** *vb.* aiutare.

**aide,** *n.* aiutante *m.*

**ail,** *vb.* èssere malato.

**ailing,** *adj.* malato.

**ailment,** *n.* malattìa *f.*

**aim, 1.** *n.* mira; (purpose) scòpo. **2.** *vb.* (point) puntare; (direct) dirìgere; (look toward) mirare.

**aimless,** *adj.* senza scòpo.

**aimlessly,** *adv.* senza scòpo.

**air, 1.** *n.* ària *f.* **2.** *vb.* aerare.

**air base,** *n.* base aèrea *f.*

**airborne,** *adj.* aviotrasportato.

**air-condition,** *vb.* istallare un impianto di condizionamento d'ària in.

**air-conditioned,** *adj.* ad ària condizionata.

**air-conditioning,** *n.* condizionamento dell'ària *m.*

**aircraft,** *n.* aèreo *m.*

**aircraft-carrier,** *n.* portaèrei *m.*

**air fleet,** *n.* flotta aèrea *f.*

**air gun,** *n.* fucile ad ària compressa *m.*

**airing,** *n.* (walk) passeggiata *f.*

**air line,** *n.* aviolìnea *f.*

**air liner,** *n.* aeroplano *m.*

**air mail,** *n.* posta aèrea *f.*

**airplane,** *n.* aeroplano *m.*

**airport,** *n.* aeropòrto *m.*, aeroscalo *m.*; (for seaplanes) idroscalo *m.*

**air pressure,** *n.* pressione dell'ària *f.*

**air raid,** *n.* attacco aèreo *m.*

**air-sick,** *adj.* be a., sentir nàusea (in un aeroplano).

**airtight,** *adj.* impermeàbile all'ària.

**airy,** *adj.* arioso.

**aisle,** *n.* passaggio *m.* (church) navata *f.*

**ajar,** *adj.* socchiuso.

**akin,** *adj.* affine.

**alacrity,** *n.* alacrità *f.*

**alarm, 1.** *n.* allarme *m.* **2.** *vb.* allarmare, spaventare.

**alarmist,** *n.* allarmista *m.*

**albino,** *n. and adj.* albino (*m.*).

**album,** *n.* album *m.*

**albumen,** *n.* albume *m.*

**alcohol,** *n.* àlcool, àlcole *m.*

**alcoholic,** *adj.* alc(o)òlico.

**alcove,** *n.* alcòva *f.*

**ale,** *n.* birra *f.*

**alert,** **1.** *n.* allarme *m.* **2.** *adj.* vigilante; (keen) acuto. **3.** *vb.* avvertire.

**alfalfa,** *n.* alfalfa *f.*

**algebra,** *n.* àlgebra *f.*

**alias,** *adv.* àlias.

**alibi,** *n.* àlibi *m.*

**alien,** *n.* and *adj.* alièno *m.* (foreign) straniero *m.*, forestiero *m.*

**alienate,** *vb.* alienare.

**alight,** *vb.* (dismount) smontare; (get down) scéndere.

**align,** *vb.* allineare.

**alike,** **1.** *adj.* sìmile. **2.** *adv.* similmente.

**alimentary,** *adj.* alimentare.

**alimentary canal,** *n.* canale alimentàrio *m.*

**alive,** *adj.* vivente; (be a.) vivere.

**alkali,** *n.* àlcali *m.*

**alkaline,** *adj.* alcalino.

**all,** *adj.* tutto; (above a.) sopratutto; (a. at once) tutt'a un tratto; (a. the same) nondimeno; (a. of you) voi tutti; (not at a.) niente affatto.

**allay,** *vb.* alleviare; (lessen) diminuire.

**allegation,** *n.* allegazione *f.*

**allege,** *vb.* allegare.

**allegiance,** *n.* fedeltà *f.*

**allegory,** *n.* allegorìa, *f.*

**allergy,** *n.* allergìa *f.*

**alleviate,** *vb.* alleviare.

**alley,** *n.* vìcolo *m.*; (in garden) viale *m.*

**alliance,** *n.* alleanza *f.*

**allied,** *adj.* alleato; (related) affine.

**alligator,** *n.* alligatore *m.*

**allocate,** *vb.* assegnare.

**allot,** *vb.* assegnare, divìdere.

**allotment,** *n.* assegnazione *f.*

**allow,** *vb.* (permit) perméttere; (admit) amméttere; (grant) concédere; (allow for) far débito conto di.

**allowance,** *n.* (money) assegno *m.*; (permission) permesso *m.*; (reduction) riduzione *f.*

**alloy,** **1.** *n.* lega *f.* **2.** *vb.* mescolare.

**all right,** *interj.* va bène.

**allude,** *vb.* allùdere.

**allure,** *vb.* affascinare, adescare.

**alluring,** *adj.* adescatore, seducènte.

**allusion,** *n.* allusione *f.*

**ally,** **1.** *n.* alleato *m.* **2.** *vb.* alleare.

**almanac,** *n.* almanacco *m.*

**almighty,** *adj.* onnipotente.

**almond,** *n.* màndorla *f.*

**almond-tree,** *n.* màndorlo *m.*

**almost,** *adv.* quasi.

**alms,** *n.* elemòsina *f.*(sg.)

**aloft,** *adv.* in alto.

**alone,** **1.** *adj.* solo; (let a.) lasciate in pace. **2.** solamente.

**along,** *prep.* lungo; (come a.!) venite dunque!

**aloof,** **1.** *adj.* riservato. **2.** *adv.* in disparte.

**aloud,** *adv.* ad alta voce.

**alpaca,** *n.* alpaca *m.*

**alphabet,** *n.* alfabèto *m.*

**alphabetical,** *adj.* alfabètico.

**alphabetize,** *vb.* méttere in òrdine alfabètico.

**Alps,** *n.* Alpi *f.pl.*

**already,** *adv.* già, di già.

**also,** *adv.* anche.

**altar,** *n.* altare *m.*

**alter,** *vb.* alterare.

**alteration,** *n.* alterazione *f.*

**alternate,** **1.** *n.* sostituto *m.* **2.** *adj.* alternativo. **3.** *vb.* alternare.

**alternating current,** *n.* corrente alternata *f.*

**alternative,** **1.** *n.* alternativa *f.* **2.** *adj.* alternativo.

**although,** *conj.* benchè, quantunque, sebbene.

**altitude,** *n.* altitùdine *f.*

**alto,** *n.* contralto *m.*

**altogether,** *adv.* completamente.

**altruism,** *n.* altruismo *m.*

**alum,** *n.* allume *m.*

**aluminum,** *n.* allumìnio *m.*

**always,** *adv.* sèmpre.

**amalgam,** *n.* amàlgama *m.*

**amalgamate,** *vb.* amalgamare.

**alongside,** **1.** *adv.* accanto. **2.** *prep.* accanto a.

**amass,** *vb.* ammassare.

**amateur,** *n.* dilettante *m.* and *f.*

**amaze,** *vb.* meravigliare, stupire; (be amazed) meravigliarsi, stupirsi.

**amazement,** *n.* meravìglia *f.*, stupore *m.*

**amazing,** *adj.* meraviglioso.

**ambassador,** *n.* ambasciatore *m.*

**amber,** *n.* ambra *f.*

**ambidextrous,** *adj.* ambidèstro.

**ambiguity,** *n.* ambiguità *f.*

**ambiguous,** *adj.* ambiguo.

**ambition,** *n.* ambizione *f.*

**ambitious,** *adj.* ambizioso.

**ambulance,** *n.* ambulanza *f.*

**ambulatory,** *n. and adj.* ambulatòrio (*m.*).

**ambush, 1.** *n.* imboscata *f.* **2.** *vb.* tendere un'imboscata a.

**ameliorate,** *vb.* migliorare.

**amenable,** *adj.* responsàbile, governàbile, dòcile.

**amend,** *vb.* emendare, corréggere, migliorare.

**amendment,** *n.* emendamento *m.*

**amenity,** *n.* amenità *f.*

**America,** *n.* Amèrica *f.*

**American,** *n. and adj.* americano *m.*

**amethyst,** *n.* ametista *f.*

**amiable,** *adj.* amàbile.

**amicable,** *adj.* amichévole.

**amid,** *prep.* fra, tra, in mèzzo a.

**amidships,** *adv.* nel mezzo della nave.

**amiss,** *adv.* che non va bene; **(be a.)** non andar bene.

**amity,** *n.* amicìzia *f.*

**ammonia,** *n.* ammonìaca *f.*

**ammunition,** *n.* munizione *f.*

**amnesia,** *n.* amnesìa *f.*

**amnesty,** *n.* amnistìa *f.*

**amoeba,** *n.* amèba *f.*

**among,** *prep.* fra, tra.

**amoral,** *adj.* amorale.

**amorous,** *adj.* amoroso.

**amorphous,** *adj.* amorfo.

**amortize,** *vb.* ammortizzare.

**amount, 1.** *n.* somma *f.*, quantità *f.* **2.** *vb.* ammontare.

**ampere,** *n.* ampère *m.*

**amphibian,** *n.* anfìbio *m.*

**amphibious,** *adj.* anfìbio.

**amphitheater,** *n.* anfiteatro *m.*

**ample,** *adj.* àmpio.

**amplify,** *vb.* ampliare, amplificare.

**amputate,** *vb.* amputare.

**amputee,** *n.* amputato *m.*, mutilato *m.*

**amuse,** *vb.* divertire.

**amusement,** *n.* divertimento *m.*

**an,** *art.* un *m.*, una *f.*

**anachronism,** *n.* anacronismo *m.*

**analogous,** *adj.* anàlogo.

**analogy,** *n.* analogìa *f.*

**analysis,** *n.* anàlisi *f.*

**analyst,** *n.* analista *m.*

**analytic,** *adj.* analìtico.

**analyze,** *vb.* analizzare.

**anarchy,** *n.* anarchìa *f.*

**anatomy,** *n.* anatomìa *f.*

**ancestor,** *n.* antenato *m.*

**ancestral,** *adj.* degli antenati.

**ancestry,** *n.* lignàggio *m.*

**anchor, 1.** *n.* àncora *f.* **2.** *vb.* ancorare.

**anchorage,** *n.* ancoràggio *m.*

**anchovy,** *n.* acciuga *f.*

**ancient,** *adj.* antico.

**and,** *conj.* e; (before vowels) ed.

**anecdote,** *n.* anèddoto *m.*

**anemia,** *n.* anemìa *f.*

**anesthesia,** *n.* anestesìa *f.*

**anesthetic,** *n. and adj.* anestètico (*m.*).

**anesthetist,** *n.* anestetista *m.*

**anew,** *adv.* di nuòvo.

**angel,** *n.* àngelo *m.*

**anger,** *n.* ira *f.*, ràbbia *f.*

**angle, 1.** *n.* àngolo *m.* **2.** *vb.* (fish) pescare.

**angry,** *adj.* adirato, arrabbiato; **(get a.)** adirarsi, arrabbiarsi.

**anguish,** *n.* angòscia *f.*

**angular,** *adj.* angolare.

**aniline,** *n.* anilìna *f.*

**animal,** *n. and adj.* animale (*m.*).

**animate,** *vb.* animare.

**animated,** *adj.* animato, **animated cartoon,** *n.* disegno animato *m.*

**animation,** *n.* animazione *f.*

**animosity,** *n.* animosità *f.*

**animus,** *n.* ànimo *m.*

**anise,** *n.* ànice *m.*

**ankle,** *n.* cavìglia *f.*

**annals,** *n.* annali *m.(pl.)*

**annex, 1.** *n.* annèsso *m.* **2.** *vb.* annèttere.

**annexation,** *n.* annessione *f.*

**annihilate,** *vb.* annichilire.

**anniversary,** *n.* anniversàrio *m.*

**annotate,** *vb.* annotare.

**annotation,** *n.* annotazione *f.*

**announce,** *vb.* annunziare.

**announcement,** *n.* annùnzio *m.*

**announcer,** *n.* annunciatore *m.*, annunziatrice *f.*

**annoy,** vb. infastidire.
**annoyance,** n. fastìdio m.
**annual,** n. and adj. ànnuo (m.), annuale (m.).
**annuity,** n. annualità f.
**annul,** vb. annullare.
**anode,** n. ànodo m.
**anoint,** vb. ùngere.
**anomalous,** adj. anòmalo.
**anomaly,** n. anomalìa f.
**anonymous,** adj. anònimo.
**another,** adj. un altro m., un'altra f.; (**one a.**) l'un l'altro.
**answer,** 1. n. risposta f. 2. vb. rispóndere.
**answerable,** adj. responsàbile.
**ant,** n. formica f.
**antacid,** 1. n. antàcido m. 2. adj. antiàcido.
**antagonism,** n. antagonismo m.
**antagonist,** n. antagonista m.
**antagonistic,** adj. ostile.
**antagonize,** vb. réndere ostile.
**antarctic,** n. and adj. antàrtico (m.).
**antecedent,** n. antecedènte.
**antedate,** vb. precédere.
**antelope,** n. antìlope f.
**antenna,** n. antenna f.
**anterior,** adj. anteriore.
**anteroom,** n. anticàmera f.
**anthem,** n. (church music) antìfona f.; (**national a.**) inno nazionale m.
**anthology,** n. antologìa f.
**anthracite,** n. antracite f.
**anthropological,** adj. antropològico.
**anthropology,** n. antropologìa f.
**antiaircraft,** adj. antiaèreo.
**antibody,** n. anticòrpo m.
**antic,** n. buffonata f.
**anticipate,** vb. anticipare.
**anticipation,** n. anticipazione f.
**anticlerical,** adj. anticlericale.
**anticlimax,** n. delusione f.
**antidote,** n. antìdoto m.
**antimony,** n. antimònio m.
**antipathy,** n. antipatìa f.
**antiquated,** adj. antiquato.
**antique,** 1. n. oggetto antico m. 2. adj. antico.
**antiquity,** n. antichità f.
**antiseptic,** n. and adj. antisèttico (m.).
**antisocial,** adj. antisociale.
**antitoxin,** n. antitossina f.
**antler,** n. palco m.
**anvil,** n. incùdine f.

**anxiety,** n. ànsia f., ansietà f.
**anxious,** adj. ansioso.
**any,** 1. adj. (in questions, for "some") del, dello, dell' m.sg., della, dell' f.sg., dei, degli m.pl., delle f.pl.; (**not . . . any**) non . . . nessun; (no matter which) non impòrta quale; (every) ogni. 2. pron. (any of it, any of them, with verb) ne.
**anybody,** pron. qualcuno; (after negative) nessuno; (no matter who) non importa chi.
**anyhow,** adv. in qualche manièra, a ogni modo.
**anyone,** pron. see anybody.
**anything,** pron. qualcosa, qualche còsa; (after negation) niènte; (no matter) non impòrta che còsa.
**anyway,** adv. see anyhow.
**anywhere,** adv. non impòrta dove.
**apart,** adv. a parte.
**apartment,** n. appartamento m.
**apathetic,** adj. apàtico.
**apathy,** n. apatìa f.
**ape,** n. scìmmia f.
**aperture,** n. apertura f.
**apex,** n. àpice m.
**aphorism,** n. aforismo m.
**apiary,** n. apiàrio m.
**apiece,** adj. l'uno, cadaùno.
**apogee,** n. apogèo m.
**apologetic,** adj.; (**be a.**) scusarsi.
**apologize for,** vb. scusarsi di.
**apology,** n. (defense) apologìa f.; (excuse) scusa f.
**apoplectic,** adj. apoplèttico.
**apoplexy,** n. apoplessìa f.
**apostate,** n. apòstata m.
**apostle,** n. apòstolo m.
**apostolic,** adj. apostòlico.
**appall,** vb. spaventare.
**apparatus,** n. apparato m., apparècchio m.
**apparel,** 1. n. vèste f., vestimento m. 2. vb. vestire.
**apparent,** adj. apparènte.
**apparition,** n. apparizione f.
**appeal,** 1. n. appèllo m. 2. vb. appellare.
**appear,** vb. parere; (become visible) apparire; (seem) sembrare; (be evident) risultare.
**appearance,** n. apparènza f.; (looks) aspètto m.
**appease,** vb. placare, acquetare.

**appeasement,** *n.* appaciamento *m.*

**appeaser,** *n.* placatore *m.*

**appellant,** *n.* appellante *m.*

**appellate,** *adj.* d'appèllo.

**appendage,** *n.* appendice *f.*

**appendectomy,** *n.* appendectomia *f.*

**appendicitis,** *n.* appendicite *f.*

**appendix,** *n.* appendice *f.*

**appetite,** *n.* appetito *m.*

**appetizer,** *n.* antipasto *m.*

**appetizing,** *adj.* gustoso.

**applaud,** *vb.* applaudire.

**applause,** *n.* applàuso *m.*

**apple,** *n.* pomo *m.*, mela *f.*

**applesauce,** *n.* (lit.) consèrva di mele *f.*; (nonsense) fròttola *f.*

**apple-tree,** *n.* melo *m.*

**appliance,** *n.* apparécchio *m.*

**appliances,** *n.* (electric) elettrodomèstici *m.pl.*

**applicable,** *adj.* applicàbile.

**applicant,** *n.* richiedènte *m.*

**application,** *n.* (putting on) applicazione *f.*; (request) domanda *f.*

**appliqué** *adj.* applicato; (**a. work**) ricamo applicato *m.*

**apply,** *vb.* (put on) applicare; (request) richièdere, fare una domanda.

**appoint,** *vb.* (a person) nominare; (time, place) fissare, stabilire.

**appointment,** *n.* (nomination) nòmina *f.*; (date) appuntamento *m.*

**apportion,** *vb.* distribuire.

**apposition,** *n.* apposizione *f.*

**appraisal,** *n.* stima *f.*

**appraise,** *vb.* stimare.

**appreciable,** *adj.* apprezzàbile.

**appreciate,** *vb.* apprezzare, tenere in giusto conto.

**appreciation,** *n.* apprezzamento *m.*

**apprehend,** *vb.* (fear) temere; (catch) arrestare.

**apprehension,** *n.* timore *m.*

**apprehensive,** *adj.* timoroso.

**apprentice,** *n.* apprendista *m.*

**apprise,** *vb.* informare.

**approach,** **1.** *n.* accèsso *m.* **2.** *vb.* avvicinarsi a.

**approachable,** *adj.* avvicinàbile.

**approbation,** *n.* approvazione *f.*

**appropriate,** **1.** *adj.* appro-

priato. **2.** *vb.* (take for oneself) appropriarsi; (set aside funds) stanziare.

**appropriation,** *n.* stanziamento *m.*

**approval,** *n.* approvazione *f.*

**approve,** *vb.* approvare.

**approximate,** **1.** *vb.* approssimare. **2.** *adj.* approssimativo.

**approximately,** *adv.* approssimativamente.

**approximation,** *n.* approssimazione *f.*

**appurtenance,** *n.* appartenènza *f.*

**apricot,** *n.* albicòcca *f.*

**April,** *n.* aprile *m.*

**apron,** *n.* grembiule *m.*

**apropos,** *adv.* a propòsito.

**apse,** *n.* àbside *f.*

**apt,** *adj.* atto; (quick at) pronto a.

**aptitude,** *n.* attitùdine *f.*

**Apulia,** *n.* le Pùglie *f.pl.*

**Apulian,** *adj.* pugliese.

**aquarium,** *n.* acquàrio *m.*

**aquatic,** *adj.* acquàtico.

**aqueduct,** *n.* acquedotto *m.*

**aqueous,** *adj.* àcqueo.

**aquiline,** *adj.* aquilino.

**Arab,** *n.* Àrabo *m.*

**Arabic,** *adj.* àrabo.

**arable,** *adj.* aràbile.

**arbiter,** *n.* àrbitro *m.*

**arbitrary,** *adj.* arbitràrio.

**arbitrate,** *vb.* arbitrare.

**arbitration,** *n.* arbitrato *m.*

**arbitrator,** *n.* àrbitro *m.*

**arbor,** *n.* pergolato *m.*

**arboreal,** *adj.* arbòreo.

**arc,** *n.* arco *m.*

**arcade,** *n.* gallerìa *f.*

**arch,** *n.* arco *m.*

**archaeology,** *n.* archeologia *f.*

**archaic,** *adj.* arcàico.

**archbishop,** *n.* arcivéscovo *m.*

**archdiocese,** *n.* arcidiòcesi *f.*

**archduke,** *n.* arciduca *m.*

**archer,** *n.* arcière *m.*

**archery,** *n.* tiro dell'arco *m.*

**archipelago,** *n.* arcipèlago *m.*

**architect,** *n.* architetto *m.*

**architectural,** *adj.* architettònico.

**architecture,** *n.* architettura *f.*

**archives,** *n.* archìvio *m.*(*sg.*)

**archway,** *n.* pòrtico *m.*

**arctic,** *adj.* àrtico.

**ardent,** *adj.* ardènte.

**ardor,** *n.* ardore *m.*

**arduous,** *adj.* àrduo.

**area,** *n.* àrea *f.*

**arena,** *n.* arena *f.*

**Argentine, 1.** *n.* Argentina *f.* **2.** *adj.* argentino.

**argue,** *vb.* (draw a conclusion) arguire; (quarrel) bisticciarsi.

**argument,** *n.* (in debate) argomento *m.*; (quarrel) bisticcio *m.*

**argumentative,** *adj.* litigioso.

**aria,** *n.* ària *f.*

**arid,** *adj.* àrido.

**arise,** *vb.* (get up) levarsi; (come into being) nàscere.

**aristocracy,** *n.* aristocrazia *f.*

**aristocrat,** *n.* aristocràtico *m.*

**aristocratic,** *adj.* aristocràtico.

**arithmetic,** *n.* aritmètica *f.*

**ark,** *n.* arca *f.*

**arm, 1.** *n.* (body part) bràccio *m.*; (weapon) arma *f.* **2.** *vb.* armare.

**armament,** *n.* armamento *m.*

**armchair,** *n.* poltrona *f.*

**armful,** *n.* bracciata *f.*

**armhole,** *n.* òcchio della mànica *m.*

**armistice,** *n.* armistìzio *m.*

**armor,** *n.* armatura *f.*

**armored,** *adj.* blindato.

**armory,** *n.* armerìa *f.*; magazzino *m.*

**armpit,** *n.* ascèlla *f.*

**arms,** *n.* (weapons) armi *f.pl.*

**army,** *n.* esèrcito *m.*

**arnica,** *n.* àrnica *f.*

**aroma,** *n.* aròma *m.*

**aromatic,** *adj.* aromàtico.

**around, 1.** *adv.* intorno. **2.** *prep.* intorno a.

**arouse,** *vb.* svegliarsi.

**arraign,** *vb.* accusare.

**arrange,** *vb.* ordinare, disporre, sistemare; (music) ridurre.

**arrangement,** *n.* ordinamento *m.*; (music) riduzione *f.*

**array, 1.** *n.* òrdine *m.*, sèrie *f.* **2.** *vb.* ordinare.

**arrears,** *n.* indietrato *m.* (*sg.*)

**arrest, 1.** *n.* arrèsto *m.* **2.** *vb.* arrestare.

**arrival,** *n.* arrivo *m.*

**arrive,** *vb.* arrivare, giùngere.

**arrogance,** *n.* arroganza *f.*

**arrogant,** *adj.* arrogante.

**arrogate,** *vb.* arrogarsi.

**arrow,** *n.* fréccia *f.*, strale *m.*

**arrowhead,** *n.* punta di fréccia *f.*

**arsenal,** *n.* arsenale *m.*

**arsenic,** *n.* arsènico *m.*

**arson,** *n.* incèndio doloso *m.*

**art,** *n.* arte *f.*; **(fine arts)** bèlle arti *f.pl.*

**arterial,** *adj.* arteriale.

**arteriosclerosis,** *n.* arterioscleròsi *f.*

**artery,** *n.* artèria *f.*

**artesian well,** *n.* pozzo artesiano *m.*

**artful,** *adj.* astuto.

**arthritis,** *n.* artrite *f.*

**artichoke,** *n.* carciòfo *m.*

**article,** *n.* artìcolo *m.*

**articulate, 1.** *adj.* articolato. **2.** *vb.* articolare.

**articulation,** *n.* articolazione *f.*

**artifice,** *n.* artifìcio *m.*

**artificial,** *adj.* artificiale.

**artificiality,** *n.* artificialità *f.*

**artillery,** *n.* artiglierìa *f.*

**artisan,** *n.* artigiano *m.*

**artist,** *n.* artista *m.*, *f.*

**artistic,** *adj.* artìstico.

**artistry,** *n.* arte *f.*

**artless,** *adj.* ingènuo, senz' arte.

**as,** *prep. and conj.* come; **(as if)** quasi.

**asbestos,** *n.* asbèsto *m.*

**ascend,** *vb.* salire.

**ascendancy,** *n.* supremazìa *f.*

**ascendant,** *adj.* suprèmo.

**ascent,** *n.* salita *f.*

**ascertain,** *vb.* accertarsi.

**ascetic, 1.** *n. and adj.* ascètico (*m.*).

**ascribe,** *vb.* ascrìvere.

**ash,** *n.* (tree) fràssino *m.*

**ashamed,** *adj.* vergognoso; **(be a. of)** vergognarsi di.

**ashen,** *adj.* di cénere.

**ashes,** *n.* cénere *f.* (*sg.*)

**ashore,** *adv.* a tèrra.

**ash-tray,** *n.* portacéneri *m.*

**Asia,** *n.* Asia *f.*

**Asiatic,** *adj.* asiàtico.

**aside,** *adv.* a parte.

**ask,** *vb.* (question) domandare; (request) chièdere; (invite) invitare.

**askance,** *adv.* sospettosamente.

**asleep,** *adj.* addormentato; **(fall a.)** addormentarsi.

**asparagus,** *n.* aspàrago *m.*, spàragi *m.pl.*

**aspect,** *n.* aspètto *m.*

**asperity,** *n.* asperità *f.*

**aspersion,** *n.* denigrazione *f.*

**asphalt,** *n.* asfalto *m.*

**asphyxia,** *n.* asfissìa *f.*

**asphyxiate,** *vb.* asfissiare.

**aspirant**, n. aspirante m.

**aspirate**, **1.** n. aspirata f.
**2.** adj. aspirato. **3.** vb.
aspirare.

**aspiration**, n. aspirazione f.

**aspirator**, n. aspiratore m.

**aspire**, vb. aspirare.

**aspirin**, n. aspirina f.

**ass**, n. àsino m.

**assail**, vb. assalire, attaccare.

**assailable**, adj. assalibile.

**assailant**, n. assalitore m.

**assassin**, n. assassino m.

**assassinate**, vb. assassinare.

**assassination**, n. assassinio m.

**assault**, **1.** n. assalto m. **2.**
vb. assaltare.

**assay**, **1.** n. saggio m. **2.** vb.
saggiare, assaggiare.

**assemblage**, n. riunione f.

**assemble**, vb. (bring together)
riunire; (come together) riunirsi.

**assembly**, n. riunione f., as-
sembléa f.; (autos, etc.)
montàggio m.

**assent**, **1.** n. assènso m. **2.**
vb. assentire.

**assert**, vb. asserire.

**assertion**, n. asserzione f.

**assertive**, adj. dogmàtico.

**assertiveness**, n. dogmaticità f.

**assess**, vb. (a fine) fissare (una
multa); (property) stimare.

**assessor**, n. assessore m.

**asset**, n. (possession) bène m.;
(in accounting) attivo m.

**asseverate**, vb. asseverare.

**asseveration**, n. asseverazione f.

**assiduous**, adj. assìduo.

**assiduously**, adv. assiduamente.

**assign**, vb. assegnare.

**assignable**, adj. assegnàbile.

**assignation**, n. assegnazione
f.; (date) appuntamento m.

**assigned**, adj. addetto.

**assignment**, n. assegnamento m., assegnazione f., incàrico m.;(school) cómpito m.

**assimilate**, vb. assimilare.

**assimilation**, n. assimilazione f.

**assimilative**, adj. assimilativo.

**assist**, vb. aiutare.

**assistance**, n. aiuto m.

**assistant**, n. and adj. assistènte (m.).

**associate**, vb. associare, tr.;
associarsi, intr.

**association**, n. associazione f.

**assonance**, n. assonanza f.

**assort**, vb. assortire.

**assorted**, adj. assortito.

**assortment**, n. assortimento
m.

**assuage**, vb. (pain) mitigare;
(desire) soddisfare.

**assume**, vb. assùmere; (appropriate) arrogarsi; (feign)
fingere; (suppose) supporre.

**assuming**, adj. arrogante,
presuntuoso.

**assumption**, n. supposizione
f.; (eccles.) Ascensione f.

**assurance**, n. assicurazione f.

**assure**, vb. assicurare.

**assured**, adj. assicurato, sicuro.

**assuredly**, adv. sicuramente.

**aster**, n. astro m.

**asterisk**, n. asterisco m.

**astern**, adv. a poppa.

**asteroid**, n. asteròide m.

**asthma**, n. asma m.

**astigmatism**, n. astigmatismo m.

**astir**, adv. in mòto.

**astonish**, vb. sorprèndere,
meravigliare.

**astonishment**, n. sorpresa f.,
meraviglia f.

**astound**, vb. stupire; (be
astounded) stupirsi.

**astral**, adj. astrale.

**astray**, **1.** adj. sviato. **2.** vb.
(go a.) sviarsi.

**astride**, adv. a cavalcioni;
prep. a cavalcioni di.

**astringent**, adj. astringènte.

**astrology**, n. astrologia f.

**astronomy**, n. astronomìa f.

**astute**, adj. astuto.

**asunder**, adv. (in twain) in
due; (in pieces) a pèzzi.

**asylum**, n. (refuge) rifùgio
m.; (madhouse) manicòmio m.

**at**, prep. (time, place price)
ad (before vowels), a (before
vowels or consonants); (at
someone's house, shop, etc.)
da.

**ataxia**, n. atassìa f.

**atheist**, n. àteo m.

**athlete**, n. atlèta m.

**athletic**, adj. atlètico.

**athletics**, n. atletismo m.

**athwart**, adv. attravèrso.

**Atlantic**, adj. atlàntico.

**Atlantic Ocean**, n. Ocèano
atlàntico m.

**atlas**, n. atlante m.

**atmosphere**, n. atmosfèra f.

**atmospheric**, adj. atmosfèrico.

**atoll,** *n.* atóllo *m.*

**atom,** *n.* àtomo *m.*

**atomic,** *adj.* atòmico.

**atomize,** (liquids), *vb.* nebulizzare.

**atonal,** *adj.* atonale.

**atone for,** *vb.* espiare.

**atonement,** *n.* espiazione *f.*

**atrocious,** *adj.* atroce.

**atrocity,** *n.* atrocità *f.*

**atrophy,** *n.* atrofìa *f.*

**atropine,** *n.* atropina *f.*

**attach,** *vb.* attaccare.

**attaché,** *n.* addetto *m.*

**attachment,** *n.* (lit.) attaccamento *m.*; (liking) affezione *f.*; (equipment) accessòrio *m.*

**attack, 1.** *n.* attacco *m.* **2.** *vb.* attaccare.

**attacker,** *n.* assalitore *m.*

**attain,** *vb.* raggiùngere.

**attainable,** *adj.* raggiungìbile.

**attainment,** *n.* raggiungimento *m.*

**attempt, 1.** *n.* tentativo *m.* **2.** *vb.* tentare.

**attendance,** *n.* assistèuza *f.*

**attend,** *vb.* (give heed to) prestare attenzione a; (medical) curarsi di.; (serve) servire; (meeting) assìstere a; (lectures) frequentare; (see to) occuparsi di.

**attendant,** *n. and adj.* assistènte (*m.*).

**attention,** *n.* attenzione *f.*; (pay a.) fare attenzione.

**attentive,** *adj.* attènto.

**attentively,** *adv.* attentamente.

**attenuate,** *vb.* attenuare.

**attest,** *vb.* attestare.

**attic,** *n.* soffitta *f.*

**attire, 1.** *n.* abbigliamento *m.* **2.** *vb.* abbigliare.

**attitude,** *n.* atteggiamento *m*; (take an a.) atteggiarsi

**attorney,** *n.* procuratore *m.*

**attract,** *vb.* attrarre.

**attraction,** *n.* attrazione *f.*

**attractive,** *adj.* attraènte.

**attributable,** *adj.* attribuìbile.

**attribute,** *vb.* attribuire.

**attribution,** *n.* attribuzione *f.*

**attrition,** *n.* attrizione *f.*

**attune,** *vb.* armonizzare; (an instrument) accordare.

**auction,** *n.* vèndita all'asta *f.*

**auctioneer,** *n.* banditore *m.*

**audacious,** *adj.* audace.

**audacity,** *n.* audàcia *f.*

**audible,** *adj.* udìbile.

**audience,** *n.* (listeners) udìtòrio *m.*; (interview) udiènza *f.*

**audit, 1.** *n.* verifica *f.*, contròllo *m.* **2.** *vb.* verificare, controllare.

**audition,** *n.* audizione *f.*

**auditor,** *n.* uditore *m.*, uditrice *f.*; (accounts) revisore *m.*, controllore *m.*

**auditorium,** *n.* auditòrio *m.*

**auditory,** *adj.* uditivo.

**auger,** *n.* succhièllo *m.*, trivèllo *m.*

**augment,** *vb.* aumentare.

**augur,** *vb.* augurare.

**August,** *n.* agosto *m.*

**aunt,** *n.* zìa *f.*

**auspice,** *n.* auspicio *m.*

**auspicious,** *adj.* favorévole.

**austere,** *adj.* austèro.

**austerity,** *n.* austerità *f.*

**Austria,** *n.* Àustria *f.*

**Austrian,** *adj.* austrìaco.

**authentic,** *adj.* autèntico.

**authenticate,** *vb.* autenticare.

**authenticity,** *n.* autenticità *f.*

**author,** *n.* autore *m.*

**authoritarian,** *adj.* autoritàrio.

**authoritative,** *adj.* autorévole.

**authoritatively,** *adv.* autorevolmente.

**authority,** *n.* autorità *f.*

**authorization,** *n.* autorizzazione *f.*

**authorize,** *vb.* autorizzare.

**auto,** *n.* àuto *f.*

**autobiography,** *n.* autobiografìa *f.*

**autocracy,** *n.* autocrazìa *f.*

**autocrat,** *n.* autòcrate *m.*

**autograph,** *n.* autògrafo *m.*

**automatic,** *adj.* automàtico.

**automatically,** *adv.* automaticamente.

**automaton,** *n.* autòma *m.*

**automobile,** *n.* automòbile *f.*

**automotive,** *adj.* automobilìstico.

**autonomous,** *adj.* autònomo.

**autonomy,** *n.* autonomìa *f.*

**autopsy,** *n.* autopsìa *f.*

**autumn,** *n.* autunno *m.*

**auxiliary,** *n. and adj.* ausiliare (*m.*).

**avail,** *vb.* servire; (be of no a.) non servire a nulla.

**available,** *adj.* disponìbile.

**avalanche,** *n.* valanga *f.*

**avarice,** *n.* avarìzia *f.*

**avaricious,** *adj.* avaro.

**avenge,** *vb.* vendicare.

**avenger,** *n.* vendicatore *m.*

**avenue,** *n.* viale *m.*

**average, 1.** *n.* mèdia *f.* **2.** *adj.* mèdio. **3.** *vb.* fare la mèdia di.

**averse,** *adj.* avvèrso.

**aversion,** *n.* avversione *f.*

**avert,** *vb.* impedire.

**aviary,** *n.* aviàrio *m.*, uccellièra *f.*

**aviation,** *n.* aviazione *f.*

**aviator,** *n.* aviatore *m.*

**aviatrix,** *n.* aviatrice *f.*

**avid,** *adj.* àvido.

**avocation,** *n.* divertimento *m.*

**avoid,** *vb.* evitare, scansare; **(so as to a.)** a scanso di.

**avoidable,** *adj.* evitàbile.

**avoidance,** *n.* scanso *m.*

**avow,** *vb.* confessare.

**avowal,** *n.* confessione *f.*

**avowedly,** *adv.* lo confèsso.

**await,** *vb.* aspettare.

**awake, 1.** *adj.* sveglio. **2.**

*vb.* svegliare, *tr.*; svegliarsi, *intr.*

**awaken,** *vb.* see **awake.**

**award, 1.** *n.* prèmio *m.* **2.** *vb.* conferire; **(a. a prize to)** premiare.

**aware,** *adj.* consapévole, cònscio.

**awash,** *adv.* al livèllo dell'acqua.

**away,** *adv.* via, lontano; **(go a.)** andàrsene.

**awe, 1.** *n.* terrore *m.*, soggezione *f.* **2.** *vb.* ispirare terrore a.

**awesome,** *adj.* tremèndo.

**awful,** *adj.* terribile.

**awhile,** *adv.* per un momento.

**awkward,** *adj.* gòffo; **(difficult)** difficile.

**awning,** *n.* tènda *f.*

**awry,** *adv.* di travèrso.

**axe,** *n.* àscia *f.*

**axiom,** *n.* assiòma *m.*

**axis,** *n.* asse *m.*

**axle,** *n.* asse *m.*

**azure,** *adj.* azzurro.

# B

**babble, 1.** *n.* balbettìo *m.* **2.** *vb.* balbettare.

**babbler,** *n.* balbuziènte *m.*

**babe,** *n.* bimbo *m.*; **(girl)** ragazza *f.*

**baboon,** *n.* babbuino *m.*

**baby,** *n.* bimbo *m.*; **(b.- carriage)** carrozzèlla *f.*

**babyish,** *adj.* bambinesco. infantile.

**bachelor,** *n.* scàpolo *m.*; **(degree)** baccellière *m.*

**bacillus,** *n.* bacillo *m.*

**back, 1.** *n.* dòsso *m.*, dòrso *m.*, schièna *f.* **2.** *adj.* posteriore. **3.** *vb.* **(go backwards)** indietreggiare; **(support)** appoggiare, sostenere, spalleggiare; **(b. down)** cèdere. **4.** *adv.* indiètro.

**backbone,** *n.* spina dorsale, *f.*

**backer,** *n.* sostenitore *m.*

**backfire,** *vb.* scoppiare.

**background,** *n.* sfondo *m.*

**backhand,** *n.* rovèscio *m.*

**backing,** *n.* appòggio *m.*, sostegno *m.*

**backlog,** *n.* risèrve *f.pl.*

**back out,** *vb.* ritirarsi.

**backstage,** *n.* retroscèna *f.*

**backward, 1.** *adj.* stùpido. **2.** *adv.* indiètro.

**backwardness,** *n.* stupidità *f.*

**backwards,** *adv.* indiètro.

**backwater,** *n.* acqua stagnante *f.*

**backwoods,** *n.* retrotèrra *f.*

**bacon,** *n.* pancetta *f.*

**bacteria,** *n.* battèri *m.pl.*

**bacteriologist,** *n.* batteriòlogo *m.*

**bacteriology,** *n.* batteriologìa *f.*

**bacterium,** *n.* battèrio *m.*

**bad,** *adj.* cattivo.

**badge,** *n.* emblèma *f.*, distintivo *m.*

**badger,** *n.* tasso *m.*

**badly,** *adv.* male, malamente.

**badness,** *n.* cattivèria *f.*

**bad-tempered**, *adj.* di cattivo umore.

**baffle**, *vb.* (hinder) impedire; (perplex) rèndere perplèsso.

**bafflement**, *n.* perplessità *f.*

**bag**, **1.** *n.* sacco *m.*, borsa *f.*; (woman's purse) borsetta *f.* **2.** *vb.* (get) ottenere; (**put in a b.**) insaccare.

**baggage**, *n.* bagàglio *m.*

**baggy**, *adj.* gónfio.

**bagpipe**, *n.* cornamusa *f.*, zampogna *f.*

**bail**, *n.* cauzione *f.*, garanzìa *f.*

**bailiff**, *n.* usciere *m.*

**bail out**, *vb.* (set free) fornire garanzìa per; (empty out water) vuotare.

**bait**, *n.* esca *f.*

**bake**, *vb.* cuòcere al forno.

**baker**, *n.* fornaio *m.*

**bakery**, *n.* forno *m.*

**baking**, *n.* cottura al forno *m.*

**balance**, **1.** *n.* (equilibrium) equilìbrio *m.*; (comm.) saldo *m.*; (scales) bilància *f.* **2.** *vb.* bilanciare; (weigh) pesare; (make of equal weight) equilibrare; (comm.) saldare.

**balcony**, *n.* balcone *m.*

**bald**, *adj.* calvo.

**baldness**, *n.* calvìzie *f.sg.*

**bale**, *n.* balla *f.*

**balk**, *vb.* (hinder) impedire; (refuse to move) essere ritroso.

**balky**, *adj.* ritroso.

**ball**, *n.* palla *f.*; (bullet) pallòttola *f.*; (dance) ballo *m.*

**ballad**, *n.* ballata *f.*

**ballade**, *n.* ballata *f.*

**ballast**, *n.* zavorra *f.*

**ball bearing**, *n.* cuscinetto a sfere *m.*

**ballerina**, *n.* ballerina *f.*

**ballet**, *n.* ballo *m.*

**ballistics**, *n.* balìstica *f.*

**balloon**, *n.* pallone *m.*

**ballot**, *n.* (voting) votazione *f.*; (paper) scheda *f.*

**ballroom**, *n.* sala da ballo *f.*

**balm**, *n.* bàlsamo *m.*

**balmy**, *adj.* balsàmico.

**balsam**, *n.* bàlsamo *m.*

**balustrade**, *n.* balaùstra *f.*, balaustrata *f.*

**bamboo**, *n.* bambù *m.*

**ban**, **1.** *n.* proibizione *f.* **2.** *vb.* proibire.

**banal**, *adj.* banale.

**banana**, *n.* banana *f.*

**band**, *n.* (group, including musical band) banda *f.*;

(headband) benda *f.*; (ribbon) striscia *f.*

**bandage**, *n.* benda *f.*

**bandanna**, *n.* fazzoletto multicolore *m.*

**bandbox**, *n.* cappellièra *f.*

**bandit**, *n.* bandito *m.*

**bandmaster**, *n.* capobanda *m.*, maestro di banda *m.*

**bandsman**, *n.* bandista *m.*

**bandstand**, *n.* palco della banda musicale *f.*

**baneful**, *adj.* dannoso.

**bang**, **1.** *n.* (hair-do) frangia *f.*; (blow) colpo *m.* **2.** *vb.* sbàttere. **3.** *interj.* pum!

**banish**, *vb.* bandire, esiliare.

**banishment**, *n.* bando *m.*, esilio *m.*

**banister**, *n.* ringhiera *f.*

**bank**, **1.** *n.* (institution) banca *f.*, banco *m.*; (edge of water) riva *f.* **2.** *vb.* (rely on) contare su; (airplane) inclinare.

**bankbook**, *n.* libretto di depòsito *m.*

**banker**, *n.* banchière *m.*

**banking**, **1.** *n.* operazioni bancàrie *f.pl.* **2.** *adj.* bancàrio.

**bank note**, *n.* banconota *f.*

**bankrupt**, **1.** *adj.* fallito. **2.** *vb.* far fallire; (**go b.**) fallire.

**bankruptcy**, *n.* fallimento *m.*, bancarotta *f.*

**banner**, *n.* bandièra *f.*

**banquet**, *n.* banchetto *m.*

**banter**, **1.** *n.* scherzo *m.*, cèlia *f.* **2.** *vb.* scherzare, celiare.

**baptism**, *n.* battésimo *m.*

**baptismal**, *adj.* battesimale.

**Baptist**, *n.* battista *m.*

**baptistery**, *n.* battistèro *m.*

**baptize**, *vb.* battezzare.

**bar**, **1.** *n.* sbarra *f.*; (obstacle) ostàcolo *m.*; (for drinks) bar *m.* **2.** *vb.* sbarrare; ostacolare.

**barb**, *n.* punta ricurva *f.*

**barbarian**, *n.* bàrbaro *m.*

**barbarism**, *n.* barbàrie *f.*; (gramm.) barbarismo.

**barbarous**, *adj.* bàrbaro.

**barbecue**, **1.** *n.* animale arrostito intèro *m.* **2.** *vb.* arrostire intèro.

**barber**, *n.* barbière *m.*, parrucchière *m.*

**barbiturate**, *n.* barbitùrico *m.*

**bare**, **1.** *adj.* nudo, scopèrto. **2.** *vb.* scoprire.

**bareback**, *adv.* sènza sèlla.

**barefoot**, *adj.* scalzo.

**barely**, *adv.* appena.

**bareness**, *n.* nudità *f.*

**bargain**, **1.** *n.* affare *m.*; (cheap purchase) occasione *f.* **2.** *vb.* mercanteggiare.

**barge**, *n.* chiatta *f.*

**baritone**, *n. and adj.* baritono (*m.*).

**barium**, *n.* bàrio *m.*

**bark**, **1.** *n.* (of tree) scorza *f.*, corteccia *f.*; (of dog) abbaiamento *m.* **2.** *vb.* abbaiare.

**barley**, *n.* orzo *m.*

**barn**, *n.* granaio *m.*

**barnacle**, *n.* cirrìpede *m.*

**barnyard**, *n.* cortile *m.*

**barometer**, *n.* baròmetro *m.*

**barometric**, *adj.* baromètrico.

**baron**, *n.* barone *m.*

**baroness**, *n.* baronessa *f.*

**baronial**, *adj.* baronale.

**baroque**, *adj.* baròcco.

**barracks**, *n.* casèrma *f.sg.*

**barrage**, *n.* fuoco di sbarramento *m.*

**barred**, *adj.* sbarrato; (excluded) escluso; (forbidden) vietato.

**barrel**, *n.* barile *m.*

**barren**, *adj.* stèrile.

**barrenness**, *n.* sterilità *f.*

**barricade**, *n.* barricata *f.*

**barrier**, *n.* barrièra *f.*

**barroom**, *n.* béttola *f.*, bar *m.*

**barter**, **1.** *n.* baratto *m.* **2.** *vb.* barattare.

**base**, **1.** *n.* base *f.* **2.** *adj.* basso. **3.** *vb.* basare.

**baseball**, *n.* baseball *m.*

**baseboard**, *n.* zòccolo *m.*

**Basel**, *n.* Basilèa *f.*

**basement**, *n.* cantina *f.*

**baseness**, *n.* bassezza *f.*

**bashful**, *adj.* tìmido.

**bashfully**, *adv.* timidamente.

**bashfulness**, *n.* timidezza *f.*

**basic**, *adj.* fondamentale.

**basin**, *n.* (wash) catino *m.*; (river) bacino *m.*

**basis**, *n.* base *f.*

**bask**, *vb.* riscaldarsi, godersi.

**basket**, *n.* cesta *f.*

**basketball**, *n.* pallacanestro *m.*

**bass**, *n.* (voice) basso *m.*; (fish) pesce pèrsico *m.*

**bassinet**, *n.* culla *f.*

**bassoon**, *n.* fagòtto *m.*

**bastard**, *n. and adj.* bastardo (*m.*).

**baste**, *vb.* (sewing) imbastire; (cooking) ammorbidire.

**bat**, *n.* (animal) pipistrèllo *m.*; (baseball) bastone *m.*

**batch**, *n.* infornata *f.*

**bate**, *vb.* diminuire.

**bath**, *n.* bagno *m.*

**bathe**, *vb.* (*tr.*) bagnare; (*intr.*) fare il bagno.

**bather**, *n.* bagnante *m. or f.*

**bathing resort**, *n.* stazione balneare *f.*

**bathrobe**, *n.* vestàglia *f.*

**bathroom**, *n.* stanza da bagno *f.*

**bathtub**, *n.* vasca da bagno *f.*

**baton**, *n.* (military) bastone *m.*; (conductor's) bacchetta *f.*

**battalion**, *n.* battaglione *m.*

**batter**, **1.** *n.* (cooking) pasta *f.* **2.** *vb.* bàttere.

**battery**, *n.* batterìa *f.*, pila *f.*

**batting**, *n.* (cotton b.) imbottitura di cotone *f.*

**battle**, **1.** *n.* battàglia *f.* **2.** *vb.* combàttere.

**battlefield**, *n.* campo di battàglia *m.*

**battleship**, *n.* nave da guèrra *f.*

**bauxite**, *n.* bauxite *m.*

**bawl**, *vb.* urlare; (b. out) sgridare.

**bay**, **1.** *n.* (geography) bàia *f.*; (plant) làuro *f.*; (howl) latrato; (at b.) a bada. **2.** *adj.* (color) baio. **3.** *vb.* latrare; abbaiare.

**bayonet**, *n.* baionetta *f.*

**bazaar**, *n.* bazàr *m.*

**be**, *vb.* èssere; (health) stare.

**beach**, *n.* spiàggia *f.*, lido *m.*

**beachhead**, *n.* tèsta di sbarco *f.*

**beacon**, *n.* faro *m.*

**bead**, **1.** *n.* grano *m.* **2.** *vb.* ornare di grani.

**beading**, *n.* ornamento di grani *m.*

**beady**, *adj.* a forma di grano.

**beak**, *n.* becco *m.*

**beaker**, *n.* recipiènte *m.*

**beam**, **1.** *n.* (construction) trave *f.*; (light) raggio *m.* **2.** *vb.* irradiare, risplèndere.

**beaming**, *adj.* raggiante, risplendènte.

**bean**, *n.* fagiòlo *m.*, fava *f.*

**bear**, **1.** *n.* (animal) orso *m.* **2.** *vb.* (carry) portare; (endure) sopportare; (give birth to) partorire.

**bearable**, *adj.* sopportàbile.

**beard**, *n.* barba *f.*

**bearded**, *adj.* barbuto.

**beardless,** *adj.* imbèrbe.

**bearer,** *n.* portatore *m.*

**bearing,** *n.* (behavior) condotta *f.*; (position) orientamento *m.*; (machinery) cuscinetto *m.*

**bearskin,** *n.* pèlle d'orso *f.*

**beast,** *n.* bèstia *f.*

**beat,** **1.** *n.* bàttito *m.* **2.** *vb.* bàttere; (conquer) vìncere.

**beaten,** *adj.* battuto.

**beatify,** *vb.* beatificare.

**beating,** *n.* percosse *f.pl.*; (defeat) disfatta *f.*

**beatitude,** *n.* beatitùdine *f.*

**beau,** *n.* (fop) damerino *m.*; (wooer) corteggiatore.

**beautiful,** *adj.* bèllo; (excellent) eccellènte.

**beautifully,** *adv.* in bel modo, bène, eccellentemente.

**beautify,** *vb.* abbellire.

**beauty,** *n.* bellezza *f.*; **(b.-parlor)** salone di bellezza *m.*

**beaver,** *n.* castòro *m.*

**becalm,** *vb.* abbonacciare.

**because,** *conj.* perché; **(b. of)** a causa di.

**beckon,** *vb.* far cenno, accennare.

**become,** *vb.* divenire, diventare; (be suitable for) convenire a; (be attractive for) star bène a.

**becoming,** *adj.* grazioso.

**bed,** *n.* lètto *m.*; (for animals) lettièra *f.*

**bedbug,** *n.* cìmice *f.*

**bedclothes,** *n.* lenzuòla *f.pl.*

**bedding,** *n.* letterecci *m.pl.*

**bedfellow,** *n.* compagno di lètto *m.*

**bedizen,** *vb.* ornare.

**bedridden,** *adj.* degènte.

**bedroom,** *n.* stanza da lètto *f.*

**bedside,** *n.*; **(at the b. of)** al capezzale di.

**bedspread,** *n.* copèrta da lètto *f.*

**bedstead,** *n.* lettièra *f.*

**bedtime,** *n.* ora d'andare a lètto *m.*

**bee,** *n.* ape *f.*

**beef,** *n.* bue *m.*

**beefsteak,** *n.* bistecca *f.*

**beehive,** *n.* alveare *m.*

**beer,** *n.* birra *f.*

**beeswax,** *n.* cera *f.*

**beet,** *n.* barbabiètola *f.*

**beetle,** *n.* scarafàggio *m.*

**befall,** *vb.* accadere, capitare.

**befit,** *vb.* convenire a.

**befitting,** *adj.* conveniènte.

**before,** **1.** *adv.* (in front) avanti, davanti; (earlier) prima. **2.** *prep.* avanti, davanti a, prima di. **3.** *conj.* prima che.

**beforehand,** *adv.* prima, in anticipo.

**befriend,** *vb.* aiutare.

**befuddle,** *vb.* confóndere.

**beg,** *vb.* (ask alms) mendicare; (request) chièdere; (implore) pregare; implorare.

**beget,** *vb.* generare.

**beggar,** *n.* mendicante *m.*

**beggarly,** *adj.* meschino.

**begin,** *vb.* cominciare, incominciare, iniziare, principiare.

**beginner,** *n.* principiante *m.*

**beginning,** *n.* princìpio *m.*, cominciamento *m.*, inizio *m.*

**begrudge,** *vb.* invidiare.

**beguile,** *vb.* ingannare.

**behalf,** *n.* favore *m.*; (on behalf of) da parte di; (in behalf of) a favore di.

**behave,** *vb.* comportarsi, condursi.

**behavior,** *n.* comportamento *m.*, condotta *f.*

**behead,** *vb.* decapitare.

**behind,** **1.** *adv.* indiètro. **2.** *prep.* diètro a.

**behold,** *vb.* vedere.

**beige,** *adj.* avana.

**being,** *n.* èssere *m.*; (existence) esistènza *f.*

**bejewel,** *vb.* ornare di gioièlli.

**belated,** *adj.* tardivo.

**belch,** **1.** *n.* rutto *m.* **2.** *vb.* ruttare.

**belfry,** *n.* campanile *m.*

**Belgian,** *n.* and *adj.* bèlga.

**Belgium,** *n.* il Bèlgio *m.*

**belie,** *vb.* smentire.

**belief,** *n.* credènza *f.*, opinione *f.*, fede *f.*

**believable,** *adj.* credìbile.

**believe,** *vb.* crédere; (make believe) fìngere.

**believer,** *n.* credènte *m.*

**belittle,** *vb.* denigrare.

**bell,** *n.* (house) campanèllo *m.*; (church) campana *f.*

**bellboy,** *n.* camerière *m.*

**bell buoy,** *n.* bòa a campana *f.*

**bellicose,** *adj.* bellicoso, battaglièro.

**belligerence,** *n.* belligeranza *f.*

**belligerent,** *adj.* belligerante, bellicoso.

**belligerently,** *adv.* bellicosamente.

**bellow, 1.** *n.* mùgghio *m.*, muggito *m.* **2.** *vb.* muggire, mugghiare.

**bellows,** *n.* (large) màntice *m.*; (small) soffietto *m.*

**bell-tower,** *n.* campanile *m.*

**belly,** *n.* vèntre *m.*, pancia *f.*

**belong,** *vb.* appartenere.

**belongings,** *n.* possessi *m.pl.* proprietà *f.sg.*

**beloved,** *adj.* amato, diletto.

**below,** *adv. and prep.* sotto.

**belt,** *n.* cintura *f.*

**bench,** *n.* banco *m.*

**bend,** *vb.* piegare; (curve) curvare.

**beneath,** *adv. and prep* sotto.

**benediction,** *n.* benedizione *f.*

**benefactor,** *n.* benefattore *m.*

**benefactress,** *n.* benefattrice *f.*

**beneficent,** *adj.* benèfico.

**beneficial,** *adj.* vantaggioso, salutare.

**beneficiary,** *n.* beneficiàrio *m.*

**benefit, 1.** *n.* beneficio *m.*, vantaggio *m.* **2.** *vb.* beneficare, trarre vantaggio da (*intr.*).

**benevolence,** *n.* benevolènza *f.*

**benevolent,** *adj.* benevolo, caritatévole.

**benevolently,** *adv.* benevolmente, caritatevolmente.

**benign,** *adj.* benigno.

**benignity,** *n.* benignità *f.*

**bent,** *adj.* piegato, curvo.

**benzine,** *n.* benzina *f.*

**bequeath,** *vb.* legare.

**bequest,** *n.* legato *m.*

**berate,** *vb.* sgridare.

**bereave,** *vb.* orbare, privare.

**bereavement,** *n.* pèrdita *f.*

**beriberi,** *n.* beri-bèri *m.*

**Bern,** *n.* Berna *f.*

**berry,** *n.* bacca *f.*

**berth,** *n.* cuccetta *f.*

**beseech,** *vb.* supplicare.

**beseeching,** *adj.* supplichévole.

**beseechingly,** *adv.* supplichevolmente.

**beset,** *vb.* assalire, assediare.

**beside,** *prep.* accanto a.

**besides, 1.** *adv.* inoltre. **2.** *prep.* oltre.

**besiege,** *vb.* assediare.

**besieger,** *n.* assediante *m.*

**besmirch,** *vb.* insudiciare; (dishonor) disonorare.

**best, 1.** *adj.* il migliore. **2.** *adv.* il mèglio. **3.** *vb.* vincere.

**bestial,** *adj.* bestiale.

**bestir oneself,** *vb.* scuòtersi.

**best man,** *n.* testimone dello sposo *m.*

**bestow,** *vb.* conferire.

**bestowal,** *n.* concessione *f.*

**bet, 1.** *n.* scommessa *f.* **2.** *vb.* scomméttere.

**betake (oneself),** *vb.* recarsi, andare.

**betoken,** *vb.* significare.

**betray,** *vb.* tradire.

**betrayal,** *n.* tradimento *m.*

**betroth,** *vb.* fidanzare.

**betrothal,** *n.* fidanzamento *m.*

**better, 1.** *adj.* migliore. **2.** *adv.* mèglio. **3.** *vb.* migliorare.

**between,** *prep.* fra, tra.

**bevel,** *n.* inclinazione *f.*

**beverage,** *n.* bevanda *f.*

**bewail,** *vb.* lamentare, piàngere.

**beware,** *vb.* guardarsi.

**bewilder,** *vb.* confóndere, rèndere perplèsso.

**bewildered,** *adj.* confuso, perplèsso.

**bewildering,** *adj.* sconcertante.

**bewilderment,** *n.* confusione *f.* perplessità *f.*

**bewitch,** *vb.* ammaliare, stregare.

**beyond, 1.** *adv.* al di là, oltre. **2.** *prep.* al di là di, oltre.

**biannual,** *adj.* biennale.

**bias, 1.** *n.* parzialità *f.*, pregiudizio *m.* **(on the b.)** in sbieco. **2.** *vb.* predisporre.

**bib,** *n.* bavaglino *m.*

**Bible,** *n.* Bìbbia *f.*

**Biblical,** *adj.* bìblico.

**bibliography,** *n.* bibliografìa *f.*

**bicarbonate,** *n.* bicarbonato *m.*

**bicentennial,** *adj.* bicentennale.

**biceps,** *n.* bicìpite *m.*

**bicker,** *vb.* litigare, bisticciarsi.

**bicycle,** *n.* bicicletta *f.*

**bicyclist,** *n.* ciclista *m.* or *f.*

**bid, 1.** *n.* (offer) offèrta *f.*; (invitation) invito *m.* **2.** *vb.* (offer) offrire; (command) comandare.

**bidder,** *n.* offerènte *m.*

**bide,** *vb.* aspettare.

**biennial,** *adj.* biennale.

**bier,** *n.* bara *f.*

**bifocal,** *adj.* bifocale.

**big,** adj. grande, gròsso; (pregnant) gràvida f.; **(b. shot)** pèzzo gròsso m.

**bigamist,** n. bìgamo m.

**bigamous,** adj. bìgamo.

**bigamy,** n. bigamìa f.

**bigot,** n. bigòtto m.

**bigoted,** adj. bigòtto.

**bigotry,** n. bigotterìa f., bigottismo m.

**bilateral,** adj. bilaterale.

**bile,** n. bile f.

**bilingual,** adj. bilingue

**bilious,** adj. (pertaining to bile) biliare; (temperament) bilioso.

**bill,** n. (bird) becco m.; (money) biglietto m.; (sum owed) conto m.; (legislative) progètto di legge m.; **(b. of fare)** lista f.

**billboard,** n. cartèllo pubblicitàrio m.

**billet,** 1. n. allòggio m. 2. vb. alloggiare.

**billfold,** n. portafògli m.

**billiard ball** n. palla da biliardo f.

**billiards,** n. biliardo m.sg.

**billion,** n. bilione m.

**bill of health,** n. certificato mèdico m.

**bill of lading,** n. polizza di càrico f.

**bill of sale,** n. manifèsto di vèndita m.

**billow,** n. maroso m.

**bimetallic,** adj. bimetàllico.

**bimonthly,** adj. (twice a month) bimensile, quindicinale; (every two months) bimestrale.

**bin,** n. recipiènte m.

**bind,** vb. legare; (oblige) obbligare; (a book) rilegare.

**bindery,** n. legatorìa f.

**binding,** 1. n. (book) rilegatura f. 2. adj. obbligatòrio.

**binocular,** 1. n. binòcolo m. 2. adj. binoculare.

**biochemistry,** n. biochìmica f.

**biographer,** n. biògrafo m.

**biographical,** adj. biogràfico.

**biography,** n. biografìa f.

**biological,** adj. biològico.

**biologically,** adv. biologicamente.

**biology,** n. biologìa f.

**bipartisan,** adj. di tutti e due i partiti.

**biped,** n. and adj. bìpede (m.)

**bird,** n. uccèllo m.

**birdlike,** adj. come un uccèllo.

**bird of prey,** n. uccèllo di rapina m.

**birth,** n. nàscita f.

**birthday,** n. compleanno m.

**birthmark,** n. vòglia f.

**birthplace,** n. luògo di nàscita m.

**birth rate,** n. natalità f.

**birthright,** n. diritto di primogenitura f.

**biscuit,** n. (roll) panino m.; (cracker) biscòtto m.

**bisect,** vb. bisecare.

**bishop,** n. véscovo m.

**bishopric,** n. vescovato m., diòcesi f.

**bismuth,** n. bismuto m.

**bison,** n. bisonte m.

**bit,** n. (piece) pèzzo m.; **(a b. of)** un po' di; (harness) mòrso m.

**bitch,** n. cagna f.

**bite,** 1. n. mòrso m. 2. vb. mòrdere.

**biting,** adj. pungènte.

**bitter,** adj. amaro.

**bitterly,** adv. amaramente.

**bitterness,** n. amarezza f.

**bivouac,** n. bivacco m.

**biweekly,** adj. (twice a week) bisettimanale; (every two weeks) quindicinale.

**black,** adj. nero.

**blackberry,** n. mòra f.

**blackbird,** n. mèrlo m.

**blackboard,** n. lavagna f.

**blacken,** vb. annerire.

**black eye,** n. òcchio pesto m.

**blackguard,** n. mascalzone m.; furfante m.

**blackmail,** 1. n. ricatto m. 2. vb. ricattare.

**blackmailer,** n. ricattatore m.

**black market,** n. mercato nero m.

**blackout,** n. oscuramento m.

**blacksmith,** n. fabbro ferraio m.

**bladder,** n. vescica f.

**blade,** n. (of cutting tool) lama f.; (grass) filo d'erba m.

**blame,** 1. n. biàsimo m. 2. vb. biasimare.

**blameless,** adj. innocènte.

**blanch,** vb. impallidire.

**bland,** adj. blando.

**blank,** 1. n. (empty space) spàzio bianco m.; (form) mòdulo m. 2. adj. (page) bianco; (empty) vuòto.

**blanket,** n. copèrta f.

**blare, 1.** n. squillo m. **2.** vb. squillare.

**blaspheme,** vb. bestemmiare.

**blasphemer,** n. bestemmiatore m.

**blasphemous,** adj. émpio.

**blasphemy,** n. bestémmia f.

**blast, 1.** n. (of wind) ràffica f.; (explosion) esplosione f. **2.** vb. far saltare.

**blatant,** adj. clamoroso, rumoroso.

**blaze, 1.** n. fiamma f.; (fire) fuòco m. **2.** vb. fiammeggiare.

**bleach,** vb. imbiancare.

**bleachers,** n. tribune f.pl.

**bleak,** adj. squàllido.

**bleakness,** n. squallore m.

**bleed,** vb. sanguinare.

**blemish,** n. màcchia f.

**blend, 1.** n. mescolanza f. **2.** vb. mescolare.

**bless,** vb. benedire.

**blessed,** adj. benedetto, beato.

**blessing,** n. benedizione f.

**blight, 1.** n. malattìa f. **2.** vb. **be blighted,** ammalare.

**blind, 1.** adj. cièco. **2.** vb. accecare.

**blindfold, 1.** n. benda f. **2.** adj. bendato. **3.** vb. bendare.

**blindly,** adv. ciecamente.

**blindness,** n. cecità f.

**blink,** vb. sbàttere le pàlpebre.

**blinker,** n. (signal) lampeggiatore m.

**bliss,** n. beatitùdine f.

**blissful,** adj. beato.

**blissfully,** adv. beatamente.

**blister,** n. vescica f.

**blithe,** adj. gaio, gioioso.

**blizzard,** n. tempèsta di neve f.

**bloat,** vb. gonfiare.

**bloc,** n. blòcco m.

**block, 1.** n. blòcco m., ostàcolo m. **2.** vb. bloccare, ostacolare.

**blockade,** n. blòcco m.

**blond,** adj. biondo.

**blood,** n. sangue m.

**bloodhound,** n. cane poliziòtto m.

**bloodless,** adj. esangue, senza sangue.

**blood plasma,** n. plasma del sangue m.

**blood poisoning,** n. avvelenamento del sangue m.

**blood pressure,** n. pressione del sangue f.

**bloodshed,** n. spargimento di sangue m.

**bloodshot,** adj. infiammato.

**bloodthirsty,** adj. sanguinàrio.

**bloody,** adj. sanguinoso.

**bloom, 1.** n. fiore m. **2.** vb. fiorire.

**blossom, 1.** n. fiore m. **2.** vb. fiorire.

**blot, 1.** n. màcchia f. **2.** vb. macchiare; (dry ink) asciugare.

**blotch,** n. (spot) màcchia f.; sgòrbio m.

**blotchy,** adj. macchiato.

**blotter,** n. carta assorbente f.

**blouse,** n. blusa f.

**blow, 1.** n. colpo m. **2.** vb. soffiare.

**blowout,** n. scòppio d'un pneumàtico m.

**blubber, 1.** n. (whale fat) grasso di balena f. **2.** vb. (snivel) piagnucolare.

**bludgeon,** n. mazza f.

**blue,** adj. azzurro, blu; (gloomy) triste.

**bluebird,** n. uccèllo azzurro m.

**blueprint,** n. eliotìpia f.; (plan) piano m.

**bluff, 1.** n. (cliff) rupe scoscesa f.; (cards) bluff m.; (trickery) inganno m. **2.** adj. franco. **3.** vb. bluffare, ingannare.

**bluffer,** n. bluffatore m.

**bluing,** n. anile m.

**blunder, 1.** n. errore m.; svista f. **2.** vb. sbagliare.

**blunderer,** n. stordito m.

**blunt,** adj. (dull) ottuso; (curt) rude.

**bluntly,** adv. ottusamente, rudemente.

**bluntness,** n. ottusità f.

**blur, 1.** n. confusione f. **2.** vb. rèndere indistinto.

**blurred,** adj. indistinto.

**blush, 1.** n. rossore m. **2.** vb. arrossire.

**bluster, 1.** n. millanterìa f. **2.** vb. millantare.

**boar,** n. vèrro m.

**board, 1.** n. (plank) asse f., tàvola f.; (food) vitto m.; (committee) comitato m.; (council) consiglio m.; (of ship) bordo m. **2.** vb. (go on b.) andare a bordo.

**boarder,** n. pensionante m.

**boarding house,** n. pensione f.

**boast, 1.** *n.* vanto *m.*, vanteria *f.* **2.** *vb.* vantare, *tr.*

**boaster,** *n.* vantatore *m.*

**boastful,** *adj.* vanaglorioso.

**boastfulness,** *n.* vanteria *f.*

**boat,** *n.* barca *f.*, battèllo *m.*

**boathouse,** *n.* tettòia per barche.

**boatswain,** *n.* nostròmo *m.*

**bob,** *vb.* tagliare corto.

**bobbin,** *n.* bobina *f.*

**bobby pin,** *n.* forcina *f.*

**bode,** *vb.* presagire.

**bodice,** *n.* busto *m.*

**bodily,** *adj.* corpòreo.

**body,** *n.* còrpo *m.*

**bodyguard,** *n.* guàrdia del còrpo *f.*

**bog, 1.** *n.* pantano *m.*, palude *f.* **2.** *vb.* **(b. down)** impantanarsi.

**Bohemian,** *n.* *and* *adj.* boemo (*m.*).

**boil, 1.** *n.* (med.) forùncolo *m.* **2.** *vb.* bollire.

**boiler,** *n.* caldaia *f.*

**boisterous,** *adj.* impetuoso, turbolènto.

**boisterously,** *adv.* impetuosamente.

**bold,** *adj.* ardito; **(be b.)** ardire.

**boldface,** *n.* (type) caràtteri grassi *m.pl.*

**boldly,** *adv.* arditamente.

**boldness,** *n.* ardimento *m.*

**Bolivian,** *adj.* boliviano.

**bologna,** *n.* salsìccia *f.*, salame *m.*

**bolster,** *vb.* appoggiare.

**bolster up,** *vb.* tenere su.

**bolt, 1.** *n.* catenàccio *m.* **2.** *vb.* (shut) chiùdere a catenàccio; (run away) fuggire.

**bomb,** *n.* bomba *f.*

**bombard,** *vb.* bombardare.

**bombardier,** *n.* bombardière *m.*

**bombardment,** *n.* bombardamento *m.*

**bomber,** *n.* bombardière *m.*

**bombproof,** *adj.* a pròva di bomba.

**bombshell,** *n.* bomba *f.*

**bombsight,** *n.* traguardo di puntamento *m.*

**bonbon,** *n.* dolce *m.*

**bond,** *n.* legame *m.*, obbligazione *f.*, vìncolo *m.*, buòno *m.*

**bondage,** *n.* servitù *f.*

**bonded,** *adj.* vincolato.

**bone,** *n.* òsso *m.*

**boneless,** *adj.* sènza òssa.

**bonfire,** *n.* falò *m.*

**bonnet,** *n.* (headdress) cappèllo *m.*; (motor-car) còfano *m.*

**bonus,** *n.* gratificazione *f.*

**bony,** *adj.* ossuto.

**book,** *n.* libro *m.*

**bookbinder,** *n.* legatore *m.*

**bookbindery,** *n.* legatoria *f.*

**bookcase,** *n.* scaffale *m.*

**bookkeeper,** *n.* contàbile *m.*

**bookkeeping,** *n.* contabilità *f.*

**booklet,** *n.* libretto *m.*

**bookseller,** *n.* libraio *m.*

**bookstore,** *n.* librerìa *f.*

**boom,** *n.* prosperità *f.*

**boon,** *n.* dono *m.*

**boor,** *n.* zòtico *m.*

**boorish,** *adj.* zòtico.

**boost, 1.** *n.* (increase) accrescimento *m.*; (push) spinta *f.* **2.** *vb.* (increase) accrèscere; (push) spìngere; (praise) lodare.

**booster,** *n.* (telephone) amplificatore *m.*; (person) entusiasta *m.*

**boot,** *n.* stivale *m.*

**bootblack,** *n.* lustrascarpe *m.*

**booth,** *n.* tènda *f.*

**booty,** *n.* bottino *m.*

**border, 1.** *n.* confine *m.*, frontièra *f.* **2.** *vb.* confinare.

**borderline, 1.** *n.* linea di confine *f.* **2.** *adj.* marginale.

**bore, 1.** *n.* (hole) foro *m.*; (annoyance) seccatura *f.* **2.** *vb.* (make a hole) forare; (annoy) seccare.

**boredom,** *n.* nòia *f.*

**boric,** *adj.* bòrico.

**boring, 1.** *n.* (hole) foro. **2.** *adj.* seccante.

**born,** *adj.* nato; **(be b.)** nàscere.

**borough,** *n.* borgo *m.*

**borrow,** *vb.* prèndere in prestito.

**borrower,** *n.* chi prende a prèstito.

**bosom,** *n.* pètto *m.*, seno *m.*

**boss,** *n.* padrone *m.*

**bossy,** *adj.* spadroneggiante.

**botanical,** *adj.* botànico.

**botany,** *n.* botànica *f.*

**botch,** *vb.* rabberciare.

**both,** *adj.* and *pron.* ambedue.

**bother, 1.** *n.* fastidio *m.* **2.** *vb.* infastidire.

**bothersome,** *adj.* fastidioso.

**bottle,** *n.* bottiglia *f.*

**bottom,** *n.* fondo *m.*

**bottomless,** *adj.* sènza fondo.

**boudoir,** *n.* salottino *m.*

**bough,** *n.* ramo *m.*

**bouillon,** *n.* bròdo *m.*

**boulder,** *n.* sasso *m.*

**boulevard,** *n.* viale *m.*

**bounce, 1.** *n.* rimbalzo **2.** *vb.* rimbalzare.

**bound, 1.** *n.* limite; (jump) balzo *m.*, salto *m.* **2.** *vb.* balzare, saltare.

**boundary,** *n.* confine *m.*

**bound for,** *adj.* diretto a.

**boundless,** *adj.* illimitato.

**boundlessly,** *adv.* illimitatamente.

**bounteous,** *adj.* liberale.

**bounty,** *n.* liberalità *f.*

**bouquet,** *n.* mazzo di fiori *m.*

**bourgeois,** *adj.* borghese.

**bout,** *n.* (boxing) assalto *m.*

**bovine,** *adj.* bovino.

**bow, 1.** *n.* (for arrows, violin) arco *m.*; (greeting) inchino *m.*; (of boat) pròra *f.* **2.** *vb.* inchinarsi.

**bowels,** *n.* budella *f.pl.*, intestini *m.pl.*

**bowl, 1.** *n.* (vessel) scodèlla *f.* **2.** *vb.* giocare alle bocce.

**bowlegged,** *adj.* colle gambe ad archetto.

**bowler,** *n.* giocatore di bocce *m.*

**bowling,** *n.* giòco delle bocce *f.*

**box, 1.** *n.* scàtola *f.*, cassetta *f.*; (theater) palco *m.*; (P.O.) casèlla postale *f.* **2.** *vb.* fare del pugilato.

**boxcar,** *n.* vagone mèrci *m.*

**boxer,** *n.* pugilatore *m.*

**boxing,** *n.* pugilato *m*

**box office,** *n.* botteghino *m.*

**boy,** *n.* ragazzo *m.*, fanciullo *m.*

**boycott, 1.** *n.* boicottàggio *m.* **2.** *vb.* boicottare.

**boyhood,** *n.* fanciullezza *f.*

**boyish,** *adj.* fanciullesco.

**boyishly,** *adv.* fanciullescamente.

**brace, 1.** *n.* sostegno *m.* **2.** *vb.* sostenere.

**bracelet,** *n.* braccialetto *m.*

**bracket,** *n.* mènsola *f.*; (group) gruppo *m.*; (typography) parèntesi quadra *f.*

**brag,** *vb.* millantare.

**braggart,** *n.* millantatore *m.*

**braid, 1.** *n.* tréccia *f.* **2.** *vb.* intrecciare.

**brain,** *n.* cervèllo *m.*

**brainy,** *adj.* intelligènte.

**brake, 1.** *n.* freno *m.* **2.** *vb.* frenare.

**bran,** *n.* crusca *f.*

**branch,** *n.* ramo *m.*; (comm.) succursale *f.*

**brand,** *n.* marca *f.*

**brandish,** *vb.* brandire.

**brand-new,** *adj.* nuovissimo.

**brandy,** *n.* acquavite *f.*

**brash,** *adj.* impertinènte.

**brass,** *n.* ottone *m.*

**brassière,** *n.* reggipètto *m.*, reggiseno *m.*

**brat,** *n.* marmòcchio *m.*

**bravado,** *n.* bravata *f.*

**brave,** *adj.* coraggioso.

**bravery,** *n.* coràggio *m.*

**brawl,** *n.* lite *f.*, rissa *f.*

**brawn,** *n.* tòrza muscolare *f.*

**bray, 1.** *n.* ràglio *m.* **2.** *vb.* ragliare.

**brazen,** *adj.* di ottone; (insolent) insolènte.

**Brazil,** *n.* il Brasile *m.*

**Brazilian,** *adj.* brasiliano.

**breach,** *n.* bréccia *f.*; (of law) violazione *f.*

**bread,** *n.* pane *m.*

**breadth,** *n.* larghezza *f.*, ampiezza *f.*

**break, 1.** *n.* rottura *f.*; interruzione *f.* **2.** *vb.* rómpere.

**breakable,** *adj.* rompibile.

**breakage,** *n.* rottura *f.*

**breaker,** *n.* frangènte *m.*

**breakfast,** *n.* prima colazione *f.*

**breakneck,** *adv.* a rompicollo.

**breakwater,** *n.* frangi-onde *m.*

**breast,** *n.* seno *m.*, mammèlla *f.*, poppa *f.*; (chest) pètto *m.*

**breath,** *n.* fiato *m.*, respiro *m.*

**breathe,** *vb.* respirare.

**breathing,** *n.* respiro *m.*

**breathless,** *adj.* sènza fiato; ansante.

**breathlessly,** *adv.* ansando.

**breeches,** *n.* brache *f.pl.*, pantaloni *m.pl.*

**breed, 1.** *n.* razza *f.* **2.** *vb.* (beget) generare; (train) educare; (raise) allevare.

**breeder,** *n.* generatore *m.*, allevatore *m.*

**breeding,** *n.* educazione *f.*

**breeze,** *n.* brezza *f.*

**breezy,** *adj.* (windy) ventoso; (cool) fresco.

**brevity,** *n.* brevità *f.*

**brew,** *vb.* fabbricare la birra.

**brewer**, *n.* birraio *m.*, fabbricante di birra *m.*

**brewery**, *n.* fabbrica di birra *f.*

**briar**, *n.* rovo *m.*

**bribe**, *vb.* corrómpere.

**briber**, *n.* corruttore *m.*

**bribery**, *n.* corruzione *f.*

**brick**, *n.* mattone *m.*

**bricklayer**, *n.* muratore *m.*

**bricklaying**, *n.* muratura *f.*

**bricklike**, *adj.* come un mattone.

**bridal**, *adj.* nuziale.

**bride**, *n.* sposa *f.*

**bridegroom**, *n.* sposo *m.*

**bridesmaid**, *n.* danigèlla d'onore *f.*

**bridge**, *n.* ponte *m.*

**bridged**, *adj.* connèsso.

**bridgehead**, *n.* tèsta di ponte *f.*

**bridle**, *n.* brìglia *f.*

**brief**, *adj.* bréve.

**brief case**, *n.* borsa *f.*

**briefly**, *adv.* brevemente.

**briefness**, *n.* brevità *f.*

**brier**, *n.* rovo *m.*

**brig**, *n.* brigantino *m.*

**brigade**, *n.* brigata *f.*

**bright**, *adj.* chiaro; luminoso.

**brighten**, *vb.* illuminare.

**brightness**, *n.* chiarore *m.*

**brilliance**, *n.* splendore *m.*

**brilliant**, *adj.* brillante.

**brim**, *n.* (cup) orlo *m.*; (hat) tesa *f.*

**brine**, *n.* acqua salata *f.*

**bring**, *vb.* portare; apportare; (**b. about**) causare.

**brink**, *n.* orlo *m.*; bordo *m.*

**briny**, *adj.* salato.

**brisk**, *adj.* vivace.

**brisket**, *n.* (meat) pètto *m.*

**briskly**, *adv.* vivacemente.

**briskness**, *n.* vivacità *f.*

**bristle**, **1.** *n.* sétola *f.* **2.** *vb.* arruffare.

**bristly**, *adj.* setoloso.

**Britain**, *n.* (**Great B.**) la Gran Bretagna *f.*

**British**, *adj.* britànnico.

**Briton**, *n.* Brètone *m.*

**brittle**, *adj.* fràgile.

**broad**, *adj.* largo, àmpio.

**broadcast**, **1.** *n.* trasmissione radiofònica *f.* **2.** *vb.* trasméttere.

**broadcaster**, *n.* trasmettitore *m.*

**broadcloth**, *n.* popelina *f.*

**broaden**, *vb.* allargare.

**broadly**, *adv.* largamente.

**broadminded**, *adv.* spregiudicato.

**broadside**, *n.* bordata *f.*

**brocade**, *n.* broccato *m.*

**brocaded**, *adj.* di broccato.

**broil**, *vb.* mettere alla graticola.

**broiler**, *n.* gratìcola *f.*

**broke**, *adj.* al verde.

**broken**, *adj.* rotto.

**broken-hearted**, *adj.* scorato.

**broker**, *n.* sensale *m.*

**brokerage**, *n.* senseria *f.*

**bronchial**, *adj.* bronchiale.

**bronchitis**, *n.* bronchite *f.*

**bronze**, *n.* bronzo *m.*

**brooch**, *n.* spilla *f.*

**brood**, **1.** *n.* covata *f.*, famiglia *f.* **2.** *vb.* covare.

**brook**, *n.* ruscèllo *m.*

**broom**, *n.* scopa *f.*

**broomstick**, *n.* mànico della scopa *f.*

**broth**, *n.* bròdo *m.*

**brothel**, *n.* bordèllo *m.*

**brother**, *n.* fratèllo *m.*

**brotherhood**, *n.* fratellanza *f.*

**brother-in-law**, *n.* cognato *m.*

**brotherly**, *adj.* fratèrno.

**brow**, *n.* fronte *f.*

**brown**, *adj.* bruno.

**browse**, *vb.* brucare.

**bruise**, **1.** *n.* ammaccatura *f.* **2.** *vb.* ammaccare.

**brunette**, *n.* bruna *f.*

**brunt**, *n.* urto *m.*

**brush**, **1.** *n.* spàzzola *f.*; (artist's) pennèllo *m.* **2.** *vb.* spazzolare; (**b. against**) sfiorare.

**brushwood**, *n.* màcchia *f.*

**brusque**, *adj.* brusco.

**brusquely**, *adv.* bruscamente.

**brutal**, *adj.* brutale.

**brutality**, *n.* brutalità *f.*

**brutalize**, *vb.* abbrutire.

**brute**, *n.* and *adj.* bruto (*m.*).

**bubble**, *n.* bolla *f.*

**buck**, *n.* dàino *m.*; (male) màschio *m.*

**bucket**, *n.* sécchia *f.*

**buckle**, **1.** *n.* fibbia *f.* **2.** *vb.* affibbiare.

**buckram**, *n.* tela da fusto *f.*

**bucksaw**, *n.* sega intelaiata *f.*

**buckshot**, *n.* pallinacci *m.pl.*

**buckwheat**, *n.* grano saraceno *m.*

**bud**, **1.** *n.* gèmma *f.* **2.** *vb.* gemmare.

**budge**, *vb.* muòversi.

**budget**, *n.* preventivo *m.*

**buffalo**, *n.* bùfalo *m.*

**buffer**, *n.* respingènte *m.*; (**b. state**) stato cuscinetto *m.*

**buffet**, 1. *n.* (slap) schiaffo *m.*; (eating place) caffè *m.* 2. *vb.* schiaffeggiare.

**buffoon**, *n.* buffone *m.*

**bug**, *n.* insètto *m.*

**bugle**, *n.* bùccina *f.*

**build**, *vb.* costruire, fabbricare.

**builder**, *n.* costruttore *m.*

**building**, *n.* edifìcio *m.*

**bulb**, *n.* (of plant) bulbo *m.*; (electric light) lampadina *f.*

**bulge**, 1. *n.* protuberanza *f.* 2. *vb.* gonfiarsi.

**bulk**, *n.* volume *m.*, massa *f.*

**bulkhead**, *n.* paratìa *f.*

**bulky**, *adj.* voluminoso.

**bull**, *n.* tòro *m.*

**bulldog**, *n.* molòsso *m.*

**bulldozer**, *n.* livellatrice *f.*

**bullet**, *n.* pallòttola *f.*

**bulletin**, *n.* bollettino *m.*

**bulletproof**, *adj.* a pròva di fucile.

**bullfinch**, *n.* ciuffolòtto *m.*

**bullion**, *n.* (gold) oro in lingotti *m.*

**bully**, *n.* prepotènte *m.*

**bulwark**, *n.* baluardo *m.*

**bum**, *n.* vagabondo *m.*

**bumblebee**, *n.* calabrone *m.*

**bump**, 1. *n.* urto *m.* 2. *vb.* urtare.

**bumper**, *n.* respingènte *m.*

**bun**, *n.* panino *m.*

**bunch**, *n.* mazzo *m.*, gràppolo *m.*

**bundle**, *n.* fàscio *m.*

**bungalow**, *n.* bungalò *m.*

**bungle**, *vb.* abborracciare.

**bunion**, *n.* infiammazione del pòllice del piède *f.*

**bunk**, *n.* (bed) cuccetta *f.*; (nonsense) fròttole *f.pl.*

**bunny**, *n.* coniglietto *m.*

**bunting**, *n.* stamigna *f.*

**buoy**, *n.* bòa *f.*

**buoyant**, *adj.* che può galleggiare; (cheerful) allegro.

**burden**, *n.* fardèllo *m.*; (**b. of proof**) ònere della pròva *m.*

**burdensome**, *adj.* opprimènte, oneroso.

**bureau**, *n.* uffìcio *m.*

**burglar**, *n.* ladro *m.*

**burglarize**, *vb.* rubare.

**burglary**, *n.* furto *m.*

**burial**, *n.* sepoltura *f.*

**burlap**, *n.* canovàccio rozzo *m.*

**burly**, *adj.* corpulento.

**burn**, 1. *n.* bruciatura *f.* 2. *vb.* bruciare, àrdere.

**burner**, *n.* bècco *m.*

**burning**, *adj.* bruciante, ardènte.

**burnish**, *vb.* brunire.

**burrow**, 1. *n.* tana *f.* 2. *vb.* scavare.

**burst**, 1. *n.* scatto *m.* 2. *vb.* scoppiare; (dash) scattare; (**b. forth**) prorómpere.

**bury**, *vb.* seppellire.

**bus**, *n.* àutobus *m.*; (**trolley bus**) fìlobus *m.*; (de luxe bus) pullman *m.*; (**b. line**) autolinea *f.*

**bush**, *n.* cespuglio *m.*

**bushel**, *n.* mòggio *m.*

**bushy**, *adj.* cespuglioso; (thick) folto.

**busily**, *adv.* attivamente.

**business**, *n.* affare *m.*; affari *m.pl.*

**businesslike**, *adj.* pràtico.

**businessman**, *n.* uòmo d'affari *m.*

**businesswoman**, *n.* dònna d'affari *f.*

**bust**, *n.* busto *m.*

**bustle**, *n.* tramestìo *m.*

**busy**, *adj.* occupato, affaccendato, attivo.

**busybody**, *n.* faccendière *m.*

**but**, 1. *prep.* eccètto, salvo. 2. *conj.* ma.

**butcher**, 1. *n.* macellaio *m.* 2. *vb.* macellare.

**butchery**, *n.* macèllo *m.*

**butler**, *n.* maggiordòmo *m.*

**butt**, *n.* estremità *f.*; (of gun) càlcio *m.*

**butter**, *n.* burro *m.*

**buttercup**, *n.* ranùncolo *m.*

**butterfat**, *n.* grasso del latte *m.*

**butterfly**, *n.* farfalla *f.*

**buttermilk**, *n.* sièro *m.*

**buttock**, *n.* nàtica *f.*

**button**, *n.* bottone *m.*

**buttonhole**, *n.* occhièllo *m.*

**buttress**, *n.* contraffòrte *m.*

**buxom**, *adj.* grassòccio.

**buy**, *vb.* comprare.

**buyer**, *n.* compratore *m.*

**buzz**, 1. *n.* ronzìo *m.* 2. *vb.* ronzare.

**buzzard**, *n.* poiana *f.*

**buzzer**, *n.* campanèllo *m.*

**buzz saw**, *n.* sega circolare *f.*

**by**, *prep.* (through) per;

(near) près**so** a; (at) a;
(indicating agent) da.
**by-and-by**, adv. fra pòco.
**bygone**, adj. passato.
**by-law**, n. legge particolare f.

**by-pass**, vb. evitare.
**by-product**, n. prodotto secondàrio m.
**bystander**, n. spettatore m.
**byway**, n. viòttolo m.

# C

**cab**, n. tassì m.
**cabaret**, n. ritròvo notturno m.
**cabbage**, n. càvolo m.
**cabin**, n. capanna f.; (on boat) cabina f.
**cabinet**, n. (furniture) stipo m.; (politics) gabinetto m.
**cabinetmaker**, n. stipettaio m.
**cable**, n. cavo m.
**cablegram**, n. cablogramma m.
**cableway**, n. funivìa f.
**cache**, n. nascondìglio m.
**cachet**, n. sigìllo m.
**cackle**, 1. n. vèrso m. 2. vb. cantare.
**cacophony**, n. cacofonìa f.
**cactus**, n. cacto m.
**cad**, n. vigliacco m.
**cadaver**, n. cadàvero m.
**cadaverous**, adj. cadavèrico m.
**cadet**, n. cadetto m.
**cadence**, n. cadènza f.
**cadmium**, n. càdmio m.
**cadre**, n. quadro m.
**café**, n. caffè m.
**caffeine**, n. caffeìna f.
**cage**, 1. n. gàbbia f. 2. vb. ingabbiare.
**caisson**, n. cassone m.
**cajole**, vb. lusingare.
**cake**, n. tòrta f., focàccia f.
**calamitous**, adj. calamitoso.
**calamity**, n. calamità f.
**calcify**, vb. calcificare.
**calcium**, n. càlcio m.
**calculable**, adj. calcolàbile.
**calculate**, vb. calcolare.
**calculating**, adj. calcolatore; (c. machine) màcchina calcolatrice f.
**calculation**, n. càlcolo m.
**calculus**, n. càlcolo m.
**caldron**, n. caldaia f.
**calendar**, n. calendàrio m.

**calf**, n. vitèllo m.
**calfskin**, n. pèlle di vitèllo f.
**caliber**, n. càlibro m.
**calico**, n. calicò m.
**caliper**, n. càlibro m.
**calisthenic**, adj. ginnàstico.
**calisthenics**, n. ginnàstica f.
**calk**, vb. calafatare.
**calker**, n. calafato m.
**call**, 1. n. chiamata f., appèllo m. 2. vb. chiamare.
**calligraphy**, n. calligrafìa f.
**calling**, n. vocazione f., professione f.
**calling card**, n. biglietto di visita m.
**callous**, adj. calloso; (unfeeling) insensìbile.
**callousness**, n. callosità f., insensibilità f.
**callow**, adj. inespèrto.
**callus**, n. callo m.
**calm**, 1. n. calma f. 2. adj. calmo. 3. vb. calmare.
**calmly**, adv. con calmo.
**calmness**, n. calma f.
**caloric**, adj. calòrico.
**calorie**, n. calorìa f.
**calorimeter**, n. calorìmetro m.
**calumniate**, vb. calunniare.
**calumny**, n. calùnnia f.
**Calvary**, n. Calvàrio m.
**calve**, vb. partorire.
**calyx**, n. càlice m.
**camaraderie**, n. cameratismo m.
**cambric**, n. cambrì m.
**camel**, n. cammèllo m.
**camelia**, n. camèlia f.
**camel's hair**, n. peli di cammèllo m.pl.
**cameo**, n. cammèo m.
**camera**, n. màcchina fotogràfica f.
**camouflage**, 1. n. camuffamento m., mimetismo m.

**2.** *vb.* camuffare, mimetizzare.

**camp, 1.** *n.* accampamento *m.* **2.** *vb.* accamparsi; (sport) campeggiare.

**campaign,** *n.* campagna *f.*

**camper,** *n.* campeggiatore *m.*

**camping,** *n.* campéggio *m.*

**camphor,** *n.* cànfora *f.*

**campus,** *n.* città universitària *f.*

**can, 1.** *n.* (tin) scàtola *f.*; (large) bidone *m.* **2.** *vb.* (be able) potere.

**Canada,** *n.* il Canadà *m.*

**Canadian,** *adj.* canadese.

**canal,** *n.* canale *m.*

**canalize,** *vb.* canalizzare.

**canapé,** *n.* crostino *m.*

**canard,** *n.* fròttola *f.*

**canary,** *n.* canarino *m.*

**Canary Islands,** *n.* Canàrie *f.pl.*

**cancel,** *vb.* annullare, cancellare, disdire.

**cancellation,** *n.* annullamento *m.*

**cancer,** *n.* cancro *m.*

**candelabrum,** *n.* candelabro *m.*

**candid,** *adj.* càndido, franco.

**candidacy,** *n.* candidatura *f.*

**candidate,** *n.* candidato *m.*

**candidly,** *adv.* candidamente, francamente.

**candidness,** *n.* franchezza *f.*, candore *m.*

**candied,** *adj.* candito.

**candle,** *n.* candela *f.*

**candlestick,** *n.* candeliere *m.*

**candor,** *n.* candore *m.*

**cane,** *n.* bastone *m.*; (plants) canna *f.*

**canine,** *adj.* canino.

**canister,** *n.* scàtola *f.*

**canker,** *n.* cancro *m.*

**cankerworm,** *n.* bruco *m.*

**canned,** *adj.* in scàtola.

**canner,** *n.* fabbricante di consèrve alimentari *m.*

**cannery,** *n.* stabilimento di consèrve alimentari *m.*

**cannibal,** *n.* cannibale *m.*

**canning,** *n.* preparazione di consèrve alimentari *f.*

**cannon,** *n.* cannone *m.*

**cannonade,** *n.* cannoneggiamento *m.*

**cannoneer,** *n.* cannonière *m.*

**cannot,** *vb.* non potere.

**canny,** *adj.* astuto.

**canoe,** *n.* canòa *f.*

**canon,** *n.* (rule, law) cànone *m.*; (person) canònico *m.*

**canonical,** *adj.* canònico.

**canonize,** *vb.* canonizzare.

**can-opener,** *n.* apriscàtole *m.*

**canopy,** *n.* baldacchino *m.*

**cant,** *n.* ipocrisìa *f.*

**can't,** *vb.* non potere.

**cantaloupe,** *n.* mellone *m.*

**canteen,** *n.* cantina *f.*

**canter,** *vb.* andare al piccolo galòppo.

**cantonment,** *n.* accantonamento *m.*

**canvas,** *n.* canovàccio *m.*

**canvass, 1.** *n.* esame *m.* **2.** *vb.* esaminare.

**canyon,** *n.* burrone *m.*

**cap,** *n.* berretto *m.*

**capability,** *n.* capacità *f.*

**capable,** *adj.* capace, àbile.

**capably,** *adv.* abilmente.

**capacious,** *adj.* spazioso.

**capacity,** *n.* capacità *f.*

**caparison, 1.** *n.* bardatura *f.* **2.** *vb.* bardare.

**cape,** *n.* cappa *f.*

**caper, 1.** *n.* capriòla *f.* **2.** *vb.* far capriòle.

**capillary,** *adj.* capillare.

**capital, 1.** *n.* (money) capitale *m.*; (city) capitale *f.* **2.** *adj.* capitale.

**capitalism,** *n.* capitalismo *m.*

**capitalist,** *n.* capitalista *m.*

**capitalistic,** *adj.* capitalistico.

**capitalization,** *n.* capitalizzazione *f.*

**capitalize,** *vb.* capitalizzare.

**capitulate,** *vb.* capitolare.

**capon,** *n.* cappone *m.*

**caprice,** *n.* capriccio *m.*

**capricious,** *adj.* capriccioso.

**capriciously,** *adv.* capricciosamente.

**capriciousness,** *n.* capricciosità *f.*

**capsize,** *vb.* capovòlgere.

**capsule,** *n.* càpsula *f.*

**captain,** *n.* capitano *m.*

**caption,** *n.* titolo *m.*

**captious,** *adj.* capzioso.

**captivate,** *vb.* affascinare.

**captive,** *n. and adj.* prigionièro (*m.*).

**captivity,** *n.* prigionìa *f.*

**captor,** *n.* catturatore *m.*

**capture, 1.** *n.* cattura *f.* **2.** *vb.* catturare.

**car**, *n.* carro *m.*, vettura *f.*; (auto) automòbile *f.*; (railroad) vagone *f.*

**caracul**, *n.* lince persiana *f.*

**carafe**, *n.* caraffa *f.*

**caramel**, *n.* caramèlla *f.*

**carat**, *n.* carato *m.*

**caravan**, *n.* carovana *f.*

**caraway**, *n.* carvi *m.*

**carbide**, *n.* carburo *m.*

**carbine**, *n.* carabina *f.*

**carbohydrate**, *n.* idrato di carbònio *m.*

**carbon**, *n.* carbònio *m.*

**carbon dioxide**, *n.* biòssido di carbònio *m.*

**carbon monoxide**, *n.* monòssido di carbònio *m.*

**carbon paper**, *n.* carta al carbone *f.*

**carbuncle**, *n.* carbónchio *m.*

**carburetor**, *n.* carburatore *m.*

**carcass**, *n.* carcassa *f.*

**card**, *n.* carta *f.*, biglietto *m.*; (filing) schedina *f.*

**cardboard**, *n.* cartone *m.*; (thin) cartoncino *m.*

**cardiac**, *adj.* cardìaco.

**cardigan**, *n.* golf *m.*

**cardinal**, *adj. and n.* cardinale *m.*

**care**, **1.** *n.* cura *f.* **2.** *vb.* curarsi; **(take c. of)** curare.

**careen**, *vb.* carenare.

**career**, *n.* carrièra *f.*

**carefree**, *adj.* sènza preoccupazioni.

**careful**, *adj.* accurato, attento.

**carefully**, *adv.* accuratamente, attentamente.

**carefulness**, *n.* accuratezza, attenzione.

**careless**, *adj.* spensierato, trascurato.

**carelessly**, *adv.* spensieratamente, trascuratamente.

**carelessness**, *n.* spensieratezza *f.*, trascuratezza *f.*

**caress**, **1.** *n.* carezza *f.* **2.** *vb.* accarezzare.

**caretaker**, *n.* guardiano *m.*

**cargo**, *n.* càrico *m.*

**caricature**, *n.* caricatura *f.*

**caries**, *n.* càrie *f.*

**carillon**, *n.* cariglione *m.*

**carload**, *n.* carrettata *f.*

**carnal**, *adj.* carnale.

**carnation**, *n.* garòfano *m.*

**carnival**, *n.* carnevale *m.*

**carnivorous**, *adj.* carnìvoro.

**carol**, **1.** *n.* canto di Natale *m.* **2.** *vb.* cantare.

**carouse**, *vb.* far baldòria.

**carousel**, *n.* carosèllo *m.*

**carpenter**, *n.* falegname *m.*

**carpet**, *n.* tappeto *m.*

**carpeting**, *n.* stoffa per tappeti *f.*

**carriage**, *n.* (vehicle) vettura *f.*; (transportation) traspòrto *m.*

**carrier**, *n.* portatore *m.*

**carrier pigeon**, *n.* piccione viaggiatore *m.*

**carrot**, *n.* caròta *f.*

**carry**, *vb.* portare; **(c. on)** continuare; **(c. out)** eseguire; **(c. through)** condurre a buon fine.

**cart**, *n.* carro *m.*

**cartage**, *n.* traspòrto *m.*

**cartel**, *n.* cartèllo *m.*

**carter**, *n.* carrettière *m.*

**cartilage**, *n.* cartilàgine *f.*

**carton**, *n.* scàtola di cartone *f.*

**cartoon**, *n.* (sketch) cartone *m.*; (picture) disegno *m.*

**cartridge**, *n.* cartùccia *f.*

**carve**, *vb.* (art) scolpire; (meat) tagliare, trinciare.

**carver**, *n.* scultore *m.*

**carving**, *n.* scultura *f.*

**carving-knife**, *n.* trinciante *m.*

**cascade**, *n.* cascata *f.*

**case**, *n.* (instance) caso *m.*; (state of things) caso *m.*; (law) càusa *f.*; (packing) cassa *f.*; (holder) astùccio *m.*; **(in any c.)** in ogni caso.

**cash**, **1.** contanti *m.pl.* **2.** *vb.* (cheque) riscuòtere.

**cashier**, *n.* cassière *m.*; (cashier's desk) cassa *f.*

**cashmere**, *n.* casimiro *m.*

**casing**, *n.* copertura *f.*

**casino**, *n.* casino *m.*

**cask**, *n.* barile *m.*

**casket**, *n.* cassettina *f.*

**casserole**, *n.* casseruòla *f.*

**cast**, **1.** *n.* (throw) gètto *m.* **2.** *vb.* gettare; (metal) fóndere.

**castanets**, *n.* nàcchere *f.pl.*

**castaway**, *n.* nàufrago *m.*

**caste**, *n.* casta *f.*

**caster**, *n.* fonditore *m.*

**castigate**, *vb.* castigare.

**cast iron**, *n.* ghisa *f.*

**castle**, *n.* castèllo *m.*

**castoff**, *adj.* abbandonato.

**casual**, *adj.* (accidental)

**casuale;** (nonchalant) indifferente.

**casually,** adv. casualmente, indifferentemente.

**casualness,** n. indifferenza f.

**casualty,** n. (accident) disgràzia f.; (injured person) ferito m.

**cat,** n. gatto m., gatta f.

**cataclysm,** n. cataclisma m.

**catacomb,** n. catacomba f.

**catalogue,** n. catàlogo m.

**catapult,** n. catapulta f.

**cataract,** n. cateratta f.

**catarrh,** n. catarro m.

**catastrophe,** n. catàstrofe f.

**catch,** vb. afferrare; (sickness) prèndere.

**catcher,** n. chi afferra, chi prende.

**catchword,** n. parola di richiamo f.

**catchy,** adj. melodioso.

**catechism,** n. catechismo m.

**catechize,** vb. catechizzare.

**categorical,** adj. categòrico.

**category,** n. categoria f.

**cater,** vb. provvedere a.

**caterpillar,** n. bruco m.

**catgut,** n. minugia f.pl.

**catharsis,** n. catarsi f.

**cathartic,** adj. purgativo.

**cathedral,** n. cattedrale f.

**cathode,** n. càtodo m.

**Catholic,** adj. cattòlico.

**Catholicism,** n. cattolicismo m.

**cat nap,** n. pisolino m.

**catsup,** n. salsa di pomodoro f.

**cattle,** n. bestiame m.

**cattleman,** n. bovaro m.

**catwalk,** n. ballatòio m.

**cauliflower,** n. cavolfiore m.

**causation,** n. causalità f.

**cause, 1.** n. càusa f. **2.** vb. causare, cagionare.

**causeway,** n. strada selciata f.

**caustic,** adj. càustico, sarcàstico.

**cauterize,** vb. cauterizzare.

**cautery,** n. cautèrio m.

**caution, 1.** n. cautèla f. **2.** vb. ammonire.

**cautious,** adj. càuto.

**cavalcade,** n. cavalcata f.

**cavalier,** n. cavalière m.

**cavalry,** n. cavalleria f.

**cave,** n. cavèrna f.

**cave-in,** n. crollo m.

**cavern,** n. cavèrna f.

**caviar,** n. caviale m.

**cavity,** n. cavità f.

**caw,** vb. gracchiare.

**cayman,** n. caimano m.

**cease,** vb. cessare.

**ceaseless,** adj. incessante.

**cedar,** n. cedro m.

**cede,** vb. cédere.

**ceiling,** n. soffitto m.

**celebrant,** n. celebrante m.

**celebrate,** vb. celebrare.

**celebrated,** adj. (famous) cèlebre.

**celebration,** n. celebrazione f.

**celebrity,** n. celebrità f.

**celerity,** n. celerità f.

**celery,** n. sèdano m.

**celestial,** adj. celèste.

**celibacy,** n. celibato m.

**celibate,** adj. cèlibe.

**cell,** n. (room) cèlla f.; (biology) cèllula f.

**cellar,** n. cantina f.

**cellist,** n. violoncellista m.

**cello,** n. violoncèllo m.

**cellophane,** n. cellòfane f.

**cellular,** adj. cellulare.

**celluloid,** n. cellulòide f.

**cellulose,** n. cellulosa f.

**Celtic,** adj. cèltico.

**cement, 1.** n. cemento m. **2.** vb. cementare.

**cemetery,** n. cimitèro m., camposanto m.

**censor, 1.** n. censore m. **2.** vb. censurare.

**censorious,** adj. censòrio.

**censorship,** n. censura f.

**censure,** n. censura f.

**census,** n. censimento m.

**cent,** n. centèsimo m.

**centenary,** adj. and n. centenàrio m.

**centennial,** adj. and n. centennale m.

**center,** n. cèntro m.

**centerpiece,** n. centro da tàvola m.

**centigrade,** adj. centìgrado.

**central,** adj. centrale.

**centralize,** vb. centralizzare.

**century,** n. sècolo m.

**century plant,** n. àgave f.

**ceramic,** adj. ceràmico.

**ceramics,** n. ceràmica f.

**cereal,** n. and adj. cereale m.

**cerebral,** adj. cerebrale.

**ceremonial,** adj. cerimoniale.

**ceremonious,** adj. cerimonioso.

**ceremony,** n. cerimònia f.

**certain,** adj. cèrto.

**certainly,** adv. certamente.

**certainty,** n. certezza f.

**certificate,** n. certificato m.

**certification,** n. certificazione f.

**certify,** vb. certificare.

**certitude,** n. certezza f.

**cervical,** adj. cervicale.

**cervix,** n. cervice f.

**cessation,** n. cessazione f.

**cession,** n. cessione f.

**cesspool,** n. pozzo nero m.

**chafe,** vb. (warm) riscaldare; (irritate) irritare.

**chaff, 1.** n. pula f., lòppa f.; (banter) cèlia f. **2.** vb. celiare.

**chagrin,** n. crùccio m.

**chain, 1.** n. catena f. **2.** vb. incatenare.

**chain reaction,** n. reazione a catena f.

**chair,** n. sèdia f.

**chairman,** n. presidènte m.

**chairmanship,** n. presidènza f.

**chairwoman,** n. presidènte f.

**chalice,** n. càlice f.

**chalk,** n. gesso m.

**chalky,** adj. gessoso.

**challenge, 1.** n. sfida f. **2.** vb. sfidare.

**challenger,** n. sfidatore m.

**chamber,** n. càmera f.; (chamber-pot) vaso da nòtte m.

**chamberlain,** n. ciambellano m.

**chambermaid,** n. camerièra f.

**chamber music,** n. mùsica da càmera f.

**chameleon,** n. camaleonte m.

**chamois,** n. camòscio m.

**champ,** vb. ròdere.

**champagne,** n. sciampagna f.

**champion,** n. campione m.

**championship,** n. campionato m.

**chance, 1.** n. caso m.; (opportunity) occasione f.; (by c.) per caso. **2.** adj. fortùito.

**chancel,** n. còro m.

**chancellery,** n. cancellerìa f.

**chancellor,** n. cancellière m.

**chandelier,** n. lampadàrio m.

**change, 1.** n. cambio m.,

cambiamento m., mutamento m.; (small coins) moneta spicciola f.; (money due) rèsto m. **2.** vb. cambiare, mutare.

**changeability,** n. mutabilità f.

**changeable,** adj. mutévole.

**changer,** n. (money-changer) cambiavalute m.

**channel,** n. canale m.

**chant, 1.** n. canto m. **2.** vb. cantare.

**chaos,** n. càos m.

**chaotic,** adj. caòtico.

**chap, 1.** n. (on skin) screpolatura f.; (fellow) tìzio m. **2.** vb. screpolare.

**chapel,** n. cappèlla f.

**chaplain,** n. cappellano m.

**chapter,** n. capitolo m.

**char,** vb. carbonizzare.

**character,** n. caràttere m.

**characteristic, 1.** n. caratterìstica f. **2.** adj. caratterìstico.

**characteristically,** adv. caratteristicamente.

**characterization,** n. caratterizzazione f.

**characterize,** vb. caratterizzare.

**charcoal,** n. carbone di legna m.

**charge, 1.** n. (load) càrico m.; (attack; gun) càrica f. (price) prèzzo m.; (custody) custòdia f. **2.** vb. (load) caricare; (set a price) far pagare.

**charger,** n. cavallo da guerra m.

**chariot,** n. carro m.

**charioteer,** n. auriga m.

**charitable,** adj. caritatévole.

**charitableness,** n. carità f.

**charitably,** adv. caritatevolmente.

**charity,** n. carità f.

**charlatan,** n. ciarlatano m.

**charlatanism,** n. ciarlatanismo m.

**charm, 1.** n. incanto m.; fàscino m.; (good-luck c.) portafortuna m. **2.** vb. incantare, affascinare.

**charmer,** n. incantatore m., incantatrice f.

**charming,** adj. affascinante m.

**chart,** n. (map) carta f.; (graph) gràfico m.

**charter.,** n. carta f.

**charwoman**, *n.* domèstica *f.*

**chase**, **1.** *n.* càccia *f.* **2.** *vb.* cacciare.

**chaser**, *n.* cacciatore *m.*

**chasm**, *n.* abisso *m.*

**chassis**, *n.* telaio *m.*

**chaste**, *adj.* casto.

**chasten**, *vb.* castigare.

**chasteness**, *n.* castità *f.*

**chastise**, *vb.* castigare, punire.

**chastisement**, *n.* castigo *m.*, punizione *f.*

**chastity**, *n.* castità *f.*

**chat**, **1.** *n.* chiàcchiera *f.* **2.** *vb.* chiacchierare.

**château**, *n.* castèllo *m.*

**chattel**, *n.* bène mòbile *m.*

**chatter**, **1.** *n.* chiàcchiera *f.* **2.** *vb.* chiacchierare.

**chatterbox**, *n.* chiacchierone *m.*

**chauffeur**, *n.* autista *m.*

**cheap**, *adj.* a buòn mercato, econòmico.

**cheapen**, *vb.* (prices) calare; (depreciate) deprezzare.

**cheaply**, *adv.* a buòn mercato, economicamente.

**cheapness**, *n.* buòn mercato *m.*

**cheat**, *vb.* ingannare, truffare.

**cheater**, *n.* ingannatore *m.*, truffatore *m.*

**check**, **1.** *n.* (restraint) freno *m.*; (verification) contròllo *m.*; (theater) contromarca *f.*; (clothes, luggage) scontrino *m.*; (bill) conto *m.*; (bank) assegno *m.* **2.** *vb.* (restrain) frenare; (verify) controllare; (luggage) registrare.

**checker**, *n.* scacco *m.*

**checkerboard**, *n.* scacchièra *f.*

**checkers**, *n.* dama *f.*

**checkmate**, *n.* scacco matto *m.*

**cheek**, *n.* guància *f.*

**cheer**, **1.** *n.* applàuso *m.* **2.** *vb.* applaudire; (**c. up**) rallegrare, *tr.*

**cheerful**, *adj.* allegro.

**cheerfulness**, *n.* allegrìa *f.*

**cheerless**, *adj.* triste.

**cheery**, *adj.* allegro.

**cheese**, *n.* càcio *m.*, formàggio *m.*

**cheesecloth**, *n.* garza *f.*

**cheesy**, *adj.* di qualità inferiore.

**chef**, *n.* cuòco *m.*

**chemical**, *adj.* chìmico.

**chemically**, *adv.* chimicamente.

**chemist**, *n.* chìmico *m.*

**chemistry**, *n.* chìmica *f.*

**chenille**, *n.* ciniglia *f.*

**cheque**, *n.* assegno *m.*

**cherish**, *vb.* tener caro.

**cherry**, *n.* ciliègia *f.*

**cherry-tree**, *n.* ciliègio *m.*

**cherub**, *n.* cherubino *m.*

**chess**, *n.* scacchi *m.pl.*

**chessboard**, *n.* scacchièra *f.*

**chessman**, *n.* scacco *m.*

**chest**, *n.* (box) cassa *f.*; (body) pètto *m.*

**chestnut**, *n.* (nut) castagna *f.*; (tree) castagno *m.*

**chevron**, *n.* gallone *m.*

**chew**, *vb.* masticare.

**chewer**, *n.* masticatore *m.*

**chic**, *adj.* alla mòda.

**chicanery**, *n.* sofisma *m.*

**chick**, *n.* pulcino *m.*

**chicken**, *n.* pollo *m.*

**chicken-hearted**, *adj.* tìmido.

**chicken-pox**, *n.* varicèlla *f.*

**chicory**, *n.* cicòria *f.*

**chide**, *vb.* rimproverare, sgridare.

**chief**, **1.** *n.* capo *m.* **2.** *adj.* principale.

**chiefly**, *adv.* principalmente.

**chieftain**, *n.* capo *m.*

**chiffon**, *n.* mussolina leggerìssima *f.*

**chilblain**, *n.* gelone *m.*

**child**, *n.* bambino *m.*, bambina *f.*

**childbirth**, *n.* parto *m.*

**childhood**, *n.* infànzia *f.*

**childish**, *adj.* infantile.

**childishness**, *n.* infantilità *f.*

**childless**, *adj.* sènza figli.

**childlessness**, *n.* stato di èssere sènza figli *m.*

**childlike**, *adj.* infantile.

**chill**, **1.** *n.* freddo *m.* (shiver) brìvido *m.* **2.** *vb.* raffreddare.

**chilliness**, *n.* freddo *m.*

**chilly**, *adj.* freddo, gèlido.

**chime**, **1.** *n.* scampanìo *m.* **2.** *vb.* scampanare.

**chimney**, *n.* camino *m.*

**chimney-sweep**, *n.* spazzacamino *m.*

**chimpanzee**, *n.* scimpanzè *m.*

**chin**, *n.* mento *m.*

**China**, *n.* (la) Cina *f.*

**china,** n. porcellana f.

**chinchilla,** n. cinciglia f.

**Chinese,** adj. cinese.

**chink,** n. crèpa f.

**chintz,** n. indiana f.

**chip, 1.** n. schéggia f. 2. vb. scheggiare.

**chiropodist,** n. callista m.

**chiropractor,** n. callista m.

**chirp, 1.** n. cinguettìo m. 2. vb. cinguettare.

**chisel, 1.** n. cesèllo m. 2. vb. cesellare.

**chivalrous,** adj. cavalleresco.

**chivalry,** n. cavallerìa f.

**chive,** n. cipolla f.

**chloride,** n. cloruro m.

**chlorine,** n. clòro m.

**chloroform,** n. clorofòrmio m.

**chlorophyll,** n. clorofilla f.

**chock full,** adj. pieno zeppo.

**chocolate,** n. cioccolato m.

**choice, 1.** n. scelta f. 2. adj. scelto.

**choir,** n. còro m.

**choke,** vb. soffocare, strangolare.

**choker,** n. cravatta f.

**choler,** n. còllera f.

**cholera,** n. colèra f.

**choleric,** adj. collèrico.

**choose,** vb. scégliere.

**chop, 1.** n. (meat) costoletta f. 2. vb. tagliare.

**chopper,** n. (knife) mannaia f.

**choppy,** adj. (of sea) corto.

**chopstick,** n. bacchetta f.

**choral,** adj. corale.

**chord,** n. (string) còrda f.; (harmony) accòrdo m.

**chore,** n. faccènda di casa f.

**choreographer,** n. coreògrafo m.

**choreography,** n. coreografìa f.

**chorister,** n. corista m.

**chortle,** vb. ridacchiare.

**chorus,** n. còro m.

**chowder,** n. minestra di pesce f.

**Christ,** n. Cristo m.

**christen,** vb. battezzare.

**Christendom,** n. cristianità f.

**christening,** n. battésimo m.

**Christian,** n. and adj. cristiano.

**Christianity,** n. cristianésimo m.

**Christmas,** n. Natale m.

**chromatic,** adj. cromàtico.

**chrome, chromium,** n. cròmo m.

**chromosome,** n. cromosòma m.

**chronic,** adj. crònico.

**chronically,** adv. cronicamente.

**chronicle,** n. crònaca f.

**chronological,** adj. cronològico.

**chronology,** n. cronologìa f.

**chrysalis,** n. crisàlide f.

**chrysanthemum,** n. crisantèmo m.

**chubby,** adj. grassetto.

**chuck,** vb. (cluck) chiocciare; (throw) lanciare.

**chuckle,** vb. ridere sotto voce.

**chug, 1.** n. sbuffo m. 2. vb. sbuffare.

**chum,** n. compagno m.

**chummy,** adj. intimo.

**chunk,** n. pèzzo m.

**chunky,** adj. tozzo.

**church,** n. chièsa f.

**churchman,** n. prète m.

**churchyard,** n. cimitèro m., camposanto m.

**churn,** n. zàngola f.

**chute,** n. canale di scolo m.

**cicada,** n. cicala f.

**cider,** n. sidro m.

**cigar,** n. sigaro m.

**cigarette,** n. sigaretta f.

**cilia,** n. ciglio m.

**ciliary,** adj. ciliare.

**cinch,** n. còsa chiara f.

**cinchona,** n. cincona f.

**cinder,** n. brùscolo m.

**cinema,** n. cinema m., cinematògrafo m.

**cinematic,** adj. cinematogràfico.

**cinnamon,** n. (tree) cinnamòmo m.; (spice) cannèlla f.

**cipher,** n. (zero) zèro m.; (figure, secret writing) cifra f.

**circle,** n. (figure) cérchio m.; (group) circolo m.

**circuit,** n. circùito m.; (**short c.**) corto circùito m.

**circuitous,** adj. indiretto.

**circuitously,** adv. indirettamente.

**circular,** n. and adj. circolare (m.).

**circularize,** vb. mandare dei circolari a.

**circulate,** vb. circolare.

**circulation,** n. circolazione f.

**circulatory,** adj. circolatòrio.

**circumcise,** vb. circoncìdere.

**circumcision,** n. circoncisione f.

**circumference,** n. circonferènza f.

**circumlocution,** n. circonlocuzione f.

**circumscribe,** vb. circonscrìvere.

**circumspect,** adj. circospètto.

**circumstance,** n. circostanza f.

**circumstantial,** adj. circostanziale; (detailed) particolareggiato.

**circumstantially,** adv. circostanziatamente.

**circumvent,** vb. circonvenire, impedire.

**circumvention,** n. circonvenzione f.

**circus,** n. circo m.

**cirrhosis,** n. cirròsi f.

**cistern,** n. cistèrna f., serbatòio m.

**citadel,** n. cittadèlla f.

**citation,** n. citazione f.

**cite,** vb. citare.

**citizen,** n. cittadino m.. cittadina f.

**citizenry,** n. cittadinanza f.

**citizenship,** n. cittadinanza f.

**citric,** adj. cìtrico.

**city,** n. città f.; (little c.) cittadina f.

**civic,** adj. cìvico.

**civil,** adj. civile.

**civilian,** n. and adj. civile.

**civility,** n. civiltà f.

**civilization,** n. civiltà f.

**civilize,** vb. civilizzare.

**civilized,** adj. civile.

**clabber,** n. quagliata f.

**clad,** adj. vestito.

**claim,** 1. n. reclamo m. 2. vb. reclamare.

**claimant,** n. reclamante m.

**clairvoyance,** n. chiaroveggènza f.

**clairvoyant,** n. and adj. chiaroveggènte m. and f.

**clamber,** vb. arrampicarsi.

**clammy,** adj. freddo e ùmido.

**clamor,** n. clamore m.

**clamorous,** adj. clamoroso.

**clamp,** n. grappa f.

**clan,** n. clan m., tribù f.; (clique) cricca f.

**clandestine,** adj. clandestino.

**clandestinely,** adv. clandestinamente.

**clang,** n. fragore m.

**clangor,** n. clangore m.

**clap,** vb. (applaud) applaudire; (hands) bàttere le mani.

**clapboard,** n. tégola di legno f.

**clapper,** n. battàglio m.

**claret,** n. claretto m.

**clarification,** n. chiarificazione f.

**clarify,** vb. chiarificare.

**clarinet,** n. clarinetto m.

**clarinetist,** n. clarinettista m.

**clarion,** n. chiarina f.

**clarity,** n. chiarità f.

**clash,** 1. n. urto m. 2. vb. urtarsi.

**clasp,** 1. n. gàncio m.; (hand) stretta di mano f.; (embrace) abbraccio m. 2. vb. agganciare, stringere, abbracciare.

**class,** 1. n. classe f.; (social) cèto m. 2. vb. classificare.

**classic, classical,** adj. clàssico.

**classicism,** n. classicismo m.

**classifiable,** adj. classificabile; (secret) segreto.

**classification,** n. classificazion. f.

**classify,** vb. classificare.

**classmate,** n. compagno di classe m.

**classroom,** n. àula f.

**clatter,** n. rumore m.

**clause,** n. clàusola f.

**claustrophobia,** n. claustrofobìa f.

**claw,** n. artiglio m., ràffio m.

**claw-hammer,** n. martello a ràffio m.

**clay,** n. argilla f., creta f.

**clayey,** adj. argilloso.

**clean,** 1. adj. pulito, netto. 2. vb. pulire.

**clean-cut,** adj. netto.

**cleaner,** n. pulitore m.

**cleanliness, cleanness,** n. pulizia f.

**cleanse,** vb. pulire.

**clear,** 1. adj. chiaro. 2. vb. (clear up) chiarire; (profit) guadagnare; (pass beyond) sorpassare; (weather, refl.) schiarirsi; (leave free) sgomberare.

**clearance,** n. permesso di partire m.

**clear-cut,** adj. netto.

**clearing,** n. radura f.

**clearing house,** n. stanza di compensazione f.

**clearly,** adv. chiaramente.

**clearness,** n. chiarezza f.

**cleat,** n. bietta f.

**cleavage**, n. fessura f., scissione f.

**cleave**, vb. fèndere.

**cleaver**, n. mannaia f.

**clef**, n. chiave f.

**cleft**, n. fenditura f.

**clemency**, n. clemènza f.

**clench**, vb. stringere.

**clergy**, n. clèro m.

**clergyman**, n. ecclesiàstico m.

**clerical**, adj. clericale.

**clericalism**, n. clericalismo m.

**clerk**, n. (clergyman) ecclesiàstico m.; (employee) impiegato m.

**clerkship**, n. posto d'impiegato m.

**clever**, adj. àbile, ingegnoso.

**cleverly**, adv. abilmente, ingegnosamente.

**cleverness**, n. abilità f., ingegnosità f.

**clew**, n. filo m.

**cliché**, n. luògo comune m.

**click**, n. rumore secco m.

**client**, n. cliènte m.

**clientele**, n. clientèla f.

**cliff**, n. rupe f.

**climactic**, adj. culminante.

**climate**, n. clima m.

**climatic**, adj. climàtico.

**climax**, n. cùlmine m.

**climb**, vb. scalare, arrampicarsi su.

**climber**, n. arrampicatore f.; (social) arrivista m. or f.

**clinch**, vb. (grasp) afferrare; (confirm) confermare; (conclude) conclùdere.

**cling**, vb. aderire.

**clinic**, n. clìnica f.

**clinical**, adj. clìnico.

**clinically**, adv. clinicamente.

**clip**, 1. n. gàncio m. 2. vb. (hair) tagliare; (wool) tosare; (plants) cimare.

**clipper**, n. tosatore m.

**clipping**, n. tosatura f.

**clique**, n. cricca f.

**cloak**, n. mantèllo m.; (cloakroom) guardaròba f.

**clock**, n. orològio m.; (two o'clock) le due.

**clockwise**, adj. and adv. destròrso.

**clockwork**, n. meccanismo d'orologeria m.

**clod**, n. zòlla f.; (person) tànghero m.

**clog**, 1. n. (wooden shoe) zòccolo m. 2. vb. ingombrare.

**cloister**, n. chiòstro m.

**close**, 1. adj. (closed) chiuso;

(narrow) stretto; (near) vicino; (secret) riservato; (compact) servato. 2. vb. chiùdere. 3. adv. vicino. 4. prep. (c. to) vicino a.

**closely**, adv. da vicino.

**closeness**, n. prossimità f.; (weather) pesantezza f.; (secrecy) riservatezza f.

**closet**, n. (toilet) gabinetto m.; (clothes) armàdio m.

**closure**, n. chiusura f.

**clot**, 1. n. grumo m. 2. vb. raggrumarsi.

**cloth**, n. stòffa f., tela f.

**clothe**, vb. vestire.

**clothes**, n. vestiti m.pl.

**clothespin**, n. fermabianche ria m.

**clothier**, n. pannaiòlo m.

**clothing**, n. vestiti m.pl.

**cloud**, 1. n. nùvola f., nube f. 2. vb. (c. over) rannuvolarsi.

**cloudburst**, n. acquazzone m.

**cloudiness**, n. nuvolosità f.

**cloudless**, adj. senza nùvole, sereno.

**cloudy**, adj. nuvoloso.

**clout**, 1. n. (blow) colpo m.; (rag) stràccio m. 2. vb. picchiare.

**clove**, n. chiodo di garòfano m.

**clover**, n. trifòglio m.

**clown**, n. pagliàccio m.

**clownish**, adv. pagliaccesco.

**cloy**, vb. saziare.

**club**, 1. n. (group) cìrcolo m.; (stick) bastone m. 2. vb. bastonare.

**clubfoot**, n. piede stòrto m.

**clubs**, n. (cards) fiori m.pl.

**clue**, n. filo m.

**clump**, n. gruppo m.

**clumsiness**, n. goffàggine f.

**clumsy**, adj. goffo.

**cluster**, 1. n. gràppolo m.; (people) gruppo m. 2. vb. raggruppare.

**clutch**, 1. n. (claw) artìglio m.; (automobile) frizione f. 2. vb. afferrare.

**clutter**, vb. ingombrare.

**coach**, 1. n. (carriage) carrozza f.; (horse-drawn) còcchio m.; (train) vagone m.; (sports) allenatore m. 2. vb. (sports) allenare; (school) dare lezioni private a.

**coachman**, n. cocchière m.

**coagulate**, vb. coagulare.

**coagulation**, n. coagulazione f.

**coal,** n. carbone fòssile m.

**coalesce,** vb. coalizzarsi.

**coalition,** n. coalizione f.

**coal oil,** n. petròlio m.

**coal tar,** n. catrame m.

**coarse,** adj. grossolano.

**coarsen,** vb. rèndere grossolano.

**coarseness,** n. grossolanità f.

**coast,** n. còsta f.

**coastal,** adj. costièro.

**coaster,** n. (ship) nave costièra f.

**coast guard,** n. milìzia guardacòste f.

**coat,** n. (of suit) giacca f.; (overcoat) sopràbito m.

**coating,** n. strato m.

**coat of arms,** n. insegna f., stèmma m.

**coax,** vb. blandire.

**cobalt,** n. cobalto m.

**cobbler,** n. ciabattino m., calzolaio m.

**cobblestone,** n. ciòttolo m.

**cobra,** n. còbra m.

**cobweb,** n. ragnatelo m.

**cocaine,** n. cocaina f.

**cock,** 1. n. (rooster) gallo m.; (male) maschio m.; (of gun) cane m.; (tap) rubinetto m.

**cocker spaniel,** n. cocker m.

**cockeyed,** adj. (lit.) stràbico; (crazy) matto, pazzo.

**cockhorse,** n. cavallo a dóndolo m.

**cockpit,** n. carlinga f.

**cockroach,** n. blatta f.

**cocksure,** adj. presuntuoso.

**cocktail,** n. coctèl m.

**cocky,** adj. impudènte.

**cocoa,** n. cacao m.

**coconut,** n. (tree) còcco m.; (nut) noce di còcco f.

**cocoon,** n. bòzzolo m.

**cod,** n. merluzzo m.

**C.O.D.,** adv. contro assegno.

**coddle,** vb. vezzeggiare.

**code,** n. (law) còdice m.; (secret) cifrario m.

**codeine,** n. codeìna f.

**codfish,** n. merluzzo m.

**codify,** vb. codificare.

**cod-liver oil,** n. òlio di fégato di merluzzo m.

**coeducation,** n. insegnamento misto m.

**coeducational,** adj. misto.

**coequal,** adj. coeguale.

**coerce,** vb. costrìngere.

**coercion,** n. coercizione f.

**coercive,** adj. coercitivo.

**coexist,** vb. coesìstere.

**coffee,** n. caffè m.

**coffer,** n. còfano m., scrigno m.

**coffin,** n. cassa da mòrto f.

**cog,** n. dente m.; (**cog railway**) ferrovia a dentièra f.

**cogent,** adj. convincènte.

**cogitate,** vb. cogitare.

**cognizance,** n. conoscènza f.; (legal) competènza f.

**cognizant,** adj. competènte.

**cogwheel,** n. ruòta dentata f.

**cohere,** vb. èssere coerènte.

**coherent,** adj. coerènte.

**cohesion,** n. coesione f.

**cohesive,** adj. coesivo.

**cohort,** n. coòrte f.

**coiffure,** n. pettinatura f.

**coil,** 1. n. spira f.; (electr.) bobina f.; (**induction c.**) bobina d'induzione f. 2. vb. arrotolare.

**coin,** 1. n. moneta f. 2. vb. coniare.

**coinage,** n. cònio m.

**coincide,** vb. coincìdere.

**coincidence,** n. coincidènza f.

**coincident,** adj. coincidènte.

**coincidental,** adj. coincidènte.

**coincidentally,** adv. per coincidènza.

**colander,** n. colatòio m.

**cold,** 1. n. (temperature) freddo m.; (med.) raffreddore m. 2. adj. freddo; (**it is c.**) fa freddo; (**feel c.**) aver freddo.

**cold-blooded,** adj. a sangue freddo.

**coldly,** adv. freddamente.

**coldness,** n. freddezza f.

**collaborate,** vb. collaborare.

**collaboration,** n. collaborazione f.

**collaborator,** n. collaboratore m.

**collapse,** 1. n. cròllo m.; (med.) collasso m. 2. vb. crollare.

**collar,** n. colletto m.; (dog's, priest's) collare m.

**collarbone,** n. clavìcola f.

**collate,** vb. collazionare.

**collateral,** n. and adj. collaterale m.

**collation,** n. (comparison) confronto m.; (meal) merènda f.

**colleague,** n. collèga m.

**collect,** vb. raccògliere; (money) riscuòtere.

**collection,** n. raccòlta f.,

collezione f., (church) quès-tua f.

**collective,** adj. collettivo.

**collectively,** adv. collettiva-mente.

**collector,** n. (art) collezioni-sta m.; (tickets) controllore m.

**college,** n. università f.

**collegiate,** adj. universitàrio.

**collide,** vb. scontrarsi.

**colliery,** n. minièra di carbo-ne f.

**collision,** n. scontro m.

**colloquial,** adj. colloquiale.

**colloquialism,** n. colloqui-alismo m.

**colloquially,** adv. colloquial-mente.

**colloquy,** n. collòquio m.

**collusion,** n. collusione f.

**Cologne,** n. Colònia f.

**colon,** n. (writing) due punti m.pl.

**colonel,** n. colonnèllo m.

**colonial,** adj. coloniale.

**colonist,** n. colòno m.

**colonization,** n. colonizza-zione f.

**colonize,** vb. colonizzare.

**colony,** n. colònia f.

**color,** 1. n. colore m. 2. vb. colorire.

**coloration,** n. colorazione f.

**colored,** adj. di colore.

**colorful,** adj. pittoresco.

**coloring,** n. coloritura f.

**colorless,** adj. sènza colore.

**colossal,** adj. colossale.

**colt,** n. puledro m.

**column,** n. colonna f.

**columnist,** n. cronista m.

**coma,** n. còma m.

**comb,** 1. n. pèttine m.; (rooster) cresta f. 2. vb. pet-tinare.

**combat,** 1. n. combattimen-to m. 2. vb. combàttere.

**combatant,** n. combattènte m.

**combative,** adj. battaglièro.

**combination,** n. combina-zione f.

**combination lock,** n. serra-tura a combinazioni f.

**combine,** vb. combinare.

**combustible,** adj. combu-stìbile.

**combustion,** n. combustione f.

**come,** vb. venire; (**c. about**) accadere; (**c. across**) incon-trare, trovare; (**c. away**) andàrsene; (**c. back**) tor-

nare; (**c. down**) scéndere; (**c. in**) entrare; (**c. out**) uscire; (**c. up**) salire.

**comedian,** n. còmico m.

**comedienne,** n. attrice cò-mica f.

**comedy,** n. commèdia f.

**come in!,** interj. avanti!

**comely,** adj. grazioso.

**comet,** n. cometa f.

**comfort,** 1. n. confòrto m. 2. vb. confortare, consolare.

**comfortable,** adj. còmodo.

**comfortably,** adv. comoda-mente.

**comforter,** n. confortatore m., consolatore m.

**comfortingly,** adv. in modo consolatore.

**comfortless,** adj. sconsolato.

**comic, comical,** adj. còmico.

**comic book,** n. giornalino a fumetti m.

**comic strip,** n. fumetto m.

**coming,** n. venuta f.

**comma,** n. virgola f.

**command,** 1. n. comando m. 2. vb. comandare.

**commandeer,** vb. requisire.

**commander,** n. comandante m.

**commander in chief,** n. comandante in capo m.

**commandment,** n. coman-damento m.

**commemorate,** vb. comme-morare.

**commemoration,** n. com-memorazione f.

**commemorative,** adj. com-memorativo.

**commence,** vb. cominciare.

**commencement,** n. comin-ciamento m.

**commend,** vb. raccomandare, lodare.

**commendable,** adj. lodévole.

**commendably,** adv. lodevol-mente.

**commendation,** n. lòde f.

**commensurate,** adj. com-misurato.

**comment,** 1. n. commento m. 2. vb. commentare.

**commentary,** n. commento m.

**commentator,** n. (radio) cronista m.

**commerce,** n. commèrcio m.

**commercial,** adj. commer-ciale.

**commercialism,** n. commer-cialismo m.

**commercialize,** *vb.* commercializare.

**commercially,** *adv.* commercialmente.

**commiserate,** *vb.* commiserare.

**commissary,** *n.* commissariato *m.*

**commission, 1.** *n.* (committee, percentage) commissione *f.*; (assignment) incàrico *m.*; mandato *m.* **2.** *vb.* incaricare.

**commissioner,** *n.* commissàrio *m.*

**commit,** *vb.* commèttere.

**commitment,** *n.* impegno *m.*

**committee,** *n.* comitato *m.*, commissione *f.*

**commodious,** *adj.* spazioso.

**commodity,** *n.* mèrce *f.*

**common,** *adj.* comune; (vulgar) volgare.

**commonly,** *adv.* comunemente.

**commonness,** *n.* volgarità *f.*

**commonplace, 1.** *n.* luògo comune *m.* **2.** *adj.* banale.

**commonwealth,** *n.* repùbblica *f.*

**commotion,** *n.* commozione *f.*

**communal,** *adj.* comunale.

**commune,** *vb.* comunicare.

**communicable,** *adj.* comunicàbile.

**communicant,** *n.* comunicante *m.*

**communicate,** *vb.* comunicare.

**communication,** *n.* comunicazione *f.*

**communicative,** *adj.* comunicativo.

**communion,** *n.* comunione *f.*; (take c.) comunicarsi.

**communiqué,** *n.* comunicato *m.*

**communism,** *n.* comunismo *m.*

**communist,** *n.* comunista *m.* or *f.*

**communistic,** *adj.* comunìstico.

**community,** *n.* comunità *f.*

**commutation,** *n.* commutazione *f.*; (c. ticket) biglietto d'abbonamento *m.*

**commute,** *vb.* commutare; (travel) viaggiare regolarmente.

**compact, 1.** *n.* accòrdo *m.*, patto *m.* **2.** *adj.* compatto.

**compactness,** *n.* compattezza *f.*

**companion,** *n.* compagno *m.*, compagna *f.*

**companionable,** *adj.* sociévole.

**companionship,** *n.* compagnìa *f.*

**company,** *n.* compagnìa *f.*, società *f.*

**comparable,** *adj.* paragonàbile, comparàbile.

**comparative,** *adj.* comparativo.

**comparatively,** *adv.* comparativamente.

**compare,** *vb.* paragonare, confrontare, comparare.

**comparison,** *n.* paragone *m.*, confronto *m.*

**compartment,** *n.* scompartimento *m.*

**compass,** *n.* (naut.) bùssola *f.*; (geom.) compasso *m.*

**compassion,** *n.* compassione *f.*

**compassionate,** *adj.* compassionévole.

**compassionately,** *adv.* compassionevolmente.

**compatible,** *adj.* compatìbile.

**compatriot,** *n.* compatriòta *m.*, compaesano *m.*

**compel,** *vb.* costrìngere.

**compensate,** *vb.* compensare.

**compensation,** *n.* compènso *m.*

**compensatory,** *adj.* compensativo.

**compete,** *vb.* compètere, concórrere, gareggiare.

**competence,** *n.* competènza *f.*

**competent,** *adj.* competènte.

**competently,** *adv.* competentemente.

**competition,** *n.* concorso *m.*, gara *f.*; (comm.) concorrènza *f.*

**competitive,** *adj.* di concorso, di concorrènza.

**competitor,** *n.* concorrènte *m.*

**compile,** *vb.* compilare.

**complacency,** *n.* contentezza di sè stesso *f.*

**complacent,** *adj.* contento di sè stesso.

**complain,** *vb.* lagnarsi, dolersi.

**complainer,** *n.* piagnucolone *m.*

**complainingly,** *adv.* lagnàndosi.

**complaint,** *n.* lagnanza *f.*; (sickness) malattìa *f.*

**complement,** n. complemento m.

**complete, 1.** adj. complèto. **2.** vb. completare.

**completely,** adv. completamente.

**completeness,** n. completezza f.

**completion,** n. completamento m.

**complex,** n. and adj. complèsso (m.).

**complexion,** n. colorito m.

**complexity,** n. complessità f.

**compliance,** n. obbedienza f.

**compliant,** adj. obbediènte.

**complicate,** vb. complicare.

**complicated,** adj. complicato.

**complication,** n. complicazione f.

**complicity,** n. complicità f.

**compliment, 1.** n. complimento m. **2.** vb. complimentare, felicitare.

**complimentary,** adj. gratùito.

**comply,** vb. obbedire.

**component,** n. and adj. componènte (m.).

**comport oneself,** vb. comportarsi.

**compose,** vb. comporre.

**composed,** adj. (made of) composto di; (calm) calmo.

**composer,** n. compositore m.

**composite,** adj. composto.

**composition,** n. composizione f.

**compost,** n. concime m.

**composure,** n. compostezza f.; calma f.

**compote,** n. consèrva f.

**compound,** n. and adj. composto m.

**comprehend,** vb. comprèndere.

**comprehensible,** adj. comprensibile.

**comprehension,** n. comprensione f.

**comprehensive,** adj. comprensivo.

**compress,** vb. comprìmere.

**compressed,** adj. comprèsso.

**compression,** n. compressione f.

**compressor,** n. compressore m.

**comprise,** vb. comprèndere.

**compromise, 1.** n. compromesso m. **2.** vb. accomodarsi; (endanger) compromèttere.

**compromiser,** n. chi fa un compromesso m.

**compulsion,** n. costrizione f.

**compulsive,** adj. coercitivo; (involuntary) involontàrio.

**compulsory,** adj. obbligatòrio.

**compunction,** n. compunzione f.

**computation,** n. computazione f.

**compute,** vb. computare.

**comrade,** n. camerata m.

**comradeship,** n. cameratismo m.

**concave,** adj. concavo.

**conceal,** vb. celare.

**concealment,** n. celamento m.

**concede,** vb. concèdere.

**conceit,** n. vanità f.

**conceited,** adj. vanitoso.

**conceivable,** adj. concepìbile.

**conceivably,** adv. concepibilmente.

**conceive,** vb. concepire.

**concentrate,** vb. concentrare.

**concentration,** n. concentrazione f., concentramento m.

**concentration camp,** n. campo di concentramento m.

**concept,** n. concètto m.

**concern, 1.** n. (affair) affare m.; (interest) interèsse m.; (firm) aziènda f.; (worry) ansietà f. **2.** vb. concèrnere, interessare, riguardare; (**be concerned with**) interessarsi di; (**be concerned over**) inquietarsi di.

**concerning,** prep. riguardo a, concernènte.

**concert, 1.** n. concèrto m. **2.** vb. concertare.

**concession,** n. concessione f.

**conch-shell,** n. conchìglia f.

**concierge,** n. portinaio m.; (c.'s office) portinerìa f.

**conciliate,** vb. conciliare.

**conciliation,** n. conciliazione f.

**conciliator,** n. conciliatore m.

**conciliatory,** adj. conciliatìvo.

**concise,** adj. conciso.

**concisely,** adv. concisamente.

**conciseness, concision,** n. concisione f.

**conclave,** n. conclave m.

**conclude,** vb. conclùdere.

**conclusion,** n. conclusione f.

**conclusive,** adj. conclusivo.

**conclusively,** adv. conclusivamente.

**concoct,** vb. concuòcere.

**concoction,** n. concozione f.

**concomitant**, *adj.* concomitante.

**concord**, *n.* accòrdo *m.*

**concordant**, *adv.* concòrde.

**concordat**, *n.* concordato *m.*

**concourse**, *n.* concorso *m.*

**concrete**, 1. *n.* cemento *m.* 2. *adj.* concrèto.

**concretely**, *adv.* concretamente.

**concreteness**, *n.* concretezza *f.*

**concubine**, *n.* concubina *f.*

**concur**, *vb.* (events) concórrere; (persons) essere d'accòrdo.

**concurrence**, *n.* concorrènza *f.*; (agreement) consènso *m.*

**concurrent**, *adj.* concorrènte.

**concussion**, *n.* concussione *f.*

**condemn**, *vb.* condannare.

**condemnable**, *adj.* condannàbile.

**condemnation**, *n.* condanna *f.*

**condensation**, *n.* condensazione *f.*

**condense**, *vb.* condensare.

**condenser**, *n.* condensatore *m.*

**condescend**, *vb.* accondiscéndere.

**condescendingly**, *adv.* con accondiscendènza.

**condescension**, *n.* accondiscendènza *f.*

**condiment**, 1. *n.* condimento *m.* 2. *vb.* condire.

**condition**, 1. *n.* condizione *f.* 2. *vb.* condizionare.

**conditional**, *adj.* condizionale.

**conditionally**, *adv.* condizionalmente.

**condole**, *vb.* condolersi.

**condolence**, *n.* condoglianza *f.*

**condone**, *vb.* condonare.

**conduce**, *vb.* condurre, tèndere.

**conducive**, *adj.* tendènte.

**conduct**, 1. *n.* condotta *f.* 2. *vb.* condurre.

**conductive**, *adj.* conduttivo.

**conductivity**, *n.* conduttività *f.*

**conductor**, *n.* conduttore *m.*; (orchestra) direttore *m.*; (train) capotreno *m.*; (train, bus) bigliettàrio *m.*

**conduit**, *n.* condotto *m.*

**cone**, *n.* còno *m.*

**confection**, *n.* (dress) confezione *f.*; (candy) confetto *m.*; confettura *f.*

**confectioner**, *n.* confettière *m.*; (**c. shop**) confetteria *f.*

**confectionery**, *n.* (store) confetteria *f.*

**confederacy**, *n.* confederazione *f.*

**confederate**, 1. *n.* confederato *m.* 2. *vb.* confederarsi.

**confederation**, *n.* confederazione *f.*

**confer**, *vb.* conferire.

**conference**, *n.* conferènza *f.*

**confess**, *vb.* confessare.

**confession**, *n.* confessione *f.*

**confessional**, *n. and adj.* confessionale (*m.*).

**confessor**, *n.* confessore *m.*

**confetti**, *n.* coriàndoli *m.pl.*

**confidant**, *n.* confidènte *m.*

**confidante**, *n.* confidènte *f.*

**confide**, *vb.* confidare.

**confidence**, *n.* confidènza *f.*

**confident**, *adj.* confidènte.

**confidential**, *adj.* confidenziale.

**confidentially**, *adv.* in confidènza.

**confidently**, *adv.* confidentemente.

**confine**, *vb.* confinare.

**confirm**, *vb.* confermare.

**confirmation**, *n.* conferma *f.*

**confiscate**, *vb.* confiscare.

**confiscation**, *n.* confisca *f.*

**conflagration**, *n.* conflagrazione *f.*

**conflict**, 1. *n.* conflitto *m.* 2. *vb.* venire a conflitto.

**conform**, *vb.* conformarsi.

**conformation**, *n.* conformazione *f.*

**conformer, conformist**, *n.* conformista *m.*

**conformity**, *n.* conformità *f.*

**confound**, *vb.* confóndere.

**confront**, *vb.* confrontare.

**confuse**, *vb.* confóndere.

**confusion**, *n.* confusione *f.*

**congeal**, *vb.* congelare.

**congealment**, *n.* congelamento *m.*

**congenial**, *adj.* simpàtico.

**congenital**, *adj.* congènito.

**congenitally**, *adv.* congenitamente.

**congestion**, *n.* congestione *f.*

**conglomerate**, 1. *n. and adj.* conglomerato (*m.*). 2. *vb.* conglomerare.

**conglomeration**, *n.* conglomerazione *f.*

**congratulate**, *vb.* felicitare, congratularsi con.

**congratulation**, *n.* felicitazione *f.*, congratulazione *f.*

**congratulatory**, *adj.* congratulatòrio.

**congregate**, *vb.* congregarsi.

**congregation**, *n.* congregazione *f.*

**congress**, *n.* congrèsso *f.*, parlamento *m.*

**congressional**, *adj.* parlamentare.

**conic**, *adj.* cònico.

**conjecture**, **1.** *n.* congettura *f.* **2.** *vb.* congetturare.

**conjugal**, *adj.* coniugale.

**conjugate**, *vb.* coniugare.

**conjugation**, *n.* coniugazione *f.*

**conjunction**, *n.* congiunzione *f.*

**conjunctive**, *adj.* congiuntivo.

**conjunctivitis**, *n.* congiuntivite *f.*

**conjure**, *vb.* scongiurare.

**connect**, *vb.* collegare, connèttere; (transport) coincìdere.

**connection**, *n.* collegamento *m.*, connessione *f.*; (transport) coincidènza *f.*

**connivance**, *n.* connivènza *f.*

**connive**, *vb.* essere connivènte.

**connoisseur**, *n.* conoscitore *m.*

**connotation**, *n.* connotazione *f.*

**connote**, *vb.* connotare.

**connubial**, *adj.* connubiale.

**conquer**, *vb.* vincere, conquistare.

**conquerable**, *adj.* vincìbile, conquistàbile.

**conqueror**, *n.* vincitore *m.*, conquistatore *m.*

**conquest**, *n.* conquista *f.*

**conscience**, *n.* coscienza *f.*

**conscientious**, *adj.* coscienzioso.

**conscientiously**, *adv.* coscienziosamente.

**conscious**, *adj.* cònscio, consapévole.

**consciously**, *adv.* consciamente.

**consciousness**, *n.* coscienza *f.*

**conscript**, *n.* coscritto *m.*

**conscription**, *n.* coscrizione *f.*

**consecrate**, *vb.* consacrare.

**consecration**, *n.* consacrazione *f.*

**consecutive**, *adj.* consecutivo.

**consecutively**, *adv.* consecutivamente.

**consensus**, *n.* consènso *m.*

**consent**, **1.** *n.* consènso *m.* **2.** *vb.* consentire, acconsentire.

**consequence**, *n.* conseguènza *f.*

**consequent**, *adj.* conseguènte.

**consequential**, *adj.* conseguenziale.

**consequently**, *adv.* conseguentemente, per conseguènza.

**conservation**, *n.* conservazione *f.*

**conservative**, *n. and adj.* conservatore (*m.*).

**conservatism**, *n.* conservatorismo *m.*

**conservatory**, *n.* conservatòrio *m.*

**conserve**, *vb.* conservare.

**consider**, *vb.* considerare.

**considerable**, *adj.* considerévole, consideràbile; (a fair amount) parécchio.

**considerably**, *adv.* considerabilmente.

**considerate**, *vb.* premuroso.

**considerately**, *adv.* premurosamente.

**consideration**, *n.* considerazione *f.*

**considering**, *adv.* considerando.

**consign**, *vb.* consegnare.

**consignment**, *n.* consegna *f.*

**consist**, *vb.* consìstere.

**consistency**, *n.* consistènza *f.*

**consistent**, *adj.* coerènte.

**consolation**, *n.* consolazione *f.*

**console**, *vb.* consolare.

**consolidate**, *vb.* consolidare.

**consommé**, *n.* bròdo ristretto *m.*

**consonant**, *n. and adj.* consonante (*f.*).

**consort**, *n.* consòrte *m. and f.*

**conspicuous**, *adj.* cospìcuo.

**conspicuously**, *adv.* cospicuamente.

**conspicuousness**, *n.* cospicuità *f.*

**conspiracy**, *n.* congiura *f.*

**conspirator**, *n.* congiurato *m.*

**conspire**, *vb.* congiurare.

**constancy**, *n.* costanza *f.*

**constant**, *adj.* costante.

**constantly**, *adv.* costantemente.

**constellation**, *n.* costellazione *f.*

**consternation,** *n.* costernazione *f.*

**constipated,** *adj.* stìtico.

**constipation,** *n.* stitichezza *f.*

**constituency,** *n.* votanti
*m.pl.*

**constituent,** *adj.* costituènte.

**constitute,** *vb.* costituire.

**constitution,** *n.* costituzione *f.*

**constitutional,** *adj.* costituzionale.

**constrain,** *vb.* costrìngere.

**constraint,** *n.* costrizione *f.*

**constrict,** *vb.* costrìngere.

**construct,** *vb.* costruire.

**construction,** *n.* costruzione
*f.*; (interpretation) interpretazione *f.*

**constructive,** *adj.* costruttivo.

**constructively,** *adv.* costruttivamente.

**constructor,** *n.* costruttore *m.*

**construe,** *vb.* interpretare.

**consul,** *n.* cònsole *m.*

**consular,** *adj.* consolare.

**consulate,** *n.* consolato *m.*

**consulship,** *n.* consolato *m.*

**consult,** *vb.* consultare.

**consultant,** *n.* consultatore *m.*

**consultation,** *n.* consultazione *f.*, consulto *m.*

**consume,** *vb.* consumare.

**consumer,** *n.* consumatore *m.*

**consummate,** *adj.* consumato.

**consummation,** *n.* consumazione *f.*

**consumption,** *n.* consumo
*m.*; (tuberculosis) tisi *f.*; tu-
berculosi *f.*

**consumptive,** *adj.* tìsico.

**contact, 1.** *n.* contatto *m.*
**2.** *vb.* venire a contatto con.

**contagion,** *n.* contàgio *m.*

**contagious,** *adj.* contagioso.

**contain,** *vb.* contenere.

**container,** *n.* recipiènte *m.*

**contaminate,** *vb.* contaminare.

**contemplate,** *vb.* contemplare.

**contemplation,** *n.* contemplazione *f.*

**contemplative,** *adj.* contemplativo.

**contemporary,** *adj.* contemporàneo.

**contempt,** *n.* disprèzzo *m.*

**contemptible,** *adj.* spregévole.

**contemptuous,** *adj.* sprezzante.

**contemptuously,** *adv.* sprezzantemente.

**contend,** *vb.* contèndere; (affirm) sostenere.

**contender,** *n.* contendènte *m.*

**content, 1.** *n.* contento *m.*
**2.** *vb.* accontentare.

**contented,** *adj.* contento.

**contention,** *n.* contenzione *f.*

**contentment,** *n.* contenta-
mento *m.*

**contest, 1.** *n.* contesa *f.*,
gara *f.* **2.** *vb.* contestare.

**contestable,** *adj.* contestàbile.

**contestant,** *n.* gareggiante *m.*

**context,** *n.* contèsto *m.*

**contiguous,** *adj.* contìguo.

**continence,** *n.* continènza *f.*

**continent,** *n. and adj.* continènte (*m.*).

**continental,** *adj.* continentale.

**contingency,** *n.* contingènza
*f.*

**contingent,** *adj.* contingènte.

**continual,** *adj.* contìnuo.

**continuation,** *n.* continuazione *f.*

**continue,** *vb.* continuare.

**continuity,** *n.* continuità *f.*

**continuous,** *adj.* contìnuo.

**continuously,** *adv.* continuamente.

**contort,** *vb.* contòrcere.

**contortion,** *n.* contorsione *f.*

**contortionist,** *n.* contorsionista *m.*

**contour,** *n.* contorno *m.*

**contraband,** *n.* contrabbando *m.*

**contract, 1.** *n.* contratto *m.*
**2.** *vb.* contrarre; (agree, undertake) contrattare.

**contraction,** *n.* contrazione
*f.*

**contractor,** *n.* contrattatore
*m.*, imprenditore *m.*

**contradict,** *vb.* contraddire.

**contradictable,** *adj.* contrad-
dicìbile.

**contradiction,** *n.* contraddizione *f.*

**contradictory,** *adj.* contraddittòrio.

**contralto,** *n.* contralto *m.*

**contraption,** *n.* congegno *m.*

**contrary,** *adj.* contràrio.

**contrast, 1.** *n.* contrasto *m.*
**2.** *vb.* contrastare, *intr.*

**contribute,** *vb.* contribuire;
(newspaper) collaborare.

**contribution,** *n.* contributo
*m.*, contribuzione *f.*

**contributive,** *adj.* contributivo.

**contributor,** *n.* contributore *m.*; (newspaper) collaboratore *m.*

**contributory,** *adj.* contribùtòrio.

**contrite,** *n.* contrito.

**contrition,** *n.* contrizione *f.*

**contrivance,** *n.* congegno *m.*

**contrive,** *vb.* (invent) inventare; (bring about) effettuare.

**control,** **1.** *n.* controllo *m.* **2.** *vb.* controllare.

**controllable,** *adj.* controllàbile.

**controller,** *n.* controllore *m.*

**controversial,** *adj.* controvèrso.

**controversy,** *n.* controvèrsia *f.*

**contusion,** *n.* contusione *f.*

**conundrum,** *n.* indovinèllo *m.*

**convalesce,** *vb.* rimèttersi in salute.

**convalescence,** *n.* convalescènza *f.*

**convalescent,** *adj.* convalescènte.

**convene,** *vb.* convenire.

**convenience,** *n.* conveniènza *f.*

**convenient,** *adj.* conveniènte.

**conveniently,** *adv.* conveni.entemente.

**convent,** *n.* convènto *m.*

**convention,** *n.* convenzione *f.*; (meeting) congrèsso *m.*

**conventional,** *adj.* convenzionale.

**conventionally,** *adv.* convenzionalmente.

**converge,** *vb.* convèrgere.

**convergence,** *n.* convergènza *f.*

**convergent,** *adj.* convergènte.

**conversant with,** *adj.* versato in, pràtico di.

**conversational,** *adj.* di conversazione.

**conversationalist,** *n.* conversatore *m.*

**converse,** **1.** *adj.* convèrso. **2.** *vb.* conversare.

**conversely,** *adv.* per convèrso.

**convert,** *vb.* convertire.

**converter,** *n.* convertitrice *f.*

**convertible,** *adj.* convertìbile.

**convex,** *adj.* convèsso.

**convey,** *vb.* trasmèttere, trasportare.

**conveyance,** *n.* trasporto *m.*; (property) trapasso di proprietà *m.*

**conveyor,** *n.* trasportatore *m.*

**convict,** **1.** *n.* condannato *m.* **2.** *vb.* dichiarare colpévole.

**conviction,** *n.* (belief) convinzione *f.*; (law) condanna *f.*

**convince,** *vb.* convìncere.

**convincing,** *adj.* convincènte.

**convincingly,** *adv.* in modo convincènte.

**convivial,** *adj.* conviviale.

**convocation,** *n.* convocazione *f.*

**convoke,** *vb.* convocare.

**convoy,** **1.** *n.* convòglio *m.* **2.** *vb.* convogliare.

**convulse,** *vb.* mèttere in convulsioni.

**convulsion,** *n.* convulsione *f.*

**convulsive,** *adj.* convulsivo.

**cook,** **1.** *n.* cuòco *m.* **2.** *vb.* cucinare.

**cookbook,** *n.* libro di cucina *m.*

**cookie,** *n.* biscòtto *m.*

**cool,** **1.** *adj.* fresco. **2.** *vb.* rinfrescare.

**cooler,** *n.* frigorìfero *m.*

**coolness,** *n.* fresco *m.*; (fig.) indifferènza *f.*

**coop,** *n.* stìa *f.*

**cooper,** *n.* bottaio *m.*

**cooperate,** *vb.* cooperare.

**cooperation,** *n.* cooperazione *f.*

**cooperative,** **1.** *n.* cooperativa *f.* **2.** *adj.* cooperativo.

**cooperatively,** *adv.* cooperativamente.

**coordinate,** *vb.* coordinare.

**coordination,** *n.* coordinazione *f.*

**coordinator,** *n.* coordinatore *m.*

**cop,** *n.* poliziòtto *m.*

**cope,** *vb.* lottare; (**c. with**) tener tèsta a.

**copious,** *adj.* copioso.

**copiously,** *adv.* copiosamente.

**copiousness,** *n.* copiosità *f.*, còpia *f.*

**copper,** *n.* rame *m.*

**copperplate,** *n.* calligrafia *f.*

**copy,** **1.** *n.* còpia *f.*; (of book) esemplare *m.* **2.** *vb.* copiare.

**copyist,** *n.* copista *m.*

**copyright,** *n.* diritti d'autore *m.pl.*

**coquetry,** *n.* civetteria *f.*

**coquette, 1.** n. civetta f. **2.** vb. civettare.

**coral,** n. corallo m.

**cord,** n. còrda f.

**cordial,** n. and adj. cordiale (m.).

**cordiality,** n. cordialità f.

**cordially,** adv. cordialmente.

**cordon,** n. cordone m.

**cordovan,** n. cordovano m.

**core,** n. (fruit) tórsolo m.; (heart) cuòre m.

**cork,** n. sùghero m.; (of bottle) tappo m.

**corkscrew,** n. cavatappi m. (sg.)

**corn,** n. (grain) granturco m.; (on foot) callo m.

**corn-plaster,** n. callifugo m.

**cornea,** n. còrnea f.

**corner, 1.** n. àngolo m., canto m. **2.** vb. (comm.) accaparrare.

**cornerstone,** n. piètra angolare f.

**cornet,** n. cornetta f.

**cornetist,** n. cornettista m.

**cornice,** n. cornicione m.

**cornstarch,** n. farina di granturco f.

**cornucopia,** n. cornucòpia m. or f.

**corollary,** n. corollàrio m.

**coronary,** adj. coronàrio.

**coronation,** n. incoronazione f.

**coronet,** n. (noble's) corona nobiliare f.; (headdress) diadèma m.

**corporal, 1.** n. caporale m. **2.** adj. corporale.

**corporate,** adj. corporato.

**corruption,** n. corruzione f.

**corruptive,** adj. corruttivo.

**corsage,** n. fiori m.pl.

**corset,** n. busto m.

**Corsican,** adj. còrso.

**cortège,** n. cortèo m.

**corvette,** n. corvetta f.

**cosmetic,** n. and adj. cosmètico (m.).

**cosmic,** adj. còsmico.

**cosmopolitan,** adj. cosmopolita.

**cosmos,** n. còsmo m.

**cost, 1.** n. costo m. **2.** vb. costare.

**costliness,** n. costosità f.

**costly,** adj. costoso.

**costume,** n. costume m.

**costumer,** n. vestiarista m.

**cot,** n. lettino m.

**coterie,** n. combriccola f., cenàcolo m.

**cotillion,** n. cotiglione m.

**cottage,** n. villetta f., casetta f.

**cotton,** n. cotone m.

**cottonseed,** n. seme di cotone m.

**couch,** n. lètto m.

**cough, 1.** n. tosse f. **2.** vb. tossire.

**could,** vb. use past or conditional of potere.

**corporation,** n. corporazione f.

**corps,** n. còrpo m.

**corpse,** n. cadàvere m.

**corpulent,** adj. corpulènto.

**corpuscle,** n. corpùscolo m.

**correct, 1.** adj. corrètto. **2.** vb. corrèggere.

**correction,** n. correzione f.

**corrective,** adj. correttivo.

**correctly,** adv. correttamente.

**correctness,** n. correttezza f.

**correlate,** vb. méttere in correlazione.

**correlation,** n. correlazione f.

**correspond,** vb. corrispóndere.

**correspondence,** n. corrispondènza f.

**correspondent,** n. and adj. corrispondènte (m.).

**corridor,** n. corridòio m.

**corroborate,** vb. corroborare.

**corroboration,** n. corroborazione f.

**corroborative,** adj. corroborativo.

**corrode,** vb. corródere.

**corrosion,** n. corrosione f.

**corrugate,** vb. corrugare.

**corrupt,** vb. corrómpere.

**corrupter,** n. corruttore m.

**corruptible,** adj. corruttibile.

**coulter,** n. vòmere m.

**council,** n. consiglio m.

**councilman,** n. consiglière m.

**counsel, 1.** n. consiglio m. **2.** vb. consigliare.

**counselor,** n. consiglière m.

**count, 1.** n. conto m.; (noble) conte m. **2.** vb. contare.

**countenance, 1.** n. viso m. **2.** vb. approvare.

**counter,** n. banco m.

**counteract,** vb. neutralizzare.

**counteraction,** n. controazione f.

**counterattack,** n. contrattacco m.

**counterbalance**, n. contrappeso m.

**counter-clockwise**, adj. and adv. sinistròrso.

**counterfeit**, 1. n. and adj. falso (m.). 2. vb. contraffare, falsificare.

**countermand**, vb. contromandare.

**counteroffensive**, n. controffensiva f.

**counterpart**, n. contropartita f.

**Counter-Reformation**, n. Controriforma f.

**countess**, n. contessa f.

**countless**, adj. innumerévole.

**country**, n. (nation) paese m.; (opposed to city) campagna f.; (native land) patria f.

**countryman**, n. (of same country) compatriòta m.; (rustic) contadino m.

**countryside**, n. campagna f.

**county**, n. contèa f.

**coupé**, n. cupè m.

**couple**, 1. n. còppia f., paio m. 2. vb. accoppiare.

**coupon**, n. tagliando m., cèdola f.

**courage**, n. coràggio m.

**courageous**, adj. coraggioso.

**courier**, n. corrière m.

**course**, n. corso m.; (for races) pista f.

**court**, 1. n. corte f. 2. vb. corteggiare, far la corte a.

**courteous**, adj. cortese.

**courtesan**, n. cortigiana f.

**courtesy**, n. cortesìa f.

**courthouse**, n. palazzo di giustizia m.

**courtier**, n. cortigiano m.

**courtly**, adj. cerimonioso.

**courtmartial**, n. corte marziale f.

**courtroom**, n. aula di udiènza f.

**courtship**, n. corteggiamento m.

**courtyard**, n. cortile m.

**cousin**, n. cugino m., cugina f.

**covenant**, n. convenzione f.

**cover**, 1. n. copertura f., (book) copertina f. 2. vb. coprire.

**covering**, n. copertura f.

**covet**, vb. bramare.

**covetous**, adj. bramoso.

**cow**, 1. n. vacca f. 2. vb. intimidire.

**coward**, n. codardo m.

**cowardice**, n. codardìa f.

**cowardly**, adj. codardo.

**cowboy**, n. vaccaro m.

**cower**, vb. rannicchiarsi.

**cow hand**, n. vaccaro m.

**cowhide**, n. vacchetta f.

**coxswain**, n. timonière m.

**coy**, adj. timido.

**cozy**, adj. còmodo.

**crab**, n. grànchio m.

**crack**, 1. n. fenditura f. 2. vb. fèndere.

**cracked**, adj. fesso.

**cracker**, n. biscòtto m.

**crackup**, n. incidènte m.

**cradle**, 1. n. culla f. 2. vb. cullare.

**craft**, n. arte f.

**craftsman**, n. artigiano m.

**craftsmanship**, n. arte f.

**crafty**, adj. furbo.

**crag**, n. picco m.

**cram**, vb. rimpinzare, infarcire.

**cramp**, n. crampo m.

**crane**, n. gru f.

**cranium**, n. crànio m.

**crank**, 1. n. (handle) manovella f.; (crackpot) pazzo m. 2. vb. girare.

**cranky**, adj. capriccioso.

**cranny**, n. fessura f.

**crapshooter**, n. giocatore di dadi m.

**craps**, n. giòco dei dadi m.

**crash**, 1. n. cròllo m. 2. vb. crollare.

**crate**, n. gabbietta da imballàggio f.

**crater**, n. cratère m.

**crave**, vb. bramare.

**craven**, adj. codardo.

**craving**, n. brama f.

**crawl**, vb. trascinarsi.

**crayon**, n. matita f.

**crazed**, adj. pazzo.

**crazy**, adj. pazzo, fòlle.

**creak**, vb. cigolare, scricchiolare.

**creaky**, adj. cigolante, scricchiolante.

**cream**, n. crèma f., panna f.

**creamery**, n. cremerìa f.

**creamy**, adj. ricco di panna.

**crease**, 1. n. pièga f. 2. vb. (fold) piegare; (crinkle) spiegazzare.

**create**, vb. creare.

**creation**, n. creazione f.

**creative**, adj. creativo.

**creator**, n. creatore m.

**creature**, n. creatura f.

**credence**, n. credènza f.

**credentials,** *n.* credenziali *f.pl.*

**credibility,** *n.* credibilità *f.*

**credible,** *adj.* credìbile.

**credit,** *n.* crédito *m.*

**creditable,** *adj.* soddisfacènte.

**creditably,** *adv.* in modo soddisfacènte.

**creditor,** *n.* creditore *m.*

**credo,** *n.* crèdo *m.*

**credulity,** *n.* credulità *f.*

**credulous,** *adj.* crèdulo.

**creed,** *n.* credo *m.*; fede *f.*

**creek,** *n.* fiumicino *m.*; **(mountain c.)** torrènte *m.*

**creep,** *vb.* strisciare, arrampicarsi.

**cremate,** *vb.* cremare.

**cremation,** *n.* cremazione *f.*

**crematory, 1.** *adj.* forno crematòrio *m.*

**creosote,** *n.* creosòto *m.*

**crepe,** *n.* crespo *m.*

**crescent,** *n.* mezzaluna *f.*

**crest,** *n.* cresta *f.*

**crestfallen,** *adj.* a cresta bassa, scoraggiato.

**cretonne,** *n.* cotonina *f.*

**crevasse,** *n.* crepàccio *m.*

**crevice,** *n.* screpolatura *f.*

**crew,** *n.* equipàggio *m.*

**crib,** *n.* lettino da bimbo *m.*

**cricket,** *n.* grillo *m.*

**crier,** *n.* banditore *m.*

**crime,** *n.* delitto *m.*

**criminal,** *n. and adj.* criminale *(m.)*.

**criminologist,** *n.* criminòlogo *m.*

**criminology,** *n.* criminologìa *f.*

**crimson,** *adj.* cremisì.

**cringe,** *vb.* piegarsi.

**crinkle,** *vb.* spiegazzare.

**cripple, 1.** *n.* sciancato *f.* *vb.* rendere sciancato.

**crippled,** *adj.* sciancato.

**crisis,** *n.* crisi *f.*

**crisp,** *adj.* crespo; (bread, etc.) croccante.

**crisscross,** *adj.* incrociato.

**criterion,** *n.* critèrio *m.*

**critic,** *n.* crìtico *m.*

**critical,** *adj.* crìtico.

**criticism,** *n.* crìtica *f.*

**criticize,** *vb.* criticare.

**critique,** *n.* crìtica *f.*

**croak,** *vb.* gracidare.

**crochet,** *vb.* lavorare all'uncinetto.

**crock,** *n.* vaso di terracotta *m.*

**crockery,** *n.* vasellame *m.*

**crocodile,** *n.* coccodrillo *m.*

**crocodile tears,** *n.* làgrime di coccodrillo *f.pl.*

**crone,** *n.* vècchia *f.*

**crony,** *n.* compare *m.*

**crook,** *n.* (bend) curvatura *f.*; (scoundrel) mascalzone *m.*

**crooked,** *adj.* stòrto.

**croon,** *vb.* canticchiare.

**crop,** *n.* raccòlta *f.*, raccòlto *m.*

**croquet,** *n.* pallamàglio *m.*

**croquette,** *n.* crocchetta *f.*, polpetta *f.*

**cross, 1.** *n.* croce *f.*; (mixture) incròcio *m.* **2.** *adj.* irritato, adirato. **3.** *vb.* attraversare; (mix) incrociare.

**crossbreed, 1.** *n.* incròcio di razze *m.* **2.** *adj.* di razza incrociata.

**cross-examine,** *vb.* esaminare in contraddittòrio.

**cross-eyed,** *adj.* stràbico.

**cross-fertilization,** *n.* ibridazione *f.*

**crossing,** *n.* incròcio *m.*; **(grade c.)** passàggio a livèllo *m.*

**cross-purposes, be at,** *vb.* fraintèndersi.

**crossroads,** *n.* crocìcchio *m.*, crocevìa *f.*

**cross section,** *n.* sezione *f.*

**crossword puzzle,** *n.* cruciverba *m.*

**crotch,** *n.* (tree) biforcazione *f.*; (human body) inforcatura *f.*

**crouch,** *vb.* accucciarsi.

**croup,** *n.* crup *m.*

**crouton,** *n.* crostino *m.*

**crow, 1.** *n.* còrvo *m.* **2.** *vb.* cantare.

**crowd, 1.** *n.* fòlla *f.* **2.** *vb.* affollare; (push) spingere.

**crown, 1.** *n.* corona *f.* **2.** *vb.* incoronare.

**crown prince,** *n.* prìncipe ereditàrio *m.*

**crow's-foot,** *n.* zampa di gallina *f.*

**crow's-nest,** *n.* còffa *f.*

**crucial,** *adj.* cruciale.

**crucible,** *n.* crogiòlo *m.*

**crucifix,** *n.* crocefisso *m.*

**crucifixion,** *n.* crocefissione *f.*

**crucify,** *vb.* crocifìggere.

**crude,** *adj.* crudo.

**crudeness,** *n.* crudezza *f.*

**crudity,** *n.* crudezza *f.*

**cruel,** *adj.* crudèle.

**cruelty,** *n.* crudeltà *f.*

**cruet,** *n.* ampollina *f.*

**cruise, 1.** *n.* crociéra *f.* **2.** *vb.* incrociare.

**cruiser,** *n.* incrociatore *m.*

**crumb,** *n.* briciola *f.*

**crumble,** *vb.* sbriciolare.

**crumple,** *vb.* spiegazzare.

**crunch,** *vb.* schiacciare rumorosamente.

**crusade,** *n.* crociata *f.*

**crusader,** *n.* crociato *m.*

**crush, 1.** *n.* fòlla *f.* **2.** *vb.* schiacciare.

**crust,** *n.* crosta *f.*

**crustacean,** *n. and adj.* crostàceo (*m.*).

**crusty,** *adj.* crostoso; (manners) irritàbile.

**crutch,** *n.* grùccia *f.*, stampèlla *f.*

**cry, 1.** *n.* grido *m.* **2.** *vb.* (shout) gridare, urlare; (weep) piàngere.

**crying,** *n.* pianto *m.*

**crypt,** *n.* cripta *f.*

**cryptic,** *adj.* breve ed oscuro.

**cryptography,** *n.* crittografìa *f.*

**crystal,** *n.* cristallo *m.*

**crystalline,** *adj.* cristallino.

**crystallize,** *vb.* cristallizzare.

**cub,** *n.* piccolo *m.*

**cubbyhole,** *n.* nascondìglio *m.*

**cube,** *n.* cubo *m.*

**cubic,** *adj.* cùbico.

**cubicle,** *n.* cubìcolo *m.*

**cubism,** *n.* cubismo *f.*

**cuckoo, 1.** *n.* cuculo *m.* **2.** *adj.* pazzo.

**cucumber,** *n.* cetriòlo *m.*

**cud,** *n.* bòlo *m.*; (chew the c.) ruminare.

**cuddle,** *vb.* accarezzare.

**cudgel,** *n.* clava *f.*, mazza *f.*

**cue, 1.** *n.* segno *m.*; (billiards) stecca *f.*

**cuff, 1.** *n.* (shirt) polsino *m.*; (blow) scapaccione *m.* **2.** *vb.* picchiare.

**cuisine,** *n.* cucina *f.*

**culinary,** *adj.* culinàrio.

**cull,** *vb.* cògliere.

**culminate,** *vb.* culminare.

**culmination,** *n.* culminazione *f.*

**culpable,** *adj.* colpévole.

**culprit,** *n.* colpévole *m.*

**cult,** *n.* culto *m.*

**cultivate,** *vb.* coltivare.

**cultivated,** *adj.* colto.

**cultivation,** *n.* coltivazione *f.*

**cultivator,** *n.* coltivatore *m.*

**cultural,** *adj.* culturale.

**culture,** *n.* cultura *f.*

**cultured,** *adj.* colto.

**cumbersome,** *adj.* ingombrante.

**cumulative,** *adj.* cumulativo.

**cunning, 1.** *n.* abilità *f.* **2.** *adj.* astuto, àbile; (attractive) attraènte, bellino.

**cup,** *n.* tazza *f.*

**cupboard,** *n.* credènza *f.*

**cupidity,** *n.* cupidìgia *f.*

**cupola,** *n.* cùpola *f.*

**curable,** *adj.* guarìbile.

**curator,** *n.* curatore *m.*

**curb,** *n.* **1.** (sidewalk) cordone *m.*; (harness) barbazzale *m.* **2.** *vb.* raffrenare.

**curbstone,** *n.* bordo di piètre *m.*

**curd,** *n.* quagliata *f.*

**curdle,** *vb.* quagliare.

**cure, 1.** *n.* cura *f.*, guarigione *f.* **2.** *vb.* guarire.

**curfew,** *n.* coprifuòco *m.*

**curio,** *n.* curiosità *f.*

**curiosity,** *n.* curiosità *f.*

**curious,** *adj.* curioso; (queer) strano.

**curl, 1.** *n.* rìcciolo *m.* **2.** *vb.* arricciare.

**curly,** *adj.* ricciuto.

**currant,** *n.* ribes *m.*

**currency,** *n.* circolazione *f.*; (money) valuta *f.*

**current,** *n. and adj.* corrènte (*f.*).

**currently,** *adv.* correntemente.

**curriculum,** *n.* currìcolo *m.*

**curry,** *vb.* (horse) strigliare.

**curse, 1.** *n.* maledizione *f.* **2.** *vb.* maledire.

**cursed,** *adj.* maledetto.

**curse-word,** *n.* bestémmia *f.*

**cursory,** *adj.* frettoloso.

**curt,** *adj.* asciutto, breve.

**curtail,** *vb.* accorciare, ridurre.

**curtain,** *n.* cortina *f.*; (theater) sipàrio *m.*

**curtsy,** *n.* riverènza *f.*

**curvature,** *n.* curvatura *f.*

**curve, 1.** *n.* curva *f.* **2.** *vb.* curvare.

**cushion,** *n.* cuscino *m.*

**cuspidor,** *n.* sputacchièra *f.*

**custard,** *n.* crema caramella *f.*

**custodian,** *n.* custòde *m.*

**custody,** *n.* custòdia *f.*

**custom,** *n.* costume *m.*, consuetùdine *f.*, uso *m.*

**customary,** *adj.* consuèto.

**customer,** *n.* cliènte *m.*; (regular c.) avventore *m.*

**customs-house, customs,** *n.* dogana *f.*

**customs-officer,** *n.* doganière *m.*

**cut, 1.** *n.* tàglio *m.* **2.** *vb.* tagliare.

**cutaneous,** *adj.* cutàneo.

**cute,** *adj.* attraènte, bellino.

**cut glass,** *n.* cristallo *m.*

**cuticle,** *n.* cutìcola *f.*

**cutlet,** *n.* costoletta *f.*

**cutlery,** *n.* posaterìa *f.*

**cutout,** *n.* interruttore *m.*

**cutter,** *n.* tagliatore *m.*; (boat) cottro *m.*

**cutthroat,** *n.* assassino *m.*

**cutting,** *n.* (railway) trincèa *f.*; (newspaper) ritàglio *m.*

**cycle, 1.** *n.* ciclo *m.*; (bicycle) bicicletta *f.* **2.** *vb.* andare in bicicletta.

**cyclist,** *n.* ciclista *m.*

**cyclone,** *n.* ciclone *m.*

**cyclotron,** *n.* ciclotrone *m.*

**cylinder,** *n.* cilindro *m.*

**cylindrical,** *adj.* cilìndrico.

**cymbal,** *n.* piatto *m.*, cinèllo *m.*

**cynic,** *n.* cìnico *m.*

**cynical,** *adj.* cìnico.

**cynicism,** *n.* cinismo *m.*

**cypress,** *n.* ciprèsso *m.*

**cyst,** *n.* ciste *f.*

# D

**dab, 1.** *n.* schizzo *m.* **2.** *vb.* sfiorare.

**dabble,** *vb.* essere un dilettante.

**dad,** *n.* babbo *m.*

**daffodil,** *n.* narciso *m.*

**daffy,** *adj.* pazzo.

**dagger,** *n.* daga *f.*, pugnale *m.*

**dahlia,** *n.* dàlia *f.*

**daily, 1.** *n.* (newspaper) giornale *m.* **2.** *adj.* giornalièro, quotidìano. **3.** *adv.* quotidianamente.

**daintiness,** *n.* squisitezza *f.*

**dainty,** *adj.* squisito, delicato.

**dairy,** *n.* latterìa *f.*

**dairymaid,** *n.* lattaia *f.*

**dairyman,** *n.* lattaio *m.*

**dais,** *n.* piattaforma *f.*

**daisy,** *n.* margherita *f.*

**dale,** *n.* valletta *f.*

**dally,** *vb.* indugiare.

**dam,** *n.* diga *f.*

**damage, 1.** *n.* danno *m.*, avarìa *f.* **2.** *vb.* danneggiare, avariare.

**damask,** *n.* damasco *m.*

**damn,** *vb.* dannare; (curse) maledire.

**damnation,** *n.* dannazione *f.*

**damp, 1.** *n.* umidità *f.* **2.** *adj.* ùmido.

**dampen,** *vb.* inumidire.

**dampness,** *n.* umidità *f.*

**damsel,** *n.* damigèlla *f.*

**dance, 1.** *n.* ballo *m.*, danza *f.*; (d. tune) ballàbile *m.* **2.** *vb.* ballare, danzare.

**dancer,** *n.* ballerino *m.*, ballerina *f.*

**dancing,** *n.* ballo *m.*

**dandelion,** *n.* radicchièlla *f.*

**dandruff,** *n.* fòrfora *f.*

**dandy, 1.** *n.* damerino *m.*, bellimbusto *m.* **2.** *adj.* òttimo.

**danger,** *n.* perìcolo *m.*

**dangerous,** *adj.* pericoloso.

**dangle,** *vb.* penzolare.

**Danish,** *adj.* danese.

**dapper,** *adj.* pìccolo e vivace.

**dappled,** *adj.* macchiettato.

**dare, 1.** *n.* sfida *f.* **2.** *vb.* osare; (challenge) sfidare.

**daredevil,** *n.* temeràrio *m.*

**daring, 1.** *n.* audàcia *f.* **2.** *adj.* audace.

**dark, 1.** *n.* oscurità *f.* **2.** *adj.* oscuro, buio, tenebroso.

**darken,** *vb.* oscurare.

**dark horse,** *n.* candidato sconosciuto *m.*

**darkness,** *n.* oscurità *f.*, buio *m.*, tènebre *f.pl.*

**darkroom,** *n.* càmera oscura *f.*

**darling,** *n. and adj.* prediletto.

**darn, 1.** *n.* rammendatura *f.* **2.** *vb.* rammendare.

**darning needle,** *n.* ago da rammendo *m.*

**dart, 1.** *n.* dardo *m.*; (movement) balzo *m.* **2.** balzare.

**dash, 1.** *n.* (energy) slàncio *m.*, scatto *m.*; (pen) tratto *m.* **2.** *vb.* (throw) gettare; (destroy) distrùggere; (rush) slanciarsi; (spurt) scattare.

**dashboard,** *n.* cruscòtto *m.*

**dashing,** *adj.* impetuoso.

**data,** *n.* dati *m.pl.*

**date, 1.** *n.* data *f.*; (appointment) appuntamento *m.*; (fruit) dàttero *m.* **2.** *vb.* datare.

**date line,** *n.* linea del cambiamento di data *f.*

**daub, 1.** *n.* imbrattatura *f.* **2.** *vb.* imbrattare.

**daughter,** *n.* figlia *f.*

**daughter-in-law,** *n.* nuòra *f.*

**daunt,** *vb.* intimidire.

**dauntless,** *adj.* intrèpido.

**dauntlessly,** *adv.* intrepidamente.

**davenport,** *n.* divano *m.*, sofaletto *m.*

**dawdle,** *vb.* indugiare.

**dawn, 1.** *n.* alba *f.* **2.** *vb.* spuntare.

**day,** *n.* giorno *m.*; (span of day) giornata *f.*

**daybreak,** *n.* alba *f.*

**daydream,** *n.* fantasticherìa *f.*

**daylight,** *n.* luce del giorno *f.*

**daylight-saving time,** *n.* ora d'estate *f.*

**daze, 1.** *n.* stupore *m.* **2.** *vb.* stupire.

**dazzle,** *vb.* abbagliare.

**deacon,** *n.* diàcono *m.*

**dead,** *n. and adj.* mòrto (*m.*).

**deaden,** *vb.* ammortire.

**dead end,** *n.* vìcolo cièco *m.*

**dead letter,** *n.* léttera mòrta *f.*

**deadline,** *n.* limite *m.*

**deadlock,** *n.* punto mòrto *m.*

**deadly,** *adj.* mortale.

**deadwood,** *n.* legno mòrto *m.*

**deaf,** *adj.* sordo.

**deafen,** *vb.* assordare.

**deaf-mute,** *n. and adj.* sordomuto (*m.*).

**deafness,** *n.* sordità *f.*

**deal, 1.** *n.* (amount) quantità *f.*; (business) affare *m.*; (cards) distribuzione *f.* **2.** *vb.* (**d. with**) trattare con; (**d. out**) distribuire.

**dealer,** *n.* negoziante *m.*

**dean,** *n.* decano *m.*

**dear,** *adj.* caro.

**dearly,** *adv.* caramente.

**dearth,** *n.* scarsezza *f.*, scarsità *f.*

**death,** *n.* mòrte *f.*

**deathless,** *adj.* immortale, imperituro.

**deathly,** *adj.* mortale.

**débâcle,** *n.* sfacèlo *m.*, disastro *m.*

**debase,** *vb.* abbassare, avvilire.

**debatable,** *adj.* discutìbile.

**debate, 1.** *n.* dibattimento *m.* **2.** *vb.* dibàttere.

**debater,** *n.* dibattènte *m.*

**debauch, 1.** *n.* òrgia *f.*, sregolatezza *f.* **2.** *vb.* pervertire.

**debenture,** *n.* obbligazione *f.*

**debilitate,** *vb.* debilitare.

**debit,** *n.* dèbito *m.*

**debonair,** *adj.* gaio.

**debris,** *n.* detriti *m.pl.*

**debt,** *n.* dèbito *m.*

**debtor,** *n.* debitore *m.*

**debunk,** *vb.* screditare.

**debut,** *n.* debutto *m.*

**debutante,** *n.* debuttante *f.*

**decade,** *n.* decènnio *m.*

**decadence,** *n.* decadènza *f.*

**decadent,** *adj.* decadènte.

**decalcomania,** *n.* decalcomanìa *f.*

**decanter,** *n.* caraffa *f.*

**decapitate,** *vb.* decapitare.

**decay, 1.** *n.* decadènza *f.*, decomposizione *f.*; (teeth) càrie *f.* **2.** *vb.* decadere, decomporre, marcire; (teeth) cariarsi.

**deceased,** *n. and adj.* deceduto *m.*, defunto *m.*

**deceit,** *n.* inganno *m.*

**deceitful,** *adj.* ingannatore.

**deceive,** *vb.* ingannare.

**deceiver,** *n.* ingannatore *m.*

**December,** *n.* dicèmbre *m.*

**decency,** *n.* (modesty) decènza *f.*; (honorable behavior) onorevolezza *f.*

**decent,** *adj.* (modest) decènte; (honorable) onorévole.

**decentralization,** *n.* decentramento *m.*

**decentralize,** *vb.* decentrare.

**deception,** *n.* inganno *m.*

**deceptive,** *adj.* ingannévole.

**decide,** *vb.* decìdere.

**deciduous,** *adj.* decìduo.

**decimal,** *adj.* decimale.

**decimate,** *vb.* decimare.

**decipher,** *vb.* decifrare.

**decision,** *n.* decisione *f.*

**decisive,** *adj.* decisivo.

**deck,** *n.* ponte *m.*

**deck-hand,** *n.* mozzo *m.*

**declaim,** *vb.* declamare.

**declamation,** *n.* declamazione *f.*

**declaration,** *n.* dichiarazione *f.*

**declarative,** *adj.* dichiarativo.

**declare,** *vb.* dichiarare.

**declension,** *n.* declinazione *f.*

**decline, 1.** *n.* decadènza *f.* **2.** *vb.* declinare; (refuse) rifiutare; (decay) decadere.

**decode,** *vb.* decifrare.

**décolleté,** *adj.* scollato.

**decompose,** *vb.* decomporre.

**decomposition,** *n.* decomposizione *f.*

**décor,** *n.* messa in scena *f.*

**decorate,** *vb.* decorare.

**decoration,** *n.* decorazione *f.*

**decorative,** *adj.* decorativo.

**decorator,** *n.* decoratore *m.*

**decorous,** *adj.* decoroso.

**decorum,** *n.* decòro *m.*

**decoy,** *vb.* attirare.

**decrease, 1.** *n.* diminuzione *f.* **2.** *vb.* diminuire.

**decree, 1.** *n.* decreto *m.* **2.** *vb.* decretare.

**decrepit,** *adj.* decrèpito.

**decry,** *vb.* deprecare.

**dedicate,** *vb.* dedicare.

**dedication,** *n.* dèdica *f.*

**deduce,** *vb.* dedurre.

**deduct,** *vb.* dedurre, sottrarre.

**deduction,** *n.* deduzione *f.*

**deductive,** *adj.* deduttivo.

**deed,** *n.* atto *m.*, fatto *m.*

**deem,** *vb.* giudicare, stimare.

**deep,** *adj.* profondo.

**deepen,** *vb.* approfondire.

**deeply,** *adv.* profondamente.

**deep-rooted,** *adj.* profondamente radicato.

**deer,** *n.* cèrvo *m.*

**deerskin,** *n.* pèlle di dàino *f.*

**deface,** *vb.* sfregiare.

**defamation,** *n.* diffamazione *f.*

**defame,** *vb.* diffamare.

**default, 1.** *n.* contumàcia *f.* **2.** *vb.* rèndersi contumace; (*comm.*) mancar di pagare.

**defaulting,** *adj.* contumace.

**defeat, 1.** *n.* sconfitta *f.*, disfatta *f.* **2.** *vb.* sconfiggere.

**defeatism,** *n.* disfattismo *m.*

**defect,** *n.* difètto *m.*, mènda *f.*

**defection,** *n.* defezione *f.*

**defective,** *adj.* difettoso.

**defend,** *vb.* difèndere.

**defendant,** *n.* imputato *m.*

**defender,** *n.* difensore *m.*

**defense,** *n.* difesa *f.*

**defenseless,** *adj.* sènza difesa.

**defensible,** *adj.* difensìbile.

**defensive,** *adj.* difensivo.

**defer,** *vb.* (put off) differire; (conform) conformarsi.

**deference,** *n.* deferènza *f.*

**deferential,** *adj.* deferènte.

**defiance,** *n.* sfida *f.*

**defiant,** *adj.* provocante.

**deficiency,** *n.* deficiènza *f.*

**deficient,** *adj.* deficiènte.

**deficit,** *n.* dèficit *m.*

**defile,** *n.* (march) sfilare; (foul) profanare.

**define,** *vb.* definire.

**definite,** *adj.* definito.

**definitely,** *adj.* definitivamente.

**definition,** *n.* definizione *f.*

**definitive,** *adj.* definitivo.

**deflate,** *vb.* sgonfiare; (*econ.*) deflazionare.

**deflation,** *n.* deflazione *f.*

**deflect,** *vb.* deflèttere.

**deform,** *vb.* deformare.

**deformed,** *adj.* deforme.

**deformity,** *n.* deformità *f.*

**defraud,** *vb.* defraudare.

**defray,** *vb.* pagare.

**defrost,** *vb.* tògliere il ghiàccio a, (**d. refrigerator**) sbrinare.

**defrosting,** *n.* (refrigerator) sbrinamento *m.*

**deft,** *adj.* dèstro, àbile.

**defy,** *vb.* sfidare.

**degenerate, 1.** *n. and adj.* degenerato (*m.*). **2.** *vb.* degenerare.

**degeneration,** *n.* degenerazione *f.*

**degradation,** *n.* degradazione *f.*

**degrade,** *vb.* degradare.

**degree,** *n.* grado *m.*; (university) làurea *f.*

**dehydrate,** *vb.* disidratare.

**deify,** *vb.* deificare.

**deign,** *vb.* degnarsi.

**deity,** *n.* deità *f.*

**dejected,** *adj.* scoraggiato.

**dejection,** *n.* scoraggiamento *m.*, abbattimento *m.*

**delay, 1.** *n.* indùgio *m.*, ritardo *m.* **2.** *vb.* indugiare, ritardare.

**delectable,** *adj.* dilettévole.

**delegate, 1.** *n.* delegato *m.* **2.** *vb.* delegare.

**delegation,** *n.* delegazione *f.*

**delete,** *vb.* cancellare.

**deliberate, 1.** adj. deliberato.
**2.** vb. deliberare.

**deliberately,** adv. deliberatamente, apposta.

**deliberation,** n. deliberazione f.

**deliberative,** adj. deliberativo.

**delicacy,** n. delicatezza f.

**delicate,** adj. delicato.

**delicious,** adj. delizioso.

**delight,** n. diletto m.

**delightful,** adj. dilettévole.

**delineate,** vb. delineare.

**delinquency,** n. delinquènza f.

**delinquent,** n. and adj. delinquente (m.)

**delirium,** n. delìrio m.

**delirious, 1.** adj. delirante.
**2.** vb. **(be d.)** delirare.

**deliver,** vb. (set free) liberare; (hand over) consegnare.

**deliverance,** n. liberazione f.

**delivery,** n. consegna f.

**delouse,** vb. spidocchiare.

**delude,** vb. delùdere.

**deluge,** n. dilùvio m.

**delusion,** n. delusione f.

**de luxe,** adj. di lusso.

**delve,** vb. scavare.

**demagogue,** n. demagògo m.

**demand, 1.** n. domanda f., richièsta f. **2.** vb. domandare, richièdere, esìgere.

**demarcation,** n. demarcazione f.

**demean (oneself),** vb. abbassarsi.

**demeanor,** n. condotta f.

**demented,** adj. demènte.

**demerit,** n. demèrito m.

**demigod,** n. semidio m.

**demilitarize,** vb. smilitarizzare.

**demise,** n. mòrte f.

**demobilization,** n. smobilitazione f.

**demobilize,** vb. smobilitare.

**democracy,** n. democrazia f.

**democrat,** n. democràtico m.

**democratic,** adj. democràtico.

**demolish,** vb. demolire.

**demolition,** n. demolizione f.

**demon,** n. demònio m.

**demonstrable,** adj. dimostràbile.

**demonstrate,** vb. dimostrare.

**demonstration,** n. dimostrazione f.

**demonstrative,** adj. dimostrativo.

**demonstrator,** n. dimostratore m.

**demoralize,** vb. demoralizzare.

**demote,** vb. degradare.

**demur,** vb. obiettare.

**demure,** adj. modesto.

**den,** n. tana f., covo m.

**denaturalize,** vb. snaturare.

**denature,** vb. denaturare.

**denial,** n. diniègo m.

**Denmark,** n. Danimarca f.

**denomination,** n. denominazione f.; (church) sètta f.

**denominator,** n. denominatore m.

**denote,** vb. denotare.

**dénouement,** n. scioglimento m.

**denounce,** vb. denunciare.

**dense,** adj. dènso.

**density,** n. densità f.

**dent,** n. incavo m.

**dental,** adj. dentale.

**dentifrice,** n. dentifrìcio m.

**dentist,** n. dentista m.

**dentistry,** n. odontoiatrìa f.

**denture,** n. dentièra f.

**denude,** vb. denudare.

**denunciation,** n. denùncia f.

**deny,** vb. negare.

**deodorant,** n. and adj. deodorante (m.)

**deodorize,** vb. deodorare.

**depart,** vb. partire.

**department,** n. dipartimento m.

**departmental,** adj. dipartimentale.

**departure,** n. partènza f.

**depend,** vb. dipèndere.

**dependability,** n. fidatezza f.

**dependable,** adj. fido.

**dependence,** n. dipendènza f.

**dependent,** n. and adj. dipendènte (m.)

**depict,** vb. dipìngere.

**depiction,** n. rappresentazione f.

**deplete,** vb. esaurire.

**deplorable,** adj. deplorévole.

**deplore,** vb. deplorare.

**depopulate,** vb. spopolare.

**deport,** vb. deportare.

**deportation,** n. deportazione f.

**deportment,** n. condotta f.

**depose,** vb. deporre.

**deposit, 1.** n. depòsito. **2.** vb. depositare.

**deposition,** n. deposizione f.

**depositor,** n. depositante m., correntista m.

**depository,** n. depòsito m.

**depot,** n. (military) depòsito m.; (railroad) stazione f.

**deprave,** vb. depravare.

**depravity,** n. depravazione f.

**deprecate,** vb. deprecare.

**depreciate,** vb. deprezzare.

**depreciation,** n. deprezzamento m

**depredation,** n. depredamento m.

**depress,** vb. deprimere.

**depression,** n. depressione f.

**deprivation,** n. privazione f.

**deprive,** vb. privare.

**depth,** n. profondità f.

**depth charge,** n. bomba di profondità f.

**deputy,** n. deputato m.

**derail,** vb. deragliare.

**derange,** vb. far impazzire.

**deranged,** adj. impazzito.

**derelict,** adj. derelitto.

**dereliction,** n. negligènza del dovere f.

**deride,** vb. deridere.

**derision,** n. derisione f.

**derisive,** adj. derisivo.

**derivation,** n. derivazione f.

**derivative,** adj. derivativo.

**derive,** vb. derivare.

**dermatology,** n. dermatologia f.

**derogatory,** adj. derogatòrio.

**derrick,** n. gru f.

**descend,** vb. scéndere.

**descendant,** n. discendènte m.

**descent,** n. discesa f.

**describe,** vb. descrivere.

**description,** n. descrizione f

**descriptive,** adj. descrittivo.

**desecrate,** vb. desecrare.

**desensitize,** vb. desensibilizzare.

**desert, 1.** n. desèrto m.; (merit) mèrito m. **2.** vb. disertare.

**deserter,** n. disertore m.

**desertion,** n. diserzione f.

**deserve,** vb. meritare.

**deserving,** adj. meritévole.

**design, 1.** n. disegno m. **2.** vb. disegnare.

**designate,** vb. designare.

**designation,** n. designazione f.

**designedly,** adv. intenzionalmente.

**designer,** n. disegnatore m.

**designing,** adj. astuto.

**desirability,** n. desiderabilità f.

**desirable,** adj. desideràbile.

**desire, 1.** n. desidèrio m. **2.** vb. desiderare.

**desirous,** adj. desideroso.

**desist,** vb. desìstere.

**desk,** n. scrivanìa f.

**desolate, 1.** adj. desolato. **2.** vb. desolare.

**desolation,** n. desolazione f.

**despair, 1.** n. disperazione f. **2.** vb. disperare.

**despatch, dispatch, 1.** n. spedizione f.; (speed) prontezza f. **2.** vb. spedire.

**desperado,** n. disperato m.

**desperate,** adj. disperato.

**desperation,** n. disperazione

**despicable,** adj. spregévole.

**despise,** vb. disprezzare, spregiare.

**despite,** prep. malgrado.

**despondent,** adj. abbattuto.

**despot,** n. dèspota m.

**despotic,** adj. dispòtico.

**despotism,** n. dispotismo m.

**dessert,** n. dessert m. (French pronunciation)

**destination,** n. destinazione f.

**destine,** vb. destinare.

**destiny,** n. destino m.

**destitute,** adj. destituito.

**destitution,** n. destituzione f.

**destroy,** vb. distrùggere.

**destroyer,** n. cacciatorpedinière m.

**destructible,** adj. distruttìbile.

**destruction,** n. distruzione f.

**destructive,** adj. distruttivo.

**desultory,** adj. saltuàrio.

**detach,** vb. staccare, distaccare.

**detachment,** n. distacco m.; (mil.) distaccamento m.

**detail, 1.** n. dettaglio m. **2.** vb. dettagliare.

**detain,** vb. detenere.

**detect,** vb. scoprire.

**detection,** n. scoprimento m.

**detective,** n. detective m. (English pron.)

**detention,** n. detenzione f.

**deter,** vb. distògliere.

**detergent,** n. and adj. detergènte (m.)

**deteriorate,** vb. deteriorare.

**deterioration,** n. deteriorazione f.

**determination**, n. determinazione f.

**determine**, vb. determinare.

**determined**, adj. risoluto.

**determinism**, n. determinismo m.

**detest**, vb. detestare.

**detestation**, n. detestazione f.

**dethrone**, vb. detronizzare.

**detonate**, vb. detonare.

**detonation**, n. detonazione f.

**detour**, n. deviazione f.

**detract**, vb. detrarre.

**detriment**, n. detrimento m., danno m.

**detrimental**, adj. dannoso.

**devaluate**, vb. svalutare.

**devastate**, vb. devastare.

**devastation**, n. devastazione f.

**develop**, vb. sviluppare.

**developer**, n. sviluppatore m.

**development**, n. sviluppo m.

**deviate**, vb. deviare.

**deviation**, n. deviazione f.

**device**, n. congegno m.

**devil**, n. diàvolo m.

**devilish**, adj. diabòlico.

**devious**, adj. dèvio.

**devise**, vb. escogitare.

**devitalize**, vb. devitalizzare.

**devoid**, adj. privo.

**devote**, vb. dedicare.

**devoted**, adj. devòto.

**devotee**, n. entusiasta m. or f.

**devotion**, n. devozione f.

**devour**, vb. divorare.

**devout**, adj. devòto.

**dew**, n. rugiada f.

**dewy**, adj. rugiadoso.

**dexterity**, n. destrezza f.

**dexterous**, adj. dèstro.

**diabetes**, n. diabète f.

**diabolic**, adj. diabòlico.

**diadem**, n. diàdema m.

**diagnose**, vb. diagnosticare.

**diagnosis**, n. diàgnosi f.

**diagnostic**, adj. diagnòstico.

**diagonal**, adj. diagonale.

**diagonally**, adv. diagonalmente.

**diagram**, n. diagramma m.

**dial**, 1. n. quadrante m.; (telephone) disco combinatore m. 2. vb. (telephone) formare (un nùmero).

**dialect**, n. dialètto m.

**dialogue**, n. diàlogo m.

**diameter**, n. diàmetro m.

**diametrical**, adj. diametrale.

**diamond**, n. diamante m.

**diaper**, n. pannilino m., pannolino m.

**diaphragm**, n. diaframma m.

**diarrhea**, n. diarrèa f.

**diary**, n. diàrio m.

**diathermy**, n. diatermìa f.

**diatribe**, n. diatriba f.

**dice**, n. dadi m.pl.

**dickens (the)**, interj. diàmine!

**dicker**, vb. mercanteggiare.

**dictaphone**, n. dittàfono m.

**dictate**, vb. dettare.

**dictation**, n. dettatura f.

**dictator**, n. dittatore m.

**dictatorial**, adj. dittatoriale.

**dictatorship**, n. dittatura f.

**diction**, n. dizione f.

**dictionary**, n. dizionàrio m.

**didactic**, adj. didàttico.

**die**, 1. n. (gaming cube) dado m.; (stamper) stampo m. 2. vb. morire.

**die-hard**, adj. oltremodo conservatore.

**diet**, n. dièta f., regime m.

**dietary**, adj. dietètico.

**dietetic**, adj. dietètico.

**dietetics**, n. dietètica f.

**dietitian**, n. dietista m.

**differ**, vb. differire.

**difference**, n. differènza f.

**different**, adj. differènte, divèrso.

**differential**, adj. differenziale.

**differentiate**, vb. differenziare.

**difficult**, adj. difficile.

**difficulty**, n. difficoltà f.

**diffident**, adj. tìmido.

**diffuse**, 1. adj. diffuso. 2. vb. diffóndere.

**diffusion**, n. diffusione f.

**dig**, vb. scavare.

**digest**, vb. digerire.

**digestible**, adj. digerìbile.

**digestion**, n. digestione f.

**digestive**, adj. digestivo.

**digitalis**, n. digitale f.

**dignified**, adj. dignitoso.

**dignify**, vb. dignificare.

**dirnitary**, n. dignitàrio m.

**dignity**, n. dignità f.

**digress**, vb. digredire.

**digression**, n. digressione f.

**dike**, n. diga f.

**dilapidated**, adj. dilapidato.

**dilapidation**, n. dilapidazione f.

**dilate**, vb. dilatare.

**dilatory**, adj. dilatòrio.

**dilemma**, n. dilemma f.

**dilettante,** n. dilettante m.
**diligence,** n. diligènza f.
**diligent,** adj. diligènte.
**dill,** n. aneto m.
**dilute,** vb. diluire.
**dilution,** n. diluzione f.
**dim, 1.** adj. oscuro. **2.** vb. oscurare.
**dimension,** n. dimensione f.
**diminish,** vb. diminuire, menomare.
**diminution,** n. diminuzione f.
**diminutive,** n. and adj. diminutivo.
**dimness,** n. oscurità f.
**dimple,** n. fossetta f.
**din,** n. rumore m.
**dine,** vb. pranzare.
**diner, dining-car,** n. vagone ristorante m.
**dinginess,** n. súdicio.
**dinner,** n. pranzo m.
**dinosaur,** n. dinosàuro m.
**diocese,** n. diòcesi f.
**dioxide,** n. biòssido m.
**dip,** vb. immèrgere, tuffare.
**diphtheria,** n. difterite f.
**diploma,** n. diplòma m.
**diplomacy,** n. diplomazìa f.
**diplomat,** n. diplomàtico m.
**diplomatic,** adj. diplomàtico.
**dipper,** n. mèstolo m.
**dire,** adj. terrìbile.
**direct, 1.** adj. dirètto. **2.** vb. dirìgere.
**direct current,** n. corrènte contìnua f.
**direction,** n. direzione f., sènso m.
**directional,** adj. direttivo.
**directive,** adj. direttivo.
**directly,** adv. direttamente, immediatamente.
**directness,** n. franchezza f.
**director,** n. direttore m.
**directorate,** n. direttorato m.
**directory,** n. guida f.; (**telephone d.**) elènco telefònico m.
**dirge,** n. canto funebre m.
**dirigible,** n. and adj. dirigìbile (m.)
**dirt,** n. sudiciume m.
**dirty,** adj. súdicio, sporco.
**disability,** n. incapacità f.
**disable,** vb. rèndere incapace.
**disabled,** adj. invàlido.
**disabuse,** vb. disingannare.
**disadvantage,** n. svantàggio m.

**disagree,** vb. discordare, dissentire.
**disagreeable,** adj. sgradévole, antipàtico.
**disagreement,** n. dissènso m.
**disappear,** vb. sparire, scomparire.
**disappearance,** n. scomparsa f.
**disappoint,** vb. delùdere.
**disappointment,** n. delusione f.
**disapproval,** n. disapprovazione f.
**disapprove,** vb. disapprovare.
**disarm,** vb. disarmare.
**disarmament,** n. disarmo m.
**disarrange,** vb. scompigliare.
**disarray,** n. scompìglio m.
**disassemble,** vb. smontare.
**disaster,** n. disastro m.
**disastrous,** adj. disastroso.
**disavow,** vb. disconóscere.
**disavowal,** n. disconoscimento m.
**disband,** vb. sbandare.
**disbar,** vb. cancellare dall'albo dell'avvocatura.
**disbelieve,** vb. non credere.
**disburse,** vb. sborsare.
**discard,** vb. scartare.
**discern,** vb. discèrnere, scòrgere.
**discerning,** adj. penetrante.
**discernment,** n. giudizio m.
**discharge, 1.** n. scàrico m.; (gun) scàrica f.; (mil., job) licenziamento m. **2.** vb. scaricare; (mil., job) licenziare.
**disciple,** n. discépolo m.
**disciplinary,** adj. disciplinare.
**discipline, 1.** n. disciplina f. **2.** vb. disciplinare.
**disclaim,** vb. disconóscere.
**disclaimer,** n. disconoscimento m.
**disclose,** vb. rivelare.
**disclosure,** n. rivelazione f.
**discolor,** vb. scolorire.
**discoloration,** n. scolorimento m.
**discomfiture,** n. sconfitta f.
**discomfort,** n. disàgio m.
**disconcert,** vb. sconcertare.
**disconnect,** vb. sconnèttere.
**disconsolate,** adj. sconsolato.
**discontent, 1.** n. scontènto m. **2.** vb. scontentare.
**discontented,** adj. scontènto.
**discontinue,** vb. interrómpere, sospèndere.

**discord,** *n.* discòrdia *f.*; (music) disaccòrdo *m.*

**discordant,** *adj.* discordante.

**discount,** 1. *n.* sconto *m.* 2. *vb.* scontare.

**discourage,** *vb.* scoraggiare.

**discouragement,** *n.* scoraggiamento *m.*

**discourse,** 1. *n.* discorso *m.* 2. *vb.* discórrere.

**discourteous,** *adj.* scortese.

**discourtesy,** *n.* scortesìa *f.*

**discover,** *vb.* scoprire.

**discoverer,** *n.* scopritore *m.*

**discovery,** *n.* scopèrta *f.*

**discredit,** 1. *n.* discrédito *m.* 2. *vb.* screditare.

**discreditable,** *adj.* disonorévole.

**discreet,** *adj.* discreto.

**discrepancy,** *n.* discrepanza *f.*

**discrepant,** *adj.* discrepante.

**discretion,** *n.* discrezione *f.*

**discriminate,** *vb.* discriminare.

**discrimination,** *n.* discriminazione *f.*

**discursive,** *adj.* digressivo.

**discuss,** *vb.* discútere.

**discussion,** *n.* discussione *f.*

**disdain,** 1. *n.* disdegno *m.* 2. *vb.* disdegnare.

**disdainful,** *adj.* disdegnoso.

**disease,** *n.* malattìa *f.*

**disembark,** *vb.* sbarcare.

**disembarkation,** *n.* sbarco *m.*

**disembodied,** *adj.* incorpòreo.

**disenchantment,** *n.* disincanto *m.*

**disengage,** *vb.* disimpegnare.

**disentangle,** *vb.* districare.

**disfavor,** *n.* sfavore *m.*

**disfigure,** *vb.* disfigurare.

**disfranchise,** *vb.* privare della franchigia.

**disgorge,** *vb.* vomitare; (*intr.*) sgorgare.

**disgrace,** 1. *n.* disgràzia *f.*, sfavore *m.*, disonore *m.* 2. *vb.* disonorare.

**disgraceful,** *adj.* disonorante.

**disgruntled,** *adj.* scontento.

**disguise,** 1. *n.* travestimento *m.* 2. *vb.* travestire.

**disgust,** 1. *n.* disgusto *m.* 2. *vb.* disgustare.

**dish,** *n.* piatto *m.*

**dishcloth,** *n.* strofinàccio (per piatti) *m.*

**dishearten,** *vb.* scoraggiare.

**dishonest,** *adj.* disonèsto.

**dishonesty,** *n.* disonestà *f.*

**dishonor,** 1. *n.* disonore *m.* 2. *vb.* disonorare.

**dishonorable,** *adj.* disonorévole.

**dish-towel,** *n.* asciugapiatti *m.*

**disillusion,** 1. *n.* disillusione *f.* 2. *vb.* disillúdere.

**disinfect,** *vb.* disinfettare.

**disinfectant,** *n.* disinfettante *m.*

**disinherit,** *vb.* diseredare.

**disintegrate,** *vb.* disintegrare.

**disinterested,** *adj.* disinteressato.

**disjointed,** *adj.* sconnèsso.

**disk,** *n.* disco *m.*

**dislike,** 1. *n.* antipatìa *f.* 2. *vb.* non piacere (with English subject as indirect object).

**dislocate,** *vb.* slogare.

**dislodge,** *vb.* sloggiare.

**disloyal,** *adj.* sleale.

**disloyalty,** *n.* slealtà *f.*

**dismal,** *adj.* melancònico.

**dismantle,** *vb.* smantellare.

**dismay,** 1. *n.* costernazione *f.* 2. *vb.* costernare.

**dismember,** *vb.* smembrare.

**dismiss,** *vb.* congedare, diméttere.

**dismissal,** *n.* congedo *m.*

**dismount,** *vb.* smontare.

**disobedience,** *n.* disubbidiènza *f.*

**disobedient,** *adj.* disobbediènte.

**disobey,** *vb.* disubbidire.

**disorder,** 1. *n.* disòrdine *m.* 2. *vb.* disordinare.

**disorderly,** *adj.* disordinato.

**disorganize,** *vb.* disorganizzare.

**disown,** *vb.* disconóscere.

**disparage,** *vb.* disprezzare.

**disparate,** *adj.* disparato.

**disparity,** *n.* disparità *f.*

**dispassionate,** *adj.* spassionato.

**dispatch,** see **despatch**.

**dispatcher,** *n.* speditore *m.*

**dispel,** *vb.* dissipare.

**dispensable,** *adj.* dispensàbile.

**dispensary,** *n.* dispensàrio *m.*

**dispensation,** *n.* dispensazione *f.*

**dispense,** *vb.* dispensare; (**d. from**) esentare da.

**dispersal,** *n.* dispersione *f.*

**disperse,** *vb.* dispèrdere.

**displace**, *vb.* spostare.

**displaced person**, *n.* rifugiato *m.*

**displacement**, *n.* spostamento *m.*; (ship) dislocamento *m.*

**display**, 1. *n.* esibizione *f.*; (showing off) ostentazione *f.* 2. *vb.* esibire, ostentare.

**displease**, *vb.* dispiacere (a).

**displeasure**, *n.* dispiacere *m.*

**disposable**, *adj.* disponibile.

**disposal**, *n.* disposizione *f.*

**dispose**, *vb.* disporre.

**disposition**, *n.* disposizione *f.*

**dispossess**, *vb.* spodestare.

**disproof**, *n.* confutazione *f.*

**disproportion**, *n.* sproporzione *f.*

**disproportionate**, *adj.* sproporzionato.

**disprove**, *vb.* confutare.

**disputable**, *adj.* disputàbile.

**dispute**, 1. *n.* disputa *f.* 2. *vb.* disputare.

**disqualification**, *n.* squalìfica *f.*

**disqualify**, *vb.* squalificare.

**disregard**, 1. *n.* indifferènza *f.*, 2. *vb.* trascurare.

**disrepair**, *n.* dilapidazione *f.*

**disreputable**, *adj.* disonorévole.

**disrespect**, *n.* mancanza di rispètto *f.*

**disrespectful**, *adj.* irrispettoso.

**disrobe**, *vb.* svestirsi.

**disrupt**, *vb.* causare una scissione in.

**dissatisfaction**, *n.* insoddisfazione *f.*

**dissatisfy**, *vb.* non soddisfare.

**dissection**, *n.* dissezione *f.*

**dissect**, *vb.* dissecare.

**dissemble**, *vb.* dissimulare.

**disseminate**, *vb.* disseminare.

**dissension**, *n.* dissènso *m.*

**dissent**, 1. *n.* dissènso *m.* 2. *vb.* dissentire.

**dissertation**, *n.* dissertazione *f.*

**disservice**, *n.* disservizio *m.*

**dissimilar**, *adj.* dissìmile.

**dissipate**, *vb.* dissipare.

**dissipated**, *adj.* dissoluto.

**dissipation**, *n.* dissipazione *f.*, dissolutezza *f.*

**dissociate**, *vb.* dissociare.

**dissolute**, *adj.* dissoluto.

**dissoluteness**, *n.* dissolutezza *f.*

**dissolution**, *n.* dissoluzione *f.*

**dissolve**, *vb.* dissòlvere, sciògliere.

**dissonance**, *n.* dissonanza *f.*

**dissonant**, *adj.* dissonante.

**dissuade**, *vb.* dissuadere.

**distance**, *n.* distanza *f.*

**distant**, *adj.* distante, lontano; (be d.) distare.

**distaste**, *n.* disgusto *m.*

**distasteful**, *adj.* disgustoso.

**distemper**, *n.* indisposizione *f.*

**distend**, *vb.* distèndere.

**distill**, *vb.* distillare.

**distillation**, *n.* distillazione *f.*.

**distiller**, *n.* distillatore *m.*

**distillery**, *n.* distillatòrio *m.*

**distinct**, *adj.* distinto.

**distinction**, *n.* distinzione *f.*

**distinctive**, *adj.* distintivo.

**distinctly**, *adv.* distintamente.

**distinguish**, *vb.* distìnguere.

**distort**, *vb.* distòrcere.

**distract**, *vb.* distrarre.

**distraction**, *n.* distrazione *f.*

**distraught**, *adj.* pazzo.

**distress**, 1. *n.* afflizione *f.* 2. *vb.* afflìggere.

**distribute**, *vb.* distribuire.

**distribution**, *n.* distribuzione *f.*

**distributor**, *n.* distributore *m.*

**district**, *n.* distretto *m.*

**distrust**, 1. *n.* sfiducia *f.* 2. *vb.* non fidarsi di.

**distrustful**, *adj.* sospettoso.

**disturb**, *vb.* disturbare.

**disturbance**, *n.* disturbo *m.*

**disunite**, *vb.* disunire.

**disuse**, *n.* disuso *m.*

**ditch**, *n.* fosso *m.*, fossato *m.*

**ditto**, *n.* lo stesso *m.*

**diva**, *n.* diva *f.*

**divan**, *n.* divano *m.*

**dive**, 1. *n.* tuffo *m.* 2. *vb.* tuffarsi.

**dive-bomber**, *n.* picchiatore *m.*, tuffatore *m.*

**diver**, *n.* tuffatore *m.*

**diverge**, *vb.* divèrgere.

**divergence**, *n.* divergènza *f.*

**divergent**, *adj.* divergènte.

**diverse**, *adj.* divèrso.

**diversion**, *n.* diversione *f.*

**diversity**, *n.* diversità *f.*

**divert**, *vb.* (turn away) stornare; (amuse) divertire.

**divest**, *vb.* spogliare.

**divide,** *vb.* divìdere.

**dividend,** *n.* dividèndo *m.*

**divine, 1.** *adj.* divino. **2.** *vb.* divinare.

**divinity,** *n.* divinità *f.*

**divisible,** *adj.* divisìbile.

**division,** *n.* divisione *f.*, scissione *f.*

**divorce, 1.** *n.* divòrzio *m.* **2.** *vb.* divorziare.

**divorcée,** *n.* divorziata *f.*

**divulge,** *vb.* divulgare.

**dizziness,** *n.* vertìgine *f.*, stordimento *m.*

**dizzy,** *adj.* vertiginoso, stordito.

**do,** *vb.* fare; **(how do you do?)** come sta?

**docile,** *adj.* dòcile.

**dock,** *n.* bacino *m.*

**docket,** *n.* etichetta *f.*; (legal) elenco *m.*

**dockyard,** *n.* arsenale *m.*

**doctor,** *n.* dottore *m.*, mèdico *m.*

**doctorate,** *n.* dottorato *m.*

**doctrinaire,** *adj.* dottrinàrio.

**doctrine,** *n.* dottrina *f.*

**document, 1.** *n.* documento *m.* **2.** *vb.* documentare.

**documentary,** *adj.* documentàrio.

**documentation,** *n.* documentazione *f.*

**dodge,** *vb.* elùdere, schivare.

**doe,** *n.* cèrva *f.*

**doeskin,** *n.* pelle di cèrva *f.*

**dog,** *n.* cane *m.*

**dogged,** *adj.* ostinato, tenace.

**doggerel,** *n.* versucci *m.pl.*

**doghouse,** *n.* canile *m.*

**dogma,** *n.* dògma *m.*

**dogmatic,** *adj.* dogmàtico.

**dogmatism,** *n.* dogmatismo *m.*

**doily,** *n.* tovagliolino *m.*

**doldrum,** *n.* **(in the d.s)** *adj.* calmo.

**dole,** *n.* elemòsina *f.* **2.** *vb.* **(d. out)** distribuire.

**doleful,** *adj.* triste.

**doll,** *n.* bàmbola *f.*, pupàttola *f.*

**dollar,** *n.* dòllaro *m.*

**dolorous,** *adj.* doloroso.

**dolphin,** *n.* delfino *m.*

**domain,** *n.* domìnio *m.*

**dome,** *n.* cùpola *f.*

**domestic,** *adj.* domèstico.

**domesticate,** *vb.* domesticare.

**domicile,** *n.* domicìlio *m.*

**dominance,** *n.* predomìnio *m.*

**dominant,** *adj.* dominante.

**dominate,** *vb.* dominare.

**domination,** *n.* dominazione *f.*

**domineer,** *vb.* spadroneggiare.

**dominion,** *n.* dominio *m.*

**domino,** *n.* dòmino *m.*

**don,** *vb.* indossare.

**donate,** *vb.* donare.

**donation,** *n.* donazione *f.*

**done,** *adj.* fatto; (food) còtto.

**donkey,** *n.* àsino *m.*, somaro *m.*

**don't,** *vb.* non fare.

**doom, 1.** *n.* (condemnation) condanna *f.*; (fate) destino *m.* **2.** *vb.* condannare.

**doomsday,** *n.* giorno del giudìzio universale *m.*

**door,** *n.* pòrta *f.*; (auto) portièra *f.*

**doorman,** *n.* portinaio *m.*

**door-mat,** *n.* stuoìno *m.*

**doorstep,** *n.* gradino della pòrta *m.*

**doorway,** *n.* vano della pòrta *m.*

**dope,** *n.* (drug) narcòtico *m.*; (fool) imbecìlle *m.*

**dormant,** *adj.* inattivo.

**dormer,** *n.* abbaìno *m.*

**dormitory,** *n.* dormitòrio *m.*

**dosage,** *n.* dosatura *f.*

**dose, 1.** *n.* dòse *f.* **2.** *vb.* dosare.

**dossier,** *n.* incartamento *m.*

**dot,** *n.* punto *m.*

**dotage,** *n.* rimbambimento *m.*

**dote,** *vb.* esser rimbambito; **(d. upon)** adorare.

**double, 1.** *n.* adj. dóppic (*m.*). **2.** *vb.* doppiare.

**double-breasted,** *adj.* a dóppio pètto.

**double-cross,** *vb.* ingannare.

**double-dealing,** *n.* duplicità *f.*

**double time,** *n.* passo di càrica *m.*

**doubly,** *adv.* doppiamente.

**doubt, 1.** *n.* dùbbio *m.* **2.** *vb.* dubitare.

**doubtful,** *adj.* dùbbio, dubbioso.

**doubtless,** *adv.* sènza dùbbio.

**dough,** *n.* pasta *f.*

**dour,** *adj.* severo.

**douse,** *vb.* spègnere.

**dove,** *n.* colombo *m.*

**dowager,** *n.* vècchia ricca e tirànnica *f.*

**dowdy,** *adj.* sciatto.

**dowel**, *n.* tassèllo *m.*

**down, 1.** *n.* (on face: bird) pelùria *f.*; (feathers) piumino *m.* **2.** *adv.* giù. **3.** *prep.* giù per.

**downcast**, *adj.* abbassato.

**downfall**, *n.* rovina *f.*

**downhearted**, *adj.* scoraggiato.

**downhill**, *adv.* in discesa.

**down payment**, *n.* anticipo *m.*

**downpour**, *n.* rovèscio di pioggia *m.*

**downright**, *adj.* chiaro, completo.

**downstairs**, *adv.* giù per le scale.

**downtown**, *n.* centro della città *m.*

**downtrodden**, *adj.* opprèsso.

**downward**, *adv.* in giù.

**downy**, *adj.* coperto di pelùria.

**dowry**, *n.* dòte *f.*

**doze, 1.** *n.* sonnellino *m.,* pisolino *m.* **2.** *vb.* sonnecchiare.

**dozen**, *n.* dozzina *f.*

**drab**, *adj.* grigio.

**draft, 1.** *n.* (plan) abbozzo *m.*; (money) tratta *f.*; (ship) pescàggio *m.*; (air) corrènte d'aria *f.*; (military service) servizio militare *m.* **2.** *vb.* (draw up) redigere.

**draftee**, *n.* rècluta *f.*

**draftsman**, *n.* disegnatore *m.*

**drafty**, *adj.* pièno di corrènti d'ària.

**drag**, *vb.* trascinare.

**dragnet**, *n.* giàcchio *m.*

**dragon**, *n.* dragone *m.*

**drain, 1.** *n.* fogna *f.* **2.** *vb.* scolare.

**drainage**, *n.* drenàggio *m.*

**dram**, *n.* dramma *m.*

**drama**, *n.* dramma *m.*

**dramatic**, *adj.* drammàtico.

**dramatics**, *n.* drammàtica *f.*

**dramatist**, *n.* drammaturgo *m.*

**dramatize**, *vb.* drammatizzare.

**dramaturgy**, *n.* drammaturgia *f.*

**drape, 1.** *n.* drappéggio *m.* **2.** *vb.* drappeggiare.

**drapery**, *n.* drappéggio *m.*

**drastic**, *adj.* dràstico.

**draught**, see **draft**.

**draw**, *vb.* (pull) tirare; (pic-

ture) disegnare; **(d. back)** ritirarsi; **(d. up)** stèndere.

**drawback**, *n.* svantàggio *m.*

**drawbridge**, *n.* ponte levatòio *m.*

**drawer**, *n.* cassetto *m.*

**drawing**, *n.* (picture) disegno *m.*; (lottery) sortéggio *m.*

**drawl**, *vb.* parlare lentamente.

**dray**, *n.* carro *m.*

**drayhorse**, *n.* cavallo da tiro *m.*

**drayman**, *n.* carrettière *m.*

**dread, 1.** *n.* timore *m.* **2.** *vb.* temere.

**dreadful**, *adj.* terrìbile.

**dreadfully**, *adv.* terribilmente.

**dream, 1.** *n.* sogno *m.* **2.** *vb.* sognare.

**dreamer**, *n.* sognatore *m.*

**dreamy**, *adj.* vago.

**dreary**, *adj.* fosco.

**dredge, 1.** *n.* draga *f.* **2.** *vb.* dragare.

**dregs**, *n.* fèccia *f.sg.*

**drench**, *vb.* inzuppare.

**dress, 1.** *n.* vestito *m.,* àbito *m.* **2.** *vb.* vestire.

**dresser**, *n.* credènza *f.*

**dressing**, *n.* (food) condimento *m.*; (medical) bende *f.pl.*

**dressing gown**, *n.* vestàglia *f.*

**dressmaker**, *n.* sarta da dònna *f.*

**dress rehearsal**, *n.* pròva generale *f.*

**drier**, *n.* essiccatòio *m.*

**drift, 1.** *n.* deriva *f.* **2.** *vb.* andare alla deriva.

**driftwood**, *n.* legno flottante *m.*

**drill, 1.** *n.* (tool) tràpano *m.*; (practice) esercitazione *f.* **2.** *vb.* trapanare; esercitare.

**drink, 1.** *n.* bevanda *f.* bìbita *f.* **2.** *vb.* bere.

**drinkable**, *adj.* bevìbile.

**drip**, *vb.* gocciolare.

**dripping**, *n.* gocciamento *m.*

**drive, 1.** *n.* (ride) passeggiata in carrozza *f.*; (avenue) viale *m.* **2.** *vb.* costrìngere; (auto) guidare.

**drivel, 1.** *n.* bava *f.* **2.** *vb.* sbavare.

**driver**, *n.* conducènte *m.*; autista *m.*

**driveway**, *n.* viale *m.*

**drizzle, 1.** *n.* pioggerella *f.* **2.** *vb.* piovigginare.

**dromedary,** *n.* dromedàrio *m.*

**drone, 1.** *n.* (bee) fuco *m.* (hum) ronzìo *m.* **2.** *vb.* ronzare.

**droop,** *vb.* abbattersi.

**drop, 1.** *n.* góccia *f.* **2.** *vb.* (fall) cadere; (let fall) lasciar cadere.

**dropper,** *n.* contagocce *m.*

**dropsy,** *n.* idropisìa *f.*

**drought,** *n.* siccità *f.*

**drove,** *n.* mandra *f.*

**drown,** *vb.* annegare.

**drowse,** *vb.* sonnecchiare, assopirsi.

**drowsiness,** *n.* sonnolènza *f.*

**drowsy,** *adj.* sonnolènto.

**drudge,** *vb.* lavorare duramente.

**drudgery,** *n.* lavoro monòtono *m.*

**drug,** *n.* dròga *f.*

**druggist,** *n.* farmacista *m.*

**drug store,** *n.* farmacìa *f.*

**drum,** *n.* tamburo *m.*

**drum major,** *n.* tamburo maggiore *m.*

**drummer,** *n.* tamburo *m.*

**drumstick,** *n.* (*lit.*) bacchetta del tamburo *m.*; (chicken) gamba di pollo *f.*

**drunk,** *adj.* ubbriaco.

**drunkard,** *n.* ubbriacone *m.*

**drunken,** *adj.* ubbriaco.

**drunkenness,** *n.* ubbriachezza *f.*

**dry, 1.** *adj.* secco, asciutto. **2.** *vb.* seccare, asciugare.

**dry cell,** *n.* pila a secco *f.*

**dry-clean,** *vb.* pulire a secco.

**dry-cleaner,** *n.* tintore *m.*

**dry-cleaning,** *n.* pulitura a secco *f.*

**dry dock,** *n.* bacino di carenàggio *m.*

**dry goods,** *n.* stoffe *f.pl.*; tessuti *m.pl.*

**dryness,** *n.* secchezza *f.*

**dual,** *n. and adj.* duale (*m.*)

**dualism,** *n.* dualismo *m.*

**dubious,** *adj.* dùbbio.

**duchess,** *n.* duchessa *f.*

**duchy,** *n.* ducato *m.*

**duck, 1.** *n.* ànitra *f.* **2.** *vb.* tuffare.

**duct,** *n.* canale *m.*

**ductile,** *adj.* dùttile.

**dud,** *n.* bomba inesplòsa *f.*; (failure) fiasco *m.*

**due,** *adj.* dèbito, dovuto; (fall due) scadere.

**duel, 1.** *n.* duèllo *m.* **2.** *vb.* duellare.

**duelist,** *n.* duellante *m.*

**dues,** *n.* quòta *f.*; (tax) diritti *m.*

**duet,** *n.* duetto *m.*

**duffle bag,** *n.* zàino *m.*

**dugout,** *n.* trincèa *f.*

**duke,** *n.* duca *m.*

**dukedom,** *n.* ducato *m.*

**dulcet,** *adj.* armonioso.

**dull, 1.** *adj.* monòtono, ottuso, insulso. **2.** *vb.* ottùndere.

**dullard,** *n.* stùpido *m.*

**dullness,** *n.* monotonìa *f.*, ottusità *f.*

**duly,** *adv.* debitamente.

**dumb,** *adj.* muto; (stupid) sciocco.

**dumbfound,** *vb.* sbalordire.

**dumbwaiter,** *n.* calapranzi *m.*, calapiatti *m.*

**dummy,** *n.* fantòccio *m.*

**dump,** *vb.* scaricare.

**dumpling,** *n.* gnòcco *m.*

**dun,** *adj.* grìgio fosco.

**dunce,** *n.* stolto *m.*

**dune,** *n.* duna *f.*

**dung,** *n.* stèrco *m.*, ietame *m.*

**dungarees,** *n.* tuta *f.sg.*

**dungeon,** *n.* prigione sotterrànea *f.*

**dunk,** *vb.* tuffare, inzuppare.

**dupe,** *n.* credulone *m.*

**duplex,** *n.* dóppio.

**duplicate,** *vb.* duplicare.

**duplication,** *n.* duplicazione *f.*

**duplicity,** *n.* duplicità *f.*

**durable,** *adj.* duràbile.

**durability,** *n.* durabilità *f.*

**duration,** *n.* durata *f.*

**duress,** *n.* coercizione *f.*

**during,** *prep.* durante.

**dusk,** *n.* crepùscolo *m.*

**dusky,** *adj.* fosco.

**dust,** *n.* pólvere *m.*; (sweepings) spazzatura *f.*

**dustpan,** *n.* paletta per spazzature *f.*

**dusty,** *adj.* polveroso.

**Dutch,** *adj.* olandese.

**Dutchman,** *n.* olandese *m.*

**dutiful,** *adj.* obbediènte.

**dutifully,** *adv.* con ubbidiènza.

**duty,** *n.* dovere *m.*; (tax) imposta *f.*

**dwarf,** *n.* nano *m.*
**dwell,** *vb.* abitare; **(d. upon)** diffóndersi su.
**dweller,** *n.* abitante *m.*
**dwelling,** *n.* abitazione *f.*, dimora *f.*
**dwindle,** *vb.* diminuire.
**dye, 1.** *n.* tintura *f.* **2.** *vb.* tíngere.
**dyer,** *n.* tintore *m.*

**dyestuff,** *n.* matèria colorante *f.*
**dynamic,** *adj.* dinàmico.
**dynamics,** *n.* dinàmica *f.*
**dynamite,** *n.* dinamite *f.*
**dynamo,** *n.* dìnamo *f.*
**dynasty,** *n.* dinastìa *f.*
**dysentery,** *n.* dissenterìa *f.*
**dyspepsia,** *n.* dispepsìa *f.*
**dyspeptic,** *adj.* dispèptico.

# E

**each,** *adj.* ogni.
**each one,** *pron.* ciascuno, cadaùno.
**each other,** *pron.* l'un l'altro; or use reflexive.
**eager,** *adj.* bramoso, impaziènte.
**eagerly,** *adv.* bramosamente, impazientemente.
**eagerness,** *n.* brama *f.*, impaziènza *f.*
**eagle,** *n.* àquila *f.*
**eaglet,** *n.* aquilòtto *m.*
**ear,** *n.* orécchio *m.*; **(grain)** spiga *f.*
**earache,** *n.* mal d'orecchi. (*m.*)
**eardrum,** *n.* tìmpano *m.*
**earl,** *n.* conte *m.*
**early,** *adv.* di buon'ora, prèsto.
**earmark,** *vb.* riservare.
**earn,** *vb.* guadagnare; **(deserve)** meritare.
**earnest,** *adj.* sèrio; **(in e.)** sul sèrio.
**earnestly,** *adv.* seriamente.
**earnestness,** *n.* serietà *f.*
**earnings,** *n.* guadagni *m.pl.*
**earphone,** *n.* cùffia *f.*
**earring,** *n.* orecchino *m.*
**earshot,** *n.* portata di voce *f.*
**earth,** *n.* tèrra *f.*
**earthenware,** *n.* stovíglie *f.pl.*
**earthly,** *adj.* terreno.
**earthquake,** *n.* terremòto *m.*
**earthworm,** *n.* lombrico *m.*
**earthy,** *adj.* terreno.
**ease, 1.** *n.* agio *m.*, còmodo *m.* **2.** *vb.* sollevare.
**easel,** *n.* cavalletto *m.*

**easily,** *adv.* facilmente.
**easiness,** *n.* facilità *f.*
**east,** *n.* èst *m.*, oriènte *m.*
**Easter,** *n.* Pasqua *f.*
**easterly,** *adj.* ad est, da est.
**eastern,** *adj.* orientale.
**eastward,** *adv.* vèrso èst.
**easy,** *adj.* fàcile.
**easygoing,** *adj.* noncurante.
**eat,** *vb.* mangiare.
**eatable,** *adj.* mangiàbile.
**eaves,** *n.* gronda *f.sg.*
**eavesdrop,** *vb.* origliare.
**ebb, 1.** *n.* riflusso *m.*; **(ebb-tide)** bassa marèa *f.* **2.** *vb.* rifluire.
**ebony,** *n.* èbano *m.*
**ebullient,** *adj.* esuberante.
**eccentric,** *adj.* eccèntrico.
**eccentricity,** *n.* eccentricità *f.*
**ecclesiastic,** *n. and adj.* ecclesiàstico (*m.*)
**ecclesiastical,** *adj.* ecclesiàstico.
**echelon,** *n.* scaglione *m.*
**echo, 1.** *n.* èco *m.* **2.** *vb.* echeggiare.
**eclipse, 1.** *n.* eclissi *f.* **2.** *vb.* eclissare.
**economic,** *adj.* econòmico.
**economical,** *adj.* econòmico.
**economics,** *n.* economìa polìtica *f.*
**economist,** *n.* economista *m.*
**economize,** *vb.* economizzare.
**economy,** *n.* economìa *f.*
**ecru,** *adj.* (colore di) seta cruda.
**ecstasy,** *n.* èstasi *f.*
**eczema,** *n.* eczèma *f.*

**eddy**, *n.* vòrtice *m.*

**edge**, *n.* bordo *m.*, màrgine *m.*; orlo *m.*

**edging**, *n.* orlatura *f.*

**edgy**, *adj.* irritàbile.

**edible**, *adj.* mangiàbile.

**edict**, *n.* editto *m.*

**edifice**, *n.* edifìcio *m.*

**edify**, *vb.* edificare.

**edit**, *vb.* (journal) dirìgere; (book) curare l'edizione di.

**edition**, *n.* edizione *f.*

**editor**, *n.* (journal) direttore *m.*

**editorial**, **1.** *n.* artìcolo di fondo *m.* **2.** *adj.* editoriale.

**educate**, *vb.* educare.

**education**, *n.* educazione *f.*

**educational**, *adj.* educativo.

**educator**, *n.* educatore *m.*

**eel**, *n.* anguilla *f.*

**efface**, *vb.* cancellare.

**effect**, **1.** *n.* effètto *m*; (in e.) effettivamente. **2.** *vb.* effettuare.

**effective**, *adj.* effettivo.

**effectively**, *adv.* effettivamente.

**effectiveness**, *n.* effettività *f.*

**effectual**, *adj.* efficace.

**effeminate**, *adj.* effeminato.

**effervescence**, *n.* effervescènza *f.*

**effete**, *adj.* effeminato.

**efficacious**, *adj.* efficace.

**efficacy**, *n.* efficàcia *f.*

**efficiency**, *n.* efficiènza *f.*

**efficient**, *adj.* efficiènte.

**efficiently**, *adv.* efficientemente.

**effigy**, *n.* effìgie *f.*

**effort**, *n.* sforzo *m.*; (make an e.) sforzarsi.

**effortless**, *adj.* sènza sforzo.

**effrontery**, *n.* sfrontatezza *f.*

**effulgent**, *adj.* risplendènte.

**effusive**, *adj.* espansivo.

**egg**, *n.* uòvo *m.*

**eggplant**, *n.* melanzana *f.*

**ego**, *n.* ìo *m.*

**egoism**, *n.* egoìsmo *m.*

**egotism**, *n.* egotismo *m.*

**egotist**, *n.* egotista *m.*

**Egypt**, *n.* l'Egitto *m.*

**Egyptian**, *adj.* egiziano.

**eight**, *num.* òtto.

**eighteen**, *num.* diciòtto.

**eighteenth**, *adj.* diciottèsimo, decimottavo.

**eighth**, *adj.* ottavo.

**eightieth**, *num.* ottantèsimo.

**eighty**, *num.* ottanta.

**either**, **1.** *pron.* l'uno o

l'altro. **2.** *conj.* o; od; sia; (either . . . or) o . . . . o; sia . . . . che.

**ejaculate**, *vb.* (med.) ciaculare; (fig.) esclamare.

**eject**, *vb.* espèllere.

**ejection**, *n.* espulsione *f.*

**eke out**, *vb.* supplire a.

**elaborate**, **1.** *adj.* elaborato. **2.** *vb.* elaborare.

**elapse**, *vb.* trascórrere.

**elastic**, *n. and adj.* elàstico (*m.*)

**elasticity**, *n.* elasticità *f.*

**elate**, *vb.* esaltare.

**elated**, *adj.* esaltato.

**elation**, *n.* esaltazione *f.*

**elbow**, *n.* gòmito *m.*

**elbowroom**, *n.* spàzio lìbero *m.*

**elder**, **1.** *n.* (older person) maggiore *m.*; (tree) sambuco *m.* **2.** *adj.* maggiore.

**elderberry**, *n.* frutto del sambuco *m.*

**elderly**, *adj.* vècchio.

**eldest**, *adj.* (il) maggiore.

**elect**, *vb.* elèggere.

**election**, *n.* elezione *f.*

**electioneer**, *vb.* cercare voti.

**elective**, *adj.* elettivo.

**electorate**, *n.* votanti *m.pl.*

**electric**, **electrical**, *adj.* elèttrico.

**electric eel**, *n.* anguilla elèttrica *f.*; gimnòto *m.*

**electrician**, *n.* elettricista *m.*

**electricity**, *n.* elettricità *f.*

**electrocution**, *n.* elettrocuzione *f.*

**electrode**, *n.* elèttrodo *m.*

**electrolysis**, *n.* elettròlisi *f.*

**electron**, *n.* elettrone *m.*

**electronic**, *adj.* elettrònico.

**electronics**, *n.* elettrònica *f.*

**electroplating**, *n.* galvanoplàstica *f.*

**elegance**, *n.* eleganza *f.*

**elegant**, *adj.* elegante.

**elegiac**, *adj.* elegìaco.

**elegy**, *n.* elegìa *f.*

**element**, *n.* elemento *m.*

**elemental**, **elementary**, *adj.* elementare.

**elephant**, *n.* elefante *m.*

**elephantine**, *adj.* elefantesco.

**elevate**, *vb.* elevare.

**elevation**, *n.* elevazione *f.*

**elevator**, *n.* ascensore *m.*

**eleven**, *num.* ùndici.

**eleventh**, *adj.* undicèsimo.

**elf**, *n.* folletto *m.*

**elfin**, *adj.* di folletto.

**elicit,** vb. cavar fuòri.

**eligibility,** n. eleggibilità f.

**eligible,** adj. eleggibile.

**eliminate,** vb. eliminare.

**elimination,** n. eliminazione f.

**elixir,** n. elisìr m.

**elk,** n. alce m.

**elm,** n. olmo m.

**elocution,** n. elocuzione f.

**elongate,** vb. allungare.

**elope,** vb. fuggire.

**eloquence,** n. eloquènza f.

**eloquent,** adj. eloquènte.

**eloquently,** adv. eloquentemente.

**else, 1.** adj. altro. **2.** adv. altrimenti.

**elsewhere,** adv. altrove.

**elucidate,** vb. elucidare.

**elude,** vb. elùdere.

**emaciated,** adj. emaciato.

**emanate,** vb. emanare.

**emancipate,** vb. emancipare.

**emancipation,** n. emancipazione f.

**emancipator,** n. emancipatore m.

**emasculate,** vb. castrare.

**embalm,** n. imbalsamare.

**embankment,** n. àrgine m.

**embargo,** n. embargo m.

**embark,** vb. imbarcare.

**embarrass,** vb. imbarazzare.

**embarrassment,** n. imbarazzo m.

**embassy,** n. ambasciata f.

**embellish,** vb. abbellire.

**embellishment,** n. abbellimento m.

**embers,** n. brace f.sg.

**embezzle,** vb. appropriarsi fraudolentemente.

**embitter,** vb. amareggiare.

**emblazon,** vb. adornare, illustrare.

**emblem,** n. emblèma m.

**emblematic,** adj. emblemàtico.

**embody,** vb. incorporare.

**emboss,** vb. stampare in rilièvo.

**embrace, 1.** n. abbràccio m.; (sexual) amplèsso m. **2.** vb. abbracciare.

**embroider,** vb. ricamare.

**embroidery,** n. ricamo m.

**embroil,** vb. imbrogliare.

**embryo,** n. embrione m.

**embryology,** n. embriologia f.

**embryonic,** adj. embrionale.

**emend,** vb. emendare.

**emerald,** n. smeraldo m.

**emerge,** vb. emèrgere.

**emergency,** n. emergènza f.

**emergent,** adj. emergènte.

**emery,** n. smeriglio m.

**emetic,** n. and adj. emètico (m.)

**emigrant,** n. and adj. emigrante (m.)

**emigrate,** vb. emigrare.

**emigration,** n. emigrazione f.

**eminence,** n. eminènza f.

**eminent,** adj. eminènte.

**emissary,** n. emissàrio m.

**emit,** vb. eméttere.

**emollient,** n. and adj. emolliènte (m.)

**emolument,** n. emolumento m.

**emotion,** n. emozione f.

**emotional,** adj. emotivo; (easily moved) emozionàbile.

**emperor,** n. imperatore m.

**emphasis,** n. ènfasi f.

**emphasize,** vb. méttere in rilièvo.

**emphatic,** adj. enfàtico.

**empire,** n. impèro m.

**empirical,** adj. empìrico.

**employ, 1.** n. impiègo m., servizio m. **2.** vb. impiegare.

**employed,** adj. addetto.

**employee,** n. impiegato m., impiegata f.

**employer,** n. datore di lavoro m.; (boss) padrone m.

**employment,** n. impiègo m.

**empower,** vb. autorizzare.

**empress,** n. imperatrice f.

**emptiness,** n. vuòto m.

**empty, 1.** adj. vuòto. **2.** vb. vuotare.

**emulate,** vb. emulare.

**emulsion,** n. emulsione f.

**enable,** vb. méttere in grado di.

**enact,** vb. decretare.

**enactment,** n. decreto m.

**enamel, 1.** n. smalto m. **2.** vb. smaltare.

**enamor,** vb. innamorarsi.

**encampment,** n. accampamento m.

**encamp,** vb. accamparsi.

**encephalitis,** n. encefalite f.

**encephalon,** n. encèfalo m.

**enchant,** vb. incantare.

**enchanting,** adj. incantévole.

**enchantment,** n. incanto m.

**encircle,** vb. accerchiare.

**enclose,** vb. rinchiùdere; (with letter) acclùdere.

**enclosure,** n. recinto m.

**encompass**, vb. (surround) circondare; (cause) causare.

**encounter**, vb. 1. n. incontro m. 2. incontrare.

**encourage**, vb. incoraggiare, confortare.

**encouragement**, n. incoraggiamento m.

**encroach upon**, vb. usurpare.

**encyclical**, n. enciclica f.

**encyclopaedia**, n. enciclopedia f.

**endear**, vb. rèndere caro.

**endearment**, n. carezza f.

**endeavor**, 1. n. sforzo m. 2. vb. sforzarsi.

**endanger**, vb. méttere in pericolo.

**end**, 1. n. fine f., tèrmine m.; (aim) scòpo m. 2. adj. ùltimo. 3. vb. finire, terminare.

**endemic**, adj. endèmico.

**ending**, n. fine f.; (gramm.) desinènza f.

**endless**, adj. sènza fine.

**endocrine**, adj. endòcrino.

**endorse**, vb. firmare; (cheques, etc.) girare.

**endorsement**, n. girata f.

**endow**, vb. dotare.

**endowment**, n. dotazione f.

**endurance**, n. sopportazione f.

**endure**, vb. sopportare; (last) durare.

**enduring**, adj. durévole.

**enema**, n. clistère m.; (colonic irrigation) enteroclisma m.

**enemy**, n. and adj. nemico (m.)

**energetic**, adj. enèrgico.

**energy**, n. energìa f.

**enervate**, vb. snervare.

**enervation**, n. snervamento m.

**enfold**, vb. avvòlgere.

**enforce**, vb. eseguire.

**enforcement**, n. esecuzione f.

**enfranchise**, vb. affrancare.

**engage**, vb. (hire) prèndere a nolo; (attention) attrarre; (to get married) fidanzare.

**engaged**, adj. (to get married) fidanzato.

**engagement**, n. (to get married) fidanzamento m.; (date) appuntamento m.

**engaging**, adj. attraènte.

**engender**, vb. generare.

**engine**, n. màcchina f.; (locomotive) locomotiva f.

**engineer**, n. ingegnère m.; (train driver) macchinista m.

**engineering**, n. ingegneria f., gènio m.

**England**, n. Inghilterra f.

**English**, adj. inglese.

**Englishman**, n. Inglese m.

**Englishwoman**, n. Inglese f.

**engrave**, vb. incìdere.

**engraver**, n. incisore m.

**engraving**, n. incisione f.

**engross**, vb. (absorb) assorbire; (copy) copiare.

**enhance**, vb. aumentare, accréscere.

**enigma**, n. enimma m.

**enigmatic**, adj. enimmàtico.

**enjoin**, vb. (command) ingiùngere; (forbid) vietare.

**enjoy**, vb. godere.

**enjoyable**, adj. godìbile, piacévole.

**enjoyment**, n. godimento m.

**enlace**, vb. allacciare.

**enlarge**, vb. ingrandire.

**enlargement**, n. ingrandimento m.

**enlarger**, n. ingranditore m.

**enlighten**, vb. illuminare.

**enlightenment**, n. chiarimento m.

**enlist**, vb. arrolare.

**enlisted man**, n. uòmo di truppa m.

**enlistment**, n. arrolamento m.

**enliven**, vb. ravvivare.

**enmesh**, vb. invilluppare.

**enmity**, n. inimicizia f.

**ennoble**, vb. annobilire.

**ennui**, n. nòia f.

**enormity**, n. enormità f.

**enormous**, adj. enòrme.

**enough**, 1. adj. sufficiènte. 2. adv. abbastanza. 3. vb. (be e.) bastare.

**enrage**, vb. far arrabbiare.

**enrapture**, vb. estasiare.

**elusive**, adv. elusivo.

**enrich**, vb. arricchire.

**enroll**, vb. iscrìvere, registrare; (mil.) arruolare.

**enrollment**, n. iscrizione f., registrazione f.

**ensemble**, n. insième m.

**enshrine**, vb. méttere in un reliquàrio.

**ensign**, n. (flag) bandièra f., insegna f.; (rank) alfière m.

**enslave**, vb. asservire.

**ensnare,** vb. prèndere in tràppola.

**ensue,** vb. (follow) seguire; (happen) accadere.

**entail,** vb. comportare, richièdere.

**entangle,** vb. imbrogliare.

**enter,** vb. entrare.

**enterprise,** n. impresa f.

**enterprising,** adj. avventuroso.

**entertain,** vb. trattenére; (guests) accògliere; (amuse) divertire.

**entertainment,** n. trattenimento m.; (amusement) divertimento m.

**enthrall,** vb. incantare.

**enthusiasm,** n. entusiasmo m.

**enthusiast,** n. entusiasta m.

**enthusiastic,** adj. entusiàstico.

**entice,** vb. adescare.

**entire,** adj. intero.

**entirely,** adj. interamente.

**entirety,** n. totalità f.

**entitle,** vb. intitolare; (authorize) autorizzare.

**entity,** n. entità f.

**entomb,** vb. seppellire.

**entrails,** n. interiora f.pl.

**entrain,** vb. prèndere il treno.

**entrance,** n. entrata f., ingrèsso m.

**entrant,** n. concorrènte m.

**entrap,** vb. intrappolare.

**entreat,** vb. supplicare.

**entreaty,** n. sùpplica f.

**entrench,** vb. trincerare.

**entrepreneur,** n. imprenditore m.

**entrust,** vb. affidare.

**entry,** n. entrata f., ingrèsso m.

**enumerate,** vb. enumerare.

**enumeration,** n. enumerazione f.

**enunciate,** vb. enunciare.

**enunciation,** n. enunciazione f.

**envelop,** vb. avviluppare.

**envelope,** n. busta f.

**enviable,** adj. invidiàbile.

**envious,** adj. invidioso.

**environment,** n. ambiènte m.

**environs,** n. dintorni m.pl.

**envisage,** vb. figurarsi.

**envoy,** n. inviato m.

**envy,** 1. n. invidia f. 2. vb. invidiare.

**eon,** n. eternità f.

**ephemeral,** adj. effimero.

**epic,** 1. n. epopèa f. 2. adj. èpico.

**epicure,** n. epicurèo m.

**epidemic,** 1. n. epidemìa f. 2. adj. epidèmico.

**epidermis,** n. epidèrmide f.

**epigram,** n. epigramma m.

**epilepsy,** n. epilessìa f.

**epilogue,** n. epìlogo m.

**episode,** n. episòdio m.

**epistle,** n. epistola f.

**epitaph,** n. epitàffio m.

**epithet,** n. epìteto m.

**epitome,** n. epitome f.

**epitomize,** vb. epitomare.

**epoch,** n. època f.

**equable,** adj. èquo.

**equal,** 1. adj. uguale, pari. 2. vb. uguagliare.

**equality,** n. uguaglianza f.

**equalize,** vb. uguagliare.

**equanimity,** n. equanimità f.

**equate,** vb. uguagliare.

**equation,** n. equazione f.

**equator,** n. equatore m.

**equatorial,** adj. equatoriale.

**equestrian,** adj. equèstre.

**equidistant,** adj. equidistante.

**equilateral,** adj. equilaterale.

**equilibrate,** vb. equilibrare.

**equilibrium,** n. equilibrio m.

**equinox,** n. equinòzio m.

**equip,** vb. corredare, fornire.

**equipment,** n. equipàggio m., corrèdo m.

**equitable,** adj. èquo.

**equity,** n. equità f.

**equivalent,** adj. equivalente; (be e.) equivalere.

**equivocal,** adj. equìvoco.

**equivocate,** vb. giocare sull'equìvoco.

**era,** n. èra f.

**eradicate,** vb. sradicare.

**eradicator,** n. sradicatore m.

**erase,** vb. cancellare, raschiare.

**eraser,** n. raschino m., cancellino m.

**erasure,** n. cancellatura f.

**erect,** 1. adj. erètto. 2. vb. erìgere, costruire.

**erection,** n. erezione f., costruzione f.

**erectness,** n. posizione erètta f.

**ermine,** n. ermellino m.

**erode,** vb. eródere.

**erosion,** n. erosione f.

**erosive,** adj. erosivo.

**erotic,** adj. eròtico.

**err,** vb. errare.

**errand,** *n.* commissione *f.*

**errant,** *adj.* errante.

**erratic,** *adj.* erràtico.

**erroneous,** *adj.* erròneo.

**error,** *n.* errore *m.*

**erudite,** *adj.* erudito.

**erudition,** *n.* erudizione *f.*

**erupt,** *vb.* eruttare.

**eruption,** *n.* eruzione *f.*

**escalator,** *n.* scala mòbile *f.*

**escapade,** *n.* scappata *f.*

**escape,** **1.** *n.* fuga *f.*, scampo *m.* **2.** *vb.* sfuggire, scappare.

**escapism,** *n.* desidèrio di sfuggire alla realtà *m.*

**eschew,** *vb.* evitare.

**escort,** **1.** *n.* scòrta *f.* **2.** *vb.* scortare.

**escutcheon,** *n.* scudo *m.*

**Eskimo pie,** *n.* eschimese *f.*

**esophagus,** *n.* esòfago *m.*

**esoteric,** *adj.* esotèrico.

**especial,** *adj.* speciale.

**especially,** *adv.* specialmente.

**espionage,** *n.* spionàggio *m.*

**espousal,** *n.* sposalìzio *m.*

**espouse,** *vb.* sposare.

**essay,** **1.** *n.* saggio *m.* **2.** *vb.* provare.

**essayist,** *n.* saggista *m.*

**essence,** *n.* essènza *f.*

**essential,** *adj.* essenziale.

**essentially,** *adv.* essenzialmente.

**establish,** *vb.* stabilire.

**establishment,** *n.* stabilimento *m.*

**estate,** *n.* (inheritance) patrimònio *m.*; (possessions) bèni *m.pl.*; (condition) condizione *f.*, stato *m.*

**esteem,** **1.** *n.* stima *f.*

**estimable,** *adj.* stimàbile.

**estimate,** **1.** *n.* valutazione *f.*, stima *f.* **2.** *vb.* valutare, stimare.

**estimation,** *n.* stima *f.*, valutazione *f.*

**estrange,** *vb.* alienare.

**estuary,** *n.* estuàrio *m.*

**etching,** *n.* acquafòrte *f.*

**eternal,** *adj.* etèrno.

**eternity,** *n.* eternità *f.*

**ether,** *n.* ètere *m.*

**ethereal,** *adj.* etèreo.

**ethical,** *adj.* ètico.

**ethics,** *n.* ètica *f.*

**etiquette,** *n.* galatèo *m.*

**etymology,** *n.* etimologìa *f.*

**eucalyptus,** *n.* eucalitto *m.*

**eugenic,** *adj.* eugènico.

**eugenics,** *n.* eugenètica *f.*

**eulogize,** *vb.* elogiare.

**eulogy,** *n.* elògio *m.*

**eunuch,** *n.* eunuco *m.*

**euphonious,** *adj.* eufònico.

**Europe,** *n.* Europa *f.*

**European,** *n.* and *adj.* europèo (*m.*)

**euthanasia,** *n.* eutanasìa *f.*

**evacuate,** *vb.* evacuare.

**evade,** *vb.* evitare, elùdere.

**evaluate,** *vb.* valutare.

**evaluation,** *n.* valutazione *f.*

**evanescent,** *adj.* evanescènte.

**evangelist,** *n.* evangelista *m.*

**evaporate,** *vb.* evaporare.

**evaporation,** *n.* evaporazione *f.*

**evasion,** *n.* evasione *f.*

**evasive,** *adj.* evasivo.

**eve,** *n.* vigìlia *f.*

**even,** **1.** *adj.* pari, giusto, uniforme. **2.** *adv.* anche, perfino.

**evening,** *n.* sera *f.*

**evenness,** *n.* uniformità *f.*

**event,** *n.* avvenimento *m.*

**eventful,** *adj.* pièno di avvenimenti.

**eventual,** *adj.* finale.

**ever,** *adv.* sèmpre, mai.

**everglade,** *n.* palude *f.*

**evergreen,** *adj.* sempreverde.

**everlasting,** *adj.* sempiterno.

**every,** *adj.* ogni.

**everybody,** *pron.* ognuno.

**everyday,** *adj.* quotidiano.

**everyone,** *pron.* ognuno.

**everything,** *pron.* tutto.

**everywhere,** *adv.* dappertutto.

**evict,** *vb.* espèllere.

**eviction,** *n.* espulsione *f.*

**evidence,** *n.* evidènza *f.*

**evident,** *adj.* evidènte; (**be e.**) risultare.

**evidently,** *adv.* evidentemente.

**evil,** **1.** *n.* male *m.* **2.** *adj.* cattivo.

**evince,** *vb.* manifestare.

**eviscerate,** *vb.* sviscerare.

**evoke,** *vb.* evocare.

**evolution,** *n.* evoluzione *f.*

**evolutionist,** *n.* evoluzionista *m.*

**evolve,** *vb.* evòlvere.

**ewe,** *n.* pècora *f.*

**exact,** **1.** *adj.* esatto. **2.** *vb.* esìgere.

**exactly,** *adv.* esattamente.

**exaggerate,** *vb.* esagerare.

**exaggeration,** *n.* esagerazione *f.*

**exalt,** *vb.* esaltare.

**exaltation,** *n.* esaltazione *f.*

**examination,** *n.* esame *m.*

**examine,** *vb.* esaminare.

**example,** *n.* esèmpio *m.*

**exasperate,** *vb.* esasperare.

**exasperation,** *n.* esasperazione *f.*

**excavate,** *vb.* scavare.

**excavation,** *n.* scavo *m.*

**exceed,** *vb.* eccèdere, superare.

**exceedingly,** *adv.* estremamente.

**excel,** *vb.* eccèllere, superare.

**excellence,** *n.* eccellènza *f.*

**Excellency,** *n.* Eccellènza *f.*

**excellent,** *adj.* eccellènte.

**except, 1.** *vb.* eccettuare. **2.** *prep.* eccètto, salvo, tranne; **(e. for)** all'infuòri di.

**exception,** *n.* eccezione *f.*

**exceptional,** *adj.* eccezionale.

**excerpt,** *n.* brano *m.*

**excess,** *n.* eccèsso *m.*

**excessive,** *adj.* eccessivo.

**exchange, 1.** *n.* scàmbio *m.* **2.** *vb.* scambiare.

**exchangeable,** *adj.* scambiàbile.

**excise,** *n.* dàzio *m.*

**excitable,** *adj.* eccitàbile.

**excite,** *vb.* eccitare.

**excitement,** *n.* eccitamento *m.,* eccitazione *f.*

**exclaim,** *vb.* esclamare.

**exclamation,** *n.* esclamazione *f.*

**exclamation point or mark,** *n.* punto esclamativo.

**exclude,** *vb.* esclùdere.

**exclusion,** *n.* esclusione *f.*

**exclusive,** *adj.* esclusivo.

**excogitate,** *vb.* escogitare.

**excommunicate,** *vb.* scomunicare.

**excommunication,** *n.* scomùnica *f.*

**excoriate,** *vb.* escoriare.

**excrement,** *n.* escremento *m.*

**excruciating,** *adj.* tormentoso.

**exculpate,** *vb.* scolpare.

**excursion,** *n.* escursione *f.*

**excusable,** *adj.* scusàbile.

**excuse, 1.** *n.* scusa *f.* **2.** *vb.* scusare.

**execrable,** *adj.* escràbile.

**execute,** *vb.* eseguire; (kill legally) giustiziare.

**execution,** *n.* esecuzione *f.;* (legal killing) esecuzione capitale *f.*

**executioner,** *n.* bòia *m.,* carnéfice *m.*

**executive, 1.** *n.* amministratore *m.* **2.** *adj.* esecutivo.

**executor,** *n.* esecutore *m.*

**exemplary,** *adj.* esemplare.

**exemplify,** *vb.* esemplificare.

**exempt, 1.** *adj.* esènte. **2.** *vb.* esentare.

**exercise, 1.** *n.* esercìzio *m.* **2.** *vb.* esercitare.

**exert,** *vb.* esercitare.

**exertion,** *n.* sforzo *m.*

**exhale,** *vb.* esalare.

**exhaust,** *vb.* esaurire.

**exhaustion,** *n.* esaurimento *m.*

**exhaustive,** *adj.* esauriènte.

**exhibit, 1.** *n.* mostra *f.* **2.** *vb.* esibire, mostrare.

**exhibition,** *n.* esibizione *f.,* mostra *f.*

**exhibitionism,** *n.* esibizionismo *m.*

**exhilarate,** *vb.* esilarare.

**exhort,** *vb.* esortare.

**exhortation,** *n.* esortazione *f.*

**exhume,** *vb.* esumare.

**exigency,** *n.* esigènza *f.*

**exile, 1.** *n.* esilio *m.;* (person) fuoruscito *m.* **2.** *vb.* esiliare.

**exist,** *vb.* esìstere.

**existence,** *n.* esistènza *f.*

**existent,** *adj.* esistènte.

**exit,** *n.* uscita *f.*

**exodus,** *n.* èsodo *m.*

**exonerate,** *vb.* esonerare.

**exorbitant,** *adj.* esorbitante.

**exorcise,** *vb.* esorcizzare; (chase away) scacciare.

**exotic,** *adj.* esòtico.

**expand,** *vb.* espàndere.

**expanse,** *n.* distesa *f.*

**expansion,** *n.* espansione *f.*

**expansive,** *adj.* espansivo.

**expatiate,** *vb.* diffóndersi.

**expatriate,** *n.* espatriato *m.*

**expect,** *vb.* aspettarsi.

**expectancy,** *n.* aspettativa *f.*

**expectation,** *n.* aspettativa *f.*

**expectorate,** *vb.* espettorare.

**expediency,** *n.* opportunità *f.*

**expedient, 1.** *n.* espediènte *m.* **2.** *adj.* espediènte, opportuno.

**expedite,** *vb.* sbrigare.

**expedition,** *n.* spedizione *f.*

**expel,** *vb.* espèllere.

**expend,** *vb.* spèndere, consumare.

**expenditure,** *n.* spesa *f.*

**expense,** *n.* spesa *f.*

**expensive,** *adj.* costoso.

**expensively,** *adv.* costosaménte.

**experience, 1.** *n.* esperiènza *f.* **2.** *vb.* esperimentare.

**experienced,** *adj.* espèrto.

**experiment, 1.** *n.* esperiménto *m.* **2.** *vb.* sperimentare.

**experimental,** *adj.* sperimentale.

**expert,** *n. and adj.* espèrto (*m.*).

**expiate,** *vb.* espiare.

**expiration,** *n.* espirazione *f.*

**expire,** *vb.* espirare, morire.

**explain,** *vb.* spiegare.

**explanation,** *n.* spiegazione *f.*

**explanatory,** *adj.* esplicativo.

**expletive, 1.** *n.* bestémmia *f.* **2.** *adj.* espletivo.

**explicit,** *adj.* esplicito.

**explode,** *vb.* esplòdere, scoppiare.

**exploit,** *vb.* sfruttare.

**exploitation,** *n.* sfruttaménto *m.*

**exploration,** *n.* esplorazione *f.*

**exploratory,** *adj.* esploratòrio.

**explore,** *vb.* esplorare.

**explorer,** *n.* esploratore.

**explosion,** *n.* esplosione *f.*, scòppio *m.*

**explosive,** *n. and adj.* esplosivo (*m.*).

**exponent,** *n.* esponènte *m.*

**export, 1.** *n.* esportazione *f.* **2.** *vb.* esportare.

**exportation,** *n.* esportazione *f.*

**expose,** *vb.* esporre.

**exposé,** *n.* esposto *m.*, esposizione *f.*

**exposition,** *n.* esposizione *f.*

**expository,** *adj.* espositivo.

**expostulate,** *vb.* far rimostranze.

**exposure,** *n.* esposizione *f.*, rivelazione *f.*; (photography) pòsa *f.*

**expound,** *vb.* esporre.

**express, 1.** *n.* esprèsso; (train) direttìssimo *m.* **2.** *adj.* esprèsso. **3.** *vb.* esprìmere.

**expressage,** *n.* spese di traspòrto *f. pl.*

**expression,** *n.* espressione *f.*; (outlet) sfògo *m.*

**expressive,** *adj.* espressivo.

**expressly,** *adv.* espressaménte.

**expressman,** *n.* impiegato della compagnìa di traspòrti *m.*

**expropriate,** *vb.* espropriare.

**expulsion,** *n.* espulsione *f.*

**expunge,** *vb.* espùngere.

**expurgate,** *vb.* espurgare.

**exquisite,** *adj.* squisito.

**extant,** *adj.* esistènte.

**extemporaneous,** *adj.* estemporàneo.

**extend,** *vb.* estèndere; (in time) prolungare; prorogare.

**extension,** *n.* estensione *f.*; (in time) prolungamento *m.*, pròroga *f.*

**extensive,** *adj.* esteso.

**extensively,** *adv.* estesaménte.

**extent,** *n.* estensione *f.*, distesa *f.*

**extenuate,** *vb.* estenuare.

**exterior,** *adj.* esteriore.

**exterminate,** *vb.* sterminare.

**extermination,** *n.* sterminio *m.*

**external,** *adj.* estèrno; (foreign) èstero.

**extinct,** *adj.* estinto.

**extinction,** *n.* estinzione *f.*

**extinguish,** *vb.* estìnguere.

**extirpate,** *vb.* estirpare.

**extol,** *vb.* estòllere.

**extort,** *vb.* estòrcere.

**extortion,** *n.* estorsione *f.*

**extortioner,** *n.* ricattatore *m.*

**extra,** *adj.* extra, aggiunto, straordinàrio.

**extra-,** *prefix* estra-, stra-.

**extract, 1.** *n.* estratto. **2.** *vb.* estrarre.

**extraction,** *n.* estrazione *f.*; (race) stirpe *f.*

**extradite,** *vb.* estradare.

**extradition,** *n.* estradizione *f.*

**extraneous,** *adj.* estràneo.

**extraordinary,** *adj.* straordinàrio.

**extravagance,** *n.* stravaganza *f.*, prodigalità *f.*

**extravagant,** *adj.* stravagante, pròdigo.

**extravaganza,** *n.* rivista frìvola *f.*

**extreme,** *adj.* estrèmo.

**extremely,** *adv.* estremaménte.

**extremity,** *n.* estremità *f.*

**extricate,** *vb.* districare.

**extrovert,** *adj.* estrovertito.

**exuberant,** *adj.* esuberante.

**exudation,** *n.* essudato *m.*

**exult,** *vb.* esultare.

**exultant,** *adj.* esultante.

**eye,** *n.* òcchio *m.*

**eyeball**, *n.* glòbo dell'òcchio *m.*

**eyebrow**, *n.* sopracciglio *m.*

**eyeglass**, *n.* lènte *f.*

**eyeglasses**, *n.* occhiali *m. pl.*

**eyelash**, *n.* ciglio *m.*

**eyelet**, *n.* occhièllo *m.*

**eyelid**, *n.* pàlpebra *f.*

**eyesight**, *n.* vista *f.*

**eyewitness**, *n.* testimòne oculare *m.*

---

# F

**fable**, *n.* fàvola *f.*

**fabric**, *n.* (cloth) stòffa *f.*; (architecture) fàbbrica *f.*

**fabricate**, *vb.* fabbricare.

**fabrication**, *n.* fabbricazione *f.*; (lie) bugìa *f.*

**fabulous**, *adj.* favoloso.

**façade**, *n.* facciata *f.*

**face**, **1.** *n.* faccia *f.*, viso *m.* **2.** *vb.* fronteggiare, affrontare.

**facet**, *n.* faccetta *f.*

**facetious**, *adj.* facèto.

**face value**, *n.* valore nominale *m.*

**facial**, *adj.* faciale.

**facile**, *adj.* fàcile.

**facilitate**, *vb.* facilitare.

**facility**, *n.* facilità *f.*

**facing**, **1.** *n.* rivestitura *f.* **2.** *adv.* dirimpètto. **3.** *prep.* dirimpètto a.

**facsimile**, *n.* facsìmile *m.*

**fact**, *n.* fatto *m.*

**faction**, *n.* fazione *f.*

**factor**, *n.* fattore *m.*

**factory**, *n.* fàbbrica *f.*

**factual**, *adj.* obiettivo.

**faculty**, *n.* facoltà *f.*

**fad**, *n.* manìa *f.*

**fade**, *vb.* appassire; (lose color) impallidire.

**faeces**, *n.* fèccie *f. pl.*

**fagged**, *adj.* stanco.

**fail**, *n.* fallire, mancare; (in examination) èsser bocciato.

**failing**, **1.** *n.* debolezza *f.* **2.** *prep.* in mancanza di.

**faille**, *n.* fàglia *f.*

**failure**, *n.* fiasco *m.*, mancanza *f.*; (bankruptcy) fallimento *m.*

**faint**, **1.** *n.* svenimento *m.* **2.** *adj.* dèbole. **3.** *vb.* svenire.

**faintly**, *adv.* debolmente.

**fair**, **1.** *n.* fièra *f.* **2.** *adj.*

bèllo; (blond) biondo; (just) giusto, èquo.

**fairly**, *adv.* giustamente; (moderately) abbastanza.

**fairness**, *n.* giustezza *f.*

**fairy**, *n.* fata *f.*

**fairyland**, *n.* paese delle fate *m.*

**faith**, *n.* fède *f.*

**faithful**, *adj.* fedele.

**faithfulness**, *n.* fedeltà *f.*

**faithless**, *adj.* sènza fede.

**fake**, **1.** *n.* falso *m.* **2.** *vb.* falsificare.

**faker**, *n.* falsificatore *m.*

**falcon**, *n.* falcone *m.*

**falconry**, *n.* falconerìa *f.*

**fall**, **1.** *n.* caduta *f.*; (autumn) autunno *m.* **2.** *vb.* cadere; (fall asleep) addormentarsi; (fall due) scadere; (fall in love) innamorarsi; (fall upon) attaccare.

**fallacious**, *adj.* fallace.

**fallacy**, *n.* fallàcia *f.*

**fallible**, *adj.* fallìbile.

**fallow**, *adj.* a maggese; (f. field) maggese *m.*

**false**, *adj.* falso.

**falsehood**, *n.* bugìa *f.*

**falseness**, *n.* falsità *f.*

**falsetto**, *n.* falsetto *m.*

**falsification**, *n.* falsificazione *f.*

**falsify**, *vb.* falsificare.

**falter**, *vb.* esitare, incespicare.

**fame**, *n.* fama *f.*

**famed**, *adj.* famoso.

**familiar**, *adj.* familiare; (f. with) pràtico di.

**familiarity**, *n.* familiarità *f.*

**familiarize**, *vb.* familiarizzare.

**family**, *n.* famiglia *f.*; (f. tree) àlbero genealògico *m.*

**famine**, *n.* carestìa *f.*

**famished,** *adj.* affamato.
**famous,** *adj.* famoso.
**fan, 1.** *n.* ventàglio *m.*; (enthusiast) tifoso *m.* **2.** *vb.* sventolare.
**fanatic,** *n. and adj.* fanàtico (*m.*)
**fanatical,** *adj.* fanàtico.
**fanaticism,** *n.* fanatismo *m.*
**fanciful,** *adj.* immaginoso, capriccioso.
**fancy, 1.** *n.* immaginazione *f.* **2.** *adj.* di fantasia. **3.** *vb.* immaginare.
**fanfare,** *n.* fanfara *f.*
**fang,** *n.* zanna *f.*
**fantastic,** *adj.* fantàstico.
**fantasy,** *n.* fantasia *f.*
**far,** *adj. and adv.* lontano; (**as far as**) fino a; (**by far**) di gran lunga; (**how far?**) fin dove?; (**in so far as**) in quanto che; (**so far**) finora.
**faraway,** *adj. and adv.* lontano.
**farce,** *n.* farsa *f.*
**farcical,** *adj.* farsesco.
**fare, 1.** *n.* (price) tariffa *f.*; (passenger) passeggièro *m.*; (food) cibo *m.* **2.** *vb.* andare.
**farewell,** *n. and interj.* addìo (*m.*)
**far-fetched,** *adj.* ricercato.
**far-flung,** *adj.* esteso.
**farina,** *n.* farina *f.*
**farm,** *n.* fattoria *f.*
**farmer,** *n.* agricoltore *m.*, colòno *m.*
**farmhouse,** *n.* casa colònica *f.*
**farming,** *n.* agricultura *f.*
**farmyard,** *adj.* cortile *m.*
**far-reaching,** *adj.* esteso.
**far-sighted, be,** *vb.* aver vista lunga.
**farther,** *adv.* più lontano.
**farthest,** *adv.* il più lontano.
**fascinate,** *vb.* affascinare.
**fascination,** *n.* fàscino *m.*
**fascism,** *n.* fascismo *m.*
**fascist,** *n. and adj.* fascista (*m.* and *f.*)
**fashion,** *n.* mòda *f.*; (manner) manièra *f.*
**fashionable,** *adj.* alla mòda.
**fast, 1.** *n.* digiuno *m.* **2.** *adj.* (speedy) ràpido; (firm) fermo; (of clock) avanti. **3.** *vb.* digiunare. **4.** *adv.* (quickly) rapidamente; (firmly) fermamente.
**fasten,** *vb.* attaccare, fissare.

**fastener, fastening,** *n.* chiusura *f.*, fermatura *f.*
**fastidious,** *adj.* fastidioso.
**fat,** *n. and adj.* grasso (*m.*)
**fatal,** *adj.* fatale; (deadly) mortale.
**fatality,** *n.* fatalità *f.*
**fatally,** *adj.* fatalmente.
**fate,** *n.* fato *m.*
**fateful,** *adj.* fatale.
**father,** *n.* padre *m.*
**fatherhood,** *n.* paternità *f.*
**father-in-law,** *n.* suòcero *m.*
**fatherland,** *n.* pàtria *f.*
**fatherless,** *adj.* òrfano di padre.
**fatherly,** *adj.* paterno.
**fathom,** *n.* bràccio *m.* **2.** *vb.* scandagliare.
**fatigue, 1.** *n.* fatica *f.* **2.** *vb.* affaticare.
**fatten,** *vb.* ingrassare.
**fatty,** *adj.* grasso.
**fatuous,** *adj.* fàtuo.
**faucet,** *n.* rubinetto *m.*
**fault,** *n.* colpa *f.*; (defect) difetto *m.*, mènda *f.*
**faultfinding,** *n.* crìtica *f.*
**faultless,** *adj.* irreprensìbile.
**faultlessly,** *adv.* irreprensìbilmente.
**faulty,** *adj.* difettoso.
**favor, 1.** *n.* favore *m.* **2.** *vb.* favorire.
**favorable,** *adj.* favorévole, propìzio.
**favorite,** *n. and adj.* favorito (*m.*)
**favoritism,** *n.* favoritismo *m.*
**fawn, 1.** *n.* cerbiàttolo *m.* **2.** *vb.* (**f. upon**) adulare.
**faze,** *vb.* sconcertare.
**fear, 1.** *n.* paùra *f.*, timore *m.* **2.** *vb.* temere, aver paùra di.
**fearful,** *adj.* (person) pauroso, timoroso; (thing) spaventoso.
**fearless,** *adj.* intrèpido.
**fearlessness,** *n.* intrepidezza *f.*
**feasible,** *adj.* fattìbile.
**feast,** *n.* fèsta *f.*; (banquet) banchetto *n.*
**feat,** *n.* fatto *m.*, impresa *f.*
**feather,** *n.* penna *f.*, piuma *f.*
**feathered,** *adj.* pennuto, piumato.
**feathery,** *adj.* piumoso.
**feature,** *n.* tratto *m.*
**February,** *n.* febbraio *m.*
**fecund,** *adj.* fecondo.
**federal,** *adj.* federale.

**federation**, *n.* federazione *f.*

**fedora**, *n.* cappèllo flòscio *m.*

**fee**, *n.* (for professional services) onoràrio *m.;* (membership) quòta *f.;* (school) tassa *f.*

**feeble**, *adj.* débole.

**feeble-minded**, *adj.* débole di cervèllo.

**feebleness**, *n.* debolezza *f.*

**feed**, **1.** *n.* nutrimento *m.* **2.** *vb.* nutrire, alimentare.

**feel**, **1.** *n.* tatto *m.* **2.** *vb.* sentire.

**feeling**, *n.* sentimento *m.*

**feign**, *vb.* fingere.

**felicitate**, *vb.* felicitare.

**felicitous**, *adj.* felice.

**felicity**, *n.* felicità *f.*

**feline**, *adj.* felino.

**fell**, **1.** *adj.* malvàgio. **2.** *vb.* abbàttere.

**fellow**, *n.* indivìduo *m.;* (associate) sòcio *m.*

**fellowship**, *n.* borsa *f.*

**felon**, *n.* fellone *m.*

**felony**, *n.* fellonìa *f.*

**felt**, *n.* feltro *m.*

**female**, **1.** *n.* fémmina *f.* **2.** *adj.* femminile.

**feminine**, *adj.* femminile.

**femininity**, *n.* femminilità *f.*

**fence**, **1.** *n.* recinto *m.* **2.** *vb.* chiùdere con un recinto; (sword, foil) schermire.

**fencer**, *n.* schermidore *m.*

**fencing**, *n.* scherma *f.*

**fender**, *n.* (auto) parafango *m.*

**ferment**, **1.** *n.* fermento *m.* **2.** *vb.* fermentare.

**fermentation**, *n.* fermentazione *f.*

**fern**, *n.* felce *f.*

**ferocious**, *adj.* feroce.

**ferociously**, *adv.* ferocemente.

**ferocity**, *n.* feròcia *f.*

**ferry**, *n.* traghetto *m.*

**fertile**, *adj.* fèrtile.

**fertility**, *n.* fertilità *f.*

**fertilization**, *n.* fertilizzazione *f.*

**fertilize**, *vb.* fertilizzare.

**fertilizer**, *n.* fertilizzante *m.*

**fervency**, *n.* fervore *m.*

**fervent**, *adj.* fervente.

**fervently**, *adv.* ferventemente.

**fervid**, *adj.* fèrvido.

**fervor**, *n.* fervore *m.*

**fester**, *vb.* suppurare.

**festival**, *n.* fèsta *f.*

**festive**, *adj.* festivo.

**festivity**, *n.* festività *f.*

**festoon**, *n.* festone *m.*

**fetal**, *adj.* fetale.

**fetch**, *vb.* (go and get) andare a cercare; (bring) apportare.

**fetching**, *adj.* attraènte.

**fête**, *n.* fèsta *f.*

**fetid**, *adj.* fètido.

**fetish**, *n.* feticcio *m.*

**fetlock**, *n.* nòcca *f.*

**fetters**, *n.* ceppi *m.pl.*

**fetus**, *n.* fèto *m.*

**feud**, *n.* inimicizia *f.;* (historical) fèudo *m.*

**feudal**, *adj.* feudale.

**feudalism**, *n.* feudalismo *m.*

**fever**, *n.* fèbbre *f.*

**feverish**, *adj.* febbrile.

**feverishly**, *adv.* febbrilmente.

**few**, *adj. and pron.* pòchi *pl.*

**fiancé**, *n.* fidanzato *m.*

**fiancée**, *n.* fidanzata *f.*

**fiasco**, *n.* fiasco *m.*

**fiat**, *n.* órdine *m.*

**fib**, *n.* fandònia *f.*

**fiber**, *n.* fibra *f.*

**fibrous**, *adj.* fibroso.

**fickle**, *adj.* incostante.

**fickleness**, *n.* incostanza *f.*

**fiction**, *n.* finzione *f.;* (novel-writing) novellìstica *f.*

**fictional**, *adj.* finto.

**fictitious**, *adj.* fittizio.

**fictitiously**, *adv.* fittiziamente.

**fiddle**, **1.** *n.* violino *m.* **2.** *vb.* suonare il violino.

**fiddlesticks**, *interj.* fandònie!

**fidelity**, *n.* fedeltà *f.*

**fidget**, *vb.* agitarsi.

**fief**, *n.* fèudo *m.*

**field**, *n.* campo *m.*

**fiend**, *n.* demònio *m.*

**fiendish**, *adj.* demonìaco.

**fierce**, *adj.* feroce.

**fiery**, *adj.* focoso.

**fife**, *n.* pìffero *m.*

**fifteen**, *num.* quìndici.

**fifteenth**, *adj.* quindicésimo.

**fifth**, *adj.* quinto.

**fifty**, *num.* cinquanta.

**fig**, *n.* fico *m.*

**fight**, **1.** *n.* combattimento *m.;* (struggle) lotta *f.;* (quarrel) lite *f.* **2.** *vb.* combàttere.

**fighter**, *n.* combattènte *m.;* (plane) càccia *m.*

**figment**, *n.* finzione *f.*

**figurative**, *adj.* figurato.

**figuratively**, *adv.* figuratamente.

**figure**, **1.** *n.* figura *f.;* (of body) lìnea *f.;* (math.) cifra *f.* **2.** *vb.* figurare, calcolare.

**figurehead**, *n.* uòmo di pàglia *m.*

**figure of speech**, *n.* figura retòrica *f.*

**figurine**, *n.* figurina *f.*

**filament**, *n.* filamento *m.*

**filch**, *vb.* rubare.

**file**, **1.** *n.* (tool) lima *f.*; (row) fila *f.*; riga *f.*; (papers, etc.) filza *f.*; archìvio *m.*; (cards) schedàrio. **2.** *vb.* (tool) limare; (papers) archiviare; (**file off**) sfilare.

**filial**, *adj.* filiale.

**filigree**, *n.* filigrana *f.*

**filings**, *n.* limatura *f. sg.*

**fill**, *vb.* riempire; (tooth) otturare.

**fillet**, *n.* (band) banda *f.*; (meat) filetto *m.*; (fish) fetta *f.*

**filling**, *n.* (of tooth) otturazione *f.*

**filling station**, *n.* stazione di servizio *f.*

**film**, *n.* pellìcola *f.*

**filmy**, *adj.* velato.

**filter**, **1.** *n.* filtro *m.* **2.** *vb.* filtrare.

**filth**, *n.* sudiciume *m.*

**filthy**, *adj.* sùdicio.

**fin**, *n.* pinna *f.*

**final**, *adj.* finale.

**finale**, *n.* finale *m.*

**finalist**, *n.* finalista *m.*

**finality**, *n.* finalità *f.*

**finally**, *adv.* finalmente.

**finance**, *n.* finanza *f.*

**financial**, *adj.* finanziàrio.

**financier**, *n.* finanzière *m.*

**find**, *vb.* trovare.

**finding**, *n.* ritrovato *m.*

**fine**, **1.** *n.* multa *f.*, ammènda *f.*; (voluntary) oblazione *f.* **2.** *adj.* (beautiful) bèllo; (pure) fino; (excellent) bravo. **3.** *vb.* multare.

**fine arts**, *n.* bèlle arti *f.pl.*

**finery**, *n.* vestiti eleganti *m.pl.*

**finesse**, *n.* finezza *f.*

**finger**, *n.* dito *m.*

**fingernail**, *n.* ùnghia *f.*

**fingerprint**, *n.* impronta digitale *f.*

**finicky**, *adj.* affettato.

**finish**, **1.** *n.* fine *f.* **2.** *vb.* finire, terminare.

**finite**, *adj.* definito.

**fir**, *n.* abete *m.*

**fire**, **1.** fuòco *m.*; (burning of house, etc.) incèndio *m.* **2.**

**fix**, **1.** *n.* impìccio *m.* **2.** *vb.* acconciare; (repair) riparare;

---

*vb.* (weapon) sparare; (deprive of job) licenziare.

**firearm**, *n.* arma da fuòco *f.*

**firecracker**, *n.* petardo *m.*

**firedamp**, *n.* grisou *m.*, mètano *m.*

**fire engine**, *n.* pompa da incèndio *f.*

**fire escape**, *n.* uscita di sicurezza *f.*

**fire extinguisher**, *n.* estintore *m.*

**firefly**, *n.* lùciola *f.*

**fireman**, *n.* pompière *m.*; (locomotive) fuochista *m.*

**fireplace**, *n.* focolare *m.*

**fireproof**, *adj.* incombustìbile.

**firescreen**, *n.* parafuòco *m.*

**fireside**, *n.* cantùccio del focolare *m.*

**firewood**, *n.* legna *f.*

**fireworks**, *n.* fuòchi d'artifìcio *m.pl.*

**firm**, **1.** *n.* ditta *f.* **2.** *adj.* fermo.

**firmness**, *n.* fermezza *f.*

**first**, *adj.* primo.

**first aid**, *n.* primo soccorso *m.*

**first-class**, *adj.* di prima classe.

**first-hand**, *adj.* di prima mano.

**first-rate**, *adj.* di prima qualità.

**fiscal**, *adj.* fiscale.

**fish**, **1.** *n.* pesce *m.* **2.** *vb.* pescare.

**fisherman**, *n.* pescatore *m.*

**fishery**, *n.* peschièra *f.*

**fishhook**, *n.* amo *m.*

**fishing**, *n.* pesca *f.*

**fishmonger**, *n.* pescivéndolo *m.*

**fishwife**, *n.* pescivéndola *f.*

**fishy**, *adj.* di pesce; (strange) strano.

**fission**, *n.* fissione *f.*

**fissure**, *n.* fessura *f.*

**fist**, *n.* pugno *m.*

**fistic**, *adj.* pugilìstico.

**fit**, **1.** *n.* accèsso *m.* **2.** *adj.* adatto, idòneo. **3.** (befit) convenire a; (clothes) andar bène; (adapt) adattare.

**fitful**, *adj.* irregolare.

**fitness**, *n.* idoneità *f.*; (health) salute *f.*

**fitting**, **1.** *n.* adattamento *m.* **2.** *adj.* conveniènte.

**five**, *num.* cinque.

(set) fissare; (**f. up**) sistemare.

**fixation**, *n.* fissazione *f.*

**fixed**, *adj.* fisso.

**fixture**, *n.* infisso *m.*

**flabby**, *adj.* flòscio.

**flaccid**, *adj.* flàccido.

**flag**, *n.* bandièra *f.*; (stone) lastra di ròccia *f.*

**flagellant**, *n.* flagellante *m.*

**flagellate**, *vb.* flagellare.

**flagging**, *adj.* indebolito.

**flagon**, *n.* coppa *f.*

**flagpole**, *n.* asta di bandièra *f.*

**flagrant**, *adj.* flagrante.

**flagrantly**, *adv.* flagrantemente.

**flagship**, *n.* nave ammiràglia *f.*

**flagstone**, *n.* lastra di ròccia *f.*

**flail**, *n.* coreggiato *m.*

**flair**, *n.* fiuto *m.*; (ability) abilità *f.*

**flake**, *n.* fiòcco *m.*

**flamboyant**, *adj.* sgargiante.

**flame**, **1.** *n.* fiamma *f.*; (**burst into flames**) divampare. **2.** *vb.* fiammeggiare.

**flame thrower**, *n.* lanciafiamme *m.*

**flaming**, *adj.* fiammante.

**flamingo**, *n.* fiammingo *m.*, fenicòttero *m.*

**flank**, **1.** *n.* fianco *m.* **2.** *vb.* fiancheggiare.

**flannel**, *n.* flanèlla *f.*

**flap**, **1.** (wing) colpo *m.*; (envelope) lembo di chiusura *m.*

**flare**, *vb.* fiammeggiare.

**flare-up**, *n.* scòppio d'ira *m.*

**flash**, **1.** *n.* baleno *m.* **2.** *vb.* balenare.

**flashiness**, *n.* vistosità *f.*

**flashlight**, *n.* lampadina tascàbile *f.*

**flashy**, *adj.* vistoso.

**flask**, *n.* fiasco *m.*

**flat**, **1.** *n.* appartamento *m.*; (music) bemòlle *m.* **2.** *adj.* piatto, piano.

**flatcar**, *n.* carro piatto *m.*

**flatness**, *n.* monotonìa *f.*

**flatten**, *vb.* appiattire.

**flatter**, *vb.* adulare, lusingare.

**flatterer**, *n.* adulatore *m.*, lusingatore *m.*

**flattering**, *adj.* lusinghièro.

**flattery**, *n.* adulazione *f.*, lusinghe *f.pl.*

**flat-top**, *n.* portaèrei *m.*

**flaunt**, *vb.* ostentare.

**flavor**, **1.** *n.* (taste) sapore *m.*; (odor) aròma *m.* **2.** *vb.* insaporire.

**flavoring**, *n.* aròma artificiale *m.*

**flavorless**, *adj.* sènza sapore.

**flaw**, *n.* difètto *m.*

**flawless**, *adj.* perfètto.

**flawlessly**, *adv.* perfettamente.

**flax**, *n.* lino *m.*

**flay**, *vb.* scorticare.

**flea**, *n.* pulce *f.*

**fleck**, *n.* macchietta *f.*

**fledgling**, *n.* uccellino *m.*

**flee**, *vb.* fuggire.

**fleece**, *n.* vèllo *m.*

**fleecy**, *adj.* velloso.

**fleet**, **1.** *n.* flòtta *f.* **2.** *adj.* veloce.

**fleeting**, *adj.* fugace.

**Fleming**, *n.* fiammingo *m.*

**Flemish**, *adj.* fiammingo.

**flesh**, *n.* carne *f.*

**fleshy**, *adj.* carnoso.

**flex**, *vb.* flèttere.

**flexibility**, *n.* flessibilità *f.*

**flexible**, *adj.* flessìbile.

**flicker**, **1.** *n.* tremolìo *m.* **2.** *vb.* tremolare.

**flier**, *n.* aviatore *m.*

**flight**, *n.* volo *m.*

**flighty**, *adj.* capriccioso.

**flimsy**, *adj.* tènue.

**flinch**, *vb.* ritirarsi.

**fling**, *vb.* lanciare.

**flint**, *n.* (lighter) piètra focaia *f.*; (stone) selce *f.*

**flip**, *vb.* gettare.

**flippant**, *adj.* leggièro.

**flippantly**, *adv.* leggieramente.

**flirt**, **1.** *n.* civetta *f.* **2.** *vb.* civettare, flirtare.

**flirtation**, *n.* flirt *m.*

**float**, *vb.* galleggiare.

**flock**, **1.** *n.* gregge *m.* **2.** *vb.* affollarsi.

**flog**, *vb.* fustigare.

**flood**, **1.** *n.* inondazione *f.* **2.** *vb.* inondare.

**floodgate**, *n.* cateratta *f.*

**floodlight**, *n.* riflettore elèttrico *m.*

**floor**, *n.* pavimento *m.*; (storey) piano *m.*; (**take the f.**) prèndere la paròla.

**flooring**, *n.* pavimentazione *f.*

**floorwalker**, *n.* ispettore di magazzino *m.*

**flop**, **1.** *n.* (failure) fiasco *m.*; (thud) tonfo *m.* **2.** *vb.* muòversi goffamente; (fail) far fiasco.

**floral**, *adj.* floreale.

**Florence**, n. Firènze f.

**Florentine**, adj. fiorentino.

**florid**, adj. rubicondo.

**florist**, n. fioraio m.

**flounce**, 1. n. volante m. 2. vb. dimenarsi.

**flounder**, vb. dibàttersi.

**flour**, n. farina f.

**flourish**, vb. fiorire; (wave around) agitare.

**flow**, vb. scórrere.

**flower**, 1. n. fiore m. 2. vb. fiorire.

**flowerpot**, n. vaso per fiori m.

**flowery**, adj. fiorito.

**fluctuate**, vb. fluttuare.

**fluctuation**, n. fluttuazione f.

**flue**, n. conduttura f.

**fluency**, n. scorrevolezza f.

**fluent**, adj. scorrévole.

**fluffy**, adj. lanuginoso.

**fluid**, n. and adj. flùido (m.)

**fluidity**, adj. fluidità f.

**flunk**, vb. bocciare.

**flunkey**, n. lacchè m.

**fluorescent**, adj. fluorescènte.

**fluoroscope**, n. fluoroscòpio m.

**flurry**, n. trambusto m.

**flush**, 1. adj. a livello di. 2. vb. (f. the toilet) tirare lo sciacquone.

**flute**, n. flàuto m.

**flutter**, vb. svolazzare.

**flux**, n. flusso m.

**fly**, 1. n. mosca f. 2. vb. volare.

**foam**, 1. n. schiuma f., spuma f. 2. vb. spumare.

**focal**, adj. focale.

**focus**, n. fuòco m.

**fodder**, n. foràggio m.

**foe**, n. nemico m.

**fog**, n. foschia f.

**foggy**, adj. nebbioso.

**foil**, 1. n. (fencing) fioretto m.; (metal) fòglia f. 2. vb. frustrare.

**foist**, vb. far accettare.

**fold**, 1. n. pièga f. 2. vb. piegare.

**folder**, n. cartèlla f.

**foliage**, n. fogliame m.

**folio**, n. fòlio m.

**folk**, n. pòpolo m.

**folklore**, n. folclore m.

**folks**, n. la gènte f.

**follicle**, n. follìcolo m.

**follow**, vb. seguire; (pursue) inseguire.

**follower**, n. seguace m.

**folly**, n. follìa f.

**foment**, vb. fomentare.

**fond**, adj. amante, tènero.

**fondant**, n. fondènte m.

**fondle**, vb. accarezzare.

**fondly**, adv. teneramente.

**fondness**, n. tenerezza f., passione f.

**food**, n. cibo m., alimento m.

**foodstuffs**, n. gèneri alimentari m.pl.

**fool**, 1. n. citrullo m., sciòcco m., stolto m. 2. vb. ingannare.

**foolhardiness**, n. temerarietà f.

**foolhardy**, adj. temeràrio.

**foolish**, adj. sciòcco, stolto.

**foolproof**, adj. assolutamente sicuro.

**foolscap**, n. carta formato protocòllo f.

**foot**, n. piède m.

**footage**, n. metràggio m.

**football**, n. (soccer) càlcio m.

**foothill**, n. collina bassa f.

**foothold**, n. appòggio m., sostegno m.

**footing**, n. appòggio m., base f.

**footlights**, n. ribalta f.sg.

**footman**, n. staffière m.

**footnote**, n. nòta f.

**footprint**, n. orma f.

**footsore, be**, vb. aver male ai pièdi.

**footstep**, n. orma f.

**footstool**, n. sgabèllo m.

**fop**, n. damerino m.

**for**, 1. prep. per. 2. conj. perchè, chè.

**forage**, 1. n. foràggio m. 2. vb. predare.

**foray**, n. scorrerìa f.

**forbear**, vb. trattenersi.

**forbearance**, n. paziènza f.

**forbid**, vb. proibire, vietare.

**forbidding**, adj. repulsivo.

**force**, 1. n. fòrza f., vigore m. 2. vb. forzare.

**forceful**, adj. vigoroso.

**forcefulness**, n. vigorìa f.

**forceps**, n. fòrcipe m. (sg.)

**forcible**, adj. forzato; (powerful) potènte.

**ford**, n. guado m.

**fore**, adj. anteriore.

**fore and aft**, adv. a pròra e a poppa.

**forearm**, n. avambràccio m.

**forebears**, n. antenati m.pl.

**forebode**, vb. presentire.

**foreboding,** *n.* presentimento *m.*

**forecast, 1.** *n.* previsione *f.*
**2.** *vb.* prevedere, pronosticare.

**forecaster,** *n.* pronosticatore *m.*

**forecastle,** *n.* castello di prua *m.*

**foreclosure,** *n.* graduazione *f.*

**forefather,** *n.* antenato *m.*

**forefinger,** *n.* indice *m.*

**forefront,** *n.* primo piano *m.*

**forego,** *vb.* rinunciare a.

**foregone,** *adj.* anticipato.

**foreground,** *n.* primo piano *m.*

**forehead,** *n.* fronte *f.*

**foreign,** *adj.* straniero, èstero.

**foreigner,** *n.* straniero *m.*

**foreleg,** *n.* gamba anteriore *f.*

**foreman,** *n.* capo operaio *m.*

**foremost, 1.** *adj.* primo. **2.**
*adv.* in avanti.

**forenoon,** *n.* mattina *f.*

**forensic,** *adj.* forènse.

**forerunner,** *n.* precursore *m.*

**foresee,** *vb.* prevedere.

**foreseeable,** *adj.* prevedìbile.

**foreshadow,** *vb.* presagire.

**foresight,** *n.* previdènza *f.*

**forest,** *n.* forèsta *f.*

**forestall,** *vb.* impedire.

**forester,** *n.* silvicultore *m.*;
(guard) guàrdia forestale *f.*

**forestry,** *n.* silvicultura *f.*

**foretaste, 1.** *n.* pregustazione *f.* **2.** *vb.* pregustare.

**foretell,** *vb.* predire.

**forever,** *adv.* per sèmpre.

**forevermore,** *adv.* eternamente.

**forewarn,** *vb.* preavvertire.

**foreword,** *n.* prefazione *f.*

**forfeit,** *vb.* demeritare, pèrdere.

**forfeiture,** *n.* pèrdita *f.*

**forgather,** *vb.* riunirsi.

**forge, 1.** *n.* fucina *f.* **2.** *vb.*
(make) foggiare; (falsify)
contraffare.

**forger,** *n.* contraffattore *m.*

**forgery,** *n.* contraffazione *f.*

**forget,** *vb.* dimenticare.

**forgetful,** *adj.* diméntico.

**forget-me-not,** *n.* miosòtide
*f.*, non ti scordar di me *m.*

**forgive,** *vb.* perdonare.

**forgiveness,** *n.* perdono *m.*

**forgo,** *vb.* rinunziare a.

**fork,** *n.* forchetta *f.*; (in road)
bìvio *m.*

**forlorn,** *adj.* disperato.

**form, 1.** *n.* forma *f.*; (blank)
mòdulo *m.*

**formal,** *adj.* formale.

**formaldehyde,** *n.* formaldèide *f.*

**formality,** *n.* formalità *f.*

**formally,** *adv.* formalmente.

**format,** *n.* formato *m.*

**formation,** *n.* formazione *f.*

**formative,** *adj.* formativo.

**former, 1.** *adj.* precedènte.
**2.** *pron.* quello.

**formerly,** *adv.* anticamente,
già.

**formidable,** *adj.* formidàbile.

**formless,** *adj.* informe.

**formula,** *n.* fòrmula *f.*

**formulate,** *vb.* formulare.

**formulation,** *n.* formulazione *f.*

**forsake,** *vb.* abbandonare.

**forsythia,** *n.* forsizia *f.*

**fort,** *n.* fortezza *f.*

**forte,** *n.* fòrte *m.*

**forth,** *adv.* (out) fuòri; (onward) via; **(and so f.)** e così
via.

**forthcoming,** *adj.* pròssimo.

**forthright,** *adj.* onèsto.

**forthwith,** *adv.* immediatamente.

**fortieth,** *adj.* quarantésimo.

**fortification,** *n.* fortificazione *f.*

**fortify,** *vb.* fortificare.

**fortissimo,** *adv.* fortìssimo.

**fortitude,** *n.* fortezza *f.*

**fortnight,** *n.* quìndici giorni
*m.pl.*

**fortress,** *n.* fortezza *f.*, ròcca *f.*

**fortuitous,** *adj.* fortùito.

**fortunate,** *adj.* fortunato.

**fortune,** *n.* fortuna *f.*

**fortune-teller,** *n.* chiaroveggènte *m.*

**forty,** *num.* quaranta.

**forum,** *n.* fòro *m.*

**forward,** *adv.* avanti.

**forwardness,** *n.* presuntuosità *f.*

**fossil,** *n. and adj.* fòssile (*m.*)

**fossilize,** *vb.* fossilizzare, *tr.*

**foster,** *vb.* (raise) allevare;
(nourish) nutrire.

**foul, 1.** *adj.* spòrco; (unfair)
disonèsto. **2.** *vb.* sporcare.

**found,** *vb.* fondare.

**foundation,** *n.* (building)
fondamento *m.*; (fund) fondazione *f.*

**founder,** *n.* fondatore *m.*

**foundling,** *n.m.* trovatèllo

*m.*; **(f. hospital)** brefotròfio *m.*

**foundry,** *n.* fonderìa *f.*

**fountain,** *n.* fontana *f.*

**fountainhead,** *n.* punto d'origine *m.*

**fountain pen,** *n.* penna stilogràfica *f.*

**four,** *num.* quattro

**four-in-hand,** *n.* cravatta *f.*

**fourscore,** *num.* ottanta

**foursome,** *n.* gruppo di quattro persone *m.*

**fourteen,** *num.* quattòrdici.

**fourth,** *adj.* quarto.

**fowl,** *n.* pollo *m.*

**fox,** *n.* volpe *f.*

**foxglove,** *n.* digitale *f.*

**foxhole,** *n.* trincèa *f.*

**foxy,** *adj.* volpino.

**foyer,** *n.* ridotto *m.*

**fracas,** *n.* fracasso *m.*

**fraction,** *n.* frazione *f.*

**fracture, 1.** *n.* frattura *f.* **2.** *vb.* fratturare.

**fragile,** *adj.* fràgile.

**fragment,** *n.* frammento *m.*

**fragmentary,** *adj.* frammentàrio.

**fragrance,** *n.* fragranza *f.*

**fragrant,** *adj.* fragrante.

**frail,** *adj.* fràgile; (morally) débole.

**frailty,** *n.* debolezza *f.*

**frame, 1.** *n.* cornice *f.* **2.** *vb.* incorniciare.

**framework,** *n.* ossatura *f.*

**France,** *n.* Frància *f.*

**franchise,** *n.* diritto di voto *m.*

**frank,** *adj.* franco.

**frankfurter,** *n.* salsiccia *f.*

**frankincense,** *n.* incènso *m.*

**frankly,** *adv.* francamente.

**frankness,** *n.* franchezza *f.*

**frantic,** *adj.* frenètico.

**fraternal,** *adj.* fratèrno.

**fraternally,** *adv.* fraternamente.

**fraternity,** *n.* fraternità *f.*

**fraternize,** *vb.* fraternizzare.

**fratricide,** *n.* (act) fratricidio *m.*; (person) fratricida *m.*

**fraud,** *n.* fròde *f.*

**fraudulent,** *adj.* fraudolento.

**fraudulently,** *adv.* fraudolentemente.

**fraught,** *adj.* càrico.

**fray,** *n.* combattimento *m.*

**freak, 1.** *n.* mostruosità *f.* **2.** *adj.* mostruoso.

**freckle,** *n.* lentìggine *f.*

**freckled,** *adj.* lentigginoso.

**free, 1.** *adj.* lìbero; (without cost) gratùito. **2.** *vb.* liberare.

**freedom,** *n.* libertà *f.*

**free lance,** *n.* giornalista o politicante indipendènte *m.*

**freestone,** *adj.* spiccàgnolo.

**freeze,** *vb.* gelare.

**freezer,** *n.* frigorìfero *m.*

**freezing,** *n.* congelamento *m.*; **(f. point)** punto di congelamento *m.*

**freight,** *n.* càrico *m.*; **(f. train)** treno mèrci *m.*; **(f. station)** scalo mèrci *m.*

**freightage,** *n.* spese di trasporto *f.pl.*

**freighter,** *n.* nave mercantile *m.*

**French,** *adj.* francese.

**Frenchman,** *n.* francese *m.* or *f.*

**frenzied,** *adj.* frenètico.

**frenzy,** *n.* frenesìa *f.*

**frequency,** *n.* frequènza *f.*

**frequency modulation,** *n.* modulazione di frequènza *f.*

**frequent, 1.** *adj.* frequènte. **2.** *vb.* frequentare.

**frequently,** *adv.* frequentemente.

**fresco,** *n.* affresco *m.*

**fresh,** *adj.* fresco; (impudent) impudènte.

**freshen,** *vb.* rinfrescare.

**freshman,** *n.* matricola *f.*

**freshness,** *n.* freschezza *f.*

**fresh-water,** *adj.* d'acqua dolce.

**fret,** *vb.* tormentare, *tr.,* irritare, *tr.*

**fretful,** *adj.* irritàbile.

**fretfully,** *adv.* irritabilmente.

**fretfulness,** *n.* irritabilità *f.*

**friar,** *n.* frate *m.*

**fricassee,** *n.* fricassèa *f.*

**friction,** *n.* frizione *f.*

**Friday,** *n.* venerdì *m.*

**friend,** *n.* amico *m.,* amica *f.*

**friendless,** *adj.* sènza amici.

**friendliness,** *n.* amichevolezza *f.*

**friendly,** *adj.* amichévole, amico.

**friendship,** *n.* amicìzia *f.*

**frigate,** *n.* fregata *f.*

**fright,** *n.* spavento *m.*

**frighten,** *vb.* spaventare.

**frightful,** *adj.* spaventoso.

**frigid,** *adj.* frìgido.

**Frigid Zone,** *n.* zona glaciale *f.*

**frill,** *n.* gala *f.,* affettazione *f.*

**frilly**, *adj.* increspato.

**fringe**, *n.* frangia *f.*

**frisky**, *adj.* allegro.

**fritter**, **1.** *n.* frittèlla *f.* **2.** *vb.* (**f. away**) sciupare.

**frivolousness**, *n.* frivolezza *f.*

**frivolous**, *adj.* frivolo.

**frivolity**, *n.* frivolità *f.*

**frock**, *n.* àbito da donna *m.*

**frog**, *n.* ranocchio *m.*, rana *f.*

**frolic**, *vb.* far capriòle.

**from**, *prep.* da.

**front**, *n.* fronte *m.*; parte anteriore *f.*; davanti *m.*; (**in f.**) davanti a.; (**in f. of**) davanti a.

**frontage**, *n.* facciata *f.*

**frontal**, *adj.* frontale.

**frontier**, *n.* frontièra *f.*

**frost**, *n.* brina *f.*

**frostbite**, *n.* congelamento *m.*

**frosting**, *n.* pasta fròlla *f.*

**frosty**, *adj.* gèlido.

**froth**, *n.* schiuma *f.*, spuma *f.*

**frown**, *vb.* aggrottare le ciglia.

**frowzy**, *adj.* trascurato.

**fructify**, *vb.* fruttificare.

**frugal**, *adj.* frugale.

**frugality**, *n.* frugalità *f.*

**fruit**, *n.* frutto *m.*

**fruitful**, *adj.* fruttuoso.

**fruition**, *n.* fruizione *f.*

**fruitless**, *adj.* infruttuoso.

**frustrate**, *vb.* frustrare.

**frustration**, *n.* frustrazione *f.*

**fry**, *vb.* friggere.

**fryer**, *n.* (**chicken**) pollo gióvane *m.*

**frying-pan**, *n.* padèlla *f.*

**fuchsia**, *n.* fùcsia *f.*

**fudge**, **1.** *n.* fondènte *m.* **2.** *interj.* sciocchezze!

**fuel**, *n.* combustibile *m.*; (**motor f.**) carburante *m.*

**fugitive**, *n. and adj.* fuggitivo (*m.*)

**fugue**, *n.* fuga *f.*

**fulcrum**, *n.* fulcro *m.*

**fulfill**, *vb.* realizzare.

**fulfillment**, *n.* realizzazione *f.*

**full**, *adj.* pieno.

**fullback**, *n.* estrèmo *m.*

**full dress**, *n.* àbito da cerimònia *m.*

**fullness**, *n.* pienezza *f.*

**fully**, *adv.* pienamente.

**fulminate**, *vb.* fulminare.

**fulmination**, *n.* fulminazione *f.*

**fumble**, *vb.* lasciar cadere.

**fume**, *n.* esalazione *f.*

**fumigate**, *vb.* fumigare.

**fumigator**, *n.* fumigatore *m.*

**fun**, *n.* divertimento *m.*

**function**, **1.** *n.* funzione *f.* **2.** *vb.* funzionare.

**functional**, *adj.* funzionale.

**functionary**, *n.* funzionàrio *m.*

**fund**, *n.* fondo *m.*

**fundamental**, *adj.* fondamentale.

**funeral**, **1.** *n.* funerale *m.* **2.** *adj.* fùnebre.

**funereal**, *adj.* funèreo.

**fungicide**, *n.* fungicida *m.*

**fungus**, *n.* fungo *m.*

**funnel**, *n.* imbuto *m.*; (smoke-stack) ciminièra *f.*

**funny**, *adj.* còmico.

**fur**, *n.* pellìccia *f.*

**furious**, *adj.* furioso.

**furlough**, *n.* licènza *f.*

**furnace**, *n.* fornace *m.*, caldaia *f.*

**furnish**, *vb.* fornire; (house) ammobiliare.

**furnishings**, *n.* mobìlia *f.*

**furniture**, *n.* mòbili *m.pl.*

**furor**, *n.* furore *m.*

**furred**, *adj.* copèrto di pellìccia.

**furrier**, *n.* pellicciaio *m.*

**furrow**, *n.* solco *m.*

**furry**, *adj.* copèrto di pellìccia; (tongue) patinoso.

**further**, **1.** *adj.* ulteriore. **2.** *adv.* oltre, più avanti.

**furtherance**, *n.* appòggio *m.*

**furthermore**, *adv.* inoltre.

**fury**, *n.* fùria *f.*, furore *m.*

**fuse**, **1.** *n.* (electricity) fusìbile *m.*; (explosives) spoletta *f.* **2.** *vb.* fóndere.

**fuselage**, *n.* fusolièra *f.*

**fusillade**, *n.* fucileria *f.*

**fusion**, *n.* fusione *f.*

**fuss**, *n.* chiasso *m.*

**fussy**, *adj.* difficoltoso.

**futile**, *adj.* fùtile.

**futility**, *n.* futilità *f.*

**future**, **1.** *n.* futuro *m.*, avvenire *m.* **2.** *adj.* futuro.

**futurity**, *n.* avvenire *m.*

**fuzz**, *n.* lanùgine *f.*

**fuzzy**, *adj.* lanuginoso; (confused) confuso.

# G

**gab**, vb. chiacchierare.
**gabardine**, n. gabardina f.
**gadabout**, n. bighellone m.
**gadfly**, n. tafano m.
**gadget**, n. congegno m.
**gag**, 1. n. bavàglio m.; (joke) trovata còmica f. 2. vb. imbavagliare.
**gaiety**, n. gaiezza f.
**gaily**, vb. gaiamente.
**gain**, 1. n. guadagno m. 2. vb. guadagnare.
**gainful**, adj. lucroso.
**gainfully**, adv. lucrosamente.
**gainsay**, vb. contraddire.
**gait**, n. andatura f.
**gala**, 1. n. gala f. 2. adj. di gala.
**galaxy**, n. galàssia f.
**gale**, n. tempèsta f.
**gall**, 1. n. (bile) fièle m.; (insolence) sfacciatàggine f.; 2. vb. irritare.
**gallant**, adj. galante, coraggioso.
**gallantly**, adv. coraggiosamente.
**gallantry**, n. coràggio m.
**gall bladder**, n. vescica del fièle m.
**galleon**, n. galeone m.
**gallery**, n. galleria f.; (top g., theater) loggione m.
**galley**, n. (ship) galèa f.; (kitchen) cucina f.; (typogr.) colonna f.
**galley proof**, n. bòzze in colonna f.pl.
**Gallic**, adj. gàllico.
**gallivant**, vb. vagare.
**gallon**, n. gallone m.
**gallop**, 1. n. galòppo m. 2. vb. galoppare.
**gallows**, n. forca f.
**gallstone**, n. càlcolo biliare m.
**galore**, adv. a bizzèffe.
**galosh**, n. galòscia f.
**galvanize**, vb. galvanizzare.
**gamble**, vb. giocare d'azzardo.
**gambler**, n. giocatore d'azzardo m.
**gambling**, n. giòco d'azzardo m.

**gambol**, 1. n. salto m. 2. vb. saltare.
**game**, 1. n. giòco m.; (sports encounter) partita f.; (hunting) selvaggina f. 2. adj. coraggioso.
**gamely**, adv. coraggiosamente.
**gameness**, n. coràggio m.
**gamin**, n. monèllo m.
**gamut**, n. gamma f.
**gamy**, adj. alquanto putrefatto.
**gander**, n. pàpero m.
**gang**, n. gruppo m., squadra f.
**gangling**, adj. smilzo.
**gangplank**, n. pontile m.
**gangrene**, n. cancrena f.
**gangrenous**, adj. cancrenoso.
**gangster**, n. gangster m.
**gangway**, n. passerèlla f.
**gap**, n. apertura f.
**gape**, vb. spalancare la bocca.
**garage**, n. autorimessa f.
**garb**, n. costume m.
**garbage**, n. rifiuti f.pl.
**garble**, vb. ingarbugliare.
**garden**, n. giardino m.
**gardener**, n. giardinière m.
**gardenia**, n. gardènia f.
**gargle**, 1. n. gargarismo m. 2. vb. gargarizzare.
**gargoyle**, n. dòccia con testa grottesca f.
**garish**, adj. sgargiante.
**garland**, n. ghirlanda f.
**garlic**, n. àglio m.
**garment**, n. vestito m.
**garner**, vb. cògliere.
**garnet**, n. granato m.
**garnish**, vb. guarnire.
**garnishee**, vb. méttere il fermo su.
**garnishment**, n. guarnizione f.
**garret**, n. soffitta f.
**garrison**, n. guarnigione f.
**garrote**, n. garrotta f.
**garrulous**, adj. gàrrulo.
**garter**, n. giarrettiera f.
**gas**, n. gas m.; (gasoline) benzina f.
**gaseous**, adj. gassoso.

**gash, 1.** n. squàrcio m. **2.** vb. squarciare.

**gasket,** n. guarnizione f.

**gasless,** adj. sènza gas, sènza benzina.

**gas mask,** n. màschera antigas f.

**gasoline,** n. benzina f.

**gasp, 1.** n. boccheggiamento m. **2.** vb. boccheggiare.

**gassy,** adj. gassoso.

**gastric,** adj. gàstrico.

**gastric juice,** n. succo gàstrico m.

**gastritis,** n. gastrite f.

**gastronomical,** adj. gastronòmico.

**gastronomy,** n. gastronomìa f.

**gate,** n. (city) pòrta f.; (apartment house) portone m.; (fence) cancèllo m.

**gateway,** n. pòrta m., entrata f.

**gather,** vb. raccògliere, radunare; (infer) desùmere.

**gathering,** n. adunata f., assemblèa f.

**gaudily,** adv. vistosamente.

**gaudiness,** n. vistosità f.

**gaudy,** adj. vistoso.

**gauge, 1.** n. apparécchio misuratore m.; (track) scartamento m.; (loading g.) sàgoma f. **2.** vb. misurare, stimare.

**gaunt,** adj. magro.

**gauntlet,** n. guanto m.

**gauze,** n. garza f.

**gavel,** n. martellino m.

**gavotte,** n. gavòtta f.

**gawky,** adj. goffo.

**gay,** adj. gaio.

**gaze,** vb. guardare.

**gazelle,** n. gazzèlla f.

**gazette,** n. gazzetta f.

**gazetteer,** n. dizionàrio geogràfico m.

**gear,** n. ingranàggio m.; (harness) finimenti m.pl.; (g. lever) lèva del càmbio m.

**gearing,** n. ingranàggio m.

**gearshift,** n. càmbio di velocità m.

**gelatin,** n. gelatina f.

**gelatinous,** adj. gelatinoso.

**geld,** vb. castrare.

**gelding,** n. castrone m.

**gem,** n. gèmma f.

**gender,** n. gènere m.

**gene,** n. gène m.

**genealogical,** adj. genealògico.

**genealogy,** n. genealogìa f.

**general,** n. and adj. generale (m.)

**generality,** n. generalità f.

**generalization,** n. generalizzazione f.

**generalize,** vb. generalizzare.

**generally,** adv. generalmente.

**generalship,** n. qualità di generale f.pl.

**generate,** vb. generare.

**generation,** n. generazione f.

**generator,** n. generatore m.

**generic,** adj. genèrico.

**generosity,** n. generosità f.

**generous,** adj. generoso.

**generously,** adv. generosamente.

**genetic,** adj. genètico.

**genetics,** n. genètica f.

**Geneva,** n. Ginèvra f.

**Genevan,** adj. ginevrino.

**genial,** adj. piacévole, cordiale.

**geniality,** n. piacevolezza f., cordialità f.

**genially,** adv. piacevolmente, cordialmente.

**genital,** adj. genitale.

**genitals,** n. genitali m.pl.

**genitive,** n. and adj. genitivo (m.)

**genius,** n. gènio m.

**Genoa,** n. Gènova f.

**Genoese,** adj. genovese.

**genocide,** n. genicìdio m.

**genre,** n. gènere m.

**genteel,** adj. eccessivamente raffinato.

**gentian,** n. genziana f.

**gentile,** n. and adj. gentile (m.); non israelìtico.

**gentility,** n. raffinatezza eccessiva f.

**gentle,** adj. mite.

**gentleman,** n. signore m., gentiluòmo m.

**gentlemanly,** adj. da gentiluòmo.

**gentlemen's agreement,** n. impegno d'onore m.

**gentleness,** n. mitezza f.

**gently,** adv. mitemente, adagio.

**gentry,** n. piccola nobiltà f.; (ironical) gènte f.

**genuflect,** vb. genuflèttersi.

**genuine,** adj. genuino.

**genuinely,** adv. genuinamente.

**genuineness,** n. genuinità f.

**genus,** n. gènere m.

**geographer,** n. geògrafo m.

**geographical,** adj. geogràfico.

**geography,** n. geografìa f.

**geometric,** adj. geomètrico.

**geometry,** n. geometrìa f.

**geopolitics,** n. geopolìtica f.

**geranium,** n. gerànio m.

**germ,** n. gèrme m.

**German,** n. and adj. tedesco (m.)

**germane,** adj. rilevante.

**Germanic,** adj. germànico.

**German measles,** n. rosolìa f.

**Germany,** n. Germània f.

**germicide,** n. germicìda m.

**germinal,** adj. germinale.

**germinate,** vb. germinare.

**gestate,** vb. portare nell'ùtero.

**gestation,** n. gestazione f.

**gesticulate,** vb. gesticolare.

**gesticulation,** n. gesticolazione f.

**gesture,** n. gèsto m.

**get,** vb. (obtain) ottenere; (receive) ricévere; (take) préndere; (become) divenire, diventare; (arrive) arrivare; **(g. in)** entrare; **(g. off)** scéndere; **(g. on,** agree) intèndersi; **(g. on,** go up) montare; **(g. out)** uscire; **(g. up)** alzarsi.

**getaway,** n. fuga f.

**geyser,** n. geyser m.

**ghastly,** adj. orrèndo.

**ghost,** n. spèttro m., larva f.

**ghost writer,** n. collaboratore anònimo m.

**giant,** n. and adj. gigante (m.)

**gibberish,** n. borbottamento m.

**gibbon,** n. gibbone m.

**gibe at,** vb. beffarsi di.

**giblets,** n. rigàglie f.pl.

**giddy,** adj. stordito.

**gift,** n. dono m.

**gifted,** adj. dotato.

**gigantic,** adj. gigantesco.

**giggle,** vb. rìdere scioccamente.

**gigolo,** n. cicisbèo m.

**gild,** vb. dorare, indorare.

**gill,** n. brànchia f.

**gilt,** 1. n. doratura f. 2. adj. dorato.

**gilt-edged,** adj. sicuro.

**gimcrack,** n. cianfrusàglia f.

**gimlet,** n. succhièllo m.

**gin,** n. gin m.

**ginger,** n. zènzero m.

**gingerly,** adj. càuto.

**gingham,** n. ghìngano m.

**giraffe,** n. giraffa f.

**gird,** vb. cingere, tr.

**girder,** n. trave f.

**girdle,** n. cintura f.

**girl,** n. ragazza f., fanciulla f.

**girlish,** adj. da ragazza.

**girth,** n. circonferènza f.

**gist,** n. contenuto essenziale m.

**give,** vb. dare; **(g. back)** rèndere; **(g. in)** cédere; **(g. out)** distribuire; **(g. up)** rinunziare a.

**give-and-take,** n. scàmbio m.

**given name,** n. nome di battèsimo m.

**giver,** n. datore m., donatore m.

**gizzard,** n. ventrìglio m.

**glacé,** adj. lùcido.

**glacial,** adj. glaciale.

**glacier,** n. ghiacciaio m.

**glad,** adj. contènto, lièto.

**gladden,** vb. allietare.

**glade,** n. radura f.

**gladiolus,** n. gladiòlo m.

**gladly,** adv. lietamente, con piacere.

**gladness,** n. contentezza f.

**glamor,** n. fàscino m.

**glamorous,** adj. affascinante.

**glance,** n. sguardo m., occhiata f.

**gland,** n. glàndola f.

**glandular,** adj. glandolare.

**glare,** n. bagliore m.

**glaring,** adj. abbagliante.

**glass,** n. vetro m.; **(drinking-g.)** bicchière m.

**glass-blowing,** n. soffiatura del vetro f.

**glasses,** n. occhiali m.

**glassful,** n. bicchière m.

**glassware,** n. cristallerìe f.pl.

**glassy,** adj. vetroso, vitreo.

**glaucoma,** n. glaucòma m.

**glaze,** 1. n. (enamel) smalto m.; (varnish) vernice f. 2. vb. smaltare, verniciare.

**glazier,** n. vetraio m.

**gleam,** n. barlume m.

**glee,** n. giòia f.

**glee club,** n. còro maschile m.

**gleeful,** adj. gioioso.

**gien,** n. valletta f.

**glib,** adj. fluènte.

**glide,** vb. scivolare.

**glider,** n. aliante m.

**glimmer,** 1. n. barlume m. 2. vb. mandare una luce incèrta.

**glimmering, 1.** *n.* barlume *m.* **2.** *adj.* incèrto.

**glimpse,** *vb.* intravedere.

**glint,** *n.* riflèsso *m.*

**glisten,** *vb.* scintillare.

**glitter, 1.** *n.* scintillìo *m.* **2.** *vb.* scintillare, risplèndere.

**gloat,** *vb.* gioìre.

**global,** *adj.* globale.

**globe,** *n.* glòbo *m.*

**globular,** *adj.* globulare.

**globule,** *n.* glòbulo *m.*

**glockenspiel,** *n.* campanette *f.pl.*

**gloom,** *n.* (darkness) oscurità *f.;* (sadness) tristezza *f.*

**gloomy,** *adj.* oscuro, triste.

**glorification,** *n.* glorificazione *f.*

**glorify,** *vb.* glorificare.

**glorious,** *adj.* glorioso.

**glory, 1.** *n.* glòria *f.* **2.** *vb.* gloriàrsi.

**gloss, 1.** *n.* lucidezza *f.;* (explanation) chiòsa *f.* **2.** *vb.* lucidare; chiosare.

**glossary,** *n.* glossàrio *m.*

**glossy,** *adj.* lùcido.

**glove,** *n.* guanto *m.*

**glow, 1.** *n.* incandescènza *f.* **2.** *vb.* èssere incandescènte.

**glowing,** *adj.* incandescènte.

**glowworm,** *n.* lùcciola *f.*

**glucose,** *n.* glucòsio *m.*

**glue, 1.** *n.* còlla *f.* **2.** *vb.* incollare.

**glum,** *adj.* (frowning) accigliato; (sad) triste.

**glumness,** *n.* tristezza *f.*

**glut,** *n.* saturazione *f.*

**glutinous,** *adj.* glutinoso.

**glutton,** *n.* ghiottone *m.*

**gluttonous,** *adj.* ghiotto.

**glycerine,** *n.* glicerina *f.*

**gnarl,** *n.* nodo *m.*

**gnash,** *vb.* digrignare.

**gnat,** *n.* cùlice *m.*

**gnaw,** *vb.* ròdere.

**go,** *vb.* andare; (become) diventare; (**g. away**) andàrsene; (**g. back**) tornare; (**g. by**) passare; (**g. down**) scèndere; (**g. in**) entrare; (**g. on**) continuare; (**g. out**) uscire; (**g. up**) salire; (**g. without**) fare a meno di.

**goad, 1.** *n.* pùngolo *m.,* stìmolo *m.* **2.** *vb.* stimolare.

**goal,** *n.* mèta *f.;* (soccer) pòrta *f.*

**goal-keeper,** *n.* portière *m.*

**goat,** *n.* capra *f.*

**goatee,** *n.* barbetta *f.*

**goatherd,** *n.* capraio *m.*

**goatskin,** *n.* pèlle di capra *f.*

**gobble,** *vb.* ingollare.

**gobbler,** *n.* tacchino *m.*

**go-between,** *n.* intermediàrio *m.*

**goblet,** *n.* coppa *f.*

**goblin,** *n.* folletto *m.*

**god,** *n.* dio *m.,* iddìo *m.*

**godchild,** *n.* figliòccio *m.*

**goddess,** *n.* dèa *f.*

**godfather,** *n.* padrino *m.,* compare *m.*

**godless,** *adj.* àteo; (impious) émpio.

**godlike,** *adj.* divino.

**godly,** *adj.* devòto, pìo.

**godmother,** *n.* madrina *f.,* comare *f.*

**godsend,** *n.* dòno del cièlo *m.*

**Godspeed,** *n.* addìo *m.*

**go-getter,** *n.* arrivista *m.*

**goiter,** *n.* gozzo *m.*

**gold,** *n.* òro *m.*

**golden,** *adj.* d'òro, àureo.

**gold-filled,** *adj.* (tooth) otturato d'òro.

**goldfinch,** *n.* cardellino *m.*

**goldfish,** *n.* pesce rosso *m.*

**gold leaf,** *n.* fòglia d'òro *f.*

**goldsmith,** *n.* oréfice *m.*

**gold standard,** *n.* parità àurea *f.*

**golf,** *n.* golf *m.*

**gondola,** *n.* góndola *f.*

**gondolier,** *n.* gondolière *m.*

**gone,** *adj.* (vanished) sparito; (departed) partito.

**gong,** *n.* gong *m.*

**gonorrhea,** *n.* gonorrèa *f.*

**good, 1.** *n.* bène *m.;* (**goods**) mèrci *f.pl.* **2.** *adj.* buòno. *(m.)*

**good-by,** *n. and interj.* addìo *(m.)*

**Good Friday,** *n.* venerdì santo *m.*

**good-hearted,** *adj.* di buòn cuòre.

**good-humored,** *adj.* di buòn umore.

**good-looking,** *adj.* bellino.

**good-natured,** *adj.* di buòn temperamento.

**goodness,** *n.* bontà *f.*

**good will,** *n.* buona volontà *f.*

**goose,** *n.* òca *f.,* pàpera *f.*

**gooseberry,** *n.* ribes *m.*

**gooseneck,** *n.* collo di cigna *m.*

**goose step,** *n.* passo d'òca *m.*

**gore,** *n.* sangue *m.*

**gorge,** *n.* gola *f.*

**gorgeous,** *adj.* splèndido.

**gorilla,** *n.* gorilla *m.*

**gory,** *adj.* insanguinato.

**gosling,** *n.* paperetto *m.*

**gospel,** *n.* vangèlo *m.*

**gossamer,** *n.* garza sottile *f.*

**gossip,** 1. *n.* (talk) diceria *f.,* pettegolezzo *m.;* (person) pettègolo *m.,* pettègola *f.* 2. *vb.* pettegolare.

**gossipy,** *adj.* pettègolo.

**Gothic,** *adj.* gòtico.

**gouge,** *n.* sgòrbia *f.*

**gourd,** *n.* zucca *f.*

**gourmand,** *n.* ghiottone *m.*

**gourmet,** *n.* buongustaio *m.*

**govern,** *vb.* governare.

**governess,** *n.* governante *f.*

**government,** *n.* govèrno *m.*

**governmental,** *adj.* governativo.

**governor,** *n.* governatore *m.*

**governorship,** *n.* governatorato *m.*

**gown,** *n.* gonnèlla *f.*

**grab,** *vb.* arraffare, carpire.

**grace,** *n.* gràzia *f.*

**graceful,** *adj.* grazioso.

**gracefully,** *adv.* graziosamente.

**graceless,** *adj.* sgraziato.

**gracious,** *adj.* grazioso.

**grackle,** *n.* gràcchio *m.*

**grade,** 1. *n.* grado *m.;* (quality) qualità *f.;* (mark) voto *m.* 2. *vb.* classificare.

**grade crossing,** *n.* passàggio a livèllo *m.*

**gradual,** *adj.* graduale.

**gradually,** *adv.* gradualmente.

**graduate,** *vb.* graduare; (university) laurearsi.

**graft,** 1. *n.* innèsto *m.;* (fraud) baratteria *f.* 2. *vb.* innestare.

**graham flour,** *n.* farina integrale *f.*

**grail,** *n.* gradale *m.*

**grain,** *n.* grano *m.;* (single) chicco *m.*

**grain alcohol,** *n.* àlcole etìlico *m.*

**gram,** *n.* grammo *m.*

**grammar,** *n.* grammàtica *f.*

**grammarian,** *n.* grammàtico *m.*

**grammar school,** *n.* scuòla elementare *f.*

**grammatical,** *adj.* grammaticale.

**gramophone,** *n.* grammòfono *m.*

**granary,** *n.* granaio *m.*

**grand,** *adj.* grande, grandioso.

**grandchild,** *n.* nipote *m.* or *f.*

**granddaughter,** *n.* nipòte *f.*

**grandeur,** *n.* grandezza *f.*

**grandfather,** *n.* nònno *m.*

**grandiloquent,** *adj.* magniloquente.

**grandiose,** *adj.* grandioso.

**grandly,** *adj.* grandiosamente.

**grandmother,** *n.* nònna *f.*

**grandparents,** *n.* nònni *m.pl.*

**grandson,** *n.* nipote *m.*

**grandstand,** *n.* tribuna *f.*

**grange,** *n.* fattoria *f.*

**granger,** *n.* fattore *m.*

**granite,** *n.* granito *m.*

**granny,** *n.* vècchia *f.*

**grant,** 1. *n.* concessione *f.;* (gift) dono *m.* 2. *vb.* concèdere.

**granular,** *adj.* granulare.

**granulate,** *vb.* granulare.

**granulation,** *n.* granulazione *f.*

**granule,** *n.* granèllo *m.*

**grape,** *n.* uva *f.;* (**g. juice**) spremuta d'uva *f.*

**grapefruit,** *n.* pompèlmo *m.*

**grapeshot,** *n.* mitràglia *f.*

**grapevine,** *n.* vite *f.*

**graph,** *n.* gràfico *m.*

**graphic,** *adj.* gràfico *m.*

**graphite,** *n.* grafite *f.*

**graphology,** *n.* grafologìa *f.*

**grapple,** 1. *n.* uncino *m.,* lotta *f.* 2. *vb.* venire alle prese.

**grasp,** 1. *n.* presa *f.* 2. *vb.* afferrare.

**grasping,** *adj.* avaro.

**grass,** *n.* èrba *f.*

**grasshopper,** *n.* cavalletta *f.*

**grassy,** *adj.* erboso.

**grate,** 1. *n.* graticola *f.* 2. *vb.* (cheese, etc.) grattugiare; (irritate) irritare.

**grateful,** *adj.* grato.

**grater,** *n.* grattùgia *f.*

**gratify,** *vb.* gratificare.

**grating,** *n.* inferriata *f.*

**gratis,** 1. *adj.* gratùito. 2. *adv.* gratuitamente.

**gratitude,** *n.* gratitùdine *f.*

**gratuitous,** *adj.* gratùito.

**gratuity,** *n.* mància *f.*

**grave,** 1. *n.* tomba *f.* 2. *adj.* grave.

**gravel,** *n.* ghiaia *f.*

**gravely,** *adj.* gravemente.

**gravestone,** *n.* piètra tombale *f.*

**graveyard**, *n.* camposanto *m.*
**gravitate**, *vb.* gravitare.
**gravitation**, *n.* gravitazione *f.*
**gravity**, *n.* gravità *f.*
**gravure**, *n.* incisione *f.*
**gravy**, *n.* sugo di carne *m.*
**gray**, *adj.* grigio.
**grayish**, *adj.* grigiastro.
**gray matter**, *n.* cervèllo *m.*
**graze**, *vb.* pàscere.
**grazing**, *n.* pàscolo *m.*
**grease**, 1. *n.* grasso *m.* 2. *vb.* ùngere, lubrificare.
**greasy**, *adj.* grasso, untuoso.
**great**, *adj.* grande.
**greatness**, *n.* grandezza *f.*
**Greece**, *n.* Grècia *f.*
**greed**, *n.* cupidìgia *f.*
**greediness**, *n.* ghiottonerìa *f.*
**greedy**, *adj.* ghiottone.
**Greek**, *adj.* grèco.
**green**, *adj.* verde.
**greenery**, *n.* verzura *f.*
**greenhouse**, *n.* sèrra *f.*
**greet**, *vb.* salutare.
**greeting**, *n.* saluto *m.*
**gregarious**, *adj.* gregàrio.
**grenade**, *n.* granata *f.*
**grenadine**, *n.* granatina *f.*
**greyhound**, *n.* levrière *m.*
**grid**, *n.* graticola *f.*; (electric power) rete *f.*
**griddle**, *n.* graticola *f.*
**gridiron**, *n.* graticola *f.*
**grief**, *n.* dolore *m.*
**grievance**, *n.* lagnanza *f.*
**grieve**, *vb.* addolorare, *tr.*
**grievous**, *adj.* doloroso, grave.
**grill**, *n.* graticola *f.*
**grillroom**, *n.* rosticcerìa *f.*
**grim**, *adj.* fosco.
**grimace**, *n.* smòrfia *f.*
**grime**, *n.* sudiciume *m.*
**grimy**, *adj.* sùdicio.
**grin**, *vb.* sorrìdere da un orécchio all'altro.
**grind**, *vb.* macinare.
**grindstone**, *n.* màcina *f.*
**grip**, 1. *n.* presa *f.*; (suitcase) valìgia *f.* 2. *vb.* afferrare.
**gripe**, 1. *n.* lagnanza *f.* 2. *vb.* lagnarsi.
**grippe**, *n.* influènza *f.*
**grisly**, *adj.* orrìbile.
**grist**, *n.* grano da macinare *m.*
**gristle**, *n.* cartilàgine *f.*
**grit**, *n.* sàbbia *f.*
**grizzled**, *adj.* grìgio.
**groan**, 1. *n.* gèmito *m.* 2. *vb.* gèmere.

**grocer**, *n.* negoziante di gèneri alimentari *m.*
**grocery**, *n.* negòzio di gèneri alimentari *m.*
**grog**, *n.* gròg *m.*
**groggy**, *adj.* intontito.
**groin**, *n.* ìnguine *m.*
**groom**, *n.* palafrenière *m.*; (footman) staffière *m.*; (bridegroom) sposo *m.*
**groove**, *n.* solco *m.*
**grope**, *vb.* andare a tastoni.
**grosgrain**, *n.* grossagrana *f.*
**gross**, *adj.* grossolano; (blunder) madornale; (weight) lordo.
**grossly**, *adv.* grossolanamente; (wholly) totalmente.
**grossness**, *n.* grossolanità *f.*
**grotesque**, *adj.* grottesco.
**grotto**, *n.* grotta *f.*
**grouch**, 1. *n.* (person) brontolone *m.* 2. *vb.* brontolare.
**ground**, 1. *n.* tèrra *f.*; (reason) motivo *m.*; (basis) base *f.*; (electrical) presa di tèrra *f.* 2. *vb.* basare.
**ground hog**, *n.* marmotta *f.*
**groundless**, *adj.* sènza base.
**ground swell**, *n.* mare di fondo *m.*
**groundwork**, *n.* fondamento *m.*
**group**, 1. *n.* gruppo *m.* 2. *vb.* raggruppare, *tr.*
**grouse**, *n.* tetraone *m.*
**grove**, *n.* boschetto *m.*
**grovel**, *vb.* umiliarsi.
**grow**, *vb.* créscere; (raise) coltivare.
**growl**, 1. *n.* brontolamento *m.* 2. *vb.* brontolare.
**grown**, *adj.* maturo.
**grown-up**, *n. and adj.* adulto (*m.*)
**growth**, *n.* créscita *f.*, sviluppo *m.*
**grub**, 1. *n.* larva *f.*; (food) cibo *m.* 2. *vb.* scavare.
**grubby**, *adj.* sporco.
**grudge**, *n.* àstio *m.*
**gruel**, *n.* pappa *f.*
**gruesome**, *adj.* orrèndo.
**gruff**, *adj.* bùrbero.
**grumble**, *vb.* brontolare.
**grumpy**, *adj.* scontènto.
**grunt**, 1. *n.* grugnito *m.* 2. *vb.* grugnire.
**guarantee**, 1. *n.* garanzìa *f.* 2. *vb.* garantire.
**guarantor**, *n.* mallevadore *m.*
**guaranty**, *n.* garanzìa *f.*

**guard,** 1. *n.* guàrdia *f.* 2. *vb.* custodire, guardarsi.

**guarded,** *adj.* guardingo.

**guardhouse,** *n.* guardina *f.*

**guardian,** *n.* guardiano *m.*; (legal) tutore *m.*

**guardianship,** *n.* tutèla *f.*

**guardsman,** *n.* guàrdia *f.*

**gubernatorial,** *adj.* governatoriale.

**guerilla,** *n.* (war) guerrìglia *f.*; (fighter) guerriglière *m.*

**guess,** *vb.* indovinare.

**guesswork,** *n.* congettura *f.*

**guest,** *n.* òspite *m.*; (hotel, etc.) cliènte *m.*

**guffaw,** 1. *n.* sghignazzata *f.* 2. *vb.* sghignazzare.

**guidance,** *n.* guida *f.*

**guide,** 1. *n.* guida *f.* 2. *vb.* guidare.

**guidebook,** *n.* guida *f.*

**guidepost,** *n.* palo indicatore *m.*

**guild,** *n.* arte *f.*, corporazione *f.*

**guile,** *n.* astùzia *f.*

**guillotine,** *n.* ghigliottina *f.*

**guilt,** *n.* colpa *f.*

**guiltily,** *adv.* colpevolmente.

**guiltless,** *adj.* sènza colpa.

**guilty,** *adj.* colpévole.

**guinea fowl,** *n.* faraona *f.*

**guinea pig,** *n.* porcellino d'India *m.*

**guise,** *n.* apparènza *f.*; (shape) foggia *f.*

**guitar,** *n.* chitarra *f.*

**gulch,** *n.* burrone *m.*

**gulf,** *n.* golfo *m.*

**gull,** *n.* gabbiano *m.*

**gullet,** *n.* gola *f.*

**gullible,** *adj.* crèdulo.

**gully,** *n.* burrone *m.*

**gulp,** *vb.* inghiottire; (g. down) ingollare.

**gum,** *n.* gomma *f.*; (chew-

**ing-g.)** gomma da masticare *f.*

**gummy,** *adj.* gommoso.

**gun,** *n.* fucile *m.*; (cannon) cannone *m.*

**gunboat,** *n.* cannonièra *f.*

**gunman,** *n.* bandito armato *m.*

**gunner,** *n.* artiglière *m.*

**gunpowder,** *n.* pólvere da sparo *m.*

**gunshot,** *n.* portata di un fucile *f.*

**gunwale,** *n.* parapètto *m.*

**gurgle,** 1. *n.* gorgoglio *m.* 2. *vb.* gorgogliare.

**gush,** *vb.* sgorgare, zampillare.

**gusher,** *n.* sorgènte di petròlio *f.*

**gusset,** *n.* gherone *m.*

**gust,** *n.* ràffica *f.*; (rain) scròscio *m.*

**gustatory,** *adj.* gustativo.

**gusto,** *n.* gusto *m.*

**gusty,** *adj.* tempestoso.

**guts,** *n.* intestino *m.*, minùgia *f.*; (courage) fégato *m.*

**gutter,** *n.* (street) cunetta *f.*; (house) grondaia *f.*

**guttural,** *adj.* gutturale.

**guy,** *n.* tìzio *m.*

**guzzle,** *vb.* ingozzare.

**gym,** *n.* palèstra *f.*

**gymnasium,** *n.* palèstra *f.*; (school) ginnàsio *m.*

**gymnast,** *n.* ginnasta *m.*

**gymnastic,** *adj.* ginnàstico.

**gymnastics,** *n.* ginnàstica *f.*

**gynaecology,** *n.* ginecologìa *f.*

**gypsum,** *n.* gesso *f.*

**gypsy,** *n.* zìngaro *m.*, zìngara *f.*

**gyrate,** *vb.* turbinare.

**gyroscope,** *n.* giroscòpio *m.*

# H

**haberdasher,** *n.* merciàio *m.*

**haberdashery,** *n.* mercerìa *f.*

**habiliments,** *n.* vestimenta *f.pl.*

**habit,** *n.* abitùdine *f.*; (dress) àbito *m.*

**habitable,** *adj.* abitàbile.

**habitat,** *n.* ambiènte *f.*

**habitation,** *n.* abitazione *f.*

**habitual,** *adj.* abituale.

**habituate,** *vb.* abituare.

**habitué,** *n.* frequentatore *m.*

**hack, 1.** *n.* cavallo da dipòrto *m.* **2.** *vb.* tagliare.

**hackneyed,** *adj.* banale.

**hacksaw,** *n.* sega per metalli *f.*

**haft,** *n.* mànico *m.*

**hag,** *n.* strega *f.*

**haggard,** *adj.* sparuto.

**haggle,** *vb.* mercanteggiare.

**hag-ridden,** *adj.* tormentato da streghe.

**Hague,** *n.*; **(The H.)** l'Aia *f.*

**hail, 1.** *n.* gràndine *f.* **2.** *vb.* grandinare; **(call to)** salutare.

**Hail Mary,** *n.* avemmaria *f.*

**hailstone,** *n.* chicco di gràndine *m.*

**hailstorm,** *n.* grandinata *f.*

**hair,** *n.* capelli *m.pl.,* crine *f.*; **(single, on head)** capello *m.*; **(body, animals)** pelo *m.*

**haircut,** *n.* tàglio di capelli *m.*

**hairdo,** *n.* pettinatura *f.,* acconciatura *f.*

**hairdresser,** *n.* parrucchière *m.*

**hairline,** *n.* lìnea sottilìssima *f.*

**hairpin,** *n.* forcina *f.*

**hair-raising,** *adj.* orrèndo.

**hair's-breadth,** *n.* grossezza di un capello *f.*

**hairy,** *adj.* peloso.

**halcyon,** *adj.* felice.

**hale,** *adj.* robusto.

**half, 1.** *n.* metà *f.* **2.** *adj.* mèzzo. **3.** *adv.* a metà.

**half-and-half,** *adv.* metà e metà.

**halfback,** *n.* secondo *m.*

**half-baked,** *adj.* immaturo, imperfètto.

**half-breed,** *n.* mestìccio *m.*

**half-brother,** *n.* fratellastro *m.*

**half-dollar,** *n.* mèzzo dòllaro *m.*

**half-hearted,** *adj.* sènza entusiasmo.

**half-mast,** *adv* a mezz'asta.

**halfway,** *adv.* a mèzza via.

**half-wit,** *n.* imbecille *m.*

**halibut,** *n.* pianuzza *f.*

**hall,** *n.* sal *f.,* àula *f.*; **(hallway)** vestìbolo *m.,* corridoio *m.*

**hallmark,** *n.* màrchio *m.*

**hallow,** *vb.* santificare.

**Halloween,** *n.* la véglia di Ognissanti *f.*

**hallucination,** *n.* allucinazione *f.*

**hallway,** *n.* vestìbolo *m.,* corridoio *m.*

**halo,** *n.* aurèola *f.*

**halt, 1.** *n.* fermata *f.* **2.** *vb.* fermare, *tr.* **3.** *interj.* altl.

**halter,** *n.* cavezza *f.,* capestro *m.*

**halve,** *vb.* dimezzare.

**halyard,** *n.* drizza *f.*

**ham,** *n.* prosciutto *m.*

**Hamburg,** *n.* Amburgo *m.*

**hamlet,** *n.* vico *m.*

**hammer, 1.** *n.* martèllo *m.* **2.** *vb.* martellare.

**hammock,** *n.* amaca *f.*

**hamper, 1.** *n.* cesta *f.* **2.** *vb.* impedire.

**hamstring,** *vb.* ostacolare.

**hand,** *n.* mano *f.*

**handbag,** *n.* **(lady's)** borsetta *f.*; **(suitcase)** valigetta *f.*

**handbook,** *n.* manuale *m.*

**handcuffs,** *n.* manette *f.pl.*

**handful,** *n.* manata *f.*

**handicap,** *n.* svantàggio *m.*

**handicraft,** *n.* lavoro manuale *f.*

**handiwork,** *n.* òpera *f.*

**handkerchief,** *n.* fazzoletto *m.*

**handle, 1.** *n.* mànico *m.,* maniglia *f.,* manovèlla *f.* **2.** *vb.* maneggiare.

**handle bar,** *n.* manùbrio *m.*

**hand-made,** *adj.* fatto a mano.

**handmaid,** *n.* ancella *f.*

**handorgan,** *n.* organetto a manovèlla *m.*

**handout,** *n.* **(alms)** limòsina *f.*

**handsome,** *adj.* bèllo.

**hand-pick,** *vb.* scégliere con cura.

**hand-rail,** *n.* mancorrente *m.*

**hand-to-hand,** *adj.* còrpo a còrpo.

**handwriting,** *n.* calligrafia *f.*

**handy,** *adj.* **(person)** dèstro; **(thing)** còmodo; **(at hand)** a portata di mano.

**handy-man,** *n.* factotum *m.*

**hang,** *vb.* pèndere; **(execute)** impiccare.

**hangar,** *n.* aviorimessa *f.*

**hangdog,** *adj.* con una fàccia patibolare.

**hanger,** *n.* gàncio *m.*; **(coat-h.)** attaccapanni *m.*

**hanger-on,** *n.* seguace *m.*

**hanging,** n. (execution) impiccagione f.; (tapestry) tappezzeria f.

**hangman,** n. impiccatore m.

**hangnail,** n. pipita f.

**hangout,** n. ritròvo m.

**hang-over,** n. stanghetta f.

**hank,** n. matassa f.

**hanker,** vb. bramare.

**haphazard,** adv. a casàccio.

**happen,** vb. (take place) accadere, succèdere; (chance to be) trovarsi.

**happening,** n. avvenimento m.

**happily,** adv. felicemente.

**happiness,** n. felicità f.

**happy,** adj. felice.

**happy-go-lucky,** adj. spensierato.

**harakiri,** n. karakiri m.

**harangue,** 1. n. arringa f. 2. vb. arringare.

**harass,** vb. annoiare.

**harbinger,** n. precursore m.

**harbor,** n. (refuge) rifùgio m.; (port) pòrto m.

**hard,** 1. adj. duro; (difficult) difficile. 2. adv. fortemente, duramente.

**hard-bitten,** adj. tenace.

**hard-boiled,** adj. sòdo.

**hard coal,** n. antracite f.

**harden,** vb. indurire.

**hard-headed,** adj. pràtico.

**hard-hearted,** adj. di cuòre duro.

**hardiness,** n. robustezza f.

**hardly,** adv. (with difficulty) stentatamente; (scarcely) appena; (**h. ever**) quasi mai.

**hardness,** n. durezza f.

**hardship,** n. avversità f.

**hardware,** n. ferramenta f.pl.

**hardwood,** n. legno duro m.

**hardy,** adj. robusto.

**hare,** n. lèpre f.

**hare-brained,** adj. scervellato.

**hare-lip,** n. labbro leporino m.

**harem,** n. àrem m.

**hark,** vb. ascoltare.

**Harlequin,** n. Arlecchino m.

**harlot,** n. meretrice f.

**harm,** 1. n. danno m. 2. vb. danneggiare, nuòcere.

**harmful,** adj. dannoso, nocivo.

**harmless,** adj. innòcuo, innocènte.

**harmonic,** adj. armònico.

**harmonica,** n. armònica f.

**harmonious,** adj. armonioso.

**harmonize,** vb. armonizzare.

**harmony,** n. armonia f.

**harness,** 1. n. bardatura f. 2. vb. bardare.

**harp,** n. arpa f.

**harpoon,** 1. n. fiòcina f. 2. vb. fiocinare.

**harpsichord,** n. clavicémbalo m.

**harridan,** n. vecchiàccia f.

**harrow,** 1. n. èrpice m. 2. vb. erpicare.

**harry,** vb. spogliare.

**harsh,** adj. aspro.

**harshness,** n. asprezza f.

**harvest,** 1. n. raccòlta f. 2. vb. raccògliere.

**hash,** n. guazzabùglio m.

**hashish,** n. hascisc m.

**hasn't,** vb. non à.

**hassock,** n. cuscino m.

**haste,** 1. n. fretta m. 2. vb. affrettarsi.

**hasten,** vb. affrettare tr.

**hastily,** adv. affrettatamente, frettolosamente.

**hasty,** adj. affrettato, frettoloso.

**hat,** n. cappèllo m.

**hatch,** 1. n. (boat) boccapòrto m. 2. vb. (hen) covare; (egg) schiudersi; aprirsi.

**hatchery,** n. vivaio m.

**hatchet,** n. accetta f.

**hate,** 1. n. òdio m. 2. vb. odiare.

**hateful,** adj. odioso.

**hatred,** n. òdio m.

**haughtiness,** n. supèrbia f.

**haughty,** adj. supèrbo.

**haul,** vb. trascinare, trasportare.

**haunch,** n. anca f.

**haunt,** vb. frequentare.

**have,** vb. avere; (**have to,** necessity) dovere.

**haven,** n. pòrto m.; (refuge) rifùgio m.

**haven't,** vb. non ò, etc.

**havoc,** n. devastazione f.

**hawk,** n. falco m.

**hawker,** n. venditore ambulante m.

**hawser,** n. alzaia f., gòmena f.

**hawthorn,** n. biancospino m.

**hay,** n. fièno m.

**hay fever,** n. asma del fièno m.

**hayfield,** n. campo da fièno m.

**hayloft,** n. fienile m.

**haystack**, *n.* cùmulo di fièno *m.*

**hazard**, **1.** *n.* rìschio *m.* **2.** *vb.* rischiare.

**hazardous**, *adj.* rischioso.

**haze**, *n.* nébbia *f.*

**hazel**, *n.* (plant) nocciòlo *m.*; (nut) nocciòla *m.*

**hazy**, *adj.* nebbioso, vago.

**he**, *pron.* egli, lùi.

**head**, *n.* tèsta *f.*, capo *m.*

**headache**, *n.* mal di tèsta *m.*

**headband**, *n.* bènda *f.*, diadèma *m.*

**headfirst**, *adv.* colla tèsta in avanti.

**headgear**, *n.* acconciatura del capo *f.*

**head-hunting**, *n.* càccia alle tèste *f.*

**heading**, *n.* tìtolo *m.*

**headlight**, *n.* fanale anteriore *m.*

**headline**, *n.* tìtolo *m.*

**headlong**, *n.* a capofitto.

**head-man**, *n.* capo *m.*

**headmaster**, *n.* direttore *m.*

**head-on**, *adj.* frontale.

**headquarters**, *n.* quartière generale *m.*

**headstone**, *n.* piètra tombale *f.*

**headstrong**, *adj.* ostinato, testardo.

**headwaters**, *n.* sorgènti *f. pl.*

**headway**, *n.* progrèsso *m.*; (trains, etc.) intervallo *m.*

**head-work**, *n.* lavoro intellettuale *m.*

**heady**, *adj.* impetuoso, inebriante.

**heal**, *vb.* guarire, risanare.

**health**, *n.* salute *f.*; (skoal) brìndisi *m.*

**healthful**, *adj.* salubre.

**healthy**, *adj.* sano.

**heap**, **1.** *n.* mùcchio *m.* **2.** *vb.* ammucchiare.

**hear**, *vb.* sentire, udire.

**hearing**, *n.* (sense) udito *m.*; (audience) udiènza *f.*

**hearken to**, *vb.* ascoltare.

**hearsay**, *n.* (by h.) per sentito dire.

**hearse**, *n.* carro fùnebre *m.*

**heart**, *n.* cuòre *m.*

**heartache**, *n.* angòscia *f.*

**heart-break**, *n.* crepacuòre *m.*

**heartbroken**, *adj.* straziato.

**heartburn**, *n.* bruciore di stòmaco *m.*

**heartfelt**, *adj.* sincèro.

**hearth**, *n.* focolare *m.*

**heartless**, *adj.* sènza cuòre.

**heart-rending**, *adj.* straziante.

**heart-sick**, *adj.* scoraggiato.

**heart-stricken**, *adj.* colpito al cuòre.

**heart-to-heart**, *adj.* ìntimo.

**hearty**, *adj.* cordiale.

**heat**, **1.** *n.* calore *m.*, caldo *m.* **2.** *vb.* riscaldare.

**heated**, *adj.* (dwelling-place) riscaldato; (discussion) infiammato.

**heater**, *n.* calorìfero *m.*

**heath**, *n.* brughièra *f.*

**heathen**, *n. and adj.* pagano *m.*

**heather**, *n.* èrica *f.*

**heat-stroke**, *n.* colpo di calore *m.*

**heat wave**, *n.* ondata di caldo *f.*

**heave**, *vb.* sollevare; (utter) eméttere.

**heaven**, *n.* cièlo *m.*

**heavenly**, *adj.* celèste.

**heavy**, *adj.* pesante.

**heavyweight**, *n. and adj.* peso màssimo (*m.*)

**Hebrew**, *n. and adj.* ebrèo (*m.*); ebràico (*m.*)

**heckle**, *vb.* fare domande imbarazzanti.

**hectare**, *n.* èttaro *m.*

**hectic**, *adj.* ètico; (wild) da impazzire.

**hectogram**, *n.* ètto *m.*, ettogramma *m.*

**hedge**, *n.* sièpe *f.*

**hedgehog**, *n.* riccio *m.*

**hedge-hop**, *vb.* volare rasentando la tèrra.

**hedgerow**, *n.* sièpe di cespùgli o di àlberi.

**hedonism**, *n.* edonismo *m.*

**heed**, *vb.* badare a, prestare attenzione a.

**heedless**, *adj.* spensierato.

**heel**, *n.* calcagno *m.*, tallone *m.*; (shoes) tacco *m.*

**hefty**, *adj.* pesante, vigoroso.

**hegemony**, *n.* egemonìa *f.*

**heifer**, *n.* giovènca *f.*

**height**, *n.* altezza *f.*; (high place) altura *f.*

**heighten**, *vb.* (raise) innalzare; (increase) accréscere.

**heinous**, *adj.* atroce.

**heir**, *n.* erède *m.*

**heir apparent,** n. erède legittimo m.

**heirloom,** n. oggètto antico di famìglia m.

**heir presumptive,** n. presunto erède m.

**helicopter,** n. elicòttero m.

**heliocentric,** adj. eliocèntrico.

**heliograph,** n. eliògrafo m.

**heliotrope,** n. eliotròpio m.

**helium,** n. èlio m.

**hell,** n. infèrno m.

**Hellenic,** adj. ellènico.

**Hellenism,** n. ellenismo m.

**hellish,** adj. infernale.

**hello,** interj. buòn giorno, buòna sera, addìo; (telephone) pronto.

**helm,** n. timone m.

**helmet,** n. èlmo m.

**helmsman,** n. timonière m.

**help,** 1. n. aiuto m. 2. vb. aiutare; (at table) servire.

**helper,** n. aiutante m.

**helpful,** adj. (person) serviziévole; (thing) ùtile.

**helpfulness,** n. utilità f.

**helping,** n. porzione f.

**helpless,** adj. impotènte.

**helter-skelter,** adv. a casàccio.

**hem,** 1. n. orlo m. 2. vb. orlare.

**hematite,** n. ematite f.

**hemisphere,** n. emisfèrio m.

**hemlock,** n. cicuta f.

**hemoglobin,** n. emoglobina f.

**hemophilia,** n. emofilìa f.

**hemorrhage,** n. emorragìa f.

**hemorrhoid,** n. emorròide f.

**hemp,** n. cànapa f.

**hemstitch,** n. orlo a giorno m.

**hen,** n. gallina f.

**hence,** adv. (time, place) di qui; (therefore) quindi.

**henceforth,** adv. d'òra in pòi.

**henchman,** n. bravo m.

**henna,** n. ennè m.

**henpecked,** adj. dominato dalla móglie.

**hepatic,** adj. epàtico.

**hepatica,** n. epàtica f.

**her,** 1. adj: suo, di lèi. 2. pron. (direct) la; (indirect) le; (alone, stressed, or with prep.) lèi.

**herald,** n. araldo m.

**heraldic,** adj. aràldico.

**heraldry,** n. aràldica f.

**herb,** n. èrba f.

**herbaceous,** adj. erbàceo.

**herbarium,** n. erbàrio m.

**herculean,** adj. ercùleo.

**herd,** n. gregge m., mandra f.

**here,** adv. qui; **(h. is)** ècco.

**hereabout,** adv. qui vicino.

**hereafter,** adv. d'òra in pòi.

**hereby,** adv. con questo.

**hereditary,** adj. ereditàrio.

**heredity,** n. eredità f.

**herein,** adv. qui dentro.

**heresy,** n. eresìa f.

**heretic,** n. erètico m.

**heretical,** adj. erètico.

**hereto,** adv. a questo.

**heretofore,** adv. finora.

**herewith,** adv. con questo.

**heritage,** n. eredità f.

**hermetic,** adj. ermètico.

**hermit,** n. eremita m.

**hermitage,** n. eremitàggio m., romitàggio m.

**hernia,** n. èrnia f.

**hero,** n. eròe m.

**heroic,** adj. eròico.

**heroically,** adv. eroicamente.

**heroin,** n. eroìna f.

**heroine,** n. eroìna f.

**heroism,** n. eroismo m.

**heron,** n. airone m.

**herpes,** n. èrpete m.

**herring,** n. aringa f.

**herringbone,** n. lisca d'arenga f.

**hers,** pron. suo, di lèi.

**herself,** pron. sè stessa.

**hesitancy,** n. esitazione f.

**hesitant,** adj. esitante.

**hesitate,** vb. esitare.

**hesitation,** n. esitazione f.

**heterodox,** adj. eterodòsso.

**heterodoxy,** n. eterodossìa f.

**heterogeneous,** adj. eterogèneo.

**hew,** vb. tagliare.

**hexagon,** n. esàgono m.

**heyday,** n. apogèo m.

**hi!** interj. ciao.

**hiatus,** n. iato m.

**hibernate,** vb. svernare.

**hibernation,** n. ibernazione f.

**hibiscus,** n. ibisco m.

**hiccup,** n. singulto m.

**hickory,** n. noce americano m.

**hide,** 1. n. pèlle f. 2. vb. nascóndere, tr.

**hideous,** adj. spaventoso.

**hide-out,** n. nascondìglio m.

**hierarchical,** adj. geràrchico.

**hierarchy,** n. gerarchìa f.

**hieroglyphic,** *adj.* geroglìfico.

**high,** *adj.* alto, elevato; (in price) caro.

**highbrow,** *n. and adj.* intellettuale *m.* or *f.*

**high-handed,** *adj.* arbitràrio.

**high-hat,** *vb.* trattare dall'alto in basso.

**highland,** *n.* regione montuosa *f.*

**highlight,** *vb.* méttere in rilièvo.

**highly,** *adv.* altamente, estremamente.

**high-minded,** *adj.* magnànimo.

**Highness,** *n.* Altezza *f.*

**high school,** *n.* licèo *m.*, ginnàsio *m.*

**high seas,** *n.* alto mare *m.* (*sg.*)

**high-strung,** *adj.* eccitàbile.

**high tide,** *n.* alta marèa *f.*

**highway,** *n.* strada maestra *f.*; (**h. robber**) grassatore *m.*

**hike, 1.** *n.* gita a pièdi *f.* **2.** *vb.* fare una gita a pièdi.

**hilarious,** *adj.* ilare.

**hilarity,** *n.* ilarità *f.*

**hill,** *n.* collina *f.*

**hilt,** *n.* èlsa *f.*

**him,** *pron.* (direct) lo; (indirect) gli; (alone, stressed, or with prep.) lùi.

**himself,** *pron.* sè stesso; (*refl.*) si.

**hind, 1.** *n.* cèrva *f.*, dàina *f.* **2.** *adj.* posteriore.

**hinder,** *vb.* impedire, ostacolare.

**hindmost,** *adj.* ùltimo.

**hindrance,** *n.* impedimento *m.*, ostàcolo *m.*, intràlcio *m.*

**hinge,** *n.* càrdine *m.*, gànghero *m.*

**hint, 1.** *n.* cenno *m.* **2.** *vb.* accennare.

**hinterland,** *n.* retrotèrra *f.*

**hip,** *n.* anca *f.*, fianco *m.*

**hippodrome,** *n.* ippòdromo *m.*

**hippopotamus,** *n.* ippopòtamo *m.*

**hire, 1.** *n.* nòlo *m.* **2.** *vb.* noleggiare.

**hireling,** *n.* mercenàrio *m.*

**his,** *adj. and pron.* suo, di lùi.

**hiss, 1.** *n.* sibilo *m.* **2.** *vb.* sibilare.

**historian,** *n.* stòrico *m.*

**historic, historical,** *adj.* stòrico.

**history,** *n.* stòria *f.*

**histrionic,** *adj.* istriònico.

**histrionics,** *n.* istriònica *f.*

**hit, 1.** *n.* colpo *m.*; (success) successo *m.* **2.** *vb.* colpire; percuòtere; picchiare.

**hitch, 1.** *n.* (obstacle) ostàcolo *m.* **2.** *vb.* attaccare.

**hither,** *adv.* qua.

**hitherto,** *adv.* finora.

**hive,** *n.* alveare *m.*

**hives,** *n.* eruzione cutànea *f.*

**hoard, 1.** *n.* ammasso *m.* **2.** *vb.* ammassare.

**hoarse,** *adj.* fiòco, ràuco.

**hoax, 1.** *n.* inganno *m.* **2.** *vb.* ingannare.

**hobble,** *vb.* zoppicare.

**hobby,** *n.* passione *f.*

**hobby-horse,** *n.* cavallo a dòndolo *m.*

**hobgoblin,** *n.* folletto *m.*

**hobnail,** *n.* chiòdo gròsso *m.*

**hobnob with,** *vb.* frequentare.

**hobo,** *n.* vagabondo *m.*

**hock,** *vb.* impegnare.

**hockey,** *n.* hockey *m.*

**hocus-pocus,** *n.* inganno *m.*

**hod,** *n.* sécchia *f.*

**hodge-podge,** *n.* miscùglio *m.*

**hoe, 1.** *n.* zappa *f.* **2.** *vb.* zappare.

**hog,** *n.* pòrco *m.*, maiale *m.*

**hog-tie,** *vb.* legare sicuramente.

**hogshead,** *n.* botte *f.*

**hoist,** *vb.* innalzare.

**hold, 1.** presa *f.*; (boat) stiva *f.* **2.** *vb.* tenere; (contain) contenere; (h. up, support) règgere.

**holder,** *n.* recipiènte *m.*; (**cigarette-h.**) portasigarette *m.*

**holdup,** *n.* grassazione *f.*

**hole,** *n.* buco *m.*

**holiday,** *n.* giorno festivo *m.*; vacanza *f.*, fèsta *f.*

**holiness,** *n.* santità *f.*

**Holland,** *n.* Olanda *f.*

**hollow,** *n. and adj.* cavo (*m.*).

**holly,** *n.* agrifòglio *m.*

**hollyhock,** *n.* malvaròsa *f.*

**holocaust,** *n.* olocàusto *m.*

**holster,** *n.* fondina *f.*

**holy,** *adj.* santo.

**holy day,** *n.* fèsta ecclesiàstica *f.*

**Holy See,** *n.* Santa Sede *f.*

**Holy Spirit**, n. Spirito Santo m.

**Holy Week**, n. settimana santa f.

**homage**, n. omàggio m.

**home**, **1.** n. casa f. **2.** adj. casalingo. **3.** adv. a casa.

**homeland**, n. pàtria f.

**homeless**, adj. sènza tètto.

**homelike**, adj. casalingo.

**homely**, adj. brutto.

**home-made**, adj. fatto in casa.

**home rule**, n. autonomìa f.

**homesick, be**, vb. soffrire di nostalgia.

**homesickness**, n. nostalgìa f.

**home-spun**, adj. filato in casa.

**homestead**, n. fattorìa f.

**homeward**, adv. vèrso casa.

**homework**, n. lavoro di casa m.

**homicide**, n. (act) omicìdio m.; (person) omicida m.

**homily**, n. omelìa f.

**homing pigeon**, n. piccione viaggiatore m.

**hominy**, n. semolino di gran-turco f.

**homogeneous**, adj. omogè-neo.

**homogenize**, vb. omogeniz-zare.

**homonym**, n. omònimo m.

**homonymous**, adj. omòni-mo.

**homosexual**, adj. omoses-suale.

**hone**, n. còte f.

**honest**, adj. onèsto.

**honestly**, adv. onestamente.

**honesty**, n. onestà f.

**honey**, n. mièle m.

**honey-bee**, n. ape da miéle f.

**honeycomb**, n. favo m.

**honeymoon**, n. luna di miéle m.

**honeysuckle**, n. caprifòglio m.

**honor**, **1.** n. onore m. **2.** vb. onorare.

**honorable**, adj. onorévole.

**honorary**, adj. onoràrio.

**hood**, n. cappùccio m.; (auto) còfano m.

**hoodlum**, n. teppista m.

**hoodwink**, vb. ingannare.

**hoof**, n. zòccolo m.

**hook**, **1.** n. uncino m.; (fish-h.) amo m. **2.** vb. uncinare; (catch) prèndere all'amo.

**hookworm**, n. anchilòstoma m.

**hoop**, n. cérchio m.

**hoot**, vb. (auto horn) sonare.

**hop**, **1.** n. (plant) lùppolo m.; (jump) salto m. **2.** vb. saltare.

**hope**, **1.** n. speranza f. **2.** vb. sperare.

**hopeful**, adj. pieno di spe-ranza.

**hopeless**, adj. disperato.

**hopelessness**, n. dispera-zione f.

**horde**, n. òrda f.

**horehound**, n. marrùbio m.

**horizon**, n. orizzonte m.

**horizontal**, adj. orizzontale.

**hormone**, n. ormone m.

**horn**, n. còrno m.; (auto) clàcson m.

**hornet**, n. calabrone m.

**horny**, adj. calloso.

**horoscope**, n. oròscopo m.

**horrendous**, adj. orrèndo.

**horrible**, adj. orribile.

**horrid**, adj. òrrido.

**horrify**, vb. far inorridire; (be horrified) inorridire.

**horror**, n. orrore m.

**horse**, n. cavallo m.; (cav-alry) cavallerìa f.

**horseback, on**, adv. a cavallo.

**horsefly**, n. mosca cavallina f.

**horsehair**, n. crine di cavallo f.

**horseman**, n. cavalière m.

**horsemanship**, n. equita-zione f.

**horseplay**, n. giòco rozzo m.

**horse-power**, n. cavallo-vapore m.

**horse-radish**, n. ràfano m.

**horseshoe**, n. fèrro di cavallo m.

**horsewhip**, n. frustino m.

**hortatory**, adj. esortativo.

**horticulture**, n. orticultura f.

**hose**, n. (tube) tubo flessìbile m.; (stockings) calze f.pl.

**hosiery**, n. calzetterìa f.

**hospitable**, adj. ospitale.

**hospital**, n. ospedale m.

**hospitality**, n. ospitalità f.

**hospitalization**, n. ospeda-lizzazione f.

**hospitalize**, vb. ospedalizzare.

**host**, n. (giver of hospitality) òspite m.; (innkeeper) òste m.; (crowd) moltitùdine f.; (Eucharist) òstia f.

**hostage,** *n.* ostàggio *m.*

**hostel,** *n.* albèrgo *m.*

**hostelry,** *n.* albèrgo *m.*

**hostess,** *n.* òspite *f.*

**hostile,** *adj.* ostile.

**hostility,** *n.* ostilità *f.*

**hot,** *adj.* caldo; (on water faucets) C.

**hotbed,** *n.* terreno concimato *m.*; (fig.) focolare *m.*

**hot dog,** *n.* salsìccia *f.*

**hotel,** *n.* albèrgo *m.*

**hot-headed,** *adj.* eccitàbile.

**hothouse,** *n.* sèrra *f.*

**hound,** *n.* cane *m.*

**hour,** *n.* ora *f.*

**hourglass,** *n.* orològio a pólvere *m.*

**hourly,** *adv.* ogni ora.

**house,** *n.* casa *f.*; (legislative) càmera *f.*

**housefly,** *n.* mosca *f.*

**household,** *n.* famiglia *f.*

**housekeeper,** *n.* massaia *f.*

**housekeeping,** *n.* economia domestica *f.*

**housemaid,** *n.* domèstica *f.*

**housewife,** *n.* massaia *f.*

**housework,** *n.* lavoro domèstico *m.*

**hovel,** *n.* tugùrio *m.*

**hover,** *vb.* volteggiare.

**how,** *adv.* come; **(h. far)** fin dove; **(h. long)** fino a quando; **(h. many, h. much)** quanto.

**however,** *adv.* comunque, però, tuttavia.

**howitzer,** *n.* òbice *m.*

**howl,** **1.** *n.* urlo *m.* **2.** *vb.* urlare.

**howsoever,** *adv.* comunque.

**hub,** *n.* mòzzo *m.*; (fig.) cèntro *m.*

**hubbub,** *n.* tumulto *m.*

**huckleberry,** *n.* vaccìnio *m.*

**huddle,** **1.** *n.* consultazione *f.* **2.** *vb.* rannicchiarsi; **(go into a h.)** tenere una consultazione.

**hue,** *n.* colore *m.*

**huff,** *n.* petulanza *f.*

**hug,** **1.** *n.* abbràccio *m.* **2.** *vb.* abbracciare.

**huge,** *adj.* immane.

**hulk,** *n.* carcassa *f.*

**hull,** **1.** *n.* (boat) scafo *m.*; (fruit) bùccia *f.*

**hullabaloo,** *n.* chiasso *m.*

**hum,** **1.** ronzìo *m.* **2.** *vb.* (insect) ronzare; (sing) canticchiare.

**human,** *adj.* umano.

**humane,** *adj.* umanitàrio.

**humanism,** *n.* umanésimo *m.*

**humanist,** *n.* umanista *m.*

**humanitarian,** *adj.* umanitàrio.

**humanity,** *n.* umanità *f.*

**humanly,** *adv.* umanamente.

**humble,** **1.** *adj.* ùmile. **2.** *vb.* umiliare.

**humbug,** *n.* impostura *f.*

**humdrum,** *adj.* monòtono.

**humid,** *adj.* ùmido.

**humidify,** *vb.* inumidire.

**humidity,** *n.* umidità *f.*

**humidor,** *n.* scàtola per inumidire i sigari *f.*

**humiliate,** *vb.* umiliare.

**humiliation,** *n.* umiliazione *f.*

**humility,** *n.* umiltà *f.*

**humor,** *n.* umore *m.*; (wit) umorismo *m.*

**humorist,** *n.* umorista *m.*

**humorous,** *adj.* umorìstico.

**hump,** *n.* gobba *f.*

**humpback,** *n.* gobbo *m.*, gobba *f.*

**humus,** *n.* humus *m.*

**hunch,** **1.** *n.* gobba *f.*; (suspicion) sospètto *m.* **2.** *vb.* curvare, *tr.*

**hunchback,** *n.* gobbo *m.*, gobba *f.*

**hundred,** *num.* cènto; (group of a hundred) centinaio *n.m.*

**hundredth,** *adj.* centésimo.

**Hungarian,** *adj.* ungherese.

**Hungary,** *n.* Ungheria *f.*

**hunger,** *n.* fame *f.*

**hungry, be,** *vb.* aver fame.

**hunk,** *n.* pèzzo *m.*

**hunt,** **1.** *n.* càccia *f.* **2.** *vb.* cacciare; **(h. for)** cercare.

**hunter,** *n.* cacciatore *m.*

**hunting,** *n.* càccia *f.*

**huntress,** *n.* cacciatrice *f.*

**hurdle,** **1.** *n.* (hedge) sièpe *f.*; (obstacle) ostàcolo *m.* **2.** *vb.* saltare.

**hurl,** *vb.* lanciare, scagliare.

**hurrah for,** *interj.* viva, evviva (often written W).

**hurricane,** *n.* uragano *m.*

**hurry,** **1.** *n.* fretta *f.* **2.** *vb.* affrettare *tr.*

**hurt,** **1.** *n.* darno *m*; (wound) ferita *f.* **2.** *vb.* far male a.

**hurtful,** *adj.* dannoso.

**hurtle,** *vb.* precipitarsi.

**husband,** *n.* marito *m.*

**husbandry,** *n.* amministrazione *f.*

**hush, 1.** *vb.* far tacere. **2.** *interj.* zittol.

**husk,** *n.* bùccia *f.*

**husky,** *adj.* (strong) fòrte; (hoarse) ràuco.

**hustle, 1.** *n.* frétta *f.* **2.** *vb.* (shove) spìngere; (hurry) affrettare, *tr.*

**hut,** *n.* casùpola *f.*

**hutch,** *n.* coniglièra *f.*

**hyacinth,** *n.* giacinto *m.*

**hybrid,** *adj.* ìbrido.

**hydrangea,** *n.* ortènsia *f.*

**hydrant,** *n.* idrante *m.*

**hydraulic,** *adj.* idràulico.

**hydrochloric,** *adj.* idroclòrico.

**hydroelectric,** *adj.* idroelèttrico.

**hydrogen,** *n.* idrògeno *m.*

**hydrophobia,** *n.* idrofobìa *f.*

**hydroplane,** *n.* idrovolante *m.*

**hydrotherapy,** *n.* idroterapèutica *f.*

**hyena,** *n.* ièna *f.*

**hygiene,** *n.* igiène *f.*

**hygienic,** *adj.* igiènico.

**hymn,** *n.* inno *m.*

**hymnal,** *n.* innàrio *m.*

**hyperacidity,** *n.* iperacidità *f.*

**hyperbole,** *n.* ipèrbole *f.*

**hypercritical,** *adj.* ipercrìtico.

**hypersensitive,** *adj.* ipersensitivo.

**hypertension,** *n.* ipertensione *f.*

**hyphen,** *n.* tratto d'unione *m.*

**hyphenate,** *vb.* scrìvere con tratto d'unione.

**hypnosis,** *n.* ipnòsi *f.*

**hypnotic,** *adj.* ipnòtico.

**hypnotism,** *n.* ipnotismo *m.*

**hypnotize,** *vb.* ipnotizzare.

**hypochondria,** *n.* ipocondrìa *f.*

**hypochondriac,** *n. and adj.* ipocondrìaco (*m.*)

**hypocrisy,** *n.* ipocrisìa *f.*

**hypocrite,** *n.* ipòcrita *m.*

**hypocritical,** *adj.* ipòcrito.

**hypodermic,** *adj.* ipodèrmico.

**hypotenuse,** *n.* ipotenusa *f.*

**hypothesis,** *n.* ipòtesi *f.*

**hypothetical,** *adj.* ipotètico.

**hysteria, hysterics,** *n.* isterismo *m.*

**hysterical,** *adj.* istèrico.

# I

**I,** *pron.* ìo.

**iambic,** *adj.* giàmbico.

**ice,** *n.* ghiàccio *m.*

**ice-berg,** *n.* borgognone *m.*

**ice-box,** *n.* ghiacciaia *f.*

**ice-cream,** *n.* gelato *m.*

**ice-skate,** *n.* pàttino *m.*

**ichthyology,** *n.* ittiologia *f.*

**icing,** *n.* pasta fròlla *f.*

**icon,** *n.* icòne *f.*

**icy,** *adj.* diàccio.

**idea,** *n.* idèa *f.*

**ideal,** *adj.* ideale.

**idealism,** *n.* idealismo *m.*

**idealist,** *n.* idealista *m.*

**idealistic,** *adj.* idealìstico.

**idealize,** *vb.* idealizzare.

**ideally,** *adv.* idealmente.

**identical,** *adj.* idèntico.

**identifiable,** *adj.* identificàbile.

**identification,** *n.* identificazione *f.*

**identify,** *vb.* identificare.

**identity,** *n.* identità *f.*

**ideology,** *n.* ideologìa *f.*

**idiocy,** *n.* idiozìa *f.*

**idiom,** *n.* idiòma *m.*

**idiot,** *n.* idiòta *m.*

**idiotic,** *adj.* idiòta.

**idle,** *adj.* ozioso.

**idleness,** *n.* òzio *m.*

**idol,** *n.* ìdolo *m.*

**idolater,** *n.* idolatra *m. or f.*

**idolatry,** *n.* idolatrìa *f.*

**idolize,** *vb.* idolatrare.

**idyl,** *n.* idìllio *m.*

**idyllic,** *adj.* idìllico.

**if,** *conj.* se; **(as if)** quasi.

**ignite,** *vb.* accèndere.

**ignition,** *n.* accensione *f.*

**ignition key**, *n.* chiavetta d'accensione *f.*

**ignoble**, *adj.* ignòbile.

**ignominious**, *adj.* ignominioso.

**ignoramus**, *n.* ignorantone *m.*

**ignorance**, *n.* ignoranza *f.*

**ignorant**, *adj.* ignorante, ignaro.

**ignore**, *vb.* trascurare.

**ill**, *adj.* malato.

**illegal**, *adj.* illegale.

**illegible**, *adj.* illeggìbile.

**illegibly**, *adv.* illeggibilmente.

**illegitimacy**, *adj.* illegittimità *f.*

**illegitimate**, *adj.* illegìttimo.

**illicit**, *adj.* illécito.

**illiteracy**, *n.* analfabetismo *m.*

**illiterate**, *n. and adj.* analfabèta (*m. or f.*)

**illness**, *n.* malattìa *f.*, malore *m.*

**illogical**, *adj.* illògico.

**ill-omened**, *adj.* infàusto.

**illuminate**, *vb.* illuminare.

**illumination**, *n.* illuminazione *f.*

**illusion**, *n.* illusione *f.*

**illusive, illusory**, *adj.* illusòrio.

**illustrate**, *vb.* illustrare.

**illustration**, *n.* illustrazione *f.*

**illustrative**, *adj.* illustrativo.

**illustrious**, *adj.* illustre.

**ill will**, *n.* cattiva volontà *f.*

**image**, *n.* immàgine *f.*

**imagery**, *n.* figure retòriche *f.pl.*

**imaginable**, *adj.* immaginàbile.

**imaginary**, *adj.* immaginàrio.

**imagination**, *n.* fantasìa *f.*, immaginazione *f.*

**imaginative**, *adj.* immaginativo.

**imagine**, *vb.* immaginare, *tr.*, figurarsi.

**imbecile**, *n. and adj.* imbecille (*m. or f.*)

**imitate**, *vb.* imitare.

**imitation**, *n.* imitazione *f.*

**imitative**, *adj.* imitativo.

**immaculate**, *adj.* immacolato.

**immanent**, *adj.* immanènte.

**immaterial**, *adj.* immateriale.

**immature**, *adj.* immaturo.

**immediate**, *adj.* immediato.

**immediately**, *adv.* immediatamente, sùbito.

**immense**, *adj.* immènso.

**immerse**, *vb.* immèrgere.

**immigrant**, *n. and adj.* immigrante.

**immigrate**, *vb.* immigrare.

**imminent**, *adj.* imminènte.

**immobile**, *adj.* immòbile.

**immobilize**, *vb.* immobilizzare.

**immoderate**, *adj.* immoderato.

**immodest**, *adj.* immodèsto, impùdico.

**immodesty**, *n.* immodèstia *f.*, impudicizia *f.*

**immoral**, *adj.* immorale.

**immorality**, *n.* immoralità *f.*

**immorally**, *adv.* immoralmente.

**immortal**, *adj.* immortale.

**immortality**, *n.* immortalità *f.*

**immortalize**, *vb.* immortalare.

**immovable**, *adj.* immòbile.

**immune**, *adj.* immune, esento.

**immunity**, *n.* immunità *f.*

**immunize**, *vb.* immunizzare.

**immutable**, *adj.* immutàbile.

**impact**, *n.* urto *m.*

**impair**, *vb.* menomare.

**impale**, *vb.* impalare.

**impart**, *vb.* impartire.

**impartial**, *adj.* imparziale.

**impatience**, *n.* impaziènza *f.*

**impatient**, *adj.* impaziènte.

**impatiently**, *adv.* impazientemente.

**impeach**, *vb.* imputare.

**impede**, *vb.* impedire.

**impediment**, *n.* impedimento *m.*

**impel**, *vb.* impèllere.

**impenetrable**, *adj.* impenetràbile.

**impenitent**, *adj.* impenitènte.

**imperative**, *n. and adj.* imperativo (*m.*)

**imperceptible**, *adj.* impercettibile.

**imperfect**, *adj.* imperfètto.

**imperfection**, *n.* imperfezione *f.*, mènda *f.*

**imperial**, *adj.* imperiale.

**imperialism**, *n.* imperialismo *m.*

**imperil**, *vb.* méttere in perìcolo.

**imperious,** *adj.* imperioso.

**impersonal,** *adj.* impersonale.

**impersonate,** *vb.* impersonare, contraffare.

**impersonation,** *n.* contraffazione *f.*

**impersonator,** *n.* impersonatore *m.*

**impertinence,** *n.* impertinènza *f.*

**impertinent,** *adj.* impertinènte.

**impervious,** *adj.* impèrvio.

**impetuous,** *adj.* impetuoso.

**impetus,** *n.* impeto *m.*

**implacable,** *adj.* implacàbile.

**implant,** *vb.* impiantare.

**implement,** *n.* strumento *m.*

**implicate,** *vb.* implicare.

**implication,** *n.* implicazione *f.*

**implicit,** *adj.* implìcito.

**implied,** *adj.* implìcito.

**implore,** *vb.* implorare.

**imply,** *vb.* implicare; (suggest) suggerire; (insinuate) insinuare.

**impolite,** *adj.* scortese.

**imponderable,** *adj.* imponderàbile.

**import, 1.** *n.* importazione *f.*; (meaning) significato *m.* **2.** *vb.* importare.

**importance,** *n.* importanza *f.*

**important,** *adj.* importante; **(be i.)** importare.

**importation,** *n.* importazione *f.*

**importune, 1.** *adj.* importuno. **2.** *vb.* importunare.

**impose,** *vb.* imporre.

**imposition,** *n.* imposizione *f.*

**impossibility,** *n.* impossibilità *f.*

**impossible,** *adj.* impossìbile.

**impotence,** *n.* impotènza *f.*

**impotent,** *adj.* impotènte.

**impoverish,** *vb.* impoverire.

**impregnable,** *adj.* inespugnàbile.

**impregnate,** *vb.* impregnare, ingravidare.

**impresario,** *n.* impresàrio *m.*

**impress,** *vb.* (imprint) imprimere; (affect) impressionare.

**impression,** *n.* impressione *f.*

**impressive,** *adj.* impressionante.

**imprison,** *vb.* imprigionare.

**imprisonment,** *n.* prigionìa *f.*

**improbable,** *adj.* improbàbile.

**impromptu, 1.** *n.* improvviso *m.* **2.** *adj.* improvvisato; estemporàneo.

**improper,** *adj.* impròprio, sconveniènte.

**improve,** *vb.* migliorare.

**improvement,** *n.* miglioramento *m.*

**improvise,** *vb.* improvvisare.

**imprudent,** *adj.* imprudènte.

**impugn,** *vb.* impugnare.

**impulse,** *n.* impulso *m.*

**impulsive,** *adj.* impulsivo.

**impunity,** *n.* impunità *f.*

**impure,** *adj.* impuro.

**impurity,** *n.* impurità *f.*

**impute,** *vb.* imputare.

**in,** *prep.* in; (within, of time) entro.

**inadvertent,** *adj.* inavvertùto.

**inalienable,** *adj.* inalienàbile.

**inane,** *adj.* inano.

**inaugural,** *adj.* inaugurale; (speech) discorso inaugurale *n.m.*

**inaugurate,** *vb.* inaugurare.

**inauguration,** *n.* inaugurazione *f.*

**incandescence,** *n.* incandescènza *f.*

**incandescent,** *adj.* incandescènte.

**incantation,** *n.* incantamento *m.*

**incapacitate,** *vb.* rèndere incapace.

**incapacity,** *n.* incapacità *f.*

**incarcerate,** *vb.* incarcerare.

**incarnate,** *adj.* incarnato.

**incarnation,** *n.* incarnazione *f.*

**incendiary,** *n.* ana eg. incendiàrio (*m*).

**incense,** *n.* incènso *m.*

**incentive,** *n.* incentivo *m.*

**inception,** *n.* inizio *m.*

**incessant,** *adj.* incessante.

**incest,** *n.* incèsto *m.*

**inch,** *n.* pòllice *m.*

**incidence,** *n.* incidènza *f.*

**incident,** *n.* incidènte *m.*

**incidental,** *adj.* incidentale.

**incidentally,** *adv.* incidentalmente.

**incipient,** *adj.* incipiènte.

**incise,** *vb.* incìdere.

**incision,** *n.* incisione *f.*

**incisive,** adj. incisivo.

**incisor,** n. dènte incisivo m.

**incite,** vb. incitare.

**inclination,** n. inclinazione f.

**incline, 1.** n. pendìo m. **2.** vb. inclinare; (fig.) propèndere.

**inclined,** adj. (disposed) propènso.

**inclose,** vb. rinchiùdere; (in letter) acclùdere.

**include,** vb. inclùdere.

**including,** prep. compreso (adj., agrees with following noun)

**inclusive,** adj. inclusivo.

**incognito,** n. incògnito f.

**income,** n. rèddito m.

**incomparable,** adj. incomparàbile.

**inconsiderate,** adj. strafottènte; villano

**inconvenience, 1.** n. scomodità f. **2.** vb. incomodare.

**inconvenient,** adj. incòmodo.

**incorporate,** vb. incorporare, tr.

**incorrigible,** adj. incorreggìbile.

**increase, 1.** n. aumento m. **2.** vb. accréscere, aumentare.

**incredible,** adj. incredìbile.

**incredulity,** n. incredulità f.

**incredulous,** adj. incrèdulo.

**increment,** n. incremento m.

**incriminate,** vb. incriminare.

**incrimination,** n. incriminazione f.

**incrust,** vb. incrostare.

**incubator,** n. incubatrice f.

**inculcate,** vb. inculcare.

**incumbency,** n. durata in càrica f.

**incumbent, 1.** n. titolare m. **2.** adj. incombènte.

**incur,** vb. incòrrere in.

**incurable,** adj. incuràbile.

**indebted,** adj. indebitato.

**indeed,** adv. davvero.

**indefatigable,** adj. infaticàbile.

**indefinite,** adj. indefinito.

**indefinitely,** adv. indefinitamente.

**indelible,** adj. indelèbile.

**indemnify,** vb. indennizzare.

**indemnity,** n. indennità f.

**indent,** vb. dentellare; (paragraph) collocare in dentro; (coastline) frastagliare.

**indentation,** n. dentellatura f.

**independence,** n. indipendènza f.

**independent,** adj. indipendènte.

**index,** n. ìndice m.

**India,** n. Ìndia f.

**Indian, 1.** n. indiano f. (American Indian) pellirossa m. **2.** adj. indiano; dei pellirossa.

**indicate,** vb. indicare.

**indication,** n. indicazione f.

**indicative,** n. and adj. indicativo (m.)

**indicator,** n. indicatore m.

**indict,** vb. accusare.

**indictment,** n. accusa f.

**indifference,** n. indifferènza f.

**indifferent,** adj. indifferènte.

**indigenous,** adj. indìgeno.

**indigent,** adj. indigènte.

**indigestion,** n. indigestione f.

**indignant,** adj. indignato.

**indignation,** n. indignazione f.

**indignity,** n. indegnità f., sgarberìa f.

**indirect,** adj. indiretto.

**indiscreet,** adj. indiscreto.

**indiscretion,** n. indiscrezione f.

**indispensable,** adj. indispensàbile.

**indisposed,** adj. indisposto.

**indisposition,** n. indisposizione f.

**individual, 1.** n. individuo m. **2.** adj. individuale.

**individuality,** n. individualità f.

**individually,** adj. individualmente.

**indivisible,** adj. indivisìbile.

**indoctrinate,** vb. addottrinare.

**indolent,** adj. indolènte.

**Indonesia,** n. Indonèsia f.

**indoor,** adj. da eseguirsi in casa.

**indoors,** adv. in casa.

**indorse,** vb. firmare; (check, etc.) girare.

**induce,** vb. indurre.

**induct,** vb. (into army) arruolare.

**induction,** n. induzione f.

**inductive,** adj. induttivo.

**indulge,** vb. indùlgere.

**indulgence,** n. indulgènza f.

**indulgent,** adj. indulgènte.

**industrial,** adj. industriale.

**industrialist,** n. industriale m.

**industrious,** adj. industrioso, operoso.

**industry,** n. indùstria f.

**inebriate, 1.** n. ubbriacone m. **2.** vb. inebbriare.

**ineligible,** adj. ineleggibile, inàbile.

**inept,** adj. inètto.

**inert,** adj. inèrte.

**inertia,** n. inèrzia f.

**inevitable,** adj. inevitàbile.

**inexplicable,** adj. inesplicàbile.

**infallible,** adj. infallìbile.

**infamous,** adj. infame.

**infamy,** n. infàmia f.

**infancy,** n. infànzia f.

**infant,** n. infante m.

**infantile,** adj. infantile.

**infantry,** n. fanteria f.

**infantryman,** n. fante m.

**infatuate,** vb. infatuare.

**infect,** vb. infettare.

**infected,** adj. infètto.

**infection,** n. infezione f.

**infectious,** adj. infettivo.

**infer,** vb. inferire, desùmere.

**inference,** n. inferènza f.

**inferior,** adj. inferiore.

**inferiority,** n. inferiorità f.; **(i. complex)** complesso d'i.

**infernal,** adj. infernale.

**inferno,** n. infèrno m.

**infest,** vb. infestare.

**infidel,** n. and adj. infedele; miscredènte.

**infidelity,** n. infedeltà f.

**infiltrate,** vb. infiltrare, tr.

**infinite,** n. and adj. infinito (m.)

**infinitesimal,** adj. infinitesimale.

**infinitive,** n. infinito m.

**infinity,** n. infinità f.

**infirm,** adj. infermo; (weak) débole; (unsure) irresoluto.

**infirmary,** n. infermeria f.

**infirmity,** n. infermità f.

**inflame,** vb. infiammare.

**inflammable,** adj. infiammàbile.

**inflammation,** n. infiammazione f.

**inflammatory,** adj. infiammatòrio.

**inflate,** vb. gonfiare.

**inflation,** n. gonfiamento m.; (financial) inflazione f.

**inflection,** n. inflessione f.; (grammar) flessione f.

**inflict,** vb. infliggere.

**infliction,** n. inflizione f.

**influence,** n. influenza f., inflùsso m.

**influential,** adj. influènte.

**influenza,** n. influènza f.

**inform,** vb. informare.

**informal,** adj. senza cerimònie.

**information,** n. informazioni f.pl.

**infringe,** vb. infràngere.

**infuriate,** vb. far infuriare; (become infuriated) infuriare.

**ingenious,** adj. ingegnoso.

**ingenuity,** n. ingegnosità f.

**ingredient,** n. ingrediènte m.

**inhabit,** vb. abitare.

**inhabitant,** n. abitante m.

**inhale,** vb. inalare.

**inherent,** adj. inerènte.

**inherit,** vb. ereditare.

**inheritance,** n. eredità f., retàggio m.

**inhibit,** vb. inibire.

**inhibition,** n. inibizione f.

**inhuman,** adj. inumano.

**inimical,** adj. nemico.

**inimitable,** adj. inimitàbile.

**iniquity,** n. iniquità f.

**initial,** n. and adj. iniziale (f.)

**initiate,** vb. iniziare.

**initiation,** n. iniziazione f.

**initiative,** n. iniziativa f.

**inject,** vb. iniettare.

**injection,** n. iniezione f.

**injunction,** n. ingiunzione f.

**injure,** vb. (harm) danneggiare, nuòcere; (wound) ferire.

**injurious,** adj. dannoso, nocivo.

**injury,** n. danno m., ferita f.

**injustice,** n. ingiustizia f.

**ink,** n. inchiòstro m.

**inland, 1.** adj. intèrno; **2.** adv. vèrso l'intèrno.

**inlet,** n. pòrto m., canale m.

**inmate,** n. paziènte m.

**inn,** n. locanda f.

**inner,** adj. interiore, intèrno.

**innermost,** adj. più intimo.

**innocence,** n. innocènza f.

**innocent,** adj. innocènte.

**innocuous,** adj. innòcuo.

**innuendo,** n. insinuazione f.

**innumerable,** adj. innumerévole.

**inoculate,** vb. inoculare.

**inoculation,** n. inoculazione f.

**inquest,** n. inchièsta f.

**inquire**, vb. informarsi.

**inquiry**, n. ricerca d'informazioni f., investigazione f., inchièsta f.

**inquisition**, n. inquisizione f.

**inquisitive**, adj. eccessivamente curioso.

**inroad**, n. incursione f.

**insane**, adj. insano, pazzo.

**insanity**, n. insània f., pazzìa f.

**inscribe**, vb. iscrìvere.

**inscription**, n. iscrizione f.

**insect**, n. insètto m.

**insecticide**, n. pólvere insetticida m.

**insensible**, adj. insensìbile.

**insensitive**, adj. insensìbile.

**insensitivity**, n. insensibilità f.

**inseparable**, adj. inseparàbile.

**insert**, **1.** n. cosa inserita f. **2.** vb. inserire.

**insertion**, n. inserzione f.

**inside**, **1.** n. intèrno m. **2.** adj. intèrno, interiore. **3.** adv., prep. dentro.

**insidious**, adj. insidioso.

**insight**, n. penetrazione f.

**insignia**, n. insegne f.pl.

**insignificance**, n. insignificanza f.

**insignificant**, adj. insignificante.

**insinuate**, vb. insinuare.

**insinuation**, n. insinuazione f.

**insipid**, adj. insìpido; (dull) insulso.

**insist**, vb. insìstere.

**insistence**, n. insistènza f.

**insistent**, adj. insistènte.

**insolence**, n. insolènza f.

**insolent**, adj. insolènte.

**insolently**, adv. insolentemente.

**insomnia**, n. insònnia f.

**inspect**, vb. ispezionare.

**inspection**, n. ispezione f.

**inspector**, n. ispettore m.

**inspiration**, n. ispirazione f.

**inspire**, vb. ispirare.

**install**, vb. installare; (a person) insediare.

**installation**, n. installazione f.; (of a person) insediamento m.; (industrial) impianto m.

**installment**, n. (payment) rata f.; (story, etc.) puntata f.

**instance**, n. istanza f.; (ex-ample) esèmpio m.; (request) richièsta f.; **(for i.)** per esèmpio.

**instant**, **1.** n. istante m., àttimo m. **2.** adj. immediato; (date) corrènte.

**instantaneous**, adj. istantàneo.

**instantly**, adv. immediatamente.

**instead**, adv. invece; **(i. of)** invece di.

**instigate**, vb. istigare.

**instill**, vb. istillare.

**instinct**, n. istinto m.

**instinctive**, adj. istintivo.

**institute**, n. istituto m.

**institution**, n. istituzione f.

**instruct**, vb. istruire.

**instruction**, n. istruzione f.

**instructive**, adj. istruttivo.

**instructor**, n. istruttore m.

**instructress**, n. istruttrice f.

**instrument**, n. strumento m.

**instrumental**, adj. strumentale.

**insufferable**, adj. insoffrìbile.

**insufficient**, adj. insufficiènte.

**insular**, adj. insulare.

**insulate**, vb. isolare.

**insulation**, n. isolamento m.

**insulator**, n. isolatore m.

**insulin**, n. insulina f.

**insult**, **1.** n. insulto m., ingiùria f. **2.** vb. insultare, ingiurare.

**insulting**, adj. insultante, ingiurioso.

**insuperable**, adj. insuperàbile.

**insurance**, n. assicurazione f.

**insure**, vb. assicurare, tr.

**insurgent**, n. and adj. ribèlle (m.)

**insurrection**, n. insurrezione f.

**intact**, adj. intatto.

**intangible**, adj. intangìbile.

**integral**, adj. integrale.

**integrate**, vb. integrare.

**integrity**, n. integrità f.

**intellect**, n. intellètto m.

**intellectual**, adj. intellettuale.

**intelligence**, n. intelligènza f.

**intelligent**, adj. intelligènte.

**intelligentsia**, n. intellighènzia f.

**intelligible**, adj. intelligìbile.

**intend**, vb. aver intenzione di.

**intense**, adj. intènso.

**intensify**, vb. intensificare.

**intensive**, *adj.* intensivo.

**intent**, 1. *n.* intènto *m.*, intendimento *m.* 2. *adj.* intènto; (i. on) intènto a.

**intention**, *n.* intenzione *f.*, propòsito *m.*

**intentional**, *adj.* intenzionale.

**intentionally**, *adv.* intenzionalmente, apposta.

**inter**, *vb.* seppellire.

**intercede**, *vb.* intercèdere.

**intercept**, *vb.* intercettare.

**intercourse**, *n.* rappòrto *m.*

**interdict**, 1. *n.* interdetto *m.* 2. *vb.* interdire.

**interest**, 1. *n.* interèsse *m.* 2. *vb.* interessare; (be interested in) interessarsi di.

**interesting**, *adj.* interessante.

**interfere**, *vb.* (i. in) immischiarsi in, intervenire in; (i. with) ostacolare.

**interference**, *n.* ingerènza *f.*; (physics) interferènza *f.*

**interim**, 1. *n.* frattèmpo *m.* 2. *adj.* provvisòrio.

**interior**, *n. and adj.* interiore (*m.*)

**interject**, *vb.* inframettere.

**interjection**, *n.* interiezione *f.*

**interlude**, *n.* interlùdio *m.*

**intermarry**, *vb.* fare matrimoni misti.

**intermediary**, *n. and adj.* intermediàrio (*m.*)

**intermediate**, *adj.* intermèdio.

**interment**, *n.* sepoltura *f.*

**intermission**, *n.* intermissione *f.*, intervallo *m.*

**intermittent**, *adj.* intermittènte.

**intern**, *vb.* internare.

**internal**, *adj.* intèrno.

**international**, *adj.* internazionale.

**internationalism**, *n.* internazionalismo *m.*

**interne**, *n.* mèdico intèrno *m.*

**interpose**, *vb.* interporre.

**interpret**, *vb.* interpretare.

**interpretation**, *n.* interpretazione *f.*

**interpreter**, *n.* intèrprete *m.*

**interrogate**, *vb.* interrogare.

**interrogation**, *n.* interrogazione *f.*

**interrogative**, *adj.* interrogativo.

**interrupt**, *vb.* interròmpere.

**interruption**, *n.* interruzione *f.*

**intersect**, *vb.* intersecare, *tr.*; (cross) incrociarsi.

**intersection**, *n.* intersezione *f.*; (crossing) incrócio *m.*

**intersperse**, *vb.* cospàrgere.

**interval**, *n.* intervallo *m.*

**intervene**, *vb.* intervenire.

**intervention**, *n.* intervènto *m.*

**interview**, 1. *n.* intervista *f.* 2. *vb.* intervistare.

**intestine**, *n. and adj.* intestino (*m.*)

**intimacy**, *n.* intimità *f.*

**intimate**, *adj.* intimo.

**intimidate**, *vb.* intimidire.

**intimidation**, *n.* intimidazione *f.*

**into**, *prep.* in.

**intolerant**, *adj.* intollerante.

**intonation**, *n.* intonazione *f.*

**intone**, *vb.* intonare.

**intoxicate**, *vb.* (poison) intossicare; (get drunk) inebriare.

**intoxication**, *n.* intossicazione *f.*, ubbriachezza *f.*

**intravenous**, *adj.* endovenoso.

**intrepid**, *adj.* intrèpido.

**intrepidity**, *n.* intrepidità *f.*

**intricacy**, *n.* complicazione *f.*

**intricate**, *adj.* intricato, complicato.

**intrigue**, 1. *n.* intrigo *m.*; (love affair) tresca *f.* 2. *vb.* intrigare.

**intrinsic**, *adj.* intrìnseco.

**introduce**, *vb.* introdurre; (persons) presentare.

**introduction**, *n.* introduzione *f.*, presentazione *f.*

**introductory**, *adj.* introduttivo.

**introspection**, *n.* introspezione *f.*

**introvert**, *adj.* introvertito.

**intrude**, *vb.* intrùdere, *tr.*

**intruder**, *n.* intruso *m.*

**intuition**, *n.* intuizione *f.*

**intuitive**, *adj.* intuitivo.

**inundate**, *vb.* inondare.

**invade**, *vb.* invàdere.

**invader**, *n.* invasore *m.*

**invalid**, *n. and adj.* invàlido (*m.*)

**invariable**, *adj.* invariàbile.

**invasion**, *n.* invasione *f.*

**invective**, *n.* invettiva *f.*

**inveigle**, *vb.* sedurre, adescare.

**invent**, *vb.* inventare.
**invention**, *n.* invenzione *f.*
**inventive**, *adj.* inventivo.
**inventor**, *n.* inventore *m.*
**inventory**, *n.* inventàrio *m.*
**inverse**, *adj.* invèrso.
**invertebrate**, *n.* and *adj.* invertebrato (*m.*).
**invest**, *vb.* investire.
**investigate**, *vb.* investigare.
**investigation**, *n.* investigazione *f.*
**investment**, *n.* investimento *m.*
**inveterate**, *adj.* inveterato.
**invidious**, *adj.* odioso.
**invigorate**, *vb.* invigorire.
**invincible**, *adj.* invincìbile.
**invisible**, *adj.* invisìbile.
**invitation**, *n.* invito *m.*
**invite**, *vb.* invitare.
**invocation**, *n.* invocazione *f.*
**invoice**, **1.** *n.* fattura *f.* **2.** *vb.* fatturare.
**invoke**, *vb.* invocare.
**involuntary**, *adj.* involontàrio.
**involve**, *vb.* coinvòlgere, implicare.
**involved**, *adj.* complicato.
**invulnerable**, *adj.* invulneràbile.
**inward**, **1.** *adj.* ìntimo. **2.** *adv.* vèrso l'intèrno.
**inwardly**, *adv.* intimamente.
**iodine**, *n.* iòdio *m.*
**Iran**, *n.* Iran *m.*
**Iraq**, *n.* Iràk *m.*
**irate**, *adj.* irato.
**ire**, *n.* ira *f.*
**Ireland**, *n.* Irlanda *f.*
**iridium**, *n.* irìdio *m.*
**iris**, *n.* ìride *f.*; (flower) ìris *f.*
**Irish**, *adj.* irlandese.
**irk**, *vb.* infastidire.
**iron**, **1.** *n.* fèrro *m.*; (flat-i.) fèrro da stiro. **2.** *adj.* di fèrro, fèrreo. **3.** *vb.* stirare.
**ironical**, *adj.* irònico.
**ironworks**, *n.* ferrièra *f.sg.*
**irony**, *n.* ironìa *f.*
**irrational**, *adj.* irrazionale.
**irrefutable**, *adj.* irrefutàbile.

**irregular**, *adj.* irregolare.
**irregularity**, *n.* irregolarità *f.*
**irrelevant**, *adj.* non pertinènte.
**irreprehensible**, *adj.* irreprensìbile.
**irreprehensibly**, *adv.* irreprensibilmente.
**irresistible**, *adj.* irresistìbile.
**irresponsible**, *adj.* irresponsàbile.
**irreverent**, *adj.* irriverènte.
**irrevocable**, *adj.* irrevocàbile.
**irrigate**, *vb.* irrigare.
**irrigation**, *n.* irrigazione *f.*
**irritability**, *n.* irritabilità *f.*
**irritable**, *adj.* irritàbile.
**irritant**, *adj.* irritante.
**irritate**, *vb.* irritare.
**irritation**, *n.* irritazione *f.*
**island**, *n.* ìsola *f.*
**isolate**, *vb.* isolare.
**isolation**, *n.* isolamento *m.*; (politics) isolazione *f.*
**isolationist**, *n.* isolazionista *m.*
**isosceles**, *adj.* isòscele.
**Israel**, *n.* Isràele *m.*
**Israelite**, **1.** *n.* israelita *m.* **2.** *adj.* israelìtico.
**issuance**, *n.* emissione *f.*
**issue**, **1.** *n.* (offspring) pròle *f.*; (bonds, etc.) emissione *f.*; (river) foce *f.*; (magazine) nùmero *m.* **2.** *vb.* (come out) uscire; (publish) pubblicare.
**isthmus**, *n.* istmo *m.*
**it**, *pron.* ciò; (subject) esso; (direct object) lo, la.
**Italian**, *adj.* italiano.
**Italic**, *adj.* itàlico.
**italics**, *n.* corsivo *m.sg.*
**Italy**, *n.* Itàlia *f.*
**itch**, **1.** *n.* prudore *m.*, prurito *m.* **2.** *vb.* prùdere, prurire.
**item**, *n.* artìcolo *m.*
**itemize**, *vb.* elencare.
**itinerant**, *adj.* girovago.
**itinerary**, *n.* itineràrio *m.*
**its**, *adj.* suo.
**itself**, *pron.* esso stesso.
**ivory**, *n.* avòrio *m.*
**ivy**, *n.* èdera *f.*

# J

**jab,** *vb.* pugnalare.

**jack,** *n.* binda *f.*, cricco *m.*, martinèllo *m.*

**jack-of-all-trades,** *n.* factotum *m.*

**jackal,** *n.* sciacallo *m.*

**jackass,** *n.* àsino *m.*

**jacket,** *n.* giacca *f.*, giacchetta *f.*

**jack-knife,** *n.* coltèllo a serramànico *m.*

**jade,** *n.* giada *f.*

**jaded,** *adj.* sfinito.

**jagged,** *adj.* seghettato.

**jaguar,** *n.* il giaguaro *m.*

**jail,** *n.* càrcere *m.*, prigione *f.*

**jailer,** *n.* carcerière *m.*

**jam,** *n.* marmellata *f.*; (trouble) impiccio *m.*

**jamb,** *n.* stìpite *m.*

**jangle,** *n.* rumore aspro *m.*

**janitor,** *n.* bidèllo *m.*

**January,** *n.* gennaio *m.*

**Japan,** *n.* il Giappone *m.*

**Japanese,** *adj.* giapponese.

**jar, 1.** *n.* giara *f.*; (glass) bottìglia *f.* **2.** *vb.* scuòtere; (displease) offèndere.

**jargon,** *n.* gèrgo *m.*

**jasmine,** *n.* gelsomino *m.*

**jaundice,** *n.* itterìzia *f.*

**jaunt,** *n.* escursione *f.*

**javelin,** *n.* giavellòtto *m.*

**jaw,** *n.* mascèlla *f.*

**jay,** *n.* ghiandaia *f.*

**jaywalk,** *vb.* attraversare la strada all'infuòri dei passaggi pedonali.

**jazz,** *n.* jazz *m.* (pronounced giazz)

**jealous,** *adj.* geloso.

**jealousy,** *n.* gelosìa *f.*

**jeer (at),** *vb.* beffarsi (di).

**jelly,** *n.* gelatina *f.*

**jelly-fish,** *n.* medusa *f.*

**jeopardize,** *vb.* méttere in perìcolo.

**jeopardy,** *n.* perìcolo *m.*

**jerk, 1.** *n.* strattone *m.*, sbalzellone *m.* **2.** *vb.* tirare con strattoni.

**jerkin,** *n.* giustacuòre *m.*

**jerky,** *adj.* a sbalzelloni.

**jersey,** *n.* màglia *f.*

**Jerusalem,** *n.* Gerusalèmme *f.*

**jest, 1.** *n.* scherzo *m.* **2.** *vb.* scherzare.

**jester,** *n.* buffone *m.*

**Jesuit,** *n.* gesuita *m.*

**Jesus Christ,** *n.* Gesù Cristo *m.*

**jet, 1.** *n.* (black substance) giavazzo *m.*; (emission) gètto *m.*; (plane) reattore *m.*, aviogètto *m.* **2.** *adj.* a reazione. **3.** *vb.* sgorgare.

**jetsam,** *n.* mèrci gettate in mare.

**jettison,** *vb.* gettare in mare.

**jetty,** *n.* mòlo *m.*

**Jew,** *n.* ebrèo *m.*, giudèo *m.*

**jewel,** *n.* gioièllo *m.*

**jeweler,** *n.* gioiellière *m.*

**jewelry,** *n.* gioiellerìa *f.*

**Jewish,** *adj.* ebrèo, ebràico.

**jib, 1.** *n.* fiòcco *m.* **2.** *vb.* (horse) recalcitrare; (refuse) rifiutarsi.

**jibe, 1.** *n.* bèffa *f.* **2.** *vb.* (**j. at**) beffarsi di.

**jiffy,** *n.* istante *m.*

**jig,** *n.* giga *f.*

**jilt,** *vb.* abbandonare.

**jingle,** *vb.* tintinnare.

**jinx,** *n.* malaugùrio *m.*

**jittery,** *adj.* nervoso.

**job,** *n.* impiègo *m.*, occupazione *f.*

**jobber,** *n.* commerciante all'ingròsso *m.*

**jockey,** *n.* fantino *m.*

**jocular,** *adj.* umorìstico.

**jocund,** *adj.* giocondo.

**jog,** *vb.* scuòtere.

**joggle,** *n.* caletta *f.*

**join, 1.** *n.* congiunzione *f.* **2.** *vb.* congiùngere; (associate with) associarsi con; (**j. up**) arruolarsi.

**joiner,** *n.* (carpenter) falegname *m.*

**joint, 1.** *n.* giuntura *f.*, articolazione *f.* **2.** *adj.* congiunto, collettivo.

**jointly,** *adv.* collettivamente, congiuntamente.

**joist,** *n.* travicèllo *m.*

**joke, 1.** *n.* schèrzo *m.*; (trick) burla *f.* **2.** *vb.* scherzare.

**joker,** *n.* burlone *m.*

**jolly**, *adj.* allegro.
**jolt, 1.** *n.* scòssa *f.*, sobbalzo *m.* **2.** *vb.* sobbalzare.
**jonquil**, *n.* giunchìglia *f.*
**jostle**, *vb.* spingere.
**jounce, 1.** *n.* sobbalzo *m.* **2.** *vb.* sobbalzare.
**journal**, *n.* giornale *m.*
**journalism**, *n.* giornalismo *m.*
**journalist**, *n.* giornalista *m.*
**journey, 1.** *n.* viàggio *m.* **2.** *vb.* viaggiare.
**journeyman**, *n.* operaio espèrto *m.*
**jovial**, *adj.* gioviale.
**jowl**, *n.* guància *f.*
**joy**, *n.* giòia *f.*
**joyful**, *adj.* gioioso.
**joyous**, *adj.* gioioso.
**jubilant**, *adj.* giubilante.
**jubilee**, *n.* giubilèo *m.*
**Judaism**, *n.* giudaismo *m.*
**judge, 1.** *n.* giùdice *m.* **2.** *vb.* giudicare.
**judgment**, *n.* giudìzio *m.*
**judicial**, *adj.* giudiziàrio; (impartial) imparziale.
**judiciary, 1.** *n.* magistratura *f.* **2.** *adj.* giudiziària.
**judicious**, *adj.* giudizioso.
**jug**, *n.* bròcca *f.*
**juggle**, *vb.* far giòchi di prestìgio.
**jugular**, *adj.* giugulare.

**juice**, *n.* succo *m.*
**juicy**, *adj.* succoso.
**July**, *n.* lùglio *m.*
**jumble**, *n.* confusione *f.*
**jump, 1.** *n.* salto *m.* **2.** *vb.* saltare.
**juncture**, *n.* giuntura *f.*
**junction**, *n.* bìvio *m.*, diramazione *f.*, biforcazione *f.*
**June**, *n.* giugno *m.*
**jungle**, *n.* giungla *f.*
**junior**, *adj.* minore; (in names) iuniore.
**juniper**, *n.* ginepro *m.*
**junk**, *n.* ròba da chiòdi *f.*
**junket**, *n.* (food) giuncata *f.*; (trip) escursione *f.*
**jurisdiction**, *n.* giurisdizione *f.*
**jurisprudence**, *n.* giurisprudènza *f.*
**jurist**, *n.* giurista *m.*
**juror**, *n.* giurato *m.*
**jury**, *n.* giurìa *f.*
**just, 1.** *adj.* giusto. **2.** *adv.* pròprio; (**j. now**) or'ora.
**justice**, *n.* giustìzia *f.*
**justifiable**, *adj.* giustificàbile.
**justification**, *n.* giustificazione *f.*
**justify**, *vb.* giustificare.
**jut**, *vb.* proiettarsi, spòrgere.
**jute**, *n.* iuta *f.*
**juvenile**, *adj.* giovanile.

# K

**kale**, *n.* càvolo *m.*
**kaleidoscope**, *n.* caleidoscòpio *m.*
**kangaroo**, *n.* canguro *m.*
**karakul**, *n.* lince persiana *f.*
**karat**, *n.* carato *m.*
**keel**, *n.* chìglia *f.*
**keen**, *adj.* acuto.
**keep**, *vb.* conservare, serbare, mantenere, tenere; (stay) tenersi.
**keeper**, *n.* custòde *m.*
**keepsake**, *n.* ricòrdo *m.*
**keg**, *n.* barletto *m.*
**kennel**, *n.* canile *m.*
**kerchief**, *n.* fazzoletto *m.*

**kernel**, *n.* gherìglio *m.*; (*fig.*) nòcciolo *m.*
**kerosene**, *n.* petròlio raffinato *m.*
**ketchup**, *n.* salsa di pomodoro *f.*
**kettle**, *n.* péntola *f.*
**kettledrum**, *n.* tìmpano *m.*
**key**, *n.* chiave *f.*; (piano) tasto *m.*; (musical structure) tonalità *f.*
**keyboard**, *n.* tastièra *f.*
**keyhole**, *n.* buco della serratura *f.*
**khaki**, *n.* cachi *m.*

**kick, 1.** n. càlcio m. **2.** vb. tirar calci (a).

**kid, 1.** n. (goat) capretto m.; (child) ragazzo m., ragazza f. **2.** vb. prèndere in giro.

**kidnap,** vb. rapire.

**kidnapper,** n. rapitore m.

**kidnapping,** n. rapimento m.

**kidney,** n. rène f.; (as food) rognone m.

**kidney bean,** n. fagiuòlo reniforme m.

**kill,** vb. uccidere.

**killer,** n. uccisore m.

**kiln,** n. fornace f.

**kilocycle,** n. chilociclo m.

**kilogram,** n. chilogramma m.; chilo m.; (abbr.) kg.

**kilometer,** n. chilòmetro m.; (abbr.) km.

**kilowatt,** n. chilowatt m.; (abbr.) kw.

**kilt,** n. gonnellino m.

**kimono,** n. chimono f.

**kin,** n. parentela f.

**kind, 1.** n. gènere m., razza f. **2.** adj. gentile.

**kindergarten,** n. giardino d'infànzia m.

**kindle,** vb. accèndere.

**kindling,** n. legna minuta f.

**kindly,** adj. benèvolo.

**kindness,** n. gentilezza f.

**kindred, 1.** n. parentela f. **2.** adj. imparentato; (alike) affine.

**kinetic,** adj. cinètico.

**king,** n. re m.

**kingdom,** n. regno m.

**kink,** n. nodo m.

**kiosk,** n. chiòsco m.

**kiss, 1.** n. bàcio m. **2.** vb. baciare.

**kitchen,** n. cucina f.

**kite,** n. aquilone m.; (bird) nibbio m.

**kitten,** n. gattino m.

**kleptomania,** n. cleptomanìa f.

**kleptomaniac,** n. cleptòmane m.

**knack,** n. facoltà f.

**knapsack,** n. zàino m.

**knead,** vb. impastare.

**knee,** n. ginòcchio m.

**knee-cap,** n. rotèlla del ginócchio f.

**kneel,** vb. inginocchiarsi.

**knell,** n. rintocco m.

**knickers,** n. (ladies' underwear) mutande da dònna f.pl.

**knife,** n. coltèllo m.

**knight,** n. cavalière m.; (chess) cavallo m.

**knit,** vb. lavorare a maglia; (k. one's brows) aggrottare le ciglia.

**knock,** vb. **1.** n. bussata f. **2.** bussare; (strike) colpire; (k. down) abbàttere.

**knot,** n. nodo m.

**knotty,** adj. nodoso.

**know,** vb. (from outside in) conoscere; (from inside out) sapere; (k. how to) sapere.

**knowledge,** n. conoscènza f.; (without the k. of) all'insaputa di.

**knuckle,** n. nòcca f.

**kodak,** n. kodak f.

**Korea,** n. Corèa f.

# L

**label,** n. etichetta f.

**labor, 1.** n. lavoro m.; (workers) manodòpera f. **2.** vb. lavorare.

**laboratory,** n. laboratòrio m.

**laborer,** n. lavoratore m.

**laborious,** adj. laborioso.

**labor union,** n. sindacato operaio m.

**laburnum,** n. avornièllo m.

**labyrinth,** n. labirinto m.

**lace,** n. merletto m., pizzo m.

**lacerate,** vb. lacerare.

**laceration,** n. lacerazione f.

**lack, 1.** n. mancanza f. **2.** vb. mancare.

**lackadaisical,** adj. lànguido.

**lackey,** n. lacchè m.

**laconic,** adj. lacònico.

**lacquer,** 1. *n.* lacca *f.* 2. *vb.* laccare.

**lactic,** *adj.* làttico *m.*

**lactose,** *n.* lattòsio *m.*

**lacy,** *adj.* leggèro come merletti.

**lad,** *n.* ragazzo *m.*

**ladder,** *n.* scala a piuòli *f.;* (stocking) cordiglièra *f.*

**ladies,** *n.* signore *f.pl.*

**ladle,** *n.* méstola *f.,* ramaiuòlo *f.*

**lady,** *n.* signora *f.*

**ladybug,** *n.* coccinèlla *f.*

**lag,** 1. *n.* ritardo *m.* 2. *vb.* indugiare.

**lag behind,** *vb.* restare indiètro.

**lagoon,** *n.* laguna *f.*

**lair,** *n.* covo *m.,* tana *f.*

**laity,** *n.* laicato *m.*

**lake,** 1. *n.* lago *m.* 2. *adj.* lacuale.

**lamb,** 1. *n.* agnèllo *m.;* (meat) abbàcchio *m.*

**lame,** *adj.* zòppo.

**lament,** 1. *n.* lamento *m.* 2. *vb.* lamentare.

**lamentable,** *adj.* lamentévole.

**lamentation,** *n.* lamentazione *f.*

**laminate,** *vb.* laminare.

**lamp,** *n.* làmpada *f.*

**lampoon,** *n.* pasquinata *f.*

**lance,** 1. *n.* lància *f.* 2. *vb.* tagliare colla lancetta *f.*

**lancet,** *n.* lancetta *f.*

**land,** 1. *n.* tèrra *f.;* (country) paese *m.* 2. *vb.* (from boat) sbarcare; (plane) atterrare.

**landholder,** *n.* proprietàrio di tèrra *m.*

**landing,** *n.* sbarco *m.;* (plane) atterràggio *m.*

**landlady,** *n.* padrona *f.*

**landlord,** *n.* padrone *m.*

**landmark,** *n.* monumento *m.*

**landscape,** *n.* paesaggio *m.*

**landslide,** *n.* frana *f.*

**landward,** *adv.* vèrso tèrra.

**lane,** *n.* viòttolo *m.*

**language,** *n.* lingua *f.;* (manner of talking) linguaggio *m.*

**languid,** *adj.* lànguido.

**languish,** *vb.* languire.

**languor,** *n.* languore *m.*

**lanky,** *adj.* alto e smilzo.

**lanolin,** *n.* lanolina *f.*

**lantern,** *n.* lantèrna *f.*

**lap,** 1. *n.* grembo *m.* 2. *vb.* lambire.

**lapel,** *n.* risvòlta *f.*

**lapin,** *n.* coniglio *m.*

**lapse,** 1. *n.* (mistake) errore *m.;* (time) percorso *m.* 2. *vb.* decadere.

**larceny,** *n.* furto *m.*

**lard,** *n.* strutto *m.*

**large,** *adj.* grande.

**largely,** *adv.* in gran parte.

**largo,** *n., adj.* largo *adv.* largo (*m.*)

**lariat,** *n.* làccio *m.*

**lark,** *n.* allòdola *f.;* (fun) divertimento *m.*

**larkspur,** *n.* consòlida reale *f.*

**larva,** *n.* larva *f.*

**laryngitis,** *n.* laringite *f.*

**larynx,** *n.* laringe *f.*

**lascivious,** *adj.* lascivo.

**lash,** 1. *n.* frusta *f.,* sfèrza *f.* 2. *vb.* frustare, sferzare.

**lass,** *n.* ragazza *f.*

**lassitude,** *n.* lassitùdine *f.*

**lasso,** *n.* làccio *m.*

**last,** 1. *n.* forma *f.* 2. *adj.* ùltimo. 3. *vb.* durare.

**lasting,** *adj.* durévole.

**latch,** *n.* saliscendi *m.*

**late,** 1. *adj.* tardo, tardivo. 2. *adv.* tardi; (delayed) in ritardo.

**lately,** *adv.* recentemente.

**latent,** *adj.* latènte.

**lateral,** *adj.* laterale.

**lath,** *n.* listéllo *m.*

**lathe,** *n.* tórnio *m.*

**lather,** *n.* schiuma *f.*

**Latin,** *n. and adj.* latino (*m.*)

**latitude,** *n.* latitùdine *f.*

**Latium,** *n.* Làzio *m.;* (**of L.**) laziale

**latrine,** *n.* latrina *f.*

**latter,** 1. *adj.* recènte. 2. *pron.* (opposed to *former*) questo.

**lattice,** *n.* grata *f.*

**laud,** *vb.* lodare.

**laudable,** *adj.* lodévole.

**laudanum,** *n.* làudano *m.*

**laudatory,** *adj.* laudativo.

**laugh,** 1. *n.* riso *m.* 2. *vb.* rìdere; (**l. at**) deridere.

**laughable,** *adj.* ridìcolo.

**laughter,** *n.* riso *m.;* (**burst of l.**) risata *f.*

**launch,** 1. *n.* lància *f.* 2. *vb.* (throw) lanciare; (boat) varare.

**launching,** *n.* varo *m.*

**launder,** *vb.* lavare.

**laundress,** *n.* lavandaia *f.*

**laundry,** *n.* (clothes) bucato *m.;* (establishment) lavanderìa *f.*

**laundryman,** *n.* lavandaio *m.*

**laureate,** *adj.* laureato.

**laurel,** *n.* allòro *m.*, làuro *m.*

**lava,** *n.* lava *f.*

**lavallière,** *n.* pendènte *m.*

**lavatory,** *n.* latrina *f.*

**lavender,** *n.* lavanda *f.*

**lavish, 1.** *adj.* pròdigo. **2.** *vb.* prodigare.

**law,** *n.* legge *f.*, diritto *m.*

**lawful,** *adj.* legale, legìttimo.

**lawless,** *adj.* sènza legge.

**lawn,** *n.* prato *m.*

**lawsuit,** *n.* càusa *f.*

**lawyer,** *n.* avvocato *m.*

**lax,** *adj.* rilassato.

**laxative,** *n. and adj.* lassativo (*m.*), purgante (*m.*).

**laxity,** *n.* rilassamento *m.*

**lay, 1.** *adj.* làico. **2.** *vb.* méttere, porre, depórre.

**layer,** *n.* strato *m.*

**layman,** *n.* làico *m.*

**lazy,** *adj.* pigro.

**lead, 1.** *n.* direzione *f.* (metal) piombo *m.* **2.** *vb.* menare; condurre.

**leaden,** *adj.* di piombo, plùmbeo.

**leader,** *n.* capo *m.*; (Fascist) duce *m.*

**leadership,** *n.* guida *f.*

**lead pencil,** *n.* matita *f.*

**leaf,** *n.* fòglia *f.*

**leaflet,** *n.* fogliolina *f.*

**leafy,** *adj.* fogliuto.

**league,** *n.* lega *f.*

**League of Nations,** *n.* Società delle Nazioni *f.*

**leak, 1.** *n.* falla *f.* **2.** *vb.* (lose water) pèrdere; (let water in) far acqua.

**leakage,** *n.* infiltrazione *f.*; (loss) pèrdita *f.*

**leaky,** *adj.* che pèrde, che à falle.

**lean, 1.** *adj.* magro. **2.** *vb.* appoggiare, *tr.*

**leap, 1.** *n.* salto *m.* **2.** *vb.* saltare.

**leap year,** *n.* anno bisestile *m.*

**learn,** *vb.* imparare.

**learnèd,** *adj.* dòtto.

**learning,** *n.* dottrina *f.*

**lease, 1.** *n.* affitto *m.*; (contract) contratto d'affitto *m.* **2.** *vb.* affittare.

**leash,** *n.* guinzàglio *m.*

**least, 1.** *adj.* mìnimo. **2.** *adv.* minimamente.

**leather,** *n.* cuòio *m.*; (artificial l.) similcuòio *m.*

**leathery,** *adj.* tiglioso.

**leave, 1.** *n.* (departure) commiato, *m.*, congedo *m.*; (permission) permesso *m.*; (furlough) licènza *f.* **2.** *vb.* lasciare; (depart) partire; (go away) andàrsene; (l. out) omèttere.

**leaven,** *n.* lièvito *m.*

**lecherous,** *adj.* lascivo.

**lecture,** *n.* conferènza *f.*

**lecturer,** *n.* conferenzière *m.*

**ledge,** *n.* ripiano *m.*

**ledger,** *n.* libro mastro *m.*

**lee,** *n.* sottovènto *m.*

**leech,** *n.* sanguisuga *f.*

**leek,** *n.* pòrro *m.*

**leer,** *vb.* guardare lascivamente.

**leeward,** *adv.* sottovènto.

**left, 1.** *n.* sinistra. **2.** *adj.* sinistro; (departed) partito. **3.** *adv.* a sinistra.

**leftist,** *adj.* di sinistra.

**left-over,** *n.* avanzo *m.*

**leg,** *n.* gamba *f.*

**legacy,** *n.* làscito *m.*

**legal,** *adj.* legale.

**legalize,** *vb.* legalizzare.

**legation,** *n.* legazione *f.*

**legend,** *n.* leggènda *f.*

**legendary,** *adj.* leggendàrio.

**Leghorn,** *n.* Livorno *f.*

**legible,** *adj.* leggìbile.

**legion,** *n.* legione *f.*

**legislate,** *vb.* fare leggi.

**legislation,** *n.* legislazione *f.*

**legislator,** *n.* legislatore *m.*

**legislature,** *n.* parlamento *m.*

**legume,** *n.* legume *m.*

**leisure,** *n.* àgio *m.*, riposo *m.*, còmodo *m.*

**leisurely,** *adj.* còmodo.

**lemon,** *n.* limone *m.*

**lemonade,** *n.* limonata *f.*

**lend,** *vb.* prestare.

**length,** *n.* lunghezza *f.*

**lengthen,** *vb.* allungare, *tr.*

**lengthwise,** *adv.* per il lungo.

**lengthy,** *adj.* molto lungo.

**lenient,** *adj.* clemente.

**lens,** *n.* lènte *f.*

**Lent,** *n.* quarésima *f.*

**Lenten,** *adj.* di quarésima.

**lentil,** *n.* lenticchia *f.*

**lento,** *adv.* lènto.

**leopard,** *n.* leopardo *m.*

**leper,** *n.* lebbroso *m.*

**leprous,** *adj.* lebbroso.

**leprosy,** *n.* lebbra *f.*

**lesion,** *n.* lesione *f.*

**less,** 1. *adj.* minore. 2. *adv. and prep.* meno.

**lessen,** *vb.* diminuire.

**lesser,** *adj.* minore.

**lesson,** *n.* lezione *f.*

**lest,** *conj.* affinchè . . . non.

**let,** *vb.* (allow) lasciare, perméttere; (lease) affittare; (**l. alone**) lasciar stare; (**l. up**) diminuire.

**letdown,** *n.* allentamento *m.*

**lethal,** *adj.* letale.

**lethargic,** *adj.* letàrgico.

**lethargy,** *n.* letargia *f.*

**letter,** *n.* léttera *f.*

**letterhead,** *n.* carta intestata *f.*

**lettuce,** *n.* lattuga *f.*

**leukemia,** *n.* leucèmia *f.*

**levee,** *n.* diga *f.*

**level,** 1. *n.* livèllo *m.* 2. *adj.* orizzontale, equilibrato. 3. *vb.* livellare.

**lever,** *n.* lèva *f.*

**levity,** *n.* leggerezza *f.*

**levy,** 1. *n.* lèva *f.*; (tax) imposta *f.* 2. *vb.* arruolare; (tax) imporre.

**lewd,** *adj.* impùdico.

**lexicon,** *n.* lèssico *m.*

**liability,** *n.* responsabilità *f.*

**liable,** *adj.* responsàbile, soggètto.

**liaison,** *n.* (mil.) collegamento *m.*; (love affair) relazione *f.*

**liar,** *n.* bugiardo *m.*

**libation,** *n.* libagione *f.*

**libel,** 1. *n.* libèllo *m.* 2. *vb.* diffamare.

**libelous,** *adj.* diffamatòrio.

**liberal,** *n. and adj.* liberale (*m.*).

**liberalism,** *n.* liberalismo *m.*

**liberality,** *n.* liberalità *f.*

**liberate,** *vb.* liberare.

**libertine,** *n. and adj.* libertino (*m.*).

**liberty,** *n.* libertà *f.*

**libidinous,** *adj.* libidinoso.

**libido,** *n.* libido *f.*

**librarian,** *n.* bibliotecàrio *m.*

**library,** *n.* bibliotèca *f.*

**libretto,** *n.* libretto *m.*

**license,** *n.* licènza *f.*, permesso *m.*; (driver's) patènte *f.*

**licentious,** *adj.* licenzioso.

**lick,** *vb.* leccare.

**licorice,** *n.* liquirìzia *f.*

**lid,** *n.* copèrchio *m.*; (eye) pàlpebra *f.*

**lie,** 1. *n.* bugìa *f.*; menzogna *f.* 2. *vb.* (tell untruths) mentire; (recline) giacere.

**lien,** *n.* sequèstro *m.*

**lieutenant,** *n.* tenènte *m.*; (**second l.**) sottotenènte *m.*

**life,** 1. *n.* vita *f.* 2. *adj.* (**for l.**) vitalìzio.

**life-boat,** *n.* barca di salvatàggio *f.*

**life-buoy,** *n.* salvagente *m.*

**life-guard,** *n.* bagnino *m.*

**life insurance,** *n.* assicurazione sulla vita *f.*

**lifeless,** *adj.* sènza vita.

**life-preserver,** *n.* (belt) cintura di salvatàggio *f.*; salvagènte *m.*

**life-time,** *n.* durata della vita *f.*

**lift,** 1. *n.* ascensore *m.* 2. *vb.* sollevare.

**ligament,** *n.* legamento *m.*

**ligature,** *n.* legatura *f.*

**light,** 1. *n.* luce *f.* 2. *adj.* luminoso; (not heavy) leggièro. 3. *vb.* accèndere; (**l. up**) illuminare, *tr.*

**lighten,** *vb.* (make less heavy) alleggerire; (flash) lampeggiare.

**lighter,** *n.* (cigar, cigarette) accendisìgaro *m.*

**light-house,** *n.* faro *m.*

**lightly,** *adv.* leggieramente.

**lightness,** *n.* leggerezza *f.*

**lightning,** *n.* lampo *m.*, fùlmine *m.*; (**l.-rod**) parafùlmine *m.*

**lightship,** *n.* nave faro *f.*

**lignite,** *n.* lignite *f.*

**Ligurian,** *adj.* lìgure.

**like,** 1. *adj.* simile. 2. *vb.* (use piacere with English subject as indirect object). 3. *prep.* come.

**likeable,** *adj.* amàbile, simpàtico.

**likelihood,** *n.* probabilità *f.*

**likely,** *adj.* probàbile.

**liken,** *vb.* assomigliare.

**likeness,** *n.* somiglianza *f.*

**likewise,** *adv.* similmente.

**lilac,** *n.* lillà *m.*

**lilt,** *n.* canto *m.*

**lily,** *n.* giglio *m.*

**lily of the valley,** *n.* mughetto *m.*

**limb,** *n.* (of body) arto *m.*; mèmbro *m.*; (of tree) ramo *m.*

**limber,** *vb.* rendere flessìbile.

**limbo,** *n.* limbo *m.*

**lime,** *n.* calce *f.*; (**bird-l.**) vìschio *f.*; (fruit) limone *f.*; (tree) tiglio *m.*

**limelight,** n. bagliore m.

**limestone,** n. pietra calcare f.

**lime-water,** n. acqua di calce f.

**limit, 1.** n. lìmite m. **2.** vb. limitare.

**limitation,** n. limitazione f.

**limited,** n. (train) ràpido m.

**limitless,** adj. illimitato.

**limousine,** n. limousine f.

**limp, 1.** n. zoppicamento m. **2.** adj. fiacco, flessibile. **3.** vb. zoppicare.

**limpid,** adj. lìmpido.

**linden,** n. tìglio m.

**line, 1.** n. (cloth) tela di lino f.; (household l.) biancheria f. **2.** adj. di lino.

**lineage,** n. lignàggio m., stirpe f.

**lineal,** adj. diretto.

**linear,** adj. lineare.

**linen, 1.** n. (cloth) tela di lino f.; (household l.) biancheria f. **2.** adj. di lino.

**liner,** n. (boat) transatlàntico m.

**linger,** vb. indugiare.

**lingerie,** n. lingerìa f.

**linguist,** n. linguista m.

**linguistic,** adj. linguìstico.

**linguistics,** n. linguìstica f.

**liniment,** n. linimento m.

**lining,** n. fòdera f.

**link, 1.** n. (bond) legame m. vìncolo m.; (in chain) anèllo m. **2.** vb. collegare, tr.

**linoleum,** n. linòleum m.

**linseed,** n. seme di lino m.

**lint,** n. filàccia inglese f.

**lion,** n. leone m.

**lip,** n. labbro m.

**lip-stick,** n. rossetto m.

**liquefy,** vb. liquefare, tr.

**liqueur,** n. liquore m.

**liquid,** n. and adj. lìquido (m.)

**liquidate,** vb. liquidare.

**liquidation,** n. liquidazione f.

**liquor,** n. liquore m.

**lira,** n. lira f.

**lisp, 1.** n. pronùncia blesa f. **2.** vb. essere bleso.

**lisping,** adj. bleso.

**lisle,** n. filo di cotone mercerizzato m.

**list, 1.** n. lista f., elenco m., ruòlo m.; (slant) inclinazione f. **2.** vb. elencare; (slant) inclinarsi.

**listen (to),** vb. ascoltare.

**listless,** adj. svogliato.

**litany,** n. litanìa f.

**liter,** n. litro m.

**literacy,** n. letteratezza f.

**literal,** adj. letterale.

**literary,** adj. letteràrio.

**literate,** adj. letterato.

**literature,** n. letteratura f.

**lithe,** adj. flessuoso.

**lithograph, 1.** n. litografìa f. **2.** vb. litografare.

**lithography,** n. litografìa f.

**litigant,** n. litigante m.

**litigation,** n. càusa f.

**litmus,** n. tornasole m.

**litter, 1.** n. (mess) disórdine m.; (stretcher) barella f.; (animal's bed) lettièra f.; (kittens, puppies) figliata f. **2.** vb. méttere in confusione; (have kittens) figliare

**little, 1.** n. poco m. **2.** adj. piccolo m. **3.** adv. poco.

**liturgical,** adj. litùrgico.

**liturgy,** n. liturgìa f.

**live, 1.** adj. vivo. **2.** vb. vìvere.

**livelihood,** n. vita f.

**lively,** adj. vivace, brioso.

**liven,** vb. ravvivare, tr.

**liver,** n. fègato m.

**livery,** n. livrèa f.

**livestock,** n. bestiame m.

**livid,** adj. lìvido.

**living, 1.** n. vita f. **2.** adj. vivènte.

**lizard,** n. lucèrtola f.

**lo,** interj. ècco.

**load, 1.** n. càrico m. **2.** vb. caricare

**loaf, 1.** n. pagnòtta f., pane m. **2.** vb. oziare.

**loafer,** n. bighellone m.; (slipper) pantòfola f.

**loam,** n. terrìccio m.

**loan, 1.** n. prèstito m. **2.** vb. prestare.

**loath,** adj. riluttante.

**loathe,** vb. abominare.

**loathing,** n. ripugnanza f.

**loathsome,** adj. schifoso.

**lobby,** n. corridoio m.

**lobe,** n. lòbo m.

**lobster,** n. aragosta f.

**local, 1.** n. (train) òmnibus m.; accelerato m. **2.** adj. locale.

**locale,** n. località f.

**locality,** n. località f.

**localize,** vb. localizzare.

**locate,** vb. collocare; (find) trovare; (**be located**) trovarsi.

**location,** n. situazione f.

**lock,** 1. *n.* serratura *f.*; (canal) chiusa *f.* 2. *vb.* chiùdere a chiave.

**locker,** *n.* armadietto *m.*

**locket,** *n.* medaglione *m.*

**lockjaw,** *n.* tètano *m.*

**locksmith,** *n.* fabbro di serrature *m.*

**locomotion,** *n.* locomozione *f.*

**locomotive,** *n.* locomotiva *f.*, locomotore *m.*

**locust,** *n.* locusta *f.*

**locution,** *n.* locuzione *f.*

**lode,** *n.* filone *m.*

**lodge,** 1. *n.* casetta *f.* 2. *vb.* alloggiare.

**lodger,** *n.* òspite *m.*

**lodging,** *n.* allòggio *m.*

**loft,** *n.* solaio *m.*; (warehouse) magazzino *m.*

**lofty,** *adj.* alto.

**log,** *n.* ciòcco *m.*, ceppo *m.*; (tree-trunk) tronco d'àlbero *m.*

**loge,** *n.* lòggia *f.*

**logic,** *n.* lògica *f.*

**logical,** *adj.* lògico.

**loin,** *n.* lombo *m.*; (food) lombata *f.*

**loiter,** *vb.* andare a zonzo.

**Lombard,** *adj.* lombardo.

**Lombardy,** *n.* Lombardìa *f.*

**London,** *n.* Londra *f.*; (of L.) londinese.

**lone, lonely, lonesome,** *adj.* solitàrio.

**loneliness,** *n.* solitùdine *f.*

**long,** 1. *adj.* lungo. 2. *vb.* (l. for) bramare. 3. *adv.* lungamente.

**longevity,** *n.* longevità *f.*

**longing,** *n.* brama *f.*

**longitude,** *n.* longitùdine *f.*

**longitudinal,** *adj.* longitudinale.

**long-lived,** *adj.* longèvo.

**look,** 1. *n.* sguardo *m.*; (appearance) aspètto *m.* 2. *vb.* guardare; (l. out, take care) badare, vigilare.

**loom,** *n.* telaio *m.*

**looking glass,** *n.* spècchio *m.*

**loop,** *n.* càppio *m.*, làccio *m.*

**loophole,** *n.* feritòia *f.*; (way out) scappatòia *f.*

**loose,** 1. *adj.* sciòlto. 2. *vb.* sciògliere.

**loosen,** *vb.* allentare, *tr.*, sciògliere, *tr.*

**loot,** *n.* bottino *m.*

**lop off,** *vb.* mozzare.

**lopsided,** *adj.* mal equilibrato.

**loquacious,** *adj.* loquace.

**lord,** *n.* signore *m.*

**lordship,** *n.* signorìa *f.*

**lorry,** *n.* autocarro *m.*

**lose,** *vb.* pèrdere; (mislay) smarrire.

**loss,** *n.* pèrdita *f.*

**lot,** *n.* (fate) sòrte *f.*; (drawing) sortéggio *m.*; (group) lotto *m.*; (land) terreno *m.*; (a l. of, lots of) molto *adj.*

**lotion,** *n.* lozione *f.*

**lottery,** *n.* lotterìa *f.*

**lotus,** *n.* lòto *m.*

**loud,** 1. *adj.* alto, fòrte. 2. *adv.* fòrte.

**loud-speaker,** *n.* altoparlante *m.*

**lounge,** 1. *n.* divano *m.*, salone *m.* 2. *vb.* andare a zonzo.

**louse,** *n.* pidòcchio *m.*

**lout,** *n.* zoticone *m.*

**louvre,** *n.* ventilatore *m.*

**lovable,** *adj.* amàbile.

**love,** 1. *n.* amore *m.* 2. *vb.* amare.

**lovely,** *adj.* bèllo, leggiadro.

**lover,** *n.* amante *m. or f.*

**low,** 1. *adj.* basso. 2. *vb.* mugghiare.

**lowbrow,** *adj.* poco intelligènte.

**lower,** 1. *adj.* inferiore. 2. *vb.* abbassare, *tr.*

**lowly,** *adj.* ùmile.

**loyal,** *adj.* leale.

**loyalist,** *n.* lealista *m.*

**loyalty,** *n.* lealtà *f.*

**lozenge,** *n.* losanga *f.*; (pastille) pasticca *f.*

**lubricant,** *n.* and *adj.* lubrificante (*m.*)

**lubricate,** *vb.* lubrificare.

**lucid,** *adj.* chiaro.

**luck,** *n.* fortuna *f.*, sòrte *f.*; (bad l.) sfortuna *f.*

**lucky,** *adj.* fortunato.

**lucrative,** *adj.* lucrativo.

**ludicrous,** *adj.* ridìcolo.

**lug,** *vb.* trascinare.

**luggage,** *n.* bagagli *m. pl.*

**lukewarm,** *adj.* tièpido.

**lull,** *vb.* cullare.

**lullaby,** *n.* ninna-nanna *f.*

**lumbago,** *n.* lombàggine *f.*

**lumber,** *n.* legname *m.*

**luminous,** *adj.* luminoso.

**lump,** 1. *n.* massa *f.*, protuberanza *f.* 2. *vb.* ammassare.

**lumpy,** adj. pieno di protu-
beranze.
**lunacy,** n. pazzìa f.
**lunar,** adj. lunare.
**lunatic,** n. and adj. lunàtico
(m.)
**lunch,** n. colazione f.
**luncheon,** n. colazione f.
**lung,** n. polmone m.
**lunge,** vb. lanciarsi.
**lurch,** vb. traballare.
**lure,** vb. adescare.
**lurid,** adj. sensazionale.
**lurk,** vb. nascóndersi.
**luscious,** adj. saporoso.
**lush,** adj. lussureggiante.
**lust,** n. concupiscènza f.

**luster,** n. lustro m.
**lustful,** adj. concupiscènte.
**lustrous,** adj. rilucènte.
**lusty,** adj. vigoroso.
**lute,** n. liuto m.
**Lutheran,** adj. luterano.
**luxuriant,** adj. lussureggiante, rigoglioso.
**luxurious,** adj. lussuoso.
**luxury,** n. lusso m.
**lying,** adj. menzognèro, bugiardo, mendace.
**lymph,** n. linfa f.
**lynch,** vb. linciare.
**lyre,** n. lira f.
**lyric,** adj. lìrico.
**lyricism,** n. liricismo m.

# M

**macabre,** adj. màcabro.
**macaroni,** n. pasta asciutta
f., maccheroni m.pl.
**machine,** n. màcchina f.
**machine gun,** n. mitragliatrice f.
**machinery,** n. meccanismo m.
**machinist,** n. macchinista m.
**mackerel,** n. sgombro m.
**mackinaw,** n. impermeàbile
m.
**mad,** adj. pazzo; (angry) furioso.
**madam,** n. signora f.
**madcap,** n. and adj. scervellato (m.).
**madden,** vb. far impazzire.
**madrigal,** n. madrigale m.
**magazine,** n. periòdico m.,
rivista f.
**magic, 1.** n. magìa f. **2.**
adj. màgico.
**magician,** n. mago m.
**magistrate,** n. magistrato m.
**magistrature,** n. magistratura f.
**magnanimous,** adj. ma-
gnànimo.
**magnate,** n. magnate m.
**magnesium,** n. magnèsio m.
**magnet,** n. magnète m.
**magnetic,** adj. magnètico.
**magnificence,** n. magnificènza f.
**magnificent,** adj. magnìfico.

**magnify,** vb. ingrandire.
**magnitude,** n. grandezza f.
**mahogany,** n. mògano m.
**maid,** n. domèstica f.; (old
m.) zitèlla f.
**maiden,** n. fanciulla f.
**mail, 1.** n. pòsta f. **2.** vb.
impostare.
**mail-box,** n. buca per lettere
f.
**mailman,** n. postino m.
**maim,** vb. storpiare.
**main,** adj. principale.
**mainland,** n. tèrra ferma
f.
**mainspring,** n. molla principale f.
**maintain,** vb. mantenere; (in
argument) sostenere.
**maintenance,** n. mantenimento m.
**maize,** n. granturco m.
**majestic,** adj. maestoso.
**majesty,** n. maestà f.
**major,** n. and adj. maggiore
(m.).
**majority,** n. maggioranza f.
**make,** vb. fare.
**make-believe, 1.** n. finta f.
**2.** adj. finto. **3.** vb. fìngere.
**maker,** n. fattore m.
**makeshift,** n. espediènte m.
**make-up,** n. belletto m.
**malady,** n. malattìa f.
**malaria,** n. malària f.

**male**, *n.* and *adj.* màschio (*m.*).

**malevolent**, *adj.* malèvolo.

**malice**, *n.* malevolènza *f.*

**malicious**, *adj.* maligno.

**malign**, 1. *adj.* maligno. 2. *vb.* diffamare.

**malignant**, *adj.* maligno.

**malleable**, *adj.* malleàbile.

**malnutrition**, *n.* cattiva nutrizione *f.*

**malt**, *n.* malto *m.*

**maltreat**, *vb.* maltrattare.

**mammal**, *n.* mammífero *m.*

**man**, *n.* uòmo *m.*

**manage**, *vb.* amministrare, dirigere.

**management**, *n.* amministrazione *f.*, direzione *f.*

**manager**, *n.* amministratore *m.*, direttore *m.*

**mandate**, *n.* mandato *m.*

**mandatory**, *adj.* obbligatòrio.

**mandolin**, *n.* mandolino *m.*

**mane**, *n.* crinièra *f.*

**maneuver**, 1. *n.* manòvra *f.* 2. *vb.* manovrare.

**manganese**, *n.* manganese *m.*

**manger**, *n.* mangiatoia *f.*

**mangle**, *vb.* tritare.

**manhood**, *n.* virilità *f.*

**mania**, *n.* manìa *f.*

**maniac**, *n.* and *adj.* manìaco (*m.*).

**manicure**, *n.* manicure *f.*

**manifest**, 1. *adj.* manifèsto. 2. *vb.* manifestare.

**manifesto**, *n.* manifèsto *m.*

**manifold**, *adj.* moltéplice.

**manipulate**, *vb.* manipolare.

**mankind**, *n.* umanità *f.*

**manly**, *adj.* virile.

**manner**, *n.* manièra *f.*, mòdo *m.*

**mannerism**, *n.* manierismo *m.*

**mansion**, *n.* palazzo *m.*

**manslaughter**, *n.* omicìdio *m.*

**mantelpiece**, *n.* cornice *f.*

**mantle**, *n.* mantèllo *m.*

**Mantua**, *n.* Màntova *f.*

**Mantuan**, *n.* and *adj.* mantovano (*m.*).

**manual**, *n.* and *adj.* manuale (*m.*).

**manufacture**, *n.* fabbricazione *f.*

**manufacturer**, *n.* fabbricante *m.*

**manufacturing**, *adj.* industriale.

**manure**, *n.* concime *m.*

**manuscript**, *n.* and *adj.* manoscritto (*m.*).

**many**, *adj.* molti *m.pl.*; molte *f.pl.*

**map**, *n.* carta *f.*

**maple**, *n.* àcero *m.*

**mar**, *vb.* danneggiare, guastare.

**marble**, *n.* marmo *m.*

**march**, 1. *n.* màrcia *f.* 2. *vb.* marciare.

**March**, *n.* marzo *m.*

**mare**, *n.* cavalla *f.*

**margarine**, *n.* margarina *f.*

**margin**, *n.* màrgine *m.*

**marginal**, *adj.* marginale.

**marinate**, *vb.* marinare.

**marine**, *adj.* marino, marìttimo.

**mariner**, *n.* marinaio *m.*

**marionette**, *n.* marionetta *f.*

**marital**, *adj.* maritale.

**maritime**, *adj.* marìttimo.

**mark**, 1. *n.* segno *m.* 2. *vb.* marcare, segnare.

**market**, *n.* mercato *m.*

**market place**, *n.* piazza del mercato *m.*

**marmalade**, *n.* marmellata *f.*

**maroon**, *n.* (color) marrone *m.*

**marquee**, *n.* pensilina *f.*

**marquis**, *n.* marchese *m.*

**marriage**, *n.* matrimònio *m.*

**marrow**, *n.* midollo *m.*

**marry**, *vb.* sposare, *tr.*; (woman) maritare, *tr.*

**Marseilles**, *n.* Marsiglia *f.*

**marsh**, *n.* palude *f.*

**marshal**, *n.* maresciallo *m.*

**martial**, *adj.* marziale.

**martinet**, *n.* tiranno *m.*

**martyr**, *n.* màrtire *m.*

**martyrdom**, *n.* martírio *m.*

**marvel**, 1. *n.* meraviglia *f.* 2. *vb.* meravigliarsi.

**marvelous**, *adj.* meraviglioso.

**mascara**, *n.* kohl *m.*

**mascot**, *n.* portafortuna *m.*

**masculine**, *adj.* maschile.

**mash**, *vb.* schiacciare.

**mask**, 1. *n.* màschera *f.* 2. *vb.* mascherare.

**mason**, *n.* muratore *m.*

**masquerade**, 1. *n.* mascherata *f.* 2. *vb.* mascherarsi.

**mass**, *n.* massa *f.*; (church) messa *f.*

**massacre**, 1. *n.* massacro *m.* 2. *vb.* massacrare.

**massage**, 1. *n.* massaggio *m.* 2. *vb.* massaggiare.

**masseur**, *n.* massaggiatore *m.*

**massive**, *adj.* massiccio.

**mass meeting**, *n.* assemblèa *f.*

**mast**, *n.* àlbero *m.*

**master**, *n.* (boss) padrone *m.*; (great artist) maestro *m.*; (workman) mastro *m.*

**master-key**, *n.* comunèlla *f.*

**masterpiece**, *n.* capolavoro *m.*

**mastery**, *n.* padronanza *f.*

**masticate**, *vb.* masticare.

**mat**, *n.* stuòia *f.*

**match**, **1.** *n.* (light) fiammìfero *m.*; (contest) incontro *m.*; (equal) uguale *m.*; (marriage) matrimònio *m.* **2.** *vb.* uguagliare.

**mate**, **1.** *n.* (spouse) consòrte *m.* or *f.*; (pal) compagno *m.*; (second in command) secondo *m.*; (assistant) assistènte *m.* **2.** *vb.* accoppiare, *tr.*

**material**, *n. and adj.* materiale (*m.*).

**materialism**, *n.* materialismo *m.*

**materialize**, *vb.* materializzare.

**maternal**, *adj.* matèrno.

**maternity**, *n.* maternità *f.*

**mathematical**, *adj.* matemàtico.

**mathematics**, *n.* matemàtica *f.*

**matinée**, *n.* mattinata *f.*

**matriarchy**, *n.* matriarcato *m.*

**matrimony**, *n.* matrimònio *m.*

**matter**, **1.** *n.* matèria *f.*; (pus) pus *m.* **2.** *vb.* importare.

**mattress**, *n.* materasso *m.*

**mature**, **1.** *adj.* maturo. **2.** *vb.* maturare; (fall due) scadere.

**maturity**, *n.* maturità *f.*; (financial) scadènza *f.*

**maudlin**, *adj.* piagnucoloso.

**maul**, *vb.* percuòtere.

**mausoleum**, *n.* mausolèo *m.*

**maxim**, *n.* màssima *f.*

**maximum**, *n. and adj.* màssimo (*m.*).

**may**, *vb.* potere.

**May**, *n.* màggio *m.*

**maybe**, *adv.* forse.

**mayhem**, *n.* danni *m.pl.*

**mayonnaise**, *n.* maionese *m.*

**mayor**, *n.* sìndaco *m.*

**maze**, *n.* labirinto *m.*

**me**, *pron.* me, mi.

**meadow**, *n.* prato *m.*

**meager**, *adj.* magro, scarso.

**meal**, *n.* pasto *m.*; (flour) farina *f.*

**mean**, **1.** *n.* mèdia *f.* **2.** *adj.* (in the middle) mèdio; (base) meschino, spregévole. **3.** *vb.* significare, voler dire.

**meaning**, *n.* significato *m.*

**means**, *n.* mèzzo *m. sg.*

**meantime**, **meanwhile**, *n.* frattèmpo *m.*

**measles**, *n.* morbillo *m.*

**measure**, **1.** *n.* misura *f.* **2.** *vb.* misurare.

**measurement**, *n.* misuramento *m.*

**measuring**, *adj.* misuratore.

**meat**, *n.* carne *f.*

**mechanic**, *n.* meccànico *m.*

**mechanical**, *adj.* meccànico.

**mechanism**, *n.* meccanismo *m.*

**mechanize**, *vb.* meccanizzare.

**medal**, *n.* medàglia *f.*

**meddle**, *vb.* immischiarsi.

**mediaeval**, *adj.* medioevale.

**median**, *adj.* mediano.

**mediate**, *vb.* fare da intermediàrio.

**mediator**, *n.* intermediàrio *m.*

**medical**, *adj.* mèdico.

**medicate**, *vb.* medicare.

**medicine**, *n.* medicina *f.*

**mediocre**, *adj.* mediòcre.

**mediocrity**, *n.* mediocrità *f.*

**meditate**, *vb.* meditare.

**meditation**, *n.* meditazione *f.*

**Mediterranean**, *n. and adj.* mediterràneo (*m.*).

**medium**, **1.** *n.* mèzzo *m.* **2.** *adj.* mèdio.

**medley**, *n.* miscùglio *m.*

**meek**, *adj.* mite.

**meekness**, *n.* mitezza *f.*

**meet**, *vb.* incontrare *tr.*

**meeting**, *n.* riunione *f.*, assemblèa *f.*; (**m. -place**) ritròvo *m.*

**megaphone**, *n.* megàfono *m.*

**melancholy**, **1.** *n.* malinconìa *f.* **2.** *adj.* malincònico, melancònico.

**mellow**, *adj.* maturato.

**melodious**, *adj.* melodioso.

**melodrama**, *n.* melodramma *m.*

**melody**, *n.* melodìa *f.*

**melon**, *n.* mellone *m.*

**melt**, *vb.* fóndere *tr.*, sciògliere, *tr.*

**member,** *n.* sòcio *m.*, mèmbro *m.*

**membership,** *n.* (persons) affiliati *m.pl.*

**membrane,** *n.* membrana *f.*

**memento,** *n.* ricòrdo *m.*

**memoir,** *n.* memòria *f.*

**memorable,** *adj.* memoràbile.

**memorandum,** *n.* memorandum *m.*

**memorial, 1.** *n.* monumento *m.*, memoriale *m.* **2.** *adj.* commemorativo.

**memorize,** *vb.* imparare a memòria.

**memory,** *n.* memòria *f.*

**menace, 1.** *n.* minàccia *f.* **2.** *vb.* minacciare.

**menagerie,** *n.* serràglio *m.*

**mend,** *vb.* accomodare.

**mendacious,** *adj.* mendace.

**mendicant, 1.** *n.* mèndico *m.* **2.** *adj.* mendicante.

**menial,** *adj.* servile.

**menopause,** *n.* menopàusa *f.*

**menstruation,** *n.* mestruazione *f.*; régole *f.pl.*

**mental,** *adj.* mentale.

**mentality,** *n.* mentalità *f.*

**menthol,** *n.* mentòlo *m.*

**mention, 1.** *n.* menzione *f.* **2.** *vb.* menzionare.

**menu,** *n.* lista *f.*

**mercantile,** *adj.* mercantile.

**mercenary,** *adj.* mercenàrio.

**merchandise,** *n.* mercanzìa *f.*

**merchant,** *n.* mercante *m.*

**merchant marine,** *n.* marina mercantile *f.*

**merciful,** *adj.* pietoso.

**merciless,** *adj.* spietato.

**mercury,** *n.* mercùrio *m.*

**mercy,** *n.* pietà *f.*, misericòrdia *f.*

**mere,** *adj.* mèro, sémplice.

**merely,** *adj.* meramente, semplicemente.

**merge,** *vb.* assorbire.

**merger,** *n.* fusione *f.*

**meringue,** *n.* meringa *f.*

**merit, 1.** *n.* mèrito *m.* **2.** *vb.* meritare.

**meritorious,** *adj.* meritòrio.

**mermaid,** *n.* sirena *f.*

**merriment,** *n.* allegrezza *f.*

**merry,** *adj.* allegro.

**merry-go-round,** *n.* carosèllo *m.*

**mesh, 1.** *n.* (fabric) màglia *f.* **2.** *vb.* (gears) ingranare.

**mesmerize,** *vb.* ipnotizzare.

**mess,** *n.* pasticcio *m.*, confusione *f.*; (soldiers' meals) ràncio *m.*

**message,** *n.* messàggio *m.*, ambasciata *f.*

**messenger,** *n.* messaggèro *m.*

**messy,** *adj.* confuso, disordinato.

**metabolism,** *n.* metabolismo *m.*

**metal,** *n.* metallo *m.*

**metallic,** *adj.* metàllico.

**metamorphosis,** *n.* metamòrfosi *f.*

**metaphysics,** *n.* metafìsica *f.*

**meteor,** *n.* metèora *f.*

**meteorology,** *n.* meteorologìa *f.*

**meter,** *n.* (recording device) contatore *m.*; (unit of measure) mètro *m.*

**method,** *n.* mètodo *m.*

**meticulous,** *adj.* meticoloso.

**metric,** *adj.* mètrico.

**metropolis,** *n.* metròpoli *f.*

**metropolitan,** *adj.* metropolitano.

**mettle,** *n.* coràggio *m.*

**Mexican,** *adj.* messicano.

**Mexico,** *n.* il Mèssico *m.*

**mezzanine,** *n.* mezzanino *f.*

**microbe,** *n.* micròbio *m.*

**microfilm,** *n.* mìcrofilm *m.*

**microphone,** *n.* micròfono *m.*

**microscope,** *n.* microscòpio *m.*

**microscopic,** *adj.* microscòpico.

**mid-,** *adj.* mèdio.

**middle, 1.** *n.* mèzzo *m.* **2.** *adj.* mèdio, intermèdio, mèzzo.

**middle-aged,** *adj.* di mèzza età.

**Middle Ages,** *n.* medioèvo *m.*

**middle class,** *n.* borghesìa *f.*, ceto mèdio *m.*, classe mèdia *f.*

**midget,** *n.* nano *m.*

**midnight,** *n.* mezzanòtte *f.*

**midriff,** *n.* diaframma *m.*

**midwife,** *n.* levatrice *f.*

**mien,** *n.* aspètto *m.*, cera *f.*

**might, 1.** *n.* potènza *f.* **2.** *vb.* use conditional of potere.

**mighty,** *adj.* potènte.

**migraine,** *n.* emicrània *f.*

**migrate,** *vb.* migrare.

**migration,** *n.* migrazione *f.*

**migratory,** *adj.* migratòrio.

**Milan,** *n.* Milano *f.*

**Milanese,** *adj.* milanese.

**mild,** *adj.* mite.

**mildew,** *n.* muffa bianca *f.*

**mildness,** *n.* mitezza *f.*

**mile,** *n.* mìglio *m.*

**mileage,** *n.* chilometràggio *m.*

**milestone,** *n.* piètra miliare *f.*

**militant,** *adj.* militante.

**militarism,** *n.* militarismo *m.*

**military,** *adj.* militare.

**militia,** *n.* milizia *f.*

**milk,** **1.** *n.* latte *m.* **2.** *vb.* mùngere.

**milk-bar,** *n.* latterìa *f.*

**milkman,** *n.* lattaio *m.*

**milky,** *adj.* làtteo.

**mill,** **1.** *n.* mulino *m.*; (factory) fàbbrica *f.* **2.** *vb.* macinare.

**miller,** *n.* mugnaio *m.*

**millimeter,** *n.* millìmetro *m.*

**milliner,** *n.* modista *m. or f.*

**millinery,** *n.* modisterìa *f.*

**million,** *n.* milione *m.*

**millionaire,** *n.* milionàrio *m.*

**mimic,** **1.** *n.* imitatore *m.* **2.** *adj.* imitato. **3.** *vb.* imitare.

**mince,** *vb.* triturare.

**mind,** **1.** *n.* mente *f.*, ànimo *m.* **2.** *vb.* badare a; (obey) ubbidire a; **(never m.)** non impòrta.

**mindful,** *adj.* mèmore.

**mine,** **1.** *n.* minièra *f.*; (explosive) mina *f.* **2.** *adj.* mìo. **3.** *vb.* minare.

**mine field,** *n.* campo minato *m.*

**miner,** *n.* minatore *m.*

**mineral,** *n. and adj.* minerale *(m.).*

**mine-sweeper,** *n.* nave spazzamine *f.*

**mingle,** *vb.* mescolare, *tr.*

**miniature,** *n.* miniatura *f.*

**minimize,** *vb.* ridurre al mìnimo.

**minimum,** *n. and adj.* mìnimo *(m.).*

**minimum wage,** *n.* salàrio mìnimo *m.*

**mining,** **1.** *n.* coltivazione delle minière *f.* **2.** *adj.* mineràrio.

**minister,** **1.** *n.* ministro *m.* **2.** *vb.* ministrare.

**ministry,** *n.* ministèro *m.*

**mink,** *n.* visone *m.*

**minnow,** *n.* pesciolino *m.*

**minor,** **1.** (person under 21) minorènne. **2.** *adj.* minore, minorènne.

**minority,** *n.* minoranza *f.*; (age) minorità *f.*

**minstrel,** *n.* menestrèllo *m.*

**mint,** **1.** *n.* (plant) menta *f.*; (coin factory) zecca *f.* **2.** *vb.* coniare.

**minus,** *prep.* meno.

**minute,** **1.** *n.* minuto *m.*; **(of meeting)** verbale *m.* **2.** *adj.* minuto.

**miracle,** *n.* miràcolo *m.*

**miraculous,** *adj.* miracoloso.

**mirage,** *n.* miràggio *m.*

**mire,** *n.* fango *m.*

**mirror,** *n.* spècchio *m.*

**mirth,** *n.* allegrìa *f.*

**misadventure,** *n.* disgràzia *f.*

**misappropriate,** *vb.* appropriare indebitamente.

**misbehave,** *vb.* comportarsi male.

**miscellaneous,** *adj.* miscellàneo.

**mischief,** *n.* cattivèria *f.*, malìzia *f.*

**mischievous,** *adj.* cattivo, malizioso.

**misconstrue,** *vb.* fraintèndere.

**miscreant,** *n. and adj.* miscredènte.

**misdemeanor,** *n.* contravvenzione *f.*

**miser,** *n.* avaro *m.*

**miserable,** *adj.* mìsero.

**miserly,** *adj.* avaro.

**misery,** *n.* misèria *f.*

**misfit,** *n.* persona inadatta *f. m.*

**misfortune,** *n.* sfortuna *f.*

**misgiving,** *n.* apprensione *f.*, dùbbio *m.*

**mishap,** *n.* disgràzia *f.*

**mislay,** *vb.* smarrire.

**mislead,** *vb.* ingannare.

**misplace,** *vb.* smarrire.

**misplaced,** *adj.* fuòri di propòsito.

**mispronounce,** *vb.* pronunziar male.

**miss,** **1.** *n.* (unsuccessful shot) colpo mancato *m.* **2.** *vb.* mancare, pèrdere; (feel the lack of) sentire la mancanza di.

**Miss,** *n.* signorina *f.*

**missile,** *n.* mìssile *m.*

**mission,** *n.* missione *f.*

**missionary,** *n. and adj.* missionàrio *(m.).*

**misspell,** *vb.* scrivere scorrettamente.

**mist,** *n.* nébbia *f.*

**mistake,** **1.** *n.* sbàglio *m.* **2.** *vb.* sbagliare.

**mistaken,** *adj.* errato, erròneo, sbagliato.

**mister,** *n.* signore *m.*

**mistletoe,** *n.* vìschio *m.*

**mistreat,** *vb.* maltrattare, bistrattare.

**mistress,** n. padrona f.; (lover) amante f.
**mistrust,** 1. n. sfidùcia f. 2. vb. diffidare di.
**misty,** adj. nebbioso.
**misunderstand,** vb. fraintèndere.
**misuse,** vb. abusare di.
**mite,** n. (coin) òbolo m.; (small piece) pezzettino m.; (tot) piccino m.
**mitigate,** vb. mitigare.
**mitten,** n. guanto m.
**mix,** vb. mescolare, tr.
**mixture,** n. mescolanza f., mistura f.
**mix-up,** n. confusione f.
**moan,** 1. n. gèmito m. 2. vb. gèmere.
**moat,** n. fòssa f.
**mob,** n. fòlla f., plebàglia f.
**mobile,** adj. mòbile.
**mobilization,** n. mobilitazione f.
**mobilize,** vb. mobilitare.
**mock,** 1. adj. finto. 2. vb. deridere, beffarsi di, schernire.
**mockery,** n. derisione f., scherno m.
**mode,** n. (way) mòdo m.; (fashion) mòda f.
**model,** 1. n. modèllo m. 2. vb. modellare.
**moderate,** 1. adj. moderato. 2. vb. moderare.
**moderation,** n. moderazione f.
**modern,** adj. modèrno.
**modernize,** vb. modernare, tr.
**modest,** adj. modèsto.
**modesty,** n. modèstia f.
**modify,** vb. modificare.
**modish,** adj. alla mòda.
**modulate,** vb. modulare.
**moist,** adj. ùmido.
**moisten,** vb. inumidire.
**moisture,** n. umidità f.
**molar,** adj. molare.
**molasses,** n. melassa f.
**mold,** 1. n. forma f., stampo m.; (must) muffa f. 2. vb. formare, modellare.
**mole,** n. (animal) talpa f.; (pier) mòlo m.
**molecule,** n. molècola f.
**molest,** vb. molestare.
**mollify,** vb. ammollire.
**molten,** adj. fuso.
**moment,** n. momènto m.
**momentary,** adj. momentàneo.

**momentous,** adj. importante.
**monarch,** n. monarca m.
**monarchy,** n. monarchìa f.
**monastery,** n. monastèro m.
**Monday,** n. lunedì m.
**monetary,** adj. monetàrio.
**money,** n. denaro m.
**money-order,** n. vàglia m.
**mongrel,** n. and adj. bastardo (m.).
**monitor,** n. monitore m.
**monk,** n. mònaco m.
**monkey,** n. scimmia f.
**monocle,** n. mondòcolo m.
**monologue,** n. monòlogo m.
**monoplane,** n. monoplano m.
**monopolize,** vb. monopolizzare.
**monopoly,** n. monopòlio m.
**monosyllable,** n. monosillabo m.
**monotone,** n. tono uniforme m.
**monotonous,** adj. monòtono.
**monotony,** adj. monotonìa f.
**monoxide,** n. monòssido m.
**monsoon,** n. monsone m.
**monster,** 1. n. mostro m. 2. adj. (huge) immènso.
**monstrosity,** n. mostruosità f.
**monstrous,** adj. mostruoso.
**month,** n. mese m.
**monthly,** adj. mensile.
**monument,** n. monumento m.
**monumental,** adj. monumentale.
**mood,** n. stato d'ànimo m.
**moody,** adj. triste.
**moon,** n. luna f.
**moonlight,** n. chiaro di luna m.
**moor,** 1. n. brughièra f. 2. vb. ormeggiare.
**mooring,** n. orméggio m.
**moot,** adj. discusso.
**mop,** n. scopa di stracci f.
**moral,** n. and adj. morale (f.).
**morale,** n. morale m.
**moralist,** n. moralista m.
**morality,** n. moralità f.
**morally,** adv. moralmente.
**morbid,** adj. morboso.
**more,** adv. più; (m. and m.) sempre più.
**moreover,** adv. per di più.
**mores,** n. costumi m.pl.
**morgue,** n. càmera mortuària f.
**morning,** n. mattina f., mattino m.
**moron,** n. imbecille m.

**morose,** adj. poco sociévole.

**morphine,** n. morfina f.

**Morse code,** n. còdice Morse m.

**morsel,** n. (food) boccone m.; (piece) frammento m.

**mortal,** n. and adj. mortale (m.).

**mortality,** n. mortalità f.

**mortar,** n. calcina f.

**mortgage, 1.** n. ipotèca f. **2.** vb. ipotecare.

**mortician,** n. imprenditore di pompe funebri m.

**mortify,** vb. mortificare.

**mortuary,** adj. mortuàrio.

**mosaic,** n. mosàico m.

**mosquito,** n. zanzara f.; **(m. net)** zanzarièra f.

**moss,** n. mùschio m.

**most, 1.** adj. la maggior parte di. **2.** adv. maggiormente.

**mostly,** adv. per lo più.

**moth,** n. tarma f.

**mother,** n. madre f., mamma f.

**mother-in-law,** n. suòcera f.

**motif,** n. motivo m.

**motion,** n. mòto m.; (parliamentary) mozione f.

**motionless,** adj. immòbile.

**motion-picture,** n. pellìcola f.

**motivate,** vb. motivare.

**motive, 1.** n. motivo m. **2.** adj. motore; **(m. power)** fòrza motrice.

**motley,** n. eterogèneo, multicolore.

**motor,** n. motore m.

**motorboat,** n. motoscafo m.

**motorcycle,** n. motocicletta f.

**motorist,** n. automobilista m.

**motorize,** vb. motorizzare.

**motorized farming,** n. motocultura f.

**motto,** n. motto m.

**mound,** n. tùmulo m.

**mount,** vb. montare, salire.

**mountain,** n. montagna f., monte m.

**mountaineer,** n. montanaro m.

**mountainous,** adj. montagnoso, montuoso.

**mountebank,** n. ciarlatano m.

**mourn,** vb. piàngere.

**mournful,** adj. doloroso.

**mourning,** n. lutto m.

**mouse,** n. sòrcio m., tòpo m.

**mouth,** n. bocca f.

**mouthpiece,** n. (instrument)

**imboccatura** f.; (spokesman) portavoce m.

**movable,** adj. mòbile.

**move, moving, 1.** n. (household goods) traslòco m. **2.** vb. muòvere, tr.

**movement,** n. movimento m.

**movie,** n. cinema m., film m.

**moving,** adj. commovènte.

**mow,** vb. falciare.

**Mr.,** n. Sig. m. (abbr. for Signore).

**Mrs.,** n. Sra. f. (abbr. for Signora).

**much,** adj. and adv. molto.

**mucilage,** n. gomma lìquida f.

**muck,** n. letame m., melma f.

**mucous,** adj. mucoso.

**mucus,** n. muco m.

**mud,** n. fango m., lòto m.

**muddy,** adj. fangoso.

**muff, 1.** n. manicotto m. **2.** vb. sbagliare.

**muffle,** vb. (wrap up) imbaccuccare, tr.; (silence) attutire.

**muffler,** n. (scarf) sciarpa f.; (auto) silenziatore dello scàrico m.

**mug,** n. coppa f.

**mulatto,** n. mulatto m.

**mule,** n. mulo m.

**multicolored,** adj. multicolore.

**multiple,** adj. mùltiplo.

**multiplication,** n. moltiplicazione f.

**multiplicity,** n. moltiplicità f.

**multiply,** vb. moltiplicare, tr.

**multitude,** n. moltitùdine f.

**mummy,** n. mùmmia f.

**mumps,** n. orecchioni m. pl.

**munch,** vb. sgranocchiare.

**Munich,** n. Mònaco di Bavièra m.

**municipal,** adj. municipale.

**munificent,** adj. munifcènte.

**munition,** n. munizione f.

**mural,** adj. murale.

**murder,** n. assassìnio m.

**murderer,** n. assassino m.

**murmur, 1.** n. mormorìo m. **2.** vb. mormorare.

**muscle,** n. mùscolo m.

**muscular,** adj. muscolare.

**muse, 1.** n. musa f. **2.** vb. meditare.

**museum,** n. musèo m.

**mushroom,** n. fungo m.

**music,** n. mùsica f.

**musical,** *adj.* musicale.
**musical comedy,** *n.* operetta *f.*, rivista *f.*
**musician,** *n.* musicista *f.*
**muslin,** *n.* mussolina *f.*
**must,** *n.* use present of dovere.
**mustache,** *n.* baffi *m.pl.*
**mustard,** *n.* sènape *f.*, mostarda *f.*
**muster, 1.** *n.* rivista *f.* **2.** *vb.* radunare.
**musty,** *adj.* ammuffito.
**mutation,** *n.* mutazione *f.*
**mute,** *adj.* muto.
**mutilate,** *vb.* mutilare.
**mutiny, 1.** *n.* ammutinamento. **2.** *vb.* ammutinarsi.
**mutter,** *vb.* borbottare.

**mutton,** *n.* carne di montone *f.*
**mutual,** *adj.* mùtuo.
**muzzle,** *n.* (gun) bocca *f.*; (animal's mouth) muso *m.*; (mouthcovering) museruòla *f.*
**my,** *adj.* mìo.
**myopia,** *n.* miopìa *f.*
**myriad, 1.** *n.* miriade *f.* **2.** *adj.* innumerévole.
**myrtle,** *n.* mirto *m.*
**myself,** *pron.* me stesso; (**I m.**) ìo stesso.
**mysterious,** *adj.* misterioso.
**mystery,** *n.* mistèro *f.*
**mystic,** *adj.* mìstico.
**mystify,** *vb.* mistificare.
**myth,** *n.* mito *m.*
**mythical,** *adj.* mìtico.
**mythology,** *n.* mitologìa *f.*

# N

**nag, 1.** *n.* ronzino *m.* **2.** *vb.* tormentare.
**nail, 1.** *n.* chiòdo *m.* **2.** *vb.* inchiodare.
**naïve,** *adj.* ingènuo.
**naked,** *adj.* nudo.
**name, 1.** *n.* nome *m.*; (**family n.**) cognome *m.* **2.** *vb.* chiamare; (nominate) nominare.
**namely,** *adv.* cioè.
**namesake,** *n.* omònimo *m.*
**nap, 1.** *n.* pisolino *m.*, sonnellino *m.* **2.** *vb.* sonnecchiare.
**naphtha,** *n.* nafta *f.*
**napkin,** *n.* tovagliòlo *m.*
**Naples,** *n.* Nàpoli *f.*
**narcissus,** *n.* narciso *m.*
**narcotic,** *n. and adj.* narcòtico (*m.*).
**narrate,** *vb.* narrare.
**narrative, 1.** *n.* racconto *m.* **2.** *adj.* narrativo.
**narration,** *n.* narrazione *f.*
**narrow,** *adj.* stretto.
**nasal,** *adj.* nasale.
**nasty,** *adj.* disgustoso, antipàtico.
**natal,** *adj.* natale.
**nation,** *n.* nazione *f.*
**national,** *adj.* nazionale.

**nationalism,** *n.* nazionalismo *m.*
**nationality,** *n.* nazionalità *f.*
**nationalization,** *n.* nazionalizzazione *f.*
**nationalize,** *vb.* nazionalizzare.
**native, 1.** *n.* indigeno *m.* **2.** *adj.* nativo, indigeno.
**nativity,** *n.* natività *f.*
**natural,** *adj.* naturale.
**naturalist,** *n.* naturalista *m.*
**naturalize,** *vb.* naturalizzare.
**naturalness,** *n.* naturalezza *f.*
**nature,** *n.* natura *f.*
**naughty,** *adj.* birichino.
**nausea,** *n.* nàusea *f.*
**nauseous,** *adj.* nauseante.
**nautical,** *adj.* nàutico.
**naval,** *adj.* navale.
**nave,** *n.* navata *f.*
**navel,** *n.* ombellico *m.*
**navigable,** *adj.* navigàbile.
**navigate,** *vb.* navigare.
**navigation,** *n.* navigazione *f.*
**navigator,** *n.* navigatore *m.*
**navy,** *n.* marina *f.*
**navy yard,** *n.* arsenale *m.*
**Neapolitan,** *adj.* napoletano.
**near, 1.** *adj., adv.* vicino. **2.** *prep.* vicino a.
**nearby,** *adv.* vicino.

**nearly,** adv. quasi.
**near-sighted,** adj. miope.
**neat,** adj. lindo.
**neatness,** n. lindezza f.
**nebula,** n. nebulosa f.
**nebulous,** adj. nebuloso.
**necessary,** adj. necessàrio; (be n.) bisognare, volerci.
**necessity,** n. necessità f.
**neck,** n. collo m.
**necklace,** n. collana f.
**necktie,** n. cravatta f.
**nectar,** n. nèttare m.
**need,** 1. n. bisogno m. 2. vb. aver bisogno di.
**needful,** adj. necessàrio.
**needle,** n. ago m.; (phonograph) puntina f.
**needless,** adj. inùtile.
**needy,** adj. bisognoso.
**nefarious,** adj. nefàrio.
**negative,** 1. n. negativa f. 2. adj. negativo.
**neglect,** vb. trascurare.
**négligée,** n. vestàglia f.
**negligent,** adj. trascurato.
**negligible,** adj. trascuràbile.
**negotiate,** vb. negoziare.
**negotiation,** n. negoziazione f.
**Negro,** n. negro m.
**neighbor,** n. vicino m., pròssimo m.
**neighborhood,** n. vicinanza f.
**neither,** conj. nè.
**neon,** n. nèon m.
**neophyte,** n. neòfita m.
**nephew,** n. nipote m.
**nepotism,** n. nepotismo m.
**nerve,** n. nèrvo m.; (effrontery) sfrontatezza f.
**nervous,** adj. nervoso.
**nest,** n. nido m.
**nestle,** vb. annidarsi.
**net,** n. rete f.
**netting,** n. rete f.
**network,** n. rete f.
**neuralgia,** n. nevralgìa f.
**neurology,** n. neurologìa f.
**neurotic,** adj. nevròtico.
**neutral,** n. and adj. nèutro (m.).
**neutrality,** n. neutralità f.
**never,** adv. mai.
**nevertheless,** adv. nondimeno.
**new,** adj. nuòvo.
**news,** n. notìzie f.pl.
**news-boy,** n. giornalaio m.
**newscast,** n. radiocorrière m.
**newspaper,** n. giornale m.
**newsreel,** n. attualità f.pl.
**next,** adj. pròssimo, seguènte.
**nibble,** vb. rosicchiare.

**nice,** adj. gentile, buòno.
**nick,** n. tacca f.
**nickel,** n. nìchel m.
**nickname,** n. nomìgnolo m.
**nicotine,** n. nicotìna f.
**niece,** n. nipote f.
**niggardly,** adj. taccagno.
**night,** n. nòtte f.
**nightgown,** n. usignuòlo m.
**night club,** n. ritròvo notturno m.
**nightly,** adv. ogni nòtte.
**nightgown,** n. camìcia da nòtte f.
**nightmare,** n. ìncubo m.
**night-stick,** n. clava f.
**nimble,** adj. àgile.
**nine,** num. nòve.
**nineteen,** num. diciannòve.
**nineteenth,** adj. dècimo nòno, diciannovèsimo.
**ninetieth,** adj. novantèsimo.
**ninety,** num. novanta.
**ninth,** adj. nòno.
**nip,** n. pizzicotto m.
**nipple,** n. capézzolo m.
**nitrate,** n. nitrato m.
**nitrogen,** n. nitrògeno m.
**no,** 1. adj. nessuno. 2. interj. nò.
**nobility,** n. nobiltà f.
**noble,** n. and adj. nòbile (m.).
**nobleman,** n. nobiluòmo m.
**nobly,** adv. nobilmente.
**nobody,** pron. nessuno.
**nocturnal,** adj. notturno.
**nocturne,** n. notturno m.
**nod,** 1. n. cenno del capo m. 2. fare un cenno col capo.
**node,** n. nòdo m.
**noise,** n. rumore m.
**noiseless,** adj. silenzioso.
**noisome,** adj. puzzolènte.
**noisy,** adj. rumoroso.
**nomad,** n. nòmade m.
**nominal,** adj. nominale.
**nominate,** vb. nominare, designare.
**nomination,** n. nòmina f.
**nominee,** n. designato m., candidato m.
**nonchalant,** adj. incurante.
**noncombatant,** n. and adj. non combattènte (m.).
**non-commissioned officer,** n. sottufficiale m.
**noncommittal,** adj. che non si compromette.
**nondescript,** adj. sènza caratteristiche speciali.
**none,** adj. and pron. nessuno.
**nonentity,** n. nullità f.
**nonpartisan,** adj. nèutro.

**nonresident**, *adj.* non resi-dènte.

**nonsense**, *n.* assurdità *f.*, fandònie *f.pl.*

**nonstop**, *adj.* sènza fermate.

**noodles**, *n.* tagliatèlle *f.pl.*

**nook**, *n.* cantùccio *m.*

**noon**, *n.* mezzogiorno *m.*

**noose**, *n.* nodo scorsoio *m.*

**nor**, *conj.* nè.

**norm**, *n.* nòrma *f.*

**normal**, *adj.* normale.

**normally**, *adv.* normalmente.

**north**, **1.** *n.* nord *m.* **2.** *adj.* settentrionale.

**northeast**, *n.* nord-èst *m.*

**northern**, *adj.* settentrionale.

**North Pole**, *n.* polo nord *m.*

**northwest**, *n.* nord-òvest *m.*

**Norway**, *n.* Norvègia *f.*

**Norwegian**, *adj.* norvegese.

**nose**, *n.* naso *m.*

**nosebleed**, *n.* emorragìa na-sale *f.*

**nose dive**, *n.* picchiata *f.*

**nostalgia**, *n.* nostalgìa *f.*

**nostril**, *n.* narice *f.*

**nostrum**, *n.* rimèdio empìri-co *m.*

**not**, *adv.* non.

**notable**, *adj.* notévole.

**notary**, *n.* notaio *m.*

**notation**, *n.* notazione *f.*

**notch**, **1.** *n.* tacca *f.* **2.** *vb.* intaccare.

**note**, **1.** *n.* nòta *f.*; (short letter) biglietto *m.* **2.** *vb.* notare.

**note-book**, *n.* agènda *f.*, taccuino *m.*

**noted**, *adj.* nòto.

**noteworthy**, *adj.* rimar-chévole.

**nothing**, *pron.* niènte, nulla.

**notice**, **1.** *n.* avviso *m.*, at-tenzione *f.* **2.** *vb.* osservare.

**noticeable**, *adj.* notévole.

**notification**, *n.* notificazio-ne *f.*, avviso *m.*

**notify**, *vb.* notificare.

**notion**, *n.* nozione *f.*

**notoriety**, *n.* notorietà *f.*

**notorious**, *adj.* famigerato, notòrio.

**notwithstanding**, *prep.* no-nostante.

**noun**, *n.* sostantivo *m.*

**nourish**, *vb.* nutrire.

**nourishment**, *n.* nutrimento *m.*

**novel**, **1.** *n.* romanzo *m* **2.** *adj.* originale.

**novelist**, *n.* romanzière *m.*

**novelty**, *n.* novità *f.*

**November**, *n.* novèmbre *m.*

**novena**, *n.* novèna *f.*

**novice**, *n.* novìzio *m.*

**Novocaine**, *n.* novocaìna *f.*

**now**, *adv.* ora, adèsso.

**nowhere**, *adv.* in nessun luògo.

**nozzle**, *n.* imboccatura *f.*

**nuance**, *n.* sfumatura *f.*

**nuclear**, *adj.* nucleare.

**nucleus**, *n.* nùcleo *m.*

**nude**, *adj.* nudo.

**nugget**, *n.* pepita *f.*

**nuisance**, *n.* fastìdio *m.*, seccatura *f.*

**nullify**, *vb.* annullare.

**number**, **1.** *n.* nùmero *m.* **2.** *vb.* numerare

**numerical**, *adj.* numèrico.

**numerous**, *adj.* numeroso

**nun**, *n.* mònaca *f.*, suòra *f.*

**nuncio**, *n.* nùnzio *m.*

**nuptial**, *adj.* nuziale.

**nurse**, **1.** *n.* (hospital) infer-mièra *f.*; (wet-nurse) nutrice *f.*, bàlia *f.*; (baby-tender) bambinaia *f.* **2.** *vb.* curare.

**nursery**, *n.* stanza dei bam-bini *f.*; (plants) vivaio *m.*

**nurture**, *vb.* allevare, curare.

**nut**, *n.* nocciòla *f.*

**nut-cracker**, schiaccianoci *m.*

**nutrition**, *n.* nutrizione *f.*

**nutritious**, *adj.* nutriènte.

**nutshell**, *n.* gùscio di noce *m.*

**nylon**, *n.* nàilon *m.*

**nymph**, *n.* ninfa *f.*

# O

**oak**, *n.* quèrcia *f.*

**oar**, *n.* remo *m.*

**oasis**, *n.* oasi *f.*

**oath**, *n.* (solemn) giuramento *m.*; (swear-word) bestémmia *f.*

**oatmeal**, *n.* fiocchi d'avena *m.pl.*

**oats,** n. avéna f.sg.

**obdurate,** adj. ostinato.

**obedience,** n. obbediènza f.

**obedient,** adj. obbediènte.

**obeisance,** n. riverènza f.

**obelisk,** n. obelisco m.

**obese,** adj. obèso.

**obey,** vb. ubbidire.

**obituary,** n. necrològio m.

**object, 1.** n. oggètto m. **2.** vb. opporsi, obiettare.

**objection,** n. obiezione f.

**objectionable,** adj. offensivo.

**objective,** n. and adj. obiettivo m.

**obligation,** n. òbbligo m., obbligazione f.

**obligatory,** adj. obbligatòrio.

**oblige,** vb. obbligare.

**obliging,** adj. serviziévole.

**oblique,** adj. obliquo.

**obliterate,** vb. cancellare.

**oblivion,** n. oblìo m.

**oblong,** adj. oblungo.

**obnoxious,** adj. odioso.

**obscene,** adj. oscèno.

**obscure,** adj. oscuro.

**obsequious,** adj. ossequioso.

**observance,** n. osservanza f.

**observation,** n. osservazione f.

**observatory,** n. osservatòrio m.

**observe,** vb. osservare.

**observer,** n. osservatore m.

**obsession,** n. ossessione f.

**obsolete,** adj. caduto in disuso.

**obstacle,** n. ostàcolo m.

**obstetrical,** adj. ostètrico.

**obstetrician,** n. ostètrico m.

**obstinate,** adj. ostinato.

**obstreperous,** adj. clamoroso, chiassoso.

**obstruct,** vb. ostruire, ostacolare.

**obstruction,** n. ostruzione f.

**obtain,** vb. ottenere.

**obtrude,** vb. intrùdersi.

**obtuse,** adj. ottuso.

**obviate,** vb. evitare.

**obvious,** adj. òvvio.

**occasion, 1.** n. occasione f. **2.** vb. cagionare.

**occasional,** adj. occasionale.

**occasionally,** adv. di quando in quando.

**Occident,** n. occidente m.

**occidental,** adj. occidentale.

**occult,** adj. occulto.

**occupant,** n. occupante m., inquilino m.

**occupation,** n. occupazione f., professione f.

**occupy,** vb. occupare.

**occur,** vb. accadere, succèdere.

**occurrence,** n. avvenimento m.

**ocean,** n. oceàno m.

**o'clock,** n. ora f.

**octagon,** n. ottàgono m.

**octave,** n. ottava f.

**October,** n. ottobre m.

**octopus,** n. ottòpode m.

**ocular,** adj. oculare.

**oculist,** n. oculista m.

**odd,** adj. (numbers) dispari; (queer) strano.

**oddity,** n. stranezza f.

**odds,** n. probabilità f.

**odious,** adj. odioso.

**odor,** n. odore m.

**of,** prep. di; (from) da.

**off,** adv. vìa.

**offend,** vb. offèndere.

**offender,** n. offensore m.; (accused) imputato m.

**offense,** n. offesa f.

**offensive, 1.** n. offensiva f. **2.** adj. offensivo.

**offer, 1.** n. offèrta f. **2.** vb. offrire.

**offering,** n. offèrta f.

**offhand,** adv. estemporaneamente.

**office,** n. ufficio m.; (dentist's, doctor's) gabinetto m.; (**o. supplies**) oggetti di cancelleria m.pl.

**officer,** n. ufficiale.

**official,** n. and adj. ufficiale (m.).

**officiate,** vb. officiare.

**officious,** adj. inframmettènte.

**offshore,** adv. vicino alla tèrra.

**offspring,** n. pròle f.

**often,** adv. spesso.

**oil, 1.** n. òlio m. **2.** vb. ùngere, lubrificare.

**oil-cloth,** n. tela cerata f.

**oily,** adj. oleoso.

**ointment,** n. unguènto m.

**old,** adj. vècchio.

**old-fashioned,** adj. passato di mòda.

**olfactory,** adj. olfattòrio.

**oligarchy,** n. oligarchìa f.

**olive,** n. (tree) olivo m.; (fruit) oliva f.

**omelet,** n. frittata f.

**omen,** n. presàgio m.

**ominous,** adj. infàusto.

**omission,** n. omissione f.

**omit,** vb. omèttere.

**omnibus,** n. àutobus m.

**omnipotent**, *adj.* onnipotènte.

**on**, *adv. and prep.* su, sopra.

**once**, *adv.* una vòlta; (formerly) un tèmpo.

**one**, *num.* uno.

**oneself**, *pron.* sè stesso (*sg.*); sè stessi (*pl.*).

**one-sided**, *adj.* unilaterale.

**one-way**, *adj.* (fare) di corsa sémplice; (street) a sènso ùnico.

**onion**, *n.* cipolla *f.*

**onion-skin**, *n.* carta velina *f.*

**only**, 1. *adj.* ùnico. 2. *adv.* solamente, soltanto; (but) ma.

**onslaught**, *n.* attacco *m.*

**onus**, *n.* ònere *m.*

**onward**, *adv.* avanti.

**ooze**, 1. *n.* melma *f.* 2. *vb.* trasudare.

**opacity**, *n.* opacità *f.*

**opal**, *n.* opale *m.*

**opaque**, *adj.* opaco.

**open**, 1. *adj.* apèrto. 2. *vb.* aprire.

**opening**, *n.* (breach) apertura *f.*; (start) inìzio *m.*; inaugurazione *f.*

**opera**, *n.* òpera *f.*

**opera-glasses**, *n.* binòcolo da teatro *m.*(*sg.*)

**operate**, *vb.* operare.

**operatic**, *adj.* lìrico.

**operation**, *n.* operazione *f.*

**operative**, *adj.* operativo.

**operator**, *n.* operatore *m.*

**operetta**, *n.* operetta *f.*

**ophthalmic**, *adj.* oftàlmico.

**opinion**, *n.* opinione *f.*, parere *m.*

**opponent**, *n.* antagonista *m.*

**opportunism**, *n.* opportunismo *m.*

**opportunity**, *n.* occasione *f.*

**oppose**, *vb.* opporre, *tr.*

**opposite**, 1. *n. and adj.* opposto (*m.*). 2. *adv.* dirimpètto. 3. *prep.* dirimpètto a.

**opposition**, *n.* opposizione *f.*

**oppress**, *vb.* opprimere.

**oppression**, *n.* oppressione *f.*

**oppressive**, *adj.* oppressivo.

**oppressor**, *n.* oppressore *m.*

**optic**, *adj.* òttico.

**optician**, *n.* òttico *m.*

**optics**, *n.* òttica *f.*

**optimism**, *n.* ottimismo *m.*

**optimistic**, *adj.* ottimìstico.

**option**, *n.* opzione *f.*

**optional**, *adj.* facoltativo.

**optometry**, *n.* optometrìa *f.*

**opulence**, *n.* opulènza *f.*

**opulent**, *adj.* opulènto.

**or**, *conj.* o (before *o*, od); sìa, ossìa.

**oracle**, *n.* oràcolo *m.*

**oral**, *adj.* orale.

**orange**, *n.* (tree) arància *m.*; (fruit) arància *f.*

**orangeade**, *n.* aranciata *f.*

**oration**, *n.* orazione *f.*

**orator**, *n.* oratore *m.*

**oratory**, *n.* oratòria *f.*

**orbit**, *n.* òrbita *f.*

**orchard**, *n.* òrto *m.*, frutteto *m.*

**orchestra**, *n.* orchèstra *f.*

**orchid**, *n.* orchidèa *f.*

**ordain**, *vb.* ordinare.

**ordeal**, *n.* ordàlia *f.*; (fig.) pròva *f.*

**order**, 1. *n.* òrdine *m.* 2. *vb.* ordinare.

**orderly**, *adj.* ordinato.

**ordinance**, *n.* ordinanza *f.*

**ordinary**, *adj.* ordinàrio.

**ordination**, *n.* ordinazione *f.*

**ore**, *n.* minerale *m.*

**organ**, *n.* òrgano *m.*

**organdy**, *n.* organza *f.*

**organic**, *adj.* orgànico.

**organism**, *n.* organismo *m.*

**organist**, *n.* organista *m.*

**organization**, *n.* organizzazione *f.*

**organize**, *vb.* organizzare.

**orgy**, *n.* òrgia *f.*

**orient**, *vb.* orientare.

**Orient**, *n.* Oriènte *m.*

**Oriental**, *adj.* orientale.

**orientation**, *n.* orientazione *f.*

**origin**, *n.* orìgine *f.*

**original**, *adj.* originale; (former) primitivo.

**originality**, *n.* originalità *f.*

**ornament**, 1. *n.* ornamento *m.* 2. *vb.* ornare.

**ornamental**, *adj.* ornamentale.

**ornate**, *adj.* ornato.

**ornithology**, *n.* ornitologìa *f.*

**orphan**, *n. and adj.* òrfano (*m.*).

**orphanage**, *n.* orfanotròfio *m.*

**orthodox**, *adj.* ortodòsso.

**orthography**, *n.* ortografìa *f.*

**orthopedic**, *adj.* ortopèdico.

**oscillate**, *vb.* oscillare.

**osmosis**, *n.* osmòsi *f.*

**ostensible**, *adj.* ostensìbile.

**ostentation**, *n.* ostentazione *f.*

**ostentatious**, *adj.* ostentato.

**ostracize**, *vb.* ostracizzare.

**ostrich**, *n.* struzzo *m.*

**other,** *adj.* altro.

**otherwise,** *adv.* altrimenti.

**ouch,** *interj.* ahi!

**ought,** *vb.* use conditional of dovere.

**ounce,** *n.* óncia *f.*

**our,** *adj.* nòstro.

**ours,** *pron.* nòstro.

**ourselves,** *pron.* noi stessi *m.*, noi stesse *f.*

**oust,** *vb.* espèllere.

**ouster,** *n.* espulsione *f.*

**out,** *adv.* fuòri.

**out of,** *prep.* fuòri di; (motion) fuòri da.

**outbreak,** *n.* scòppio *m.*

**outburst,** *n.* scòppio *m.*

**outcast,** *v.* pària *m.*

**outcome,** *n.* evènto *m.*

**outdoors,** *adv.* all'apèrto.

**outer,** *adj.* esteriore.

**outfit,** 1. *n.* corredo *m.* 2. *vb.* corredare, fornire.

**outgrowth,** *n.* risultato *m.*

**outing,** *n.* escursione *f.*, gita *f.*

**outlandish,** *adj.* curioso, strano.

**outlaw,** *n.* bandito *m.*

**outlet,** *n.* sbocco *m.*, sfògo *m.*; (electrical) presa elèttrica *f.*

**outline,** *n.* schizzo *m.*

**outlive,** *vb.* sopravvìvere a.

**out-of-date,** *adj.* arretrato.

**outpost,** *n.* avampósto *m.*

**output,** *n.* produzione *f.*

**outrage,** *n.* oltràggio *m.*

**outrageous,** *adj.* oltraggioso.

**outrank,** *vb.* precèdere.

**outright,** *adv.* completamente.

**outrun,** *vb.* oltrepassare.

**outside,** 1. *n.* and *adj.* estèrno (*m.*). 2. *adv.* fuòri 3. *prep.* fuòri di; (except) all'infuòri di.

**outskirts,** *n.* sobbórghi *m.pl.*, perifería *f.*

**outward,** 1. *adj.* esteriore. 2. *adv.* vèrso l'estèrno.

**outwardly,** *adv.* esteriormente.

**oval,** *n.* and *adj.* ovale (*m.*).

**ovary,** *n.* ovàia *f.*

**ovation,** *n.* ovazione *f.*

**oven,** *n.* forno *m.*

**over,** *adv.* and *prep.* sopra; (**o. again**) di nuòvo; (**o. and o.**) ripetutamente.

**overbearing,** *adj.* prepotènte.

**overcoat,** *n.* sopràbito *m.*

**overcome,** *vb.* sopraffare, superare.

**overdue,** *adj.* scaduto.

**overflow,** *vb.* straripare, traboccare.

**overhaul,** *vb.* rimèttere a nuòvo.

**overhead,** 1. *n.* spese ordinàrie *f.pl.* 2. *adj.* and *adv.* in alto.

**overlook,** *vb.* omèttere, trascurare.

**overnight,** 1. *adj.* notturno. 2. *adv.* durante la nòtte.

**overpass,** *n.* cavalcavia *m.*

**overpower,** *vb.* vincere.

**overrule,** *vb.* decìdere contro; (law) cassare.

**overrun,** *vb.* invàdere.

**oversee,** *vb.* sorvegliare.

**oversight,** *n.* negligènza *f.*

**overstuffed,** *adj.* imbottito.

**overt,** *adj.* apèrto.

**overtake,** *vb.* raggiùngere.

**overthrow,** 1. *n.* sconvolgimento *m.* 2. *vb.* sconvòlgere, sovvertire.

**overtime,** *adj.* straordinàrio.

**overture,** *n.* sinfonìa *f.*

**overturn,** *vb.* capovòlgere.

**overweight,** *n.* peso eccessivo *m.*

**overwhelm,** *vb.* sopraffare.

**overwork,** 1. *n.* lavoro eccessivo *m.* 2. *vb.* lavorare troppo.

**owe,** *vb.* dovere.

**owing,** *adj.* dovuto; (**o. to**) dovuto a.

**owl,** *n.* civetta *f.*, gufo *m.*; (**owl service**) servizio notturno *m.*

**own,** 1. *adj.* pròprio. 2. *vb.* possedere.

**owner,** *n.* possessore *m.*

**ox,** *n.* bue *m.*

**oxygen,** *n.* ossìgeno *m.*

**oyster,** *n.* òstrica *f.*

# P

**pa**, *n.* babbo *m.*
**pace**, *n.* passo *m.*
**pacific**, *adj.* pacifico.
**pacifier**, *n.* pacificatore *m.*
**pacifism**, *n.* pacifismo *m.*
**pacifist**, *n.* pacifista *m.*
**pacify**, *vb.* pacificare.
**pack**, **1.** *n.* pacco *m.*; (gang) banda *m.*; (cards) mazzo *m.*; (dogs) muta *f.* **2.** *vb.* imballare; (suitcases) fare le valigie.
**package**, *n.* pacco *m.*
**packing**, *n.* imballàggio *m.*
**pact**, *n.* patto *m.*
**pad**, **1.** *n.* cuscinetto *m.* **2.** *vb.* imbottire.
**padding**, *n.* imbottitura *f.*
**paddle**, **1.** *n.* remo *m.* **2.** *vb.* remare; (splash) guazzare; (spank) sculacciare.
**paddock**, *n.* campo *m.*
**padlock**, *n.* lucchetto *m.*
**Padua**, *n.* Pàdova *f.*
**Paduan**, *adj.* padovano.
**pagan**, *n.* and *adj.* pagano (*m.*).
**page**, **1.** *n.* pàgina *f.*; (servant) pàggio *m.* **2.** *vb.* chiamare.
**pageant**, *n.* cortèo *m.*
**pagoda**, *n.* pagòda *f.*
**pail**, *n.* sécchia *f.*
**pain**, *n.* dolore *m.*, pena *f.*
**painful**, *adj.* doloroso.
**painstaking**, *adj.* coscienzoso.
**paint**, **1.** *n.* colore *m.*; (makeup) belletto *m.* **2.** *vb.* dipingere. ·
**painter**, *n.* pittore *m.*
**painting**, *n.* pittura *f.*, dipinto *m.*
**pair**, *n.* paio *m.*
**pajamas**, *n.* pigiama *m.pl.*
**palace**, *n.* palazzo *m.*
**palatable**, *adj.* gustoso.
**palate**, *n.* pàlato *m.*
**palatial**, *adj.* magnifico.
**pale**, **1.** *adj.* pàllido. **2.** *vb.* impallidire.
**paleness**, *n.* pallidezza *f.*
**palette**, *n.* tavolòzza *f.*
**pall**, *vb.* perder sapore *m.*
**pallbearer**, *n.* persona che règge i cordoni *f.*
**pallid**, *adj.* pàllido.

**palm**, *n.* palma *f.*
**palpitate**, *vb.* palpitare.
**paltry**, *adj.* meschino.
**pamper**, *vb.* trattare con indulgènza.
**pamphlet**, *n.* opùscolo *m.*
**pan**, **1.** *n.* padèlla *f.* **2.** *vb.* criticare aspramente; (**p. out**) riuscire.
**panacea**, *n.* panacèa *f.*
**pan-cake**, *n.* frittèlla *f.*
**pane**, *n.* (**p. of glass**) vetro *m.*
**panel**, *n.* pannèllo *m.*
**pang**, *n.* spàsimo *m.*
**panic**, *n.* pànico *m.*
**panorama**, *n.* panorama *m.*
**pant**, *vb.* anelare, ansare.
**panther**, *n.* pantèra *f.*
**pantomime**, *n.* pantomima *f.*
**pantry**, *n.* dispènsa *f.*
**pants**, *n.* pantaloni *m.pl.*
**papa**, *n.* papà *m.*
**papal**, *adj.* papale.
**paper**, *n.* carta *f.*; (**newsp.**) giornale *m.*; (**wall-p.**) carta da parati *f.*
**paper-hanger**, *n.* tappezzière in carta *m.*
**par**, *n.* pari *f.*
**parable**, *n.* paràbola *f.*
**parachute**, *n.* paracadute *m.*
**parade**, *n.* parata *f.*
**paradise**, *n.* paradiso *m.*
**paradox**, *n.* paradòsso *m.*
**paraffin**, *n.* paraffina *f.*
**paragraph**, *n.* paràgrafo *m.*
**parakeet**, *n.* pappagallo *m.*
**parallel**, *n.* and *adj.* parallèlo (*m.*).
**paralysis**, *n.* paràlisi *f.*
**paralyze**, *vb.* paralizzare.
**paramount**, *adj.* suprèmo.
**paraphrase**, **1.** *n.* paràfrasi *f.* **2.** *vb.* parafrasare.
**parasite**, *n.* parassita *f.*
**parcel**, *n.* pacco *m.*
**parch**, *vb.* inaridire.
**parchment**, *n.* pergamena *f.*
**pardon**, **1.** *n.* perdono *m.* **2.** *vb.* perdonare.
**pare**, *vb.* (nails) tagliare; (fruit) sbucciare.
**parent**, *n.* genitore *m.*
**parentage**, *n.* paternità *f.*
**parenthesis**, *n.* parèntesi *f.*
**pariah**, *n.* pària *m.*

parish, *n.* parròcchia *f.*; (**p. priest**) pàrroco *m.*

Paris, *n.* Parigi *f.*

Parisian, *adj.* parigino.

parity, *n.* parità *f.*

park, **1.** *n.* parco *m.* **2.** *vb.* parcare.

parking, *n.* postéggio *m.* parcamento *m.*; (**p. area**) autoparchéggio *m.*;(**p. lights**) luci di città *f.pl.*

parkway, *n.* viale *m.*; (super-highway) autostrada *f.*

parley, *n.* **1.** parlamento *m.* **2.** *vb.* parlamentare.

parliament, *n.* parlamento *m.*

parliamentary, *adj.* parlamentare.

parlor, *n.* salòtto *m.*

Parmesan, *adj.* parmigiano.

parochial, *adj.* parrocchiale.

parody, *n.* **1.** parodìa *f.* **2.** *vb.* parodiare.

parole, *n.* paròla d'onore *f.*

paroxysm, *n.* parossismo *m.*

parrot, *n.* pappagallo *m.*

parsimony, *n.* parsimònia *f.*

parsley, *n.* prezzémolo *m.*

parson, *n.* pàrroco *m.*

part, **1.** *n.* parte *f.* **2.** *vb.* separare, *tr.*

partake, *vb.* partecipare.

partial, *adj.* parziale.

partiality, *n.* parzialità *f.*

participant, *n.* partecipante *m.*

participate, *vb.* partecipare.

participation, *n.* partecipazione *f.*

participle, *n.* particìpio *m.*

particle, *n.* particèlla *f.*

particular, *adj.* particolare; (fussy) esigente.

parting, *n.* separazione *f.*

partisan, *n. and adj.* partigiano (*m.*).

partition, *n.* partizione *f.*; (wall) muro divisòrio *m.*

partly, *adv.* in parte.

partner, *n.* compagno *m.*, sòcio *m.*

part of speech, *n.* parte del discorso *f.*

partridge, *n.* pernice *f.*

party, *n.* (political) partito *m.*; (social) ricevimento *m.*; (legal) parte in càusa *f.*; (person) individuo *m.*; (group) gruppo *m.*

pass, **1.** *n.* passo *m.* **2.** *vb.* passare; (auto) sorpassare; (exam.) superare; (go beyond) oltrepassare.

passable, *adj.* (road) praticàbile; (work) passàbile.

passage, *n.* passaggio *m.*

passé, *adj.* fuòri di mòda; (faded) appassito.

passenger, *n.* passeggèro *m.*

passer-by, *n.* passante *m.*

passing, *n.* (auto) sorpasso *m.*

passion, *n.* passione *f.*

passionate, *adj.* appassionato.

passive, *n. and adj.* passivo (*m.*).

passport, *n.* passapòrto *m.*

past, *n. and adj.* passato (*m.*).

paste, **1.** *n.* pasta *f.*, còlla *f.* **2.** *vb.* incollare.

pasteurize, *vb.* pasteurizzare.

pastille, *n.* pastiglia *f.*, sticca *f.*

pastime, *n.* passatèmpo *m.*

pastor, *n.* pastore *m.*

pastry, *n.* pasticceria *f.*

pastry shop, *n.* pasticcerìa *f.*

pasture, *n.* pàscolo *m.*

pasty, **1.** *n.* pasticcio *m.* **2.** *adj.* (color) pàllido.

pat, **1.** *n.* colpetto *m.*; (butter, etc.) panetto *m.* **2.** *vb.* bàttere leggiermente.

patch, **1.** *n.* pèzza *f.* **2.** *vb.* rappezzare, rattoppare.

patchwork, *n.* raffazzonamento *m.*

patent, **1.** *n.* brevetto *m.* **2.** *vb.* brevettare.

patent leather, *n.* pèlle verniciata *f.*

paternal, *adj.* patèrno.

paternity, *n.* paternità *f.*

path, *n.* sentiero *m.*, pista *f.*

pathetic, *adj.* patètico.

pathology, *n.* patologìa *f.*

pathos, *n.* pàtos *m.*

patience, *n.* paziènza *f.*

patient, *adj.* paziènte.

patio, *n.* cortile *m.*

patriarch, *n.* patriarca *f.*

patrimony, *n.* patrimònio *m.*

patriot, *n.* patriòta *m.*

patriotic, *adj.* patriòttico.

patriotism, *n.* patriottismo *m.*

patrol, *n.* pattùglia *f.*

patrolman, *n.* poliziòtto *m.*

patron, *n.* patròno *m.*

patronage, *n.* patronato *m.*

patronize, *vb.* comprare da.

pattern, *n.* modèllo *m.*

pauper, *n.* pòvero *m.*

pause, *n.* pàusa *f.*

pave, *vb.* pavimentare.

pavement, *n.* selciato *m.*

pavilion, *n.* padiglione *m.*

**paw,** *n.* zampa *f.*

**pawn, 1.** *n.* pegno *m.*; (chess) pedína *f.* **2.** impegnare.

**pay, 1.** *n.* paga *f.* **2.** *vb.* pagare; (**pay in**) versare.

**payment,** *n.* pagamento *m.*, versamento *m.*

**pea,** *n.* pisèllo *m.*

**peace,** *n.* pace *f.*

**peaceable,** *adj.* pacífico.

**peaceful,** *adj.* tranquillo.

**peach,** *n.* (tree) pèsco *m.*; (fruit) pèsca *f.*

**peacock,** *n.* pavone *m.*

**peak,** *n.* cima *f.*, picco *m.*

**peal, 1.** *n.* scampanìo *m.* **2.** *vb.* scampanare.

**peanut,** *n.* aràchide *f.*

**pear,** *n.* (tree) **pero** *m.*; (fruit) pera *f.*

**pearl,** *n.* pèrla *f.*

**peasant,** *n.* contadino *m.*

**pebble,** *n.* ciòttolo *m.*

**peck,** *vb.* beccare.

**peculiar,** *adj.* (special) peculiare; (queer) strano.

**peculiarity,** *n.* peculiarità *f.*

**pecuniary,** *adj.* pecuniàrio.

**pedagogue,** *n.* pedagògo *m.*

**pedagogy,** *n.* pedagogìa *f.*

**pedal, 1.** *n.* pedale *m.* **2.** *vb.* pedalare.

**pedant,** *n.* pedante *m.*

**peddle,** *vb.* vèndere al minuto.

**peddler,** *n.* venditore ambulante *m.*

**pedestal,** *n.* piedestallo *m.*

**pedestrian, 1.** *n.* pedone *m.* **2.** *adj.* pedèstre; (pertaining to pedestrians) pedonale.

**pediatrician,** *n.* pediàtra *m.*

**pedigree,** *n.* genealogìa *f.*

**peek,** *vb.* sbirciare.

**peel,** *vb.* sbucciare, pelare.

**peep, 1.** *n.* occhiata *f.* **2.** *vb.* (look) dare un' occhiata; (appear) spuntare.

**peer, 1.** *n.* pari *m.* **2.** *vb.* guardare curiosamente.

**peevish,** *adj.* stizzoso.

**peg,** *n.* piuòlo *m.*

**pelt, 1.** *n.* (skin) pèlle *f.* **2.** *vb.* assalire.

**pelvis,** *n.* pèlvi *f.*

**pen,** *n.* penna *f.*; (fountain p.) p. stilogràfica. *vb.* scrivere.

**penalty,** *n.* pena *f.*

**penance,** *n.* penitènza *f.*

**penchant,** *n.* inclinazione *f.*

**pencil,** *n.* làpis *m.*, matita *f.*

**pendant,** *n.* pendènte *m.*

**pending, 1.** *adj.* pendènte. **2.** *prep.* in attesa di.

**penetrate,** *vb.* penetrare.

**penetration,** *n.* penetrazione *f.*

**penicillin,** *n.* penicillina *f.*

**peninsula,** *n.* penìsola *f.*

**penitence,** *n.* penitènza *f.*

**penitent,** *n. and adj.* penitènte (*m.*)

**pen-knife,** *n.* temperino *m.*

**penniless,** *adj.* al verde.

**penny,** *n.* sòldo *m.*

**pension,** *n.* pensione *f.*

**pensive,** *adj.* pensoso.

**pent-up,** *adj.* rinchiuso.

**penury,** *n.* penùria *f.*

**people,** *n.* (folks) gènte *f.*; (nation) pòpolo *m.*

**pepper,** *n.* pepe *m.*

**per,** *prep.* per.

**perambulator,** *n.* carrozzèlla *f.*

**perceive,** *vb.* scòrgere.

**per cent,** *adv.* per cènto.

**percentage,** *n.* percentuale *f.*

**perceptible,** *adj.* percettìbile.

**perception,** *n.* percezione *f.*

**perch,** **1.** *n.* (fish) pesce pèrsico *m.*; (pole) pèrtica *f.*; (for birds) posatóio *m.* **2.** *vb.* (roost) appollaiarsi.

**perdition,** *n.* perdizione *f.*

**peremptory,** *adj.* perentòrio.

**perennial,** *adj.* perènne.

**perfect, 1.** *adj.* perfètto. **2.** *vb.* perfezionare.

**perfection,** *n.* perfezione *f.*

**perforation,** *n.* perforazione *f.*

**perform,** *vb.* eseguire; (a play) rappresentare; (sing) cantare; (instrumental music) suonare.

**performance,** *n.* esecuzione *f.*, rappresentazione *f.*

**perfume, 1.** *n.* profumo *m.* **2.** *vb.* profumare.

**perfunctory,** *adj.* casuale.

**perhaps,** *adv.* forse; (**p. even**) magari.

**peril,** *n.* perìcolo *m.*

**perilous,** *adj.* pericoloso.

**perimeter,** *n.* perìmetro *m.*

**period,** *n.* perìodo *m.*

**periodic,** *adj.* periòdico.

**periodical,** *n. and adj.* periòdico (*m.*).

**periphery,** *n.* periferìa *f.*

**perish,** *vb.* perire.

**perishable,** *adj.* deperìbile.

**perjure oneself,** *vb.* spergiurare.

**perjury**, *n.* spergiuro *m.*

**permanent**, *adj.* permanènte.

**permeate**, *vb.* permeare.

**permissible**, *adj.* permissìbile.

**permission**, *n.* permesso *m.*

**permit**, 1. *n.* permesso *m.* 2. *vb.* permèttere.

**pernicious**, *adj.* pernicioso.

**perpendicular**, *n. and adj.* perpendicolare (*m.*).

**perpetrate**, *vb.* perpetrare.

**perpetual**, *adj.* perpètuo.

**perplex**, 1. *adj.* perplèsso. 2. *vb.* rèndere perplèsso.

**perplexity**, *n.* perplessità *f.*

**persecute**, *vb.* perseguitare.

**persecution**, *n.* persecuzione *f.*

**perseverance**, *n.* perseveranza *f.*

**persevere**, *vb.* perseverare.

**persist**, *vb.* persìstere.

**persistent**, *adj.* persistènte.

**person**, *n.* persona *f.*

**personage**, *n.* personàggio *m.*

**personal**, *adj.* personale.

**personality**, *n.* personalità *f.*

**personally**, *adv.* personalmente.

**personnel**, *n.* personale *m.*

**perspective**, *n.* prospettiva *f.*

**perspiration**, *n.* sudore *m.*

**perspire**, *vb.* sudare.

**persuade**, *vb.* persuadere.

**persuasive**, *adj.* persuasivo.

**pertain**, *vb.* appartenere.

**pertinent**, *adj.* pertinènte.

**perturb**, *vb.* perturbare.

**peruse**, *vb.* scórrere.

**pervade**, *vb.* pervàdere.

**perverse**, *adj.* pervèrso.

**perversion**, *n.* perversione *f.*

**pervert**, *vb.* pervertire.

**pessimism**, *n.* pessimismo *m.*

**pestilence**, *n.* pestilènza *f.*

**pet**, 1. *n. and adj.* favorito (*m.*); (animal) animale domèstico *m.* 2. *vb.* vezzeggiare.

**petal**, *n.* pètalo *m.*

**petition**, *n.* petizione *f.*

**petrify**, *vb.* pietrificare.

**petrol**, *n.* benzina *f.*

**petroleum**, *n.* petròlio *m.*

**petticoat**, *n.* sottana *f.*

**petty**, *adj.* meschino, piccolo.

**petulance**, *n.* petulanza *f.*

**petulant**, *adj.* petulante.

**pew**, *n.* banco in chièsa *m.*

**phantom**, *n.* fantasma *m.*

**pharmacist**, *n.* farmacista *m.*

**pharmacy**, *n.* farmacìa *f.*

**phase**, *n.* fase *f.*

**pheasant**, *n.* fagiano *m.*

**phenomenal**, *adj.* fenomenale.

**phenomenon**, *n.* fenòmeno *m.*

**philanthropy**, *n.* filantropìa *f.*

**philately**, *n.* filatèlica *f.*

**philosopher**, *n.* filòsofo *m.*

**philosophical**, *adj.* filosòfico.

**philosophy**, *n.* filosofìa *f.*

**phlegm**, *n.* flèmma *m.*

**phlegmatic**, *adj.* flemmàtico.

**phobia**, *n.* fobìa *f.*

**phonetic**, *adj.* fonètico.

**phonograph**, *n.* grammòfono *m.*

**phosphorus**, *n.* fòsforo *m.*

**photoelectric**, *adj.* fotoelèttrico.

**photogenic**, *adj.* fotogènico.

**photograph**, 1. *n.* fotografìa *f.* 2. *vb.* fotografare.

**photographer**, *n.* fotògrafo *m.*

**photography**, *n.* fotografìa *f.*

**photostat**, *n.* riproduzione anastàtica *f.*

**phrase**, *n.* frase *f.*

**physical**, *adj.* fìsico.

**physician**, *n.* mèdico *m.*

**physicist**, *n.* fìsico *m.*

**physics**, *n.* fìsica *f.*

**physiology**, *n.* fisiologìa *f.*

**physiotherapy**, *n.* fisioterapìa *f.*

**physique**, *n.* fìsico *m.*

**pianist**, *n.* pianista *m.*

**piano**, *n.* pianofòrte *m.*

**picayune**, *adj.* meschino.

**piccolo**, *n.* ottavino *m.*

**pick**, 1. *n.* piccone *m.* 2. *vb.* (gather) raccògliere; (select) scégliere.

**picket**, *n.* picchetto *m.*

**pickle**, *n.* salamòia *f.*; (trouble) impìccio *m.*

**pickpocket**, *n.* borsaiòlo *m.*

**picnic**, *n.* gita *f.*

**picture**, *n.* quadro *m.*

**picturesque**, *adj.* pittoresco.

**pie**, *n.* tòrta *f.*

**piece**, *n.* pèzzo *m.*

**Piedmont**, *n.* Piemonte *m.*

**Piedmontese**, *adj.* piemontese.

**pier**, *n.* (dock) banchina *f.*, mòlo *m.*; (pillar) pilone *m.*

**pierce**, *vb.* forare, traforare.

**piety**, *n.* pietà *f.*

**pig**, *n.* pòrco *m.*, maiale *m.*

**pigeon**, *n.* piccione *m.*

**pigeonhole**, *n.* casèlla *f.*

**pigment,** *n.* pigmènto *m.*

**pile, 1.** *n.* (heap) ammasso *m.*, mucchio *m.*; (post) palafitta *f.* **2.** *vb.* ammucchiare.

**pilfer,** *vb.* rubacchiare.

**pilgrim,** *n.* pellegrino *m.*

**pilgrimage,** *n.* pellegrinàggio *m.*

**pill,** *n.* pìllola *f.*

**pillage, 1.** *n.* saccheggio *m.* **2.** *vb.* saccheggiare.

**pillar,** *n.* pilastro *m.*, pilone *m.*

**pillow,** *n.* guanciale *m.*

**pillowcase,** *n.* fèdera *f.*

**pilot,** *n.* pilòta *m.*

**pimple,** *n.* forùncolo *m.*

**pin,** *n.* spillo *m.*

**pinch, 1.** *n.* pizzicòtto *m.* **2.** *vb.* pizzicare.

**pine, 1.** *n.* pino *m.* **2.** *vb.* languire.

**pineapple,** *n.* ananàs *m.*

**ping-pong.** *n.* tennis da tàvola *m.*

**pink,** *adj.* ròsa.

**pinnacle,** *n.* pinnàcolo *m.*

**pint,** *n.* pinta *f.*

**pioneer,** *n.* pionière *m.*

**pious,** *adj.* pio.

**pipe,** *n.* tubo *m.*; (tobacco) pipa *f.*

**piper,** *n.* pìffero *m.*

**piquant,** *adj.* piccante.

**pirate,** *n.* pirata *m.*

**pistol,** *n.* pistola *f.*

**piston,** *n.* pistone *m.*, stantuffo *m.*

**pit,** *n.* buca *f.*

**pitch, 1.** *n.* (tar) pece *f.*; (throw) làncio *m.*; (music) tòno *m.* **2.** *vb.* (hurl) lanciare.

**pitchblende,** *n.* pechblenda *f.*, uraninite *f.*

**pitcher,** *n.* bròcca *f.*; (thrower) lanciatore *m.*

**pitchfork,** *n.* forca *f.*

**pitfall,** *n.* tràppola *f.*

**pitiful,** *adj.* pietoso.

**pitiless,** *adj.* spietato.

**pity,** *n.* pietà *f.*; (shame) peccato *m.*; **(what a p.)** che peccato!

**pivot,** *n.* pèrnio *m.*

**placard,** *n.* cartèllo *m.*

**placate,** *vb.* placare.

**place, 1.** *n.* posto *m.*, luògo *m.*; **(take p.)** aver luògo, accadere. **2.** *vb.* méttere; porre.

**placid,** *adj.* plàcido.

**plagiarism,** *n.* plàgio *m.*

**plague,** *n.* pèste *f.*

**plain, 1.** *n.* pianura *f.* **2.** *adj.* (clear) chiaro; (simple) sémplice, modèsto.

**plaintiff,** *n.* attore *m.*

**plan, 1.** *n.* piano *m.*, progètto *m.*, (map) pianta *f.* **2.** *vb.* progettare.

**plane, 1.** *n.* piano *m.*; (airplane) aeroplano *m.*; (carpenter's) pialla *f.* **2.** *vb.* pillare.

**planet,** *n.* pianeta *m.*

**planetarium,** *n.* planetàrio *m.*

**planetary,** *adj.* planetàrio.

**plank,** *n.* asse *f.*, tàvola *f.*

**plant, 1.** *n.* pianta *f.*; (factory; installation) impianto *m.* **2.** *vb.* piantare.

**plantation,** *n.* piantagione *f.*

**planter,** *n.* piantatore *m.*; (plantation owner) propriètàrio di piantagione *m.*

**plasma,** *n.* plasma *m.*

**plaster, 1.** *n.* intònaco *m.*; (medical) empiastro *m.* **2.** *vb.* intonacare.

**plastic, 1.** *n.* plàstica *f.* **2.** *adj.* plàstico.

**plate,** *n.* piatto *m.*; (photographic) lastra *f.*; (auto) targa *f.*

**plateau,** *n.* altopiano *m.*

**platform,** *n.* piattaforma *f.*

**platinum,** *n.* plàtino *m.*

**platitude,** *n.* banalità *f.*

**platoon,** *n.* drappèllo *m.* plotone *m.*

**platter,** *n.* piatto grande *m.*

**plaudit,** *n.* applàuso *m.*

**plausible,** *adj.* plausìbile.

**play, 1.** *n.* (game) giòco *m.*; (joke) schèrzo *m.*; (theater) dramma *m.* **2.** *vb.* giocare; (on stage) recitare; (instrument) suonare.

**player,** *n.* (game) giocatore *m.*; (instrument) suonatore *m.*

**playful,** *adj.* scherzoso.

**playground,** *n.* campo per ricreazione *m.*

**playmate,** *n.* compagno di giòchi *m.*

**playwright,** *n.* drammaturgo *m.*

**plea,** *n.* preghièra *f.*; (excuse) scusa *f.*

**plead,** *vb.* esortare, implorare; (give as excuse) addurre come scusa.

**pleasant,** *adj.* piacévole.

**please, 1.** *vb.* piacere a. **2.** *adv.*, *interj.* per favore.

**pleasing,** *adj.* piacévole, grato.

**pleasure,** *n.* piacere *m.*

**pleat**, n. pièga f.

**plebiscite**, n. plebiscito m.

**pledge**, 1. n. pegno m. 2. vb. impegnare.

**plentiful**, adj. abbondante.

**plenty**, 1. n. abbondanza. 2. adj. **p. of**, molto.

**pleurisy**, n. pleurite f.

**pliable, pliant**, adj. pieghévole.

**pliers**, n. pinze f.pl., pinzette f.pl.

**plight**, n. situazione f.

**plot**, 1. n. (conspiracy) complòtto m.; (story) intréccio m.; (land) appezzamento m.; (plan) pianta f.

**plow**, 1. n. aratro m. 2. vb. arare.

**pluck**, 1. n. fégato m. 2. vb. cògliere.

**plug**, 1. n. tappo m.; (electric) spina f. 2. vb. tappare.

**plum**, 1. n. (tree) susino m.; (fruit) susina f., prugna f.

**plumage**, n. piumàggio m.

**plumber**, n. trombàio m., stagnino m.; idràulico m.

**plume**, n. penna f.

**plump**, adj. grassòccio.

**plunder**, 1. n. bottino m., prèda f. 2. vb. saccheggiare, predare.

**plunge**, 1. n. tuffare. 2. vb. tuffare, tr.

**plural**, n. and adj. plurale (m.).

**plus**, prep. più.

**plutocrat**, n. plutòcrate m.

**pneumatic**, adj. pneumàtico.

**pneumonia**, n. polmonite f.

**poach**, vb. (hunt illegally) andare a càccia di fròdo; (eggs) cuòcere in camìcia; (poached eggs) uòva affogate.

**poacher**, n. cacciatore di fròdo m.

**pocket**, 1. n. tasca f. 2. vb. intascare.

**pocket-book**, n. portafògli m.

**pocket-size**, adj. tascàbile.

**pod**, n. baccèllo m.

**podiatry**, n. cura dei pièdi f.

**poem**, n. poesìa f., poèma m.

**poet**, n. poèta m.

**poetic**, adj. poètico.

**poetry**, n. poesìa f.

**poignant**, adj. doloroso.

**point**, 1. n. punto m. 2. vb. puntare; (**p. to**) indicare; (**p. out**) additare.

**pointed**, adj. acuto.

**pointless**, adj. privo di senso.

**poise**, n. equilibrio m.

**poison**, 1. n. veleno m. 2. vb. avvelenare.

**poisonous**, adj. velenoso.

**poke**, vb. spingere; (fire) attizzare.

**Poland**, n. Polònia f.

**polar**, adj. polare.

**pole**, n. (post) palo m.; (rod) pèrtica f.; (wagon) timone m.; (electrical, geographical) pòlo m.

**police**, n. polizìa f.

**policeman**, n. vìgile, m., poliziòtto m.

**policy**, n. polìtica f.; (insurance) polizza f.

**polish**, 1. n. (material) lùcido m.; (gloss) lucidatura f. 2. vb. lucidare.

**Polish**, adj. polacco m.

**polite**, adj. cortese.

**politeness**, n. cortesìa f.

**politic, political**, adj. polìtico.

**politician**, n. polìtico m.

**politics**, n. politica f.

**poll**, 1. n (head) tèsta f.; (voting) votazione f.; (**p. tax**) testàtico m. 2. vb. (get, in voting) ottenere.

**pollen**, n. pòlline m.

**pollute**, vb. contaminare.

**polonaise**, n. polacca f.

**polygamy**, n. poligamìa f.

**polygon**, n. polìgono m.

**pomp**, n. pompa f., fasto m.

**pompous**, adj. pomposo, fastoso.

**poncho**, n. impermeàbile m.

**pond**, n. stagno m.

**ponder**, vb. ponderare.

**ponderous**, adj. ponderoso.

**pontiff**, n. pontéfice m.

**pontoon**, n. pontone m.

**pony**, n. cavallino m.

**pool**, n. stagno m.; (money) fondo comune m.

**poor**, adj. pòvero.

**pop**, 1. n. scòppio m.; (father) babbo m. 2. vb. scoppiettare.

**pope**, n. papa m.

**popular**, adj. popolare.

**popularity**, n. popolarità f.

**population**, n. popolazione f.

**porcelain**, n. porcellana f.

**porch**, n. veranda f.; (church) pòrtico m.

**pore**, n. pòro m.

**pork**, n. maiale m.

**pornography**, n. pornografìa f.

**porous,** *adj.* poroso.

**port,** *n.* pòrto *m.*

**portable,** *adj.* portàtile.

**portal,** *n.* portale *m.*

**portend,** *vb.* presagire.

**portent,** *n.* presàgio *m.*

**porter,** *n.* facchino *m.,* porta-bagagli *m.;* (hotel) portière *m.*

**portfolio,** *n.* cartella *f.,* porta-fòglio *m.*

**porthole,** *n.* oblò *m.*

**portico,** *n.* pòrtico *m.*

**portion,** *n.* porzione *f.*

**portly,** *adj.* corpulènto.

**portrait,** *n.* ritratto *m.*

**portray,** *vb.* ritrattare.

**Portugal,** *n.* il Portogallo *m.*

**Portuguese,** *adj.* portoghese.

**pose, 1.** *n.* pòsa *f.* **2.** *vb.* posare; **(p. as)** atteggiarsi a.

**position,** *n.* posizione *f.*

**positive,** *adj.* positivo.

**possess,** *vb.* possedere.

**possession,** *n.* possèsso *m.*

**possessive,** *adj.* possessivo.

**possessor,** *n.* possessore *m.*

**possibility,** *n.* possibilità *f.*

**possible,** *adj.* possibile.

**possibly,** *adv.* possibilmente, forse.

**post, 1.** *n.* (pole) palo *m.;* (place) posto *m.;* (mail) pòsta *f.* **2.** *vb.* (put up) affiggere; (mail) impostare.

**postage,** *n.* affrancatura *f.;* **(p. -stamp)** francobollo *m.*

**postal,** *adj.* postale.

**post-card,** *n.* cartolina postale *f.*

**roster,** *n.* cartello *m.*

**poste restante,** *adv.* fermo pòsta.

**posterior, 1.** *n.* culo *m.* **2.** *adj.* posteriore.

**posterity,** *n.* posterità *f.,* pòsteri *m.pl.*

**post-graduate,** *n., adj.* di perfezionamento *m.*

**post-mark,** *n.* timbro postale *m.*

**postman,** *n.* postino *m.*

**post office,** *n.* ufficio postale *m.*

**postpone,** *vb.* posporre, rimandare.

**postscript,** *n.* poscritto *m.*

**posture,** *n.* posizione *f.*

**pot,** *n.* pèntola *f.*

**potassium,** *n.* potàssio *m.*

**potato,** *n.* patata *f.*

**potent,** *adj.* potènte.

**potential,** *n. and adj.* potenziale *n.*

**pot-hole,** *n.* buca *f.*

**potion,** *n.* pozione *f.*

**pottery,** *n.* stoviglie *f.pl.*

**pouch,** *n.* borsa *f.*

**poultry,** *n.* pollame *m.*

**pound, 1.** *n.* libbra *f.;* **(p. sterling)** sterlina *f.* **2.** *vb.* pestare.

**pour,** *vb.* versare; **(p. off)** travasare.

**poverty,** *n.* povertà *f.,* misèria *f.*

**powder, 1.** *n.* pólvere *m.;* **(face-p.)** cìpria *f.;* **(p.-puff)** fiòcco da cipria *m.* **2.** *vb.* polverizzare; (one's face) incipriare, *tr.*

**power,** *n.* potere *m.,* potènza *f.*

**powerful,** *adj.* possènte.

**powerless,** *adj.* impotènte.

**practicable,** *adj.* praticàbile.

**practical,** *adj.* pràtico.

**practically,** *adv.* praticamente.

**practice, 1.** *n.* pràtica *f.* **2.** *vb.* praticare, esercitare, *tr.*

**practiced,** *adj.* espèrto.

**practitioner,** *n.* professionista *m.*

**pragmatic,** *adj.* prammàtico.

**prairie,** *n.* prateria *f.*

**praise, 1.** *n.* lòde *f.* **2.** *vb.* lodare.

**prank,** *n.* birichinata *f.,* burla *f.*

**pray,** *vb.* pregare.

**prayer,** *n.* preghiera *f.*

**preach,** *vb.* predicare.

**preacher,** *n.* predicatore *m.*

**preamble,** *n.* preàmbolo *m.*

**precarious,** *adj.* precàrio.

**precaution,** *n.* precauzione *f.*

**precede,** *vb.* precèdere.

**precedence,** *n.* precedènza *f.*

**precedent,** *n.* precedènte *m.*

**precept,** *n.* precètto *m.*

**precinct,** *n.* precinto *m.*

**precious,** *adj.* prezioso.

**precipice,** *n.* precipìzio *m.*

**precipitate,** *vb.* precipitare.

**precise,** *adj.* preciso.

**precision,** *n.* precisione *f.*

**preclude,** *vb.* preclùdere.

**precocious,** *adj.* precoce.

**precursor,** *n.* precursore *m.*

**predatory,** *adj.* predatòrio, di prèda.

**predecessor,** *n.* predecessore *m.*

**predestination**, n. predestinazione f.

**predicament**, n. impiccio m.

**predicate**, n. predicato m.

**predict**, vb. predire.

**predilection**, n. predilezione f.

**predispose**, vb. predisporre.

**predominant**, adj. predominante.

**prefabricated**, adj. prefabbricato.

**preface**, n. prefazione f.

**prefect**, n. prefetto m.

**prefer**, vb. preferire.

**preferable**, adj. preferìbile.

**preference**, n. preferènza f.

**prefix**, n. prefisso m.

**pregnancy**, n. gravidanza f.

**pregnant**, adj. gràvida f. incinta f.; (animals only) prègna f.

**prehistoric**, adj. preistòrico.

**prejudice**, 1. n. pregiudizio m. 2. vb. pregiudicare.

**prejudiced**, adj. pregiudicato.

**preliminary**, adj. preliminare.

**prelude**, n. prelùdio m.

**premature**, adj. prematuro.

**premeditate**, vb. premeditare.

**premier**, n. primo ministro m.

**première**, n. prima f.

**premise**, n. premessa f.

**premium**, n. prèmio m.

**premonition**, n. premonizione f.

**prenatal**, adj. prenatale.

**preparation**, n. preparazione f.

**preparatory**, adj. preparatòrio.

**prepare**, vb. preparare.

**preponderant**, adj. preponderante.

**preposition**, n. preposizione f.

**preposterous**, adj. assurdo.

**prerequisite**, n. primo requisito m.

**prerogative**, n. prerogativa f.

**prescribe**, vb. prescrìvere.

**prescription**, n. prescrizione f.

**presence**, n. presènza f.

**present**, 1. n. dono m., regalo m., omàggio m. 2. adj. presènte; (be p.) assìstere. 3. vb. presentare; regalare.

**presentable**, adj. presentàbile.

**presentation**, n. presentazione f.

**presently**, adv. fra pòco, immediatamente.

**preservation**, n. conservazione f.

**preservative**, adj. conservativo.

**preserve**, vb. preservare, conservare, serbare.

**preside**, vb. presièdere.

**presidency**, n. presidènza f.

**president**, n. presidènte m.

**press**, 1. n. prèssa f.; (newspapers) stampa f. 2. vb. prèmere; strìngere; (urge) insistere.

**pressing**, adj. urgènte.

**pressure**, n. pressione f.

**pressure cooker**, n. pèntola a pressione f.

**prestige**, n. prestìgio m.

**presume**, vb. presùmere.

**presumption**, n. presunzione f.

**presumptuous**, adj. presuntuoso.

**presumptuousness**, n. presuntuosità f.

**presuppose**, vb. presupporre.

**pretend**, vb. fìngere, far finta; (claim) pretèndere.

**pretense**, n. finta f.

**pretension**, n. pretesa f.

**pretentious**, adj. pretenzioso.

**pretext**, n. pretèsto m.

**pretty**, adj. grazioso, bellino.

**prevail**, vb. prevalere.

**prevalent**, adj. prevalènte.

**prevent**, vb. impedire.

**prevention**, n. prevenzione f.

**preventive**, adj. preventivo.

**preview**, n. anteprima f.

**previous**, adj. precedènte.

**prey**, n. prèda f.

**price**, n. prèzzo m.

**priceless**, adj. inestimàbile.

**prick**, vb. pùngere.

**pride**, n. orgòglio m.

**priest**, n. prète m.

**prim**, adj. affettato.

**primary**, adj. primàrio.

**prime**, adj. primo, principale.

**prime minister**, n. primo ministro m.

**primitive**, adj. primitivo.

**prince**, n. prìncipe m.

**princess**, n. principessa f.

**principal**, 1. n. capo m., direttore m. 2. adj. principale.

**principally**, adv. principalmente.

**principle**, n. princìpio m.

**print**, 1. n. stampa f.; (impression) impronta *f.* **2.** *vb.* stampare.

**printing,** *n.* stampa *f.*; (press-run) tiratura *f.*

**printing-press,** *n.* màcchina per stampare *f.*

**priority,** *n.* priorità *f.*

**prism,** *n.* prisma *m.*

**prison,** *n.* prigione *f.*

**prisoner,** *n.* prigionièro *m.*

**privacy,** *n.* intimità *f.,* solitùdine *f.*

**private, 1.** *n.* soldato sémplice *m.* **2.** *adj.* privato.

**privation,** *n.* privazione *f.*

**privet,** *n.* ligustro *m.*

**privilege,** *n.* privilègio *m.*

**privy,** *n.* latrina *f.*

**prize, 1.** *n.* prèmio *m.* **2.** *vb.* apprezzare.

**probability,** *n.* probabilità *f.*

**probable,** *adj.* probàbile.

**probate, 1.** *n.* omologazione *f.* **2.** *vb.* omologare.

**probation,** *n.* pròva *f.*

**probe,** *vb.* sondare.

**probity,** *n.* probità *f.*

**problem,** *n.* problèma *m.*

**procedure,** *n.* procedimento *m.*; (legal) procedura *f.*

**proceed,** *vb.* procèdere.

**process,** *n.* procèsso *m.*

**procession,** *n.* processione *f.*

**proclaim,** *vb.* proclamare.

**proclamation,** *n.* proclamazione *f.*

**procrastinate,** *vb.* procrastinare.

**procure,** *vb.* procurare.

**prodigal,** *adj.* pròdigo.

**prodigy,** *n.* prodìgio *m.*

**produce,** *vb.* produrre.

**product,** *n.* prodotto *m.*

**production,** *n.* produzione *f.*

**productive,** *adj.* produttivo.

**profane, 1.** *adj.* profano. **2.** *vb.* profanare.

**profanity,** *n.* bestémmia *f.pl.*

**profess,** *vb.* professare.

**profession,** *n.* professione *f.*

**professional, 1.** *n.* professional *m.* **2.** *adj.* professionale.

**professor,** *n.* professore *m.*

**proficient,** *adj.* espèrto.

**profile,** *n.* profilo *m.*

**profit, 1.** *n.* guadagno, *m.* profitto *m.,* vantàggio *m.* **2.** *vb.* approfittare.

**profitable,** *adj.* vantaggioso *m.*

**profiteer,** *n.* pescecane *m.*

**profound,** *adj.* profondo.

**profoundly,** *adv.* profondamente.

**profundity,** *n.* profondità *f.*

**profuse,** *adj.* profuso.

**prognosis,** *n.* prògnosi *f.*

**program,** *n.* programma *m.*

**progress, 1.** *n.* progrèsso *m.* **2.** *vb.* progredire.

**progressive,** *adj.* progressivo.

**prohibit,** *vb.* proibire.

**prohibition,** *n.* proibizione *f.,* divièto *m.*

**prohibitive,** *adj.* proibitivo.

**project, 1.** *n.* progètto *m.* **2.** *vb.* (plan) progettare; (stick out) spòrgere.

**projectile,** *n.* proièttile *m.*

**projection,** *n.* proiezione *f.*

**projector,** *n.* proiettore *m.*

**prolific,** *adj.* prolìfico.

**prologue,** *n.* pròlogo *m.*

**prolong,** *vb.* prolungare.

**prolongation,** *n.* prolungamento *m.*

**prominent,** *adj.* prominènte.

**promiscuous,** *adj.* promìscuo.

**promise, 1.** *n.* promessa *f.* **2.** *vb.* prométtere.

**promote,** *vb.* promuòvere.

**promotion,** *n.* promozione *f.*

**prompt,** *adj.* pronto.

**prompter,** *n.* suggeritore *m.*

**promulgate,** *vb.* promulgare.

**pronoun,** *n.* pronome *m.*

**pronounce,** *vb.* pronunciare.

**pronunciation,** *n.* pronùncia *f.*

**proof,** *n.* pròva *f.*; (printing) bòzze *f.pl.*

**proof-read,** *vb.* corrèggere le bòzze di.

**prop, 1.** *n.* puntèllo *m.* **2.** *vb.* puntellare.

**propaganda,** *n.* propaganda *f.*

**propagate,** *vb.* propagare.

**propel,** *vb.* spingere innanzi.

**propeller,** *n.* èlica *f.*

**propensity,** *n.* propensione *f.*

**proper,** *adj.* pròprio.

**property,** *n.* proprietà *f.*

**prophecy,** *n.* profezìa *f.*

**prophesy,** *vb.* profetizzare.

**prophet,** *n.* profèta *m.*

**prophetic,** *adj.* profètico.

**propitious,** *adj.* propìzio.

**proponent,** *n.* proponènte *m.*

**proportion,** *n.* proporzione *f.*

**proportionate,** *adj.* proporzionato.

**proposal,** *n.* propòsta *f.*

**propose,** *vb.* proporre, *tr.*

**proposition**, *n.* propòsta *f.*

**proprietor**, *n.* proprietàrio *m.*

**propriety**, *n.* conveniènza *f.*

**prosaic**, *adj.* prosàico.

**proscribe**, *vb.* proscrìvere.

**prose**, *n.* pròsa *f.*

**prosecute**, *vb.* intentare giudizio contro.

**prospect**, *n.* prospètto *m.*

**prospective**, *adj.* prospettivo.

**prosper**, *vb.* prosperare.

**prosperity**, *n.* prosperità *f.*

**prosperous**, *adj.* pròspero.

**prostitute**, *n.* prostituta *f.*

**prostrate**, 1. *adj.* prostrato. 2. *vb.* prostrare.

**protect**, *vb.* protèggere.

**protection**, *n.* protezione *f.*

**protective**, *adj.* protettivo.

**protector**, *n.* protettore *m.*

**protégé**, *n.* protètto *m.*

**protein**, *n.* proteìna *f.*

**protest**, 1. *n.* protèsta *f.* 2. *vb.* protestare.

**Protestant**, *n. and adj.* protestante (*m.*).

**Protestantism**, *n.* protestantésimo *m.*

**protocol**, *n.* protocòllo *m.*

**proton**, *n.* protone *m.*

**protract**, *vb.* protrarre.

**protrude**, *vb.* spìngere fuòri, *tr.*

**protuberance**, *n.* protuberanza *f.*

**proud**, *adj.* orgoglioso.

**prove**, *vb.* comprovare.

**proverb**, *n.* provèrbio *m.*

**proverbial**, *adj.* proverbiale.

**provide**, *vb.* provvedere.

**provided**, *conj.* purchè.

**providence**, *n.* provvidènza *f.*

**province**, *n.* provìncia *f.*

**provincial**, *adj.* provinciale.

**provision**, *n.* provvista *f.*

**provocation**, *n.* provocazione *f.*

**provoke**, *vb.* provocare.

**prowess**, *n.* prodezza *f.*

**prowl**, *vb.* vagare intorno.

**proximity**, *n.* prossimità *f.*

**proxy**, *n.* (person) procuratore *m.*; (document) procura *f.*

**prudence**, *n.* prudènza *f.*

**prudent**, *adj.* prudènte.

**prune**, *n.* prugna secca *f.*

**pry**, *vb.* ficcare il naso.

**psalm**, *n.* salmo *m.*

**pseudonym**, *n.* pseudònimo *m.*

**psychiatrist**, *n.* psichiatra *m.*

**psychiatry**, *n.* psichiatrìa *f.*

**psychoanalysis**, *n.* psicoanàlisi *f.*

**psychological**, *adj.* psicològico.

**psychology**, *n.* psicologìa *f.*

**psychosis**, *n.* psi còsi *f.*

**ptomaine**, *n.* ptomaina *f.*

**public**, *n. and adj.* pùbblico (*m.*).

**publication**, *n.* pubblicazione *f.*

**publicity**, *n.* pubblicità *f.*

**publish**, *vb.* pubblicare.

**publisher**, *n.* editore *m.*

**pudding**, *n.* budino *m.*

**puddle**, *n.* pozzànghera *f.*

**puff**, 1. *n.* sbuffo *m.*; (powder-p.) fiòcco da cìpria *m.* 2. *vb.* sbufiare.

**pugnacious**, *adj.* pugnace.

**pull**, 1. *n.* tirata *f.* 2. *vb.* tirare.

**pulley**, *n.* puléggia *f.*

**pulmonary**, *adj.* polmonare.

**pulp**, *n.* polpa *f.*

**pulpit**, *n.* pùlpito *m.*

**pulsate**, *vb.* pulsare.

**pulse**, *n.* polso *m.*

**pump**, 1. *n.* pompa *f.* 2. *vb.* pompare.

**pumpkin**, *n.* zucca *f.*

**pun**, *n.* freddura *f.*

**punch**, 1. *n.* (drink) pònce *m.*; (blow) pugno *m.* 2. *vb.* (make hole) perforare; (hit) colpire; dar pugni a.

**punctual**, *adj.* puntuale.

**punctuate**, *vb.* punteggiare.

**punctuation**, *n.* punteggiatura *f.*

**puncture**, 1. *n.* puntura *f.*; (tire) foratura *f.* 2. *vb.* forare.

**pungent**, *adj.* pungènte.

**punish**, *vb.* punire.

**punishment**, *n.* punizione *f.*

**punitive**, *adj.* punitivo.

**puny**, *adj.* dèbole.

**pupil**, *n.* alunno *m.*; scolaro *m.*

**puppet**, *n.* burattino *m.*

**puppy**, *n.* cùcciolo *m.*

**purchase**, 1. *n.* compra *f.*; (grasp) presa *f.* 2. *vb.* comprare.

**pure**, *adj.* puro.

**purée**, *n.* passato *m.*

**purgative**, *n. and adj.* purgante (*m.*).

**purge**, 1. *n.* purga *f.* 2. *vb.* purgare.

**purify**, vb. purificare.
**puritanical**, adj. da puritano.
**purity**, n. purezza f., purità f.
**purple**, n. pórpora f.
**purport**, **1.** n. significato m. **2.** vb. use future of verb which in English is dependent on "purport".
**purpose**, n. fine m., scòpo m., propòsito m.; (**on p.**) appòsta.
**purposely**, adv. appòsta.
**purse**, n. borsa f.
**pursue**, vb. inseguire, perseguire.

**pursuit**, n. inseguimento m.
**push**, **1.** n. spinta f. **2.** vb. spìngere.
**put**, vb. méttere, porre, ficcare; (**p. back**) riméttere; (**p. down**, suppress) sopprimere; (**p. in**) inserire; (**p. off**) rimandare; (**p. on**) indossare; (**p. out**, extinguish) spégnere; (**p. up with**) soffrire.
**putrid**, adj. pùtrido.
**puzzle**, n. indovinello m.; (**cross-word p.**) crucivèrba m.
**pyjamas**, n. pigiama m. pl
**pyramid**, n. pirâmide f.

# Q

**quadrangle**, n. quadrângolo m.
**quadruped**, n. quadrùpede m.
**quail**, **1.** n. quàglia f. **2.** vb. scoraggiarsi.
**quaint**, adj. strano.
**quake**, **1.** n. trèmito m. **2.** vb. tremare.
**qualification**, n. qualificazione f., qualifica f., requisito m.
**qualified**, adj. idòneo.
**qualify**, vb. qualificare; (be fit) essere idòneo.
**quality**, n. qualità f.
**qualm**, n. nàusea f.; (fig.) scrùpolo m.
**quandary**, n. perplessità f.
**quantity**, n. quantità f., somma f.
**quarantine**, n. quarentena f.
**quarrel**, **1.** n. lite f. **2.** vb. litigare.
**quarry**, n. cava f.
**quarter**, **1.** n. (one fourth) quarto m.; (region; mercy) quartière m.; (three months) trimèstre m.
**quarterly**, adj. trimestrale.
**quartet**, n. quartetto m.
**quartz**, n. quarzo m.
**quaver**, vb. tremolare.
**queen**, n. regina f.

**queer**, adj. strano.
**quell**, vb. sopprimere.
**quench**, vb. estinguere; (**q. one's thirst**) dissetare.
**query**, **1.** n. domanda f. **2.** vb. domandare.
**quest**, n. ricerca f.
**question**, **1.** n. domanda f., questione f. **2.** vb. interrogare; (doubt) dubitare di.
**questionable**, adj. dùbbio.
**question mark**, n. punto interrogativo m.
**questionnaire**, n. questionàrio m.
**quick**, **1.** adj. ràpido, pronto, svelto. **2.** adv. prèsto.
**quicken**, vb. affrettare, tr.
**quicksand**, n. banco mòbile di sàbbia m.
**quiet**, **1.** n. quiète f. **2.** adj. quièto; (be, keep q.) tacere.
**quilt**, n. trapunta f., coltrone m., imbottita f.
**quinine**, n. chinino m.
**quintet**, n. quintètto m.
**quip**, n. motto m.
**quit**, vb. (leave) lasciare; (stop) cessare, sméttere; (resign) diméttersi.
**quite**, adv. completamente, proprio.
**quiver**, **1.** n. farètra f. **2.** vb. tremare; (shiver) rabbrividire.

**quixotic,** *adj.* donchisciottesco.
**quiz,** 1. *n.* esame *m.* 2. *vb.* esaminare.

**quorum,** *n.* quorum *m.*
**quota,** *n.* quòta *f.*
**quotation,** *n.* citazione *f.*
**quote,** *vb.* citare.

---

# R

**rabbi,** *n.* rabbino *m.*
**rabbit,** *n.* coniglio *m.*
**rabble,** *n.* plebàglia *f.*, volgo *m.*
**rabid,** *adj.* rabbioso.
**rabies,** *n.* ràbbia *f.*
**race,** 1. *n.* (contest) corsa *f.*; (breed) razza *f.* 2. *vb.* córrere.
**race-track,** *n.* ippòdromo *m.*
**rack,** 1. *n.* (torture) ruòta *f.*; (for feed) rastrellièra *f.*; (luggage) reticella *f.*; (railroad) cremaglièra *f.* 2. *vb.* torturare.
**racket,** *n.* (tennis) racchetta *f.*; (uproar) frastuòno *m.*, baccano *m.*
**radar,** *n.* (instrument) radiotelèmetro *m.*; (science) radiotelemetrìa *f.*
**radiance,** *n.* fulgore *m.*
**radiant,** *adj.* raggiante.
**radiate,** *vb.* irradiare, *ir.*
**radiation,** *n.* irradiazione *f.*
**radiator,** *n.* radiatore *m.*
**radical,** *n. and adj.* radicale (*m.*)
**radio,** 1. *n.* ràdio *f.* 2. *adj.* (pertaining to r.) radiofònico.
**radioactive,** *adj.* radioattivo.
**radish,** *n.* ramolàccio *m.*, ravanèllo *m.*
**radium,** *n.* ràdio *m.*
**radius,** *n.* ràggio *m.*
**raffle,** *n.* lotterìa *f.*
**raft,** *n.* zàttera *f.*
**rafter,** *n.* travicèllo *m.*
**rag,** *n.* céncio *m.*, stràccio *m.*
**ragamuffin,** *n.* straccione *m.*
**rage,** 1. *n.* ràbbia *f.* 2. *vb.* infuriare.
**ragged,** *adj.* cencioso.
**raid,** *n.* incursione *f.*

**rail,** *n.* rotaia *f.*; (bar) sbarra *f.*
**railcar,** *n.* automotrice *f.*; (electric r.) elettromotrice *f.*
**railing,** *n.* ringhièra *f.*
**railroad,** 1. *n.* ferrovìa *f.* 2. *adj.* (pertaining to railroads) ferroviàrio.
**rain,** 1. *n.* piòggia *f.* 2. *vb.* piòvere; (r. cats and degs) diluviare.
**rainbow,** *n.* arcobaleno *m.*
**raincoat,** *n.* impermeàbile *m.*
**rainfall,** *n.* precipitazione atmosfèrica *f.*
**rainy,** *adj.* piovoso.
**raise,** *vb.* (bring up) allevare; (erect) erìgere; (grow) coltivare; (increase) aumentare; (hoist) innalzare; (lift) levare; (collect) raccògliere; (intensify) alzare.
**raisin,** *n.* uva secca *f.*; (sultana r.) uva sultanina *f.*
**rake,** 1. *n.* rastrèllo *m.* 2. *vb.* rastrellare.
**rally,** 1. *n.* (recovery) ricùpero di fòrze *m.*; (meeting) raduno *m.* 2. *vb.* riunire, *ir.*
**ram,** 1. *n.* (animal) montone *m.*; (post) battipalo *m.* 2. *vb.* bàttere; cacciare.
**ramble,** *vb.* divagare.
**ramp,** *n.* piano inclinato *m.*
**rampart,** *n.* bastione *m.*
**ranch,** *n.* fattorìa *f.*
**rancid,** *adj.* ràncido.
**rancor,** *n.* rancore *m.*
**random,** *n.* (at r.) a casàccio.
**range,** 1. *n.* (distance) portata *f.*; (mountains) catena *f.*; (scope) estensione *f.*; (sphere) sfèra *f.*; (stove)

cucina econòmica *f*. **2**. *vb*.
(arrange) disporre; (vary)
variare.

**rank, 1.** *n*. rango *m.*; (line)
fila *f.*; (position) grado *m.*

**ransack,** *vb*. frugare dappertutto.

**ransom, 1.** *n*. riscatto *m*.
**2**. *vb*. riscattare.

**rap, 1.** *n*. colpo *m.*, picchio
*m*. **2**. *vb*. colpire, picchiare.

**rape,** *vb*. violare. ·

**rapid,** *adj*. ràpido.

**rapport,** *n*. rappòrto *m*.

**rapture,** *n*. èstasi *f*.

**rare,** *adj*. raro; (underdone)
pòco còtto.

**rarely,** *adv*. raramente.

**rascal,** *n*. briccone *m*.

**rash, 1.** *n*. eruzione *f*. **2**.
*adj*. inconsiderato.

**raspberry,** *n*. lampone *m.*;
(Bronx cheer) pernàcchia *f*.

**rat,** *n*. ratto *m*.

**rate, 1.** *n*. (price) prèzzo *m.*;
(speed) velocità *f*. **2**. *vb*.
classificare, tirar.

**rather,** *adv*. piuttosto.

**ratify,** *vb*. ratificare.

**ratio,** *n*. rapporto *m*.

**ration, 1.** *n*. razione *f.*;
**(r.-card)** tèssera annonària
*f*. **2**. *vb*. razionare.

**rational,** *adj*. razionale.

**rattle,** *n*. ràntolo *m.*, rumore
secco *m*.

**raucous,** *adj*. ràuco.

**ravage, 1.** *n*. devastazione
*f*. **2**. *vb*. devastare.

**rave,** *vb*. delirare.

**ravel,** *n*. groviglio *m*.

**raven, 1.** *n*. corvo *m*. **2**.
*adj*. corvino.

**ravenous,** *adj*. affamato.

**raw,** *adj*. grezzo, crudo.

**ray,** *n*. ràggio *m*.

**rayon,** *n*. ràion *m*.

**razor,** *n*. rasòio *m*.

**reach, 1.** *n*. portata *f*. **2**.
*vb*. (get to) arrivare a; raggiùngere; (extend) allungare.

**react,** *vb*. reagire.

**reaction,** *n*. reazione *f*.

**reactionary,** *adj*. reazionàrio.

**reactor,** *n*. reattore *m*.

**read,** *vb*. lèggere.

**reader,** *n*. (person) lettore
*m.*; (book) libro di lettura
*m*.

**readily,** *adj*. prontamente.

**reading,** *n*. lettura *f*.

**ready,** *adj*. pronto; **(r.-
made)** già fatto.

**real,** *adj*. reale, vero.

**realist,** *n*. realista *m*.

**reality,** *n*. realtà *f*.

**realization,** *n*. realizzazione
*f*.

**realize,** *vb*. (make real)
realizzare; (be, become
aware of) rèndersi conto di.

**really,** *adv*. realmente, veramente, davvero.

**realm,** *n*. reame *m.*, regno *m*.

**reap,** *vb*. mietere, raccògliere.

**rear, 1.** *n*. (back) parte
posteriore *f.*; **(r.-guard)**
retroguàrdia *f*. **2**. *vb*. (bring
up) allevare; (raise) alzare;
(erect) èrgere, (lift)
sollevare; (of horse) impennarsi.

**rear-view mirror,** *n*. spècchio retrovisore *m*.

**reason, 1.** *n*. ragione *f*. **2**.
*vb*. ragionare.

**reasonable,** *adj*. ragionévole.

**reassure,** *vb*. rassicurare.

**rebate,** *n*. sconto *m*.

**rebel, 1.** *n*. and *adj*. ribèlle
(*m.*). **2**. *vb*. ribellarsi.

**rebellion,** *n*. ribellione *f*.

**rebellious,** *adj*. ribèlle.

**rebirth,** *n*. rinàscita *f*.

**reborn, be,** *vb*. rinàscere.

**rebound, 1.** *n*. rimbalzo *m*.
**2**. *vb*. rimbalzare.

**rebuff,** *n*. ripulsa *f*.

**rebuild,** *vb*. ricostruire.

**rebuke, 1.** *n*. rimpròvero
*m*. **2**. *vb*. rimproverare.

**rebuttal,** *n*. confutazione *f*.

**recalcitrant,** *adj*. ricalcitrante.

**recall,** *vb*. richiamare.

**recapitulate,** *vb*. ricapitolare.

**recede,** *vb*. recèdere.

**receipt,** *n*. ricevuta *f.*; (document) quietanza *f*.

**receive,** *vb*. ricévere.

**receiver,** *n*. ricevitore *m*.

**recent,** *adj*. recènte.

**recently,** *adv*. recentemente.

**receptacle,** *n*. ricettàcolo *m.*,
recipiènte *m*.

**reception,** *n*. accogliènza *f.*;
(party) ricevimento *m*.

**receptive,** *adj*. ricettivo.

**recess,** *n*. (in wall) rientranza
*f.*; (vacation) vacanze *f*.

**recipe,** *n*. ricètta *f*.

**recipient,** *n*. ricevènte *m*.

**reciprocate,** *vb*. ricambiare.

**recitation,** *n*. recitazione *f*.

**recite,** *vb.* recitare.

**reckless,** *adj.* avventato.

**reckon,** *vb.* (count) contare; (deem) stimare; (think) pensare.

**reclaim,** *vb.* redìmere; (land) bonificare.

**reclamation,** *n.* bonìfica *f.*

**recline,** *vb.* reclinare.

**recognition,** *n.* riconoscimento *m.*

**recognize,** *vb.* riconóscere.

**recoil,** *vb.* indietreggiare.

**recollect,** *vb.* ricordare, rammentarsi.

**recommend,** *vb.* raccomandare.

**recommendation,** *n.* raccomandazione *f.*

**recompense,** 1. *n.* ricompènsa *f.* 2. *vb.* ricompensare.

**reconcile,** *vb.* riconciliare.

**recondition,** *vb.* riparare.

**reconsider,** *vb.* riprèndere in esame.

**reconstruct,** *vb.* ricostruire.

**record,** 1. *n.* memoria *f.* ricordo *m.*, registro *m.*; (top achievement) primato *m.*; (phonograph) disco *m.*; (**r. library**) discoteca *f.*; (**r. player**) giradischi *m.* 2. *vb.* registrare; (phonograph) incidere.

**recording,** *n.* incisione *f.*

**recount,** *vb.* (tell) raccontare; (count again) contare di nuòvo.

**recourse,** *n.* ricorso *m.*; (**have r.**) ricórrere.

**recover,** *vb.* ricuperare.

**recovery,** *n.* ricùpero *f.*; (medical) guarigione *f.*

**recruit,** 1. *n.* rècluta *f.* 2. *vb.* reclutare.

**rectangle,** *n.* rettàngolo *m.*

**rectifier,** *n.* rettificatrice *f.*

**rectify,** *vb.* rettificare.

**recuperate,** *vb.* ricuperare.

**recur,** *vb.* ricórrere, ritornare.

**red,** *adj.* rosso.

**redeem,** *vb.* redìmere.

**redeemer,** *n.* redentore *m.*

**redemption,** *n.* redenzione *f.*

**redress,** *n.* riparazione *f.*

**reduce,** *vb.* ridurre.

**reduction,** *n.* riduzione *f.*

**reed,** *n.* canna *f.*; (for instrument) ància *f.*

**reef,** *n.* scòglio *m.*

**reel,** 1. *n.* (bobbin) naspo *m.*; (spool) rocchetto *m.*;

(dance) trescone *m.* 2. *vb.* traballare; (**r. off**) dipanare.

**refer,** *vb.* riferire, *tr.*

**referee,** *n.* àrbitro *m.*

**reference,** *n.* allusione *f.*, riferimento *m.*; (**cross-r.**) rimando *m.*; (**r. room**) sala di consultazione *f.*

**refill,** *vb.* riempire di nuòvo.

**refine,** *vb.* raffinare.

**refinement,** *n.* raffinatezza *f.*

**reflect,** *vb.* riflèttere.

**reflection,** *n.* riflessione *f.*, riflèsso *m.*

**reflex,** *n.* riflèsso *m.*

**reform,** 1. *n.* riforma. 2. *vb.* riformare.

**reformation,** *n.* riforma *f.*

**refractory,** *adj.* ribèlle.

**refrain,** *vb.* trattenere, *tr.*

**refresh,** *vb.* rinfrescare, ristorare.

**refreshment,** *n.* ristòro *m.*

**refrigerator,** *n.* frigorìfero *m.*

**refuge,** *n.* rifùgio *m.*; (**take r.**) rifugiarsi.

**refugee,** *n.* rifugiato *m.*

**refund,** *vb.* restituire.

**refusal,** *n.* rifiuto *m.*

**refuse,** 1. *n.* (waste matter) rifiuti *m.pl.* 2. *vb.* rifiutare.

**refutation,** *n.* confutazione *f.*

**refute,** *vb.* confutare.

**regain,** *vb.* ritornare a.

**regal,** *adj.* regale.

**regard,** 1. *n.* riguardo *m.*, rispètto *m.* 2. *vb.* (look at) guardare; (concern) riguardare; (consider) considerare.

**regarding,** *prep.* riguardo a.

**regardless,** *adv.* ciò nonostante; (**r. of**) malgrado.

**regent,** *n.* reggènte *m.*

**regime,** *n.* regime *m.*

**regiment,** *n.* reggimento *m.*

**region,** *n.* regione *f.*

**register,** 1. *n.* registro *m.* 2. *vb.* registrare.

**registration,** *n.* registrazione *f.*

**regret,** 1. *n.* rimpianto *m.*, rincrescimento *m.* 2. *vb.* rimpiàngere, rincréscere (with English subject in dative).

**regular,** *adj.* regolare.

**regularity,** *n.* regolarità *f.*

**regulate,** *vb.* regolare.

**regulation,** *n.* regolamento *m.*

**regulator,** *n.* regolatore *m.*

**rehabilitate**, *vb.* riabilitare.

**rehearsal**, *n.* pròva *f.*

**rehearse**, *vb.* provare.

**reign**, 1. *n.* regno *m.* 2. *vb.* regnare.

**reimburse**, *vb.* rimborsare.

**rein**, *n.* rèdina *f.*

**reincarnation**, *n.* nuòva incarnazione *f.*

**reindeer**, *n.* rènna *f.*

**reinforce**, *vb.* rinforzare.

**reinforcement**, *n.* rinfòrzo *m.*

**reinstate**, *vb.* rimèttere.

**reiterate**, *vb.* reiterare.

**reject**, *vb.* rigettare, respìngere.

**rejoice**, *vb.* rallegrare, *tr.*

**rejoin**, *vb.* (answer) replicare; (join again) ricongiùngersi.

**rejoinder**, *n.* rèplica *f.*

**rejuvenate**, *vb.* ringiovanire.

**relapse**, 1. *n.* ricaduta *f.* 2. *vb.* ricadere.

**relate**, *vb.* (tell) narrare; (connected with) riferirsi a; riguardare; (connect) méttere in relazione.

**related**, *adj.* affine, connèsso.

**relation**, *n.* (story) narrazione *f.*; (connection) rappòrto *m.*; relazione *f.*; (person) parènte *m.*

**relationship**, *n.* rappòrto *m.*; (kinship) parentela *f.*

**relative**, 1. *n.* parènte *m.* 2. *adj.* relativo.

**relativity**, *n.* relatività *f.*

**relax**, *vb.* allentare, *tr.*

**relay**, *vb.* ritrasméttere.

**release**, 1. *n.* liberazione *f.* 2. *vb.* liberare, sprigionare.

**relent**, *vb.* aver pietà.

**relevant**, *adj.* pertinènte.

**reliable**, *adj.* fededegno.

**reliant**, *adj.* fidènte.

**relic**, *n.* avanzo *m.*; (religious) reliquia *f.*

**relief**, *n.* sollièvo *m.*; (social work) assistènza *f.*; (diversion) diversivo *m.*; (replacement) càmbio *m.*; (help) soccorso *m.*

**relieve**, *vb.* sollevare; (help) soccórrere; (free) liberare; (alleviate) alleviare.

**religion**, *n.* religione *f.*

**religious**, *adj.* religioso.

**relinquish**, *vb.* abbandonare.

**relish**, 1. *n.* gusto *m.*; (sauce) condimento *m.* 2. *vb.* gustare.

**reluctance**, *n.* riluttanza *f.*

**reluctant**, *adj.* riluttante.

**rely**, *vb.* confidare.

**remain**, *vb.* restare, rimanere.

**remainder**, *n.* rèsto *m.*

**remark**, 1. *n.* osservazione *f.* 2. *vb.* osservare.

**remarkable**, *adj.* notévole, rimarchévole.

**remedy**, 1. *n.* rimèdio *m.* 2. *vb.* rimediare a.

**remember**, *vb.* ricordarsi di.

**remembrance**, *n.* ricòrdo *m.*

**remind**, *vb.* rammentare.

**reminiscence**, *n.* reminiscènza *f.*

**remiss**, *adj.* negligènte.

**remit**, *n.* (send) spedire; (forgive) rimèttere.

**remittance**, *vb.* spedizione *f.*

**remnant**, *n.* rèsto *m.*, rimanènte *m.*

**remorse**, *n.* rimòrso *m.*

**remote**, *adj.* remòto.

**removable**, *adj.* amovìbile.

**removal**, *n.* rimozione *f.*

**remove**, *vb.* tògliere, rimuòvere.

**renaissance**, *n.* rinascimento *m.*

**rend**, *vb.* strappare.

**render**, *vb.* rèndere.

**rendezvous**, *n.* appuntamento *m.*

**rendition**, *n.* esecuzione *f.*

**renege**, *vb.* rifiutare.

**renew**, *vb.* rinnovare.

**renewal**, *n.* rinnovamento *m.*

**renounce**, *vb.* rinunciare a.

**renovate**, *vb.* rimodernare.

**renown**, *n.* rinomanza *f.*

**renowned**, *adj.* rinomato.

**rent**, *n.* affitto *m.*, pigione *f.* 2. *vb.* affittare, noleggiare.

**rental**, *n.* nolèggio *m.*

**repair**, 1. *n.* riparazione *f.* 2. *vb.* riparare.

**reparation**, *n.* riparazione *f.*

**repatriate**, *vb.* rimpatriare.

**repay**, *vb.* ripagare, rimborsare.

**repeat**, 1. *n.* (music) ripresa *f.* 2. *vb.* ripètere, replicare.

**repel**, *vb.* respìngere.

**repent**, *vb.* pentirsi di.

**repentance**, *n.* pentimento *m.*

**repercussion**, *n.* ripercussione *f.*

**repertoire**, *n.* repertòrio *m.*

**repetition**, *n.* ripetizione *f.*; (theater) rèplica *f.*

**replace**, vb. sostituire, rimpiazzare.

**replenish**, vb. riempire di nuovo.

**reply**, 1. n. risposta f.; (rebuttal) rèplica f. 2. vb. rispóndere; replicare.

**report**, 1. n. (bang) detonazione f.; (news) notizia f.; (rumor) voce f.; (memoir) rappòrto m. 2. vb. dare notizia di; (complain of) denunciare.

**reporter**, n. cronista m., giornalista m.

**repose**, 1. n. ripòso m. 2. vb. riposare.

**reprehend**, vb. riprèndere.

**reprehensible**, adj. riprensìbile.

**represent**, vb. rappresentare.

**representation**, n. rappresentazione f.

**representative**, 1. n. deputato m. 2. adj. rappresentativo.

**repress**, vb. reprìmere.

**repression**, vb. repressione f.

**reprimand**, 1. n. rimpròvero m. 2. vb. rimproverare.

**reprisal**, n. rappresàglia f.

**reproach**, 1. n. rimpròvero m. 2. vb. rimproverare.

**reproduce**, vb. riprodurre, tr.

**reproduction**, n. riproduzione f.

**reproof**, n. rimpròvero m.

**reprove**, vb. rimproverare.

**reptile**, n. rèttile m.

**republic**, n. repùbblica f.

**republican**, adj. repubblicano.

**repudiate**, vb. ripudiare.

**repudiation**, n. ripùdio m.

**repulse**, 1. n. ripulsa f. 2. vb. respingere.

**repulsive**, adj. repellènte.

**reputation**, n. riputazione f.

**repute**, vb. riputare.

**request**, 1. n. richièsta f., domanda f. 2. vb. richièdere, domandare.

**require**, vb. richièdere, esìgere.

**requirement**, n. esigènza f., requisito m.

**requisite**, 1. n. requisito m. 2. adj. necessàrio.

**requisition**, 1. n. requisizione f. 2. vb. requisire.

**rescind**, vb. rescìndere.

**rescue**, 1. n. liberazione f. 2. vb. liberare.

**research**, n. ricerche f.pl.

**resemble**, vb. rassomigliare a.

**resent**, vb. offèndersi di.

**reservation**, n. risèrva f.; (tickets) prenotazione f.

**reserve**, 1. n. risèrva f. 2. vb. riservare; (tickets) prenotare.

**reservoir**, n. serbatòio m.

**reside**, vb. risièdere, abitare.

**residence**, n. residènza f., abitazione f.

**resident**, 1. n. abitante m. 2. adj. residènte.

**residue**, n. residuo m.

**resign**, vb. dimèttersi; (r. oneself, give up hope) rassegnarsi.

**resignation**, n. dimissione f.; (loss of hope) rassegnazione f.

**resist**, vb. resìstere.

**resistance**, n. resistènza f.

**resolute**, adj. risoluto.

**resolution**, n. risoluzione f.

**resolve**, 1. n. decisione f. 2. vb. risòlvere, sciògliere; (decide) decidersi.

**resonance**, n. risonanza f.

**resonant**, adj. risonante.

**resort**, 1. n. (recourse) ricorso m.; (vacation place) stazione f.; luògo di soggiorno m. 2. vb. ricórrere.

**resound**, vb. risonare.

**resource**, n. risorsa f.

**respect**, 1. n. rispètto m. 2. vb. rispettare.

**respectable**, adj. rispettàbile.

**respectful**, adj. rispettoso.

**respective**, adj. rispettivo.

**respiration**, n. respirazione f.

**respite**, n. trégua f.

**respond**, vb. rispóndere.

**response**, n. risposta f.

**responsibility**, n. responsabilità f.

**responsible**, adj. responsàbile.

**responsive**, adj. responsivo.

**rest**, 1. n. (remainder) rimanènte m.; (repose) ripòso m. 2. vb. riposare.

**restaurant**, n. ristorante m., ristoratore m., trattoria f.; (r.-keeper) trattore m.

**restful**, adj. riposante.

**restitution**, n. restituzione f.

**restless**, adj. irrequièto.

**restoration,** *n.* restaurazione *f.*

**restore,** *vb.* restaurare.

**restrain,** *vb.* trattenere.

**restraint,** *n.* contròllo *m.*

**restrict,** *vb.* restringere.

**restriction,** *n.* restrizione *f.*

**result,** **1.** *n.* risultato *m.* **2.** *vb.* risultare.

**resume,** *vb.* riassùmere, riprèndere.

**résumé,** *n.* riassunto *m.*

**resurgent,** *adj.* risorgènte.

**resurrect,** *vb.* esumare.

**resurrection,** *n.* risurrezione *f.*

**retail,** **1.** *adv.* al minuto, al dettàglio. **2.** *vb.* véndere al minuto, véndere al dettàglio.

**retain,** *vb.* ritenere, conservare.

**retake,** *vb.* riprèndere.

**retaliate,** *vb.* ricambiare.

**retaliation,** *n.* rappresàglia *f.*

**retard,** *vb.* ritardare.

**retention,** *n.* ritenzione *f.*; (remembering ability) memòria *f.*

**reticence,** *n.* reticènza *f.*

**reticent,** *adj.* reticènte.

**retina,** *n.* rètina *f.*

**retinue,** *n.* sèguito *m.*

**retire,** *vb.* ritirare, *tr.*

**retort,** *vb.* replicare, ribàttere.

**retract,** *vb.* (pull back) ritrarre; (withdraw) ritrattare.

**retreat,** **1.** *n.* ritirata *f.* **2.** *vb.* ritirarsi.

**retribution,** *n.* retribuzione *f.*

**retrieve,** *vb.* ricuperare.

**retroactive,** *adj.* retroattivo *m.*

**retrospect,** *n.* sguardo retrospettivo *m.*

**retrospective,** *adj.* retrospettivo *m.*

**return,** **1.** *n.* ritorno *m.*; (r. ticket) biglietto d'andata e ritorno *m.* **2.** *vb.* tornare; ritornare.

**reunion,** *n.* riunione *f.*

**reunite,** *vb.* riunire.

**reveal,** *vb.* rivelare.

**revel,** **1.** *n.* (noisy good time) baldòria *f.*; (drunken rout) gozzovìglia *f.* **2.** *vb.* far baldòria; gozzovigliare.

**revelation,** *n.* rivelazione *f.*

**revelry,** *n.* baldòria *f.*

**revenge,** **1.** *n.* vendetta *f.* **2.** *vb.* vendicare.

**revenue,** *n.* entrata *f.*

**reverberate,** *vb.* riverberare.

**revere,** *vb.* riverire.

**reverence,** *n.* riverènza *f.*

**reverend,** *adj.* reverèndo.

**reverent,** *adj.* riverènte.

**reverie,** *n.* fantasticheria *f.*

**reverse,** **1.** *n.* rovèscio *m.*, contràrio *m.*; (auto) marcia indiètro *f.* **2.** *vb.* rovesciare; (direction) invertire.

**revert,** *vb.* ritornare.

**review,** **1.** *n.* rivista *f.*, riesame *m.*; (book r.) recensione *f.* **2.** *vb.* passare in rivista; riesaminare; (book) recensire.

**revise,** *vb.* rivedere.

**revision,** *n.* revisione *f.*

**revival,** *n.* ravvivamento *m.*; (theater) ripresa *f.*

**revive,** *vb.* ravvivare.

**revocation,** *n.* rèvoca *f.*

**revoke,** *vb.* revocare.

**revolt,** **1.** *n.* rivòlta. **2.** *vb.* rivoltare, *tr.*

**revolution,** *n.* rivoluzione *f.*; (turn) giro *m.*

**revolutionary,** *adj.* rivoluzionàrio.

**revolve,** *vb.* girare.

**revolver,** *n.* rivoltèlla *f.*

**reward,** **1.** *n.* ricompènsa *f.* **2.** *vb.* ricompensare.

**rhetoric,** *n.* rettòrica *f.*

**rhetorical,** *adj.* rettòrico.

**rheumatic,** *adj.* reumàtico.

**rheumatism,** *n.* reumatismo *m.*

**rhinoceros,** *n.* rinoceronte *m.*

**rhubarb,** *n.* rabàrbaro *m.*

**rhyme,** **1.** *n.* rima *f.* **2.** *vb.* rimare.

**rhythm,** *n.* ritmo *m.*

**rhythmical,** *adj.* rìtmico.

**rib,** *n.* còstola *f.*

**ribbon,** *n.* nastro *m.*

**rice,** *n.* riso *m.*

**rich,** *adj.* ricco.

**riches,** *n.* ricchezza *f.*

**rid,** *vb.* sbarazzare.

**riddle,** *n.* enimma *m.*

**ride,** **1.** *n.* corsa *f.* **2.** *vb.* (on horse) cavalcare; (other transport) andare.

**rider,** *n.* cavalière *m.*

**ridge,** *n.* (between furrows) pòrca *f.*; (mountain) cresta *f.*

**ridicule, 1.** *n.* ridìcolo *m.*
**2.** *vb.* derìdere.

**ridiculous,** *adj.* ridìcolo.

**rifle,** *n.* fucile *m.*

**rig, 1.** *n.* equipàggio *m.;*
(ship) atrezzatura *f.* **2.**
*vb.* equipaggiare; attrezzare.

**right, 1.** *n.* (side) dèstra
*f.;* (justice) giusto *m.* **2.**
*adj.* (side) dèstro; (straight)
diretto; (correct) corrètto;
(be r.) aver ragione. **3.** *vb.*
(set upright) drizzare; (correct) corrèggere.

**righteous,** *adj.* giusto.

**righteousness,** *n.* giustìzia
*f.*

**right of way,** *n.* precedènza
*f.*

**rigid,** *adj.* rìgido.

**rigidity,** *n.* rigidezza *f.*

**rigor,** *n.* rigore *m.*

**rigorous,** *adj.* rigoroso.

**rim,** *n.* bordo *m.*, orlo *m.*

**ring, 1.** *n.* (circle) cérchio
*m.;* (for finger) anèllo *m.;*
(boxing) quadrato *m.;* (on
bell) suòno *m.*, scampanellata
*f.* **2.** *vb.* sonare; **(r. out)**
risonare; **(form a r. around)**
accerchiare.

**rinse,** *vb.* risciacquare.

**riot, 1.** *n.* tumulto *m.* **2.**
*vb.* tumultuare.

**rip,** *vb.* strappare.

**ripe,** *adj.* maturo.

**ripen,** *vb.* maturare.

**ripple,** *n.* increspatura *f.*

**rise, 1.** *n.* (increase) aumènto *m.;* (origin) origine *f.*
**2.** *vb.* alzarsi, levarsi, sorgere.

**risk, 1.** *n.* rischio *m.* **2.** *vb.*
arrischiare, rischiare.

**rite,** *n.* rito *m.*

**ritual,** *n. and adj.* rituale
*(m.)*

**rival, 1.** *n. and adj.* rivale.
**2.** *vb.* rivaleggiare con.

**rivalry,** *n.* rivalità *f.*

**river,** *n.* fiume *m.*

**rivet, 1.** *n.* chiòdo ribadito
*m.* **2.** *vb.* ribadire.

**road, 1.** *n.* cammino *m.*,
strada *f.*, via *f.* **2.** *adj.*
(pertaining to roads) stradale.

**roam,** *vb.* vagare.

**roar, 1.** *n.* ruggito *m.* **2.** *vb.*
ruggire.

**roast, 1.** *n.* arròsto *m.* **2.**
*vb.* arrostire.

**roasting** (of coffee), *n.* torrefazione *f.*

**rob,** *vb.* derubare; **(r. completely)** svaligiare.

**robber,** *n.* ladrone *m.*

**robbery,** *n.* furto *m.*

**robe,** *n.* vèste *f.*

**robin,** *n.* pettirosso *m.*

**robot,** *n.* autòma *m.*

**robust,** *adj.* robusto.

**rock, 1.** *n.* ròccia *f.;* (fortress) ròcca; **(pertaining
to r.)** roccioso. **2.** *vb.*
dondolare.

**rocker,** *n.* (rocking-chair)
sèdia a dòndolo *f.*

**rocket,** *n.* razzo *m.*

**rocky,** *adj.* roccioso.

**rod,** *n.* verga *f.*

**rodent,** *n.* roditore *m.*

**roe,** *n.* cèrva *f.*

**rogue,** *n.* briccone *m.*

**roguish,** *adj.* bricconesco.

**rôle,** *n.* ruòlo *m.*

**roll, 1.** *n.* ròtolo *m.;* (bread)
panino *m.;* (list) ruòlo *m.;*
(of ship) rullio *m.* **2.** *vb.*
rotolare; (ship) rullare.

**roller,** *n.* rotèlla *m.*, rullo *m.*

**roller-bearing,** *n.* cuscinetto
a rotolamento *m.*

**Roman,** *adj.* romano.

**Rome,** *n.* Roma *f.*

**romance,** *n.* romanzo *m.*

**romantic,** *adj.* romàntico.

**romp,** *vb.* giocare vigorosa-
mente.

**roof,** *n.* tètto *m.*

**room,** *n.* (in house) càmera
*f.*, stanza *f.;* (space) posto
*m.*, spàzio *f.*

**roommate,** *n.* compagno di
stanza *m.*, compagna di
stanza *f.*

**rooster,** *n.* gallo *m.*

**root,** *n.* radice *f.*

**rope,** *n.* còrda *f.;*, fune *f.*

**rosary,** *n.* rosàrio *m.*

**rose,** *n.* ròsa *f.*

**rosin,** *n.* rèsina *f.*

**rosy,** *adj.* ròseo.

**rot, 1.** *n.* putrefazione *f.*
**2.** *vb.* marcire, imputridire,
tr.

**rotary,** *adj.* rotatòrio.

**rotate,** *vb.* rotare.

**rotation,** *n.* rotazione *f.*

**rotten,** *adj.* pùtrido.

**rouge,** *n.* rossetto *m.*

**rough,** *adj.* rùvido, rozzo.

**round, 1.** *n.* giro *m.* **2.** *adj.*
rotondo, tondo. **3.** *adv.*
intorno. **4.** *prep.* intorno a.

**rouse,** *vb.* svegliare, risvegliare.

rout, n. rotta f.
route, n. percorso m.
routine, n. abitùdini fisse f.pl.
rove, vb. errare.
row, 1. n. (fight) lite f.; (uproar) baccano m.; (series) fila f.; (boat ride) remata f. 2. vb. (raise a row) litigare; (use oars) remare.
rowboat, n. battèllo a remi m.
rowdy, adj. litigioso.
royal, adj. reale, règio.
royalty, n. regalità f.
rub, 1. n. fregata f. 2. vb. fregare, strofinare.
rubber, n. gomma f.; (over-shoe) scarpa di gomma f.
rubbish, n. scarti m.pl.; (nonsense) fandònie f.pl.
ruby, n. rubino m.
rudder, n. timone m.
ruddy, adj. rubicondo.
rude, adj. rude.
rudiment, n. rudimento m.
rue, vb. pentirsi di.
ruffian, n. malfattore m.
ruffle, 1. n. increspatura f. 2. vb. increspare.
rug, n. (for floor) tappeto m.; (blanket) copèrta f.
rugged, adj. scabroso.
ruin, 1. n. rovina f.; (remain) rùdere m. 2. vb. rovinare.
ruinous, adj. ravinoso.
rule, 1. n. règola f. 2. vb. regolare; (reign) regnare.

ruler, n. (lawgiver) sovrano m.; (measuring-stick) règolo m.
rum, n. rum m.
rumble, 1. n. brontolìo m. 2. vb. brontolare.
rumor, n. dicerìa f., voce f.
run, 1. n. (in stocking) cordiglièra f. 2. vb. córrere; (work) funzionare; (flow) scórrere; (r. across) incontrare; (r. away) fuggire; (r. into) investire.
run-down, adj. indebolito.
rung, n. piuòlo m.
runner, n. corridore m.
runway, n. pista f.
rupture, n. rottura f.
rural, adj. rurale.
rush, 1. n. afflusso m.; (hurry) fretta f.; (reed) giunco m. 2. vb. affluire; precipitarsi.
Russia, n. Rùssia f.
Russian, adj. russo.
rust, 1. n. rùggine f. 2. vb. arrugginire, tr.
rustic, n. and adj. rùstico (m.).
rustle, 1. n. fruscìo m. 2. vb. frusciare.
rust-proof, adj. inossidàbile.
rusty, adj. arrugginito, rugginoso.
rut, n. solco m.
ruthless, adj. spietato.
rye, n. ségale f.

# S

Sabbath, n. giorno di ripòso m.
saber, n. sciàbola f.
sable, n. zibellino m.
sabotage, 1. n. sabotàggio m. 2. vb. sabotare.
saboteur, n. sabotatore m.
saccharine, 1. n. saccarina f. 2. adj. saccarino.
sachet, n. sacchetto di profumo m.
sack, 1. n. sacco m.; (pillage) sacchèggio m. 2. vb. (dis-charge) licenziare; (plunder) saccheggiare.
sacrament, n. sacramento m.
sacred, adj. sacro.
sacrifice, 1. n. sacrificio m. 2. vb. sacrificare.
sacrilege, n. sacrilègio m.
sacrilegious, adj. sacrilego.
sacristan, n. sagrestano m.
sacristy, n. sagrestìa f.
sad, adj. triste.
sadden, vb. rattristare.

**saddle,** 1. *n.* sèlla *f.* 2. *vb.* sellare.

**sadism,** *n.* sadìsmo *m.*

**safe,** 1. *n.* cassafòrte *m.* 2. *adj.* sicuro, salvo; (**s. and sound**) sano e salvo.

**safeguard,** 1. *n.* salvaguàrdia *f.* 2. *vb.* salvaguardare.

**safety,** *n.* sicurezza *f.*

**safety island,** *n.* isolòtto salvagente *m.*

**safety-pin,** *n.* spillo di sicurezza *f.*

**sage,** *n. and adj.* sàggio (*m.*)

**sail,** 1. *n.* vela *f.* 2. *vb.* navigare; (depart) salpare.

**sailboat,** *n.* battèllo a vela *m.*

**sailor,** *n.* marinaio *m.*

**saint,** *n.* santo *m.*

**sake,** *n.* motivo *m.*

**salad,** *n.* insalata *f.*

**salary,** *n.* stipèndio *m.*

**sale,** *n.* véndita *f.*, spàccio *m.*

**salesman,** *n.* commesso di negòzio *m.*; (**traveling s.**) commesso viaggiatore *m.*

**saliva,** *n.* saliva *f.*

**salmon,** *n.* salmone *m.*

**salon,** *n.* salone *m.*

**salt,** 1. *n.* sale *m.* 2. *adj.* salso. 3. *vb.* salare.

**salty,** *adj.* salso, salato.

**salutation,** *n.* saluto *m.*, salutazione *f.*

**salute,** 1. *n.* saluto *m.* 2. *vb.* salutare.

**salvage,** 1. *n.* salvatàggio *m.* 2. *vb.* salvare.

**salvation,** *n.* salvezza *f.*

**salve,** *n.* unguento *m.*

**same,** *adj.* stesso.

**sample,** *n.* campione *m.*; (**s. fair**) fièra campionària *f.*

**sanatorium,** *n.* sanatòrio *m.*

**sanctify,** *vb.* santificare.

**sanction,** 1. *n.* sanzione *f.* 2. *vb.* sanzionare.

**sanctity,** *n.* santità *f.*

**sanctuary,** *n.* santuàrio *m.*

**sand,** *n.* rena *f.*, sàbbia *f.*

**sandal,** *n.* sàndalo *m.*

**sandwich,** *n.* sandwich *m.*, tramezzino *m.*

**sandy,** *adj.* renoso, sabbioso.

**sane,** *adj.* sano.

**sanguinary,** *adj.* sanguinàrio.

**sanitary,** *adj.* igiènico, sanitàrio.

**sanitation,** *n.* igiène *f.*

**sanity,** *n.* sanità *f.*

**Santa Claus,** *n.* Befana *f.* (old woman who brings presents on Twelfth Night).

**sap,** 1. *n.* linfa *f.*; (fool) citrullo *m.* 2. *vb.* (weaken) indebolire.

**sapphire,** *n.* zaffiro *m.*

**sarcasm,** *n.* sarcasmo *m.*

**sarcastic,** *adj.* sarcàstico.

**sardine,** *n.* sardèlla *f.*

**Sardinia,** *n.* Sardegna *f.*

**Sardinian,** *adj.* sardo.

**sash,** *n.* cintura *f.*

**satellite,** *n.* satèllite *m.*

**satin,** *n.* raso *m.*

**satire,** *n.* sàtira *f.*

**satirize,** *vb.* satireggiare.

**satisfaction,** *n.* soddisfazione *f.*

**satisfactory,** *adj.* soddisfacènte.

**satisfy,** *vb.* soddisfare.

**saturate,** *vb.* saturare.

**saturation,** *n.* saturazione *f.*

**Saturday,** *n.* sàbato *m.*

**sauce,** *n.* salsa *f.*

**saucer,** *n.* piattino *m.*

**saucy,** *adj.* impertinènte.

**sausage,** *n.* salsìccia *f.*

**savage,** *n. and adj.* selvàggio (*m.*)

**save,** 1. *vb.* (preserve) salvare; (economize) risparmiare. 2. *prep.* salvo.

**savings,** *n.* rispàrmio *m.*; (**s.-bank**) cassa di rispàrmio *f.*

**savior,** *n.* salvatore *m.*

**savor,** 1. *n.* sapore *m.* 2. *vb.* sapere.

**savory,** *adj.* saporito.

**saw,** 1. *n.* sega *f.*; (proverb) provèrbio *m.* 2. *vb.* segare.

**say,** *vb.* dire; (**s. again**) ridire.

**saying,** *n.* provèrbio *m.*

**scab,** *n.* crosta *f.*; (non-striker) crumiro *m.*

**scaffold,** *n.* patibolo *m.*

**scaffolding,** *n.* impalcatura *f.*

**scald,** 1. *n.* scottatura *f.* 2. *vb.* scottare.

**scale,** 1. *n.* scala *f.*; (balance) bilància *f.*; (fish, etc.) squama *f.*; (music) gamma *f.* 2. *vb.* scrostare; (climb) arrampicarsi su.

**scalp,** *n.* pèlle del crànio *f.*

**scan,** *vb.* scrutare; (poetry) scandire.

**scandal,** *n.* scàndalo *m.*; (gossip) maldicènza *f.*

**scandalous,** *adj.* scandaloso.

**scant,** *adj.* scarso.

**scar, 1.** *n.* cicatrice *f.* **2.** *vb.* cicatrizzare, *tr.*

**scarce,** *adj.* scarso; **(be s.)** scarseggiare.

**scarcely,** *adv.* appena.

**scarcity,** *n.* scarsità *f.*

**scare, 1.** *n.* spavento *m.* **2.** *vb.* spaventare.

**scarecrow,** *n.* spauràcchio *m.*

**scarf,** *n.* sciarpa *f.*

**scarlet,** *n. and adj.* scarlatto (*m.*).

**scarlet fever,** *n.* scarlattina *f.*

**scathing,** *adj.* mordace.

**scatter,** *vb.* spàrgere.

**scavenger,** *n.* spazzino *m.*

**scene,** *n.* scèna *f.*

**scenery,** *n.* paesàggio *m.*

**scent,** *n.* odore *m.,* fiuto *m.;* profumo *m.;* (track) pista *f.*

**schedule,** *n.* oràrio *m.*

**scheme,** *n.* progètto *m.*

**scholar,** *n.* dòtto *m.,* erudito *m.*

**scholarship,** *n.* borsa di stùdio *f.;* (knowledge) erudizione *f.*

**school,** *n.* scuòla *f.*

**sciatica,** *n.* sciàtica *f.*

**science,** *n.* sciènza *f.*

**scientific,** *adj.* scientìfico.

**scientist,** *n.* scienziato *m.*

**scissors,** *n.* fòrbici *f.pl.*

**scoff,** *vb.* schernire, farsi beffe.

**scold,** *vb.* sgridare.

**scolding,** *n.* ramanzina *f.*

**scoop, 1.** *n.* cucchiàia *f.,* ramaiuòlo *m.* **2.** *vb.* travasare.

**scope,** *n.* (extent) portata *f.;* (outlet) stògo *m.*

**scorch,** *vb.* bruciare.

**score, 1.** *n.* (points) punti *m.pl.;* (twenty) ventina *f.;* (music) partitura *f.* **2.** *vb.* segnare.

**scorn, 1.** *n.* disprèzzo *m.* disdegno *m.* **2.** *vb.* disprezzare, disdegnare.

**scornful,** *adj.* sprezzante, disdegnoso.

**Scotch,** *adj.* scozzese.

**Scotland,** *n.* Scòzia *f.*

**scour,** *vb.* lavare strofinando.

**scourge, 1.** *n.* sfèrza *f.* **2.** *vb.* sferzare.

**scout,** *n.* esploratore *m.*

**scowl,** *vb.* aggrottare le cìglia.

**scramble, 1.** *n.* parapìglia

*m.* **2.** *vb.* (climb) arrampicarsi.

**scrambled eggs,** *n.* uòva strapazzate *f.pl.*

**scrap, 1.** *n.* pezzetto *m.;* (fight) tafferùglio *m.* **2.** *vb.* scartare; (fight) azzuffarsi.

**scrape, 1.** *n.* (trouble) impiccio *m.* **2.** *vb.* raschiare.

**scratch, 1.** *n.* graffiatura *f.* **2.** *vb.* graffiare.

**scream, 1.** *n.* strillo *m.* **2.** *vb.* strillare.

**screen, 1.** *n.* (furniture) paravènto *m.;* (sieve) crivèllo *m.;* (movie) schèrmo *m.* **2.** *vb.* (protect) protèggere; (sift) crivellare.

**screw, 1.** *n.* vite *f.* **2.** *vb.* avvitare.

**screw-driver,** *n.* cacciavite *m.*

**scribble,** *vb.* scribacchiare.

**scribe,** *n.* scriba *m.*

**scripture,** *n.* scrittura *f.*

**scroll,** *n.* ròtolo *m.*

**scrub,** *vb.* strofinare.

**scruple,** *n.* scrùpolo *m.*

**scrupulous,** *adj.* scrupoloso.

**scrutinize,** *vb.* scrutare.

**sculptor,** *n.* scultore *m.*

**sculpture,** *n.* scultura *f.*

**scythe,** *n.* falce *f.*

**sea,** *n.* mare *m.*

**seal, 1.** *n.* sigillo *m.,* suggèllo *m.* (animal) fòca *f.* **2.** *vb.* sigillare; suggellare.

**sealing-wax,** *n.* ceralacca *f.*

**seam,** *n.* cucitura *f.*

**seaport,** *n.* pòrto di mare *m.*

**search, 1.** *n.* ricerca *f.* **2.** *vb.* ricercare.

**seasick,** *adj.* **(be s.)** soffrire di mal di mare.

**seasickness,** *n.* mal di mare *m.*

**season, 1.** *n.* stagione *f.;* **(s. ticket)** bigliètto d'abbonamento *m.* **2.** *vb.* condire.

**seasoning,** *n.* condimento *m.*

**seat, 1.** *n.* (chair) sèdia *f.;* (place) posto *m.;* (headquarters) sede *f.* **2.** *vb.* far sedere.

**second,** *n. and adj.* secondo (*m.*).

**secondary,** *adj.* secondàrio.

**secret,** *n. and adj.* segreto *m.*

**secretary,** *n.* segretàrio *m.,* segretària *f.*

**sect,** *n.* sètta *f.*

**section**, n. sezione f.

**sectional**, adj. sezionale.

**secular**, adj. secolare.

**secure**, adj. sicuro.

**security**, n. sicurezza f.

**sedative**, n. and adj. sedativo (m.).

**seduce**, vb. sedurre.

**seductive**, adj. seducènte.

**see**, vb. vedere.

**seed**, n. seme m.

**seek**, vb. cercare.

**seem**, vb. parere, sembrare.

**seep**, vb. trasudare.

**seesaw**, n. altalena f.

**segment**, n. segmento m.

**segregate**, vb. segregare.

**seize**, vb. afferrare.

**seldom**, adv. di rado, raramente.

**select**, 1. adj. scelto. 2. vb. scégliere.

**selection**, n. scelta f., selezione f.

**selective**, adj. selettivo.

**self**, pron. stesso; **self-**, di sè stesso.

**selfish**, adj. egoìstico.

**selfishness**, n. egoismo m.

**sell**, vb. véndere.

**semantic**, adj. semàntico.

**semantics**, n. semàntica f.

**semester**, n. semèstre m.

**semicircle**, n. semicérchio m.

**semicolon**, n. punto e vìrgola, m.sg.

**seminary**, n. seminàrio m.

**senate**, n. senato m.

**senator**, n. senatore m.

**send**, vb. mandare, spedire, inviare.

**senile**, adj. senile.

**senior**, adj. maggiore; (father) padre.

**sensation**, n. sensazione f.

**sensational**, adj. sensazionale.

**sense**, 1. n. sènso m.; (intelligence) senno m. 2. vb. intuire.

**sensible**, adj. assennato.

**sensitive**, adj. sensitivo, sensìbile.

**sensual**, adj. sensuale.

**sentence**, 1. n. frase f., proposizione f.; (court) condanna f. 2. vb. condannare.

**sentiment**, n. sentimento m.

**sentimental**, adj. sentimentale.

**separate**, 1. adj. separato. 2. vb. separare.

**separation**, n. separazione f.

**September**, n. settèmbre m.

**sequence**, n. sèrie f.

**serenade**, n. serenata f.

**serene**, adj. sereno.

**sergeant**, n. sergènte m.

**serial**, adj. in sèrie, periòdico.

**series**, n. sèrie f.

**serious**, adj. sèrio.

**sermon**, n. sermone m.

**serpent**, n. serpènte m.

**serum**, n. sièro m.

**servant**, n. domèstico m., sèrvo m.; (servants, collectively) servitù f.

**serve**, vb. servire.

**service**, n. servìzio m.

**servile**, adj. servile.

**servitude**, n. servitù f.

**session**, n. sessione f.

**set**, 1. n. sèrie f.; (clique) cricca f. 2. adj. fisso. 3. vb. (put) méttere; (regulate) regolare; (fix) fissare; (mount) montare.

**settle**, vb. (establish) stabilire, tr.; (fix) fissare; (decide) decidere; (arrange) sistemare; (pay) saldare; (s. down to) méttersi a.

**settlement**, n. (colony) colònia f.; (hamlet) borgo m. (accounts) regolamento m.; (affairs) sistemazione f.

**settler**, n. colòno m.

**seven**, num. sètte.

**seventeen**, num. diciassètte.

**seventeenth**, adj. diciassettèsimo.

**seventh**, adj. sèttimo.

**seventieth**, adj. settantèsimo.

**seventy**, num. settanta.

**sever**, vb. staccare, tr.

**several**, adj. parecchi.

**severe**, adj. sevèro.

**severity**, n. severità f.

**sew**, vb. cucire.

**sewer**, n. fogna f.

**sex**, n. sèsso m.

**sexton**, n. sagrestano m.

**sexual**, adj. sessuale.

**shabby**, adj. (worn-out) lògoro; (mean) gretto, meschino.

**shack**, n. capanna f.

**shade**, 1. n. ombra f.; (color) tinta f.; (against light) paralume m. 2. vb. ombreggiare; (darken) oscurare.

**shadow**, n. ombra f.

**shady**, adj. ombroso.

**shaft**, n. (mine) pozzo m.;

(transmission) àlbero *m.*; (wagon) stanga *f.*; (ray) ràggio *m.*; (arrow) strale *m.*

**shaggy,** *adj.* ispido.

**shake, 1.** *n.* scòssa *f.*; (hand-s.) stretta di mano *f.* **2.** *vb.* scuòtere, *tr.*; (quiver) tremare; (s. hands with) stringere la mano a.

**shall,** *vb.* dovere; or use future tense of verb.

**shallow,** *adj.* pòco profondo.

**shame, 1.** *n.* vergogna *f.*; (pity) peccato *m.*; (what a s.) che peccato!. **2.** *vb.* gettar vergogna su.

**shameful,** *adj.* vergognoso.

**shampoo,** *n.* sciampò *m.*

**shape, 1.** *n.* forma *f.*; fòggia *f.* **2.** *vb.* formare, foggiare.

**share, 1.** *n.* parte *f.*, porzione *f.*; (stock) azione *f.* **2.** *vb.* condividere.

**shark,** *n.* pescecane *m.*

**sharp, 1.** *n.* (music) dièsis. **2.** *adj.* acuto.

**sharpen,** *vb.* aguzzare.

**sharply,** *adv.* acutamente; (harshly) aspramente.

**sharpness,** *n.* acutezza *f.*

**shatter,** *vb.* frantumare.

**shave,** *vb.* ràdere, *tr.*, fare la barba a, *tr.*

**shawl,** *n.* scialle *m.*

**she,** *pron.* ella *f.*, essa *f.*, lèi *f.*

**sheaf,** *n.* fàscio *m.*, covone *m.*

**shear,** *vb.* tosare.

**shears,** *n.* cesòie *f.pl.*

**sheath,** *n.* fòdero *m.*, guaìna *f.*

**shed, 1.** *n.* tettòia *f.* **2.** *vb.* versare; (lose) lasciar cadere.

**sheep,** *n.* pècora *f.*

**sheet,** *n.* (bed) lenzuòlo *m.*; (paper) fòglio *m.*; (metal) lastra *f.*

**shelf,** *n.* scaffale *m.*

**shell, 1.** *n.* (egg) gùscio *m.*; (pod) baccèllo *m.*; (conch) conchiglia *f.*; (explosive) bomba *f.* **2.** *vb.* bombardare.

**shellac,** *n.* gomma lacca *f.*

**shelter, 1.** *n.* ricòvero *m.* **2.** *vb.* ricoverare, *tr.*

**shepherd,** *n.* pastore *m.*

**sherbet,** *n.* sorbetto *m.*

**sherry,** *n.* vino di Xeres *m.*

**shield, 1.** *n.* scudo *m.* **2.** *vb.* protèggere.

**shift, 1.** *n.* (change) cam-

biamento *m.*; (turn) turno *m.* **2.** *vb.* cambiare.

**shin,** *n.* stinco *m.*

**shine,** *vb.* brillare, splèndere; (shoes) lucidare.

**shingles,** *n.* èrpete *f.*

**shiny,** *adj.* lùcido.

**ship, 1.** *n.* nave *f.* **2.** *vb.* spedire.

**shipment,** *n.* spedizione *f.*

**shipper,** *n.* speditore *m.*

**shipping agent,** *n.* spedizionière *m.*

**shipwreck,** *n.* naufràgio *m.*

**shirk,** *vb.* sottrarsi a.

**shirt,** *n.* camìcia *f.*

**shiver, 1.** *n.* brìvido *m.* **2.** *vb.* rabbrividire.

**shock, 1.** *n.* scòssa *f.*, urto *m.* **2.** *vb.* urtare.

**shoe, 1.** *n.* scarpa *f.* **2.** *vb.* calzare; (horse) ferrare.

**shoelace,** *n.* làccio per scarpe *m.*

**shoemaker,** *n.* calzolaio *m.*

**shoot, 1.** *n.* (sprout) germòglio *m.* **2.** *vb.* (gun) sparare; (a person) fucilare; (s. down) abbàttere.

**shop, 1.** *n.* bottega *f.*, negòzio *m.*, spàccio *m.* **2.** *vb.* far compre.

**shopping,** *n.* compre *f.pl.*, spese *f.pl.*

**shore,** *n.* spiàggia *f.*, sponda *f.*

**short,** *adj.* brève, corto; (s. circuit) corto circùito *m.*; (run s.) scarseggiare.

**shortage,** *n.* mancanza *f.*

**shorten,** *vb.* abbreviare, *tr.*

**shorthand,** *n.* stenografìa *f.*

**shortly,** *adv.* fra pòco.

**shorts,** *n.* calzoncini corti *m.pl.*

**shot,** *n.* colpo *m.*, sparo *m.*; (bullets) pallini *m.pl.*; (distance) portata *f.*

**should,** *vb.* use conditional of dovere.

**shoulder,** *n.* spalla *f.*

**shout, 1.** *n.* grido *m.* **2.** *vb.* gridare.

**shove, 1.** *n.* spinta *f.* **2.** *vb.* spìngere.

**shovel,** *n.* pala *f.*

**show, 1.** *n.* mostra *f.*, esposizione *f.*; (theater) spettàcolo *m.* **2.** *vb.* mostrare.

**shower,** *n.* (rain) acquazzone *m.*; (bath) dòccia *f.*

**shrapnel,** *n.* shràpnel *m.*

**shrewd,** *adj.* acuto, furbo.

**shriek,** 1. *n.* strillo *m.* 2. *vb.* strillare.

**shrill,** *adj.* strídulo.

**shrimp,** *n.* gamberetto *m.*; (small person) nano *m.*

**shrine,** *n.* santuàrio *m.*

**shrink,** *vb.* contrarsi; (s. from) rifuggire da.

**shroud,** *n.* sudàrio *m.*

**shrub,** *n.* arbusto *m.*

**shudder,** 1. *n.* brívido *m.* 2. *vb.* rabbrividire.

**shun,** *vb.* schivare.

**shut,** *vb.* chiúdere.

**shutter,** *n.* scuretto *m.*; (camera) otturatore *m.*

**shy,** *adj.* tímido.

**Sicilian,** *adj.* siciliano.

**Sicily,** *n.* Sicília *f.*

**sick,** *adj.* ammalato, malato.

**sickness,** *n.* malattìa *f.*

**side,** *n.* lato *m.*, fianco *m.*

**side-car,** *n.* carrozzino *m.*

**side-dish,** *n.* contorno *m.*

**sidewalk,** *n.* marciapiède *m.*

**siege,** *n.* assèdio *m.*

**sieve,** *n.* crivèllo *m.*, stàccio *m.*, vàglio *m.*

**sift,** *vb.* stacciare, crivellare.

**sigh,** 1. *n.* sospiro *m.* 2. *vb.* sospirare.

**sight,** *n.* vista *f.*

**sightseeing,** *n.* turismo *m.*

**sign,** 1. *n.* segno *m.* 2. *vb.* firmare, sottoscrivere.

**signal,** 1. *n.* segnale *m.* 2. *vb.* segnalare.

**signature,** *n.* firma *f.*

**significance,** *n.* significato *m.*

**significant,** *adj.* significativo.

**signify,** *vb.* significare.

**silence,** 1. *n.* silènzio *m.* 2. *vb.* far tacere.

**silencer,** *n.* silenziatore *m.*

**silent,** *adj.* silenzioso, zitto.

**silk,** *n.* seta *f.*

**silken, silky,** *adj.* setàceo.

**sill,** *n.* davanzale *m.*

**silly,** *adj.* sciòcco.

**silo,** *n.* silo *m.*

**silver,** 1. *n.* argènto *m.* 2. *adj.* argènteo.

**silvery,** *adj.* argentino.

**silverware,** *n.* posaterìa d'argento *m.*

**similar,** *adj.* símile.

**similarity,** *n.* somiglianza *f.*

**similarly,** *adv.* similmente.

**simple,** *adj.* sémplice.

**simplicity,** *n.* semplicità *f.*

**simplify,** *vb.* semplificare.

**simply,** *adj.* semplicemente.

**simulate,** *vb.* simulare.

**simultaneous,** *adj.* simultàneo.

**sin,** 1. *n.* peccato *m.* 2. *vb.* peccare.

**since,** 1. *prep.* sino da. 2. *conj.* da quando; (because) giacchè, poichè.

**sincere,** *adj.* sincèro.

**sincerely,** *adv.* sinceramente.

**sincerity,** *n.* sincerità *f.*

**sinew,** *n.* nèrbo *m.*

**sinful,** *adj.* peccaminoso.

**sing,** *vb.* cantare.

**singe,** *vb.* strinare.

**singer,** *n.* cantatore *m.*, cantatrice *f.*

**single,** *adj.* solo, único; (unmarried) cèlibe.

**single file,** *n.* fila indiana *f.*

**singular,** *adj.* singolare.

**sinister,** *adj.* sinistro.

**sink,** 1. *n.* acquàio *m.*, lavandino *m.* 2. *vb.* affondare; (ground) sprofondarsi.

**sinner,** *n.* peccatore *m.*

**sinuous,** *adj.* sinuoso.

**sinus,** *n.* seno frontale *m.*

**sinusitis,** *n.* sinusite *f.*

**sip,** 1. *n.* sorso *m.* 2. *vb.* sorseggiare.

**siphon,** *n.* sifone *m.*

**sir,** *n.* signore *m.*

**siren,** *n.* sirèna *f.*

**sirloin,** *n.* lombo *m.*

**sister,** *n.* sorèlla *f.*

**sister-in-law,** *n.* cognata *f.*

**sit,** *vb.* sedere.

**site,** *n.* sito *m.*

**sitting,** *n.* seduta *f.*

**situate,** *vb.* situare.

**situation,** *n.* situazione *f.*

**six,** *num.* sèi.

**sixteen,** *num.* sédici.

**sixteenth,** *adj.* sedicésimo, decimosèsto.

**sixth,** *adj.* sèsto.

**sixty,** *num.* sessanta.

**size,** *n.* grandezza *f.*; (apparel) misura *f.*

**sizing,** *n.* incollatura *f.*

**skate,** 1. *n.* pàttino *m.* 2. *vb.* pattinare.

**skein,** *n.* matassa *f.*

**skeleton,** *n.* schèletro *m.*

**skeptic,** *n.* scèttico *m.*

**skeptical,** *adj.* scèttico.

**sketch,** 1. *n.* abbozzo *m.*, schizzo *m.* 2. *vb.* abbozzare, schizzare.

**ski,** 1. *n.* sci *m.* 2. *vb.* sciare.

**skid,** 1. *n.* slittamento *m.* 2. *vb.* slittare.

**ski-lift**, *n.* seggiovìa *f.*

**skill**, *n.* abilità *f.*, destrezza *f.*

**skillful**, *adj.* àbile, dèstro.

**skim**, *vb.* (remove cream) scremare; (go over lightly) sfiorare, rasentare.

**skin**, **1.** *n.* pèlle *f.* **2.** *vb.* pelare; (fruit) sbucciare.

**skip**, *vb.* saltare.

**skirmish**, **1.** *n.* scaramùccia *f.* **2.** *vb.* scaramucciare.

**skirt**, **1.** *n.* gònna *f.*, sottana *f.* **2.** *vb.* rasentare.

**skull**, *n.* crànio *m.*

**skunk**, *n.* moffetta *f.*; (person) puzzone *m.*

**sky**, *n.* cièlo *m.*

**skylight**, *n.* lucernàrio *m.*

**skyscraper**, *n.* grattacièlo *m.*

**slab**, *n.* lastra *f.*

**slack**, *adj.* lento.

**slacken**, *vb.* rallentare.

**slacks**, *n.* calzoni *m.pl.*

**slam**, *vb.* sbàttere.

**slander**, **1.** *n.* calùnnia *f.* **2.** *vb.* calunniare.

**slang**, *n.* gèrgo *m.*

**slant**, **1.** *n.* pendìo *m.* **2.** *adj.* oblìquo. **3.** *vb.* inclinarsi.

**slap**, **1.** *n.* schiaffo *m.* **2.** *vb.* schiaffeggiare.

**slash**, **1.** *n.* squàrcio *m.* **2.** *vb.* squarciare.

**slat**, *n.* stecca *f.*

**slate**, *n.* ardèsia *f.*, lavagna *f.*

**slaughter**, **1.** *n.* massacro *m.*, carneficina *f.*, macèllo *m.* **2.** *vb.* massacrare, macellare.

**slave**, *n.* schiavo *m.*

**slavery**, *n.* schiavitù *f.*

**Slavic**, *adj.* slavo.

**slay**, *vb.* trucidare.

**sled**, *n.* slitta *f.*

**sleek**, *adj.* lìscio.

**sleep**, **1.** *n.* sonno *m.* **2.** *vb.* dormire.

**sleeper, sleeping car**, *n.* vagone lètti *m.*, carrozza lètti *m.*

**sleepy**, *adj.* sonnolento.

**sleet**, *n.* nevìschio *m.*

**sleeve**, *n.* mànica *f.*

**sleigh**, *n.* slitta *f.*

**slender**, *adj.* svelto.

**slice**, **1.** *n.* fetta *f.* **2.** *vb.* affettare.

**slide**, *vb.* scivolare, sdrucciolare.

**slide rule**, *n.* règolo calcolatore *m.*

**slight**, **1.** *n.* disprèzzo *m.* **2.** *adj.* esìguo, insufficiènte; (thin) èsile.

**slim**, *adj.* sottile.

**slime**, *n.* melma *f.*

**sling**, **1.** *n.* fionda *f.* **2.** *vb.* lanciare, scagliare.

**slink**, *vb.* andare furtivamente.

**slip**, **1.** *n.* scivolone *m.*; (mistake) errore *m.*; (paper) strìscia *f.*; (underwear) sottovèste *f.* **2.** *vb.* scivolare, sdrucciolare; (make a mistake) sbagliare.

**slipper**, *n.* pantòfola *f.*

**slippery**, *adj.* sdrucciolévole.

**slit**, *n.* fessura *f.*

**slogan**, *n.* paròla d'òrdine *f.*; (advertising) motto *m.*

**slope**, *n.* pendènza *f.*, pendìo *m.*

**sloppy**, *adj.* trasandato.

**slot**, *n.* fessura *f.*

**slot machine**, *n.* distributore automàtico *m.*

**slouch**, *vb.* stare scomposto.

**slovenly**, *adj.* trascurato.

**slow**, *adj.* lento; (behind time) indiètro, in ritardo.

**slowly**, *adv.* lentamente.

**slowness**, *n.* lentezza *f.*

**sluggish**, *adj.* lento.

**slum**, *n.* bassofondo *m.*

**slumber**, *n.* sonno *m.*

**slur**, **1.** *n.* calùnnia *f.*; (music) legatura *f.* **2.** *vb.* calunniare.

**slush**, *n.* fanghìglia *f.*

**sly**, *adj.* furbo.

**smack**, **1.** *n.* (blow) pacca *f.*; (boat) battèllo *m.* **2.** *vb.* (hit) schiaffeggiare; (taste) sapere.

**small**, *adj.* piccolo.

**smallpox**, *n.* vaiòlo *m.*

**smart**, *adj.* elegante, intelligènte.

**smash**, *vb.* fracassare, frantumare.

**smear**, *vb.* spalmare.

**smell**, **1.** *n.* odore *m.*; (stench) puzzo *m.*; (sense) fiuto *m.* **2.** *vb.* fiutare; (stink) puzzare.

**smelt**, **1.** *n.* (fish) eperlano *m.* **2.** *vb.* (melt) fóndere.

**smile**, **1.** *n.* sorriso *m.* **2.** *vb.* sorridere.

**smite**, *vb.* colpire.

**smock**, *n.* (workman's) camiciòtto *m.*; (hospital) càmice *m.*

**smoke, 1.** *n.* fumo *m.* **2.** *vb.* fumare.

**smokestack,** *n.* fumaiòlo *m.*

**smolder,** *vb.* covare.

**smooth, 1.** *adj.* levigato, lìscio. **2.** *vb.* levigare, lisciare.

**smother,** *vb.* asfissiare, soffocare.

**smug,** *adj.* contento di sè stesso.

**smuggler,** *n.* contrabbandière *m.*

**smuggling,** *n.* contrabbando *m.*

**snack,** *n.* spuntino *m.*

**snag,** *n.* ostàcolo *m.*

**snail,** *n.* lumaca *f.*

**snake,** *n.* sèrpe *m.*

**snap,** *vb.* schioccare; (break) rómpere.

**snapshot,** *n.* istantànea *f.*

**snare,** *n.* tràppola *f.*

**snarl, 1.** *n.* (growl) rìnghio *m.*; (tangle) grovìglio *m.* **2.** *vb.* ringhiare, aggrovigliare, *tr.*

**snatch,** *vb.* afferrare, ghermire.

**sneak,** *vb.* andare furtivamente.

**sneaker,** *n.* scarpa di tela *f.*

**sneer, 1.** *n.* sogghigno *m.* **2.** *vb.* sogghignare.

**sneeze, 1.** *n.* starnuto *m.* **2.** *vb.* starnutire.

**snicker,** *n.* risatina *f.*

**snob,** *n.* snob *m.*

**snore,** *vb.* russare.

**snow, 1.** *n.* neve *f.* **2.** *vb.* nevicare.

**snowdrift,** *n.* ammasso di neve *m.*

**snub,** *vb.* non salutare.

**snug,** *adj.* còmodo.

**so,** *adv.* così; (**so far,** in time) finora; (**so far,** in space) fin qui; (**so as to**) così da.

**soak,** *vb.* bagnare, inzuppare.

**soap,** *n.* sapone *m.*

**soar,** *vb.* volare in alto.

**sob, 1.** *n.* singhiozzo *m.* **2.** *vb.* singhiozzare.

**sober,** *adj.* moderato, non ubriaco; (serious) sòbrio.

**sociable,** *adj.* sociévole.

**social,** *adj.* sociale; (**s. work**) assistènza sociale *n.f.*

**socialism,** *n.* socialismo *m.*

**socialist,** *n. and adj.* socialista.

**society,** *n.* società *f.*

**sociology,** *n.* sociologìa *f.*

**sock, 1.** *n.* calzino *m.*; (blow) pugno *m.* **2.** *vb.* (hit) colpire.

**socket,** *n.* òrbita *f.*; (electric) presa *f.*

**sod,** *n.* piòta *f.*, zòlla *f.*; (with grass) zòlla erbosa *f.*

**soda,** *n.* sòda *f.*

**sodium,** *n.* sòdio *m.*

**sofa,** *n.* sofà *m.*

**soft,** *adj.* molle, mòrbido.

**soft drink,** *n.* bibita non alcoòlica *f.*

**soften,** *vb.* ammollire.

**soil, 1.** *n.* suòlo *m.*, terreno *m.* **2.** *vb.* sporcare.

**soiled,** *adj.* spòrco.

**sojourn, 1.** *n.* soggiorno *m.* **2.** *vb.* soggiornare.

**solace, 1.** *n.* consolazione *f.* **2.** *vb.* consolare.

**solar,** *adj.* solare.

**solder, 1.** *n.* saldatura *f.* **2.** *vb.* saldare.

**soldier,** *n.* soldato *m.*

**sole, 1.** *n.* (of foot, shoe) suòla *f.*; (fish) sògliola *f.* **2.** *adj.* ùnico.

**solemn,** *adj.* solènne.

**solemnity,** *n.* solennità *f.*

**solicit,** *vb.* sollecitare.

**solicitous,** *adj.* sollécito.

**solid,** *n. and adj.* sòlido (*m.*)

**solidify,** *vb.* solidificare, *tr.*

**solidity,** *n.* solidità *f.*

**solitary,** *adj.* solitàrio.

**solitude,** *n.* solitùdine *f.*

**solo,** *n.* assolo *m.*

**soloist,** *n.* solista *m. or f.*

**so long,** *interj.* ciao.

**soluble,** *adj.* solùbile.

**solution,** *n.* soluzione *f.*

**solve,** *vb.* risòlvere.

**solvent,** *n. and adj.* solvènte (*m.*)

**somber,** *adj.* fosco, sòbrio.

**some, 1.** *pron.* ne. **2.** *adj.* qualche, alcuni; (a little) un po'.

**somebody,** *pron.* qualcuno.

**somehow,** *adv.* in qualche mòdo.

**someone,** *pron.* qualcuno.

**somersault,** *n.* capriòla *f.*, salto mortale *m.*

**something,** *pron.* qualcosa, qualche cosa.

**sometime,** *adj.* (former) già.

**sometimes,** *adv.* qualche vòlta.

**somewhat,** *adv.* un po'.

**somewhere,** adv. in qualche luògo.
**son,** n. figlio m.
**song,** n. canto m., canzone f.
**son-in-law,** n. gènero m.
**soon,** adv. prèsto, fra pòco.
**soot,** n. fuliggine f.
**soothe,** vb. calmare.
**soothingly,** adv. dolcemente.
**sophisticated,** adj. sofisticato.
**soprano,** n. soprano m.
**sorcery,** n. stregonerìa f.
**sordid,** adj. sòrdido.
**sore, 1.** n. piaga f. **2.** adj. dolènte; (angry) adirato.
**sorrow, 1.** n. dolore m. **2.** vb. addolorarsi.
**sorrowful,** adj. addolorato.
**sorry,** adj. dispiacènte.
**sort, 1.** n. sòrta f. **2.** vb. assortire.
**soul,** n. ànima f.
**sound, 1.** n. suòno m. **2.** adj. sano, giusto. **3.** vb. suonare; (take soundings) sondare.
**soup,** n. minèstra f., zuppa f.
**sour,** adj. àcido; (unripe) acèrbo.
**source,** n. fonte f., sorgènte f.
**south,** n. sud m., mezzogiorno m.
**southeast,** n. sud-èst m.
**southern,** adj. meridionale.
**South Pole,** n. pòlo sud m.
**southwest,** n. sud-òvest m.
**souvenir,** n. ricòrdo m.
**sovereign,** n. and adj. sovrano (m.).
**sovereignty,** n. sovranità f.
**soviet, 1.** n. sovièt m. **2.** adj. soviètico.
**sow, 1.** n. scrofa f., tròia f. **2.** vb. seminare.
**space,** n. spàzio m.
**spacious,** adj. spazioso.
**spade,** n. vanga f.
**spaghetti,** n. spaghetti m.pl.
**Spain,** n. Spagna f.
**span, 1.** (measure) spanna f.; (bridge) ponte m. **2.** vb. stèndersi m.
**Spaniard,** n. spagnuòlo m.
**Spanish,** adj. spagnuòlo.
**spank,** vb. sculacciare.
**spanking,** n. sculacciata f.
**spar, 1.** n. àlbero m. **2.** vb. (box) fare il pugilato.
**spare, 1.** n. pèzzo di ricàmbio m. **2.** adj. (extra) di ricàmbio; (thin) magro;

(available) disponìbile. **3.** vb. aver disponìbile; (save) risparmiare.
**spark,** n. scintilla f.
**sparkle,** vb. scintillare.
**spark-plug,** n. candela d'accensione f.
**sparrow,** n. pàssero m.
**sparse,** adj. rado.
**spasm,** n. spàsimo m.
**spasmodic,** adj. spasmòdico.
**spatter, 1.** n. spruzzo m. **2.** vb. spruzzare.
**speak,** vb. parlare; **(s. ill)** sparlare.
**speaker,** n. oratore m.; (presiding officer) presidènte m.
**spear, 1.** n. lància f. **2.** vb. trafiggere.
**special,** adj. speciale.
**specialist,** n. specialista m.
**specially,** adv. specialmente.
**specialty,** n. specialità f.
**species,** n. spècie f.
**specific,** adj. specìfico.
**specify,** vb. specificare.
**specimen,** n. saggio m.
**spectacle,** n. spettàcolo m.; (pl., eyeglasses) occhiali m.pl.
**spectacular,** adj. spettacolare.
**spectator,** n. spettatore m.
**spectrum,** n. spèttro m.
**speculate,** vb. speculare.
**speculation,** n. speculazione f.
**speech,** n. discorso m.
**speechless,** adj. interdetto.
**speed, 1.** n. velocità f. **2.** vb. affrettare, tr.; **(s. up)** accelerare, tr.
**speedometer,** n. tachìmetro m.
**speedy,** adj. veloce.
**spell, 1.** n. incantésimo m. **2.** vb. scrìvere.
**spelling,** n. ortografìa f.
**spend,** vb. (money) spèndere; (time) passare.
**spendthrift,** n. sciupone m.
**sphere,** n. sfèra f.
**spice,** n. spèzie, f.pl.
**spider,** n. ragno m.; **(s.-web)** ragnatelo m.
**spike,** n. chiòdo m.
**spill,** vb. rovesciare.
**spillway,** n. scàrico m.
**spin, 1.** n. (excursion) giretto m. **2.** vb. filare; (whirl) girare.
**spinach,** n. spinaci m.pl.
**spine,** n. spina dorsale f.

**spinet,** *n.* spinetta *f.*

**spinster,** *n.* zitèlla *f.*

**spiral,** *n.* *and adj.* spirale (*m.*)

**spire,** *n.* gùglia *f.*

**spirit,** *n.* spírito *m.*

**spiritual,** *adj.* spirituale.

**spiritualism,** *n.* spiritismo *m.*

**spit,** *vb.* sputare.

**spite, 1.** *n.* dispètto *m.*; (**in s. of**) malgrado. **2.** *vb.* contrariare.

**splash, 1.** *n.* tonfo *m.*, spruzzo *m.* **2.** *vb.* spruzzare.

**splendid,** *adj.* splèndido.

**splendor,** *n.* splendore.

**splice,** *vb.* congiùngere.

**splint,** *n.* stecca *f.*

**splinter, 1.** *n.* schéggia *f.* **2.** *vb.* scheggiare, *tr.*

**split, 1.** *n.* (crack) fessura *f.*; (division) scissione *f.* **2.** **vb.** (wood) spaccare; (crack) fèndere, *tr.*; (divide) dividere, *tr.*, scindere, *tr.*

**splurge,** *vb.* spèndere molto denaro.

**spoil,** *vb.* guastare.

**spoke,** *n.* ràggio *m.*

**spokesman,** *n.* portavoce *m.*

**sponge,** *n.* spugna *f.*

**sponsor,** *n.* mallevadore *n.*; (backer) sostenitore *m.*

**spontaneity,** *n.* spontaneità *f.*

**spontaneous,** *adj.* spontàneo.

**spool,** *n.* bobina *f.*; (film) rocchetto *m.*

**spoon,** *n.* (large) cucchiaio *m.*; (small) cucchiaino *m.*

**spoonful,** *n.* cucchiaiata *f.*

**sporadic,** *adj.* sporàdico.

**spore,** *n.* spòra *f.*

**sport, 1.** *n.* sport *m.*, dipòrto *m.* **2.** *adj.* sportivo.

**sportsman,** *n.* sportivo *m.*

**spot,** *n.* (place) posto *m.*; (blot) màcchia *f.*

**spouse,** *n.* sposo *m.*, sposa *f.*

**spout, 1.** *n.* becco *m.* **2.** *vb.* spruzzare.

**sprain, 1.** *n.* stòrta *f.* **2.** *vb.* stòrcere.

**sprawl,** *vb.* sdraiarsi.

**spray,** *vb.* sprizzare, nebulizzare.

**spread, 1.** *n.* distesa *f.*; (food) banchetto *m.* **2.** *adj.* disteso, spiegato. **3.** *vb.* stèndere, *tr.*, spiegare, *tr.*; (diffuse) diffóndere, *tr.*

**spree,** *n.* baldòria *f.*

**sprig,** *n.* ramoscèllo *m.*

**sprightly,** *adj.* brioso.

**spring, 1.** *n.* (season) primavera *f.*; (source) fonte *f.*, sorgènte *f.*; (leap) salto *m.*; (metal) mòlla *f.* **2.** *vb.* sòrgere, saltare; (leap up) scattare.

**springboard,** *n.* trampolino *m.*

**sprinkle,** *vb.* cospàrgere.

**sprint, 1.** *n.* corsa veloce. **2.** *vb.* córrere velocemente.

**sprinter,** *n.* velocista *m.*

**sprout, 1.** *n.* germòglio *m.* **2.** *vb.* germogliare.

**spry,** *adj.* arzillo.

**spur, 1.** *n.* sprone *m.*, sperone *m.* **2.** *vb.* spronare.

**spurious,** *adj.* spùrio.

**spurn,** *vb.* disdegnare.

**spurt, 1.** *n.* scatto *m.* **2.** *vb.* scattare; (pour out) spruzzare.

**spy, 1.** *n.* spione *m.* **2.** *vb.* spiare; (perceive) scòrgere.

**squabble,** *n.* battibecco *m.*

**squad,** *n.* squadra *f.*

**squadron,** *n.* squadrone *m.*

**squalid,** *adj.* squàllido.

**squall,** *vb.* sbraitare.

**squalor,** *n.* squallore *m.*

**squander,** *vb.* scialacquare.

**square, 1.** *n.* quadrato *m.*; (open place) piazza *f.* **2.** *adj.* quadrato. **3.** *vb.* quadrare.

**squash, 1.** *n.* (drink) spremuta *f.*; (vegetable) zucca *f.* **2.** *vb.* spiaccicare.

**squat, 1.** *adj.* tarchiato. **2.** *vb.* accosciarsi.

**squeak, 1.** *n.* cigolìo *m.* **2.** *vb.* cigolare.

**squeamish,** *adj.* schizzinoso.

**squeeze, 1.** *n.* stretta *f.* **2.** *vb.* stríngere; (juice) sprèmere.

**squirrel,** *n.* scoiàttolo *m.*

**squirt,** *vb.* schizzare, zampillare.

**stab, 1.** *n.* pugnalata *f.* **2.** *vb.* pugnalare.

**stability,** *n.* stabilità *f.*

**stabilize,** *vb.* stabilizzare.

**stable, 1.** *n.* stalla *f.* **2.** *adj.* stàbile.

**stack, 1.** *n.* mùcchio *m.* **2.** *vb.* ammucchiare.

**stadium,** *n.* stàdio *m.*

**staff,** *n.* (stick) bastone *m.*; (personnel) personale *m.*; (music) rigo *m.*

**stag,** *n.* cèrvo *m.*

**stage,** *n.* (theater) palco-scènico *m.;* (phase) fase *f.,* stàdio *m.*

**stagger,** *vb.* barcollare.

**stagnant,** *adj.* stagnante.

**stagnate,** *vb.* stagnare.

**stain, 1.** *n.* màcchia *f.;* (color) colore *m.* **2.** *vb.* colorare; macchiare.

**staircase, stairs,** *n.* scala *f.*

**stake, 1.** *n.* (post) palo *m.;* (sum, bet) posta *f.* **2.** *vb.* rischiare; (bet) puntare.

**stale,** *adj.* raffermo.

**stalemate,** *n.* punto mòrto *m.*

**stalk,** *n.* gambo *m.*

**stall, 1.** *n.* stallo *m.;* (vendor's) banco *m.* **2.** *vb.* (stop) arrestarsi.

**stallion,** *n.* stallone *m.*

**stalwart,** *adj.* robusto.

**stamen,** *n.* stame *m.*

**stamina,** *n.* vigore *m.*

**stammer,** *vb.* balbettare.

**stamp, 1.** *n.* (adhesive) bollo *m.;* (embossed, im-pressed) timbro *m.;* (**pos-tage-s.**) francobollo *m.* **2.** *vb.* bollare, timbrare.

**stampede,** *n.* fuga precipi-tosa *f.*

**stamp pad,** *n.* cuscinetto *m.*

**stand, 1.** *n.* (position) posizione *f.;* (vendor's) padi-glione *m.;* (grandstand) tribuna *f.* **2.** *vb.* stare; (put) méttere; (suffer) soffrire, tollerare; (**s. up**) stare in pièdi.

**standard, 1.** *n.* nòrma *f.* **2.** *adj.* normale.

**standardize,** *vb.* standardiz-zare.

**standing, 1.** *n.* riputazione *f.* **2.** *adj.* permanènte; (**s. up**) in pièdi.

**standpoint,** *n.* punto di vista *m.*

**staple,** *n.* (fiber) fibra *f.;* (comm.) prodotto principale *m.*

**star,** *n.* stella *f.*

**starboard,** *n.* tribordo *m.*

**starch, 1.** *n.* àmido *m.* **2.** *vb.* inamidare.

**stare,** *vb.* guardare fisso.

**stark,** *adv.* completamente.

**start, 1.** *n.* inizio *m.;* (de-parture) partènza *f.;* (jump) sussulto *m.* **2.** *vb.* comin-ciare, iniziare; (depart) par-

tire; (jump) sussultare, tra-salire.

**startle,** *vb.* allarmare, far trasalire.

**starvation,** *n.* fame *f.*

**starve,** *vb.* morire di fame.

**state, 1.** *n.* stato *m.* **2.** *vb.* affermare.

**statement,** *n.* affermazione *f.;* (bank) rendiconto *m.;* (legal) deposizione *f.*

**stateroom,** *n.* cabina *f.*

**statesman,** *n.* uòmo di stato *m.*

**static,** *adj.* stàtico.

**station,** *n.* stazione *f.,* fatto-ria *f.*

**stationary,** *adj.* stazionàrio.

**stationer,** *n.* cartolaio *m.*

**stationery,** *n.* oggetti di cancelleria, *m.pl.;* (**s. store**) cartoleria *f.*

**station wagon,** *n.* giardi-netta *f.*

**statistics,** *n.* (science) sta-tistica *f.;* (data) statistiche *f.pl.*

**statue,** *n.* stàtua *f.*

**stature,** *n.* statura *f.*

**status,** *n.* condizione *f.*

**statute,** *n.* statuto *m.*

**staunch,** *adj.* fedele.

**stay, 1.** *n.* (sojourn) perma-nènza *f.;* (delay) sospensione *f.* **2.** *vb.* restare; (hold back) fermare.

**steadfast,** *adj.* saldo.

**steady,** *adj.* fermo, saldo.

**steak,** *n.* bistecca *f.*

**steal,** *vb.* rubare; (go fur-tively) andare di soppiatto.

**stealth,** *n.* (**by s.**) furtiva-mente.

**stealthily,** *adv.* di soppiatto.

**stealthy,** *adj.* furtivo.

**steam,** *n.* vapore *m.*

**steamboat,** *n.* piròscafo *m.*

**steamship,** *n.* piròscafo *m.*

**steel, 1.** *n.* acciàio *m.* **2.** *vb.* indurire.

**steel wool,** *n.* lana di acciaio *f.,* paglia di acciaio *f.*

**steep,** *adj.* èrto, rìpido, scosceso.

**steeple,** *n.* campanile *m.*

**steeplechase,** *n.* corsa ad ostàcoli *f.*

**steer,** *vb.* dirìgere.

**stellar,** *adj.* stellare.

**stem,** *n.* stelo *m.*

**stencil,** *n.* stampino *m.*

**stenographer,** *n.* stenògrafa *f.*

**stenography**, *n.* stenografia *f.*

**step, 1.** *n.* (pace) passo *m.*; (footprint) orma *f.*; (stair) gradino *m.* **2.** *vb.* camminare.

**stepfather**, *n.* patrigno *m.*

**stepmother**, *n.* matrigna *f.*

**stepladder**, *n.* scalèo *m.*

**stereotype**, *n.* stereotipia *f.*

**sterile**, *adj.* stèrile.

**sterility**, *n.* sterilità *f.*

**sterilize**, *vb.* sterilizzare.

**sterling**, *adj.* puro; (**pound s.**) sterlina *f.*

**stern, 1.** *n.* poppa *f.* **2.** *adj.* sevèro.

**stethoscope**, *n.* stetoscòpio *m.*

**stevedore**, *n.* stivatore *m.*

**stew, 1.** *n.* stufato *m.* **2.** *vb.* stufare.

**steward**, *n.* camerière *m.*

**stewardess**, *n.* (boat) camerièra *f.*; (plane) stewardess *f.*

**stick, 1.** *n.* bastone *m.*; *vb.* (adhere) aderire; (attach) appiccicare, attaccare; (shove) cacciare, ficcare.

**sticker**, *n.* etichetta *f.*

**sticky**, *adj.* attaccatìccio, viscoso.

**stiff**, *adj.* rìgido.

**stiffen**, *vb.* irrigidire, *tr.*

**stiffness**, *n.* rigidezza *f.*

**stifle**, *vb.* soffocare.

**stigma**, *n.* stigma *m.*

**stigmata**, *n.* stimmate *f.pl.*

**still, 1.** *n.* alambicco *m.* **2.** *adj.* calmo. **3.** *vb.* calmare. **4.** *adv.* ancora.

**still-born**, *adj.* nato mòrto.

**still life**, *n.* natura mòrta *f.*

**stillness**, *n.* quiète *f.*, calma *f.*

**stilted**, *adj.* ampolloso.

**stimulant**, *n. and adj.* stimolante (*m.*)

**stimulate**, *vb.* stimolare.

**stimulus**, *n.* stìmolo *m.*

**sting, 1.** *n.* (body-part) pungiglione *m.*; (wound) puntura *f.* **1.** *vb.* pùngere.

**stingy**, *adj.* avaro, tìrchio.

**stipulate**, *vb.* stipulare.

**stir, 1.** *n.* agitazione *f.*, commozione *f.* **2.** *vb.* agitare, *tr.*, muòvere, *tr.*

**stitch, 1.** *n.* punto *m.* **2.** *vb.* cucire.

**stock, 1.** *n.* (supply) provvista *f.*; (lineage) stirpe *f.*; (animals) bestiame *m.*; (of

gun) càlcio *m.*; (financial) azioni *f.* **2.** *vb.* tenere in magazzino.

**stockbroker**, *n.* agènte di càmbio *m.*

**stock exchange**, *n.* borsa *f.*

**stockholder**, *n.* azionista *m.*

**Stockholm**, *n.* Stoccolma *f.*

**stocking**, *n.* calza *f.*

**stockyard**, *n.* mattatòio *m.*

**stodgy**, *adj.* ottuso.

**stoic**, *n.* stòico *m.*

**stoical**, *adj.* stòico.

**stole**, *n.* stòla *f.*

**stolid**, *adj.* stòlido.

**stomach, 1.** *n.* stòmaco *m.* **2.** *vb.* tollerare.

**stone, 1.** *n.* piètra *f.*, sasso *m.* **2.** *vb.* lapidare.

**stool**, *n.* sgabèllo *m.*

**stoop**, *vb.* curvarsi; (demean oneself) abbassarsi.

**stooped**, *adj.* curvo.

**stop, 1.** *n.* fermata *f.* **2.** *vb.* fermare, *tr.*; (close) otturare; (cease) tappare; (cease) sméttere; (cease moving) sostare.

**stopgap**, *n.* temporàneo *m.*

**stop-over**, *n.* fermata intermèdia *f.*

**stopper**, *n.* tappo *m.*

**stopping**, *n.* sosta *f.*

**storage**, *n.* magazzinàggio *m.*

**store, 1.** *n.* negòzio *m.*; (supply) provvista *f.* **2.** *vb.* immagazzinare, conservare; (fill) riempire.

**storehouse**, *n.* magazzino *m.*

**storm**, *n.* tempèsta *f.*

**stormy**, *adj.* tempestoso.

**story**, *n.* racconto *m.*, stòria *f.*

**stout**, *adj.* grasso; (strong) fòrte.

**stove**, *n.* fornèllo *m.*, stufa *f.*

**straight, 1.** *adj.* diritto, rètto. **2.** *adv.* direttamente, diritto.

**straight-away**, *n.* rettilìneo *m.*

**straighten**, *vb.* raddrizzare.

**straightforward**, *adj.* franco.

**strain, 1.** *n.* tensione *f.* **2.** *vb.* sforzare, *tr.*; (filter) colare.

**strainer**, *n.* colino *m.*

**strait**, *n.* stretto *m.*

**strand, 1.** *n.* riva *f.* **2.** *vb.* arenarsi.

**strange**, *adj.* strano; (foreign) stranièro.

**stranger**, *n.* stranièro *m.*

**strangle,** *vb.* strangolare.

**strap,** *n.* cìnghia *f.*

**stratagem,** *n.* stratagèmma *m.*

**strategic,** *adj.* stratègico.

**strategy,** *n.* strategìa *f.*

**stratosphere,** *n.* stratosfèra *f.*

**stratum,** *n.* strato *m.*

**straw,** *n.* pàglia *f.;* (for drinking) cannùccia di pàglia *f.*

**strawberry,** *n.* fràgola *f.*

**stray, 1.** *adj.* smarrito *f.* **2.** *vb.* allontanarsi.

**streak,** *n.* strìa *f.*

**stream,** *n.* corrènte *f.,* fiòtto *m.*

**streamlined,** *adj.* aerodinàmico.

**street,** *n.* vìa *f.,* strada *f.*

**strength,** *n.* fòrza *f.*

**streetcar,** *n.* tram *m.*

**strengthen,** *vb.* rafforzare.

**strenuous,** *adj.* strènuo.

**streptococcus,** *n.* streptocòcco *m.*

**stress, 1.** *n.* sfòrzo *m.;* (accent) accènto *m.* **2.** *vb.* accentare.

**stretch, 1.** *n.* tratto *m.* **2.** *vb.* tèndere.

**stretcher,** *n.* barèlla *f.*

**strew,** *vb.* cospàrgere.

**stricken,** *adj.* colpito.

**strict,** *adj.* sevèro.

**stride, 1.** *n.* passo lungo *m.* **2.** *vb.* camminare a passi lunghi.

**strident,** *adj.* stridulo.

**strife,** *n.* conflitto *m.*

**strike, 1.** *n.* (workers') sciòpero *m.* **2.** *vb.* scioperare; (hit) colpire.

**strike-breaker,** *n.* crumiro *m.*

**string, 1.** *n.* filo *m.,* còrda *f.* **2.** *vb.* infilare.

**string bean,** *n.* fagiòlo *m.*

**stringent,** *adj.* rigoroso.

**strip, 1.** *n.* striscia *f.* **2.** *vb.* spogliare, *tr.*

**stripe,** *n.* lista *f.,* striscia *f.*

**strive,** *vb.* sforzarsi.

**stroke, 1.** *n.* colpo *m.* **2.** *vb.* accarezzare.

**stroll, 1.** *n.* passeggiata *f.* **2.** *vb.* passeggiare.

**stroller,** *n.* passeggiatore *m.*

**strong,** *adj.* fòrte.

**stronghold,** *n.* roccafòrte *f.*

**structure,** *n.* struttura *f.*

---

**struggle, 1.** *n.* lotta *f.* **2.** *vb.* lottare.

**strut,** *vb.* pavoneggiarsi.

**stub,** *n.* mozzicone *m.;* (check-book) madre *f.*

**stubborn,** *adj.* testardo.

**stucco,** *n.* stucco *m.*

**student,** *n.* studènte *m.,* studentessa *f.*

**studious,** *adj.* studioso.

**study, 1.** *n.* stùdio *m.* **2.** *vb.* studiare.

**stuff, 1.** *n.* (cloth) stoffa *f.;* (junk) ròba *f.* **2.** *vb.* rimpinzare, imbottire; (food) infarcire.

**stuffed,** *adj.* ripieno.

**stuffing,** *n.* ripièno *m.*

**stumble,** *vb.* inciampare.

**stump,** *n.* (tree) ceppo *m.;* (arm, leg) moncone *m.*

**stun,** *vb.* stordire.

**stunt,** *n.* impresa fuòri del consuèto *f.*

**stupendous,** *adj.* stupèndo.

**stupid,** *adj.* stùpido.

**stupidity,** *n.* stupidità *f.*

**stupor,** *n.* stupore *m.*

**sturdy,** *adj.* gagliardo.

**stutter,** *vb.* tartagliare.

**Stuttgart,** *n.* Stoccarda *f.*

**sty,** *n.* porcile *m.;* (eye) orzaiòlo *m.*

**style,** *n.* stile *m.*

**stylish,** *adj.* di mòda.

**suave,** *adj.* blando.

**subconscious,** *adj.* subcosciènte.

**subdue,** *vb.* soggiogare.

**subject, 1.** *n.* soggètto *m.;* (of king) suddito *m.* **2.** *adj.* soggètto. **3.** *vb.* sottoporre, assoggettare.

**subjugate,** *vb.* soggiogare.

**subjunctive,** *n. and adj.* congiuntivo (*m.*)

**sublimate, 1.** *n. and adj.* sublimato (*m.*) **2.** *vb.* sublimare.

**sublime,** *adj.* sublime.

**submarine, 1.** *n.* sommergìbile *m.* **2.** *adj.* sottomarino.

**submerge,** *vb.* sommèrgere.

**submersion,** *n.* sommersione *f.*

**submission,** *n.* sottomissione *f.*

**submit,** *vb.* sottomèttere, *tr.*

**subnormal,** *adj.* subnormale.

**subordinate,** *n. and adj.*
subordinato (*m.*)

**subscribe,** *vb.* (write name)
sottoscrivere; (take regularly) abbonarsi; (agree with) aderire.

**subscription,** *n.* abbonamento *m.*

**subsequent,** *adj.* successivo.

**subservient,** *adj.* servile.

**subside,** *vb.* diminuire; (building) sprofondarsi; (earth) cédere; (water) abbassarsi.

**subsidy,** *n.* sussìdio *m.*

**substance,** *n.* sostanza *f.*

**substantial,** *adj.* sostanziale.

**substitute,** **1.** *n.* sostituto *m.* **2.** *vb.* sostituire.

**substitution,** *n.* sostituzione *f.*

**subterfuge,** *n.* sotterfùgio *m.*

**subtle,** *adj.* sottile.

**subtract,** *vb.* sottrarre.

**suburb,** *n.* sobborgo *m.*

**subvention,** *n.* sovvenzione *f.*

**subversive,** *adj.* sovversivo.

**subvert,** *vb.* sovvertire.

**subway,** *n.* metropolitana *f.*

**succeed,** *vb.* (come after) succédere a; (be successful) riuscire.

**success,** *n.* successo *m.*; riuscita *f.*

**successful,** *adj.* riuscito.

**succession,** *n.* successione *f.*, sèrie *f.*

**successive,** *adj.* successivo.

**successor,** *n.* successore *m.*

**succor,** **1.** *n.* soccorso *m.* **2.** *vb.* soccórrere.

**succumb,** *vb.* soccómbere.

**such,** *adj.* tale.

**suck,** *vb.* succhiare.

**suction,** *n.* aspirazione *f.*

**sudden,** *adj.* improvviso.

**suds,** *n.* schiuma *f.*

**sue,** *vb.* citare in giudizio.

**suffer,** *vb.* soffrire.

**suffice,** *vb.* bastare.

**sufficient,** *adj.* sufficiènte.

**suffocate,** *vb.* soffocare.

**sugar,** *n.* zùcchero *m.*

**suggest,** *vb.* suggerire.

**suggestion,** *n.* suggerimento *m.*

**suicide,** *n.* suicidio *m.*; (commit s.) suicidarsi.

**suit,** **1.** *n.* (clothes) àbito *m.*; (cards) colore *m.*; (request) domanda *f.*; (law)

càusa *f.* **2.** *vb.* convenire a, andar bène a.

**suitable,** *adj.* conveniènte.

**suitcase,** *n.* valìgia *f.*

**suite,** *n.* sèrie *f.*; (followers) sèguito *m.*; (music) suite *f.*

**suitor,** *n.* corteggiatore *m.*

**sullen,** *adj.* cupo.

**sultana raisin,** *n.* uva sultanina *f.*

**sum,** **1.** *n.* somma *f.* **2.** *vb.* sommare; (**s. up**) riassùmere.

**summarize,** *vb.* riassùmere.

**summary,** *n. and adj.* sommàrio (*m.*)

**summer,** **1.** *n.* estate *f.* **2.** *adj.* estivo.

**summit,** *n.* sommità *f.*, cima *f.*, vetta *f.*

**summon,** *vb.* chiamare, citare.

**summons,** *n.* chiamata *f.*; (court) citazione *f.*

**sumptuous,** *adj.* sontuoso.

**sun,** *n.* sole *m.*

**sunburn,** *n.* abbronzatura *f.*

**sunburned,** *adj.* abbronzato.

**Sunday,** *n.* doménica *f.*

**sunken,** *adj.* infossato.

**sunny,** *adj.* solatio.

**sunshine,** *n.* sole *m.*

**superb,** *adj.* supèrbo.

**superficial,** *adj.* superficiale.

**superfluous,** *adj.* supèrfluo.

**super-highway,** *n.* autostrada *f.*

**superhuman,** *adj.* sovrumano.

**superintendent,** *n.* sovrintendènte *m.*

**superior,** *adj.* superiore.

**superiority,** *n.* superiorità *f.*

**superlative,** *n. and adj.* superlativo (*m.*)

**superman,** *n.* superuòmo *m.*

**supernatural,** *adj.* soprannaturale.

**supersede,** *vb.* soppiantare.

**superstition,** *n.* superstizione *f.*

**superstitious,** *adj.* superstizioso.

**supervise,** *vb.* sorvegliare.

**supper,** *n.* cena *f.*

**supplant,** *vb.* soppiantare.

**supplement,** *n.* supplemento *m.*

**supply,** **1.** *n.* fornitura *f.*, provvista *f.* **2.** *vb.* fornire, provvedere.

**support,** **1.** *n.* sostegno *m.* **2.** *vb.* appoggiare, sostenere.

**suppose,** *vb.* supporre.
**suppress,** *vb.* sopprimere.
**suppression,** *n.* soppressione *f.*
**supreme,** *adj.* suprèmo.
**sure,** *adj.* sicuro.
**surely,** *adv.* sicuramente.
**surety,** *n.* sicurezza *f.*
**surf,** *n.* frangènti *m.pl.*
**surface,** *n.* superfície *f.*
**surge,** *vb.* ondare.
**surgeon,** *n.* chirurgo *m.*
**surgery,** *n.* chirurgia *f.*
**surmise, 1.** *n.* congettura *f.* **2.** *vb.* congetturare.
**surmount,** *vb.* sormontare.
**surname,** *n.* cognome *m.*
**surpass,** *vb.* sorpassare.
**surplus,** *n.* avanzo *m.*
**surprise, 1.** *n.* sorpresa *f.* **2.** *vb.* sorprèndere.
**surrender,** *vb.* (hand over) cédere; (yield) arrèndersi.
**surround,** *vb.* circondare.
**surroundings,** *n.* dintorni *m.pl.*
**surveillance,** *n.* sorveglianza *f.*
**survey, 1.** *n.* esame *m.;* (geographical) rilevamento *m.* **2.** *vb.* esaminare.
**surveyor,** *n.* agrimensore *m.*
**survival,** *n.* sopravvivènza *f.*
**survive,** *vb.* sopravvivere.
**susceptible,** *adj.* suscettìbile.
**suspect, 1.** *adj.* sospètto. **2.** *vb.* sospettare.
**suspend,** *vb.* sospèndere.
**suspense,** *n.* incertezza *f.*
**suspension,** *n.* sospensione *f.*
**suspension bridge,** *n.* ponte sospeso *m.*
**suspicion,** *n.* sospètto *m.*
**suspicious,** *adj.* sospettoso; (questionable) sospètto.
**sustain,** *vb.* sostenere.
**swallow, 1.** *n.* (bird) róndine *f.;* (food) boccone *m.;* (drink) sorso *m.* **2.** *vb.* inghiottire.
**swamp, 1.** *n.* palude *f.* **2.** *vb.* inondare.
**swan,** *n.* cigno *m.*
**swap, 1.** *n.* baratto *m.* **2.** *vb.* barattare.
**swarm, 1.** *n.* sciame *m.* **2.** *vb.* sciamare; (be crowded) formicolare.
**sway,** *vb.* oscillare; (influence) dominare.
**swear,** *vb.* giurare; (curse) bestemmiare; (s.-word) be- stémmia *f.*

**sweat, 1.** *n.* sudore *m.* **2.** *vb.* sudare.
**sweater,** *n.* golf *m.*
**Swede,** *n.* svedese *m.*
**Sweden,** *n.* Svèzia *f.*
**Swedish,** *adj.* svedese.
**sweep,** *vb.* spazzare.
**sweet,** *adj.* dolce.
**sweetheart,** *n.* innamorato *m.,* innamorata *f.*
**sweetness,** *n.* dolcezza *f.*
**swell, 1.** *adj.* magnìfico. **2.** *vb.* gonfiare, *tr.*
**swelter,** *vb.* sudare.
**swift,** *adj.* veloce.
**swim,** *vb.* nuotare.
**swindle,** *vb.* truffare.
**swindler,** *n.* truffatore *m.*
**swine,** *n.* pòrco *m.*
**swing, 1.** *n.* (children's) altalena *f.* **2.** *vb.* dòndolare, penzolare.
**swirl,** *vb.* turbinare.
**Swiss,** *adj.* svìzzero.
**switch, 1.** *n.* (rod) verga *f.;* (railway) scàmbio *m.;* (electric) interruttore *m.* **2.** *vb.* (whip) sferzare; (s. on) accèndere; (s. off) spègnere.
**switchboard,** *n.* centralino *m.*
**Switzerland,** *vb.* Svìzzera *f.*
**sword,** *n.* spada *f.*
**sword-fish,** *n.* pesce spada *m.*
**syllable,** *n.* sìllaba *f.*
**symbol,** *n.* sìmbolo *m.*
**symbolic,** *adj.* simbòlico.
**sympathetic,** *adj.* sensìbile.
**sympathize,** *vb.* simpatiz- zare.
**sympathy,** *n.* simpatìa *f.*
**symphonic,** *adj.* sinfònico.
**symphony,** *n.* sinfonìa *f.;* (s. orchestra) orchèstra sinfònica *f.*
**symptom,** *n.* sìntomo *m.*
**symptomatic,** *adj.* sinto- màtico.
**synchronous,** *adj.* sìncrono.
**synchronize,** *vb.* sincroniz- zare.
**syndicate,** *n.* consòrzio *m.*
**synonym,** *n.* sinònimo *m.*
**synonymous,** *adj.* sinònimo.
**synthesis,** *n.* sìntesi *f.*
**synthetic,** *adj.* sintètico.
**syphilis,** *n.* sìfilide *f.*
**syphilitic,** *adj.* sifilìtico.
**syringe,** *n.* siringa *f.*
**syrup,** *n.* sciròppo *m.*
**system,** *n.* sistèma *m.*
**systematic,** *adj.* sistemàtico.

# T

**tabernacle,** *n.* tabernàcolo *m.*

**table,** *n.* tàvola *f.*

**tablecloth,** *n.* tovàglia *f.*

**tablespoon,** *n.* cucchiaio *m.*

**tablespoonful,** *n.* cucchiaiata *f.*

**tablet,** *n.* tavoletta *f.;* (pastille) pasticca *f.*

**tack,** **1.** *n.* bulletta *f.* **2.** *vb.* attaccare; (turn) virare.

**tact,** *n.* tatto *m.*

**tag,** *n.* etichetta *f.*

**tail,** *n.* coda *f.*

**tailor,** *n.* sarto *m.*

**take,** *vb.* prèndere; (carry) portare; (lead) condurre.

**tale,** *n.* racconto *m.*

**talent,** *n.* talènto *m.*

**talk,** **1.** *n.* discorso *m.* **2.** *vb.* parlare.

**talkative,** *adj.* loquace.

**tall,** *adj.* alto.

**tallow,** *n.* sego *m.*

**tame,** **1.** *adj.* addomesticato, mansuèto. **2.** *vb.* addomesticare, domare.

**tamper,** *vb.* immischiarsi.

**tan,** **1.** *n.* (sun) abbronzatura *f.* **2.** *adj.* castagno. **3.** *vb.* abbronzare; (leather) conciare.

**tangible,** *adj.* tangìbile.

**tangle,** **1.** *n.* garbùglio *m.* **2.** *vb.* ingarbugliare.

**tank,** *n.* serbatòio *m.;* (armored vehicle) carro armato *m.*

**tap,** **1.** *n.* (blow) colpetto *m.;* (faucet) rubinetto *m.* **2.** *vb.* percuòtere.

**tape,** *n.* nastro *m.*

**tape recorder,** *n.* magnetòfono *m.*, registratore magnètico *m.*

**tapestry,** *n.* tappezzerìa *f.*

**tar,** **1.** *n.* catrame *m.* **2.** *vb.* incatramare.

**target,** *n.* bersàglio *m.*

**tariff,** *n.* tariffa *f.*

**tarnish,** **1.** *n.* appannatura *f.* **2.** *vb.* appannare, *tr.*

**tart,** **1.** *n.* tòrta *f.;* (harlot) puttana *f.* **2.** *adj.* acre.

**task,** *n.* còmpito *m.*, incàrico *m.*

**taste,** **1.** *n.* gusto *m.* **2.** *vb.* gustare.

**tasty,** *adj.* gustoso, saporito, saporoso.

**taunt,** *vb.* schernire.

**taut,** *adj.* teso.

**tavern,** *n.* osterìa *f.*, tavèrna *f.*

**tax,** *n.* imposta *f.*, tassa *f.*

**taxi,** *n.* tassì *m.*

**taxpayer,** *n.* contribuènte *m.*

**tea,** *n.* thè (tè) *m.*

**teach,** *vb.* insegnare.

**teacher,** *n.* insegnante *m.* or *f.*, maestro *m.*, maestra *f.*

**team,** *n.* squadra *f.*

**tea-pot,** *n.* teièra *f.*

**tear,** **1.** *n.* làgrima *f.* **2.** *vb.* strappare.

**tease,** *vb.* tormentare.

**teaspoon,** *n.* cucchiaino da thè *m.*

**technical,** *adj.* tècnico.

**technique,** *n.* tècnica *f.*

**tedious,** *adj.* tedioso.

**tedium,** *n.* tèdio *m.*

**telegram,** *n.* telegramma *m.*

**telegraph,** **1.** *n.* telègrafo *m.* **2.** *vb.* telegrafare.

**telephone,** **1.** *n.* telèfono *m.;* (t.-call) telefonata *f.* **2.** *vb.* telefonare.

**telescope,** *n.* telescòpio *m.*

**teletype,** *n.* telescrivènte *f.*

**televise,** *vb.* trasmettere per televisione.

**television,** *n.* televisione *f.;* (t. screen) teleschermo *m.;* (t. set) televisore *m.*

**tell,** *vb.* raccontare.

**teller,** *n.* cassière *m.*

**temper,** **1.** *n.* (anger) còllera *f.* **2.** *vb.* temperare.

**temperament,** *n.* temperamento *m.*

**temperamental,** *adj.* capriccioso.

**temperance,** *n.* temperanza *f.*

**temperate,** *adj.* temperato.

**temperature,** *n.* temperatura *f.*

**tempest,** *n.* tempèsta *f.*

**tempestuous,** *adj.* tempestoso.

**temple**, *n.* tèmpio *m.*; (forehead) tèmpia *f.*

**temporary**, *adj.* provvisòrio.

**tempt**, *vb.* tentare.

**temptation**, *n.* tentazione *f.*

**ten**, *num.* dièci.

**tenant**, *n.* inquilino *m.*

**tend**, *vb.* tèndere; (care for) curare.

**tendency**, *n.* tendènza *f.*

**tender**, 1. *n.* carro di scòrta *m.* 2. *adj.* tènero. 3. *vb.* offrire.

**tenderly**, *adv.* teneramente.

**tenderness**, *n.* tenerezza *f.*

**tendon**, *n.* tèndine *m.*

**tennis**, *n.* tènnis *m.*

**tenor**, *n.* tenore *m.*

**tense**, *adj.* teso.

**tension**, *n.* tensione *f.*

**tent**, *n.* tènda *f.*

**tentative**, 1. *n.* tentativo *m.* 2. *adj.* sperimentale, tentativo.

**tenth**, *adj.* dècimo.

**term**, *n.* perìodo *m.*; (school) trimèstre *m.*

**terminal**, *adj.* terminale.

**terminate**, *vb.* terminare.

**terminus**, *n.* capolìnea *m.*, tèrmine *m.*

**terrace**, *n.* terrazza *f.*

**terrible**, *adj.* terrìbile.

**terribly**, *adv.* terribilmente.

**terrify**, *vb.* atterrire.

**territory**, *n.* territòrio *m.*

**terror**, *n.* terrore *m.*

**test**, 1. *n.* pròva *f.* 2. *vb.* provare, collaudare.

**testament**, *n.* testamento *m.*

**testify**, *vb.* testimoniare.

**testimony**, *n.* testimonianza *f.*

**text**, *n.* tèsto *m.*

**textile**, 1. *n.* tessuto *m.* 2. *adj.* tèssile.

**texture**, *n.* tessitura *f.*

**than**, *prep.* (before nouns, pronouns) di; (elsewhere) che.

**thank**, *vb.* ringraziare.

**thankful**, *adj.* grato.

**that**, 1. *adj.* quel, quello, quella. 2. *pron.* quello, quella. 3. *conj.* che.

**the**, *def. art.* il, lo, la, l'; i, gli, gli, le.

**theater**, *n.* teatro *m.*

**thee**, *pron.* te, ti.

**theft**, *n.* furto *m.*

**their**, *adj.* loro.

**theirs**, *pron.* loro.

**them**, *pron.* li, le; loro.

**theme**, *n.* tèma *m.*

**themselves**, *pron.* si, sè; essi stessi.

**then**, *adv.* (at that time) allora; (therefore) dunque; (afterward) pòi.

**thence**, *adv.* di là.

**theologian**, *n.* teòlogo *m.*

**theology**, *n.* teologìa *f.*

**theoretical**, *adj.* teòrico.

**theory**, *n.* teorìa *f.*

**therapy**, *n.* terapìa *f.*

**there**, *adv.* lì, là; ci, vi.

**therefore**, *adv.* perciò.

**thermometer**, *n.* termòmetro *m.*

**these**, *adj. and pron.* questi *m.pl.*, queste *f.pl.*

**they**, *pron.* loro; essi *m.pl.*; esse *f.pl.*

**thick**, *adj.* spesso, folto, dènso, fitto.

**thicken**, *vb.* infoltire, condensare.

**thickness**, *n.* spessore *m.*

**thief**, *n.* ladro *m.*

**thigh**, *n.* còscia *f.*

**thimble**, *n.* ditale *m.*

**thin**, *adj.* sottile; (meager) magro.

**thing**, *n.* còsa *f.*

**thingumajig**, *n.* còso *m.*

**think**, *vb.* pensare.

**thinker**, *n.* pensatore *m.*

**third**, *adj.* tèrzo.

**thirst**, *n.* sete *f.*

**thirsty**, *adj.*; (be t.) aver sete.

**thirteen**, *num.* trédici.

**thirteenth**, *adj.* tredicésimo, dècimotèrzo.

**thirtieth**, *adj.* trentésimo.

**thirty**, *num.* trenta.

**this**, *adj. and pron.* questo *m.sg.*, questa *f.sg.*; (this man) questi *pron.m.sg.*

**thorough**, *adj.* complèto.

**those**, 1. *adj.* quei, quegli *m.pl.*; quelle *f.pl.* 2. *pron.* quelli *m.pl.*; quelle *f.pl.*

**thou**, *pron.* tu.

**though**, 1. *adv.* però. 2. *conj.* sebbène.

**thought**, *n.* pensièro *m.*

**thoughtful**, *adj.* pensoso; (careful) attènto.

**thousand**, *num.* mille.

**thread**, 1. *n.* filo *m.* 2. *vb.* infilare.

**threat**, *n.* minàccia *f.*

**threaten**, *vb.* minacciare.

**three**, *num.* tre.

**thrift**, n. economìa f.

**thrill**, n. frèmito m.

**thrive**, vb. prosperare.

**throat**, n. gola f.

**throne**, n. tròno m.

**through, 1.** adj. (direct) dirètto. **2.** prep. per, attravèrso; (**go t., pass t.**) attraversare.

**throughout**, adv. dappertutto, completamente.

**throw**, vb. gettare, lanciare, buttare.

**thrust, 1.** n. spinta f. **2.** vb. spìngere.

**thumb**, n. pòllice m.

**thunder, 1.** n. tuòno m. **2.** vb. tuonare.

**Thursday**, n. giovedì m.

**thus**, adv. così.

**thwart**, vb. frustrare.

**thy**, adj. tuo.

**ticket**, n. biglietto m.

**tickle**, vb. solleticare.

**ticklish**, adj. delicato.

**tide**, n. marèa f.

**tidy, 1.** adj. ordinato. **2.** vb. ordinare.

**tie, 1.** n. (bond) legame m.; (neck-tie) cravatta f. **2.** vb. legare; (make equal score) èssere pari con.

**tier**, n. fila f.

**tiger**, n. tigre m.

**tight**, adj. stretto, teso; (drunk) ubriaco.

**tighten**, vb. stríngere.

**tile**, n. tègola f.

**till, 1.** n. cassetto m. **2.** vb. coltivare. **3.** prep. fino a; sino a. **4.** conj. finché.

**tilt, 1.** n. inclinazione f. **2.** vb. inclinare.

**timber**, n. legname m.

**time**, n. tèmpo m.; (o'clock) ora f.; (occasion) vòlta f.

**timetable**, n. oràrio m.

**timid**, adj. tìmido.

**timidity**, n. timidezza f.

**timidly**, adv. timidamente.

**tin**, n. stagno m.; (metal can) latta f.

**tint**, n. tinta f.

**tiny**, adj. minùscolo.

**tip, 1.** n. (end) punta f.; (reward) mància f. **2.** vb. (tilt) inclinare; (give money to) dare una mància a.

**tire, 1.** n. pneumàtico m. **2.** vb. stancare.

**tired**, adj. stanco.

**tissue**, n. tessuto m.; (facial) fazzoletti detergenti m.pl.

**title**, n. tìtolo m.

**to**, prep. a, ad (before a and, optionally, before other vowels).

**toast, 1.** n. pane abbrustolito m.; (health) brìndisi m. **2.** vb. abbrustolire; (drink health) brindare.

**tobacco**, n. tabacco m.

**today**, n. and adv. òggi (m.).

**toe**, n. dito del piède m.; (**big t.**) pòllice m.

**together**, adv. insième.

**toil, 1.** n. fatica f. **2.** vb. faticare.

**toilet**, n. latrina f., gabinetto m.

**token**, n. segno m.; (metal) gettone m.

**tolerance**, n. tolleranza f.

**tolerant**, adj. tollerante.

**tolerate**, vb. tollerare.

**tomato**, n. pomodoro m.

**tomb**, n. tomba f.

**tomorrow**, n. and adv. domani (m.).

**ton**, n. tonnellata f.

**tone**, n. tòno m.

**tongue**, n. lingua f.

**tonic**, n. and adj. tònico (m.); (music) tònica f.

**tonight**, adv. stasera.

**tonsil**, n. tonsilla f.

**too**, adv. (also) anche; (excessively) troppo.

**tool**, n. utensile m.

**too many, too much**, adj. troppo.

**totter**, vb. barcollare.

**tooth**, n. dènte m.

**toothache**, n. mal di denti m.

**toothbrush**, n. spazzolino per i denti m.

**top, 1.** n. sommità f. **2.** vb. superare.

**topcoat**, n. sopràbito m.

**topic**, n. argomento m.

**topical**, adj. d'attualità.

**topsy-turvy**, adv. sottosopra.

**torch**, n. fiàccola f.

**torment, 1.** n. tormento m. **2.** vb. tormentare.

**torrent**, n. torrènte m.

**torture, 1.** n. tortura f. **2.** vb. torturare.

**toss**, vb. buttare, agitare, tr.

**total**, n. and adj. totale m.

**totalitarian**, adj. totalitàrio.

**touch, 1.** n. tocco m. **2.** vb. toccare.

**tough**, adj. (meat) tiglioso; (hard) difficile.

**tour, 1.** *n.* viàggio *m.* **2.** *vb.* viaggiare.

**touring, tourism,** *n.* turismo *m.*

**tourist,** *n.* **1.** *n.* turista *m. or f.* **2.** *adj.* turìstico.

**tournament,** *n.* concorso *m.*

**tow,** *vb.* rimorchiare.

**toward,** *prep.* vèrso.

**towel,** *n.* asciugatòio *m.*; **(hand-t.)** asciugamani *m.*

**tower,** *n.* torre *f.*

**town,** *n.* città *f.*; **(small t.)** cittadina *f.*

**toy, 1.** *n.* giocàttolo *m.*, trastullo *m.* **2.** *vb.* trastullarsi.

**trace, 1.** *n.* tràccia *f.* **2.** *vb.* rintracciare.

**track,** *n.* binàrio *m.*; **(for running)** pista *f.*

**tract,** *n.* tratto *m.*

**tractor,** *n.* trattrice *f.*

**trade, 1.** *n.* commèrcio *m.* **2.** *vb.* commerciare.

**trader,** *n.* commerciante *m.*

**tradition,** *n.* tradizione *f.*

**traditional,** *adj.* tradizionale.

**traffic,** *n.* tràffico *m.*

**trafficator,** *n.* fréccia *f.*

**traffic light,** *n.* semàforo *m.*

**tragedy,** *n.* tragèdia *f.*

**tragic,** *adj.* tràgico.

**trail,** *n.* sentièro *m.*

**trailer,** *n.* rimòrchio *m.*; **(house-t.)** carovana *f.*; **(t. truck)** autotreno *m.*

**train, 1.** *n.* treno *m.* **2.** *vb.* allenare.

**traitor,** *n.* traditore *m.*

**tram,** *n.* tram *m.*

**tramway, 1.** *n.* tranvìa *f.* **2.** *adj.* tranviàrio.

**tramp,** *n.* vagabondo *m.*

**tranquil,** *adj.* tranquillo.

**tranquillity,** *n.* tranquillità *f.*

**transaction,** *n.* operazione *f.*

**transfer, 1.** *n.* trasferimento *m.* **2.** *vb.* trasferire.

**transfix,** *vb.* trafìggere.

**transform,** *vb.* trasformare.

**transfusion,** *n.* trasfusione *f.*

**transition,** *n.* transizione *f.*

**translate,** *vb.* tradurre.

**translation,** *n.* traduzione *f.*

**transmit,** *vb.* trasméttere.

**transparent,** *adj.* trasparènte.

**transport, 1.** *n.* traspòrto *m.* **2.** *vb.* trasportare.

**transportation,** *n.* traspòrto *m.*

**trap,** *n.* tràppola *f.*

**trash,** *n.* cianfrusàglia *f.*

**travel, 1.** *n.* viàggio *m.*; **t. agency,** agenzia viaggi *f.* **2.** *vb.* viaggiare.

**traveler,** *n.* viaggiatore *m.*

**tray,** *n.* vassòio *m.*

**treacherous,** *adj.* proditòrio; **(deceptive)** ingannévole.

**tread, 1.** *n.* passo *m.* **2.** *vb.* calpestare.

**treason,** *n.* tradimento *m.*

**treasure,** *n.* tesòro *m.*

**treasurer,** *n.* tesorière *m.*

**treasury,** *n.* tesòro *m.*

**treat,** *vb.* trattare.

**treatise,** *n.* trattato *m.*

**treatment,** *n.* trattamento *m.*

**treaty,** *n.* trattato *m.*

**tree,** *n.* àlbero *m.*

**tremble,** *vb.* tremare.

**tremendous,** *adj.* tremèndo.

**trench,** *n.* trincèa *f.*

**trend,** *n.* tendènza *f.*

**trespass,** *n.* violazione di confine *f.*

**trial,** *n.* pròva *f.*; **(law)** procèsso *m.*

**triangle,** *n.* triàngolo *m.*

**tribulation,** *n.* tribolazione *f.*

**tributary,** *n. and adj.* tributàrio (*m.*); **(river)** affluènte *m.*

**tribute,** *n.* tributo *m.*

**trick, 1.** *n.* tiro *m.*; trucco *m.* **2.** *vb.* ingannare.

**tricky,** *adj.* ingannévole.

**trifle,** *n.* bazzècola *f.*

**trigger,** *n.* grilletto *m.*

**trim, 1.** *adj.* ordinato. **2.** *vb.* **(clip)** cimare; **(make neat)** ordinare.

**trinket,** *n.* nìnnolo *m.*

**trip, 1.** *n.* viàggio *m.* **2.** *vb.* incespicare.

**triple,** *adj.* trìplice. **2.** *vb.* triplicare, *tr.*

**trite,** *adj.* trito.

**triumph, 1.** *n.* trionfo *m.* **2.** *vb.* trionfare.

**triumphal,** *adj.* trionfale.

**triumphant,** *adj.* trionfante.

**trivial,** *adj.* meschino.

**trolley-bus,** *n.* filobus *m.*; **(t.-b. line)** filovia *f.*

**trolley-car,** *n.* tram *m.*

**troop,** *n.* truppa *f.*

**trophy,** *n.* trofèo *m.*

**tropic,** *n.* tròpico *m.*

**tropical,** *adj.* tròpico.

**trot, 1.** *n.* tròtto *m.* **2.** *vb.* trottare.

**trouble, 1.** *n.* guaio *m.*; **(jam)** impìccio *m.*; **(bother)**

disturbo *m.*; fastidio *m.* **2.** *vb.* disturbare, infastidire.

**troublesome,** *adj.* fastidioso.

**trough,** *n.* trògolo *m.*

**trousers,** *n.* calzoni *m.pl.*

**trousseau,** *n.* corredo nuziale *m.*

**trout,** *n.* tròta *f.*

**truce,** *n.* trégua *f.*

**truck,** *n.* camione *m.*, autocarro *m.*

**true,** *adj.* vero; (loyal) fedele.

**truly,** *adv.* veramente; (**yours t.**) Vostro devmo.

**trumpet,** *n.* tromba *f.*

**trumpeter,** *n.* trombettière *m.*

**trunk,** *n.* (tree) tronco *m.*; (luggage) baùle *m.*

**trust,** *n.* fidùcia *f.*; (comm.) consòrzio *m.*

**trustworthy,** *adj.* fededegno.

**truth,** *n.* verità *f.*

**truthful,** *adj.* verídico.

**try,** *vb.* provare, tentare.

**tryst,** *n.* appuntamento *m.*

**tub,** *n.* vasca *f.*

**tube,** *n.* tubo *m.*; (radio) vàlvola *f.*

**tuberculosis,** *n.* tuberculòsi *f.*

**tuck, 1.** *n.* pièga *f.* **2.** *vb.* rimboccare.

**Tuesday,** *n.* martedì *m.*

**tuft,** *n.* ciuffo *m.*

**tug,** *vb.* tirare.

**tug-boat,** *n.* rimorchiatore *m.*

**tuition,** *n.* (fee) tassa scolàstica *f.*

**tulip,** *n.* tulipano *m.*

**tumble, 1.** *n.* capitómbolo *m.* **2.** *vb.* capitombolare.

**tumor,** *n.* tumore *m.*

**tumult,** *n.* tumulto *m.*

**tuna,** *n.* tonno *m.*

**tune, 1.** *n.* melodìa *f.* **2.** *vb.* accordare; (**t. in**) sintonizzare.

**tuneful,** *adj.* melodioso.

**tunnel, 1.** *n.* gallerìa *f.*, traforo *m.* **2.** *vb.* traforare.

**turban,** *n.* turbante *m.*

**turbine,** *n.* turbina *f.*

**turbo-jet,** *n.* turboreattore *m.*

**turbo-prop,** *n.* turbo-èlica *f.*

**turf,** *n.* piòta *f.*

**Turin,** *n.* Torino *f.*

**Turinese,** *adj.* torinese.

**Turk,** *N.* Turco *m.*

**turkey,** *n.* tacchino *m.*

**Turkey,** *n.* Turchìa *f.*

**Turkish,** *adj.* turco.

**turmoil,** *n.* confusione *f.*

**turn, 1.** *n.* giro *m.*; (vehicle) svòlta *f.*; (time around) turno *m.* **2.** *vb.* girare.

**turnip,** *n.* rapa *f.*

**turret,** *n.* torretta *f.*

**turtle,** *n.* tartaruga *f.*

**Tuscan,** *adj.* toscano.

**Tuscany,** *n.* Toscana *f.*

**tutor,** *n.* insegnante privato *m.*

**twelfth,** *adj.* dodicésimo.

**twelve,** *num.* dódici.

**twentieth,** *adj.* ventésimo.

**twenty,** *num.* venti.

**twice,** *adv.* due vòlte.

**twig,** *n.* ramoscèllo *m.*

**twilight,** *n.* crepùscolo *m.*

**twin,** *n.* gemèllo *m.*

**twine,** *n.* spago *m.*

**twinkle,** *vb.* luccicare.

**twist,** *vb.* tòrcere, *tr.*

**two,** *num.* due.

**type, 1.** *n.* tipo *m.* **2.** *vb.* dattilografare.

**typewriter,** *n.* màcchina da scrivere *f.*

**typhoid fever,** *n.* febbre tifoidèa *f.*

**typhus,** *n.* tifo *m.*

**typical,** *adj.* típico.

**typist,** *n.* dattilògrafa *f.*

**tyranny,** *n.* tirannìa *f.*

**tyrant,** *n.* tiranno *m.*

# U

**udder,** *n.* mammèlla *f.*

**ugliness,** *n.* bruttezza *f.*

**ugly,** *adj.* brutto.

**ulcer,** *n.* úlcera *f.*

**ulterior,** *adj.* ulteriore.

**ultimate,** *adj.* último.

**umbrella,** *n.* ombrèllo *m.*

**Umbrian,** *adj.* umbro.

**umpire,** *n.* àrbitro *m.*

**un-,** **1.** *with adjectives,* non, in-. **2.** *with verbs,* s-, dis-.

**unable,** *adj.* incapace.

**unanimous,** *adj.* unànime.

**unbecoming,** *adj.* sconveniènte.

**unbounded,** *adj.* sconfinato.

**uncertain,** *adj.* incèrto.

**uncertainty,** *n.* incertezza *f.*

**uncle,** *n.* zìo *m.*

**unconscious,** *adj.* incònscio.

**uncork,** *vb.* sturare.

**uncouth,** *adj.* gòffo.

**uncover,** *vb.* scoprire, *tr.*

**under,** **1.** *adj.* inferiore. **2.** *adv. and prep.* sotto.

**underestimate,** *vb.* sottovalutare.

**undergo,** *vb.* subire.

**underground,** *adj.* sotterràneo.

**underline,** *vb.* sottolineare.

**underneath,** *adv. and prep.* sotto.

**underpass,** *n.* sottopassàggio *m.*

**undershirt,** *n.* camiciòla *f.*

**undersigned,** *adj.* sottoscritto.

**understand,** *vb.* capire.

**understanding,** *n.* comprensione *f.*

**undertake,** *vb.* intraprèndere.

**undertaker,** *n.* imprenditore di pompe fùnebri *m.*

**underwear,** *n.* sottovèsti *f. pl.*

**underworld,** *n.* malavita *f.*

**undo,** *vb.* disfare.

**undress,** *vb.* svestire, *tr.*

**undulate,** *vb.* ondeggiare.

**unearth,** *vb.* dissotterrare.

**uneasy,** *adj.* inquièto.

**unemployed,** *adj.* disoccupato.

**unequal,** *adj.* ineguale.

**uneven,** *adj.* disuguale.

**unexpected,** *adj.* inaspettato.

**unexpectedly,** *adv.* inaspettatamente.

**unfair,** *adj.* ingiusto.

**unfamiliar,** *adj.* pòco nòto.

**unfavorable,** *adj.* sfavorévole.

**unfit,** *adj.* inàbile, disadatto.

**unfold,** *vb.* spiegare, *tr.*

**unforgettable,** *adj.* indimenticàbile.

**unfortunate,** *adj.* disgraziato, sfortunate.

**unfurl,** *vb.* spiegare.

**unhappy,** *adj.* infelice.

**uniform,** **1.** *n.* divisa *f.*, uniforme *m.* **2.** *adj.* uniforme.

**unify,** *vb.* unificare.

**unilateral,** *adj.* unilaterale.

**union,** *n.* unione *f.*

**unique,** *adj.* ùnico.

**unit,** *n.* unità *f.*

**unite,** *vb.* unire.

**United Nations,** *n.* Nazioni Unite *f.pl.*

**United States,** *n.* Stati Uniti *m.pl.*

**unity,** *n.* unità *f.*

**universal,** *adj.* universale.

**universe,** *n.* univèrso *m.*

**university,** *n.* università *f.*

**unjust,** *adj.* ingiusto.

**unknown,** *adj.* ignòto, sconosciuto.

**unless,** *conj.* a meno che . . . non.

**unlike,** *adj.* dissìmile.

**unlikely,** *adj.* improbàbile.

**unload,** *vb.* scaricare.

**unlock,** *vb.* disserrare, aprire.

**unlucky,** *adj.* disgraziato, infelice.

**unmarried,** *adj.* cèlibe.

**unmask,** *vb.* smascherare.

**unpack,** *vb.* disimballare.

**unpleasant,** *adj.* spiacévole.

**unqualified,** *adj.* (unfit) incompetènte; (unreserved) incondizionato.

**unravel,** *vb.* districare, *tr.*

**unrecognizable,** *adj.* irriconoscìbile.

**unrighteous,** *adj.* iniquo.

**unseemly,** *adj.* sconveniènte.

**unsettle,** *vb.* sconvòlgere.

**unsteady,** *adj.* instàbile.

**unsuccessful,** *adj.* infruttuoso.

**untie,** *vb.* sciògliere.

**until,** **1.** *prep.* fino a, sino a. **2.** *conj.* finchè . . . non.

**untruth,** *n.* menzogna *f.*

**untruthful,** *adj.* menzognèro.

**unusable,** *adj.* inservìbile.

**unusual,** *adj.* insòlito.

**unwarranted,** *adj.* ingiustificato.

**unwell,** *adj.* indisposto.

**unwind,** *vb.* dipanare.

**unworthiness,** *n.* indegnità *f.*

**unworthy,** *adj.* indegno.

**up,** **1.** *adv.* su. **2.** *prep.* su per.

**upbraid,** *vb.* rimproverare.

**uphill, 1.** *adj.* (hard) àrduo. **2.** *adv.* all'insù.

**uphold,** *vb.* sostenere.

**upholder,** *n.* sostenitore *m.*

**upholster,** *vb.* tappezzare.

**upholsterer,** *n.* tappezzière *m.*

**upon,** *prep.* sopra, su.

**upper,** *adj.* superiore.

**upright,** *adj. and adv.* diritto.

**uprising,** *n.* sollevazione *f.*

**uproar,** *n.* baccano *m.*

**uproot,** *vb.* sradicare.

**upset, 1.** *n.* sconvolgimento *m.* **2.** *vb.* sconvòlgere.

**upside down,** *adv.* sottosopra.

**upstairs,** *adv.* su dalle scale.

**upward,** *adv.* in alto.

**urban,** *adj.* urbano.

**urchin,** *n.* monèllo *m.*

**urge,** *vb.* spìngere, sollecitare.

**urgency,** *n.* urgènza *f.*

**urgent,** *adj.* urgènte.

**urinal,** *n.* orinatòio *m.;* (public) vespasiano *m.*

**urinate,** *vb.* orinare.

**urine,** *n.* orina *f.*

**urn,** *n.* urna *f.*

**us,** *pron.* noi, ci.

**usage,** *n.* usanza *f.*

**use, 1.** *n.* uso *m.* **2.** *vb.* usare, adoperare, servirsi di.

**useful,** *adj.* ùtile.

**useless,** *adj.* inùtile.

**user,** *n.* utènte *m.*

**usher,** *n.* màschera *f.*

**usual,** *adj.* sòlito, usuale; **(as u.)** come di sòlito.

**usurp,** *vb.* usurpare.

**usury,** *n.* usura *f.*

**utensil,** *n.* utensile *m.*

**uterus,** *n.* ùtero *m.*

**utility,** *n.* utilità *f.;* (light truck) camioncino *m.*

**utilize,** *vb.* utilizzare.

**utmost,** *adj.* estrèmo.

**utter, 1.** *adj.* complèto. **2.** *vb.* proferire, emèttere.

**utterance,** *n.* espressione *f.*

**utterly,** *adv.* completamente.

**uvula,** *n.* ùgola *f.*

# V

**vacancy,** *n.* posto vacante *m.;* (hotel) stanza lìbera *f.*

**vacant,** *adj.* vacante, lìbero, vuòto.

**vacate,** *vb.* abbandonare, lasciar lìbero.

**vacation,** *n.* vacanze *f.pl.;* (rest) ripòso *m.*

**vaccinate,** *vb.* vaccinare.

**vaccination,** *n.* vaccinazione *f.*

**vaccine,** *n.* vaccino *m.*

**vacillate,** *vb.* vacillare.

**vacuous,** *adj.* vàcuo.

**vacuum,** *n.* vuòto *m.*

**vagrant,** *n. and adj.* vagabondo *(m.)*

**vague,** *adj.* vago.

**vain,** *adj.* vano; **(in v.)** invano.

**valet,** *n.* camerière *m.*

**valiant,** *adj.* valoroso.

**valid,** *adj.* vàlido.

**valise,** *n.* valigia *f.*

**valley,** *n.* valle *f.*

**valor,** *n.* valore *m.*

**valuable,** *adj.* prezioso; (expensive) costoso.

**value, 1.** *n.* valore *m.* **2.** *vb.* stimare, valutare.

**valve,** *n.* vàlvola *f.*

**vampire,** *n.* vampiro *m.*

**van,** *n.* (vehicle) carro *m.;* furgone *m.;* (front) avanguàrdia *f.;* **(moving v.)** furgone per traslòchi *m.*

**vandal,** *n.* vàndalo *m.*

**vanguard,** *n.* avanguàrdia *f.*

**vanilla,** *n.* vanìglia *f.*

**vanish,** *vb.* svanire.

**vanity,** *n.* vanità *f.*

**vanquish,** *vb.* vìncere.

**vapor,** *n.* vapore *m.*

**variance,** *n.* disaccòrdo *m.*

**variation,** *n.* variazione *f.*

**varied,** *adj.* svariato.

**variety,** *n.* varietà *f.*

**various,** *adj.* vàrio.

**varnish,** *n.* vernice *f.*

**vary,** *vb.* variare.

**vase,** *n.* vaso *m.*

**vassal,** *n.* vassallo *m*

**vast,** *adj.* vasto.

**vat,** *n.* tino *m.*

**vaudeville,** *n.* spettacolo di varietà *m.*

**vault,** **1.** *n.* (of roof) vòlta *f.;* (jump) salto. **2.** *vb.* saltare.

**veal,** *n.* vitèllo *m.*

**vegetable,** **1.** *n.* legume *m.;* (v. s) verdura *f.* **2.** *adj.* vegetale.

**vehemence,** *n.* veemènza *f.*

**vehement,** *adj.* veemènte.

**vehicle,** *n.* veicolo *m.*

**veil,** *n.* velo *m.*

**vein,** *n.* vena *f.;* (geology) filone *m.*

**velocity,** *n.* velocità *f.*

**velvet,** **1.** *n.* velluto **2.** *adj.* di velluto.

**veneer,** **1.** *n.* piallàccio *m.* **2.** *vb.* impiallacciare.

**venereal,** *adj.* venèreo.

**Venetian,** *adj.* veneziano.

**vengeance,** *n.* vendetta *f.*

**Venice,** *n.* Venèzia *f.*

**venom,** *n.* veleno *m.*

**venomous,** *adj.* velenoso.

**vent,** **1.** *n.* foro *m.;* (expression) sfògo *m.* **2.** *vb.* sfogare.

**ventilate,** *vb.* ventilare.

**ventilation,** *n.* ventilazione *f.*

**venture,** **1.** *n.* ventura *f.;* (risk) rischio *m.* **2.** rischiare; (dare) osare.

**venturesome,** *adj.* avventuroso.

**verb,** *n.* vèrbo *m.*

**verbal,** *adj.* verbale.

**verbose,** *adj.* verboso.

**verdict,** *n.* verdetto *m.*

**verge,** **1.** *n.* orlo *m.* **2.** *vb.* (v. on) confinare con.

**verify,** *vb.* verificare.

**vermilion,** *adj.* vermìglio.

**vernacular,** *n. and adj.* vernàcolo (*m.*), volgare (*m.*).

**versatile,** *adj.* versàtile.

**verse,** *n.* vèrso *m.*

**versify,** *vb.* versificare.

**version,** *n.* versione *f.*

**versus,** *prep.* contro.

**vertebrate,** *n. and adj.* vertebrato (*m.*)

**vertical,** *adj.* verticale.

**vertigo,** *n.* vertìgine *f.*

**verve,** *n.* brìo *m.*

**very,** **1.** *adj.* vero; (selfsame) stesso. **2.** *adv.* molto; or add suffix -ìssimo.

**vespers,** *n.* vèspri *m.pl.*

**vessel,** *n.* (container) recipiènte *m.;* (boat) nave *f.*

**vest,** *n.* gilè *m.,* panciòtto *m.*

**vestige,** *n.* vestìgio *m.*

**vestry,** *n.* sagrestìa *f.*

**Vesuvius,** *n.* Vesùvio *m.*

**veteran,** *n.* veterano *m.*

**veterinary,** *n. and adj.* veterinàrio (*m.*)

**veto,** **1.** *n.* vèto *m.* **2.** *vb.* vietare.

**vex,** *vb.* irritare.

**via,** *prep.* vìa.

**viaduct,** *n.* viadotto *m.*

**vibrate,** *vb.* vibrare.

**vibration,** *n.* vibrazione *f.*

**vicar,** *n.* vicàrio *m.*

**vice,** *n.* vìzio *m.*

**vicinity,** *n.* vicinanza *f.*

**vicious,** *adj.* vizioso.

**victim,** *n.* vìttima *f.*

**victor,** *n.* vincitore *m.*

**victorious,** *adj.* vittorioso.

**victory,** *n.* vittòria *f.*

**victuals,** *n.* vettovàglie *f.pl.,* vitto *m.*

**view,** *n.* vista *f.,* veduta *f.*

**vigil,** *n.* véglia *f.,* vigìlia *f.*

**vigilant,** *adj.* vigilante.

**vigor,** *n.* vigore *m.*

**vigorous,** *adj.* vigoroso.

**vile,** *adj.* vile.

**village,** *n.* villàggio *m.*

**villain,** *n.* furfante *m.;* (in play) antagonista *m.*

**vim,** *n.* brìo *m.*

**vindicate,** *vb.* rivendicare.

**vine,** *n.* vite *f.*

**vinegar,** *n.* aceto *m.*

**vineyard,** *n.* vigna *f.*

**vintage,** *n.* vendémmia *f.*

**viol, viola,** *n.* viòla *f.*

**violate,** *vb.* violare.

**violation,** *n.* violazione *f.,* contravvenzione *f.*

**violator,** *n.* violatore *m.,* contravventore *m.*

**violence,** *n.* violènza *f.*

**violent,** *adj.* violènto.

**violet,** *n.* viòla *f.*

**violin,** *n.* violino *m.*

**virgin,** *n.* vérgine *f.*

**virile,** *adj.* virile.

**virility,** *n.* virilità *f.*

**virtual,** *adj.* virtuale.

**virtue,** *n.* virtù *f.*

**virtuous,** *adj.* virtuoso.

**virus,** *n.* virus *m.*

**visa,** **1.** *n.* visto *m.* **2.** *vb.* vistare.

**viscous,** *adj.* viscoso.

**vise,** *n.* mòrsa *f.*

**visible,** *adj.* visìbile.

**vision,** *n.* visione *f.;* (of v.) visivo.

**visit, 1.** *n.* vìsita *f.* **2.** *vb.* visitare.

**visitor,** *n.* òspite *m.* or *f.*

**visual,** *adj.* visuale.

**vital,** *adj.* vitale.

**vitality,** *n.* vitalità *f.*

**vitamin,** *n.* vitamina *f.*

**vitiate,** *vb.* viziare.

**vivacious,** *adj.* vivace.

**vivid,** *adj.* vìvido.

**vocabulary,** *n.* vocabolàrio *m.*

**vocal,** *adj.* vocale.

**vociferate,** *vb.* vociare.

**vogue,** *n.* voga *f.*

**voice,** *n.* voce *f.*

**void,** *adj.* nullo; (devoid) privo.

**volcano,** *n.* vulcano *m.*

**voltage,** *n.* voltàggio *m.*

**volume,** *n.* volume *m.*

**voluntary,** *adj.* volontàrio.

**volunteer,** *n.* volontàrio *m.*

**vomit, 1.** *n.* vòmito *m.* **2.** *vb.* vomitare.

**vote, 1.** *n.* voto *m.* **2.** *vb.* votare.

**voter,** *n.* votante *m.*

**voting,** *n.* votazione *f.*

**vouch for,** *vb.* attestare.

**vow,** *n.* voto *m.*

**vowel,** *n.* vocale *f.*

**voyage, 1.** *n.* viàggio *f.* **2.** *vb.* viaggiare.

**vulgar,** *adj.* volgare.

**vulgarity,** *n.* volgarità *f.*

**vulnerable,** *adj.* vulneràbile.

# W

**wad,** *n.* batùffolo *m.;* (roll) ròtolo *m.*

**wadding,** *n.* ovatta *f.*

**wade,** *vb.* attraversare a guado.

**wag, 1.** *n.* bellumore *m.* **2.** *vb.* dimenare, scuòtere.

**wage,** *vb.* (war) fare.

**wager, 1.** *n.* scommessa *f.* **2.** *vb.* scomméttere.

**wages,** *n.* salàrio *m.*

**wagon,** *n.* carro *m.*

**wail,** *vb.* lamentarsi.

**waist,** *n.* cintura *f.,* vita *f.*

**waistcoat,** *n.* gilè *m.,* panciòtto *m.*

**wait,** *vb.* aspettare.

**waiter,** *n.* camerière *m.*

**waitress,** *n.* camerièra *f.*

**waive,** *vb.* rinunciare a.

**waiver,** *n.* rinùncia *f.*

**wake, 1.** *n.* (vigil) vèglia *f.;* (of boat) scìa *f.* **2.** *vb.* svegliare; (be awake) vegliare.

**walk, 1.** *n.* passeggiata *f.* **2.** *vb.* camminare, passeggiare.

**wall,** *n.* muro *m.*

**wallet,** *n.* portafògli *m.*

**walnut,** *n.* noce *f.*

**walrus,** *n.* trichèco *m.*

**waltz,** *n.* vàlzer *m.*

**wander,** *vb.* vagare.

**want, 1.** *n.* bisogno *m.;* (pov-

erty) misèria *f.* **2.** *vb.* desiderare.

**war,** *n.* guèrra *f.*

**ward,** *n.* pupillo *m.;* (city) rione *m.*

**ware,** *n.* mèrce *f.*

**warlike,** *adj.* guerresco.

**warm,** *adj.* caldo, caloroso.

**warmth,** *n.* calore *m.*

**warn,** *vb.* ammonire, avvertire.

**warning,** *n.* avviso *m.,* ammonimento *m.*

**warp,** *vb.* curvare, *tr.,* viziare.

**warrant,** *n.* mandato *m.*

**warrior,** *n.* guerrièro *m.*

**warship,** *n.* nave da guerra *f.*

**wash, 1.** *n.* (laundry) biancherìa *f.* **2.** *vb.* lavare.

**wash-basin,** *n.* lavabo *m.*

**washing machine,** *n.* lavabiancherìa *f.*

**washroom,** *n.* lavatòio *m.*

**wasp,** *n.* vèspa *f.*

**waste, 1.** *n.* sprèco *m.* **2.** *vb.* sprecare.

**watch, 1.** *n.* (timepiece) orològio *m.;* (guard) guàrdia *f.* **2.** *vb.* guardare.

**watchful,** *adj.* vigilante.

**watchmaker,** *n.* orologiaio *m.*

**watchman,** *n.* guardiano *m.*

**water,** 1. *n.* acqua *f.* 2. *vb.* innaffiare.

**water-color,** *n.* acquarèllo *m.*

**waterfall,** *n.* cascata *f.*

**waterproof,** *adj.* impermeàbile.

**wave,** 1. *n.* onda *f.* 2. *vb.* sventolare.

**waver,** *vb.* esitare, vacillare.

**wax,** 1. *n.* cera *f.* 2. *vb.* incerare.

**way,** *n.* vìa *f.*; (manner) manièra *f.*

**we,** *pron.* noi.

**weak,** *adj.* débole.

**weaken,** *vb.* indebolire.

**weakly,** *adv.* debolmente.

**weakness,** *n.* debolezza *f.*

**wealth,** *n.* ricchezza *f.*

**wealthy,** *adj.* ricco.

**weapon,** *n.* arma *f.*

**wear,** 1. *n.* consumo *m.* 2. *vb.* portare; (w. out) consumare; logorare.

**weary,** *adj.* stanco.

**weasel,** *n.* dònnola *f.*

**weather,** *n.* tèmpo *m.*

**weave,** *vb.* tèssere.

**weaver,** *n.* tessitore *m.*

**weaving,** *n.* tessitura *f.*

**web,** *n.* tela *f.*

**wedding,** *n.* nòzze *f.pl.*

**wedge,** 1. *n.* bietta *f.*, cùneo *m.* 2. *vb.* incuneare.

**Wednesday,** *n.* mercoledì *m.*

**weed,** *n.* erbàccia *f.*

**week,** *n.* settimana *f.*

**weekday,** *n.* giorno feriale *m.*

**week end,** *n.* fine di settimana *f.*

**weekly,** *n. and adj.* settimanale (*m.*)

**weep,** *vb.* piàngere.

**weigh,** *vb.* pesare.

**weight,** *n.* peso *m.*

**weird,** *adj.* strano.

**welcome,** *adj.* benvenuto.

**welfare,** *n.* benèssere *m.*

**well,** 1. *n.* pozzo *m.* 2. *vb.* sgorgare. 3. *adv., interj.* bène.

**well-known,** *adj.* nòto.

**west,** *n.* òvest *m.*

**western,** *adj.* occidentale.

**westward,** *adv.* vèrso òvest.

**wet,** 1. *adj.* ùmido, bagnato. 2. *vb.* inumidire.

**whale,** *n.* balena *f.*

**what,** *pron.* che?, che còsa?

**whatever,** 1. *adj.* qualunque. 2. *pron.* qualunque còsa.

**wheat,** *n.* frumento *m.*

**wheel,** *n.* ruòta *f.*

**when,** *adv.* quando.

**whence,** *adv.* donde.

**whenever,** *adv.* ogniqualvòlta.

**where,** *adv.* dove.

**wherever,** *adv.* dovunque.

**whether,** *conj.* se.

**which,** 1. *interrog. pron.*. 2. *rel. pron.* che, il quale; (after prep.) cùi; (to w.) cùi.

**whichever,** *adj. and pron.* qualunque.

**while,** *conj.* mentre.

**whim,** *n.* capriccio *m.*

**whip,** 1. *n.* frusta *f.* 2. *vb.* frustare.

**whirl,** *vb.* girare.

**whirlpool,** *n.* vòrtice *m.*

**whirlwind,** *n.* tùrbine *m.*

**whisk broom,** *n.* scopetta *f.*

**whisker,** *n.* basetta *f.*

**whiskey,** *n.* vìschi *m.*

**whisper,** 1. *n.* bisbìglio *m.* 2. *vb.* bisbigliare.

**whistle,** 1. *n.* fischio *m.* 2. *vb.* fischiare.

**white,** *adj.* bianco.

**who, whom,** *pron.* 1. *interrog.* chi. 2. *rel.* che, il quale; (after prep.) cùi.

**whoever, whomever,** *pron.* chiunque.

**whole,** *adj.* intèro, tutto.

**wholesale,** *adj., adv.* all'ingròsso.

**wholesome,** *adj.* sano.

**wholly,** *adv.* completamente.

**whom,** see who.

**whore,** *n.* puttana *f.*

**whose,** *pron.* 1. *interrog.* di chi?. 2. *rel.* cùi.

**why,** *adv.* perchè.

**wicked,** *adj.* malvàgio.

**wickedness,** *n.* malvagità *f.*

**wide,** *adj.* largo.

**widen,** *vb.* allargare, *tr.*

**widespread,** *adj.* diffuso.

**widow,** *n.* védova *f.*

**widower,** *n.* védovo *m.*

**width,** *n.* larghezza *f.*

**wield,** *vb.* règgere.

**wife,** *n.* móglie *f.*

**wig,** *n.* parrucca *f.*

**wild,** *adj.* selvàggio; (plants) selvàtico; (mad) furioso.

**wilderness,** *n.* desèrto *m.*

**wilful,** *adj.* capàrbio.

**will,** 1. *n.* volontà *f.*; (testament) testamento *m.* 2. *vb.* (leave) lasciare; (future) use future tense.

**willing,** *adj.* pronto.

**willow,** *n.* sàlice *m.*

**wilt,** *vb.* appassire.

**win,** *vb.* vincere.

**wind, 1.** *n.* vènto *m.* **2.** *vb.* avvòlgere; (watch) caricare.

**window,** *n.* finèstra *f.*

**windshield,** *n.* parabrezza *m.;* paravènto *m.;* (w.-wiper) tergicristallo *m.*

**windy,** *adj.* ventoso.

**wine,** *n.* vino *m.*

**wing,** *n.* ala *f.*

**wink,** *vb.* ammiccare.

**winner,** *n.* vincitore *m.*

**winter, 1.** *n.* invèrno *m.* **2.** *adj.* **(of w.)** invernale.

**wintry,** *adj.* invernale.

**wipe,** *vb.* asciugare.

**wire, 1.** *n.* filo *m.;* (telegram) telegramma *m.* **2.** *vb.* telegrafare.

**wireless, 1.** *n.* (radio) ràdio *f.* **2.** *adj.* sènza fili.

**wire recorder,** *n.* registratore a filo *m.*

**wisdom,** *n.* saggezza *f.*

**wise,** *adj.* sàggio.

**wish, 1.** *n.* desidèrio *m.* **2.** *vb.* desiderare.

**wit,** *n.* intelligènza *f.;* (humor) spìrito *m.* (wag) bellumore *m.*

**witch,** *n.* strega *f.*

**with,** *prep.* con.

**withdraw,** *vb.* ritirare, *tr.*

**wither,** *vb.* avvizzire.

**withhold,** *vb.* trattenere.

**within, 1.** *adv.* dentro. **2.** *prep.* entro.

**without,** *prep.* sènza.

**witness,** *n.* testimone *m.*

**witty,** *adj.* spiritoso.

**wizard,** *n.* stregone *m.*

**woe,** *n.* calamità *f.,* guaio *m.*

**wolf,** *n.* lupo *m.,* lupa *f.*

**woman,** *n.* dònna *f.*

**womb,** *n.* ùtero *m.*

**wonder, 1.** *n.* meravìglia *f.* **2.** *vb.* meravigliarsi, domandarsi.

**wonderful,** *adj.* meraviglioso.

**woo,** *vb.* corteggiare.

**wood,** *n.* legno *m.;* (forest) bosco *m.,* forèsta *f.*

**wooded,** *adj.* boscoso.

**wooden,** *adj.* di legno.

**wool,** *n.* lana *f.*

**woolen,** *adj.* di lana.

**word,** *n.* paròla *f.*

**wordy,** *adj.* verboso.

**work, 1.** *n.* lavoro *m.,* òpera *f.* **2.** *vb.* lavorare; (function) funzionare.

**worker,** *n.* lavoratore *m.*

**workman,** *n.* operaio *m.*

**world,** *n.* mondo *m.*

**worldly,** *adj.* mondano.

**world-wide,** *adj.* mondiale.

**worm,** *n.* vèrme *m.*

**worn-out,** *adj.* lògoro.

**worry, 1.** *n.* preoccupazione *f.* **2.** *vb.* preoccupare, *tr.*

**worse, 1.** *adj.* peggiore. **2.** *adv.* pèggio.

**worship, 1.** *n.* adorazione *f.,* culto *m.* **2.** *vb.* adorare.

**worst, 1.** *adj.* il peggiore. **2.** *adv.* il pèggio.

**worth, 1.** *n.* valore *m.* **2.** *adj.* **(be w.)** valere.

**worthless,** *adj.* sènza valore.

**worthy,** *adj.* degno.

**would,** *vb.* use conditional tense.

**wound, 1.** *n.* ferita *f.* **2.** *vb.* ferire.

**wrap, 1.** *n.* mantèllo *m.* **2.** *vb.* avvòlgere.

**wrapping,** *n.* involucro *m.*

**wrath,** *n.* ira *f.*

**wreath,** *n.* ghirlanda *f.*

**wreck, 1.** *n.* (ship) naufràgio *m.;* (ruin) rovina *f.* **2.** *vb.* naufragare, rovinare.

**wrench, 1.** *n.* (tool) chiave inglese *f.* **2.** *vb.* strappare.

**wrestle,** *vb.* lottare.

**wretched,** *adj.* misero.

**wring,** *vb.* tòrcere.

**wrinkle, 1.** *n.* ruga *f.* **2.** *vb.* corrugare.

**wrist,** *n.* polso *m.*

**wrist-watch,** *n.* orològio da polso *m.*

**write,** *vb.* scrìvere.

**writer,** *n.* scrittore *m.*

**writhe,** *vb.* contòrcersi.

**writing,** *n.* scrittura *f.,* scritto *m.*

**wrong, 1.** *n.* tòrto *m.* **2.** *adj.* errato; **(be w.)** aver tòrto.

# X, Y, Z

**x-rays,** *n.* raggi x (pron. ics) *m. pl.*

**xylophone,** *n.* silòfono *m.*

**yacht,** *n.* pànfilo *m.*

**yard,** *n.* cortile *m.;* (railroad) scalo di smistamento *m.;* (measure) jarda *f.*

**yarn,** *n.* filato *m.;* (tale) stòria *f.*

**yawn, 1.** *n.* sbadìglio *m.* **2.** *vb.* sbadigliare.

**year,** *n.* anno *m.*

**yearly, 1.** *adj.* annuale. **2.** *adv.* ogni anno.

**yearn,** *vb.* bramare.

**yell, 1.** *n.* urlo *m.* **2.** *vb.* urlare.

**yellow,** *adj.* giallo.

**yes,** *interj.* sì.

**yesterday,** *n. and adv.* ièri (*m.*)

**yet, 1.** *adv.* ancora. **2.** *conj.* tuttavìa.

**yield, 1.** *n.* produzione *f.* **2.** *vb.* cédere; (produce) produrre.

**yoke,** *n.* giogo *m.*

**yolk,** *n.* torlo *m.*

**you,** *pron.* tu, te, ti; voi, vi, Lei; La, Lo, Loro.

**young,** *adj.* gióvane.

**your,** *adj.* tuo; vòstro; Suo; Loro.

**yours,** *pron.* tuo; vòstro; Suo; Loro.

**yourself,** *pron.* tu stesso; te stesso, voi stessi, Lei stesso; Loro stessi.

**youth,** *n.* giovinezza *f.*

**youthful,** *adj.* giovanile.

**Yugoslav,** *adj.* jugoslavo.

**Yugoslavia,** *n.* Jugoslàvia *f.*

**zeal,** *n.* zèlo *m.*

**zealous,** *adj.* zelante.

**zebra,** *n.* zèbra *f.*

**zephyr,** *n.* zèffiro *m.*

**zest,** *n.* entusiasmo *m.*

**zinc,** *n.* zinco *m.*

**zipper,** *n.* chiusura lampo *f.*

**zone,** *n.* zòna *f.*

**zoo,** *n.* giardino zoològico *m.*

**zoological,** *adj.* zoològico.

**zoology,** *n.* zoologìa *f.*

**Zurich,** *n.* Zurigo *m.*

# Days of the Week

| Monday | lunedì |
|--------|--------|
| Tuesday | martedì |
| Wednesday | mercoledì |
| Thursday | giovedì |
| Friday | venerdì |
| Saturday | sàbato |
| Sunday | doménica |

# Months

| January | gennaio | July | lùglio |
|---------|---------|------|--------|
| February | febbraio | August | agosto |
| March | marzo | September | settèmbre |
| April | aprile | October | ottobre |
| May | màggio | November | novèmbre |
| June | giugno | December | dicèmbre |

# Weights and Measures

The Italians use the *Metric System* of weights and measures, which is a decimal system in which multiples are shown by the prefixes: *deci-* (one tenth); *centi-* (one hundredth); *milli-* (one thousandth); *deca-* (ten); *etto-* (hundred); *chilo-* (abbreviated *k.*) (thousand).

| | | |
|---|---|---|
| 1 centìmetro | = | .3937 inches |
| 1 mètro | = | 39.37 inches |
| 1 chilòmetro (abbr. *km.*) | = | .621 mile |
| | | |
| 1 centigramma | = | .1543 grain |
| 1 gramma | = | 15.432 grains |
| 1 ettogramma (abbr. *etto*) | = | 3.527 ounces |
| 1 chilogramma (abbr. *kg.*) | = | 2.2046 pounds |
| 1 tonnellata | = | 2204 pounds |
| | | |
| 1 centilitro | = | .338 ounces |
| 1 litro | = | 1.0567 quart (liquid); |
| | | .908 quart (dry) |
| 1 chilolitro | = | 264.18 gallons |

315

# Legal Holidays In Italy

| | |
|---|---|
| All Sundays | May 1, Labor Day |
| January 1, New Year's Day | June 2, Day of the Republic |
| January 6, Epiphany | June 29, Saints Peter's & Paul's Day |
| March 19, Saint Joseph's Day | August 15, Assumption of Mary |
| April 25, Liberation of Italy | November 1, All Saints' Day |
| Monday after Easter Sunday | December 8, Immaculate Conception of Mary |
| Ascension Day | December 25, Christmas |
| Corpus Christi Day | December 26 |

Most businesses are closed on the afternoon of the following traditional holidays:

> The last day before Lent (Mardi Gras)
> Thursday of Holy Week
> November 2, All Souls' Day
> December 24, Christmas Eve
> December 31, New Year's Eve

# Centuries

In Italian, centuries may be referred to by the equivalent of ordinal numeral plus the word for century: *il secolo decimottavo* "the eighteenth century," etc. For the centuries from 1200 A.D. to the present, it is also common to refer to them by the cardinal numbers for the "hundreds" present in each century-name, thus:

| | | | |
|---|---|---|---|
| il Duecènto | = | the thirteenth century | = the '200's |
| il Trecènto | = | the fourteenth century | = the '300's |
| il Quattrocènto | = | the fifteenth century | = the '400's |
| il Cinquecènto | = | the sixteenth century | = the '500's |
| il Seicènto | = | the seventeenth century | = the '600's |
| il Settecènto | = | the eighteenth century | = the '700's |
| l'Ottocènto | = | the nineteenth century | = the '800's |
| il Novecènto | = | the twentieth century | = the '900's |

# Italy

| | |
|---|---|
| Population | 50,762,000 |
| Approximate Length | 760 miles |
| Approximate Width | 100 to 150 miles |
| Square Miles | 116,294 |
| Capital | Rome (Roma) |

# Regions and Provinces

| Region | Population | Constituent-Provinces |
|---|---|---|
| Abruzzi | 1,213,002 | Chieti, L'Aquila, Pescara, Teramo |
| Basilicata | 648,085 | Matera, Potenza |
| Calabria | 2,045,215 | Catanzaro, Cosenza, Reggio Calabria |
| Campania | 4,756,094 | Avellino, Benevento, Caserta, Napoli, Salerno |
| Emilia-Romagna | 3,646,507 | Bologna, Ferrara, Forlì, Modena, Parma, Piacenza, Ravenna, Reggio Emilia |
| Friuli-Venezia Giulia | 1,205,222 | Gorizia, Trieste, Udine |
| Lazio (Latium) | 3,922,783 | Frosinone, Latina, Rieti, Roma, Viterbo |
| Liguria | 1,717,630 | Genova, Imperia, La Spezia, Savona |
| Lombardia (Lombardy) | 7,390,492 | Bergamo, Brescia, Como, Cremona, Mantova, Milano, Pavia, Sondrio, Varese |
| Marche (Marches) | 1,347,234 | Ancona, Ascoli Piceno, Macerata, Pesaro Urbino |
| Molise | 371,775 | Campobasso |
| Piemonte (Piedmont) | 3,889,962 | Alessandria, Asti, Cuneo, Novara, Torino, Vercelli |
| Puglia (Apulia) | 3,220,485 | Bari, Brindisi, Foggia, Lecce, Taranto |
| Sardegna (Sardinia) | 1,413,289 | Cagliari, Nuoro, Sassari |
| Sicilia (Sicily) | 4,711,783 | Agrigento, Caltanissetta, Catania, Enna, Messina, Palermo, Ragusa, Siracusa, Trapani |
| Trentino-Alto Adige | 785,491 | Bolzano, Trento |
| Toscana (Tuscany) | 3,267,374 | Arezzo, Firenze, Grosseto, Livorno, Lucca, Massa, Pisa, Pistoia, Siena |
| Umbria | 788,546 | Perugia, Terni |
| Valle d'Aosta | 99,754 | |
| Veneto (Venetia) | 3,833,837 | Belluno, Padova, Rovigo, Treviso, Venezia, Verona, Vicenza |

# Major Cities

| City | Population | Location |
|---|---|---|
| Roma (Rome) | 2,328,930 | W. Central |
| Milano (Milan) | 1,643,402 | N.W. |
| Napoli (Naples) | 1,198,233 | S.W. |
| Torino (Turin) | 1,096,958 | N.W. |
| Genova (Genoa) | 814,232 | N.W. |
| Palermo | 604,475 | S. (N.W. Sicily) |
| Bologna | 469,170 | N. Central |
| Firenze (Florence) | 451,730 | N. Central |
| Catania | 376,239 | S. (E. Sicily) |
| Venezia (Venice) | 353,018 | N.E. |
| Bari | 320,049 | S.E. |
| Messina | 258,118 | S. (N.E. Sicily) |
| Verona | 230,907 | N.E. |
| Padova (Padua) | 205,057 | N.E. |
| Taranto | 197,716 | S.E. |
| Cagliari | 191,439 | W. (S. Sardinia) |
| Brescia | 182,232 | N. |
| Livorno (Leghorn) | 164,808 | N.W. |
| Ferrara | 156,038 | N.E. |
| Parma | 155,132 | N. Central |
| Reggio di Calabria | 155,039 | S. |
| Modena | 147,501 | N. Central |
| La Spezia | 125,661 | N.W. |
| Reggio nell'Emilia | 119,912 | N. Central |
| Bergamo | 117,773 | N. |
| Perugia | 115,852 | Central |
| Ancona | 102,604 | E. Central |
| Pescara | 100,363 | E. Central |
| Bolzano (Bozen) | 83,956 | N. |
| Trento (Trient) | 74,766 | N. |

# Italian Family Names

In its simplest form, an Italian proper name consists of given name (*prenome*) plus family name (*cognome*): *Giovanni Rossi*. It may, however, contain more than one of each type of name: *Luigi Maria Franceschini-Petrocchi*. If more than one family name is present, both are used or else only the first: *il signor Franceschini-Petrocchi*, or *il signor Franceschini*, but not *il signor Petrocchi*.

A woman, on marrying, adds her husband's family name preceding her own: *Giuseppina Bianchi*, on marrying Mr. Bracciolini, becomes *Giuseppina Bracciolini-Bianchi*. She will often, however, be referred to simply as *la signora Bracciolini* after her marriage. The American English order for a married woman's name, given name plus maiden name plus husband's family name, is found in Italian only in an archaic construction in which the woman's maiden name is followed by *in* plus her husband's family name: *Giuseppina Bianchi in Bracciolini*.

In traditional Italian usage, a person's given name precedes his or her family name, as in English: *Giuliano Bàrtoli Pierina Cardinali*. A modern habit, of placing the family name before the given name, is by now almost universal in lists, directories and official documents, and is being used increasingly even in everyday situations: *Bàrtoli Giuliano, Cardinali Pierina*.